Copy No. 814906

00953101

782.1092 ER K
KIMBELL
81/4906

DISCARD

KT-445-878

DISCARD

B.C.H.E. LIBRARY

00108660

Verdi in the Age of Italian Romanticism

VERDI
IN THE AGE OF
ITALIAN ROMANTICISM

DAVID R. B. KIMBELL

Professor of Music, University of St Andrews

CAMBRIDGE UNIVERSITY PRESS

Cambridge

London   New York   New Rochelle
Melbourne   Sydney

Published by the Press Syndicate of the University of Cambridge
The Pitt Building, Trumpington Street, Cambridge CB2 1RP
32 East 57th Street, New York, NY 10022, U.S.A.
296 Beaconsfield Parade, Middle Park, Melbourne 3206, Australia

© Cambridge University Press 1981

First published 1981

Text set in 10/12 pt Linotron 202 Melior, printed and bound
in Great Britain at The Pitman Press, Bath

British Library Cataloguing in Publication Data Ltd

Kimbell, David R. B.
  Verdi in the Age of Italian Romanticism.
  1. Verdi, Giuseppe
  I. Title
  782.1′092′4   ML410.V4   80–40723

ISBN 0 521 23052 7

BATH COLLEGE

HIGHER EDUCATION

NEWTON PARK
LIBRARY

DISCARD

CLASS
No. 782·1092 Verk

ACC.
No. 814906

Contents

v

CONTENTS

Part IV. The operas

PREFACE

There is no shortage of admirable English-language books on Verdi. They range from the 'popular' life-and-works studies of Bonavia, Toye and Hussey, all of which can still be read with pleasure and profit, to Weaver's magisterial documentary study. Two works in particular rank among the finest achievements of musical histor-iography in the post-war period. In *The operas of Verdi*, Julian Budden has provided the first part of what one might think of as a companion study to Newman's *Wagner nights* – an opera-by-opera guide that is richly informative, authoritative and well written, and which has already become indispensable; while Frank Walker's *The man Verdi* is one of the tiny number of composers' biographies which can be described quite simply as a great book. My own indebtedness to both Budden and Walker will be obvious to all my readers, and this contribution to the Verdi literature is certainly not made in the hope of superseding them. On the contrary, it is because the fundamental books have been so well written that it seems legitimate to pursue enquiries into some of the fascinating secondary apsects of Verdi's music.

Obviously any artist's achievement is in some measure con-ditioned by the environment in which he works. In certain cases however the fact is more important than in others, and this book has been written in the belief that Verdi, certainly in his early works, is one of the most interesting of such artists. During the 1850s his practice as a composer began to be more independent, so that at the end of his long active life he was able to say of *Falstaff* that he had written it to please himself. In the 1830s and 1840s such independ-ence would have been unthinkable. Verdi's early operas belong to a flourishing tradition; they were written for a society which knew quite clearly what the social function of the composer was; and they reflect the artistic, moral and philosophical values of the age remarkably fully. These relationships – the relationships of Verdi's operas to tradition, to society, and to the cultural climate of Italian Romanticism – are the theme of this book.

Part I describes those aspects of the Italy of Verdi's youth that seem to me to have most bearing on his work as a composer. Part II, the documentary history of the early operas, shows the kind of life a successful composer of the period led. It is not a biography, clearly, since everything not related to the composition and production of operas has been omitted; but it will, I hope, tell the reader most of the things he may want to know about the genesis of the operas: about commissions and contracts; about the relationship between Verdi, his librettists and his singers; about the way the composer went to work, and his attitude to what he was doing. The third part of the book describes the musical resources Verdi brought to his task. I have tried to suggest the values and assumptions, the overall formal principles, the points of musical style which he inherited from the Italian tradition, and to show the way in which he slowly developed and transformed these things during the first fifteen years of his career as an opera composer.

The various aspects of the subject presented in the first three sections of the book are finally drawn together in Part IV, a critical study of selected operas from the period. To some extent such a selection is necessarily arbitrary. But I think most Verdians would agree that the operas I have chosen represent Verdi's best at each state of his development; and they are certainly the ones that have most bearing on the theme of this book. These are the operas that best show his progressive transformations of inherited tradition (*Macbeth, Rigoletto*); that reflect his active concern for contemporary political issues (*Nabucco, La Battaglia di Legnano*); and that reveal how fruitful for opera were the cosmopolitan literary tastes of the Italian Romantics (*Ernani, I Due Foscari, Luisa Miller* etc.).

All translations in the book, unless an attribution is specifically made, are, in principle, my own. I say 'in principle' because the books of Budden, Osborne and Walker contain many felicitous renderings, which may have lingered in my memory longer than I knew, and presented themselves to me when I thought I was doing my own work. For any such subconscious appropriations I apologize now.

It remains to acknowledge the assistance I have received in writing this book. First, to the custodians of the treasures in Italy: Messrs Ricordi of Milan, particularly the staff of the Archive at Via Salomone; Maestro Giampiero Tintori and his staff at the Museo Teatrale alla Scala, Milan; Maestro Sandro Della Libera and his staff at the Archive of the Teatro La Fenice, Venice; the library staff of the

Fondazione Giorgio Cini, Venice. All have received me kindly and rendered whatever assistance lay in their power. Most especially I thank Maestro Mario Medici and his colleagues in the Instituto di Studi Verdiani in Parma. Every scholar who has worked in Italy in recent years will have faced his share of exasperations; but under Maestro Medici's direction the Istituto di Studi Verdiani has remained a haven of old-world courtesy and dedicated scholarship, where all serious students can be confident of the warmest welcome and the most willing assistance.

The University of Edinburgh generously supported my work, financing several research visits to Italy, and granting me sabbatical leave during the academic year 1974–5. I am most grateful too for the advice and assistance of many former colleagues in Edinburgh, particularly Dr Peter Williams; Mr Michael Anderson, the Reid Music Librarian; Mr Walter Cairns, formerly of the Edinburgh University Press; and two members of the Italian department, Dr Alan Freedman (now at Salford) and Mr Brian Phillips, who were endlessly patient in helping me overcome the limitations of my own Italian. Further afield Mr Julian Budden, London; Fräulein Helga Heim of the Music Department of the Staats- und Universitätsbibliothek, Hamburg; and the staff of the Italian Institute in Hamburg rendered assistance of various kinds.

I am grateful to the Royal Musical Association for permission to reprint part of my article 'The Young Verdi and Shakespeare' which appeared in volume 101 of its *Proceedings*, and to the Istituto di Studi Musicali e Teatrale of the Università degli studi di Bologna for permission to reprint my article 'I Due Foscari' which is published in the Festschrift in honour of Mario Medici.

My last and greatest debts are personal as well as practical ones: to my mother-in-law, Frau Ilse Lübbe, in whose Hamburg flat the greater part of the book was written, and to my wife, Ingrid, without whose goading it would not have been written at all. Not content with making me write it, she has herself typed it – much of it several times – and prepared the index.

DAVID R. B. KIMBELL

Hamburg 1974 – Edinburgh 1978

PART I

The setting

1

Verdi's Italy

Politics

Verdi's early life and the greater part of his operatic career fall within that phase of Italian history known as the *risorgimento*, a movement of renewal and revivification, a 'rising-up-again' of the Italian people to nationhood, that stretched from the Italian conquests of Napoleon in 1796 to the unification of Italy in 1870. Verdi was himself keenly involved with this process of renewal in Italian society, particularly in its most dramatic decade, the 1840s; indeed his involvement was so close that the way his art developed during his early years is hardly to be understood without some knowledge of these momentous events.

When Verdi was born on 10 October 1813 at Le Roncole, a village in what is now the province of Parma in the region of Emilia, by far the greater part of Italy was still under Napoleonic rule. Some of its regions – Piedmont, Verdi's own Parma, Umbria, Tuscany, Latium – had, between 1800 and 1808, been annexed to the French Empire; Lombardy, the Veneto, and much of central Italy had been merged into a new-fangled Kingdom of Italy, dating from 1805, of which Napoleon was king; while since 1806 the nominally independent Kingdom of Naples had been a vassal state ruled over first by Joseph Bonaparte and then by Marshal Murat, Napoleon's brother-in-law.

But the Napoleonic imperium was approaching its close. Already at the end of 1812 news of the collapse of the Russian campaign had reached Italy; in 1813 followed the Battle of Leipzig. The Napoleonic rulers in Italy did what they could to disengage their own political fortunes from those of the waning emperor, and some patriotic Italians glimpsed visions of independence and perhaps even of nationhood following upon his downfall. But there was no co-ordinated popular movement to oust the French. The collapse of Napoleonic Italy was neither willed nor effected by the Italians themselves: it was the consequence of Napoleon's defeats in northern and central Europe, and was brought about by the reinvasion of northern Italy by the Austrians. It was therefore not the Italians who determined how they were henceforth to be governed: that decision was made by the powers who had defeated Napoleon – Austria, Britain, Prussia and Russia – at the Congress of Vienna in 1815.

The principle according to which this decision was made was that of legitimacy: and it was applied 'with zealous and bureaucratic punctiliousness'.[1] Neither Venice nor Genoa was permitted to resume its old tradition of republican government. But with that exception, the outcome of the Congress of Vienna was the restoration of that multitude of kings, dukes, and grand dukes whose rule had been cut short by Napoleon's conquests. Lombardy and the Veneto were absorbed into the Austrian Empire, the Savoyard monarchy was restored in Piedmont, and the Bourbon monarchy in Naples; the Pope's temporal power was re-established throughout central Italy from Rome to the Po; Austrian archdukes assumed control in Tuscany and Modena; the duchies of Parma and Lucca were restored to a nominal independence. This was the pattern of Italian government in Verdi's youth, and it was not seriously threatened for more than thirty years.

Although an antiquated political system of well-proved inefficiency was thus re-established in 1815, and although some rulers, notably the bewigged, pigtailed and powdered Victor Emmanuel I of Piedmont, re-entered into their inheritances in a manner quite ostentatiously reactionary, the period of Napoleonic rule had not vanished without trace. In almost every part of Italy something at least of the more libertarian Napoleonic code of law was preserved; and in Lombardy and the Veneto the restored Austrian authorities, initially at least, strove to rule in an even more efficient and non-repressive way than Napoleon and his representatives had done. But the crucial inheritance from Napoleon was surely something less tangible than mere legal and bureaucratic efficiency, more even than the exhilaration of being able to take one's chance in a meritocratic society. What resounds and re-echoes through the decades of the risorgimento is that vibrant enthusiasm for liberty and for heroism that Napoleon had figured forth. The autocratic arbitrariness with which he had partitioned and repartitioned the land, the monstrous slaughter in which he had involved its people, were largely forgotten. But nostalgia for the tone and the idealism of his era was a force in Italian politics throughout the risorgimento, and was a sentiment which in the early years much nourished the Carboneria and other secret societies.

On the surface, the period following the Restoration of 1815 was one of fatalistic indolence. Periodically, however, this apparent stagnation erupted into life: the discontent and animosities of the people came into focus and insurrection followed. Because the legitimist political system in Italy was an integral factor in the European balance of power, it generally happened that such insurrections were sparked off by events in other parts of Europe which looked like upsetting the prevailing equilibrium. In 1820, it was the fact that the Spanish king had been forced by his army to adopt a constitution that led the Neapolitan army to make a similar demand of King Ferdinand; this in turn provoked an uprising in Piedmont.

Santorre di Santarosa, one of the leaders of the Piedmontese revolt, described the events of 1820–1 as 'the first revolution . . . in which two Italian peoples worked together at the two extremities of our peninsula'.[2] But this was wishful thinking. What was really critical about the Italian patriotic and revolutionary movements of the period was their lack of a common idealism. The Sicilians saw the commotion in Naples as an opportunity to attempt some degree of secession for themselves, a move repellent to Neapolitan absolutists and parliamentarians alike. An army was dispatched to quell Sicily, thus leaving Ferdinand free to call in Austrian troops to re-establish absolute rule early in 1821. It was disputes and contradictory expectations within the Piedmontese army that led to the failure of their revolt, too.

A similar air of short-sighted improvisation characterizes the series of insurrections set off in 1830 by the July revolution in France. Successively in Modena, in Bologna, and in Parma, popular provisional governments were set up in the early weeks of 1831, and that in Bologna rapidly wrested from the Papal authorities all the Romagna, the Marches and Umbria. The so-called 'Italian United Provinces' was, however, an affair so very provincial that it declined to ally itself with the revolutionary movement in Modena, a 'foreign' city fully twenty miles distant, and was an easy prey for the Austrians when, in response to urgent Papal pleading, they intervened to restore legitimate rule once more.

The strength of local patriotisms, the jealous pride in local traditions, the mutual distrust between one region and the next which contributed to the failures of 1821 were among the major problems waiting to be solved by the proponents of Italian unity. Italy had been divided too long; so many cities had been for centuries centres of commerce, of intellectual and artistic life, that to sacrifice a proper local pride and some measure of independence to the greater national good came hard to them. Not a few observers sympathetic to the Italians felt that the notion of a unified nation-state was entirely utopian. Lord Burghersh, British Ambassador in Florence, felt that 'no measure could be so hurtful or unpopular as the forming of their country into one Kingdom. The different states into which it has so long been divided have separated the feelings and the interests of the people. The inhabitants of no separate country hate each other more thoroughly than those of the neighbouring states of Italy.'[3]

The failure of the revolts in and around Bologna in 1831, and of the first of the many revolutionary outbreaks organized by Mazzini, that in Genoa in 1833, has been seen by many historians as the point when the fate of Italy shifted from the hands of the 'revolutionaries' into the hands of the 'moderates'. There was, from this time up to the revolutions of 1848, perhaps less palpable unrest than before; but on the other hand the sense of a common bond uniting the various states of the peninsula, and of a common destiny to be shared, became ever stronger. It was less the political than the philosophical and cultural achievement of those years that ensured that, when the 1848 revolution came, and despite the fact that it was apparently a failure, it set in motion a train of events that could only culminate in the independence and unification of the Italian nation.

One factor that contributed to this growing sense of nationhood was the more and more widely felt hostility to Austria. While only Lombardy and the Veneto were directly ruled by Austria, the Piedmontese and the Neapolitans in 1821 and the various peoples of the Papal States in 1831 had all shared the experience of seeing popular movements forcibly suppressed by Austrian intervention. But if the Austrians were coming increasingly to be seen as the villains of the piece, the heroes were not so much those who manned the barricades – their time was not yet returned – as the men who built up Italian idealism and Italian self-awareness. Foremost among them was Mazzini, less for his ill-fated attempts to overthrow existing governments by organizing popular insurrections than for the way in which, in his writings, he proclaimed the inexorable necessity of the emergence of an Italian nation. In Mazzini's view nothing could stand in the way of the unity of a people who shared a common religion, a common way of life, and a common culture. All the towering figures of the era were in fact 'intellectuals' of one kind or another rather than activists: like Massimo D'Azeglio, who, besides being an astute politician with a detestation of the 'falsehoods' and 'daggers' he associated with Mazzini, was a novelist who saw his role in Italian life as being that of 'influencing people through a patriotically inspired literature';[4] or like Manzoni, who, not content with having produced in *I Promessi Sposi* one of the great novels of the nineteenth century, spent more than a decade refashioning it in such a way that it might contribute to the immense task of providing Italy with an accepted national language; or like Verdi himself.

That for all the predominance of 'moderation' Italy remained in a highly excitable state appeared in 1846, when the reactionary and repressive reign of Pope Gregory XVI came to an end, and Pope Pius IX was elected his successor. The new Pope's granting of an amnesty to all political prisoners was a traditional practice, and the reforms that he introduced in the administration of his realms had for the most part been urged upon his predecessor by the five powers – Austria, Britain, France, Prussia and Russia – fifteen years before. But in 1846 Italians chose to see them as dramatically libertarian gestures, and for a few years, somewhat against his will, Pius IX became one of the heroes of the patriotic movement. One of the best-known incidents linking Verdi's music with the passions of the *risorgimento* occurred in Bologna in 1846, when the Act III finale of *Ernani* was turned into a kind of topical cantata proclaiming 'A Pio nono sia gloria e onor'.[5]

By 1848 the whole of the Italian peninsula was simmering. In Piedmont, partly as a result of D'Azeglio's far-sighted persuasiveness, partly because of the increasingly assertive postures Metternich was obliged to adopt, King Charles-Albert and his ministers were preparing to challenge the Austrians; in Milan, Austrian repression was prompting a series of peaceful demonstrations, apparently a novel idea at the time; Rome and the other cities of the Papal States were still in a heady rapture over the reforms of Pius IX; throughout the poorer rural areas ever-worsening poverty had brought a desperate peasantry to the verge of revolution.

There was no waiting now for external prompting. The countless revolutions of 1848 in fact began in Italy, in Palermo, where, early in January, a popular demonstration rapidly grew into general insurrection. By February, the Neapolitan royalist troops had been expelled from virtually the whole island, and the revolution had spread to the mainland, prompting King Ferdinand II to grant a constitution. In February, too, Paris was once more in turmoil, and within weeks the unrest had spread to the very heart of the Austrian Empire. Metternich's downfall in Vienna in March 1848 signalled revolution in the Austrian provinces in Italy. The result was one of the most thrilling episodes of the *risorgimento*, the 'five days' during which the

Milanese defeated Radetzky's forces and freed Lombardy. Simultaneously the Venetian Republic was restored. In non-Austrian territories, the Grand Duke of Tuscany, King Charles-Albert of Piedmont, and even the Pope hastened to grant constitutions, though only Charles-Albert was able thereby to save his throne.

The most sensational events of the year were probably those of Rome. In April the Pope, alarmed to find himself increasingly associated with revolutionary Italian nationalist movements, delivered an encyclical in which he emphasized the universality of his apostolate, the fact that 'he embraced all kindreds, peoples and nations, with equal solicitude of paternal affection'; he also insisted on the duty which the Italian people owed to their legitimate rulers. The dismay which this pronouncement occasioned was followed in the autumn by violent action. On 15 November a government minister was assassinated by members of a secret society, and a few days later the Pope himself fled from the city in disguise to take refuge in Gaeta in the Kingdom of Naples. In the new year, after elections had been held on a basis of universal suffrage, the temporal power of the Papacy was abolished, and the Roman Republic proclaimed.

But already the forces of reaction were reclaiming the land. In Lombardy and the Veneto intense regional resentment was felt at Charles-Albert's insistence that the liberated parts of Italy, which indeed owed him not the tiniest part of their liberty, should be fused into an enlarged Kingdom of Piedmont. When his vacillation and incompetence as a military leader resulted in the reconquest of most of the Austrian territories by March 1849, the demoralization of the revolutionary movement in the North must have been complete. In the summer, after a protracted struggle, a French army sent by Napoleon III succeeded in putting down the Roman Republic, and the temporal power of the Papacy was restored. Bourbon absolutism returned to Naples, and the Grand Duke of Tuscany, under the protection of an Austrian expeditionary force, to Florence. Finally in Venice malaria and cholera made it impossible to resist the Austrian blockade any longer. By the end of the year a second restoration had been effected.

In fact, however, the situation in 1850 was very different. The Austrians had been shown to be vulnerable in the North; the Italians themselves had by now acquired a far keener sense of their national identity; the events of 1848–9, especially the defence of Rome, had revealed in the person of Garibaldi an Italian military commander of genius; and finally and decisively, Piedmont, despite the contempt

Charles-Albert had earned for his part in the recent wars, began to find a new sense of national purpose.

After his defeat at the hands of the Austrians in 1849, Charles-Albert abdicated in favour of his son Victor-Emmanuel. The new king's realism and the determination of his prime minister, D'Azeglio, succeeded in preserving for Piedmont a constitutional parliamentary monarchy throughout this demoralising period of reaction. First under D'Azeglio, and subsequently under Cavour, Piedmont gradually developed into the most enlightened and most efficiently administered state in the peninsula. As D'Azeglio himself put it, Turin, once 'the dullest, most insupportable city in the whole of Italy . . . now seems . . . the city where there is most liberty'.[6] It became a centre for exiles from other parts of Italy, and even such devout republicans as Garibaldi and Manin came to acknowledge the Kingdom of Piedmont as the natural leader in the movement for Italian independence rather than as a reactionary power that sought to exploit the patriotic movement for purposes of self-aggrandizement. This new unity of purpose ensured that the next war of independence could not be long delayed. When it did break, the speed at which the divisions imposed by legitimacy were to be swept away would astonish the world.

Artistic life

The years immediately following the Restoration of 1815 were as momentous in the history of Italy's artistic life as in its politics. During this period was formulated that distinctive Italian brand of Romanticism by which the young Verdi's artistic tastes were formed and on which his imagination was nourished. What is generally regarded as the manifesto of Italian Romanticism, Giovanni Berchet's *Lettera semiseria di Grisostomo*, appeared in 1816, and during 1817–18 the famed literary periodical *Il Conciliatore* acted as a forum for the discussion of the philosophical and technical questions associated with the new movement. Berchet and the *Conciliatore* anticipated the preoccupations of a whole era of Italian literature.

In most contexts the term 'Romanticism' is one of surpassing vagueness. But Manzoni was probably right when he observed that in Italy, and particularly 'in Milan, where it has been talked about more and for a longer time than elsewhere, the word 'Romanticism' has been adopted, if I am not mistaken . . ., to represent a combination of ideas more rational, better organized and more comprehensive than in any other place'.[7]

Manzoni was writing quite early in the history of Italian Romanticism, and at the time he had no doubt that its negative achievements outweighed the positive. Of these negative achievements he particularly emphasized 'its tendency to exclude – the use of mythology – the servile imitation of the classics – rules based not on general principles but on special cases, on the authority of the rhetoricians and not on reason, and especially the rule of the so-called dramatic unities of time and place attributed to Aristotle'.

Throughout the eighteenth century, the cult of the Antique, particularly of its mythology, and the preoccupation with harmoniousness of expression and perfection of form had been more vital issues in the literature of Italy than in that of any other nation. Such concerns had been specifically nurtured by the countless Arcadian academies in the peninsula. Already in the last decades of the century there were signs of reaction against a literary world that seemed, with the passing of the years, to become ever more precious, ever more remote from reality. It was not until after 1815, however, that the disaffection with the Arcadian classicizing tradition became a wholesale literary revolt, directed, in the name of progress and truth, against an idiom that had divorced literature from life and that in its cult of formal beauty had stood in the way of the rejuvenation of the language.

Although Italian Romanticism was so soon to develop a distinctive, national tone it was at first much stimulated by the Romantic literature of northern Europe. Indeed one of its most notable features was its cosmopolitanism. Italy had for so long been the source and pattern for so much of the artistic life of Europe that, though France might be accorded the homage due to a truly civilized nation, it had rarely occurred to Italian artists to ask what might be learned of England or of Germany. But by the early nineteenth century, when the distinction of Italian culture was by no means so obvious, this self-sufficiency was beginning to look like provincialism. Again and again the leaders of literary Romanticism emphasized the need to bring Italy back into the mainstream of European culture, especially by providing translations of the greatest foreign authors, ancient and modern.

The first to emphasize the value of such translations and the role they could play in reanimating Italy's stagnant literary life was apparently Madame de Staël, whose essay 'De l'esprit des traductions' set off a flurry of polemics when it was published in Italy in 1816. In the same year Berchet's *Lettera semiseria* proclaimed a similar idea in drastic terms: 'Homer, Shakespeare, Schiller are just as much *italiani di patria* as Dante, Ariosto and Alfieri.' Nor was this concern limited to the professional men of letters. Mazzini, in his 'Saggio sul dramma storico' (1830), a philosophical essay on the development to be wished for in the Italian theatre, emphasizes the exemplary educative value of translations – particularly, in the theatrical context, translations of Aeschylus, Shakespeare and Schiller.* The building up in the first half of the nineteenth century of a massive repertory of translations was one of the most monumental achievements of Italian Romanticism. And in the years after 1815, it was precisely this interest that made it possible for the forces of literary reaction to pose as the patriotic party, the upholders of Italy's cultural self-respect.

It was a claim that could not long be sustained. The best authors rapidly demonstrated that they were no more interested in servile imitations of Schiller or Byron than in servile imitations of Petrarch or Metastasio. Italians on the whole regarded with pronounced distaste the more bizarre manifestations of northern Romanticism, those features contemptuously described by Manzoni as 'a mishmash of witches and ghosts, a systematic disorder, a *recherché* extravagance, an abdication of common sense'. Even with Shakespeare, whose prestige among most of the Romantics was immense, who 'was by himself authority enough to counter the whole of Antiquity, of the Renaissance, of the eighteenth century',[8] Italian critics tended to play down that element which they described as 'the fantastic' in favour of the moral and the historical. Verdi himself, for choosing to make an operatic version of Shakespeare's 'fantastic' *Macbeth*, received something of a rebuke from Giuseppe Giusti, *risorgimento* Italy's finest satirical poet: 'the fantastic is something which puts the imagination to the test', Giusti wrote to him shortly after the *première*; 'the true is something which puts both the imagination and the heart to the test'.[9]

Probably a large number of Italians were simply too realistic to become really enthusiastic about the gothic apparatus of 'witches and ghosts'. They felt, like Manzoni, that such things were an affront to good sense, that they were unworthy of the attention of adult nineteenth-century men. Other aspects of Romanticism in its north European forms, notably the *Weltschmerz* of Byron and his imitators, were unacceptable to many writers on religious grounds. But

* Cf. below, p. 188.

the most interesting of the matters on which the best Italian artists parted company with the Romantics of England and Germany was in their belief that there were greater issues at hand than the joys and anguishes and imaginings of the hypersensitive individual. For most of the Italian Romantics the overriding concerns of the day were liberty and nationhood: and for this reason their literature tends not to make an exhibition of the singularities that distinguish the artist–hero from the common throng, but to emphasize those things that bind a nation together, especially religion and history. The way in which this ideal qualified the enthusiasm for north European Romanticism can best be seen in the literary essays of Mazzini, particularly in 'Byron and Goethe'. What, asks Mazzini, is the reason for the Byronic heroes' suffering and indignation?

They are alone; this is the secret of their wretchedness and impotence . . . They have never realized the conception of Humanity in the multitude that have preceded, surround and will follow after them; never thought on their own place between the past and future; on the continuity of labour that unites all the generations into one Whole . . .

. . . in our own day, we are beginning, though vaguely, to foresee this new social poetry, which will soothe the suffering soul by teaching it to rise towards God through Humanity . . .[10]

Giusti and Mazzini define quite clearly the antithesis between Italian and north European Romanticism. Against the northern artist's interest in the 'fantastic', Giusti would set the 'true'; against the Byronic (or Shakespearean or Goethean) egoism, Mazzini would set 'social poetry', the poetry of humanity. Under the circumstances it is hardly surprising that, once the battle with the classicizing Arcadians had been won, Italians began to doubt if 'Romanticism' was really an appropriate term to express their own interests and aspirations. A term that sometimes came to be preferred was *letteratura nazionale e moderna* (national and modern literature); it is more cumbersome than 'Romanticism', but it does define more clearly both the break with the Arcadian past and the contrast with Romanticism in its north European forms.

A prominent place in this national and modern literature was found for the Catholic Church. As in France, the Restoration was marked by a reaction against both the materialism of the revolutionary period and the paganism of the eighteenth century. Even those who chafed most impatiently at the restoration of the legitimate temporal powers rejoiced and assisted in the restoration of the religious authority of the Church: in Italy, 'neo-Guelphism' had no necessary connection with political reaction. Typical was the desire to reconcile the spiritual teachings of the Church with the social needs of mankind. The mood of the religious reaction was, in De Sanctis's memorable formulation, 'the famous trio, *liberty, equality, fraternity,* evangelized'.[11]

The religious preoccupations of the Italian Romantics are not necessarily to be seen in explicitly religious works. More interesting, because it overlaps more fruitfully with the political aspirations of the *risorgimento,* is the tendency to see the guiding hand of God in the course of history, the new belief in historical miracles and particularly in providence. The great events of the past are no longer to be explained in terms of human will or of material needs. At the spectacle of a Napoleon,

> . . . nui
> Chiniam la fronte al Massimo
> Fattor, che volle in lui
> Del creator suo spirito
> Più vasta orma stampar.

In the profusion of historical novels, historical plays and historical paintings that marked the Romantic era in Italy no less than in other European countries, it would probably be true to say that the interest in the remote, the mysterious, the exotic was rarely a significant factor. One should perhaps not assume that to discern the providential hand of God in the patterns of history was as important to all Italian writers as it was to Manzoni. But increasingly as the years passed history was explored for incidents and characters pertinent to the political and social needs of nineteenth-century Italy. By studying their own past Italians could discern the principles on which their aspirations to nationhood rested, they could perceive the follies and errors that had led to their present plight, and occasionally they could discover figures to act as paradigms for modern *risorgimento* man. The point at which the political objectives become supreme in this historical literature is marked by D'Azeglio;* but even the most fastidious artists proved adept at turning the Italian past into a mirror of the Italian present, as a stanza from a chorus in Manzoni's *Conte di Carmagnola* will serve to demonstrate:

> D'una terra son tutti: un linguaggio
> Parlan tutti: fratelli li dice
> Lo straniero: il comune lignaggio
> A ognun d'essi dal volto traspar.
> Questa terra fu a tutti nudrice,
> Questa terra di sangue ora intrisa,

---

* Cf. his comment quoted above, pp. 6–7.

Che natura dall'altre ha divisa,
E recinta con l'Alpe e col mar.

With this central concern of nineteenth-century Italian literature we have obviously come to the point where Italian Romanticism can best be described as the cultural arm of the *risorgimento*.

That literature should be an expression of the period and society in which it was written – that the artist was not a solitary seer conjuring exquisite artifacts out of the silence of his study, but a man who knew how to express the emotions and give form to the aspirations of the whole people – had been the most devoutly held tenet of the creed of the Italian Romantics since the days of *Il Conciliatore*. This *risorgimento*-inspired literature ran the whole gamut from simplistic propaganda to education in nationhood. At one extreme were the anti-Austrian allusions to be savoured in some of the popular theatres in Milan; at the other we might put the various treatments – by Berchet, D'Azeglio, Carducci, and of course Cammarano and Verdi – of what came to be seen as the most glorious event in the mediaeval history of Italy, the Battle of Legnano. Somewhere between these extremes was a regular flow of what one might describe as sublimated journalism. Any representative anthology of Italian verse will demonstrate the way in which the poets of the day celebrated the glorious and the tragic incidents of the *risorgimento*, from Rossetti's *La Costituzione di Napoli* and Manzoni's *Marzo 1821* onwards.

There was however one major problem for the writers who aspired to play a part in strengthening national self-awareness. D'Azeglio recalled it in his memoirs:

I was also turning over in my mind the notion of writing . . . It only remained to decide on what subject, with what purpose, in what sort of language and style I was to do it. Mere trifles! I often discussed this with Bidone, when I was in Turin. He gave me his usual advice. 'Write!' – 'But what about?' – 'Write!' – 'But the language, the style?' – 'Write!' – 'But', I said at last, 'if there is really no Italian language and no readable prose, what do I do?' 'If there is none, invent one!'[12]

A language that we would today recognize as Italian was spoken only in Tuscany. In the rest of Italy a whole range of local dialects were used for everyday purposes; many of them had their own literatures, and most of them were mutually unintelligible. In the various Italian courts and in government circles, French (Piedmont, and the Bourbon courts in Parma and Naples), German (Lombardy and the Veneto) and even ecclesiastical Latin (Rome) were used. Thanks to the achievements of Dante, Boccaccio and Petrarch in the fourteenth century, Tuscan had always enjoyed a unique prestige among the various Italian dialects, and had come to be recognized as Italy's literary language. But for the writers for whom Tuscan was not an everyday colloquial form it had become, as the centuries passed, progressively more stilted, more precious, more unfit to describe or express the common concerns of ordinary men. This was the problem that for D'Azeglio and Manzoni and their contemporaries stood in the way of that all-Italian intelligibility at which they aimed. The creation of a national language came increasingly to be seen as a necessary preliminary to the creation of an independent and unified Italy.

The greatest single contribution to the solution of the problem was doubtless that made by Manzoni with his novel *I Promessi Sposi*. During the early stages of writing, in the years after 1820, his dilemma was typical. To put literary Italian into the mouths of the peasant characters would be to deprive them of every semblance of vitality and verisimilitude; but to write for them in Milanese dialect – which he himself spoke – would be to give his book a merely provincial character that must limit its appeal in other parts of Italy. In the first version of the book, published in 1827, he attempted to mitigate this provincialism by a blending of Milanese and Tuscan elements. But despite the phenomenal success which *I Promessi Sposi* enjoyed, Manzoni remained unsatisfied. In 1827 he had visited Florence for the first time, and, entranced by the language, determined to rewrite his novel, transforming it linguistically by 'washing his linen in the Arno'. For twelve years he wrestled with the problems of Tuscan usage until between 1840 and 1842 he was able to write a revised version of what at once became Italy's greatest national book.

The urge to communicate, the artist's sense of being in fellowship with society, is one of the most admirable and impressive aspects of Italian Romanticism. In no other country did the towering achievements of music and literature provide so much spiritual nourishment and sheer pleasure for so large a proportion of the population. Verdi and Manzoni and their contemporaries believed that 'art, like truth, should be accessible to all; that, as everyone's soul is the same at bottom, so every clear beauty, every certain truth, is the domain of everyone,'[13] Stanzas from the choruses of Manzoni's plays were sung by the volunteers as they marched through the streets of Milan during the 1848 revolution; and the pleasing anecdote is told of a Genoese border guard who during Manzoni's journey to Florence in 1827 poked his head through the carriage window, and recited paragraphs of *I Promessi Sposi* by heart. The popular success enjoyed by Verdi as a composer was, we see, unique neither in degree nor in kind.

Society

It would be pretentious and superfluous to embark upon a comprehensive social anatomy of *risorgimento* Italy. Nevertheless some indication, however sketchy, of the kind of society Verdi lived in – its values, its pleasures, and, in particular, the place music held in it – seems imperative. The distinctiveness of local atmosphere, the survival of local traditions, the contrasts in the way of life between one region or city and another are notable features of life in Italy even today. In the *risorgimento* period, at a time when the Italians had shared very little history, and when each region lived under a different form of government, these contrasts were still more striking. D'Azeglio's memoirs provide a multitude of illustrations of the fact. He contrasts, for example, the nobility of Piedmont, 'active and energetic', with those of other parts of the peninsula, particularly Rome, 'an aristocracy of *non far niente*'.[14] For a man from Turin like D'Azeglio, Florence represented a 'land of exile'.[15] In later years, after experiencing life in Milan, he was oppressed by 'the regularity, the formality, the social distinctions, the Jesuitism; the absolute lack of any symptoms of energy or life' in Piedmont.[16] For the purposes of the present discussion, however, it will be sufficient to narrow the focus a little and consider not so much Verdi's Italy as Verdi's Milan.

Though by birth a subject of Maria Luigia of Parma, Verdi was as musician and man of the theatre a Milanese. It was in Milan that he had studied, and it was in Milan that he lived during the first ten years of his career. Of course during this period he paid extended visits to, and worked in, other areas of Italy. But it was Milan he belonged to; it was Milan that exerted the profound formative influence on him as man and artist.

Milan was the administrative capital of the Italian provinces of the Austrian Empire. It would therefore be easy to suppose – given present-day views on the subject of imperialism – that it was a centre of tyranny, repression and discontent. It was not. For several decades between the Restoration and 1848, Milan was the most justly and best administered, the most exuberantly creative, and, as far as one can judge, the happiest city in the peninsula. It is worth quoting D'Azeglio in this context, for though 'a professed hater of the foreigner' he could not, as a fair-minded man, refrain from attributing to the Austrians much credit for the amiable style of life in Restoration Milan. He admired the way in which

the Austrian authorities, intent perhaps on making themselves comfortable in a congenial, prosperous, rich and cheerful city, understood the art of quashing or softening the orders from Vienna and leaving the Milanese (except of course in matters of real substance) the greatest liberty to grumble, to mock the police, to give their authoritative judgement not only on the performances at La Scala, but even on politics: one just did not have to shout too loudly, but with a little prudence one could say anything . . . From 1840 to 1845 there was in Milan . . . a government so mild, so non-intimidatory, that among all the small governments of Italy there is not one which compared with the Austrian, has not been infinitely more horrible.[17]

Not surprisingly, therefore, anti-Austrian feeling was far from universal. It had to be cultivated, by the intellectuals and by the secret societies, and even in 1848 a substantial number of Italians were more sympathetically disposed to the Austrian Empire than to the prospect of a free and united Italy. The Austrian diplomat Alexander Graf von Hübner records how, in May 1848, at a time when Milan had just thrown out the Austrians and he was under a kind of house arrest, a young lady from Genoa who was living in the same house used to knock on his door whenever news was received of reverses for the Italians and 'whisper, with a rapturous expression on her face, *Grazia a Dio, siamo stati battuti*'.[18]

Hazlitt in 1826 and Liszt in 1838 were both impressed by the exuberance and enthusiasm with which the Austrian Emperor was received on his visits to Milan. The latter visit was on the occasion of his coronation in Milan Cathedral as King of Lombardy and the Veneto, and marked the apparently successful climax of the Austrian attempts to reconcile the Milanese to the Empire. And that this aim did not amount simply to blinding an ignorant populace with ostentatious pomp is clear from another incident recorded by Hübner:

I was in Milan in the years 1828 and 1838. This is my third visit. During my first stay I was too young for political observations. I only know that at that time the Milanese and the Germans enjoyed life together peaceably . . . In 1838 the Emperor Ferdinand was crowned King of Lombardy and Venetia . . . It was a time of reconciliation. On the one hand 1821 and 1830 were forgotten, on the other Silvio Pellico and the Spielberg. The emperor announced a general amnesty for all political prisoners. Milan was in a tumult of rejoicing and the salon of Prince Metternich, who accompanied the emperor on this journey, was the gathering place for the Lombard aristocracy. Besides Pasta, with Rossini at the piano, we heard Prince Belgiojoso sing, just returned home from exile. He was a tenor *di primo cartello.* – 'What a voice,' exclaimed the Princess Metternich, enraptured. – 'And what a misfortune for music,' replied Belgiojoso, 'if your husband had had me hanged.' We others, from the diplomatic staff of the Chancellor, were on the best of terms with the young man of fashion. Litta, Borromeo, d'Adda addressed us as 'Du', and overwhelmed us with civilities . . .[19]

Under the mild imperium of Austria, commercial and artistic life flourished in Milan as rarely before. Though it possessed no ancient university, and though the inherited prestige of Florence and Rome as centres of fine art could hardly be matched, Milan now confirmed that position as the centre of Italy's intellectual life which it had begun to win during the Napoleonic period. It had the most flourishing industries in Italy; its new public building schemes were the most ambitious; it was the city of Manzoni, Grossi, Porta, Pellico and Berchet, and consequently the headquarters of Italian Romanticism; its principal opera house, La Scala, had, in the opinion of most competent judges, ousted the San Carlo in Naples as the premier theatre in the peninsula. Just how stimulating and agreeable life in Restoration Milan could be is suggested by the enthusiasm of Stendhal.

I should never leave . . . if I were to follow my inclinations. I should spend all my leave in Milan. I have never met people I find so easy to take to my heart. When I am with the Milanese and when I speak Milanese, I forget that men are wicked, and all the wicked part of my own nature goes to sleep at once . . . But it is not just the men of the better sort . . . who make me regret leaving Milan; it is the *ensemble* of its ways, the naturalness of its manners, its good nature its great art of being happy, which is practised here with an additional charm, namely that the good people do not realize that it is an art, the most difficult art of all.[20]

Despite Stendhal, however, the 'great art of being happy' became an increasingly difficult one even for the Milanese. Some cultured men may be presumed to have retained this enviable facility; but deprived of the chance of taking responsibility for their own way of life, encouraged by the Austrian administration to take things easily and to enjoy themselves, a large number of well-to-do families in the city, particularly the young men, the so-called 'lions', devoted themselves not to the 'great art of being happy', but to idleness, to trivial and superficial pleasures, which became more gross as the years passed. D'Azeglio recalled that

as the House of Orleans consolidated its power in France . . . The people of Lombardy had recourse to their old consolation of eating, drinking and amusing themselves . . . During my residence in Milan, most young men spent their time in drinking and with chorus girls – they often married them! ! ! They cursed the Austrians and kept apart from them. They lived in sloth and profound ignorance. A few of the more daring involved themselves in all the secret, useless intrigues of the *Giovine Italia*.[21]

By the 1840s, according to Ghislanzoni, many of the public balls and masquerades held at the smaller Milanese theatres were little better than debauches. And as a demonstration of the political ramifications of such phenomena he recorded 'a private ball, where were assembled large numbers of people of both sexes, dressed in the very plain costume of Adam and Eve. The Austrian police were undisturbed by the scandal – Those dancers, so succinctly clad, were not the kind of people to conspire against the security of the state.'[22]

Ghislanzoni's 'history' is familiar to English readers through the extracts included by Frank Walker in his Verdi biography. The 'mordant chronicle' may be quoted a little more fully to counter the perhaps over-idealized image of Verdi's city given so far.

The streets were illuminated with oil lamps, and the flickering of the flames quite blinded the pedestrians – The Milanese boasted of the cleanliness of their city, and meanwhile the pavements were crossed by runnels which did not smell of musk. The cathedral, admired by visitors, served as a *pissoir* for the better kind of people, who, for the greater contempt of the building, were very numerous. – The city woke up about eleven in the morning; the real 'lions' did not appear in public until one o'clock in the afternoon ... Top hats towered over the heads of the elegant at the Porta Renzo and in the public gardens; but it was dangerous to approach the areas around Porta Ticinese or Porta Comasina with this symbol on one's head ...

Young men of the better class got drunk on port or madeira, and finally committed suicide by drinking absinth. This appalling beverage was introduced to Milan about 1840. – The fashion for moustaches and beards met with stubborn and fierce opposition ... Older men, public employees, and generally all the so-called responsible men shaved scrupulously from the nose to the throat. Students who wore beards or moustaches risked compromising their whole future: normally they were refused admission to the exams, or even expelled ...

It was not permitted to smoke in any public place, and before 1844, the few loafers who dared to stroll along the ramparts by the Porta Renzo or in the public gardens with a cigar in their mouths while the band was playing were regarded disapprovingly and reproached with bad manners. At the approach of a cigar, ladies pretended to swoon: at the sight of a pipe the fair and sterner sex alike were aghast ...

The ordinary people had neither newspapers nor books – their literature consisted of topical street songs – their politics were summed up in the motto; *viva nûn e porchi i sciori!** ... The pails of the milk-sellers went the round of the streets uncovered, or covered only by a layer of flies. There was a butcher in every street; the pigs and the calves brutally dragged along on

* 'Up with us and the nobs are pigs!'

carts filled the streets with the sound of their squeals . . . Little attention was paid to public hygiene.

It would be unwise to ascribe literal truthfulness to all Ghislanzoni's observations. But better than any other contemporary chronicler, he does make it clear that Milan was one of the nineteenth century's real big cities, teeming with the same multifarious life, boasting the same shocking contrasts of opulence and squalor, as Dickens's London.

Among the occasions of social intercourse the so-called *corso*, a post-prandial ride round the public gardens in a horse-drawn carriage, was virtually obligatory for the wealthier classes, a ritual of far greater significance than the comparable ride round the Hyde Park Ring in nineteenth-century London. Stendhal suggests one of the reasons why:

In all Italian cities there is a *Corso*, or general parade of high society. Is it a Spanish custom, like that of the *cicisbeo*?

In summer, on returning from the *corso*, one stops in the Corsia de' Servi to eat ices; one goes home for ten minutes, after which one goes to La Scala. It is claimed that these ten minutes are the time of the rendezvous [that is, between a married woman and her recognized gallant] and that a slight signal on the *Corso*, such as a hand rested on the carriage door, indicates whether there is a possibility of presenting oneself that evening.[23]

Cicisbeism, introduced from Spain during the period of Spanish rule in the late seventeenth century, declined slowly during the Restoration period, but certainly had not died out completely in Verdi's time. The principle of it is best explained by Hazlitt: 'It is a kind of *marriage within a marriage*; it begins with infidelity to end in constancy; it is not a state of licensed dissipation, but is a real chain of the affections, superadded to the first formal one, and that often lasts for life . . . In noble families the lover must be noble; and he must be approved by the husband.'[24]

If a marriage turned out less than ideally happy, upper-class Italians of the period set little store by the virtue of mere dutiful fidelity. No disrepute attached to the practice of cicisbeism; no secrecy was felt to be necessary. Women rode in the carriages of their lovers and were escorted by them at the opera. Indeed Stendhal tells us that in his time, when cicisbeism was still in its heyday, it was only if 'the woman really found herself without a lover that her husband did her the service of accompanying her'.[25]

One feature of social life that impressed visitors from abroad was the fact that families did not 'entertain', that invitations for dinner were virtually never given. Poor homesick Otto von Nicolai thought it was because Roman wives were too lazy to apply themselves to the modest arts that become the *Hausfrau*.[26] Stendhal suggested that in Milan they were still haunted by the 'Spanish ideas of the luxury that was to be displayed on these occasions'.[27] The most important reason we shall come to in a moment, but there is no doubt that this omission was deplored by starchier visitors.

There were however, especially in Milan, the salons, the gatherings of friends with common artistic or intellectual or political interests, in the drawing-rooms of some well-to-do and accomplished lady, who acted as hostess. The leading Milanese painter of the period, Francesco Hayez, recalled in his memoirs the evenings he spent in the Casa Traversi: 'In this house I frequently heard Guiditta Pasta, the elder Ronconi, I got to know Taglioni and many first-rate artists, and others who became famous later. – The concerts alternated with improvised snacks, so-called *risotti*, during which the atmosphere was one of unaffected gaiety.'[28]

Of these Milanese salons two were particularly celebrated in Verdi's time: that of the bizarre and sensual Russian Countess Samoyloff, and that of Clarina Maffei. Samoyloff has earned a footnote in the history of Italian music as a collector of lovers from the world of opera, and more than a footnote in the social history of Milan where her prodigality and ostentation were a byword. Admirers are said to have made ice-cream out of the asses' milk in which she bathed. But because her salon was pro-Austrian it became gradually less influential during the 1840s, and could certainly have offered nothing congenial to a man of Verdi's temperament.

The salon of Clarina Maffei was another matter. Founded in 1834, it became almost at once a centre of Milanese artistic life. Clarina's husband Andrea was himself a poet of repute, particularly admired for his translations of Schiller, and among the earlier members of the salon were Grossi, D'Azeglio, Carcano, Hayez, and from 1842, after the success of *Nabucco* had made him a national figure, Verdi himself. Verdi, indeed, rapidly became one of the most intimate members of the salon, a life-long friend of both Clarina and Andrea. In 1846 he was one of the two witnesses who supervised the legal proceedings when the Maffeis decided to separate.

From the start the Maffei salon had been tinged with anti-Austrian feelings. Austrian residents or visitors to Milan, no matter how distinguished, were never invited. And in the prevailing atmosphere of sensuousness and frivolity, of which the Samoyloff salon was a resplendent example, the Maffeis endeavoured to preserve what were seen as the old Milanese virtues – what Carcano called 'the traditions of respect and courtesy, a certain Spanish *hauteur*, tempered by Ambrosian amiability'.[29]

The love of music was virtually universal in Italy: music, specifically opera, was the favourite pastime of the greater part of the population. Milan had some half-dozen theatres in which opera was regularly performed, and this was not untypical of the greater cities in the peninsula. There were besides the marionette theatres, in which straight or parodied versions of the most popular operas were given to audiences who could not afford La Scala. In Genoa, Lady Blessington found that 'in every street, voices are heard singing the strains of Rossini with a gusto that is unknown save in the sunny south'.[30] Dickens's *vetturino* in 1846 'had a word and a smile, and a flick of his whip, for all the peasant girls, and odds and ends of the Sonnambula for all the echoes'.[31] And in the industrial town of Carrara he found that such operas as those of Bellini held the same kind of place in the hearts of Italian workers as *Messiah* did in the industrial towns of northern England: 'it is an interesting custom there, to form the chorus of labourers in the marble quarries, who are self-taught and sing by ear. I heard them in a comic opera and in an act of "Norma"; and they acquitted themselves very well . . .'[32]

It was operatic music that formed the basis of the repertory performed in the salons; opera transcriptions were played in the open air by the military bands and by the barrel-organs: organists played arias and overtures as voluntaries at Mass. In Milan, said Ghislanzoni, the opera house was the 'major preoccupation of cultivated society'. It was, observed Stendhal, 'the city's salon. There is no society except there; no open houses. Whatever the business may be, people say, "We will see you at La Scala".'[33]

The attractions of La Scala for the Milanese, the absolutely central position which it and the artists who worked there held during the *risorgimento* period, may be illustrated by these words of D'Azeglio:

I was writing [*Nicolo de' Lapi*] . . . to stir up the Italians and to call their attention to matters rather more important than the contracts of ballerinas and singers. But I hasten to admit that I did not for a moment dream of playing the dirty trick on the impresarios of emptying the great La Scala. I realized that not only did the great performers exert an irresistible tyranny over the spirits of the Milanese, but that everything related to La Scala . . . was at that time in Milan a matter of far keener interest and affection than the whole crowd of us artists or writers. And in this connection one must pay tribute to the refinement and shrewdness of the Austrian government. For years they could be said to have governed Lombardy by means of La Scala, and one has to admit that for some time they succeeded well.[34]

Theatrical censorship

Few composers have suffered more from theatrical censorship than Verdi, and few combated its absurd manifestations more stoutly. Before discussing the nature of *ottocento* opera, it will be helpful to examine the way in which all Italian dramatists of the period had their work checked, inhibited and frustrated by such censorship. In this issue those political and artistic currents described in chapter 1 converge in a bizarre but illuminating conflict of values.

From the political circumstances of Restoration Italy it naturally followed that no one set of principles applied to censorship throughout the peninsula. In Piedmont, in the Austrian territories of Lombardy and the Veneto, in the duchies and grand duchies of central Italy, in the Papal States and in the Kingdom of Naples, censorship was administered by a multitude of different authorities in a multitude of different ways. An opera or spoken drama deemed by one such authority fit for public presentation could be totally banned or severely expurgated by another. In the early years of the Restoration their relative severity was perhaps most clearly indicated by their attitude to the plays of Alfieri. When Stendhal was in Naples in 1817, he recorded in his diary:

I have been to *Saul*, at the Teatro Nuovo. This tragedy (by Alfieri) must exert some power over the *secret nationalism* of the Italians. It rouses them to transports ... My friend the marquis tells me that only three of Alfieri's tragedies are permitted here; four in Rome; five in Bologna; seven in Milan; none in Turin. Consequently to applaud them is a point of honour, and to find fault with them is the mark of an *ultra*.[1]

The Austrian authorities in Milan were, it will be seen, the mildest in the whole of Italy, though here too censorship became much more stringent after the revolution of 1848. Verdi, whose early years were spent largely in the Austrian territories, suffered comparatively little, so long as he was composing for Milan or Venice. It was when he attempted to introduce his *risorgimento* idealism or his dramatic boldness to Rome or Naples that real aggravation arose.

Censorship in all parts of Italy was concerned with three issues, political offence, religious offence and moral offence. In general it may be said that the last exercised the censors least, though even in the Austrian territories it did cause the total banning of a substantial number of romantic dramas, particularly those of Victor Hugo. The attitude on such matters is clearly stated in one of the reports of Torresani, the prefect of police in Milan: 'Theatres are designed to correct morals, and must therefore never present anything but moral themes, or, if they present vice and wickedness, it must be done in such a way that virtue appears the more glorious and beautiful as a result.'[2]

Authors of librettos for operas were required to have their choice of subject approved before they actually began writing, and such approval was occasionally withheld on moral grounds. In 1843 Verdi was refused permission by the Venetian authorities to compose an opera based on Dumas père's *Catherine Howard* on the grounds that it indulged in 'excessive atrocity'. And the same authorities were at first implacably hostile to the idea of *Le Roi s'amuse* (*Rigoletto*), deploring the fact that 'The poet Piave and the celebrated maestro Verdi were unable to find some other field in which to exhibit their talents than one of such repellent immorality and obscene triviality as the theme of the libretto entitled *La Maledizione* . . . His Excellency has therefore determined absolutely to forbid the performance of this work.'[3]

Religious offences – that is to say not simply subjects or expressions which were regarded as heretical or blasphemous, but those which in any way trespassed upon the authority of the Church, its clergy or its liturgy – were generally taken more seriously. Out of the authoritarian piety of the period came a nervous and pettifogging scrupulousness, which saw mischief on two quite opposite fronts. On the one hand was the horror of religious rebellion or unorthodoxy which led to such rules as that current in Naples that mention must never be made of Luther, Campanello, Voltaire, or Gioberti; on the other, the feeling that the Church was sullied by association with the theatre. To cite the enemies of the faith was irreligious propaganda; to cite the defenders of the faith was blasphemy. Phrases from the Bible or from the liturgy were forbidden: hence the virtual suppression of the last scene of *Stiffelio* at Trieste in 1850, for it centres upon a gospel reading, the story of the woman taken in adultery. Even the use of such words as 'angelo' and 'cielo' was looked at askance in some parts. In 1851 the Archbishop of Ferrara reported to the minister of the interior for the Papal States that he had forbidden the performance of *Luisa Miller* because of the frequent use made of the words 'angelo', 'inferno', 'cielo', 'Iddio'.

Theatrical censorship

There is no doubt however that it was on political issues that the censors were strictest. Subjects, situations, or phrases that implied disrespect toward sovereigns or established governments, expressions of patriotism or libertarianism, mention of conspiracy or assassination, were all alike regarded with distrust, and in some parts of the country, notably Rome and Naples, they might well lead to the suppression or expurgation of the libretto. One instance may be given of the kind of emendation which so many censors felt it proper to make in the interests of state security. At Rome, the censor Abate Somai found dangerously inflammatory the sentence:

> Amo la patria e intrepido
> Il mio dovere adempio!

It returned from his office emended to

> Amo la sposa e intrepido
> Il mio dovere adempio!

promoting at the performance a public reaction which, as Di Stefano observes, should have been easily foreseeable.

Before the argument is taken further, the principles according to which censorship attempted to operate may be summarized by citing the weightiest of the rules laid down for the censor in the comparatively liberal Grand Duchy of Tuscany in 1822.

Dramas based on subjects taken from the Old Testament are permitted when written by celebrated authors and in a sublime style worthy of the subject, and when the theatre and the means of the impresario provide the necessary facilities for presenting them in a dignified and fitting manner.

No performance can be permitted of a drama based on subjects taken from the history and the affairs of the Church.

It will be necessary to take the most scrupulous care to see that in the ballets, even the serious ones, nothing should be permitted which could relate to the history of the Old Testament or to that of the Church.

The general rules for the censorship of [printed] works in which are disseminated religious principles or principles that are politically subversive, or of works based on a malicious plan threatening to weaken or destroy veneration for Religion or for the Throne and which awaken in people's minds emotions hostile to either of these, will be applied more strictly to theatrical performances.

Equally to be banned from the stage are all those comedies which could offend morals and good manners and at which every class of person could not properly be present, especially those representing sinful love affairs, faithless husbands and wives, scandalous intrigues with young girls who marry or even become mothers clandestinely, before finally forcing from their parents consent for what they have done; all those, in short, in which insubordination and lack of respect in the children is seen to triumph over paternal authority.

Also to be excluded from the theatre are all those tasteless pieces in which are exhibited only crimes and atrocious deeds, such as assassination, premeditated murder, despairing suicides, and such other topics as are rendered interesting only by the singular difficulty or the barbarous circumstances attending the crime . . .

The judgement of the censor will be very sharp on performances based on stories from Italian history, and prohibit absolutely performances of a kind which could in any way offend the conscience and the principles of modern times. He should also forbid under all circumstances performances in which appear members of the royal families of Europe who lived in ages not far distant from our own.

The so-called 'dramas of feeling', generally translated from the German or the French, in which dangerous and exalted passions appear on the stage may be tolerated, but not encouraged, and the censor will forbid absolutely those which give clear evidence of tending to corrupt the heart and deprave morals . . .[4]

It need only be added that in some of the more repressive states, notably in Rome, the censors concerned themselves not only with the texts of plays and operas but also with costumes and stage designs. Their solicitude in this particular was not chiefly about whether the costumes might be immodest, but whether they might by their combination of colours make allusion to the Italian flag.

Such comprehensive principles of censorship were differently exercised in the different states. In Milan, the chief of police, Torresani, seems to have been the sole authority. In Palermo, too, censorship was largely the responsibility of the chief of police, though here he was assisted by twelve professors from the university, all of them priests or monks. The most cumbersome apparatus was certainly that in Rome. Here every theatrical work had to undergo a threefold process of examination, at the hands of an ecclesiastical censor for 'religion, morals and good manners', a political censor for 'respect for the law and persons', and a municipal censor for 'philological matters'. So cumbrous had the procedure become, so numerous were the busy bodies involved, that no fewer than forty-one copies of an opera libretto had to be submitted to the censors' office.

Nevertheless the censors' task cannot have been an easy one, especially if, like Torresani, they had broader responsibilities. The Austrian authorities in Lombardy and the Veneto, although they were keenly aware of its inflammatory potential, did in some measure rely on a flourishing theatre for keeping their Italian subjects in an amiable frame of mind. Both D'Azeglio and Ghislanzoni comment on the astute way in which the Austrians encouraged the Italians to enjoy themselves. It was no doubt this consideration that made Torresani, once Verdi had become a celebrity with *Nabucco*, such an enlightened wielder of censorial powers, not only 'refusing to clip the wings of so promising a genius' in the case of *I Lombardi*, but actually going out of his way to encourage Verdi to help make a success of the Milan revival of *Attila*, a work which, as he cannot have failed to observe, was bound to provoke a fair amount of nationalist excitement. The wholehearted enjoyment of what was going on in the theatre, even if it did occasionally boil over into a patriotic furore, was, it was calculated, less of a threat to the stability of the Empire than sullen resentment.

This was a dilemma of policy; in other cases censors were faced with a dilemma of practicability. The regulations drawn up for the Florentine censors show that particular care was taken over those subjects taken from Italian history, and those in which appeared members of the royal families of Europe. It was such considerations that led in 1849 to Verdi's being absolutely refused permission to base an opera on Guerrazzi's *L'Assedio di Firenze*. But the censors rapidly acquired expertise in manipulating what was intended to be a less blunt instrument than a total ban. Countless are the cases in which they attempted to draw the sting, whether political or religious, from a suspect work, by changing its title and the names of its characters, and transferring its action to a different country and a different period. Thus when performed in Rome, Verdi's *Giovanna d'Arco* became *Orietta di Lesbo*, Rossini's *Guillaume Tell* became *Rudolfo di Stirling*. Throughout Italy, after the failure of the wars of independence in 1848–9, *La Battaglia di Legnano* became *L'Assedio d'Arlem*; *Le Roi s'amuse* was eventually rendered respectable by being transformed into *Rigoletto*.

But here arose the censors' difficulty. For if *La Battaglia di Legnano* could be transformed into *L'Assedio d'Arlem* by the censor, equally a *Battaglia di Legnano* could be read into an *Assedio d'Arlem* by the audience. Patriotic emotions ostensibly belonging to fifteenth-century France, or eleventh-century Scotland, or wherever it might be, could very easily be transformed into comments on nineteenth-century Italy. As one Florentine censor noted in a report on Niccolini's *Ludovico il Moro*, 'the perplexity of the censor is due to the public reaction to these works of Niccolini, and the interpretation which they give them over and above their literal meaning'.[5]

The censors' solution to this problem again varied from place to place. In the Austrian territories, and in Tuscany at least, they seem to have shrugged their shoulders and accepted the situation with fair good humour. The story is told of a performance of Niccolini's

Giovanni da Procida in Florence at which the French *chargé d'affaires*, Visconte Villiers di Lanone, was moved to exclaim, 'What amazes me is that His Highness the grand duke can sit calmly in his box listening to all the insults so impertinently addressed to a friendly power.' To which the Austrian minister, Conte Lodovico di Bourbelles, replied: 'Keep calm, my friend, it is addressed to you, but the letter is for me!'[6] Elsewhere, in Rome and Naples for example, attempts to circumvent such secondary meanings were taken to grotesque lengths, particularly during the 1850s. A run of performances of *La Traviata* at the Teatro Argentino in Rome in 1859–60 was suspended after the first night, because the audience had applauded the phrase 'la crisi non le concede che poche ore', choosing to see it not just as a medical comment on Violetta's health, but also as an allusion to the impending demise of Papal government.

A particularly bizarre episode in the history of the Roman censorship occurred in 1852–3, when G. G. Belli was appointed one of the censors. Belli still enjoys the reputation of being the wittiest, most open-minded and realistic portrayer of Roman life of the period; yet his censorship, as if he were attempting to undermine the authority of the institution by the preposterousness of his zeal, was of an unparalleled pedantry. Belli's principles were such that, if strictly observed, 'all that could be recited in the theatre would be the rosary'.[7] It was during this period that *Il Trovatore* had its *première* in Rome, although Belli himself was not one of the censors who examined Cammarano's libretto. Neither politics nor religion plays a particularly significant part in *Il Trovatore*, and in any case Verdi took care not to commit himself to a Roman *première* until he was assured that the dramatic essentials of his opera would remain intact. Nevertheless the original Roman libretto provides instructive instances of the kind of petty irritations to which the artists of the period were ever subject.

Almost all the alterations made by the censors fall into the categories already distinguished – those made in the interests of morality, of religion and of politics – though there is a smaller group of alterations which, even if we assume they had some serious purpose at the time, now seem quite pointless. Thus in Luna's recitative in I.3, the phrase 'l'amorosa fiamma m'arde ogni fibra' is changed to ''l'amorosa vampa . . .' and Azucena's cantabile in III.4 begins not 'Giorni poveri vivea' but 'Ivi poveri vivea'.

The censor with responsibility for public morality must be allowed an eagle eye for improprieties. In Azucena's *racconto*

'Condotta all'era in ceppi', Cammarano had included the phrase 'fra bestemmie oscene, pungendola coi ferri', and though he neither quoted nor further particularized the 'obscene oaths', he was judged to have been too bold, and the phrase becomes 'tra i più duri oltraggi, pungendola coi ferri'. Twice Leonora's expressions of amorous abandon are either consecrated or chastened. Thus in I.4, the phrase 'Al fin ti guida Pietoso amor tra queste braccia' is modified to 'Al fin ti guida Pietoso amor alla tua sposa', though of course Leonora is not Manrico's *sposa*; and in IV.2, the bold undertaking to give Luna 'Me stessa' becomes simply 'La mano'. The most obvious emendations in this area are, however, those made with a view to expunging all mention of witches and enchantment, and substituting for them gipsies and poison. In Ferrando's aria in I.1 we have instead of 'Cingeva i simboli di maliarda', 'Mostrava al tremito l'alma bugiarda'; instead of 'Ammaliata egli era!', 'Avvelenato egli era!'; instead of 'la fatucchiera perseguitata', 'la delinquente perseguitata', etc.

On religious grounds a larger number of phrases were found objectionable. For every use of 'Dio', 'angelo', 'altare', 'inferno' more or less happy synonyms or paraphrases had to be found. Once or twice Cammarano had done more than make free with the vocabulary of the Church; he had even gone so far as to introduce ideas which, if read as literal statements rather than as examples of poetic hyperbole, could be deemed contrary to its doctrine. Thus in II.2 Manrico exclaims:

> No, che basta ad arrestarmi
> Terra e ciel non han possanza,

and in IV.*ult.* Leonora says:

> T'arrendi . . . fuggi o sei perduto!
> Nemmeno il cielo salvarti può!

Both these impugnments of divine power needed correction, becoming respectively:

> No, che basti al arrestarmi
> Niuno in terra avrà possanza,

and

> Ti arrendi . . . fuggi, o sei perduto,
> O il ciel soltanto salvarti può.

The religious censor, Antonio Ruggieri, found himself most exercised, however, when he discovered in IV.1 a chorus built around

29

the liturgical word 'Miserere', which furthermore mentioned in one sentence the 'divine bounty' and the 'infernal sojourn'.

> Miserere d'un alma già vicina
> Alla partenza che non ha ritorno!
> Miserere di lei, bontà divina,
> Preda non sia dell'infernal soggiorno!

The ineptness of his attempt to improve this has become notorious:

> Ah! pietade d'un alma già vicina
> Alla partenza che non ha ritorno;
> Ah! pietade di lei che si avvicina
> Allo splendor dell'immortal soggiorno.

The inadequacy of Cammarano's attempts to indicate something of the political and social background of *Il Trovatore* is already one of the most obvious faults of the libretto. When it left the office of C. Doria, the political censor, his shadowy hints had become even more insubstantial. Mention of 'civil guerra' (1.2), of a 'proscritto' (1.5) and of 'prigionieri . . . di Stato' (IV.1) were deleted, and phrases that appeared disrespectful of monarchy and government were paraphrased. Thus in Manrico's romanza in 1.3 the lines

> Ma s'ei quel cor possiede,
> Bello di casta fede,
> E d'ogni re maggior
> Il Trovator

became

> . . . di casta fede,
> Egli è d'ogni uom maggior
> Il Trovator

while in IV.2 the sense of the phrase in which Luna expresses his guilty conscience

> Abuso io forse del poter che pieno
> In me trasmise il prence! A tal mi traggi,
> Donna per me funesta!

is completely ignored in the censor's correction:

> Giusto è il rigor: perversa stirpe è questa,
> D'ogni delitto piena . . . Ed essa l'ama! . . .
> Donna per me funesta!

So far we have only considered the changes to individual words and phrases in Cammarano's libretto, matters which though they may sometimes weaken the sense or the liveliness of a passage do not materially damage the drama as a whole. Twice, though, the censors went further than this, requiring that no mention should be made of two of the turning-points in the story: Leonora's decision in Act I to take the veil and withdraw into a nunnery, and her suicide in Act IV. The latter incident is cryptic enough in Cammarano to start with, being suggested only in a phrase and stage-direction in scene 1, 'sicura, Presta è la mai difesa. (*I suoi occhi figgonsi ad una gemma che le fregia la mano destra)*', and retrospectively in the final scene:

> Ah! fu più rapida
> La forza del veleno
> Ch'io non pensava!

In the censored version, however, Leonora is not permitted to gaze significantly at the gem which, we take it, conceals a phial of poison; and in the final scene her words are altered to

> Ah! fu più rapida
> Ch'io non pensava . . . almeno
> Presso te spirò!

Why and how she dies are matters now left entirely to the imagination of the audience.

Quite the most ludicrous and protracted bout of censorial wriggling comes with the nunnery scene. The process begins with the message brought to Manrico in II.2, that

> Giunta la sera,
> Tratta in inganno di tua morte al grido,
> Nel vicin Chiostro della croce il velo
> Cingerà Leonora.

The censor gives the message a touch of romantic mystery:

> . . . di tua morte al grido,
> Per sempre in ermo impenetrabil loco
> Fuggirà Leonora.

Nevertheless, by the next scene both Luna and Manrico have found their way to this 'remote impenetrable spot', and the action continues as before. The stage is still dominated by the monastic buildings, a female chorus still sings of the peace of a retired life, Leonora still bids the world farewell; yet all specific mention of God, altar, rite, or veil is suppressed. The fecund evasiveness of the censor may be exemplified in a pair of juxtaposed stanzas:

Cammarano:	Censor:
Vieni e t'asconda il velo Ad ogni sguardo umano!	Vieni, a tranquilla stanza Il tuo destin ti chiama;

Auro o pensier mondano
Qui vivo più non è.
Al ciel ti volgi e il cielo
Si schiuderà per te.

Un riso, una speranza, un fior la
  terra
Non ha per me! Degg'io
Volgermi a Quei che degli
  afflitti è solo
Sostegno e dopo i penitenti
  giorni
Può fra gli eletti al mio
  perduto bene
Ricongiungermi un dì . . .
  Tergete i rai
E guidatemi all'ara!

Pace, che ogn' alma brama,
Pose quì solo il piè.
Or vieni, e la speranza
Rieda, ch'è morta in te.

Un riso, una speranza, un fior
  la terra
Non ha per me! Degg'io
In quest'asil remoto, ad ogni
  incauto
Sguardo celarmi ognor e i mesti
  giorni
Trar nel dolor, che il mio
  perduto bene
Destommi eterno in cor! . . .
  Tergete i rai
Il mio destin si compia!

The operatic experience

The easy contempt with which so many historians have described the state of music in the Italy of Verdi's youth is no new phenomenon. To the musicians from France and Germany who visited Italy at that time, operatic conventions already appeared decadent and alien, and theatrical manners wholly unacceptable to anyone with a proper appreciation of the place of art in civilized life. From Naples in 1831, Mendelssohn complained that the Italians treated music 'like an article of fashion, coldly, indifferently, scarcely concerned even with the appearance of courtesy';[1] and the experience of Berlioz's sojourn in Italy in 1831 and 1832 confirmed him in a similar opinion. 'The behaviour of audiences beyond the Alps is so humiliating to art and to artists', he averred, 'that I confess I would as soon sell pepper and cinnamon in a grocer's shop in the rue Saint-Denis as write for the Italians.'[2]

Not all, but a majority of such visiting musicians were convinced not only that the great creative days of Italian music were a thing of the past, but that even the art of performing opera was dead. Mendelssohn in 1830, and Gounod in 1840 felt that one could get a truer impression of the qualities of Italian opera in Paris or in London than in Italy. And when Dickens was in Italy in 1846 he was moved to observe: 'Our English dilettanti would be very pathetic on the subject of the national taste, if they could hear an Italian opera half as badly sung in England as we may hear the Foscari performed, tonight, in the splendid theatre of San Carlo.'[3] How tantalizing to think that one might have had a Dickensian description of a Verdi production of that period!

As the terms of Mendelssohn's and Berlioz's letters show, the root of the problem, as far as they were concerned, was that Italy had not yet come to accept the Romantic view of the artist as a man apart. His vocation did not entitle him to any special veneration, nor was the music he wrote approached with any glimmering of holy awe. It was a commodity to be used as its consumers thought fit. And if we are less impatient of such a view now than we used to be, there is no point in denying that it did lead to innumerable tasteless and trivial abuses. Changing the order of scenes or even of whole acts, omitting sections of the score to suit the convenience of one singer, and introducing movements from other works to gratify another were all malpractices rife at the time. Two specimens may be cited, for both of which the impresario Bartolomeo Merelli was responsible. In 1843, announcing a performance of Donizetti's *Fausta* to be given in Bergamo, Merelli claimed that the work had been specially revised by the composer. Nothing of the kind had in fact been done, so Merelli was obliged to play out the pretence by removing two of the numbers and in their place 'adding a cavatina by maestro Savj, and the finale of *Les Martyrs*.'[4] Verdi, who abhorred this kind of meddling, was himself the victim on the other occasion: at a Milan performance of *I Due Foscari* attended by Tsar Nicholas I in 1845, the third act was performed before the second. Certain types of piracy further undermined any aspirations a composer might have to think of an opera as a 'work of art'. Bellini complained of the habit of 'many Milanese publishers who have piano reductions of my operas orchestrated, and sell them as if they were really mine, with the result that the effect of the opera is quite ruined'.[5] One does not need to have a Wagnerian conception of the holiness of art to find such goings-on as these entirely reprehensible.

Verdi certainly could not have supposed that the musical life he knew was ideal in every respect. Indeed, at times of humiliation or distress (after the *première* of *Un Giorno di Regno*, for example), or in darker moods during the 'years in the galley', his sense of the wretchedness of the life of an Italian artist could be expressed with a bitterness which no visiting foreigner could match. Generally, however, Verdi acquiesced in the theatrical world he knew. He admired the ability and the style of its performers; he recognized that his job as a composer was to delight and to thrill an audience, and conversely that the audiences had every right to pass judgement on what was served up to them; he participated without apparent distaste in the various rituals that the theatrical etiquette of the day demanded. When he came across other traditions of performance in London or in Paris, nothing that he said or wrote suggested that he found them self-evidently superior to those in Italy. Indeed, Verdi's view was that Italian musical practice did have its own proper stylishness and validity, as this passage from a letter to Escudier shows: '[Hiller] knows nothing about the way we perform operas; because, whether you like it or not, in Italy they are performed differently than they are with you: I don't know whether they are done better or worse, but I repeat they are done differently . . . For performing Italian music (note this bizarrerie well!) I should like Italian names . . .'[6]

The repertory

For a long time the operatic year had been divided into three seasons: the Carnival season, commencing on 26 December and continuing until Lent; the Spring season, beginning after Easter and ending in June; and the Autumn season, beginning early in September and lasting until Advent. In the larger Italian cities, during the period with which we are concerned, the major opera houses tended to extend their seasons. For example, at La Scala, from 1834 onwards, the start of the Autumn season was pushed back into the middle of August. But the most interesting development during these years was the theatrical deconsecration of Lent. The German violinist and composer Spohr happened to be in Naples when this innovation took place in February 1817, and he recorded some of the incidental details in his autobiography: 'Yesterday Carnival ended, and Lent has begun. After the din of the last days of Carnival the calm that has now descended is really welcome, though the evenings do become somewhat tedious as all the theatres are closed for four days. In the San Carlo theatre this year, instead of the customary oratorios, operas will be given as usual, but without ballets, which are absolutely forbidden during this time.'[7] Thenceforth, in the principal theatres at least, the Carnival season was transformed into a Carnival and Lent season extending into March.

Not all cities could support opera houses providing three seasons of opera each year. And even in the biggest cities, where several different theatres were used for opera, it would be rare for more than one of these to be open during all three seasons. In Rome, for example, there were three theatres: the Apollo or Tordinona, the longest-established and grandest of them, which specialized in a repertory of heroic opera and sumptuous ballets; the Argentina, where both heroic and comic opera was performed and where the ballets were of a lighter kind; and the Valle for comic opera, where spoken dramatic intermezzos took the place of the ballets of the more august establishments. Of these three theatres, only the Valle opened for the Carnival, Spring and Autumn seasons; the Apollo offered only a Carnival Season, the Argentina a Carnival season and sometimes one other.[8]

This emphasis on the Carnival season was by no means a Roman speciality. Throughout Italy it was regarded as the most important of the three; the longest, socially the most brilliant, musically the most exciting. In small theatres it was often the only season; and if a great theatre fell on bad times, as La Scala did in the 1850s, it contrived at least to put on a respectable show for Carnival. The opening night of the Carnival season was the most dazzling occasion of the year, as Stendhal recorded:

Since the day when *Religion* stalked back into the land to reclaim its birthright, there is no opera performed during Advent . . . with the result that, now, the old, tense anticipation of novlity is increased a thousand-fold by deprivation of the foremost requirement of life . . . Not a woman in the whole theatre, on that evening, but is decked out in the gayest and most gorgeous of her gala-dresses . . . I should merely be wasting my time if I were to attempt a description of the wild extravagance of these carnival *premières*.[9]

In Rome – where, according to Spohr, the only music to be heard during Advent was that of the hordes of bagpipe virtuosos who descended on the city from the hills across the Naples border – the opening of the Carnival season in the Apollo theatre was marked by a splendid banquet provided by the governor of the city for the owners of the boxes (*apocati*) in the second and third tiers. No wonder Giuseppina Strepponi described Saint Stephen (26 December is St Stephen's Day) as 'a drunken saint and a bad judge [of music]'.[10]

A season of opera in a major opera house of the period would generally have consisted of between fifty and eighty performances.[11] In Naples, where opera was performed on only three days of the week, it would clearly have been less. Given the small number of singers engaged for such a season, the strain on them was considerable. It was by no means unusual to sing in five performances during a single week, and in the event of a temporary indisposition a singer could be required to make up for lost time by performing every night in the following week. This happened to Giuseppina Strepponi in October 1839, for example.[12] Under the circumstances it is hardly surprising that premature loss of voice – as in Strepponi's case – or total exhaustion towards the end of a season were common phenomena.

Nor was a single evening's performance the kind of project in which a present-day musician would lightly involve himself. For the custom of performing an opera with ballet intermezzos which Charles III had introduced to Naples in 1735 was still current throughout the peninsula, making an evening's entertainment of formidable density. Spohr was sufficiently struck by the peculiarity of the habit to describe a typical evening:

After the first act of the opera (Soliva's *Statua di bronza*) a grand heroic ballet was given which likewise rose to imposing dramatic heights by virtue of the artistry of some of the dancers, and the splendour of the sets and costumes. As it lasted nearly an hour one had entirely forgotten the first half of the opera. After the second act of the opera yet another ballet was performed, a comic one, hardly any shorter, so that the whole performance lasted from eight o'clock until twelve o'clock. What hard work for the poor musicians![13]

In one respect, however, these hard-worked musicians had things much easier than their present-day counterparts. They were not expected to master music in a wide range of idioms old and new; they were not expected to sing and play in a different musical language every night of the week. To us, one of the facts most difficult to grasp about Italian musical life in Verdi's youth is the narrowness, chronologically and nationally, of the repertory on which it was based. At La Scala in the 1830s during his student and apprentice days, the repertory was almost entirely Italian and almost entirely contemporary. The very occasional appearance of a work by Auber or Boieldieu was the only thing to break the Italian monopoly. Performances of music from a pre-Rossini generation were even rarer, the only instance at La Scala at this time being a brief run of *Don Giovanni* at the end of the Carnival/Lent season 1836. In other cities the situation was much the same: Rome had not heard a Mozart opera since 1811. Moreover, within this modern Italian repertory, the larger theatres were concentrating more and more on the tragic and heroic works. While the repertory of La Scala between 1790 and 1796 comprised 36 comic operas as against 16 heroic operas, the position forty years later, between 1830 and 1836, had been reversed. At least twice as many heroic as comic operas were now performed, even if one groups such pieces as *Don Giovanni* and *La Sonnambula* with the comedies.

The declining interest of the big theatres in comic opera was compensated for by numerous small theatres which specialized in the genre such as the Fondo in Naples, the Valle in Rome, the San Benedetto in Venice. Nor should one fail to note how many of the foreign visitors, disappointed in the quality of Italian heroic opera, enthused over these humbler comedies. Stendhal and Heine in the 1820s, Berlioz in the 1830s, Dickens in the 1840s all bear witness to the continued flourishing of the comic style and to the brilliance of the performances. 'At the Fondo', declared Berlioz, 'opera buffa is given with a zest and fire and brio that make it incomparably superior to our opéra-comique theatres.'[14]

Although the style of the Italian repertory was so homogeneous, so narrowly circumscribed, it was saved from torpidity by the regular production of newly composed works. During any season it was rare for more than five or six different operas to be performed, but during the Carnival season at least it was expected, indeed in many places it was constitutionally required, that one or two of these should be new operas, or at least new for the theatre in question. The profusion of such pieces was still, by modern standards, fantastic. In February 1846 the Allgemeine musikalische Zeitung of Leipzig published a statistical survey of Italian theatres which revealed that between 1838 and 1845, no fewer than 342 new operas had been produced. If well received, the new opera would run for about twenty or thirty performances (the same was of course true of a familiar repertory piece); of these the first three would be directed by the composer himself. This custom is commented on by Stendhal:

Traditionally, the maestro who wrote the opera is required to conduct the performance of his own music from the piano during the first three performances; I leave you to imagine the ignominious horror of this obligation if the opera should turn out to be a flop! In practice, an opera has to be absolutely detestable to be taken off before the third performance; the composer, in fact, can claim three as a right . . . More than once I have seen an opera pick up at the third performance; and in any case, organized opposition, knowing that its efforts will be comparatively useless, will necessarily be much less active at the première.[15]

Theatres and theatre etiquette

The various theatres of Italy were organized and administered in widely differing ways. To begin with, the status of the theatre differed from city to city. In some, such as Turin or Naples, it was a court theatre belonging to the crown, to which however the public was generally admitted. Elsewhere, as in Milan or Venice, the theatres were public amenities; in other cities again, for example Rome or Trieste, they were privately owned but were made available for public performances in exchange for state subventions. Some theatres, the Court Theatre in Turin and La Fenice in Venice among them, were administered by committees of noblemen or dignitaries. Others, probably a majority, were leased to an impresario, who then assumed sole responsibility for running the theatre economically and artistically. It was the impresario who commissioned new works, who engaged singers and players, and who was responsible to government, police and public for what went on in his theatre.

However adroit the impresario, there was by Verdi's time no Italian theatre capable of running itself as a viable economic enterprise without generous financial support from the sovereign or the state. This was particularly true of the two largest theatres, La Scala and the San Carlo, since the closure of their public gaming rooms, on which they had previously relied for a steady income. Stendhal reported that

In vast halls adjoining the theatres stood faro-tables and rouge-et-noir, and, the average Italian being a born gambler, the bank would usually show a more than handsome profit and so turn over enormous sums to swell the funds of the theatres. Gaming played a particularly vital role in the history of La Scala, which, situated as it is in a city with a damp winter climate, soon grew to be a general meeting-place for the whole town . . . But the Austrian authorities in Milan have prohibited gambling at La Scala, while the transitory revolution in Naples closed the tables there too, and King Ferdinand has not yet seen fit to open them again. In consequence, both these theatres are doomed, and their great musical traditions will die with them . . .[16]

Stendhal took too gloomy a view of the prospect. But certainly the amount of money spent on subsidizing the opera did now begin to mount to formidable proportions; 200,000 francs a year to La Scala in the 1820s, 350,000 a year to the San Carlo (the figures are Stendhal's).

This generous support given by the various rulers of Italy to their local opera houses was not, it must be said, normally due to a disinterested enthusiasm for public education. Since the time of the various revolutionary governments of the Napoleonic period, when the theatres had been used for public festivities to celebrate the great man's victories or even such a deed as the execution of Louis XVI – 'There was no public restraint in acclaiming the lugubrious anniversary', observes Gatti[17] – their value as political tools had been recognized in most states. But, of course, after the Restoration the political object was not unbridled enthusiasm for heroic or violent deeds, but contentment with the ordering of things as they were. D'Azeglio's assertion that at this time the Austrians governed Lombardy through La Scala has already been quoted. The kind of consideration he would presumably have had in mind is shown more precisely in a document drawn up by Monsignor Luigi Ciacchi in 1837 with the purpose of persuading the Pope of the desirability of giving more support to the opera in Rome:

The theatre, considered in the abstract, is and can only be an object of indifference to the government, an object to be tolerated, an object with no immediate connection with the heavy cares of the state.

But considered concretely, in view of the links it forges in society between the people and the government, it naturally changes its aspect, and necessarily takes its place among the beneficent concerns of the governing classes.

In order for a people to be more calm and content with the government to which it finds itself subjected, it is absolutely clear and confirmed by the experience of centuries that the means most fitting and conducive to this end is a suitably distracting theatre, decently entertaining and soberly diverting; and particularly at this time the distraction and entertainment of the people is the healthiest cure for the wounds that have been inflicted in almost every part of the world.[18]

For a time the theatres did indeed contribute to inspiring in the Italian people that quietude wished for by their governments. But because of the central position which they held in social life, they were bound in due course to become the centres of resistance to foreign domination, the hotbeds of conspiracy and, when appropriate, the scenes of demonstrations and protests. In the very nature of the case one can hardly insist upon documentary confirmation of such a claim of Gatti's as this:

there was conspiracy in the boxes, sealed by an amiable smile and a significant press of the hand between beautiful women and young gentlemen; whispered and ambiguous words were exchanged between acquaintances and friends as they passed through the corridors during the intervals in the performances: in the foyer groups of people formed as if by chance and conversed with a show of casualness: take care that not a word should leak out![19]

But almost certainly he is substantially right. At least there is no mistaking the way in which the performers and the audiences took fire when occasion demanded. Whether it was the gentlemen of Rome, on the occasion of the concessions granted by the King of Naples in January 1848, forming a chain out of their handkerchiefs as a symbol of brotherhood; or the Milanese *corps de ballet*, insisting on adorning themselves with Pius IX medallions, despite the objections of the prima ballerina Fanny Elssler; or the people of the same city surrounding La Scala in February 1857 and imposing a three-day closure as a sign of mourning for the death of Emilio Dandolo, it had become clear that the political interest in the theatre taken by the restored and generally reactionary governments after 1815 was being turned to quite different ends by the patriotic and liberal movements.

In purely physical terms the Italian theatres with which Verdi was most concerned, La Scala, La Fenice, and the San Carlo, have changed little. One need only recall that in his youth they would have been lit with oil lamps and candles, and from the 1860s onwards by gas, to be able to imagine quite clearly the picture they must have presented. Apart from the sheer beauty of the interiors of these buildings, what will most impress someone used to the type of theatre built in Britain is the fact that, except for the stalls in the pit of the theatre and the gallery right at the top, the whole of the auditorium is divided up into tiers of small boxes. Originally, in the public opera houses of seventeenth-century Venice, the grounds for designing a theatre in such a way had been largely financial. The theatre-owner could hire out a box for a season, or he could sell it (this was still the practice in the nineteenth century), and thus secure himself an income that was largely independent of the success of a particular opera. Spohr provides some further details of how the system operated:

The boxes are sold permanently, for as long as the theatre stands, to private individuals, as a result of which the owner of the theatre surrenders all his rights in them. However on entering the theatre the owners of the boxes must pay the price of admission just like everyone else. This is the same for every part of the theatre and is always very low; extortionate sums are made out of the boxes that are left to the owner of the theatre, and at the best-attended productions [large sums of money] are paid for them.[20]

Boxes became such assets for theatre-owners because they were rapidly recognized as incomparable social amenities; they came to be regarded as supernumerary drawing-rooms, salons in which acquaintances could be received and entertained. At the Teatro Argentina in Rome it was even customary for the owners to be responsible for the decoration of their own boxes, the result being 'rather absurd, but agreeably varied', according to Stendhal. He noticed 'three or four draperies which bore distant resemblance to a crown: I was told that the vanity of all the poor crowned heads who live in Rome finds consolation in this'.[21]

Indeed the status of the box-holders, the sense of precedence among them, does seem to have been a very real issue altogether. Stendhal simply records that the boxes in the second tier were most sought after because they were 'most convenient', but clearly there was more to it than this. The proximity of one's box to the royal or ducal box was a question of social status. In Rome, because of the unusually large number of diplomats, exiled royalty, and native nobility resident there, it was such a difficult question that it became necessary to issue an edict in 1837 proclaiming that from Carnival 1838 (that is, 26 December 1837) henceforth, 'the second and third tiers in all the theatres must be regarded as being of exactly equal status in every respect'.[22]

There was also a lot to be said for boxes from a purely artistic point of view, as Stendhal again explains:

since, to derive enjoyment from listening to music, the first condition is to achieve a state of imperturbable indifference concerning the figure one cuts and the part one plays in the eyes of others, and since the second condition is to feel perfectly at ease, it was a stroke of genius to have divided up the bulk of the auditorium into a hive of private and completely independent *boxes* . . . a certain degree of private self-communion is essential to savour the sublimest charms of music.[23]

But this discussion of boxes is leading us from the purely physical appearance of the theatres to the much less familiar ground of the decorum that prevailed in them.

There is no doubt that it was in the comparatively relaxed atmosphere of La Scala that the box system affected theatre etiquette most interestingly. Here, where there was normally no monarch or grand duke present to inhibit the audience, the sense that one's box was indeed one's own, that to be there was to be 'at home', was keenly felt. As a consequence one did indeed go to the theatre every night: the opera was there if one cared to listen, and if one did not, one could draw the curtain, withdraw into one's own private world, or savour the pleasures of social intercourse:

Every day I go to Signor di Brema's box at La *Scala* [writes Stendhal] – it is an entirely literary society . . . I bring these gentlemen news of France, anecdotes about the retreat from Moscow, Napoleon, the Bourbons; they pay me back with news of Italy . . . I don't know anything in Paris to compare with this box where, every evening, one sees fifteen or twenty distinguished men sit themselves down one after another; and if the conversation ceases to be interesting one listens to the music.[24]

In the *Life of Rossini*, Stendhal provides further details:

except at *premières* there are never more than two people occupying these front seats, the escorted lady and her recognized gallant and servitor, while the remainder of the box, or rather *salon*, may contain anything up to nine or ten persons, who are perpetually coming and going all the evening. Silence is observed only at *premières*; or, during subsequent performances, only while one or other of the more memorable passages is being performed. Anyone who wishes to concentrate on watching the opera right through from beginning to end goes and sits in the pit, which is vast, and luxuriously equipped with benches furnished with backrests, where the spectator can make himself exceedingly comfortable . . .[25]

Not that the pit was entirely filled with earnest devotees of the melodrama. In all the major cities it was the custom to make over the front rows to the military. Though this was probably a minor vexation in Milan, where the white uniforms of the Austrian officers occupied only two rows of seats,[26] Stendhal himself had to admit the inconvenience in Naples. There

the first eleven rows are occupied by MM. the officers of the red guards, of the blue guards, of the guards of the gate etc., etc. . . . Add to this the very large space taken up by the orchestra, and you see that the poor visitor, relegated to the middle of the room, is absolutely unable either to hear or to see.[27]

Dickens found the situation as tiresome in Genoa:

There are a great number of Piedmontese officers too, who are allowed the privilege of kicking their heels in the pit, for next to nothing: gratuitous, or cheap accommodation for these gentlemen being insisted on, by the Governor, in all public or semi-public entertainments. They are lofty critics in consequence, and infinitely more exacting than if they made the unhappy manager's fortune.[28]

The kind of social life described by Stendhal as characteristic of La Scala was less common in other Italian cities. Particularly in those opera houses attached to royal or ducal courts an altogether starchier decorum reigned. D'Azeglio records a chilling incident at the Turin opera in the late 1820s, when he had returned to his native Piedmont after some years in the less ceremonial atmosphere of Florence and Rome.

The King loved music, and was in his Number 1 Box, second row on the right, every evening from the first note. He took a frugal supper, consisting of a few rusk biscuits which he swallowed with dexterity, holding them one by one by the ends and nibbling away very quickly. Provincial visitors looked on this performance as one of the sights of Turin and used to stare at him open-mouthed. One evening I was seated on the farther side in a box of the first row on the left, near the entrance to the pit. There were two ladies with me and three or four others and we were chatting . . . All of a sudden an officer of foot guards appeared at the door of the box, saluted, and said: 'On behalf of His Majesty, I ask you to be quiet.' We stared at each other, exchanged bows with the officer, and the conversation languished . . .
This was the sort of thing that happened in the Turin of those days, and you may well believe it wasn't to my taste.[29]

Another singular feature of such court theatres in Turin and Naples, at least when the court was present, was that 'no applause or disapprobation of the performance is expressed by the audience, such demonstrations being deemed an infringement on the rules of etiquette'.[30] Consequently, whether an opera was good or bad, whether it inspired enthusiasm or contempt, the atmosphere in the theatre was much the same, as Michael Beer explained to his brother Giacomo Meyerbeer of a performance at the San Carlo in Naples:

to put it mildly the opera [Generali's *Elena e Olfredo*] was coldly received. But as one can neither applaud nor call for the composer if the court is present, it is impossible in the pit to tell how great the fiasco is. Judging from what is said, the opinion of the public is very unfavourable.[31]

Of course if the monarch gave the sign, public demonstrations of approval were permitted. Stendhal records an occasion when 'the public could scarcely restrain its desire to applaud: the king set the example, I heard the voice of His Majesty from my box, and the transports mounted to a furore which lasted three-quarters of an hour'.[32] But even a monarch's liberty to express his approval was apparently limited. After the *première* of the revised version of Bellini's *Bianca e Fernando* at Genoa in 1828, 'the king sent one of his chamberlains to thank the composer and the singers, and to say he was sorry that, as it was a formal occasion, he could not applaud; in fact yesterday evening he kept his word, reserving his applause for the one occasion when the court etiquette of the Turin theatre permits it, after the second-act duet . . .'[33]

Etiquette at the court theatres inhibited more than applause. When the king was present, the whole theatre remained brilliantly illuminated throughout the performance, destroying the illusion the stage sets and lighting were attempting to create. In Naples, the lack of curtains for the boxes, combined with this continuous bright light, made any kind of privacy in them an impossibility, and everyone had to be formally dressed for every performance. Nor was it the audience alone that suffered. Spohr tells of a curious Neapolitan custom according to which 'as the king enters his box, the curtain must be raised; so that the poor singers are put in the position of having to submit to being stared at for the whole duration of the overture, without being able to enter into the spirit of their roles'.[34]

Performance

What one would most dearly like to know about the opera houses of distant times is what a performance would really have been like. Even for a period as comparatively recent as Verdi's, with a repertory whose performing traditions have never quite died, it is extraordinarily difficult to imagine. Whether we should have been thrilled or appalled by the quality of the performances obviously we can never know. Just to try to envisage the style in which an opera would have been presented, or the merest mechanics of its production and execution, is acutely problematic.

One of the respects in which the theatre of Verdi's youth most obviously differed from that of today, or indeed from that of his own old age, was in the lack of a conductor in the modern sense of the word. We have already seen that one of the obligations normally assumed by a composer when he contracted to compose a new opera for a particular theatre was that of 'directing' the first three performances. But what exactly did 'directing' mean? And who took over when the composer had done his obligatory three performances? In one of the letters in which Verdi's pupil and assistant Emanuele Muzio describes their visit to London in 1847 for the *première* of *I Masnadieri*, we read that 'the maestro himself conducted . . . seated on a chair higher than the rest and with a baton in his hand',[35] and it seems a little old-fashioned, but entirely plausible. What he would have been doing, however, if he had been directing his *première* in Italy is by no means so clear. The difficulty lies in charting the stages of the transition from the eighteenth-century tradition in which the composer directed his operas from the keyboard to the later-nineteenth-century tradition in which he conducted, and in deciding what point in this transition we have reached when we discuss Verdi's early operas.

When Mendelssohn went to hear the *première* of a new opera by Pacini in Rome in 1831 he observed quite unambiguously that the composer appeared 'at the piano'.[36] One assumes that he directed as a continuo-player had been accustomed to direct for centuries; and if this seems a pretty pointless exercise in the 1830s one should recall that in many smaller theatres a full complement of instrumentalists could not be assembled, and that to give the music some 'body' in this way may well have been desirable. That on some occasions at least a piano was called for in a continuo capacity is clear from the scores themselves. Verdi's own *Un Giorno di Regno* includes *secco* recitatives with the accompaniment notated in figured bass. Generally, however, it is far from clear that when the composer sat himself at the piano it was in order to be able to perform in a continuo capacity. According to Pacini, what the composer actually did was 'to turn the pages for the principal cello and double-bass players . . . a custom which remained in force until 1839, and which I abolished when I produced *Saffo* . . .' (in Naples).[37] This seems very much more curious, indeed pointless, than the continuo use of the piano, of which Pacini admittedly says nothing.

Nicolai is also silent on the subject of the piano continuo in a context where he might be expected to have had something to say about it. Speaking of a performance of his *Il Templario* in Turin in 1840 he remarks simply: 'Herr Gebhard directed the orchestra . . . as is the custom, I sat at the keyboard for the three evenings.'[38]

With the better orchestras, then, the composer's task was probably limited to supervising the performance: to assisting, advising and encouraging the principal instrumentalists on whom in practice the direction of the opera fell. That at least is the implication in a letter of Donizetti's, in which he discusses the new seating arrangement adopted at La Scala during Carnival 1833–4:

The principal quartet of the orchestra being brought together in the centre, it can at will direct the rest of the instruments, and the composer, who finds himself in the middle of them, and next to the first violin, has the advantage (whenever he wishes) of giving the leader, both by word and gesture, the indication of the tempos he desires . . .[39]

He could also give the orchestra a lead interpretatively. It is reported of Mercadante, for example, when he directed an opera, that 'he contorted, he seemed inebriated, he wept, he became convulsed and furious; his emotional intensity passed like electricity to his performers'.[40]

Presumably once the composer had seen the opera launched, his place at the piano was taken by the 'maestro al cembalo'. But it is clear that the person whose responsibilities most resembled those of the modern conductor was the 'primo violino, capo e direttore d'orchestra'. Spohr describes the direction of an opera at La Scala in 1816 thus: 'Signor Rolla, an artist known even abroad through his compositions, conducted from the first violin desk. Apart from him there is no further direction, either from the piano or with a baton, but simply a prompter with the score, who whispers the text to the singers and gives the chorus a beat where necessary.'[41] What Spohr does not tell us is how exactly Rolla directed.

At La Scala with its highly drilled professional orchestra it is very possible that the first violinist directed much as Verdi himself was to do in London, from a higher seat, using his bow in the manner of a baton. But in other places, for a long time after 1815, cruder methods prevailed. Mendelssohn reported from Naples in 1831 that 'throughout the entire opera, the first violinist beats out the four beats of the bar on a tin lampstand, so that sometimes one hears more of it than of the voices (it sounds something like *obbligato* castanets, but louder)'.[42] In the same city, later in the same year, Berlioz was also taken aback by the custom: 'The highly disagreeable noise made by the conductor tapping with his bow on the desk was another point I was disposed to criticize; but I was told that without it his musicians would sometimes have been hard put to it to play in time. This was unanswerable . . .'[43]

Happily, fuller and more objective accounts of the responsibilities of the first violinist are avilable in Pietro Lichtenthal's dictionary:

1. [He must] understand the positioning of the orchestra and how to balance the number of instruments . . . 2. [He must] tune the instruments, give and maintain precise tempos not only in the orchestra, but for the actors and especially the choruses too; and if any mistakes occur in the performance, he must know how to remedy them without the public being disturbed. 3. [He must] judge the right tempo and the true sentiment of the composition in question, since its effectiveness is dependent on that. 4. [He must] maintain a precise ensemble in the orchestra, so that all the performers observe the same accents, the same *pianos* and *fortes*, the same *crescendos* and *diminuendos*, the same bowings etc. 5. [He needs] practical knowledge of the human voice, and of the characteristics of all the instruments used in the orchestra. 6. [He needs] a knowledge of harmony, to be able to correct errors in the score, and mistakes that may be made by singers and players. 7. [He must] attend rehearsals, to acquire an intimate knowledge of the compositions in question. 8. Although strictly speaking the director of the orchestra does not need to be a player of concerto class, he must nevertheless approach that, and be thoroughly accomplished on his instrument.[44]

The first Italian musician to distinguish himself as a conductor in the modern sense of the word was Angelo Mariani, and even he seems to have abandoned his violin and bow in favour of the baton only in the 1860s.[45]

I have been guilty of indulging in anachronistic priorities in beginning a discussion of the performances of *ottocento* opera with the conductor. Clearly in Verdi's youth, except perhaps when the composer himself was directing, the conductor was not the key figure he has since become. There was no question of his taking it upon himself to impose upon the rest of the cast an individual or even homogeneous 'interpretation' of the opera. He was really a member of the orchestra. His job was to maintain ensemble in the orchestra; and the orchestra's job was to accompany the singers.

Of the Italian opera orchestras of the time, two, those of Milan and Naples, were pre-eminent both in size and in accomplishment. In 1816, the orchestra of La Scala boasted 'twenty-four violins, eight double-basses and a similar number of cellos, all the usual wind instruments, trombones, "bass horn", "Turkish music" etc.'[46] In most other theatres the numbers were appreciably smaller. In Palermo, for example, the complete double woodwind and brass was matched by a string orchestra which between 1825 and 1855 averaged seventeen violins, three violas, seven or eight basses (cellos and double-basses);[47] while in Trieste the full orchestra rarely numbered more than thirty.[48]

Only one thing about the actual constitution of a Verdian orchestra would surprise the modern musician, as it surprised the foreign musicians of the time: the habit of employing more double-basses than cellos. Thus in Trieste in the early years of the century there were three double-basses in the orchestra but only one cello; at the Apollo in Rome, and in Palermo through to the 1850s at least, five double-basses to two or three cellos. Only in Milan, as far as the available evidence shows, did the number of cellos even equal that of the double-basses. Spohr commented on the effect which this had on Italian orchestration: 'As in the majority of Italian orchestras there is only one usually not exactly first-class cello to six or even eight double-basses, the use of the cellos as a middle voice which has been common since Mozart, and which in skilful hands has such a splendid effect, is here quite unknown.'[49]

Berlioz too objected to the balance even in the San Carlo orchestra, which he otherwise admired: '. . . the 'cellos played with a good singing tone, though there were too few of them (the common practice in Italy of having fewer 'cellos than double-basses has no justification, not even in the kind of music that Italian orchestras normally play)'.[50]

Some critics were determined to admire nothing about Italian music-making. Mendelssohn found the orchestra and chorus of the San Carlo theatre 'as in one of our minor middle-sized towns, only rougher and more uncertain'.[51] But the consensus of opinion was that the orchestras of Naples and Milan at least were very good in their way. Of the same Naples orchestra that Mendelssohn complained about, in the same year, Berlioz wrote: 'I went to the San Carlo and there, for the first time since coming to Italy, heard music. The orchestra, compared with those I had encountered until then, struck me as excellent. It was quite safe to listen to the wind instruments. The violins were competent, and the 'cellos played with a good singing tone.'[52]

Spohr too had been impressed by the Naples orchestra in 1816, though he had reservations: 'The performance [of Carafa's *Gabriele de' Vergi*] both on the part of the singers and of the orchestra was very precise. The latter under the exact, fiery, though rather too loud direction of Signor Festa is very well rehearsed, but has too few nuances between *piano* and *forte*; the wind instruments in particular are always too loud in *piano* sections.'[53]

The orchestra which most appealed to Spohr was that of La Scala, whose playing 'much exceeded my expectation: it was clean [rein], powerful, precise, and at the same time very composed'.[54] On several occasions during his Italian journey – in Milan, in Venice and in Naples – Spohr had occasion to comment on how well rehearsed the orchestras were; though this was not necessarily always a good thing, since if they had to learn something quickly (like a Spohr concerto) they tended to play rather inaccurately.

But whether one was disposed to accord the Milan and Naples orchestras a degree of real excellence, or only a kind of rough and ready competence, it is clear that their qualities were not to be expected in every theatre. Even in Rome, the standards would have been distinctly lower, though from 1834 onwards the impresario Alessandro Lanari did bring about spectacular improvements at the Apollo theatre. In 1831 Berlioz had described the Roman orchestras in memorable phrases: 'They were formidable and imposing in the manner of the Monégasque army, possessing every single quality which is normally considered a defect.'[55]

Notwithstanding their incompetence, however, they had preserved in a debased form the ancient skill of impromptu ornamentation. Spohr's account is the fullest:

the orchestra had been assembled out of the best musicians in Rome, but despite this was quite the worst I had yet had to accompany me. The ignorance, tastelessness and arrogant stupidity of these men defies description. They knew nothing of *piano* and *forte*; one might put up with that, but every one of them plays ornaments, as it takes his fancy, and turns on almost every note, so that the ensemble sounds more like the din an orchestra makes when it is warming up and tuning than harmonious music. It is true I did repeatedly forbid them to play any notes that were not in their parts, but ornamentation has become so much second nature to them that they simply cannot refrain from it.[56]

They still had not learned to refrain from it when Mendelssohn heard them fifteen years later. Such wholesale and indiscriminate use of ornamentation does, however, seem to have been a Roman predilection: at least it provoked no comment in other cities, and one presumes that elsewhere orchestras were more disciplined. In Naples, for example, Mendelssohn noted that 'old-fashioned ornamentation was applied to every little instrumental solo',[57] but made no mention of the ornamentation of the harmony-sustaining voices that had affronted him in Rome.

Few theatres were able to assemble their orchestras entirely from the ranks of the musical profession, as Milan and Naples did. 'At the Valle theatre in Rome,' observed Berlioz, 'the 'cellos number precisely one, a goldsmith by trade, in which respect he is more fortunate than one of his colleagues, who earns his living by repairing cane-bottomed chairs.'[58] For such orchestras the performance of an opera was as much an evening out as it was for the audience, and they were as determined to have a good time. According to an account in the Roman *Rivista Teatrale* in 1834, 'At the Valle [the orchestra] is permitted to chatter in a loud voice, to applaud the singers when the audience disapproves of them, to leave and resume their seats from time to time, straddling across the partition which separates the orchestra from the pit.'[59]

Before leaving this discussion of the orchestra, a word should perhaps be said about the *banda* that looms so large in Verdi's early operas. The *banda* was what we should describe as a military band, a woodwind and brass ensemble, which actually appeared on stage in marches, processions or ballroom scenes. It had nothing directly to do with the theatre, but would be engaged by the impresario, if the composer wished for it, from the ranks of a local military garrison. Thus the Bourbon troops garrisoned in Palermo would provide the *banda* for the opera there, and the Austrian Kinsky regiment would provide the *banda* for La Fenice in Venice. Such a *banda* would probably contain something over twenty players: there were for example twenty-two performing in the *banda* for the Teatro Argentina in Rome in 1843.

The art of singing went through at least two distinct phases in early-nineteenth-century Italy. In the first years of the century it was still dominated by the types of skill commanded and taught by the great eighteenth-century *castrati*: ease of delivery, delicacy of nuance, flexibility and brilliance of execution, imaginative and spontaneous employment of ornamentation. This tradition was not entirely dead even in Verdi's time, but it amounted to hardly more than a faint echo of a vanished age. Even those who reported on the musical scene in Italy immediately after the Restoration could not fail to observe that the style was in decline. Stendhal lamented that, as a result of Rossini's habit of writing out in full detail everything that a singer was to sing, 'the glories of *spontaneous inspiration* have been banished for ever from an art whose loveliest achievements have so often depended upon the individual interpreter and his genius for improvisation'.[60] And within a decade or so the whole concept of florid song had been called in doubt by changes in taste, so that (as Chorley later reflected) 'the modern idea of accomplishment . . . denounces a shake as beneath the dignity of a hero, – and a *roulade* to be nothing less meretricious than a dancer's *pirouette*'.[61]

The style of singing that supplanted this earlier manner was at once simpler, louder and more starkly emotional. One of its most sensational symptoms was the development of the tenor chest voice. Until about 1830 the top notes of the tenor range had always been sung falsetto. Domenico Donzelli's voice, as described in one of his own letters to Bellini, would be typical for most tenors of the day: '. . . Chest tones . . . up to the G; and it is in that range that I can declaim with equal strength and sustain all the force of the declamation. From the G to the high C, I can avail myself of a falsetto which, used with artistry and strength, is a resource for ornamentation.'[62]

But chest notes were gradually pushed higher and higher, and before the end of the decade the French tenor Gilbert Duprez had electrified audiences with his 'ut de poitrine' – an acquisition which rapidly became 'a new Golden Fleece, in pursuit of which some Argonauts lost such modest means as they might have possessed, others their genuine natural aptitude'.[63]

What connoisseurs of the older style of singing necessarily regarded as 'coarse and stentorian bawling' (Chorley) came to be an integral feature of Italian vocal art. It was accompanied by an ultimately undiscriminating use of vibrato. In the view of the doyen of early-nineteenth-century singing teachers, Manuel García, a vibrato had been incompatible with good singing, unmistakably a symptom of a deficient method. But as singers pressed their voices harder – whether to compete with the heavier orchestral writing that was now being employed, or to enable them to carry through the vast spaces and unsympathetic acoustics of the new San Carlo theatre, or simply in pursuit of greater emotional intensity – it was inevitable that most of them should, to quote Chorley once again, 'contract a habit of trembling'. Nonetheless one should guard against exaggerating the extent of the change. The demands in delicacy and brilliance still made by, say, Bellini have been quite beyond the power of all but a select handful of twentieth-century artists.

One grave reproach that has often been levelled at the opera singers of *ottocento* Italy is that of dramatic irresponsibility. When Spohr saw a production of Rossini's *L'Italiana in Algeri* in Florence he recorded: 'One listens . . . to one of the characters in a most passionate situation singing by himself for a quarter of an hour, while the others stroll about in the background, or, half-hidden in the scenery, talk and joke with their acquaintances.'[64] In the light of such comments, while many a historian has been prepared to grant the Italian singers of the period a superhuman degree of technical virtuosity, frankly few have believed that they cared for dramatic illusion or the subtler arts of characterization.

That they knew nothing, and wished to know nothing, of that modern style of producer-dominated performance in which the whole action of the drama moves in a carefully calculated, pseudo-naturalistic flow may be readily conceded. So may the fact that several aspects of stage conduct had more to do with social decorum than with drama – an obvious example being the applause and acknowledgements at the first entrance of the prima donna. But no one who has ever had anything to do with the Italians will easily believe that there was once a time when they could not be bothered to act.

How they acted, what the dramatic conventions were that prevailed in the early nineteenth century, are matters not easily defined. There is a striking absence of illuminating descriptions of their performance, and one is really obliged to resort to the scores as the only reliable source of information. From these one crucial principle emerges with unmistakable clarity: that stillness prevails in the moments of greatest passion; that dramatic action (in the sense of stage movement) is nothing more than a necessary link in an exhibition of pathetic statuary and brilliant or tension-laden tableaux. The illusion sought in the performance of this kind of opera cannot have been the naturalistic illusion of a world going by: it must have been the illusion of a gallery of pictures in which our attention is focused in turn on different characters or groups of characters in every-changing relationships.

But there is no lack of testimony – most eloquent, perhaps, in the pages of Stendhal and Chorley – to the fact that, within this statuesque framework, the singers of the period did care about characterization and did act with thrilling dramatic effect. Such things were a matter of concern from the moment a singer started to learn his role, as we see from the custom of giving him not only his part, but also a libretto, 'to enable him to perceive the character of the role' – the form of words is Count Mocenigo's in sending the part of Ernani to Carlo Guasco. And they were a matter of concern to public and critics in judging the qualities of a performance. Frank Walker cites the critic of *La Fama* writing of Napoleone Moriani, 'il tenore della bella morte': 'The extinction of life is expressed by singing that has the tints, the shuddering, of death itself; it is like a trampled narcissus that bows its head, and in whose bosom the transient echo weeps and laments'[65] – and an *Il Figaro* critic on Giuseppina Strepponi in her prime: 'The greatest triumph of la

Strepponi was in the third act, where she delivered the prayer with such deep feeling, and declaimed and sang the duet with Viscardo with such abandon, as to transport the audience, who burst into the loudest acclamation, astonished at such dramatic truth.'[66]

From a letter which Goethe's friend Wilhelm Ehlers wrote to Meyerbeer in September 1823, we can even see that in the opinion of some good judges it was not the voices of the Italians but their dramatic vitality that gave them a degree of superiority over singers from other lands:

Until the Italians came, Italian operas were performed only in translation (with a few exceptions, all of which were unsuccessful). Rossini, you, and all the other Italian composers wrote music almost all of which was so well written for the voice that acting and dramatic, declamatory delivery and so forth were no longer cared about. So it was quite natural, when almost all these operas appeared in the original language, acted and sung by the Italians with real vitality, that the demise of the German singers should follow inexorably.[67]

One other factor enhanced the dramatic vividness of Italian opera; and it may seem surprising in view of the extent to which the theatre was regarded as a centre of social intercourse. Italy was well in advance of most parts of Europe in darkening the auditorium, so as, potentially at least, to concentrate the attention on the spectacle. Hazlitt thought that 'Milton might easily have taken his idea of Pandemonium from the inside of an Italian Theatre, its heat, its gorgeousness and its gloom.'[68]

So far as one can see, then, in Verdi's youth Italian singers continued to act in what one might call the Baroque tradition, highly emotional in demeanour and gesture, but poised and architectural in movement. The sheer quality of singing had become more forceful but less agile. In this connection we may note that although in 1816 Spohr had found that Italian singers ornamented excessively and tastelessly, 'always in the same style, with embellishments we have already heard a thousand times',[69] thirty years later a simpler manner prevailed in Italy than elsewhere. When Muzio heard Jenny Lind in London in 1847 he objected to her use of ornamentation: 'We Italians are not accustomed to things of this sort, and if la Lind came to Italy she would have to abandon her mania for embellishments and sing simply, having a voice uniform and flexible enough to sustain a phrase in la Frezzolini's manner.'[70]

Information about the calibre of the choruses and the dramatic use made of them is sparse; though the remark of a critic at the Genoese *première* of *I Vespri Siciliani* in 1864, that the chorus was 'as usual

unperturbed by what was going on around them',[71] sounds ominous
Generally the choruses seem to have been neither excellent enough
nor deplorable enough to excite comment from visitors to Italy; and
unlike the orchestra, the chorus was not something about which
German musicians would get excited as a matter of course.

In purely numerical terms choruses gradually grew in importance
during the first half of the century. At the Apollo theatre in Rome, for
example, numbers slowly rose from fourteen in 1818 to thirty-six in
1855. By 1843 there were as many as seventy singers in the San Carlo
chorus.[72] One further piece of information suggests that male voices
may have predominated slightly over female: the figures for the
small Palermo chorus were eight to ten women, ten to twelve
men.[73]

One of the few interesting criticisms of Italian opera choruses
comes from Berlioz, who gives the impression that they got worse
the further south one went. At the Pergola theatre in Florence he
heard 'a large chorus . . . singing, I thought, tolerably well, with
full-bodied, incisive tone; among them a dozen boys of fourteen or
fifteen whose alto voices were particularly effective'.[74] But already
in Rome 'The choruses are rather below that of the Opéra-Comique
in point of warmth, intonation and ensemble . . .'[75] And the nadir is
reached in Naples: 'The chorus was indescribably feeble. A composer who writes for the San Carlo assured me that it is extremely
difficult if not impossible to get a decent performance of music
written in four parts. The sopranos find it hard to keep a separate
line from the tenors, so one is more or less obliged to write the two
parts in octaves.'[76]

From what has already been said about the style of operatic performances in the first part of the nineteenth century it will be clear
that there was even less room for a producer than there was for a
conductor. In so far as the performance was supervised dramatically
and visually, it was done by the librettist. One of the crosses that
Felice Romani had to bear during his collaboration with Bellini was
the task of trying to teach Rubini to act. His widow's memoirs record
his exertions at the early rehearsals of Il Pirata: 'Get up, move back,
stir yourself, gesticulate . . . No, no, not like that, . . . you're angry
now . . . a step backwards . . . clear words, . . . with an agitated voice
. . . Good Lord, don't talk rubbish! . . . make a gesture of contempt . . .
now forward threateningly . . . no, not like that . . .'[77]

The fullest contemporary account which I have come across of the
production responsibilities of the librettist is found in a contract
drawn up in Venice in 1817 between Meyerbeer and the impresario

Mazzucato for the opera *Romilda e Costanza*. Clauses 3 and 4 of the contract read:

Signor Mazzucato cannot require the opera to be performed until such time as Signor de Meyerbeer has held all the necessary music rehearsals, and Signor Rossi, author of the drama, all the necessary stage rehearsals, and until such time as the choruses and extras have been rehearsed and practised as much as necessary, the stage sets seen, the practicables tested, the properties and costumes approved.

The authors wish to be as certain about the physical appearance of the drama as about the accurate execution of the singers: for this reason Signor Mazzucato undertakes to have the stage sets belonging to the drama painted in accordance with Signor Rossi's instructions: to have costumes of the appropriate character specially prepared, both for the soloists (of whom the principals shall have entirely new ones) and for the chorus, and for the extras: the properties likewise to be new, in accordance with the instructions of Signor Rossi, and subject to his approval . . .[78]

The author of the libretto was obviously not able to accept responsibility for the staging of all later revivals of his opera. In these cases the resident librettists attached to most of the large theatres would take over.

That the performance of an opera should be an experience no less impressive visually than musically was an Italian tradition as old as opera itself. In the early nineteenth century it was probably at Milan that the art of the scenographer was most developed, and his contribution to the beauty of the opera and to its dramatic power most keenly felt. The Milanese tradition had been established in the early years of the theatre by the Galliari brothers, and their style remained exemplary well into the nineteenth century. Its distinguishing qualities were virtuosity in the handling of perspective, and the imposingly architectural qualities of the design and the colour scheme. According to Gatti, 'their knowledge of architectural styles was slight, their archaeological erudition still less, so that they conferred on all their designs, no matter for what time or place, the Greco-Roman style'.[79] Stendhal implies much the same when he tells us that

All scenery is painted with size-paint, and the set as a whole is built up on principles which are utterly different from those which are in vogue in Paris today. In Paris, it is all tinselly glitter, everything is a filigree of pretty, witty little arabesques, each enamelled in immaculate detail. But in Milan, everything is sacrificed to mass effects of form and colour, and to the *general impression*. It is David's own special genius transposed into the medium of décor.[80]

Stendhal is very informative altogether on the subject of the *décor* at La Scala in the years after the Restoration:

Each scene of the opera, and each scene of the ballets, is set in a fresh décor; and there are invariably a great many scenes, since the author relies to some extent upon the audience's appreciation of new and original sets to ensure the success of the work as a whole. No set is ever used for two distinct spectacles; if the opera or ballet should prove a failure the set, which may have been magnificent, is nevertheless ruthlessly painted out on the following day, even if it has only been seen at one single performance; for the same flats are used over and over again for new scenes . . .[81]

But as in so many other respects, Milan and Naples were exceptional among the theatres of Italy for the sumptuousness of their décor; and even in Naples its impressiveness was often detrimentally affected by the brilliant illumination of the auditorium. Of the Roman theatres, only the Apollo had its décor painted by artists of distinction, and that by no means invariably. Costumes were an even more unpredictable asset: according to Radiciotti, the soloists dressed more in accordance with their own whims, and the chorus more in accordance with what the ignorance and meanness of the impresario dictated, than with the character of the drama. Gounod saw a production of Norma at the Apollo theatre in 1840 in which 'The Roman warriors wore firemen's helmets and tunics, and yellow nankeen trousers with cherry-coloured stripes. It was utterly ridiculous and might have been a Punch and Judy show.'[82]

We have already seen that ballet was a regular part of the evening's entertainment in the Italian opera house. The fact that it might be discontinued in Lent, or that some smaller theatres might be incapable of supporting a ballet company at all, must not be taken as indicating that dancing was a superfluous or subsidiary entertainment, which would have been as little missed as today one would miss the interval music in a cinema. Balletomanes were as numerous in the house as opera-lovers, and among the most serious-minded enthusiasts for drama the ballets excited as much admiration as the opera. As a young composer of opera, Verdi, with such sensational triumphs as Nabucco, I Lombardi, Ernani and Attila, had the 1840s almost to himself. But if one had gone along to the theatre, to almost any of these clamorous successes, one would have found Verdi sharing the honours not so much with his singers as with the prima ballerinas of the day. Gatti describes an evening (20 March 1843) when Fanny Cerrito and Maria Taglioni were dancing together in I Viaggiatori all'Isola d'Amore, a ballet which was being performed in conjunction with I Lombardi:

the 'steps' executed by la Cerrito and la Taglioni aroused waves of frantic applause and unrestrained comparisons. The public called the two rivals repeatedly on to the stage against the peremptory prohibition of the police, and succeeded in getting their wishes gratified. That evening Verdi too appeared between the two dancers with la Frezzolini. Flowers and crowns for la Taglioni, jewels for la Cerrito. When the performance was over the musicians, the military [presumably the *banda*] and the chorus of La Scala carried the serenade under the balconies of the goddesses.[83]

The enthusiasm provoked by Fanny Elssler in the next few years was still more extravagant.

But there was more than giddy sensuality in this Italian enthusiasm for ballet. Stendhal's praises for the ballets of Viganò had been for their dramatic power:

I have seen Kean in London in *Othello* and *Richard III*: I thought then that I would never experience anything more alive in the theatre; but Shakespeare's most beautiful tragedy does not produce upon me half the effect of a ballet by Viganò . . .[84]

And thirty years later, at a time when the Milanese enthusiasm for Elssler seemed to have reached an almost mindless pitch, Dickens wrote of the ballet at La Scala:

there was a ballet of action performed after the opera, under the title of Prometheus; in the beginning of which, some hundred or two men and women represented our mortal race before the refinements of the arts and sciences, and loves and graces, came on earth to soften them. I never saw anything more effective. Generally speaking the pantomimic action of the Italians is more remarkable for its sudden and impetuous character than for its delicate expression; but in this case, the drooping monotony: the weary, miserable, listless, moping life, the sordid passions and desires of human creatures destitute of those elevating influences to which we owe so much, and to whose promoters we render so little: were expressed in a manner really powerful and affecting . . .[85]

Appreciation

So far in this chapter I have been concerned with describing the kind of entertainment offered by a major Italian theatre in the years of the *risorgimento*. The question that remains to be answered is, what did Italian audiences make of it; what did an opera mean to them; were the contemptuous views of Mendelssohn and Berlioz quoted at the beginning of the chapter justified?

That the box system and the repertory system in operation at the time made the opera house as much a social as an artistic amenity has already been shown in sufficient detail. Ideally the system needed an audience of Stendhals, as sensitive to the beauties of song, dance and spectacle as they were to the pleasure of witty or erudite conversation. Such audiences of course were simply not to be had:

and as a result the system was bound to be abused frequently. It was abused by people who became so engrossed in the most trivial socializing aspects of theatre life that they lost sight of its artistic purpose altogether; people like the wife of the Viceroy Rainieri, for example, who 'from her box in La Scala used to ogle all the most fashionable young men with her opera-glass. One of the lions ogled most avidly by the archduchess took pleasure in embarrassing her by assuming the most strange and far from respectable poses.'[86]

And it was abused when frequent performances of well-known operas given by casts of no special distinction led to the whole opera being regarded as a kind of *musique d'ameublement* to which virtually no attention was paid. In Milan in 1832, Berlioz went to a performance of Donizetti's *L'Elisir d'Amore* at the Cannobiana theatre:

I found the theatre full of people talking in normal voices, with their backs to the stage. The singers, undeterred, gesticulated and yelled their lungs out in the strictest spirit of rivalry. At least I presumed they did, from their wide-open mouths; but the noise of the audience was such that no sound penetrated except the bass drum. People were gambling, eating supper in their boxes, etcetera, etcetera . . .[87]

There is indeed no doubt that as a result of the manners prevailing in opera houses the habit of listening attentively to music had virtually been lost. In 1818 in Venice, Meyerbeer was present at an occasion that provides an excellent illustration of this:

During Holy Week, Cavaliere Grizzo, at his own expense . . . gave several 'academies' in the Teatro San Benedetto in aid of the poor, during the course of which Handel's *Messiah*, Haydn's *Stabat Mater* etc. were performed. As far as the notes were concerned, one couldn't say that the performances were bad, only the spirit of the players involuntarily contradicted that of the work . . . so that for anyone who had really understood the composer's intention, and who knew the good traditions of London, Vienna and Berlin, the whole thing sometimes seemed like a travesty. The only really enjoyable part of the spectacle was the sight of the elegantly dressed ladies and gentlemen in their illuminated boxes. They sat there quite crushed with boredom, but didn't dare either to yawn or to talk, since a few days before the performance Grizzo had explained, with his usual courtesy, that these compositions were masterpieces of the human spirit, that anyone who didn't enjoy them was an ass; and that anyone who was disposed to chatter during such music, the way one does during an Italian opera, could only be an ill-educated peasant.[88]

As a rule, however, one may assert with some confidence that the Italians' concern for the social aspects of opera-going did not in the slightest degree impair either their sensibility or their critical faculties. The directness and spontaneity with which these qualities manifested themselves are another point where the practice of the time diverged sharply from that of today.

Many observers were of the opinion that Italian audiences were naturally malicious, sometimes even vicious, and there seems to be some evidence that during the Restoration this maliciousness intensified. When E. Hartmann, a friend of Meyerbeer, heard an opera by Pavesi hissed from the stage of La Fenice in 1824 he wrote: 'I am really sorry for poor Pavesi, he must have been quite desperate – for as far as I can recall . . . there has never been such a vulgar exhibition at La Fenice as last St Stephen's day – it's true I have seen many operas flop, but they have never been whistled and shouted down.'[89] But during the next twenty years there was nothing uniquely dreadful in such a fate. Verdi would surely never have taken such a tragic view of the failure of *Un Giorno di Regno* had it not been for the bitterness of the personal circumstances under which it was composed. What seems to have been a typical fiasco of the 1830s and 1840s is described in one of Mendelssohn's letters with some interesting incidental reflection. The occasion was the *première* of Pacini's *Il Corsaro* in Rome in January 1831.

. . . The corsair appeared, sang his aria and was applauded, which the corsair above, and maestro below, acknowledged together . . . Then followed many other pieces, and things became tedious. The public thought so too, and as Pacini's grand finale began, those in the pit stood up, began talking loudly and laughing, and turned their backs to the stage. Mme Samoilow swooned in her box and had to be carried out. Pacini disappeared from the piano, and the curtain fell at the end of the act amid tumult. – Now followed the grand ballet *Barbe-bleu*, then the last act of the opera. As they were now really warmed up, they whistled down the whole of the ballet from beginning to end, and similarly accompanied the second act of the opera with hisses and laughter . . . I should have been angry if the music had created a furore, because it is so wretched as to be beneath criticism. But that now they should turn their backs on their darling Pacini, whom they wanted to garland on the Capitol, ape and caricature his melodies, makes me angry too, and it shows how low a composer stands in the general esteem. On another occasion they would carry him home on their shoulders – that is no compensation.[90]

Dickens too was much impressed by 'the uncommonly hard and cruel character of the audience' in Genoa, and wondered if there might not be some political ground that partially excused it: 'as there is nothing else of a public nature at which they are allowed to express the least disapprobation, perhaps they are resolved to make the most of this opportunity.'[91]

Ghislanzoni seems to confirm this when he writes: 'All the anger, the contumely, the calumnies which today erupt in political conflict gathered at that time around the heads of poets and artists; and they used to fall upon them fiercely and with deadly effect.'[92]

But for all the social brilliance of the opera house, and notwithstanding the inattention which the conventions of the day encouraged, or the hasty and heartless rejection of a composer's work to which audiences were perhaps too prone, what was really sought in the opera house and what was experienced amazingly often when the best of their composers and the best of their performers came together was an intoxicating rapture, an intensity of delight that for its spontaneity and conviviality has few parallels in the modern experience of music. During the Carnival season 1830–1 Glinka was in Milan, and recorded that

In the few performances [of La Sonnambula] given before the theatres closed, Pasta and Rubini sang with the most evident enthusiasm to support their favourite maestro; in the second act the singers themselves wept and carried their audiences along with them so that in the happy days of carnival, tears were continually being wiped away in boxes and parquet alike. Embracing Shterich in the Ambassador's box, I, too, shed tears of emotion and ecstasy.[93]

And there is a fascinating passage in Heinrich Heine's *Reisebilder* in which the poet probes a little beneath the surface of this kind of emotional scene:

A facial expression suggestive of suffering is most clearly visible in the Italians when one speaks with them of the misfortune of their homeland, and there is opportunity enough for that in Milan. That is the most painful wound in the breast of the Italians, and they wince as soon as one touches on it, even lightly. Then they have a way of moving their shoulders, which fills us with strange pity. One of my British friends regards the Italians as politically indifferent because they listen with apparent unconcern when we foreigners talk politics – about Catholic emancipation and the Turkish war; and he was so unjust as to express himself mockingly on this point to a pale Italian with a beard as black as pitch. The evening before, we had seen the production of a new opera at La Scala and listened to the scenes of slaughter which as usual had formed part of the occasion. 'You Italians', said the Briton to the pale man, 'seem to be dead to everything except music; this is the only thing still able to excite you.' 'You wrong us,' said the pale man, and moved his shoulders. 'Ah,' he sighed, 'Italy sits amid her ruins, dreaming elegiacally, and if sometimes, at the melody of some song, she awakens of a sudden and springs wildly up, this enthusiasm is not just for the song itself but rather for the old memories and emotions which the song awakened, which Italy always carries in her heart, and which now pour out in a torrent – and that is the meaning of that mad uproar which you heard in La Scala.'

Perhaps this observation affords some insight into the enthusiasm which Rossini's or Meyerbeer's operas provoke everywhere beyond the Alps. If I have even seen human madness, it was at a performance of the *Crociato in*

Egitto when the music sometimes made a transition from a soft, sad mood into one of frenzied grief. That madness is called in Italy: *furore*.[94]

Both Glinka's and Heine's words touch upon, without explicitly describing, one aspect of the Italian susceptibility to music which even now has not been wholly suppressed: the immediacy and the spontaneity with which they expressed their enjoyment or emotion. One should not imagine that the habit of withholding applause until the last note has died away, which today passes for well-mannered, was current anywhere in the early nineteenth century. Nevertheless, that the Italians' lack of inhibition was something quite different from what was to be experienced in other parts of Europe is clear from what Spohr and Meyerbeer and others had to say about it. Their habit of applauding immediately and uninhibitedly anything that had given delight was only gradually repressed in the last years of the nineteenth century during Toscanini's brilliant bullying incumbency at La Scala. In Verdi's youth it was still undiminished. The effect which that kind of conduct had on the musical and dramatic style of *ottocento* opera is one of the questions to be examined in the next chapter.

Dramatic principles and musical form in early *ottocento* opera

Opera as drama

At Mantua in the year 1607, a decade of experimental attempts by antiquarians and intellectuals to recreate the lyrical dramatic art of the Ancient Greeks was suddenly transfigured by the appearance among the votaries of the Spirit of Music. She is the protagonist in the prologue of Monteverdi's *favola in musica, Orfeo*, and this is what she sings:

> I am Music; who, with my sweet accents,
> Am able to calm every troubled heart;
> And now with noble wrath and now with love
> I can inflame even the coldest hearts.
> I am wont to sing to the golden lyre
> Giving delight to the ears of men,
> And in this way I incline their souls
> To the sonorous harmony of the heavenly lyre.
> Today I am moved to tell you of Orpheus,
> Of Orpheus who drew the wild beasts by the power of his singing
> And made Hades obedient to his prayers ...

Striggio's verses have an application far wider than he could have imagined when he wrote them. For they serve not merely as a prologue to *Orfeo*, but as a statement of the principles underlying the whole tradition of Italian opera for the next three centuries. An opera was a dramatic representation of a worthwhile story, a representation made not to the accompaniment of music, but *in* music; and the primary medium of the representation was song. It belonged to the natural inherent faculties of music to be able to soothe and uplift the spirit, but the faculty that was more particularly significant for opera was that of expressing the passions, of 'inflaming even the coldest heart, now with noble wrath, and now with love'.

Opera is drama; opera is impassioned song. While the principle that Striggio had cloaked in a classicizing allegorical form was expressed in a variety of ways down the centuries, no one working within the Italian tradition would have ventured to challenge it. It received perhaps its most trenchant statement in the words Bellini wrote to his librettist Pepoli during work on *I Puritani*: 'Carve in your head in letters of adamant: *the music drama must draw tears, inspire terror, make people die, through singing.*'[1] The dilemma inherent in this tradition was, as has always been recognized, that of determining how exactly the dramatic purpose and the musical medium were to be held in balance. Was it in fact possible for drama and music to maintain perfect equilibrium, to be wholly themselves and yet at the same time mutually dependent and mutually illuminating? If not, were Algarotti and his followers correct in asserting that the composer 'ought to be in a subordinate station', that his 'chief business is to predispose the minds of the audience for receiving the impression to be excited by the poet's verse'? Or should some artificial and schematic alternation of priorities be devised such as that of the classical *opera seria* perfected by Metastasio in the 1720s? Or should it rather be said that the function of the drama was to provide pretexts for impassioned song, that it was indeed a case of *dramma per musica* – drama *for* music?

In early-nineteenth-century Italy it was probably the last view that was most prevalent. Certainly the expression of intense and egocentric passions filled a larger proportion of the operas than ever before. In seventeenth-century Venetian opera, relief had been provided by scenes of comedy and enchantment; in Metastasian *opera seria* the sway of the passions had been suspended by sententiousness and disciplined by reason. But in the early *ottocento*, as befitted the tumultuousness of the times, the passions raged unbridled and obsessive, driving the protagonists to an irrational doom. Mazzini, as ever with his eye on a future of corporate, socialized Humanity, saw in the music of Rossini and his followers the cult of individualism at its peak:

Generally speaking, the principle of individualism ... has inspired our music, and it dominates it still. The I is king: a despotic and solitary king ... Lyrical to the point of delirium, passionate to the point of intoxication, volcanic as the soil that gave it birth, scintillating as the sun which shines down on the earth ... it leaps from one thing to another, from one passion to another, from one thought to another, from laughter to tears, from rage to love, from heaven to hell ... it has twice as much life as other living things, and a heart that beats feverishly ...[2]

And though passion was a fiercer, madder, more all-pervasive thing for the Napoleonic and post-Napoleonic generations than it had been for their forefathers, they did not yet doubt that song was the proper medium for its expression. It was by singing, not by veristic declamation nor by exploring the expressive resources of the symphony orchestra, that Bellini aspired to move his audiences to 'tears, terror, and death'.

It was also prophetic of the character of the Italian opera tradition that Monteverdi should have composed the elevated declamation of Striggio's Spirit of Music in the strict form of the strophic variation. For the vast majority of Italian opera composers strict formal patterns were part of the essence of music: they were certainly not to be sacrificed merely as a consequence of music's association with drama. Frenzied and destructive as the passions might be by which the characters of early *ottocento* opera were moved, the composer's deep-rooted instinct for clarity and precision remained basically unaffected. Musical forms had become more various since the eighteenth century, but forms they remained, distinct solo and ensemble 'numbers', in which the composer was subject to no conditions or inhibitions or pressures save those dictated by the values of his own art. No Italian composer of this period would have subscribed to Gluck's view that his proper office was to 'serve poetry'. Though his songs and ensembles expressed the passions that the librettist's text had suggested, their forms, it was felt, should be quite independent of the drama, arising from the patterns and symmetries and developments most congenial to music. The independence of dramatic action and musical form was still axiomatic to Rossini, as he explained to Wagner in 1860: 'As a matter of fact [a play], if one simply considers the rational, rapid, and regular development of the dramatic action, makes no use of conventional forms. Only how can this independence required by the literary conception be maintained in an alliance with musical form, which is wholly dependent upon convention?'[3]

With the younger generation of composers that followed Rossini, particularly with Bellini, the relationship between drama and music was once again to become more intimate and mutually dependent. Nevertheless, the dramatic principles, the musical form and much of the musical style of early *ottocento* opera were the creations of Rossini, and they carried with them well into the second half of the century the marks of his conviction that, whatever the character of the drama, the composer must preserve a measure of independence from it, must uphold his right to work as a pure musician, creating the kinds of formal patterns, the kinds of order and logic that were proper to his art. It is one of the pleasantest ironies of nineteenth-century operatic history that Rossini was an inspiration for

Schopenhauer's 'metaphysics of music', and hence, indirectly, of Wagner's *Tristan und Isolde*.

Words and music

It was a necessary consequence of this belief that the long-established distinction between the functions of recitative and those of song remained unchallenged. One of the most comprehensive theorists of *ottocento* opera, Carlo Ritorni, was still writing in 1841 in terms that might have applied equally well to the Metastasian *opera seria*.

[The arias] are like gems joined together in a piece of jewelry, and the metal which joins them is the recitative. This can be considered as the path along which the action progresses; the cantabile is the place where it stops and dwells upon a peroration of the passions ... They are by nature such different things that one must be careful not to dress the one in the attributes of the other, and to ensure that a clear line separates them.[4]

Recitative in which the action of the drama advanced and formal songs and ensembles in which the passions were expressed was the age-old recipe of Italian opera. Where Rossini and his contemporaries parted from the eighteenth-century masters was in the placing of the musical movements, which were as likely to occur at the beginning or in the middle of a scene as at the end of it, and, most strikingly, in the variousness and expansiveness of the musical forms they employed. The 'full music' (to use Metastasio's term) was taking over a larger proportion of the operatic design, and as a result the 'half-music' (the recitative) – and by extension the dramatic action – was becoming cramped. There was no longer room for the elegant and exhaustive dialogues in which classical *opera seria* had advanced the action, nor for such purely literary graces as the sententious maxims with which the action had been adorned and interpreted. Faced with a libretto by Tottola or Gaetano Rossi no one would have been moved to exclaim, as Saverio Mattei did of Metastasio, 'What philosophy! What maxims! What truths!'[5] What was required of the librettist in the early nineteenth century was that he should set up as plausibly and rapidly as possible the kinds of situation in which impassioned song could flourish. Strong situations and fierce passions had become the primary requirements of a libretto; 'you have given me verses, but not situations' was apparently a standard reproach of Rossini to his librettists.[6]

It was the search for such things that made Italian opera a more willing victim of north European Romanticism than was Italian literature. And it was the feeling that too many librettists and composers had pursued their very proper quest for situations and passions into the realms of the unnatural and the grotesque, that 'the Italian muses had yielded up their ancient seat to the Nordic harpies',[7] that prompted many of the complaints that were to be heard about the tastelessness and decadence of the form; as the classicizing librettist Luigi Torrigiani complained of Bellini: 'He has explained to me that the classic style is cold and boring ... Unnatural confrontations in the midst of forests, among tombs and such like are the situations that attract him.'[8] Even Romani, Bellini's preferred collaborator and the most admired librettist of the age, was not entirely happy about the developments in taste which he had helped bring about:

For myself, I confess, when I am most bored by the reveries of our Hugos and our Scotts, when I am most afflicted by the depressing philosophism that discolours and turns every flower of this life pale, I take refuge in the past centuries, I warm myself in the sun of ancient wisdom, and console myself for the turpitude of the present with the virtue of the past.[9]

The system would have worked best if librettists and composers had been content with simple stories, uncomplicated by intrigues and subplots, and characters who are naturally and obviously passionate and energetic. Opera is a more congenial home for the Marin Falieros and Othellos of this world than for the Jacopo Foscaris and Macbeths. Ritorni's prescription for a libretto seems eminently reasonable:

The character of a really operatic subject is that which offers incidents that can be developed easily and spontaneously, rather by means of action and a few words, than by means of long-drawn-out disputations ... The characters should be selected from among the more animated and decisive types, who do not need many words to make their hidden emotions understood, but rather speak through their actions. Then they should all have a particular colour which distinguishes them from the others, so that together they form the contrasts and the gradations of a harmonious picture ...[10]

Two works in which such principles are exhibited with rare success are the Bellini/Romani masterpieces La Sonnambula and Norma. In both cases the simplicity of the action makes it possible for the recitatives to be brief without seeming inadequate to their dramatic purpose, the emotional states of the characters can be explored fully and carefully, and as a result both operas achieve consistency of style and distinctiveness of tone. They provide in fact fine examples of that elusive concept which contemporary writers called *colorito*. Basevi describes this desideratum in the following terms:

The music finds ... in the basic idea of the drama a form of support, a focus on which, more or less, according to the genius of the composer, all the pieces making up the opera converge ... There is no doubt that the general *colorito* of an opera reveals the composer's talent better than anything else, because it shows us his faculty for synthesis. When the composer has succeeded in conceiving what is necessary to give his music – by means of the disposition of the notes, the harmonic style, the choice of instruments etc. – the desired *colorito*, then he has set a standard, established a rule, created limiting conditions to which the various numbers, the themes, the accompaniments etc. can easily be referred. From this results a *whole* which surprises and attracts the listener irresistibly; and, full of admiration, he is constrained to recognize the opera as a work of genius.[11]

The stylistic unity of *La Sonnambula* and *Norma* is by no means typical of the genre, however. When the means by which the opera occasioned delight was the expression of the passions, it was tempting to suppose that the wider and more varied the range of passions the better. Innumerable are the operas of this period in which the attempt to incorporate too wide a range of colours destroys the dramatic coherence. Perhaps still more numerous are those in which one feels that because of the conventional pattern of the scenes, the preservation of the old distinctions between 'half-music' and the various types of 'full music', it is difficult to distinguish the primary dramatic issues from the secondary ones. Under such circumstances certain critics felt that the opera as it was constituted was incapable of dealing with real dramatic themes at all: 'Who would seek in an opera for one idea?' asked Mazzini, scathingly.[12] Regardless of the complexity of the action or the density of thought underlying a particular scene, the operatic pattern demanded that recitatives be kept as brief as possible. Where the whole effort of the librettist and composer was concentrated on a single dramatic idea or a closely related group of ideas there was no harm in that. Where not, the disproportion between the constituent elements of the opera became excessive:

Instead of the opera being composed of harmoniously contrasted parts, in such a way that it is precisely the chiaroscuro of the one in relation to the others which shows us more clearly the unity, the individuality and solidity of the whole, the so-called pieces are a series of dainties, bait for gluttonous palates, which are infused at random in a little tasteless broth to keep them moist and separate, and so as not to provide completely desiccated nourishment, but with the intention that anyone can remove them from this moisture at pleasure.[13]

Several commentators observed the danger in a development that was leading to ever more elaborate and extended musical numbers and correspondingly impatient recitative. But it was Mazzini who expressed most vividly the sense that opera had become a chaotic and fragmented art, and that it could not recover any real strength until librettists and composers learned to concentrate on some unifying dramatic idea. Along with most of the composers working in the 1830s, Mazzini felt that the opera 'could only be defined by the enumeration of its parts' –

a series of cavatinas, choruses, duets, trios and finales, interrupted – not joined together – by any old recitative, which is not listened to: a mosaic, a gallery, an accumulation, more often a clash of different ideas, independent and disconnected, which swirl about like spirits in a magic circle ... a tumult, a whirl of figures and phrases and little musical concepts which remind you of those lines of Dante about the souls of the dead, about the 'words of grief', about the 'accents of wrath', about the 'shrill and hoarse voices', and about the clapping of hands which is heard in our theatres as it is at the gates of Hell. You would say it was a witches' sabbath – you would say it was the fantastic chase, across strange moors and meadows, described in a ballad by Bürger. The infernal steed carries Leonora and a dead man – Music and the Public – on its back, dragging them furiously from steep to steep to the sound of that monotonous cadence: 'The dead are riding fast'. Hurrah! Hurrah! Where are we going? What does this music mean? Where is it leading? Where is the unity? Why doesn't it stop at this point? Why does it break off that idea for this one? With what meaning? For what dominant concept? Hurrah! Hurrah! The hour is at hand. Midnight is past. The public demands its rights, its due number of motifs. Give it them; forward! They are a cavatina short, the prima donna hasn't had her rondo. Hurrah – The hour has sounded; they applaud and leave ...[14]

There is no doubt that the musicians involved in the opera – not only the composers, but the singers too – had claimed for themselves an excessive influence on the pattern and style of things, and scarcely conceded a significant role to the librettist at all. It has often been observed that Rossini's music pays scant regard to the metre or even to the meaning of some of the texts he composed. His melodic and rhythmic exuberance and his passion for 'florid song' were not content to demand their legitimate right to unfold according to the principles of musical logic: they seem on occasion to come into being as purely and exclusively musical inspirations, wholly irrelevant to the dramatic context. The ease with which Rossini 'parodied' his music, removing a piece from one context and placing it in another wholly different in mood, is a sign of the tendency of his music to go further than freedom from the drama and to topple over into irrelevance. Even Bellini, who took the dramatic element of his operas far more seriously than Rossini, and who was far more dependent on the poetic quality of his text, had no doubt that the librettist's job was to serve him, and that the composer had the right to handle the texts as he pleased. As he put it in the letter to Pepoli already cited:

... all your absurd rules, perfectly good for a topic of conversation, ... will never convince a living soul who understands something of the difficult art which must *draw tears through singing*.

If my music is beautiful and the opera pleases, you will be able to write a million letters against composers' abuse of poetry without having proved anything.[15]

And it was Bellini's own Romani who penned the most rueful evocation of the tribulations of the early *ottocento* librettist:

[The libretto] is a hasty birth, but little educated, still rough and unpolished: the composer takes charge of it and sometimes subjects it to the torture of Procrustes; he cuts it and stretches it to fit the proportions of the bed on which he has laid it: the singers surround it, and turn it this way and that, as the fancy takes them; they give it the impress of their caprices, and the rehearsal room is the Hebrus which rolls and tosses it about, lacerated as Orpheus was by the Bacchantes. If only it could return to its paternal home, like the son in the parable, and cast off the melancholy spoils acquired on its travels! It does not have the time; it is forcibly dragged to the theatre and appears on stage so ill-used, so distorted and deformed, that its own father blushes to have given it to the light. Believe me, believe me: the dangers run by a melodrama are such that if one were to tell them all the result would be one long Odyssey of misfortunes.[16]

Those who, like Mazzini, regarded opera as being urgently in need of 'reform' believed that a closer collaboration of composer and librettist was a necessary preliminary. Poetry must be the sister of music, not her slave. Mazzini looked forward to a time when 'the poets will write dramas, not verses or worse than verses, and poet and musician will not take turns insulting and tormenting one another, but will approach their work with devotion and with one accord as if it were the work of the sanctuary, the one calling on the other, sharing their inspirations'.[17]

Even Salvatore Cammarano, a working librettist of old-fashioned rather than progressive tastes, was occasionally visited by such idealistic visions.

Did I not fear the imputation of being an Utopian [he wrote to Verdi in 1849] I should be tempted to say that to achieve the highest degree of perfection in an opera it would be necessary for both the words and the music to be the product of one and the same mind: and from this ideal follows my firm opinion that when it has two authors, they must at least be like brothers, and that if Poetry should not be the servant of Music, still less should it tyrannize over her.[18]

The aspirations voiced by Mazzini and Cammarano were only to be realized by Verdi and Boito in the 1880s and 1890s. Nevertheless it would be wrong to give the impression that nothing changed in this respect in the first half of the nineteenth century. Most composers were affected by the trend towards a more mutual dependency of words and music. It was a big step from Rossini's cavalier unconcern for literary values to Bellini's fastidiousness. And it was a big step again from that to the kind of collaborations characteristic of Verdi with, say, Piave, where there is no aspect of the libretto, from the broad architectural layout of the 'sketch' to the minutest verbal details of recitatives and arias, in which the composer is not closely interested. Of course the composer is the dominant partner – despite the theoretical disclaimers of Gluck and Wagner there has never really been a time when he wasn't – but he has learned to appreciate more keenly what he owes or what he can owe to his librettist.

The structural articulation of the opera

In almost all traditions, opera has tended to a high degree of formalism. Partly because of their need to satisfy an insatiable demand for new operas, which left them little time for structural inventiveness, but more seriously because of their instinctive preference for clarity and patterning in music, Italian composers especially were prone to devise schematic designs which, with little essential modification, could serve for more or less any dramatic theme for decades on end. Around 1800, in the late works of Cimarosa and Paisiello and in the operas of Guglielmi and Zingarelli, Paer and Mayr, Italian opera was in one of its transitional periods of flux, the forms both of individual movements and of whole scenes and acts being treated with a freedom and variety unprecedented in the previous hundred years. By 1820, however, a new schematicism had come to prevail; a standard pattern was established for individual numbers and for the opera as a whole, and this became as authoritative for the Italian repertory for the next thirty or forty years as the pattern of the Metastasian *opera seria* had been a hundred years earlier. Ritorni, with some exaggeration, complained that Italian opera's 'worst defect resulted from the boring uniformity of every opera ... each of them composed of parts with a predetermined structure, and from the very same situations and words ... so that all operas are like identical twins. When you have seen one, you have seen them all.'[19]

Dramatic principles and musical form

The principal lawgiver of this new orthodoxy was 'the great reformer' Rossini[20] – which was not a little paradoxical in view of his tendency to idealize the past, and the general spiritual discomfort he felt at being part of an age whose interests revolved around 'steam, plunder, and the barricades'.[21] He has been well called 'the reluctant architect of Italian romantic opera' (by Budden), for he was in sympathy neither with the literary tastes of the younger school of librettists, nor with the new interest in attempting to synthesize text and music into a 'musico-dramatic' unity, nor yet with the way the *opera buffa* was slowly losing its hold on the repertory in favour of heroic opera. Nevertheless the authority of this blithe misfit was irresistible for two reasons. First, because as a composer he had the decisiveness and flamboyance of manner that enabled him to restore real stylishness to the Italian operatic idiom. Secondly, because his zest for movement, his sense of rhythmic animation, prompted him to revitalize the heroic opera with an infusion of *buffo* elements, so giving tangible and emphatic form to a tendency that had been 'in the air' for some years. Once a composer with a really assured style had done what everyone had long sensed was desirable, his influence became all-pervasive. As Pacini was to write: 'Everyone followed the same school, the same fashions, and as a result they were all imitators of the *great luminary* just as I was. But, good heavens, what could one do if there was no other way of making a living? If I was a follower of the great man of Pesaro, so was everyone else.'[22]

Mozart's *La Clemenza di Tito*, with its profusion of dynamic arias moving during their courses from slow to fast, and with its regular succession of ensembles, which Mazzolà has let into the Metastasian fabric to transform it into a 'vera opera', shows that there was nothing unprecedented in the interest in fusing the two mediums which so many Italian composers showed in the early *ottocento*. Similar formal procedures – *andante–allegro* aria designs, regular use of large-scale ensemble movements, combination of soloists and chorus and especially the massive grand finales – are to be found in Italy too. But until Rossini the movement of the heroic opera remained somewhat formal and ponderous. It was he who gave elegance and sparkle, as appropriate, to its lyrical style, and who, especially, filled every fibre of the music with a new kind of pulsing vitality, driving along arias and ensembles alike with a texture of dancing or marching orchestral figures, and giving the whole an orchestral colouring so bright and sharply profiled as to be almost garish.

One of the many paradoxes of Rossini's position is that while he was giving new zest to the language of Italian opera he was encouraging a regularity in its structural layout that by 1820 was to result in almost complete formal stagnation. It was not that Rossini in any way attempted to undo the achievements of the previous generation, from Piccini to Mayr. Like them he aimed to give a new dramatic vitality to the scena by incorporating a wider variety of styles and tempos into it. Like them he spread the 'full music' over a larger proportion of the scenes, drastically reducing the amount of *secco* recitative, and linking up the constituent parts rather with contributions from the chorus and orchestra. But where such composers as Cimarosa and Guglielmi applied these principles in whatever manner seemed appropriate to the dramatic task in hand, with the result that their scores show a wide variety of formal patterns, Rossini preferred to establish an 'ideal' and conventional pattern to be used regularly in the majority of full-scale scenas in his operas. This pattern was given its authoritative stamp in collaboration with the librettist Tottola during Rossini's Neapolitan period (1815–22).

According to this Rossinian scheme, the dramatic action of the opera is articulated into a series of quite substantial scenes, each of which is built round a single incident or dramatic idea and is enacted, in all essentials, by a small group of characters. Within each of these scenes the dominant dramatic theme is examined from every probable point of view, and this examination employs a standard pattern at once simple, coherent and satisfying. Initially the dramatic mood is established, or the dramatic issue stated. Next it is meditated upon by one or more of the characters involved. After this meditation, new forces are brought to bear upon the prevailing theme: they may be external, physical forces manifested in stage action, or they may be internal forces, manifested only in the transition from deliberation to decision in the mind of the protagonist. In either case, their function is to precipitate the climax of the scene, a climax in which the mood is transformed, or the dramatic issue resolved: we pass from retrospection to anticipation, from quiet thought to decisive action.

Intolerably schematic as this design may seem when thus abstracted, it was in fact particularly apt for the fluid yet architectural medium of music. The variousness of pace and mood in the music could diversify the regularity of the structure, and at the same time derive from that structure much of its own formal security. Moreover, the great singers of the period found that the design enabled them at each of their appearances on stage to exhibit the whole range of their art, declamatory, lyrical and virtuosic. The dramatic mood was established in an orchestral and/or recitative introduction; it was mused over in a lyrical aria, the cantabile; it was subtly or violently reorientated in a declamatory transition, the *tempo di mezzo*; and finally it was transformed into action in the brilliant concluding aria, the cabaletta.

In the solo scenes of an opera this regularity of form tends to be obscured by an apparently arbitrary variety of terminology – scena, aria, cavatina, *sortita*, rondo etc. This variety of terminology is in part a survival from the time before Rossini when a genuine variety of forms were used in opera, and in part a reflection of the placing of the scene within the opera as a whole. After Rossini such terms tell us nothing about the form of the scene, only about its position. The cavatina, for example, is the aria in the scene in which a principal singer makes his or her first appearance, hence its other name, the (aria di) *sortita*; the rondo, a term becoming rare by 1840, is a principal singer's final aria. In terms of structure and style there is little or nothing to distinguish them from one another or from 'arias'. All these types employ the pattern described above.

So congenial was this pattern to Rossini and his followers, so precisely did its contrasts of style and its gathering momentum seem to reconcile the interests of form and those of drama, that it was applied to the ensemble scenes as regularly as to the solo ones. Such ensembles were by now as prominent a feature of the heroic opera as they had long been of the *opera buffa*. But whereas the eighteenth-century *buffo* ensemble arose from the desire to set action to music, the ensemble of the nineteenth-century heroic opera arose rather from the desire to create a musical form out of conflicts of passion. The pattern of the solo scenes was elaborated by antitheses, by statements and counterstatements, which result in a still more formal structure. Only in one respect however is the ensemble scene likely to differ structurally from the solo scene. It often happens that the cantabile is preceded by an additional movement, known as the *primo tempo*. As the dramatic action is sometimes still moving forward during this *primo tempo* it tends to have a more relaxed design. The give and take between the voices is less regular than in cantabile and cabaletta, and the cohesion is generally dependent upon a symmetrical pattern of themes in the orchestra. One should add that in the larger ensembles the term 'cabaletta' was generally replaced by 'stretta'.

Between about 1820 and the 1850s the only parts of an Italian opera which did not conform to the pattern described were the handful of single-movement pieces, whether solo or choral, and the so-called introduction, the basically choral movement that followed the orchestral sinfonia or prelude. The most convenient definition of the introduction is Stendhal's: 'the term *introduction* covers every-thing that is sung between the end of the overture and the first recitative'.[23] Ritorni however distinguishes two basic types:

The one consists of choruses – without which no modern opera commences – among which are interwoven the voices of one or more of the subsidiary characters to form one complete number . . . The other – and this is the really choice form of the introduction – admits some principal character besides and is a compound musical picture with . . . something of the character of the grand scena.[24]

He also suggests that it may have been the development of the introduction that had led to a decline in the popularity of the full-scale sinfonia or overture.

It was not merely in the organization of the individual scenes that Rossini established a pattern imitated by his successors for decades. The plan of whole acts became equally a matter of preordination and stereotype. Again Ritorni provides an authoritative contemporary account:

After the introduction it is necessary to think about the so-called *sortite* of the principal characters, which usually take the form of three cavatinas, either preceded by short recitatives or more often *ex abrupto*. These triumphal first appearances of theirs, which provoke the expected applause from the audience, and which at once make it clear what they are capable of, have therefore become so indispensable to them that, although in some scores they may go so far as to sacrifice their second-act rondo, they will virtually never sacrifice their cavatina.

The scale of composition has expanded so much that the number of pieces has been reduced proportionally, and the first act, apart from the aforemen-tioned cavatinas, the introduction and the finale, consists only of a duet or a pair of dialogued pieces . . .

The second act begins sometimes with a kind of introduction performed by the chorus and some subsidiary character . . . Thereafter the act consists of the rondos of the three principal singers, none of which will willingly be sacrificed, of a duet – in which the greatest importance will be attached to its situation, its composition and its execution – and often of an ensemble for a larger number of voices . . .

At one time . . . arias for the secondary characters were inserted; but they became tedious, and fell out of favour. Now, more judiciously, at least one song for the chorus is introduced.

Operas used to end (and at that time they had a happy ending) with a *polacca*: a cabaletta sung by the principals one after another . . . But then the prima donna . . . turned her mind to the task of appropriating the final applause for herself and chose to end the drama with her own rondo . . .

In recent operas, where the subject matter is taken from more tragic sources, it has become customary to combine the pathetic dénouement with a rondo ... [to form] what is called the grand *scena* of the protagonist.[25]

The general accuracy of Ritorni's observations may be confirmed if we set out the pattern of movements in almost any of the Italian operas composed by Rossini and his successors. Bellini's *Il Pirata* will serve as an example:

Ouverture

Act I
1. Introduzione (chorus with bass solo)
2. Recitativo e Cavatina (double aria with chorus: tenor)
3. Recitativo e Cavatina (double aria with female chorus: soprano)
4. Coro
5. Recitativo e Duetto (ariosos, *primo tempo*, cantabile, cabaletta: soprano, tenor)
6. Coro ed Aria (chorus with march, double aria: bass)
7. Recitativo, Quintetto, Finale del Atto Primo (recit. etc., cantabile, *tempo di mezzo* and *stretta*)

Act II
8. Coro d'Introduzione
9. Recitativo e Duetto (*primo tempo*, cantabile, cabaletta)
10. Duetto e Terzetto (*primo tempo a2*, cantabile *a3*, cabaletta *a3*)
11. Coro
12. Scena ed Aria (double aria: tenor)
13. Scena ed Aria (double aria: soprano)

Apart from the chorus no. 4, the preference for the term 'aria' instead of 'rondo', and the suppression of one of the bass's arias, this is exactly the scheme outlined by Ritorni. And *Il Pirata* is the work in which Romani claimed to be seeking to wean Bellini away from his dependence on 'school rules and the servility of imitation'.[26]

'L'arte di far libretti'

This discussion of the schematization of *ottocento* opera, with its tendency to reduce all dramatic themes to a stereotyped formal pattern and to typify all varieties of character, may be closed with a brief reference to one of the several satirical examinations of the conventions of *ottocento* opera. It is the work of Antonio Ghislanzoni, adapter of the Italian version of the libretto of *Aida*, and appeared in his *Capricci Letterarj* in 1870. 'L'arte di far libretti', as the work is called, itself takes the form of an opera libretto, in which the conventional forms and the conventional preoccupations of the type are deliciously travestied.

The curtain rises on 'a hall, a forest or a square, at the convenience of the scenographer', and from a distance the following chorus is heard:

> Al cominciar dell'opera,
> Siccome è nostra usanza,
> Una preghiera o un brindisi
> Cantiamo in lontananza ...
> E perchè il dotto pubblico
> Alla canzon plaudisca,
> Facciam ch'ei non capisca
> Quello che noi cantiam.
>   Dunque ... preghiam!
>   Dunque ... beviam!
> Poi tutti, senza muoverci ... fuggiam!

The principal tenor enters with a *comprimario*. A brief recitative dialogue ends:

> Or va, diletto mio – veglia da lunge ...
> Esplora il bosco, la vallata, il colle
> Mentre io canto *l'adagio* in *mi bemolle*.

Planting himself next to the prompter's box, the tenor then breaks into the first movement of his cavatina.

> Per quel destin che a gemere
> Condanna ogni tenore,
> La moglie del baritono
> Amo di immenso amore ...
> E questo ardente affetto
> Cui nulla estinguer può,
> Nel prossimo duetto
> A tutti ... e a lei dirò.

At this point the *comprimario* returns in great agitation, and sings hoarsely into the tenor's ear:

> Or che *l'adagio*
> Hai terminato
> Tenor carissimo
> Son qui tornato
> Per darti il tempo
> Di riposar.

Thanking the *comprimario*, the tenor strolls briefly about the stage, only to be summoned back by a fanfare of trumpets to the footlights, where he cries out at the top of his voice

> Nuovi prodigi il pubblico
> Dalla mia gola aspetta
> Ei vuol la cabaletta

> La cabaletta avrà.
> E griderò si forte:
> Guerra, sterminio e morte!
> Che di mie note al turbine
> La vôlta crollerà.

The tenor's cavatina is followed by the soprano's, and that by a duet for the two of them, of which the tenor's solo verse and the continuation are perhaps worth quoting:

> Non iscordar, bell' angelo,
> Che prima donna sei;
> Perchè il libretto è serio
> Morir con me tu dei ...
> In barba al Re baritono,
> Al basso e ad altri ancora,
> Infino all'ultim'ora
> Noi canterem insiem.
> Ed i maggiori applausi
> Per certo coglierem. (*rullo di timpani*)

PRIMA DONNA: O mio spavento! (*atterrito*)
TENORE: I timpani (*accorrendo*)
PRIMA DONNA: Tu pure udisti.
TENORE: Ho udito ...
PRIMA DONNA: Sempre quel suon funereo
            Precede mio marito ...

Notwithstanding Ghislanzoni's burlesque, the long survival of Rossini's pattern of opera proves that it had a fundamental strength and logic. By preserving the time-honoured distinction of half-music and full music it allowed the composer to concentrate on the task that was felt to be most intrinsically musical, that of expressing the passions in song. At the same time the elaboration of the simple aria of the eighteenth century into a musical complex constituted from recitative, cantabile, *tempo di mezzo* and cabaletta lent the pattern a new degree of dynamism, and enabled the composer to bring all the resources of his art to bear on each phase of the operatic design.

External pressures on the operatic form

Nevertheless, it would be vain to try to pretend that every aspect of the form and style of early *ottocento* opera served a strictly musical or strictly dramatic function. We have already seen that opera-going in the early nineteenth century was not, as it is today, an occasional treat: it was a social habit which had developed an etiquette wholly forgotten by the modern opera-goer, and this etiquette was reflected in certain details of the music. Some features of the *ottocento* idiom are clearly attributable to the fact that composers and singers had only a partial claim on the audience's attention. To take one simple example, if Stendhal was right in saying that at most performances silence was observed only during the more memorable passages (cf. p. 42 above), then obviously there had to be some convention by which the audience could know when those passages were likely to occur. Here, surely, we have one explanation for that schematization of the pattern of movements within the act already commented on. One such highlight in virtually every opera of the period was the prima donna's *aria di sortita*. This, it came to be felt, created the best effect if placed about a third of the way through the first act: by then the orchestra and chorus were warmed up, late-comers in the audience were settled, and a preponderance of male-voice colouring in the opening scenes could have been used to set off the soprano more effectively. And so the convention hardened: the placing of the *aria di sortita* became virtually obligatory. By the 1820s not even the most impassioned card-player, not even the most loquacious of conversationalists, need have feared that he might be unprepared for it.

But although the teeming social life in the opera house was an important factor affecting the character and form of *ottocento* opera, it was probably less crucial than the fact that every opera that Rossini, Donizetti, Bellini and the youthful Verdi composed for production in Italy formed part of an exceptionally homogeneous repertory. Today we are used to a repertory comprising the best and most representative works from a wide variety of operatic traditions. But in the 1830s, when Verdi was a student in Milan, the works that he would have heard at La Scala were exclusively modern and almost exclusively Italian. Apart from Mozart's *Don Giovanni*, which appeared for a brief run in 1836, no work from a pre-Rossini generation was performed during this decade. Modern opera and Italian opera was all audiences knew and all they wanted.

Given the nature of the Italian operatic repertory at that time, these audiences can hardly have failed to have a pretty keen sense of style. They could probably draw distinctions between a Pacini and a Mercadante that would be largely meaningless to us today; and given the hold of the operatic tradition they should have been able at once to savour the enrichments of that tradition achieved by composers of real genius. But even if one chooses to take a quite different view, to be entirely cynical about their taste and discrimination, one thing is indisputable. At the very least they regarded themselves as connoisseurs, and they recognized and exploited their authority in the theatre. As Stendhal wrote of the typical Italian audience of his day, 'These are men possessed of seven devils, determined at all costs, by dint of shrieking, stamping and battering with their canes against the backs of the seats in front, to enforce the triumph of *their* opinion, and above all, to prove that, come what may, *none but their opinion is correct.*'[27]

An audience claimed the right to pass judgement on every detail of an operatic performance, and it was by the warmth and frequency of its applause, not by the considered judgement of informed critics, that the success of a work was measured. Verdi's account of the *première* of *Attila* in Venice in 1846 is a typical composer's post-mortem: '*Attila* enjoyed a very good success. There were calls after every piece, but it was the whole of the first act that was applauded with the greatest enthusiasm. I had high hopes of the second- and third-act finales, but either I was mistaken or the public did not understand, because they were less warmly applauded ...'[28]

Given these conditions, it is clear that when he was writing an opera, the composer was not merely concerned with drama and with song. He had also to take cognizance of a social milieu in which he was competing for the audience's attention; and he had to be prepared to engage in a kind of ritual in which he sought that audience's applauding participation. It was thus impossible for early *ottocento* opera to be music drama of a kind in which every detail had some ideal significance apart from the circumstances in which it was originally performed; on the contrary, these circumstances had a direct effect on the idiom and form of the opera. The give and take between performers and listeners was much more direct and frequent than we are now accustomed to. At each stage in the opera the audience wished to pass judgement, and the composer, having done his best to soothe or stir or harrow them with his songs, submitted himself to this judgement.

The ritual of audience participation had to be provided for in the operatic form. And so the wholly rational formal scheme which I have described came to be adorned with a number of features that served no other purpose than that of making room for the ceremony of judgement-passing, that had in fact more to do with public relations than with art. As Liszt put it to Schumann, 'Rossini and his colleagues always conclude with a "votre très humble serviteur".'[29] These ritual adornments naturally gathered round the two aria or ensemble passages in the scene, the cantabile and the cabaletta.

When Spohr was in Italy in 1816–17, he was frequently moved to comment on the universal enthusiasm for Rossini that prevailed at that time. On one occasion, speaking of Rossini's 'florid song', he observes: 'Whenever these sweet trifles are well performed by the singers, the audience bursts into enraptured applause.'[30] I take it that Spohr means spontaneously and unpredictably; but it was not long before the applause for the cantabile was being deliberately manipulated. It became the custom for the end of the cantabile to be very obviously announced, by a cadenza, and for this cadenza to be succeeded by a hiatus in the musical design, which could be made as long as the audience's enthusiasm demanded. Given the gentle pace and the florid character of most cantabiles of the period, the cadenza is a perfectly congruous way of ending it – several of Chopin's nocturnes provide good examples of the same habit transferred to the instrumental medium – but we cannot doubt that in Italian opera it was also a signal in the ritual of audience participation. One of the several pieces of evidence that make this quite clear is a letter written from Rome in 1831 by Mendelssohn. Much of the letter is taken up with disparaging comments on the standard of instrumental playing in the city: one of the details Mendelssohn cites was a concert in which a flute solo had been played more than a quarter-tone sharp; 'it gave me toothache,' he wrote, 'but no one noticed it, and because there was a trill at the end, they applauded mechanically'.[31]

The situation with the cabaletta was more complex, partly because there was a purely artistic problem here. The tempo was brisk, the idiom brilliant; so how, without becoming diffuse, could the composer provide a piece sufficiently imposing to act as a consummation of the whole long and emotionally complex scene? But this was not the sole consideration. There was the audience's participation to be provided for; and there was also, despite Rossini's drastic attempts to reduce it, the singer's art of improvised ornamentation, which was assuredly not yet dead, and which would presumably come into its own at this juncture.

Rossini himself generally adopted a cabaletta form in which, after an intermediate cadence, a substantial proportion of the music was repeated. But in his later works and in those of his followers this idea was taken further. All the considerations I have mentioned were satisfied by the simple and drastic step of repeating the cabaletta in its entirety. This solved the problem of proportions; and when the two statements of the cabaletta were linked by a strident orchestral din it gave the audience a space to applaud in. If they did applaud, the cabaletta repeat gave the impression of being an encore, which the singer could adorn with impromptu variation. The final stage in the cabaletta ceremony was marked by an extended *più mosso*, played by the orchestral *tutti* throughout, and comprising little but a series of cadence reiterations.

Taken all together, this process amounts to something rather different from the cadenza and hiatus that concluded the cantabile. Here we have a concept, nowadays quite unfamiliar, according to which some of the music is designed not merely as a cue for applause but actually to accompany applause. Its loudness and brashness illuminate no dramatic issue; they serve merely to stimulate the audience's enthusiasm. This fact explains that strange dichotomy which we almost always find in a cabaletta of this period. The aria itself may be composed with a keen sense of mood and even verbal nuance, but the link between the two statements and the *più mosso* at the end totally disregard such things. However low an opinion one may have of early *ottocento* opera, one can scarcely suppose that composers wrote passages of such bludgeoning monotony in order that audiences should listen to them and derive pleasure from them.

One amusing illustration of the real situation again comes from Spohr, whose first meeting with an Italian audience was at a concert in La Scala in September 1816. He describes the occasion quite fully: 'I had the pleasure of seeing that my new concerto, which I had composed in Switzerland and which was in the form of a lyrical scena, appealed very strongly to the tastes of the Italians, and especially all the lyrical passages were received with the greatest enthusiasm.'[32] It seems that at the end of each of the solo sections of his concerto Spohr was loudly applauded. This he regarded as a mixed blessing. After all, he was no mere violin virtuoso; he was an earnest German symphonist, too. He continues: 'This noisy applause, welcome and encouraging as it is for the soloist, remains nevertheless an intense annoyance to the composer. As a result of it all continuity is destroyed, the painstakingly elaborated *tuttis* go quite unnoticed, and one hears the soloist recommence in a new key, without knowing how the orchestra effected the modulation.' An Italian composer, familiar with the habits of his fellow-countrymen, knew better than to waste time in the 'painstaking elaboration' of his *tuttis*. The orchestral tumult that he released at the end of a cabaletta was, in the words of another German observer, 'a mere invitation to applause ... It is the enthusiasm of the audience set to music.'[33]

Developments in the tradition between Rossini and Verdi

In principle the structure and the dramatic purpose of Italian opera remained unchanged from Rossini's time down to Verdi's 'middle period'. In fact, though, its character did undergo a gradual transformation. One of the reasons for this was that all the major composers of the period, at some stage of their careers, showed themselves ready to stand up against and root out certain abuses that looked like becoming part of the 'tradition'.

One such abuse, the elimination of which transformed the character of Italian opera in the first half of the nineteenth century, was the unlimited licence to vary and embellish their music which the leading singers had inherited from the eighteenth-century *castrati*. A few *castrati* had of course survived the Napoleonic period and were still active in opera in the early years of the Restoration. Indeed it was as a result of his contretemps with Velluti, the last of the great operatic *castrati*, that Rossini embarked on the first and crucial stage in this reform. Velluti was the leading singer in *Aureliano in Palmira*, first performed in Milan in 1813. According to the composer's own account, Velluti embellished his songs with a profusion of *fioritura* that increased at every successive rehearsal, until by the time of the first performance, Rossini was unable to recognize his own music.

Rossini's way of dealing with this particular problem was to compose into his music such a quantity of surface decoration that the singers were fully extended in giving even a simple rendering of it. The unrelieved density of its virtuosity meant that further spontaneous adornment was neither needful nor feasible. Clearly the first obvious outcome of this reform was that music became more highly decorated, more coolly virtuosic than ever before. Nor is it likely that the habits of centuries could be stamped out overnight, even by such drastic methods as this. But in the long run Rossini was bringing closer together what composers wrote and what was performed in the theatre. He was creating a situation in which singers were becoming more directly dependent on composers, and in which they might even come to learn the habit of deference. It was this new relationship that Bellini was able to call upon when, at the time of *Il Pirata*, he was intent upon introducing a 'new style' in which song could adopt a dramatically meaningful simplicity without being threatened by the encroachment of improvised coloratura.

Dramatic principles and musical form

Another abuse to be checked during this period was the assumption of many leading singers that because the opera would normally assume such and such a form, they therefore had a right to insist that it always should; that they should be furnished with an *aria di sortita* in the first act, a 'rondo' in the second, and such other movements as became the dignity of a principal, regardless of the subject and style of the drama and whether or not such movements could be accommodated convincingly. The difficulty of departing from the accepted pattern of operatic design seems generally to have proved greater than that of breaking with a habit of style such as impromptu ornamentation. Donizetti could, from bitter experience, have vouched for the justice of Ritorni's observation that principals would not willingly renounce their second-act rondo. For in 1833 in *Lucrezia Borgia* he had attempted to conclude an opera in a different and, in the context, a more dramatically congruous way, only to be informed by the prima donna Henriette-Clémentine Méric-Lalande that without a rondo she would refuse to sing. Donizetti bowed to the inevitable and added the brilliant concluding aria 'Era desso il figlio mio'. A decade later Verdi found himself in a similar position with Sophie Loewe, over the trio finale of *Ernani*. But Verdi had that much more iron in his character than Donizetti and refused to recognize that a rondo finale was a prima donna's 'right'. At the time of *Rigoletto* he recalled the incident of the 'German woman who is now a princess and who didn't like the final trio of *Ernani*: perhaps she wanted a rondo, and meanwhile poor *Ernani* was horribly treated on the first night'.[34] Nor was it always the singers who needed to be carried when composers aimed to make such formal innovations: audiences were sometimes equally intolerant of these forms of originality. A review of the *première* of *Norma* in the Milan journal *L'Eco* reported that 'at the end of the first act, there arose not the least sign of applause ... The Public, which was certainly expecting to hear the first act close with a finale in the grand style, found itself deceived, and was much displeased to see the curtain fall after a not very effective trio.'[35]

Despite such discouraging experiences, however, composers continued to work away, undermining the commonly held view that there was something sacrosanct about the formal schemes established by Rossini. In the late 1830s a prominent 'reformer' was Mercadante, who wrote to Florimo of his *Elena da Feltre*, 'I have continued the revolution begun with *Il Giuramento* – varied the forms, abolished trivial cabalettas, exiled the crescendos; concision, less repetition, some novelty in the cadences; due regard paid to the dramatic side; the orchestration rich, without swamping the voices; long solos in the concerted numbers avoided, as they obliged the other parts to stand coldly by, to the harm of the dramatic action . . .'[36]

There were, then, throughout our period, a series of attacks on the ingrained and schematic habits of the heroic opera: the idea of reform, the determination to root out abuses, seems never to have been long absent from the thoughts of the better composers. In addition there were certain subtle reinterpretations of convention, such as Donizetti's cultivation of the slow cabaletta. All the same there can be no mistaking the fact that the spirit of these reforms was remarkably deferential. In general composers were less concerned with breaking with the habits of the style than with organizing their dramatic themes in such a way as to make the habits appear logical and dramatically motivated.

It was Bellini who showed most resourcefulness in this direction, and his librettist Romani certainly deserves some share of the credit for this. Although his musical instincts were if anything more formal and meticulous even than Rossini's, Bellini's best operas adhere to the established patterns only when he feels that they are dramatically congruous. Elsewhere, without ever giving the impression that he is flouting convention, he proves marvellously adept at contriving dramatically motivated adjustments or reappraisals. In *La Sonnambula*, for example, he characterizes the flirtatious Lisa by suppressing introspective cantabile movements and giving her nothing to sing but cabalettas. And in *Norma* there are several striking examples of a reorganization of the constituent elements of the scene, such as the Adalgisa/Pollione duet in Act I, in which the *primo tempo* and the cantabile are fused together into one emotionally fluctuating movement; or the Act II finale, in which the prima donna's 'rondo' is transformed from a showpiece into a tragic scena by what is essentially a reversal of the standard order, the 'cabaletta' preceding the cantabile. Characteristic of Bellini's approach to opera is his insistence on finding some dramatic motive for involving the chorus in the solo and ensemble scenes. In his view, the sonority, the contrasts, the articulation of the form which the chorus could provide were insufficient grounds for their involvement, unless they could be made to serve some specific dramatic purpose. Rather than bringing a chorus on to the stage in a merely formal and decorative capacity, he preferred them to sing 'di dentro', where they could fulfil the same formal purpose and yet create a degree of tension or alienation with the soloists in the foreground. On the other hand, where the subject provided the opportunity for a fuller involvement of the chorus, as for example in *La Sonnambula*, Bellini was happy to enlarge their traditional role. The unusual degree to which the chorus becomes involved in the solo arias and ensembles in this opera is a formal reflection of the fact that the individuals in this particular drama are members of a closely knit social community. Another aspect of Bellini's greater care in matching the musical forms to the advancing dramatic action is suggested by his own description of the character of *I Puritani*: 'if we wanted to count the movements there are really fourteen, but, my dear Florimo, as usual with me they are short and passionate, and the action moves forward well in them'.[37] Not only was the lyrical style being matched more carefully to the mood of the words; song had come to be regarded as reconcilable with the continuing forward movement of the drama.

But while on the one hand Bellini was matching the music to the action with a closeness that had not been approached in purely Italian opera for well over a century, he was at the same time articulating the musical forms more lucidly, making them more poised and symmetrical. Bellini's best operas mark one of the high points in the reconciliation of the claims of the dramatic action and the aspiration to perfect formal beauty which had always underlain the Italian tradition.

Bellini's major achievement in formal organization may not at this distance in time seem especially remarkable nor even necessarily admirable. It can perhaps best be defined as the application of the firm and symmetrical patterns of popular song to lyrical melodies in the freest and most refined style. Rossini had employed symmetrical 'closed' forms of lyricism only when he was specifically aiming at a folk-song-like style, as for example with Desdemona's willow-song in Act III of *Otello*. Elsewhere his cantabiles tend to sound like improvisatory, fantasia-like preludes, stringing out fragments of extravagantly florid song in a loose and erratic continuity; while the cabalettas, though their individual phrases are more clearly defined, typically assume a form that is not so much architectural as chain-like; one balanced musical sentence succeeds another, generally becoming increasingly florid as the aria proceeds. Both Bellini and Donizetti, not to mention the host of lesser masters, employed this form of aria in their early works; but from the time of *Il Pirata* onwards (1827) Bellini showed a marked, almost obsessive, preference for neatness and balance of design, features that remain exemplary for the young Verdi. His preferred form in both cantabiles and cabalettas was one in which the two quatrains of the text were composed, the one as a symmetrical thematic exposition (A^1A^2), the other as an episode and a shortened and varied reprise $(BA^{\cdot})$.

Il Pirata and its successor *La Straniera*, though hardly Bellini's masterpieces, could be said to be the operas in which his originality, his reform of the tradition from within, is epitomized. Of the latter the *Gazzetta Privilegiata di Milano* wrote:

Amid the irruption of the Rossinian torrent, it is no small thing that a young composer should signal the first steps in his career by attempting a genre that could be called new for the present period. Not only is he a restorer of Italian music, but also he – a modern Orpheus – has resuscitated the beautiful melody of Jommelli, of Marcello, of Pergolesi, with beautiful song, with splendid, elegant, pleasing instrumentation.[38]

And *I Teatri* confirmed the impression:

Seeing that for a stretch of fully sixteen or eighteen years the public was accustomed to the extremely brilliant style of Rossini, it seemed impossible to discover another style that would entice it to enjoy melodies of an altogether different workmanship. But it seems impossible to doubt that a courageous young man, also Italian, is appointed to bring about a change in our habits, almost satiated with beauty as they have been, and incapable of finding new beauty.[39]

What exactly it was in these scores that so enthralled and impressed Bellini's contemporaries is perhaps best expressed by Ritorni. It was the way in which the Rossinian brilliance had been replaced by simplicity of form and directness of utterance, the sheer wanton pleasurability by dramatic expressivity. In its broadest outlines the character of *ottocento* opera was still a creation of Rossini's: but its musical language, and especially the application of its musical language to a dramatic purpose, had been transformed before Verdi's time, largely by the work of Bellini.

What pleased above all in *Il Pirata* [wrote Ritorni] was the extending of musical significance to the recitatives, which were elevated to the richness of the arias, while the latter were humbled somewhat, contrary to the common practice, so that the transition should be natural. The tyrannical boldness of the orchestra was restrained; it was reduced to a submissive accompaniment, to a pathetic echo of the passions, only then to resume that vigour and vivacity to which modern ears are too accustomed; so that at intervals it punctuated the song, it did not disturb it. In the same way it accompanied those stage actions that were not sung. The volubility of the cantilena was concealed, shaded, broken, so that the singing of the characters did not resemble that of zither-players [*citaredi*]. In the duets and trios the poet was not asked for those strict forms which inflict torment on the ideas of the speakers; free and natural metres such as accord better with familiar conversation were tolerated, even preferred. Finally the concerted pieces and the choral finale of the first act were either removed or regulated in accordance with dramatic principles, so that many musicomanes muttered and exclaimed over Bellini's ignorance, since he had avoided those tests in which the maestro's learning is revealed.

Even in the cabalettas, though he believed he could not write them without making use of a popular taste to which he was little accustomed, he succeeded in moving the heart wonderfully, when it seemed that they were intended only to tickle the ears . . .[40]

Many connoisseurs revered Bellini as 'the restorer of Italian music'; others, of a more elegiac temperament, cherished him, as did Werfel's Marchese Gritti, as the last of the line. But the more forceful spirits of the age, those more in tune with its ambitions and aspirations, wondered if Bellini really had the energy and power to act as the representative musical figure of *risorgimento* Italy. Mazzini, for instance, though not unaffected by the beauty of Bellini's music, concluded that ultimately it was more likely 'to enfeeble, to enervate, and to make sterile the power of the human spirit than to strengthen it, to reinforce it and to make it more fruitful'. He continued: 'Today in order to bring about a revival in literature and in music it is necessary, for anyone who might aspire to be a leader, to combine the power of Byron and the active faith of Schiller. Bellini's music lacks both.'[41]

For the time being he preferred to put his faith in Donizetti. Bellini was in any case dead before Mazzini wrote his 'Filosofia'. But perhaps the most pleasing detail in this long essay is the intuition of 'him who is to come': 'the unknown young man who perhaps in some corner of our land, even while I am writing, is stirred by inspiration and revolves within himself the secret of a musical epoch.'[42] The date was 1836.

PART II

A documentary history of the early operas

Launching a career

Oberto, Conte di San Bonifacio

The story of how a nineteenth-century Italian maestro launched himself into the world of opera is generally a story of distinguished conservatory career and student productions and professorial blessings; or perhaps of fleeting associations with humble itinerant companies on short stands in the less prestigious theatres of the peninsula. Given the talent and a certain amount of good fortune, progress by such paths could be rapid. Even Bellini, in many ways the slowest starter of the older generation of composers, graduated from the *teatrino* attached to the Naples Conservatory to a triumphant *première* at La Scala in less than three years.

The early stages of Verdi's career do not conform to such a pattern at all. His musical training had not taken him to a conservatory, and either chance or his own temperament had prevented him from striking up casual relationships with such modest ensembles as those with which Rossini and Donizetti had won their spurs. Verdi's story begins with no precocious portents, no spectacular ascent to glory; rather with a long and seemingly complicated process of deliberation, self-examination and procrastination, undertaken largely in drear isolation in Busseto. It is a story of maturing self-confidence and sudden pangs of doubt; of ambitions that soared ever higher and obstacles that grew ever more vexatious. His first opera, *Oberto, Conte di San Bonifacio*, materialized only after four years of work composing, revising and composing anew. But after disappointments and delays that must at the time have seemed endless, Verdi was able to produce it in the most famous opera house in the world, in Milan's La Scala. Indeed he went on to produce all his first four operas at La Scala: it was a remarkable start for a composer who had never been regarded as precocious, and on whose youthful career the Graces had smiled so seldom. For five years Verdi's experience of the sweetnesses and anguishes of which the lot of the nineteenth-century maestro was compounded was to be acquired wholly in this one great theatre.

If we knew more about it, the story of the origins and development of *Oberto* would surely be a fascinating one. As it is, the opera provides the historian with a task that is merely frustrating, for the surviving source material is so scanty that any attempt to give a rational history of the work, and in particular an account of its relationship with the lost opera *Rocester*, will be likely to founder on conjecture and surmise.

We may best begin with Verdi's two recorded statements on the origins of *Oberto*. The first is found in a letter written on 14 May 1871 to Emilio Seletti, son of the landlord of his early student days in Milan: '*Oberto di S. Bonifacio* was adapted and expanded by Solera on the basis of a libretto entitled *Lord Hamilton* by Antonio Piazza, a government employee and afterwards writer of *feuilletons* for the *Gazzetta di Milano*.'[1]

Verdi's other account is found in the autobiographical sketch dictated to Giulio Ricordi in October 1879 for inclusion in the Italian translation of Pougin's 'Anecdotal biography': 'Massini, who it appears had great confidence in the young artist, then proposed that I should write an opera for the Teatro Filodrammatico which he directed, and forwarded to me a libretto which, subsequently, modified in part by Solera, became *Oberto, di San Bonfacio*.'[2]

The first conclusion we may draw, then, is that, as far as Verdi recalled in later life, his first surviving opera was the result of a rather curious but by no means unparalleled *rifacimento*, carried out by Solera. In this revision, Piazza's dramatic version of some now unknown episode in British history was fitted out with a new set of characters and transposed into northern Italy at the time of strife between Guelphs and Ghibellines in the early thirteenth century.

The problems arise when we attempt to reconcile this supposition with the surviving documents of the period 1835-7. Leaving aside a very early enterprise in collaboration with a librettist named Tasca,[3] which in all probability remained unrealized, we may trace the course of Verdi's work on his first operatic composition in a series of letters from Busseto to his Milanese friend Massini. From this correspondence we learn that when Verdi returned to Busseto in the summer of 1835, after completing his studies with Lavigna, he was proposing to set to work at once on an opera for Massini:

I am writing the opera (as you know) and by the time you return to Milan I hope to have sketched out all the pieces. Advise me about all the singers you have heard in the concert that by now you will have given, so that I can take into consideration the range of the voices.[4]

But sustained work on the composition was delayed until well into 1836. On 24 January Verdi had written apologetically to Massini,

I am sorry not to have kept my word to you. Before leaving Milan I had promised you to return soon to compose the opera, but at that time I was not free to do as I wished, and so I have not been able to keep my promise.

If I am appointed maestro here, the municipality grants me two months' holiday, September and October, and then (if you agree to it) I am ready to keep my promise. It will be a great piece of good fortune for me if I can write an opera, and be assured that my gratitude to you will be eternal.[5]

Despite his appointment as *maestro di musica* to the municipality of Busseto at the end of February, and the multifarious activities which this involved him in, progress on the opera must have been quite steady during the next months, for by 16 September it was virtually finished:

... I am much the same, and am awaiting a definite reply about the opera; I foresee that there may be some obstacles and for this reason am the more eager to hear from you. Meanwhile I advise you that I have finished the opera except for some short passages which will have to be altered by the librettist.[6]

Difficulties did indeed arise over the production of the opera, and when Massini found that he would not after all be able to put it on at the Teatro Filodrammatico, Verdi began to look elsewhere for a stage. Already before the end of 1836 it was rumoured in Busseto that a performance of the opera might take place at the Ducal Theatre in Parma. In a document drawn up by the Podestà and President of the Monte di Pietà to settle a protracted dispute about the scholarship which Verdi had held, we read: 'I am given to understand that he has completed a serious opera which may be performed in the Ducal Theatre.'[7] Verdi continued to entertain this hope for many months. On 21 September 1837 he was still telling Massini:

It may be possible for me to produce the opera *Rocester* at Parma this Carnival season: so I beg you to go with the bearer of this letter (who is an intimate friend of mine) to the author of the libretto, Piazza, and tell him how things stand. If Piazza should wish to change any of the verses we still have time, and indeed I would request him to extend the duet for the two women to make a more imposing piece of it.

... Oh, how I should have liked to produce *Rocester* in Milan, but I can see well enough myself that I am too far away to make all the necessary arrangements.[8]

Here we come to a first difficulty, for the opera Verdi is hoping to put on at Parma is called not *Oberto*, not even *Lord Hamilton*, but *Rocester*.

Verdi's hopes of seeing *Rocester* staged at Parma were likewise disappointed, and, his thoughts turning again to Milan, he wrote to Massini once more on 3 November:

I spent a few days at Parma waiting for the new Impresario, a certain Granci, of Lucca. Meanwhile I secured the support of the Theatre Commission and the orchestra, all of which I was able to do easily, for to tell you the truth, not owing to my merits, I enjoy some credit at Parma. I had besides found influential people who showed themselves willing to help me. The day before yesterday the Impresario finally arrived. I presented myself to him at once in the name of the Commission and without preamble he replied that it didn't suit him to risk putting on an opera of uncertain outcome ... If I hadn't been the first to speak to him I should have thought that some enemy had maligned me to him, but that wasn't possible. I returned home angry and without the slightest hope. Poor young people! What a time they have of it, studying without ever a reward! Tell me, wouldn't it be possible to speak to Merelli, to see if it could be performed at some theatre at Milan? Tell him first of all that I should like the score to be submitted for examination by musicians of standing, and if their judgement were unfavourable I should not wish the opera to be performed. You would be doing me the greatest service. Perhaps you would be able to rescue me from obscurity, and I should be eternally grateful to you. Go to see Piazza and talk it over.[9]

Bartolomeo Merelli, who enters the story of Verdi's career at this point, was the impresario both of La Scala and of the Kärntnertor Theatre in Vienna; he was one of the most influential men in the operatic world of the day, and a fateful and generally beneficent influence on the young Verdi. The obliging Massini does seem to have exercised himself on Verdi's behalf. Certainly we are abandoning the contemporary documents now to rely on Verdi's reminiscences to Ricordi in 1879, but this is the composer's own version of the next development:

[Massini] told me that he would do all he could to get my opera performed at La Scala, on the occasion of the benefit for the Pio Istituto. Count Borromeo and the lawyer Pasetti promised Massini their support, but if I am to be quite truthful I must say that I don't know that this support amounted to more than a few words of recommendation. On the other hand Massini gave himself much trouble over the affair, and in this he was strongly supported by Merighi, the professor of violoncello, who, having got to know me at the time when he played in the orchestra of the Filodrammatico, seems to have had faith in the young maestro.

At last they succeeded in making all the arrangements for the Spring season of 1839 ...[10]

But by now, and indeed throughout the relevant passages of the autobiographical sketch, it is clear that Verdi is talking not about Rocester, but about Oberto, and it is time to consider how far these two works, not to mention Lord Hamilton, are related.

The reconciliation of the recollections of 1871 and 1879 with the documents of 1835–7 is not really the impossible undertaking that Walker too conscientiously seems to think it.[11] On two occasions in later life Verdi recalled his first staged opera, Oberto, as being some kind of remodelling of an earlier work. On one of these occasions, in 1871, he stated that the original opera was called Lord Hamilton and that it had a libretto by Piazza: the documents reveal that though Piazza was indeed the librettist, the original Verdi opera was in fact called Rocester. The obvious inference is that if it existed at all – if Verdi is not accidentally confusing the issue by invoking the name of some other noble Briton who may have been the subject of an abortive operatic essay in his earliest years – Lord Hamilton was identical with Rocester; that Lord Hamilton was a character in the opera Rocester, or perhaps an alternative title. Such a hypothesis demands little strain on our credulity, especially when the only alternative appears to be the supposition that Rocester and Lord Hamilton are two different operas composed by Verdi between 1835 and 1838, both to librettos by Piazza, both taking members of the post-Renaissance British aristocracy as their leading characters, one of which, though its composition is amply documented, has disappeared without trace, while of the other there is only one solitary reference in the whole vast Verdi documentation, more than thirty years after it had been converted into Oberto, Conte di San Bonifacio.

If we accept the identity of Lord Hamilton and Rocester, we can address ourselves to the more interesting problem of how closely Rocester and Oberto are related. Apart from Verdi's statement in 1871, partly reiterated in 1879, that the Piazza opera 'became' Oberto through the agency of Solera, there is little external evidence that can be relied upon. The autograph score of Oberto, in the Ricordi archives in Milan, does, however, contain a number of valuable clues.

First, at least two movements in Act I – Riccardo's cabaletta 'Già parmi udire il fremito' and Leonora's cabaletta 'Oh potessi nel mio core' – have been recomposed. Secondly, the characters in the Act II quartet were originally named Eleonora, Cuniza, Rocester and Oberto. Verdi himself corrected 'Rocester' to 'Riccardo', but his original error is obviously an invaluable pointer. Finally there is at the end of the manuscript a kind of appendix of separate movements. Two of these were composed in the autumn of 1840 for the revival of Oberto at La Scala after the fiasco of Un Giorno di Regno.[12] But a third, a duet for Eleonora and Cuniza, numbered 11, and thus shown to precede Oberto's scena and aria 'Ei tarda ancor', appears to be a deleted rather than an additional movement. The knowledge of the existence of a duet for the sopranos in *Rocester*[13] and the absence of such a duet from the final version of *Oberto* was one of the factors which caused Walker to doubt their identity.[14]

In the light of all this the most plausible hypothesis is undoubtedly that put forward originally by Sartori,[15] that *Oberto* is nothing more than a remodelling of *Rocester*.

It seems that towards the end of 1837, acting in response to Verdi's letter of 3 November, Massini attempted to interest Merelli in *Rocester*. Merelli, while sufficiently impressed with the opera not to dismiss it out of hand, was presumably aware of certain weaknesses in the libretto, or of a lack of real interest in the theme chosen, and must have required a reworking of the libretto before he would commit himself to staging the work at La Scala. Solera was brought in to carry out this reworking. Either at the instance of Merelli or on his own initiative, Solera then decided not simply to improve the libretto but to rewrite it completely, perhaps preserving many of the lyrical verses and dialogues, but transposing the action from (let us say) seventeenth-century Britain to thirteenth-century Italy, rather as *Gustavo III* was transferred from eighteenth-century Sweden to seventeenth-century Boston and became *Un ballo in maschera*. The awkwardness of such an undertaking may help explain the untidy action of *Oberto*, and the need for a preliminary clarification of the issues in the lengthy introduction to the libretto. With Merelli's qualified interest to spur him on, and Solera's revised libretto, Verdi would have worked on *Oberto* for the rest of the winter 1837–8, finishing it in the spring as 'Folchetto' implies.[16]

Verdi went back to Milan during his 1838 holiday in September and October, and seems to have made good progress in negotiating the acceptance of his opera for performance during the forthcoming season. A letter to an unknown friend in Busseto written on 6 October 1838 summarizes the state of affairs at that time:

Where the devil did you get the idea that my opera was to be staged by the 15th of this month? I never said or wrote that ... I will frankly admit that I came to make arrangements about the opera, but the season was too far advanced, and with three operas already performed, and a cantata and another three operas already promised to the public to follow (an enormous undertaking), there was no longer time to produce mine with the necessary decorum.

It might be possible to perform it during the next Carnival season; but it is a matter of a new opera, written by a new composer, to be presented in nothing less than the first theatre in the world; I still want to think it over thoroughly. If you want the poster, you can expect it in the spring; then, if not before, you will certainly get it.[17]

Walker observes that at this juncture Verdi, although fairly certain that he could get his opera staged, seems to have been undergoing a slight crisis of confidence in himself. But his further suggestion that it may have been only now that *Rocester* was replaced by a newly composed *Oberto* seems incredible.[18] More probable would be the supposition that this was the period when some of the weaker pieces in the score were deleted or replaced by new compositions.

At last [to return to Verdi's autobiographical sketch] we succeeded in making all the arrangements for the Spring season of 1839; and in such a manner that I had the double fortune of staging my opera at La Scala on the occasion of the benefit performances for the Pio Istituto, and of having four truly outstanding performers, la Strepponi, the tenor Moriani, the baritone Giorgio Ronconi, and the bass Marini.[19]

But even here the story does not end, for in *Oberto* as we have it now there are only two male parts, the tenor, Riccardo, and the bass, Oberto.

When Moriani fell ill and the projected performances in the spring of 1839 had to be cancelled, Merelli summoned Verdi to the theatre and promised, in view of the high opinion of the music expressed by Strepponi and Ronconi, to stage the opera during the next season, provided Verdi would make the necessary revisions to suit the voices of the new company. According to the autobiographical sketch these modifications did not amount to much, certainly to nothing as drastic as the excision of a leading character.

The opera was performed by la Marini, mezzo-soprano, Salvi, tenor, and the bass, Marini; and as I have said, I was urged to alter some parts of the music for reasons of tessitura, and to write one new piece, the quartet. The dramatic context of this was suggested by Merelli himself, and I got Solera to write the verses . . .[20]

Clearly Verdi has remembered something imperfectly. Most probably, in listing the cast of the projected performances in the spring of 1839 he has thrown in together the man who should have sung Oberto, Ronconi, with the man who actually sang Oberto the following autumn, Marini. The original cast would thus have been Strepponi, one other soprano, Moriani and Ronconi; and Verdi's task during the summer of 1839 would have been simply to readjust their music for Antonietta Marini, Shaw, Salvi and Ignazio Marini, and to compose the quartet.

When at last the opera was performed on 17 November 1839 its success was considerable; Verdi's own verdict was 'Un esito non grandissimo ma abbastanza buono',[21] which is probably a modest assessment. One does not need to accept too literally the rapturous effusions of Soffredini, who reported of the overture: 'An eye-witness told me that at La Scala, after this brilliant overture there was an explosion of enthusiastic applause, and everyone gazed at one another exclaiming "Here is the Messiah",' and of the opera as a whole: 'The Scala audience applauded it enthusiastically, and ... at midnight as they left the theatre, the Milanese again said to one another "We have a Messiah".'[22] But the facts do speak for themselves.

Oberto ran to the end of the Autumn season, which Merelli found it profitable to extend, giving a total of fourteen performances. It was revived within a year, during the Autumn season 1840, for a further seventeen performances. Turin staged it as soon as possible after the Milan première during the Carnival season 1840; Genoa followed in January 1841, and Naples during the Spring season of the same year. It was produced in Barcelona in February 1842.[23] Giovanni Ricordi found the opera sufficiently impressive to purchase the ownership of it, thus inaugurating a uniquely fruitful relationship which lasted throughout Verdi's life. And finally, on the strength of the success of Oberto Merelli concluded a contract with Verdi according to the terms of which he was to compose three more operas for La Scala to be performed at eight-monthly intervals.

Un Giorno di Regno

As with Oberto, so too with Un Giorno di Regno, we depend more on later reminiscences than on contemporary documents for our knowledge of the genesis of the opera. Verdi's autobiographical recollections of 1879 are still the principal source of information:

Merelli then made me what was a very generous proposal for those days: he offered me a contract for three operas at intervals of eight months to be given at La Scala or at the theatre in Vienna of which he was also the impresario. In return he was to pay me 4,000 Austrian lire for each opera, sharing with me the proceeds from the sale of the scores. I accepted the contract straight away; and a little while later Merelli set off for Vienna, having charged the poet Rossi to provide me with the libretto; and this was to be Il Proscritto; however I was not entirely happy about it and I hadn't begun to set it to music when Merelli came back to Milan in the early months of 1840 and said that he absolutely must have a comedy for the autumn season for special reasons of repertory; he would like to find me a libretto straight away and after that I could set Il Proscritto. I didn't refuse this request, and Merelli gave me various libretti by Romani to read, all of which had lain forgotten on the shelf, either because they hadn't been successful or for some other reason. I read them over and over and didn't like any of them, but because the matter was of some urgency I chose the one which seemed to me the least bad; and that was *Il Finto Stanislao*, which was then christened *Un Giorno di Regno*.[24]

Romani's libretto had originally been written for the Bohemian composer Adalbert Gyrowetz in 1818, and was indifferently received by the Milan audiences even then. It can well be believed that Verdi undertook the composition of this uncongenial and antiquated piece with a less than ideal degree of commitment. I do not know, however, on what evidence some writers have made the claim that he cared so little about it that he neither discussed the libretto with its author nor requested any kind of alterations. At any rate, a comparison of the 1818 and 1840 librettos shows that alterations were made in plenty, whether at Verdi's instigation or not. Many extended passages of recitative dialogue were reduced in length; some scenes were deleted entirely, others put in different sequence, others replaced by newly written ones; some aria texts were rewritten too. The revised libretto does not name Romani, nor does it suggest who may have made the alterations to his original text. But Mario Rinaldi, the author of the most comprehensive study of Romani's work, believes not only that Romani himself was responsible, but that he made the revision in collaboration with Verdi: 'There is no doubt that Verdi must have met Romani often over the revision, for it is impossible to imagine that the poet would have subjected his text to so many alterations: it would have gone against his very nature, he who so loved comicality.'[25]

Whether the revised libretto really answered to Verdi's ideal conception of what an *opera buffa* should be seems uncertain: whether Verdi at this stage of his career was even potentially capable of good musical comedy we shall never know. But *Un Giorno di Regno* would surely have turned out a more tender and a more sparkling piece had Verdi been able to spend the spring and summer months of 1840 working on it in a tranquil state of mind. In fact, though, this was a distraught and ultimately tragic episode in his life.

The autobiographical sketch records that first Verdi was confined to bed with severe angina, and that hardly had he begun to convalesce from this when he realized that he had forgotten to pay 50 *scudi* owing for the rent. Not having the necessary money, and being too late to apply to his 'most excellent father-in-law Barezzi' for the sum in question, he was obliged to undergo the humiliation of getting his friend Pasetti to request from Merelli either an advance on his contract money or a short-term loan. At this point, for almost the only time in the story of Verdi's life, his first wife, Margherita, emerges from the shadows:

I don't need to go into the circumstances which made it impossible for Merelli, through no fault of his own, to advance me the 50 *scudi*. It distressed me to let pass the date when the rent was due without paying it, even if it was only for a few days, and my wife, seeing my anxiety, took the few precious things she possessed, left the house, somehow or other managed to collect together the required sum and handed it to me: I was touched by this affectionate gesture, and promised myself that I would restore everything to my wife, which I could soon have done in view of the contract which I now had.

Verdi was unable to keep his promise, however. For early in June, Margherita was smitten with an illness, possibly encephalitis, in the face of which contemporary medicine was helpless, and from which she was never to recover. Her father, Antonio Barezzi, arrived from Busseto just in time to be with her when she died. He recorded in the family diary:

Through a terrible disease, perhaps unknown to the doctors, there died in my arms at Milan, at noon on the day of Corpus Domini, my beloved daughter Margherita in the flower of her years and at the culmination of her good fortune, because married to the excellent youth Giuseppe Verdi, Maestro di Musica. I implore for her pure soul eternal peace, while weeping bitterly over this painful loss.[26]

Once the funeral rites were over, Barezzi took Verdi back to Busseto with him, where (as an old friend, Giuseppe Demaldè, recorded) he arrived grief-stricken and distraught 'to the point of nervous collapse',[27] and from where he wrote to Merelli in an attempt to release himself from his contract. Merelli – probably, to judge from subsequent relations between the two men, more by persuasiveness than by an insistence on his legal rights – nevertheless succeeded in holding Verdi to his contract; and after a period of quiet, among old friends and familiar scenes, he returned to Milan to complete the opera. We know nothing more until the fiasco of the first night on 5 September 1840.

Un Giorno di Regno needed all the help the performers could give it. It seems not to have got it. Only two of the singers, the basses Raffaele Scalese and Agostino Rovere, were really adept in the comic style; the rest had been assembled principally for the first opera of the season, Nicolai's Scott-inspired melodrama *Il Templario*, and were conspicuously less at ease in comedy. Indeed their performance was in some respects so deplorable that one reviewer, writing in *La moda*, was moved to rebuke them in no uncertain terms:

The performance of this opera provides us with the opportunity to warn *some* of the singers at present engaged at our theatre that, whatever the reception given them by the audience, whatever spirit of rivalry or jealousy may corrode their artistic soul, they must neither flaunt themselves nor show resentment of public opinion; their conduct must always be strictly proper and their sense of decorum exclude all idea of unbecoming behaviour, not to venture more severe words. One might add that, even if the opera does not please, the performers must nevertheless present it to the public with the same good will; that ceasing to sing, or simply moving the lips in the concerted pieces, shows a culpable ignorance of their proper responsibility, since the public does not lavish money on the heroes of the stage so that they can just sing whenever the fancy happens to take them; finally the indifference and carelessness of a singer, even in an unsuccessful opera, could be regarded as a principal cause for its failure.[28]

But for Verdi it seems to have been the reaction of the audience rather than the singers' indifference that remained the bitterest memory of this dreadful first night. In February 1859, during an unsuccessful run of *Simon Boccanegra* performances, also at La Scala, he wrote to Tito Ricordi:

You are amazed by the 'unbecoming conduct of the public'? It doesn't surprise me in the least. They are always happy when there is an opportunity to create a scandal! When I was twenty-five, I did have illusions, and I did believe in their courtesy; a year later the scales fell from my eyes and I saw the sort of people I had to deal with. Those who try to tell me with a kind of reproachfulness that I owe so much to this audience or to that make me laugh! It's true: at La Scala on another occasion *Nabucco* and *I Lombardi* were applauded; but whether one takes the music, or the singers, or the chorus, or the orchestra, or the staging, the fact is that altogether it was a spectacle which did no dishonour to those who applauded. Hardly more than a year before, however, this same public maltreated the opera of a poor, sick young man, who was rushed for time, and whose heart was broken by a terrible misfortune! All this they knew, but it did not restrain their rudeness. I haven't seen *Un Giorno di Regno* since then, and no doubt it is a bad opera, though who knows how many other operas no better are tolerated and perhaps even applauded. Oh, if the public then had not applauded, but had borne my opera in silence, I should not have words sufficient to thank them![29]

Nabucodonosor (Nabucco)

The fiasco of *Un Giorno di Regno* marked the lowest ebb of Verdi's whole career: the determination, the professionalism, the sense of loyalty that had just sufficed to sustain him through the awful summer months simply gave way when the Milanese audience rejected with contempt the work that had cost him so much pain. Again he determined to renounce his composing career, and this time he did succeed in extricating himself from the contract he had with Merelli. The autobiographical sketch records:

With mind tormented by my domestic misfortunes, embittered by the failure of my work, I was convinced that I could find no consolation in my art and decided never to compose again. I even wrote to the engineer Pasetti, asking him to obtain from Merelli my release from the contract.

Merelli sent for me and treated me like a capricious schoolboy – he would not allow me to be discouraged by the unhappy failure of my opera, etc., etc. But I stood my ground, so that handing me back the contract Merelli said: 'Listen, Verdi! I can't force you to write. My faith in you is undiminished: who knows whether, one of these days, you won't decide to take up your pen again? In that case, as long as you give me two months' notice before the beginning of the season, I promise that your opera shall be performed.' I thanked him, but these words did not suffice to alter my decision and I went away.[30]

Though he could not force Verdi to compose, Merelli was too resourceful a man to let himself lose sight of a musician whom he believed in simply because of the disillusion and bitterness of the moment. What he could do, until such time as Verdi came round again and was prepared to re-enter into some contractual arrangements, was to ensure that his association with La Scala was maintained. This he did promptly after the failure of *Un Giorno di Regno* by putting *Oberto* back in the repertory under Verdi's direction. Moreover, unless we are to make the improbable supposition that Verdi composed them during the last stages of work on *Un Giorno di Regno*, two new movements were composed for this revival, a cavatina for Cuniza and a duet for her and Riccardo. Apparently Merelli had breached Verdi's mood of renunciation quite expeditiously. What is more, *Oberto* was again a good success, achieving a total of seventeen performances during the season, more than Donizetti's *La Figlia del Reggimento*, more than Bellini's *Il Pirata*, and second only to Nicolai's *Il Templario*.[31]

In several ways during this winter of 1840–1, *Oberto* must have served to remind Verdi that he was not after all a despised and unwanted failure. In January he was in Genoa for a revival of the work at the Carlo Felice Theatre, and again he was at work revising and composing new movements to substitute for those with which he was dissatisfied or which did not suit the cast. After the somewhat cool reception of the opera he reported to a Busseto friend, Luigi Balestra, who had apparently helped with rewriting some of the text:

I don't know whether the 'Genoese have the curse of Euterpe on their heads', but I do know that *Oberto* did not rouse the fanaticism which it did in Milan, despite the fact that the performance was on the whole good, and as far as Marini was concerned really excellent: he sang divinely that evening. Almost all the pieces were applauded, but the quartet and the rondo, of which I had such high hopes, received very little applause, and that ceased altogether at the second performance. The piece which pleased best of all was the aria in the introduction; I have added the *banda* and it makes a diabolical din.

I am sorry not to have been able to perform your duet, which I had already composed; but it proved too difficult for Marini, and I substituted another very short one . . .[32]

Hardly was he back in Milan when he 'heard with pleasure that they wanted to perform *Oberto* at Parma during the Spring season'.[33] In the early months of 1841 he also witnessed two fellow-composers – Mazzucato with *I Due Sergenti*, and Nicolai with *Il Proscritto* – being savaged by the Milanese public not a whit less ferociously than he had been for *Un Giorno di Regno*. Perhaps in the long run this experience too helped give Verdi a more objective and stoical view of the bitterness of the previous autumn.

As it happened the projected Parma revival of *Oberto* came to nothing. But in any case by now Verdi had more compelling matters to attend to than more revivals, perhaps even more revisions, of his already much transmogrified first opera. In January 1841, a chance meeting with Merelli had led to Verdi's being given the libretto of *Nabucco*, and it was with this work, crucial alike to Verdi's personal development and to his prestige in the Italian theatre, that he was to be wholly involved for the next year or more.

The autobiographical sketch takes up the story of *Nabucco* in these terms:

. . . one winter evening on leaving the Galleria De Cristoforis I encountered Merelli, who was on his way to the theatre. It was snowing heavily and, taking me by the arm, he invited me to accompany him to his office at La Scala. On the way we talked and he told me he was in difficulties over the new opera he had to present: he had entrusted it to Nicolai but the latter was not satisfied with the libretto.

'Imagine!' said Merelli. 'A libretto by Solera! Stupendous! Magnificent! Extraordinary! Effective, grandiose dramatic situations and beautiful verses! But that pig-headed composer won't hear of it and says it's a hopeless libretto. I'm at my wits' end to know where to find another one quickly.'

'I'll help you out myself,' I replied. 'Didn't you have prepared for me *Il proscritto*? I haven't written a note of the music: I put it at your disposal.'

'Oh! that's fine – a real stroke of luck!'

Talking like this, we had reached the theatre. Merelli called Bassi, the poet, stage-manager, call-boy, librarian etc., etc., and told him to look at once in the archives for a copy of *Il proscritto*. The copy was there. At the same time Merelli picked up another manuscript and, showing it to me, exclaimed:

'Look! Here is Solera's libretto. Such a beautiful subject – and he turned it down! Take it – read it through!'

'What the deuce should I do with it? No, no, I have no wish to read librettos.'

'Go on with you! It won't do you any harm. Read it and then bring it back to me again.' And he gave me the manuscript. It was on large sheets in big letters, as was then customary. I rolled it up, said goodbye to Merelli and went home.

On the way I felt a kind of indefinable malaise, a very deep sadness, a distress that filled my heart. I got home and with an almost violent gesture threw the manuscript on the table, standing upright in front of it. The book had opened in falling on the table; without knowing how, I gazed at the page that lay before me, and read this line:

Va, pensiero, sull'ali dorate.

I ran through the verses that followed and was much moved, all the more because they were almost a paraphrase from the Bible, the reading of which had always delighted me.

I read one passage, then another. Then, resolute in my determination to write no more, I forced myself to close the booklet and went to bed. But it was no use – I couldn't get *Nabucco* out of my head. Unable to sleep, I got up and read the libretto, not once, but two or three times, so that by the morning I knew Solera's libretto almost by heart.

Still I was not prepared to relax my determination and that day I returned to the theatre and handed the manuscript back to Merelli.

'Isn't it beautiful?' he said to me.

'Very beautiful!'

'Well then – set it to music!'

'I wouldn't dream of it. I won't hear of it.'

'Set it to music! Set it to music!'

And so saying he took the libretto, thrust it into my overcoat pocket, took me by the shoulders and not only pushed me out of the room but locked the door in my face.

What was I to do?

I returned home with *Nabucco* in my pocket. One day one verse, another day another, here a note and there a phrase, little by little the opera was composed.[34]

Among the profusion of vivid detail with which Verdi evokes this distant episode of his life, two crucial points stand out. One was that fate thrust upon him precisely that part of Solera's text, the patriotic psalm-paraphrase 'Va pensiero sull'ali dorate', which he was bound to find irresistible; the other that, although set in train by this blinding moment of vision, the composition of the opera as a whole was a slow and laborious business.

The truth of the story of the fateful confrontation with 'Va pensiero' can, I think, be accepted without further comment: it is confirmed by an earlier publication, Michele Lessona's *Volere è potere*, which includes, among its thumbnail biographies of poor Italians who made good, a description of Verdi's early years. On the question of how Verdi actually composed the opera, however, Lessona contradicts the autobiographical sketch. According to Lessona, after Merelli had thrust the libretto upon Verdi

the young maestro went home with his drama, but threw it into a corner without looking at it again, and for a further five months went on reading cheap novels. [This, Lessona claimed, had been the composer's consolation after the failure of *Un Giorno di Regno*.]

Then one fine day, towards the end of May, that blessed drama came into his hands again: he read the last scene again, the scene with the death of Abigaille (which was later cut), went over to the piano almost mechanically, to that piano which had stood silent for so long, and set the scene to music. The ice was broken.

Like someone who escapes from a dark and noisome prison to breathe the fresh air of the fields, Verdi found himself once more in a congenial atmosphere. Three months from then *Nabucco* was composed, finished, and in every respect the work it is today.[35]

Despite Verdi's authentication of Lessona's account as 'la storia mia vera vera vera',[36] the version of the history of *Nabucco* in his own autobiographical sketch must be preferred. It lacks Lessona's self-contradictions and those palpable untruths which have been commented on particularly by Cavicchi and Budden;[37] such things as the absorption in bad novels from morning to night asserted in one paragraph, the daily reading of the Bible in another; or the poignant detail of the piano 'silent for so long', which is crucial to Lessona's evocation of the sudden upsurge of creative energy in the spring of 1841, but which is demonstrably false in the light of the revisions composed for *Oberto* during the autumn and winter.

Little can now be established about the progress of the opera between January and the autumn, when it was finished. But a retrospective reference to Solera, made at the time of *Ernani*, is indicative of Verdi's faith in his librettist and the comparative effortlessness of their collaboration at this time:

I have written the music for three librettos by Solera, and comparing the original, which I keep, with the printed librettos, only a very few lines will be found to be changed, and those only when Solera himself was persuaded that it was necessary. But Solera has already written five or six librettos and knows the theatre, and what is effective, and he knows the musical forms.[38]

Nevertheless a passage in the autobiographical sketch suggests that there was at least one contrarious incident:

I remember an amusing scene I had with Solera ... In the third act he had written a love duet for Fenena and Ismaele. I didn't like it, as it cooled down the action and seemed to me to detract somewhat from the Biblical grandeur which characterized the drama. One morning when Solera was with me I said so: but he was reluctant to agree, perhaps not so much because he found the comment unjust, as because it annoyed him to revise what he had already written. We argued about it, and both of us held firm to our points of view. He asked me what I wanted in place of the duet, and it was then that I suggested writing a prophecy for the prophet Zaccaria: he found the idea not bad, and with a few ifs and buts he said he would think about it and then write it. That was not what I wanted, because I knew that many, many days would pass before Solera would bring himself to write a line. I locked the door, put the key in my pocket, and half-jokingly said to Solera, 'You don't leave here until you have written the prophecy; here is the Bible, you have the words ready made.' Solera, who was a man of violent temper, did not take kindly to my joke: his eyes blazed angrily: I passed an uncomfortable moment, for the poet was a giant of a man who could have made short work of an obstinate composer, but suddenly he sat down at the table and a quarter of an hour later the prophecy was written.[39]

We cannot date the completion of the opera more precisely than autumn 1841, when, in Verdi's own words,

recalling Merelli's promise, I went to see him and announced that Nabucco was written and could therefore be performed in the next Carnival season.
Merelli declared himself ready to keep his word, but at the same time pointed out that it would be impossible to give the opera in the coming season, because the repertory was already settled and because three new operas by renowned composers were due for performance. To give a fourth opera by a composer who was almost a beginner was dangerous for everybody concerned, and above all dangerous for me. It would thus be better to wait for the spring season, for which he had no prior engagements. He assured me that good artists would be engaged. But I refused: either in the Carnival season or not at all. And I had good reasons for that, knowing it would be impossible to find two other artists so well suited to my opera as la Strepponi and Ronconi, whom I knew to be engaged and on whom I was much relying.
Merelli, although disposed to give me my way, was, as impresario, not altogether in the wrong – to give four new operas in a single season was very risky! But I had good artistic grounds for opposing him. In short, after assertions and denials, obstacles and half-promises, the bills of La Scala were posted – but Nabucco was not announced![40]

Our story has now reached December 1841, the beginning of the Carnival season, and can momentarily turn to a source much closer to the events it describes than the reminiscences of Verdi's old age. On 26th December, Verdi's brother-in-law Giovanni Barezzi, who was visiting Milan, wrote to his father to describe the to-ing and fro-ing of Verdi and his friends when *Nabucco* had been found to be missing from the repertory announced for the season:

and then [Verdi] decides to write to Merelli in rather harsh terms. Merelli resents that and shows the letter to Pasetti and says: 'See how Verdi has misunderstood this! That is not my intention, but I did it so that I should gain credit with the subscribers when, towards the end of Carnival, I put out a new placard, with the announcement of his opera. Tell Verdi, however, to show la Strepponi her part, and if she wants to sing it I'll gladly put it on.'

Pasetti sends for Verdi and they go to see la Strepponi; they explain the situation and she very willingly agrees to sing in the opera and adds: 'Come here tomorrow at half past one and I'll look through my part.'

Next day – 23rd [December] 1841, that is – Verdi and Pasetti go to see la Strepponi at the agreed time; she tries over her part at the pianoforte with Verdi and then says to him: 'I like this music very much, and I want to sing it when I make my *début*,' and at once adds: 'Let's go and see Ronconi.' They get in Pasetti's cab, which had been waiting at the door, and go to see Ronconi. La Strepponi *points out to him the beauties of the opera* and Verdi tells him the plot. Ronconi, after hearing all about it, says: 'Very well, this evening I'll speak to the impresario, and tell him that I don't want to sing in Nini's opera, but that I want to sing in yours.'[41]

In view of the part which the resentment of the singers had played in the downfall of *Un Giorno di Regno*, it was a good move of Merelli's to insist that Verdi should be able to engage their good will before embarking on a production of *Nabucco*.

The account of *Nabucco* in the autobiographical sketch continues:

Towards the end of February the rehearsals began, and twelve days after the first rehearsal with piano the first public performance took place on 9 March, with Signore Strepponi and Bellinzaghi, and Signori Ronconi, Miraglia and Derivis in the cast. With this opera it is fair to say my artistic career began.

And Verdi concludes by giving a few details about the performances: how despite the fact that the scenery and costumes were old stock – presumably touched up from Cortesi's ballet *Nabuco-donosor* – they created such an impression that the audience applauded the first scene for ten minutes; how 'at the dress rehearsal no one knew when or where the stage band was to come in. The conductor Tutsch was embarrassed. I pointed out a bar to him, and at the performances the band entered on the crescendo with such precision that the audience burst into applause.' Nor are romantic legends lacking, plausible and implausible, which the interested reader may chase up in Abbiati's biography.

But amid all the optimism and enthusiasm that accompanied the preparations for the production, there must have been tensions more acute than usual too: particularly over the prima donna, Giuseppina Strepponi. She had arrived in Milan on 16 February to start rehearsals for Donizetti's *Belisario* and for *Nabucco*; but, although she struggled to fulfil the obligations she had contracted, she was clearly in such a deplorable state of health that Merelli insisted that she undergo a thorough medical examination. This took place less than a week before the *première* of *Nabucco* on 3 March, and the outcome must have been profoundly worrying for all involved. The crucial paragraph of the medical report reads:

The said Signora Strepponi has a very delicate constitution, and her loss of weight has become very considerable. Furthermore she is tormented by frequent coughing, with an unpleasant feeling of irritation all along the trachea and the larynx, which, she says, often becomes a burning sensation, especially after the effort of singing. Her pulse is weak and rapid; in brief, she shows symptoms of light feverish reaction, with loss of appetite and appreciable prostration. In view of all that was established the undersigned doctors unanimously declared Signora Strepponi to be affected with such laryngo-tracheal inflammation as will lead to consumption unless she at once ceases to exercise her profession and submits herself to similar careful treatment and an uninterruptedly tranquil way of life.[42]

Verdi's personal esteem for the woman who was later to be his second wife was already considerable, as we shall see from the fact that it was she whom he consulted on the second night of *Nabucco* about the commission for *I Lombardi*. But under the circumstances it is hardly surprising that, professionally speaking, he saw her as a threat to the success of his opera, and seems to have made attempts to have her replaced. Donizetti, who was in Milan for the revivals of *Belisario*, mentions this incidentally in writing to his brother-in-law with a message for some Roman impresario: 'Tell him that his singer created such a furore here in *Belisario* that she was the only one who never received any applause, that her Verdi did not want her in his own opera and the management imposed her on him.'[43]

Despite the worry about Strepponi's health, however, the *première* of *Nabucco* proved to be one of the great nights in the annals of the Italian theatre. The next day the *Gazzetta Privilegiata di Milano* reported that 'the new opera composed by the young maestro Verdi on a lyric drama by Solera, entitled *Nabucodonosor*, was performed at our Gran Teatro with clamorous and total success. It is perhaps one of the few occasions on which the audience have been universally agreed in applauding the facility and fluency of the style, and a certain sustained liveliness in the musical ideas . . .'

Later in the review we read that after 'Immenso Jeovha' 'all hands applauded so that the rule of no encores might be dispensed with for once', and that when 'the drama finished, the applause did not; applause for the main performers, and in an exceptional degree for maestro Verdi, who enjoyed a real triumph, was prolonged and often repeated, in the belief that the composer should not be charged with some less than happy performances by the singers'.

Among *Nabucco*'s most fervent admirers was Donizetti, who already at rehearsals had been sufficiently impressed to write to friends in Bergamo urging them to make the journey to Milan to see the new opera. The story is well known of how during his journey to Bologna on the day after the *première* he sat musing in a corner of the coach, exclaiming from time to time, 'Oh that *Nabucco*! Beautiful! Beautiful! Beautiful!'

Numerous are the accounts of the 'Nabucodonosorization' of Milan at this time. Perhaps the earliest is Lessona's: 'The great success of *Nabucco* roused such wild enthusiasm as had never before been seen. That night Milan did not sleep, next day the new masterpiece was the topic of all conversations. The name of Verdi was in every mouth; even fashion, even cookery borrowed his name, making hats *alla Verdi*, shawls *alla Verdi*, and sauces *alla Verdi*.'[44] On a more serious level, there is no doubt that the success of *Nabucco* gave Verdi the entrée into aristocratic and literary circles in Milan.

By March, when *Nabucco* was produced, the Carnival/Lent season was nearly at an end, allowing only eight performances of the opera to be given. Naturally Merelli was eager to revive it, and brought it back again at the start of the Autumn season in August. From then until December it virtually monopolized the scene, squeezing out indifferently masters like Donizetti and Mercadante, and minor figures like Ricci and Imperatori. Fifty-seven performances of *Nabucco* alternated with a total of twenty-nine performances of the other six operas in the repertory. The critic Lambertini, writing in the *Gazzetta Privilegiata di Milano*, was obviously expressing what was generally felt when he observed that *Nabucco* was an opera which 'engages the interest more and in which the musical beauties shine more brightly the more one hears it'.

I Lombardi alla Prima Crociata

All the biographers have remarked that Verdi's sensational triumph with *Nabucco* made it a virtually automatic matter that Merelli should commission him to compose one of the *opere d'obbligo* for the following 1842–3 Carnival season. They likewise record that Merelli was bold enough to present Verdi with a contract in which the fee was not named, and to invite him to claim whatever sum he deemed fit. Verdi sought the advice of Giuseppina Strepponi, who suggested that he demand the fee that Bellini had received for *Norma* twelve years earlier, namely 6800 francs.

Merelli's generous and perspicacious dealings with the young Verdi constitute the most honourable episode in his chequered career. In this matter too, he was in all probability anticipating rather than simply acquiescing in public demand. Verdi apparently consulted Giuseppina Strepponi in her dressing room at La Scala on 10 March 1842, that is to say after the second performance of *Nabucco*;[45] and while it is possible, it is on the whole unlikely that the preliminary negotiations over the contract should all have taken place in the twenty-four hours since the Milanese had acclaimed the opera. More probably, Merelli was again trusting his intuition, and above all observing the effect that *Nabucco* made on all those involved in the production. We recall the words that Merighi the principal cellist is supposed to have spoken to Verdi as he made his way to the composer's seat: 'Maestro, I would give anything to be in your place this evening.' The triumph of the work seems never to have been in doubt among those who had worked on the production, and it was presumably during the rehearsals, seeing his faith in Verdi's talent more splendidly vindicated than he could have hoped, that Merelli invited him to compose another new opera for the next season.

As soon as one moves forward from these very earliest negotiations, one finds that nothing remains but anecdote and legend on which to base a history of *I Lombardi*: only a yarner of Abbiati's genius could make a coherent narrative of it. But of these stories one is of peculiar interest since it deals with what seems to be the first of Verdi's clashes with the censor, presumably towards the end of 1842.

It was not, as one might have expected in view of the *risorgimento* overtones of Verdi's early operas, any Austrian politician that attempted to hinder or emasculate *I Lombardi*: it was the archbishop, Cardinal Gaisruck. And the grounds for his objections were purely religious, not at all political. He took exception to the portrayal on the operatic stage of the sacrament of baptism, and to the paraphrase of the Ave Maria sung by Giselda in Act I; and he asked the chief of police, Baron Torresani, to see that they were suppressed.

Launching a career

We have seen in an earlier chapter how ambiguous was Torresani's attitude to the problem of operatic censorship. In the present case, he is said to have summoned Merelli, Verdi and Solera to his office to discuss the problem with him, though only Merelli and Solera deigned to appear. What exactly their various attitudes were, how exactly the negotiations were conducted, we do not know; but it is difficult to believe that any of the trio was really convinced of the gravity of these transgressions. Certainly very little was done; certainly *I Lombardi* escaped quite unscathed. The baptismal scene was allowed to stand, the opening words of Giselda's aria were changed from 'Ave Maria' to 'Salve Maria', and Torresani is remembered still for his remark 'I will not be the man to clip the wings of so promising a genius.' Even at his most defiantly idealistic Verdi can hardly have objected to this.

By all accounts, the triumph of *I Lombardi*, when it was first performed on 11 February 1843, was no less brilliant than that of *Nabucco*. The reputation which Verdi had earned with *Nabucco* was of itself sufficient to guarantee that the keenest interest should be excited by his next new opera, and the fact that the other *opera d'obbligo* of the season, Federico Ricci's *Vallombra*, had proved a fiasco can only have served to sharpen the opera-goer's anticipation. According to Abbiati 'the chronicles' – I think he means the old stories – 'tell of endless queues of people forming from the early hours of the afternoon in front of the still closed doors of the theatre. The inevitable trimmings of fisticuffs, swoons, bruises, and other little incidents to be charged to the enthusiasm of the faithful followers of the melodrama.'[46]

At the performance itself, we learn from the review in *Il Figaro*, 'the public, crowded into the boxes, into the pit and into the gallery, received every piece, or to be more precise every bar, with the loudest cheers, and from time to time eagerly saluted the maestro with extraordinary ovations'.[47]

Amid the profusion of suppositions, traditions and anecdotes that surround *I Lombardi*, sober documented facts are hard to come by. Most of those that do survive deal with a matter we are bound to regard as peripheral at best, namely with the dedication of the opera to the Duchess Maria Luigia of Parma. A number of grotesquely courteous letters from Verdi to Bombelles, the duchess's grand chamberlain and consort, survive to illuminate the episode. On 31 January 1843 Verdi had written from Busseto expressing his desire to 'pay homage with this new opera of his to our August Sovereign, provided that the work should be so worthy as to make the dedication permissible'.[48] Apparently unencouraged by Bombelles, on 13 February, from Milan, Verdi 'made bold to request again that you should intercede with our August Sovereign Maria Luigia for permission to humiliate her with the dedication of this, my favourite work ... My gratitude will be eternal and the benefit immense if I were to be honoured by the venerated Sovereign with a distinction such as would leave nothing wanting to ensure a brilliant career.'[49]

Clearly in Milanese society Verdi was rapidly mastering the courtier's art. His commonsense self peeps out briefly in a letter to Demaldè to whom he confides his amazement that dedicating an opera should prove to be such an arduous enterprise.[50] But he concludes the affair on 4 June 1843 in the very best style:

Flattered by the kind reception which Her Majesty deigned to accord me, and by the magnificent gift with which she honoured me, I beg Your Excellency to present to her my humble and sincere thanks.

As Her Majesty, deigning to speak about the music of *I Lombardi*, asked about the reduction for pianoforte, I advise Your Excellency that a copy will be prepared as soon as possible and I shall make it my duty to send it to you.

I thank also Your Excellency for the kindness with which you received me, which I shall always remember, and which will be an encouragement to persevere in my thorny career.[51]

The genesis of an opera – *Ernani*

In the spring of 1843 Verdi's star was still in the ascendant with the Milanese, and Merelli did his best, with 'generous offers', to persuade him to write yet another opera for La Scala. But, as Verdi remarked to an old friend, his first Oberto, Ignazio Marini, he 'did not wish to take the risk of writing another opera for Milan just yet'.[1] While the Milanese were still eager for more, Verdi felt that it would be good policy to establish his reputation in other parts of Italy.

Since the production of *Nabucco* a year before, there had been no lack of interested impresarios. But from the point of view of the historian it is a piece of singular good fortune that the first city outside Milan with which Verdi took up a contract should have been Venice. Of all the opera houses of Italy, Venice's La Fenice alone has preserved a full record of its dealings with composers, and of the productions staged there. Its theatre archive makes it possible to give an account of the genesis of *Ernani* incomparably fuller and more accurate than for any of Verdi's early Milanese operas. Here for the first time one can observe his shrewd yet conscientious way of handling contracts, his fastidious interest in the details of his librettos and in the qualities of his singers; there are even some precious hints about his idiosyncrasies as a composer. In short, the whole world of *ottocento* opera – the contracts, the collaboration between composer and librettist, the casting, the rehearsals, the *première* – is systematically documented.

It was on 19 March 1843 that the proprietors of La Fenice met to discuss arrangements for the Carnival/Lent season 1843–4. The composers to be sounded out included Mercadante, Donizetti, Pacini and Nini, but there is no doubt that the 'Presidente agli Spettacoli', Count Francesco Mocenigo, was most interested in Verdi. He had met him a year earlier in Vienna at the time of the revival of *Nabucco* at the Kärntnertor theatre and had been disappointed then at not being able to engage him for Venice. Now he recommended to his committee that they 'offer to pay Maestro Verdi the sum of 10,000 Austrian *lire* for the composition of a new opera, the libretto to be prepared at his own cost'.[2] Some of the committee thought the sum too high for a comparative beginner, though Mocenigo was sceptical about getting Verdi for less. Eventually it was decided to ask all the composers in question to state how much they would require to compose a new opera.

When he received Mocenigo's letter, Verdi was again in Vienna on the point of returning to Italy. He replied from Udine:

You will be wondering why you have not had a reply to your letter of 20 March, but I had left for Vienna, and your letter was late in reaching me from Milan. Allow me to make a few observations on the conditions indicated in your letter. I should not be able to submit the fully completed score by 15 December; I should be able to submit it complete as far as the composition is concerned, and so that all the singing parts and all the choruses could be copied from it. But as far as the orchestration is concerned, I am accustomed to do that only after the piano rehearsals have started.

Nor could I undertake to deliver the libretto during June, because it is extremely probable, indeed virtually certain, that I should not have a poet. Indeed in my opinion, the president himself should commission the libretto from that poet who has already written two for Maestro Ferrari . . .[3]

Obviously gratified that Verdi was showing interest, Mocenigo hastened to clarify the details.

On my return from Milan I found your letter directed to the presidency from Udine. As they are desirous of concluding an arrangement with you, I request you kindly to indicate what would be the lowest sum you would require for the following:
1. To produce I Lombardi alla Prima Crociata.
2. To compose a new opera seria, which would be produced as the second piece of the season.
3. To engage a librettist, excepting Peruzzini, who is already occupied with another opera.[4]

Verdi replied from Parma:

. . . I think it is not a good idea either for me or for the theatre to perform the new opera as the second of the season, especially if I Lombardi is to be given as the first. The best thing would be to leave an interval of a month between the one opera and the other. I don't mind whether the new opera is performed before or after I Lombardi. I am sorry that the poet Peruzzini cannot write the libretto; he was the one I had chosen, not knowing that two new operas were going to be written for La Fenice in the next Carnival season.
. . . It only remains to talk business; for me, to compose the new opera and produce I Lombardi, twelve thousand lire; for the poet, the amount to be fixed either by me or by the management according to the reputation he enjoys.[5]

At first sight Verdi's concern about not being able to find a librettist seems odd; one has the impression that they were hovering about him as eagerly as the impresarios. Solera, currently in Brescia, had already been in touch with Ricordi:

I am working on a libretto even more effective than *Nabucco* and *I Lombardi* ... If Verdi would like it, I promise him he will have a greater success than ever, whatever the expectations of the public; I will let him have it if he is wanting to compose for La Scala. Have a word with him about it.[6]

And notwithstanding the fate of *Un Giorno di Regno*, Romani too was making advances via his brother-in-law Isidoro Cambiasi. To him Verdi replied:

... I should count myself fortunate if I could have that unpublished libretto which you mention: indeed you would be doing me a favour if, when you write to Romani, you would ask him if it would be suitable for the company that is to sing in Venice next Carnival season, as I may very well be composing for that theatre. If so, I would come over to Turin to make all the necessary arrangements, and to pay my homage to the incomparable Romani.[7]

Probably, though, Verdi's unease about librettists reflects the fact that in his heart of hearts he knew that the time was past when he could take over and set to music the ready-written texts of the eminent literary men of the day. He had reached a stage in his development when he needed to choose a subject for himself and to fashion it himself into the dramatic shape that best answered his needs as a composer. By the time of *Ernani* he needed not so much a distinguished librettist as a kind of literary batman, willing to carry out his commands unquestioningly, and able to sense and give verbal form to the needs he was only half capable of articulating. Fortunately Venice possessed such a man in the person of Francesco Maria Piave, whose twenty-year-long collaboration with Verdi was to be inaugurated with *Ernani*.

But the meeting with Piave still lay in the future. The month of May was largely occupied with drawing up a contract satisfactory to all parties. On 1 May, Mocenigo conveyed to the mayor, Correr, the replies he had received to the preliminary enquiries of 20 March, indicating his own preference for Verdi. Receiving an endorsement from the mayor, who scribbled on the envelope, 'Verdi is necessary for every reason and is the only one I approve', Mocenigo wrote off to Verdi immediately offering him 10,000 Austrian *lire* for the production of *I Lombardi* and the composition of the new opera. The libretto was to be charged to the composer; the score, all arrangements and the libretto thereafter to belong wholly to La Fenice. By way of apology for offering a sum less than that demanded by Verdi a few days before, he added the forlorn note: 'The president is not authorized to exceed this amount.'[8]

Verdi promptly rejected the offer. From Parma on 3 May, and again on the 17th as the first letter never reached its destination, he wrote:

I cannot accept the sum which Your Excellency offers me in your letter of 1st instant. Taking into account the production of *I Lombardi*, the cost of the libretto, and the expense of travel and accommodation in Venice, I should stand to earn much less for the new opera than I did for *I Lombardi*, an amount with which I could not be satisfied next year.

I will produce *I Lombardi*, I will compose the new opera, leaving the score as the sole property of the management, I will have a libretto written at my own expense and the management or the company will pay me 12,000 (twelve thousand) Austrian *lire*. Or the ownership of the score can be left to me, the other conditions remaining, and I will be paid 6000 (six thousand) Austrian *lire*.[9]

Mocenigo acquiesced without protest, observing only that 'the increase of 2000 Austrian *lire* will be an indubitable proof of the high esteem which the president entertains of your merit and of the wish that you should compose specially for this great theatre'.[10]

A draft contract was then drawn up and sent to Verdi. Three of its nine clauses proved unacceptable. He could not agree to submit the libretto for approval

. . . because the presidency could refuse me both the first and the second libretto etc. and so we should never come to any conclusion. The presidency may be quite sure that I shall try to get a libretto written which I can feel, so that I can compose it in the best way possible. If the presidency still has no confidence in me, you get the libretto written at my expense: always provided that this expense is within my means . . .

Nor would Verdi undertake to deliver a completed score during December

. . . as I wrote in my letter from Udine, my system of working is to do the orchestration during the piano rehearsals, and the score is never completely finished until just before the dress rehearsal.

Finally he was not prepared to wait until after the third performance before being paid the last instalment of his fee, on the grounds that there might never be a third performance.[11]

The contract eventually drawn up on 28 May between Count Mocenigo, on behalf of La Fenice, and Verdi consisted of ten clauses:

1st. Maestro Verdi undertakes to compose a new *opera seria* on a specially written libretto to be performed at the Gran Teatro della Fenice during the Carnival and Lent season 1843–4.
2nd. The cost of the said libretto will be met by the composer, who undertakes to submit it for approval during the coming month of September 1843.

3rd. Maestro Verdi undertakes to have completed his score in time for it to be staged without fail on the first Saturday of February next.

4th. The composer must be in Venice on 5 December 1843 and is to remain there at least until after the third performance of his new opera has taken place; he is also to be present at all the preliminary rehearsals for it, as well as at the first performances.

5th. The composer undertakes further to produce for St Stephen's Day, 26 December, next, his opera *I Lombardi alla Prima Crociata*, and to direct all the piano and orchestral rehearsals.

6th. The libretto, the score, and the arrangements of the score will remain entirely the property of the proprietary company of the Gran Teatro della Fenice.

7th. In recompense for the obligations assumed by Maestro Verdi, the presidency of the theatre must pay him 12,000 (twelve thousand) Austrian *lire*, in three equal parts, the first when the score is delivered, the second at the first orchestral rehearsal, and the third after the first performance.

8th. All cases of unforeseeable theatrical accidents [*tutti i casi fortuiti teatrali di metodo*] will be in favour of the presidency.

9th. Should any differences arise over the production of the opera, it is expressly agreed that Maestro Verdi should submit any appeal against the decisions of the presidency to the sole political authority.

10th. The artists who are to perform Maestro Verdi's new opera will be selected by the composer from the roster of the company and agreed upon with the presidency.[12]

Verdi signed the contract on 6 June, adding the note 'always provided that the approval of the libretto does not expose me to any inconvenience whatever, as I am assured in the letter of 28 May which accompanies this contract'. Then, in his own covering letter, he raised the question which was to occupy his energies for the next two months, the choice of a subject:

... I will let the presidency know the subject of the opera as soon as possible; if I had an artist of the calibre of Ronconi, I would choose either *King Lear* or *The Corsair*, but since it will probably be necessary to depend on the prima donna I might perhaps choose *The Bride of Abydos*, or some other in which the prima donna would be the protagonist. In any case I shall choose a subject that has no connection with the subject of another score.

I have written to Cammarano, to Solera, to Bancalari in Genoa. Perhaps even some fairly distinguished Milanese poet could write me a libretto which could be really fine. If nothing comes of all these I don't know what else I could do but apply to Peruzzini.[13]

Of these letters, only that to Bancalari appears to survive:

I am contracted to compose an opera for Venice. Would you like to write the libretto for me? If you would, and if you have time, send me two or three subjects straight away because they have to be approved by the presidency.

What I would like is an imposing and at the same time passionate libretto, quite distinct from *Nabucco* and the *Crociato*. It should be very fiery, packed with action, and concise. I should add that it will have to lean heavily on the prima donna.[14]

Guglielmo Brenna, the secretary of La Fenice, reported to Mocenigo on 30 June that he had received Verdi's letter of acceptance. It is at this point that Piave appears on the scene. Observing that Peruzzini could not do the libretto, since he was already engaged on one for Samuele Levi, Brenna continues: 'But I think Piave would like to enter the lists and that he will make Verdi an offer.'[15]

The offer that Piave made Verdi was of a libretto called *Cromvello*. It derived from *Allan Cameron*, a spurious Scott novel, which was enjoying a modest currency both in its French original and in Italian translation.[16] Verdi was reserved.

Like you, I feel that *Cromvello* would be an excellent subject, but it doesn't seem to be suitable under the circumstances. For many reasons which I don't need to repeat to you, it is necessary to choose a subject in which the prima donna is the protagonist.

At the moment I could not accept your courteous offer because I am awaiting replies from other poets with whom I am engaged ... In the meantime if you would care to finish *Cromvello* it might well be suitable for me, even if not for Venice.[17]

By this time Verdi had dived into a veritable ocean of luridly romantic literature. At one moment Bulwer Lytton's *Rienzi* was the favoured subject, at the next a *Caduta dei Longobardi*. At the end of June he submitted to La Fenice a sketch of *Catherine Howard*, based on the play by Dumas *père*; within a couple of days this had been supplanted in his favour by Byron's *The Two Foscari*, 'a Venetian theme ... full of passion and ideal for music ... a most interesting subject and much more attractive than *Catterina*'.[18]

Brenna had felt doubtful about *Catherine Howard* the moment he received the synopsis. On 2 July he reported to Mocenigo: 'Verdi has forwarded the synopsis of the libretto for his opera. The subject is *Catterina Howard*. Today I shall forward it to the mayor. But I fear there is too much atrocity in it for it to be readily permitted.'[19]

The synopsis of *The Two Foscari* followed *Catherine Howard* to the mayor's and censor's offices. Both were rejected: *Catherine Howard*, as Brenna had feared, 'because of excessive atrocity'; *The Two Foscari* 'out of consideration for families living in Venice, such as the Loredano and Barbarigo families, who could be distressed by the hateful characters given to their ancestors'. In communicating the sorry news to Verdi, Brenna once more suggested a collaboration with Piave. Verdi replied:

... I am sorry that the subject of *I Due Foscari* has not been approved because I found it very convincing, and because the libretto was already commissioned and, one might say, virtually finished. It will do for me another time.

Cromvello, from what I know of him historically, is certainly a fine subject, but everything depends on the way in which it is treated. I do not know Signor Piave, but if Your Excellency assures me he is a good poet, who knows what is effective in the theatre and understands musical forms, I beg you to pass on to him the enclosed letter, doing me the favour of reading it first yourself.[20]

The testimonial to Piave's accomplishments came in two instalments. On 28 July Brenna sent Verdi a synopsis and probably some of the verses of the *Cromwell* libretto, now entitled *Allan Cameron*. A commendatory letter followed on 1 August.

. . . if the proposed sketch proves satisfactory, have no fear for the calibre of the verses. Piave is a man of letters, and although this is the first *opera seria* libretto which he has attempted to write, he is very well known as a lyric poet, and the beauty of his ideas and his spontaneity leave nothing to be desired. As far as payment is concerned, Piave asks 300 florins, but would rely entirely on my judgement if I thought that amount should be reduced. I am new to this sort of affair, and so I should be embarrassed to make a judgement. Unless you could tell me what you think it reasonable to spend; I am sure that Piave could be got to accede to your wishes, simply for the satisfaction of writing for the composer whose glorious fame today fills all Italy.[21]

With a subject apparently agreed upon, and a librettist chosen, Verdi's letters for the rest of the month are largely concerned with establishing a good working relationship with his new colleague. Words of approval and encouragement, advice and exhortation flowed from Milan to Venice. From the start Verdi's relationship with Piave was quite different from what it had been with his other librettists: one man was the experienced veteran of four La Scala *premières*, the other a novice. Piave had first been encouraged to apply himself to libretto-writing the previous winter, by Pacini, whose memoirs paint a picture of this 'man of letters' rather different from that in Brenna's letter: 'he said he had never written a quatrain in his life, and understood nothing of the art of writing a libretto'.[22] From the start Verdi sensed that he could mould Piave to be exactly the kind of librettist he wanted. The education began on 8 August:

The sketch of your drama which . . . I have now read at greater leisure, and the verses of the introduction go splendidly, and leave nothing to be desired . . . You know better than I that this sort of composition is not effective unless there is action, so always as few words as possible . . . As far as the length of the pieces is concerned, brevity is never a defect. The metres can be as you wish. I never shackle the genius of my poets, and if you cast an eye over the librettos I have set, you will see that they are set very freely, and without regard for the usual conventions. Sometimes admittedly I do venture to make some modifications, but I do this for the general effect of something, not for my own sake: it's all the same to me whether I compose a duet or an aria in one metre or another. I do recommend brevity because that is what the public likes . . .[23]

A few days later Verdi heard from Brenna, who assured him,

Piave is progressing, putting his heart and soul into the work. He has finished the first act. He gave it to Count Mocenigo to read, and he was very satisfied with it. I can assure you that the poetry is full of beautiful thoughts and energetic ideas.[24]

The contract between composer and librettist was drawn up on 17 August:

1st. Signor Francesco Piave undertakes to write for Maestro Verdi a new lyric drama for music.
2nd. The subject of the drama will be Allan Cameron, or The Flight of Charles II, King of Scotland, from the persecutions of Cromwell, based on the sketch already approved by the presidency of La Fenice and by the police authorities.
3rd. Signor Piave undertakes to deliver his work complete by 20 September next without fail.
4th. He undertakes whenever requested by Signor Verdi to change any passages of verse in the libretto which are not fully to his satisfaction.
5th. In payment for Signor Piave's poetry, Maestro Verdi undertakes to pay the said Signor Piave six hundred (600) Austrian *lire* in two equal parts; that is, 300 *lire* on delivery of the libretto, and the other 300 after the first performance.[25]

About the same time the completed first act was sent off to Verdi. The composer's letter of acknowledgement is more interesting for what it tells us of his methods of composing than for its kind words on Piave's verse:

I have received the first act, which I find excellent both poetically and in its musical form. If there should be anything to alter, it will be tiny things that can be done on the spot in a moment. If you should wish to improve the odd line or phase etc., pray do. You may be sure it won't cause me any trouble.
   I have locked away this first act because I don't want to start work on it until I have the complete libretto. That is what I usually do and I find it works better, because when I have a general conception of the whole poem the music always comes of its own accord. But don't rush with the other two acts; as long as I have them by the end of next month there will be time to compose them. Again I would urge you to give the last finale all the pathetic colouring you can.[26]

The fact that the first act of Piave's libretto was locked away does not of course mean that Verdi was not already thinking about the new opera. One consideration he was probably finding more vexatious than stimulating was the eagerness of the Fenice authorities to have a big part for the contralto prima donna Carolina Vietti, a firm favourite with Venetian audiences, Brenna had vainly attempted to arouse Verdi's interest in her back in June. Now, it seems, he or Mocenigo had requested the Milanese theatre correspondent Antonio de Val to sing her praises to Verdi. On 24 August de Val reported to Brenna: 'he has promised me that, as far as the libretto allows, he will spare no pains to treat her well. He is a sworn enemy to having a woman singing dressed up as a man.'[27]

Mocenigo himelf was in Milan at this time and took the opportunity to have a long talk with Verdi about the new opera. On 25 August he wrote to Brenna that Verdi was

satisfied with Piave's libretto, and wishes only that the third act should be fast-moving and energetic; so the dialogue must be incisive and vigorous; at the end there should be a grand aria for the soprano. His only fear is that the costumes might be drab. I am looking into the question of whether it might be possible to add some English gentlemen of Charles's party to the first act. We shall see. Maestro Verdi has decided on the title *Cromwell*.[28]

In fact, by the time Mocenigo's letter reached Venice, Piave must have finished the libretto and had the good news sent to Verdi. Verdi replied:

I have heard with great delight that you have finished the work. Just get it approved by everyone and then send it me so that I can get to work at once on the composition. Don't hesitate to make any annotations you like, as you did in the first act, because I shan't be in the least offended.

I hear that you have reduced the drama to two acts; all the better. I would only say that if the second act turns out to be longer than the first, then it would be better to keep to the original division. Think about it . . .[29]

But Verdi was never to 'get to work' on the composition of *Cromwell*. When Mocenigo read Piave's completed libretto he decided he didn't like it, and though he had the libretto sent to Verdi, he expressed his doubts quite clearly. It did not convince him in this two-act form, he wrote, 'because the opera doesn't gain in interest in the least, and because the entertainment would be very short'.[30] Rather than suggesting that Piave should be asked to rewrite the second act, he straightway proposed *Hernani* as an alternative subject.

Reading this, one cannot help suspecting a touch of collusion between Mocenigo and Verdi, going back to their 'long conversation' on 24 August. Mocenigo must have known that he could not have proposed any subject which would more effectively kill Verdi's interest in *Cromwell* than *Hernani*, the most sensational theatrical triumph of that firebrand of French Romanticism, Victor Hugo. Verdi wrote back.

This *Cromvello* certainly isn't particularly interesting, when one considers the needs of the theatre. The action is fluent, clear, altogether well organized, but miserably uneventful: the fault more of the subject perhaps than of the poet. I found the first act convincing, but the second act, instead of becoming more effective, as I had hoped, was less so.

My view (if we are going to keep to this libretto) would be to keep to the original arrangement of three acts; to devise a grand finale for the farewell of Charles; and to change the last finale, because as it stands, it isn't gripping enough: let the poet keep in mind the finale of *Beatrice* or of *Norma*.

Oh, if we could only do *Hernani*, how marvellous that would be! It's true it would mean a lot of work for the poet, but I should make it my first duty to compensate him for it, and we should certainly create a much greater effect for the public.

And then Sig. Piave has great facility in versifying, and in *Hernani* he would only need to condense and tighten up; the action is all ready-made; and it is immensely gripping.

Tomorrow I will write ... to Signor Piave setting out all the scenes of *Hernani* that seem to me suitable. I have already seen that all of Act I can be condensed into a magnificent introduction, and the act could finish where Don Carlos commands Silva to give up Hernani, who is hidden behind the portrait. The second act could be made from the fourth act of the French play. And the third act finish with the magnificent trio in which Ernani dies etc.

But if *Cromvello* should be decided on after all, the poet must take all the time necessary.

If the changes in the second act prove to be really effective, then let's do that.[31]

Piave must have been vexed at this latest development. It was some days before he was ready to reply, and when he did, via Brenna, he could not refrain from suggesting that there was more to the loss of interest in *Cromwell* than Mocenigo was professing. Piave was prepared to write *Ernani*, but not until he had a guarantee from the political censor that the subject would be permitted. He must have known how Bellini's wish to compose an *Ernani* for Venice had been frustrated by the Austrian authorities in 1831, and frankly did not believe that they would be any more accommodating now. Brenna wrote:

Piave had chosen Cromwell as a subject, and in particular the conspiracy which he himself had uncovered when he aspired to the English crown. The story was magnificent both theatrically and visually, but Count Mocenigo did not want to approve it because he feared that the police would veto his approval. Now if one is going to worry about a conspiracy in England against a mildly aristocratic republican, how can one hope for *Ernani* to be approved where there is a conspiracy against the German Emperor in which the Electors take part'.[32]

The genesis of an opera – *Ernani*

Naturally Piave wanted his 100 florins for the work done on *Cromwell* and requested 400 *lire* for the new libretto. On 20 September two further letters went from Brenna to Verdi, the first simply repeating that Piave's sketch for *Ernani* was ready and assuring him that the completed libretto would be ready by 15 November, the second going into Piave's proposed treatment of the drama in some detail. The synopsis is included and then Brenna continues:

So that he can get started Piave requests that you should let him know by return of post if you would be agreeable to writing Hernani's part for contralto; even in the original he has to be a youth of twenty. If you did that, everything else would follow naturally. Don Carlos would be the tenor, Don Rui the baritone and Don Riccardo the *basso profondo*, who . . . could be introduced into all the finales without having any arias or duets. If necessary, to get round any objections, the drama could be called *Don Carlos* or *Don Rui di Silva*. On financial matters I await your instructions and promise to make the best terms possible. Perhaps to facilitate matters you could tell me whether you think I should in your name pay Piave the hundred florins for the first libretto; for I am sure that the sound of these would have the power to moderate the demands of my good friend.[33]

Verdi replied:

. . . Your proposals on *Hernani* . . . seem to me excellent. Urge Piave to take particular care with the verses and not to omit any of those powerful phrases in the original which always make such a fine effect in the theatre.

I will write the part of Hernani for Vietti etc. Warn the poet against longueurs, especially in the recitative. And let him take care to give the baritone something in the cantabile style, for I have been assured that he sings divinely.[34]

Verdi also authorized the presidency to settle up with Piave for *Cromwell*.

Next day, a new contract was sent for Verdi's signature:

1st. Sig. Francesco Maria Piave undertakes to write a new opera libretto, apart from that already prepared in respect of the contract of last July.

2nd. The subject of the new libretto will be Victor Hugo's play *Hernani*, for the approval of which Signor Piave assumes no responsibility. Indeed he declares that he will not start work on the new libretto unless the presidency of the Teatro La Fenice, where the opera is to be produced, has previously obtained the approval of the political censor for the sketch of the said drama.

3rd. Sig. Piave undertakes to submit the sketch of the aforementioned libretto within three days of this date, and, provided it is approved within the following three days, to deliver the completed libretto by 10 November next, promising further to send to Maestro Verdi the sections of verse as they are written.

4th. In accordance with the obligations assumed in the contract of last July Maestro Verdi shall pay Signor Piave 600 (six hundred) Austrian *lire* for the libretto *Hallan Cameron* based on the novel by Sir Walter Scott. This payment is a firm offer for the libretto already completed and delivered, always provided that Sig. Piave undertakes to remodel the second act into two acts, and incorporate any changes requested by Maestro Verdi. The payment for writing the new libretto is limited to 300 Austrian *lire*, but additionally Maestro Verdi undertakes to commission a third opera libretto from Signor Piave within one year of the previous date, the subject to be chosen by the said Maestro Verdi, for payment of not less than 600 Austrian *lire*.

5th. Of the total payment of 900 lire . . . for the libretto already completed and the libretto still to be written by 10 November, 300 (three hundred) *lire* will be paid to Signor Piave as soon as the plan of the new libretto based on *Ernani* has been approved by the Theatre Committee and the political censor; a further 300 (three hundred) *lire* after the libretto has been delivered and approved; and the final three hundred (300) *lire* the day after the first performance.

6th. That in the event of the plan of the new libretto *Ernani* not receiving the sanction of the political censor the payment for the libretto already completed remains limited to 600 *lire*, payable as recorded in the contract of last July, and always provided that Signor Piave introduces the modifications as mentioned in Article 4 . . .[35]

Piave went to work at once, but hardly with a will, and still profoundly sceptical about the whole enterprise. When he submitted the plan of the libretto, it was accompanied by a very sour note:

I have been constrained to write it to please the esteemed presidency and to safeguard my own reputation; but I am bound to observe that it can never succeed to my full satisfaction since I maintain that the beautiful situations of Victor Hugo lose much of their interest when they are not properly prepared and followed through, as is unavoidable in compressing them for a musical setting; especially when it all has to be done in such haste.[36]

But Mocenigo was sanguine. Forwarding the synopsis to Verdi, he expressed his confidence that 'notwithstanding Piave's dissatisfaction I think a more than tolerable libretto can be made of it'. Moreover he was certain that the originality of the choruses would appeal strongly to Verdi.[37] Very soon Verdi too was making encouraging and approving noises.

I have received the two pieces of *Ernani*. These verses are excellent and I am very pleased with them. If you continue like this you will make a very fine libretto. These verses are much better (excuse me for saying so) than those in *Cameron*. Do please be brief and now that the action is under way don't let it drag, and don't forget those beautiful phrases in the original. And then I would beg you, at the point where Ruy appears, to leave room for a fine *cantabile*, especially as Superchi sings splendidly; besides, it is an appropriate place for one, and Victor Hugo too has these words: 'Take it, crush with your feet this mark of honour . . . tear out my white hairs etc.'

I don't understand why there has been a change of scene in the third act. I don't find it convincing, because the situation is commonplace, the action is held up, one has to have a useless chorus in the throne room, and so the effect of the scene is diminished. It seems to me that when Carlo appears and surprises the conspirators the action must move on rapidly to the end of the act. A change of scene would completely disturb the audience and hold up the action.

For the love of God don't finish with a rondo, but write a trio: and this trio really must be the best piece in the opera.

The changes you have made in the first two acts work well, but in the last two the closer we keep to Hugo, the greater will be the effect. I think those two acts are divine.

I repeat that I am very pleased with the verses I have received, and assure you that this libretto will be a success. Take courage and send me the rest of the first act quickly. I urge you, be brief and fiery . . .[38]

Obviously by this stage Verdi, even more than Mocenigo, had become quite intoxicated by the idea of an *Ernani*. It was the merest formality when, on 3 October, Mocenigo authorized the composer to substitute it for *Allan Cameron* and conceded him any extension of time that might be necessary for its completion.[39] And under these circumstances, Piave was not disposed to protest about the subject any longer. *Allan Cameron*, it should perhaps be recorded, was eventually to be set by Pacini in 1848. It seems, however, that there were still some financial problems to be sorted out. Probably Verdi had refused to commit himself to that part of the contract that required him to commission another libretto from Piave within a year; and in view of this, the librettist felt the payment offered for *Ernani* was inadequate. But Piave was soon reconciled to waiting to sort out a satisfactory arrangement until Verdi arrived in Venice. Meanwhile he worked away at the versification of *Ernani*. When Verdi received the next instalment he was rather more critical:

I have received the scene, so permit me to offer some observations which seem to me appropriate, though you will be at liberty to do as you think fit. I find it risky to have Carlo, Ernani and Ruy follow one another on to the stage without having had an extended and substantial piece of music. It is the sort of thing which the theatre public is inclined to find ridiculous. At the point when Don Carlos enters, I would write a little duet, quite delicate in style, elaborate a little on Don Carlos's love. Then when Ernani rushes in a little later, I would make the *stretta* of the piece for Carlo and Elvira . . .

Afterwards I should have a servant, or Giovanna, announce the arrival of Ruy in a sort of recitative (as in Hugo). After a few words of surprise, I should have him start the *adagio* of the concerted finale, and I should like him to be the leading figure in this great scene. Do what you like after that.

Meanwhile carry on and finish the libretto and we can sort out these little problems later. Otherwise the verses are excellent . . .[40]

Rather surprisingly, in view of the terms of the libretto contract, nothing had yet been done by either Piave or Mocenigo to ensure police approval of the subject. On 23 September Brenna had reported that Piave

has finished the first part of his libretto. This evening he will read it to Count Mocenigo, who has no fears about police approval being withheld.

In any case the count himself will tomorrow take the completed part of the libretto, and the sketch of the rest, to Councillor Brasil [?], so by the day after tomorrow I shall have some positive news for you.

If Piave gets political approval the day after tomorrow, he undertakes to have the second part complete within the next week, and the third and fourth parts well before 15 November. Proceed with your work in good spirits, then; it will surely bring you laurels in Venice not dissimilar to those which your music has earned you elsewhere.[41]

In fact, however, nearly two weeks were to pass before Mocenigo did finally submit the sketch, now entitled *D. Gomez de Silva*, to the censor. In the accompanying letter, a minor masterpiece of diplomatic humbug, he remarks:

The only difficulty that had to be overcome was that of writing the part of Carlos in such a way as to cause no political affront and yet preserve all its vigour and interest. This was the only difficulty, since, with Schiller's *Don Carlos* in the repertory of the Court Theatre in Vienna, there could be no doubt that it was possible for this character to appear in a theatrical role. To change the name of the leading character or the place of action was a thought that could not have been entertained for a moment: the drama would have lost all its strength; which really lies not in amorous intrigue, not in a conspiracy, not in a coronation . . . but rather in the importance of the character, in historical truth.

The poet, omitting the cupboard scene and the duel scene, motivating the appearance of Don Carlos in Elvira's room, giving fine expression to the courage and clemency of that sovereign in the third and fourth parts, has solved the problem fully. There is indeed a great difference between the incestuous love of Schiller's Don Carlos and the dignity, nobility of thought and purity of conduct of Piave's Don Carlos; nothing but feelings of respect and admiration can be awakened in the hearts of the audience . . .

Even the title has been changed to remove any idea that the improprieties of the French text would be retained in the Italian version . . .[42]

The police replied on 27 October, authorizing Piave to proceed with the writing of the libretto, but making it clear that there were some potentially sensitive points where they would be particularly vigilant:

. . . It is required that in the second scene of Part III, where the conspirators appear, the action should be as brief as possible, that their swords should not be drawn, and that in the third scene, when the Emperor appears among them, his act of clemency should be liberal and impressive.

It is also essential that, during the scene between the Emperor and Ernani, the poet should use expressions becoming and proper for a subject addressing his sovereign, omitting talk of blood and vengeance . . . and should moderate in a similar way all other improprieties . . .[43]

Meanwhile a difficulty had arisen between Verdi and Mocenigo. As Piave's verses gradually accumulated, and as the musical character of the new opera gradually became clearer in his mind, Verdi began to regret the undertaking he had given a month before to write the part of Ernani for Vietti. He confided to Piave his wish to write the part for a tenor, and presumably asked him to sound out Mocenigo on the question. On 26 October a letter was written to Verdi on Mocenigo's behalf.

Piave has conveyed to Count Mocenigo the desire you have expressed to entrust the role of Hernani to a tenor. His first thought was to accede to your request, but when the matter was examined more closely, insurmountable difficulties presented themselves. For Signora Vietti not to sing in the season's new opera would be contrary to the wishes of the entire city. To give her the part of Carlo would be to make a parody of a character whom it is indispensable to portray with all the dignity and sublimity possible.

Besides Vietti could represent a young man of twenty, such as Hernani, since she has a physique and figure of masculine robustness, and furthermore is distinguished by all that vibrancy of spirit with which that character must be marked; but she could not sustain the dignity of Carlo, who should no longer be in the flower of his youth.

For these reasons the Count must refuse his consent to the proposed change. But he flatters himself that the reasons given for the refusal will convince you that it will be to your advantage to make use of the talents of Signora Vietti. The Count urges you to have full confidence in her, and is certain that when you hear the sympathetic voice and the fine style of this artist you will be grateful to him for his firmness.[44]

Verdi was not grateful, however: nor, for very long, was Mocenigo firm. Ten days later he wrote to Verdi again, describing the artists engaged for the Carnival season and authorizing him to write the part of Ernani for either tenor or baritone. He also enquired whether Verdi had any good suggestions for a *basso profondo* to take the role of Silva. Verdi replied:

I don't know what artist to suggest for the basso profondo, but I think we could manage with the company as it is now. We could even make use of two tenors; but the best solution would be to give Conti the part of Ernani, Superchi that of Carlo, and Rossi that of Gomez, since in this part there is only the finale of Act I, a few pertichini,* a duet in the second act (a very powerful one with chorus); and in Act III he only has ensembles. In Act IV there's the terzetto finale, but if the poet will bear with me, we can centre all the interest on the two lovers . . . I think this will work out well, especially as everyone assures me that Superchi is a very fine singer . . .[45]

* I.e. short, unimportant solo phrases.

'If the poet will bear with me' – Piave was the most docile and amenable of men, but as yet, not having come face to face with Verdi and fallen under the spell of his personality, he was not incapable of indignation. Faced with further changes of plan in the casting, which obviously would require some far-reaching revision of work he imagined already finished, he must have ventured some mild protest to Brenna. At any rate, on 13 November Brenna wrote to Verdi that Piave had finished the fourth part except for the *stretta* of the trio and that 'before writing that, he would like to discuss it with you, so as to avoid as far as possible making alterations to work that is already finished'.[46] Piave seems also to have been a little put out because Verdi had not yet answered his last letter. Verdi replied on 15 November:

Piave will by now have received my letter ... I await the fourth act with impatience, because I could not come to Venice yet. Let him finish the trio as he thinks fit; but it seems to me that a genuine solo for Ernani would be very tedious. What are the other two to do? I would like this trio as quickly as possible because I want to compose it at leisure before I come to Venice.

From your letter I see that Piave 'would like to discuss it with me, so as to avoid as far as possible making alterations to work that is already finished'. I am the last person to want to put a poet to the trouble of changing a single line; and I have written the music for three librettos of Solera, and comparing the originals, which I keep, with the printed librettos, you will find that really very few lines have been altered, and then only when Solera himself was convinced it was necessary.

But Solera has already written five or six librettos: he knows the theatre, and what is effective, and he knows the musical forms. Signor Piave has never written one, and so it is natural that he should be wanting in these matters.

In fact what woman is going to sing one after another a grand cavatina, a duet finishing as a trio, and an entire finale, as she is expected to in the first act of *Ernani*? Signor Piave may have good reasons to offer me, but so have I, and I say that the lungs wouldn't be up to such a task. And what composer can set to music a hundred lines of recitative as there are in this third act without boring everyone? In all four acts of *Nabucco* or *I Lombardi* put together you will certainly not find more than a hundred lines of recitative.

The same could be said about many other small details. You have been very kind to me, and I do beg you to try to make Piave see the point of all these things. However little experience I may have, I do nonetheless go to the theatre all the year round, and I pay very close attention: I have been able to put my finger on the fact that many compositions would not have failed if the pieces had been better distributed, the effects better calculated, the musical forms clearer ... in short, if both the poet and the composer had had greater experience. So often a recitative a bit too long, a single phrase or sentence that would be beautiful in a book or even in a spoken drama make people laugh in an opera.

I await the last act with impatience ...[47]

The genesis of an opera – *Ernani*

Perhaps fearing that all the straight talking of this letter might have a demoralizing effect on Piave, Verdi concluded his instructions to Brenna on a more warm-hearted note:

Beg Piave to send me the poetry as quickly as possible and put him in a good humour, and assure him that *Hernani* is certain to be a success . . . If Piave wants to await my arrival in Venice, I hope that I shan't give him cause for complaint. If he wants to be certain of another hundred zwanzigers or so, do give him them. And if he still wants to write me another libretto he can do that too . . . Can I speak fairer?

By 28 November the libretto was at last ready, and the following day Mocenigo submitted it to the police. With Don Ruy Gomez de Silva's role now assigned to a *comprimario* it was no longer possible for the opera to bear his name, as Mocenigo's covering letter explained:

. . . It was deemed more appropriate to give it the title *L'Onore Castigliano* . . . so that the leading role would not devolve on the *comprimario* to whom the character of Gomez had been entrusted.

Signor Piave's fully worked-out libretto needed to be copied, but in order not to delay the production any more, I am enclosing it in the hope that the authorities will kindly return it, since the author does not even have a copy of the latest corrections, which he made on this unique original.

Though Maestro Verdi is already well advanced in the task of composing the music, it would be appreciated if the permission requested could be granted as quickly as possible, so that, if necessary, room can be made for such modifications as are required.[48]

Police approval was forthcoming on 6 December, though 'some corrections and changes had been made in agreement with the poet Francesco Maria Piave'.[49] And by this time Verdi himself was in Venice. He had announced his departure from Milan in an unprecedentedly familiar letter to Piave:

Tomorrow evening at six I shall leave for Venice, and I shall arrive on Sunday morning at about six. I shall find myself a room at the Luna or the Europa or the devil knows where else close to the post office. I don't know my way around Venice, and you do, and so taking advantage of that holy confidence which, as you have so often said, should exist between us, I beg you to come and find me; come about ten, and if I am asleep, wake me up. If you can't manage it then, I'll rummage around myself until I find you.[50]

Verdi's first impressions of Venice are recorded in a letter to Giuseppina Appiani:

Venice is beautiful, poetic, divine, but . . . I wouldn't stay here voluntarily. My *Ernani* progresses, and the poet does everything I desire. Each day I have two rehearsals for *I Lombardi*, and all of them do their best, especially Signora Loewe. The first time we met was at the first rehearsal of *I Lombardi*: we exchanged a few complimentary words and that was that; I have never

129

been to visit her, nor do I propose to, unless it is absolutely necessary. Otherwise I can only say good of her, she carries out her duties very conscientiously, and without the slightest trace of temperament.

You can laugh if you like, but I shall be in Milan as soon as *Ernani* has been produced . . .[51]

During December there is a lull in the spate of documents relating to *Ernani*. Problems could now be discussed directly; and Verdi must have been too busy to write much to friends back in Milan. Nothing else has come to light until the well-known report on the *première* of the revival of *I Lombardi*, again addressed to Appiani, and dated 'Venice, 26 December 1843, an hour after midnight':

You are eager to hear news of *I Lombardi*, so I am sending you the very latest: it is not a quarter of an hour since the curtain fell.

I Lombardi was a complete fiasco, a truly classic fiasco. Everything was disapproved of or barely tolerated, with the exception of the cabaletta of the vision. This is the simple truth of the matter, and I tell it without pleasure and without distress . . .[52]

The various surviving notes from Verdi to his friends reporting the fiasco of *I Lombardi* do not suggest what the reasons for the fiasco might have been. From subsequent developments, however, it is clear that a prime factor was the incapacity of the leading tenor, Domenico Conti. Within a day or two of the *Lombardi première*, Verdi seems to have written to Mocenigo refusing to proceed with the composition and production of *Ernani* unless a replacement could be found. On 30 December the two men met to discuss what could best be done under the circumstances, and probably on the same day Mocenigo and his committee decided that they should take legal action against the theatrical agent Giovanni Bonola 'because he has sold to the presidency the tenor Conti who is absolutely incapable of assuming the responsibilities assigned to him'.[53] The presidency feared that it might not be able to proceed with the season's performances since 'it was impossible to find a suitable replacement', and if things continued as at present, the theatre would soon be empty anyway. Next day Conti resigned, explaining that 'in view of his state of health it is impossible for him to sustain the part of principal tenor during the present 1843–4 season' and that he would 'return home hoping to derive some benefit from the quiet and from his native air'.[54]

There could have been no worse time than the start of the Carnival season in which to have to look for a first-class tenor to replace Conti. Carlo Guasco was engaged for the latter part of the season, but Mocenigo still hoped to be able to stage *Ernani* sooner rather than later. On 2 January, therefore, having heard good reports of one Raffaele Vitali, he decided that Verdi ought to go off to Verona, where Vitali was currently performing in *Nabucco*, to hear him sing. Verdi's report came on 8 January: 'I have heard Vitali, and I don't like him. With time perhaps he'll develop into a fairly good tenor, but at present he's nothing and his voice gets tired and half-way through the opera he tends to go flat'.[55]

Meanwhile, between the departure of Conti and the arrival of Guasco, things were going badly at La Fenice. The fiasco of *I Lombardi* was nothing compared with that of Pacini's *Fidanzata Corsa*, the performance of which was abandoned amidst 'an uproar of shouting', a mark of disapproval so signal even for those times that Mocenigo tendered his resignation. Though he was persuaded to continue in his position of Presidente agli Spettacoli, the next opera of the season, Levi's *Giuditta*, was hardly more successful. No wonder that, after the failure of his expedition to Verona, Verdi was starting to find his Venetian sojourn sorely trying. To his Milanese friend Pasetti he wrote on 12 January:

If I haven't written before now it is because I have nothing very comforting to tell you. Without mentioning the outcome of *I Lombardi*, I foresee that the future cannot be rosy in this theatre. The performance of the *Fidanzata* can prove that: the opera was not even finished. The singers were whistled at; insults were shouted at the presidency and especially Mocenigo, who has resigned his post as president. They even threw chrysanthemums on to the stage. What they meant by that I do not know. The tenor Conti has been released from his contract, but as yet no substitute has been found. Meanwhile *I Lombardi* continues to be performed with a real novice, Bettini, whom I have never heard.

I have tried to release myself from my contract, but without success. I am obliged to wait for Guasco, and go into production with *Ernani* in Lent. I am told Guasco's health is not good: I don't know what to say! The whole business is such a mess that one almost has to laugh. If I have a fiasco the fault won't be mine. I have done everything I can, and am not dissatisfied with my work, and if *Ernani* fails to please in Venice it will please somewhere else . . .[56]

Soon illness was added to Verdi's other worries, plunging him into one of his acutest melancholias. An undated letter to Toccagni is generally assumed to be from this time:

I write to you with tears in my eyes, and long for the time when I can leave here. Add to this a slight fever which assails me every evening and you see how well I am . . . My rooms are tolerably good and I stay in a lot, that is I stay in bed. I am composing this poor *Ernani* of mine and am not dissatisfied with it. Despite my apparent indifference I shall smash my head in if I have a fiasco; I couldn't bear the idea, especially as these Venetians are expecting I don't know what . . .

Night is coming, driving me to despair. Greet all my friends, and tell them to think of me. Wish me well, really well . . .[57]

The composition of the opera must have been completed towards the end of January: the few dates recorded in the autograph full score show that Verdi had orchestrated at least the introductory chorus before the end of the month. The scene-painter Pietro Venier was sent a descriptive listing of the scenes on 21 January; the final version of the libretto was ready a few days later and submitted to the police on the 29th. The copying of parts for the singers was also under way, firing at least part of the Fenice team with enthusiasm.[58] On 31 January, Mocenigo sent Guasco the first instalment of his role.

In accordance with the arrangement made in the contract of 28 July last year . . . we hasten to send you the part of Hernani in the drama of the same name, expressly composed by Maestro Verdi.

The presidency joins with Maestro Verdi in urging that you should study this most important role with devotion, The rehearsals with the under-studies will be starting here on 11 February, so that when you arrive in Venice there will be nothing to delay the production beyond arranging the ensembles satisfactorily.

Meanwhile we will have a copy of the new libretto prepared for you, which we will send together with the few pieces of music which are still lacking to make your part complete.[59]

The rest of the music was sent him on 2 February:

Here, Signor Guasco, is the rest of your part of Hernani, and the libretto of this new drama, which will enable you to perceive the character of the role which has been entrusted to your skill.[60]

It must have been at about this time that Sophie Loewe began to exhibit more than a sufficiency of that 'temperament' which she had concealed during the rehearsals of *I Lombardi*. The pretext for her ill will was apparently that Verdi had chosen to conclude the opera with a trio rather than with a solo aria for her. But there was worse to come for Mocenigo and Verdi than Signora Loewe's pique. Guasco, far from being exhilarated at the prospect of creating a Verdi role, was so dismayed by the demands it made on him, that he wrote to his agent Giaccone on 14 February refusing to undertake it: 'I do not feel strong enough to undertake a task of this kind at the end of the present season, so I ask you to take whatever precautionary measures may be necessary. That is all I have to say to you. I am sending you the complete part of Ernani and enclose the libretto with it.'[61]

In consternation, Giaccone at once sent the news to Mocenigo. He was, he said, the more astounded as he knew that Guasco had been studying his role right up to the previous day and had made all arrangements for the journey to Venice. He assured Mocenigo that he and 'all Guasco's acquaintances will today try every means of conciliation and do everything to persuade him of the critical position he is putting himself in . . . by this sort of conduct. It will be the complete ruin of him'.[62]

Scarcely had Mocenigo had time to express his 'surprise and displeasure', and to declare that he regarded Giaccone as entirely responsible in this affair, than Guasco changed his mind and decided that he would do the part after all. The same day, however, 18 February, the bass Meini 'declared that he did not wish to sing the part of Ruiz de Silva in Maestro Verdi's new opera *Hernani*'.[63] The dismay provoked by this news was slight. Verdi seems positively to have leapt at the chance of engaging a more congenial artist, and requested Mocenigo's permission to engage the bass Antonio Selva, 'for whom the role would be absolutely ideal'.[64]

By 27 February Verdi had completed the orchestration, and submitted the score to Mocenigo, who authorized the payment of the first instalment of Verdi's fee on the following day.[65] Later that day Verdi wrote a quick letter to Toccagni; his mood was brighter now, though he still affected grave concern at the ferocity of the Venetians:

It is a long time since I heard any news from you. It's true you were entitled to a letter from me, but I have been extraordinarily busy. Now I have pretty well finished all my work, except for the rehearsals which will start tomorrow. The first performance will be on 6 or 7 March. I don't know whether they will let us live; nevertheless, provided Guasco is all right, I am hopeful. Are you coming? Stir yourself up, old friend; run to the post; jump in the carriage, and come to Venice. Venice is really lovely for eight days. I'm in very good health now. I have finished the orchestration, and now have only the ordeal of the rehearsals . . .[66]

One friend had already arrived in Venice on 25 February, Verdi's brother-in-law Giovanni Barezzi, who in a series of letters to his father Antonio, back home in Busseto, provides us with an eye-witness account of the last stages of the work on the new opera. On 26 February he wrote:

Yesterday at ten in the morning I arrived safely in Venice, and found Verdi at once (I am with him now). He is writing away for all he is worth, and will have finished within two days. I have heard the soprano aria, which is very beautiful. I have made the acquaintance of Piave, a big, jolly young man like Solera. Guasco has arrived but doesn't know his part yet and the opera won't be staged before Tuesday . . .[67]

On the 29th:

133

The opera première will be on the 9th. The rehearsals are going well. What I have heard so far has been astonishing, perhaps even more so than Nabucco or I Lombardi.

All the Venetians are anxious to hear it. According to what I have heard at the Cafe Florian people are coming from Padua and Trieste and Verona and Bologna expressly to hear Ernani; From Padua are coming the members of the Società Mirionimi Enobattisti, who are the ones who gave him that banquet . . .[68]

The first orchestral rehearsal was on 1 March, but even at this late date not everything was ready. Verdi still had the orchestral prelude to compose, a movement he eventually completed, as the autograph shows, on 6 March. The first dress rehearsal took place on 7 March; the final dress rehearsal, attended by most of the city's chief dignitaries, on the 8th. In the early days of March, too, a week before the première according to Abbiati, Piave and Verdi had been dismayed to find that costumes and scenery were not ready, and decided that they must register a protest with Mocenigo:

Having considered the matter carefully, we, the undersigned, advise the esteemed presidency that it is quite improper to put Ernani on the stage before the scenery and costumes are completely ready; there would be the danger of a scandal, harmful both to the interests of the management and to the effect of the drama . . .[69]

The protest was, however, in vain. When the audience arrived for the first performance they found in the theatre 'a grotesque mural manifesto' (Abbiati) which explained that

the sets for the last two scenes of the first part and the first scene of the second part are not ready; in order not to delay the production of the opera, two makeshift scenes have therefore been substituted, until such time as the newly painted sets are finished.[70]

At least one onlooker, Giovanni Barezzi, had no fears for the effect such inconveniences would have on the outcome of Ernani. Apparently just before going off to the theatre for the première, he wrote to his father:

This evening will see the triumph and coronation of Verdi as the world's leading maestro. Yesterday I heard the rehearsal. All the pieces were applauded. What an uproar this evening, what a pleasure to see people coming from all over the place. Oh! here are the gondolas from the railway passing under my window, carrying more than a hundred young people from Padua. Bravo! To Ernani. You come too, to make Verdi's triumph the greater.[71]

In all material particulars Barezzi's confidence proved to be justified. The letter he wrote the following day provides one of the best descriptions we have of a Verdian première:

The genesis of an opera – Ernani

Yesterday evening we heard *Ernani*, with Guasco without a voice and appallingly hoarse, and with Loewe, who has never sung so badly out of tune as she did yesterday. The reception was very favourable. All the pieces were applauded with the exception of Guasco's cavatina . . . the fact that Guasco had no voice was the reason for that. At eight o'clock, when it should have started, nothing was ready. Guasco had been shouting for an hour without stopping, which was the reason he was hoarse. Two lots of sets were missing, costumes were missing, there were all manners of absurdities. Between the second act and the third, and between the third and the fourth, we had to wait three-quarters of an hour, because they had nothing ready. I swear they wouldn't have got to the end, if the music hadn't been as I told you yesterday.[72]

The successful *première* was a tonic to all concerned. Guasco's nerves were presumably calmed and less of his voice wasted on shouting before the curtain went up; Signora Loewe's intonation improved, and the subsequent performances enjoyed even greater success. Young Barezzi reported on 11 March that

Yesterday evening the singers performed respectably, and it was a real festival from beginning to end, enthusiasm that lasted from the first piece to the last, twenty curtain-calls, apart from the forty or fifty between the acts. This just goes to show the truth of what I wrote . . .[73]

The same day the less partial *Gazzetta Privilegiata di Venezia* confirmed that it had been 'all in all an ovation . . . a triumph, in which everyone was happy and contented'. And it is worth quoting part of a review in *Il Gondoliere* of 16 March as a choice specimen of contemporary music criticism in a more popular vein:

On the walls of our leading theatre a banner is unfurled on which, in letters of gold, is inscribed *Hernani*.

With a hundred voices people and senators applaud this Spanish bandit, conqueror of the *Lucrezias*, of the *Gemmas*, of the *Fidanzatas* and of the *Giudittas* [i.e. the other operas of the Carnival/Lent season of La Fenice].

The plot of the drama is from Hugo, its Italian dress by F. Piave, the harmonies by Verdi, the esteemed author of *I Lombardi* and of *Nabucco*.

His latest notes intoxicate, four times over, the souls even of grave aristarchs and severe matrons.

In halls, in the streets, in chambers, in cultivated assemblies the new songs are in every mouth.

Accompanying the composer in his well-earned triumphal carriage are the poet, and with the poet the singers.

There were crowns, flowers, shouts, palms for all . . . etc. etc.

With the success of the opera established, Verdi felt that it would be a gracious gesture to offer the dedication to Countess Clementina Spaun Mocenigo, wife of the long-suffering president of the theatre. She made elegant acknowledgement:

The proposal which you courteously make me in the note I have just received is a delightful surprise. If being a passionate devotee of music and a sincere admirer of one of the finest and most outstanding talents of our age entitles me to such a distinction, I can certainly claim to be that. I thank you then most warmly, and accept with the greatest pleasure the dedication of the beautiful opera *Ernani*. Pray accept the expression of my sincerest esteem and regard.[74]

The splendid success enjoyed by *Ernani* must have been the sweeter for the epic of ordeals through which Verdi had passed during the autumn and winter. The composition of *Ernani* ranks with the composition of *Nabucco*, *Macbeth* and *Rigoletto* as one of the heroic achievements of his youth: frustrations, disappointment, misfortune, illness, depression, hostility had all had to be overcome: all had failed to tarnish his imaginative vision or impair his craftsmanship. Verdi had earned his hour of glory and he relished it to the full. His last letter from Venice was to Barezzi:

Tomorrow I leave for Milan; you will have heard about the success of *Ernani* from Giovannino. The public has shown every manner of courtesy, and yesterday they escorted me home together with the band, the two presidents of the theatre and a crowd of people shouting 'Viva' at the top of their voices. Yesterday those dear young men of Venice gave a dinner for me at the Albergo Reale and tomorrow they are all accompanying me as far as Padua. When I first wrote I said I didn't like staying in Venice; tomorrow on the contrary I shall be very sorry to have to leave. Who would not be affected by such kindness? To tell you the truth I was really moved yesterday evening and I shall be even more tomorrow . . .[75]

Two overcrowded years

The young Verdi had had more than his share of personal sorrows and difficulties. His professional career, however, had been a dazzling one. With his third opera he had hoisted himself up out of the teeming ranks of petty maestros into that select company of composers whose works could expect an enthusiastic and respectful hearing in every city in Italy; and the position gained by *Nabucco* had been consolidated with two further brilliant triumphs. What is more, one can already see from the letters and other documents relating to *Ernani* that, besides an exciting musical talent, Verdi had the questing imagination, the toughness of character and an integrity uncompromised by the exigencies of theatre life that would enable him to develop infinitely far as an artist. But at this point Verdi stumbles. The next two years are confused and generally unhappy ones; their achievements not to be compared with those of the early 1840s.

The major symptom of this decline is an overcrowded routine. Hitherto in approximately seven years Verdi had composed five operas: in the next two years he composed four more – the number would have been higher had ill health not slowed him down – as well as supervising quite a number of revivals of his earlier works. Moreover this tighter routine is accompanied by increasingly profound attacks of melancholia and even of disgust with the career to which his genius devoted him.

A completely satisfactory explanation of these phenomena can hardly be hoped for. But one contributory factor cannot be overlooked. Verdi was suffering from the mutually exacerbating effect of two of the vulnerable spots in his character: one was that failing which Giuseppina Strepponi was to call, quite unequivocally, his 'love of gold'; the other a type of sensitivity which, however well performed and successful his operas were, rendered him prone to spasms of sickened disillusion with the whole world of the theatre. It looks very much as if, in the years after *Ernani*, Verdi used the latter weakness as a justification for indulging the former. Unable to resist the accumulating wealth which new contracts represented, he entered into more of them than he could properly cope with. And when enthusiasm and commitment were exhausted he could rationalize the continuing pattern: the quicker he composed, the sooner he would be financially independent, and so able to retire from an intermittently uncongenial career. But in fact, by working at a speed that gave him no leisure for reflection, that overtaxed his physical and nervous strength and consequently made it impossible to produce his best work, Verdi only succeeded in tormenting the idealist in his make-up, making the operatic career appear more, and more continuously, detestable.

The history of these years is then a confused one. Again and again Verdi's essential idealism and enthusiasm well up, but the general burden of the period is a decline; the best in him is being sapped away by ill health, disillusion and routine.

I Due Foscari

Verdi's *Copialettere*, a collection of fair copies of business letters, memoranda and accounts, preserved in five large exercise books in the Villa Verdi at Sant'Agata, comprise one of the most fascinating documentary sources for nineteenth-century musical historiography. It was on his return to Milan from Venice in March 1844 that Verdi began to keep this more systematic record of his correspondence. One of the earliest documents in the *Copialettere* (reproduced in facsimile as plate XI of the published edition) is entitled 'Argomenti d'opere': it is a memorandum in which Verdi jotted down a list of subjects for operas which he hoped to write in the next few years. The works are, in order: Shakespeare's *King Lear*, *Hamlet* and *The Tempest*, Byron's *Cain*, Hugo's *Le Roi s'amuse*, Grillparzer's *Die Ahnfrau*, Dumas's *Kean*, Euripides/Racine's *Phèdre*, Calderón's *A secreto agravio, secreta venganza*; then three works whose authors' names are indecipherable, *Atala* (Consenza or Chateaubriand), *Iñes di Castro* (Hugo?) and *Buondelmonte* (probably the version by Tedaldi-Fores); the list continues with Dennery's *Maria Giovanna*, the 'Spanish drama' *Guzmán el Bueno* (Antonio Gil y Zarata); *Giacomo* ('a subject from Sismondi's history, chapter 30'), *Arria* ('a subject from the Annals of Tacitus', Book IX); and finally Hugo's *Marion Delorme* and *Ruỳ Blas*, and *Elnava* (Cuciniello della Torre?).

It is quite an anthology of the heroes of Italian Romanticism, and Shakespeare, Byron and Hugo were indeed to be pervasive influences on Verdi's development during the next few years. But memoranda are made for future reference: at present, in the spring of 1844, two other subjects were occupying his mind. One was Byron's *The Two Foscari*, which, as we have seen, he had at one time hoped to be able to use for his Venetian début, the previous winter; the other a *Lorenzino de' Medici*, presumably based on Giuseppe Revere's play of the same name. Initially the latter seems to have been the preferred theme.

The theatre for which Verdi's next opera was destined was the Argentina in Rome. Of the circumstances of the commission and the details of the contract nothing is known, except that the impresario with whom he was now dealing, Antonio Lanari, was new to the business. On 12 April 1844 the theatrical journal *Il Pirata* reported:

Antonio Lanari, son of Alessandro Lanari, the very well-known impresario of some of the principal theatres of Italy, is himself embarking independently on the career of theatrical impresario. He has already obtained from His Excellency the Prince D. Alessandro Torlonia an eight-year lease of the Teatro Argentina in Rome, and likewise a lease of the Teatro Comunale in Faenza for the coming summer season.[1]

No doubt Lanari had gained valuable experience and established useful contacts through his father; but it was nonetheless a considerable feather in his cap to succeed in getting an opera from Verdi for his first Roman season.

Compared with the endless debate and heart-searching over the choice of Hugo's *Ernani*, the choice of *I Due Foscari* was a simple matter. Verdi and Piave submitted their first choice to the Roman censor and it was rejected out of hand; so they substituted for it their second choice, which was found acceptable. The whole history of the matter is documented in two letters from Verdi to Piave written in April.

This *Lorenzino* is very good ... Moreover Ricordi is pleased because it is not based on a French drama. My only fear is that the police won't allow it: but I will send it to Rome today and we shall see ... In case the police don't permit it, we shall have to think of an alternative in good time, and I would suggest *I Due Foscari*. I like the subject and there is already a sketch of it in Venice, sent by me to the presidency. I beg you to retrieve it from them. If you want to make any alterations to the synopsis do so, but stick close to Byron. I would ask you to divide this drama into three acts too; the second would have to finish at the death of young Foscari.[2]

A few weeks later – the letter is undated – Verdi wrote:

I told you that *Lorenzino* wouldn't be approved ... Let's not think about it just now and we will do it when circumstances are more favourable. Take good care with *I Due Foscari* ... but, for heaven's sake, eight days is a long time for sending me a synopsis that has already been made ... Do the job carefully, because it is a fine theme, delicate and very pathetic. I notice that Byron's play does not have the theatrical grandeur which one wants in an opera: rack your brains to find something which will make a bit of a stir, especially in the first act. Do get started on the verses as soon as you have sent me the programme, and let me have the first piece at once. This subject cannot possibly be prohibited ...[3]

Almost all the surviving documents relating to *I Due Foscari* are concerned with the shaping of the subject into a satisfying libretto. Rarely can a librettist's contribution have been limited so exclusively to the task of versification. The dramatic plan of the libretto Piave had inherited from an earlier collaborator of Verdi's, perhaps Romani, and the composer's letters in the summer of 1844 show that its final form was largely the result of instructions and suggestions from the composer. On 14 May Verdi acknowledged the receipt of the synopsis and some of the verses of the *Foscari* libretto.

I have just this moment received *I Due Foscari*. A beautiful drama, very beautiful, surpassingly beautiful! ... But with all the sincerity and affection that we feel for each other I will tell you my frank opinion.

The first scene works excellently, and the poetry of the first chorus is superb: perhaps it will be composed tomorrow. I find the character of the father is noble, very beautiful and skilfully handled. Likewise the character of Marina. But that of Jacopo is weak and makes little theatrical impact – besides, it is almost a secondary role: he has only a single romanza in Act I, and the whole of Act II. Believe me, my dear tomcat of a poet, it is absolutely essential to put this role in order. To start with I would give him a more energetic character, I wouldn't have him tortured, and after his tender apostrophe to Venice I would try to find something more robust and make a real aria out of it.

Allow me to observe that I don't like the handmaids of Marina in the Doge's palace. Couldn't you set Marina's aria in the Foscari's palace? Introduce the handmaids to provide consolation, give Marina an *adagio* cantabile to express her desolation over her husband, then have a servant enter to announce to Marina the torture or condemnation of Jacopo: Marina curses the Republic and determines to go to see the Doge, etc., etc. Avoid long recitatives, especially for Loredano and Barbarigo. The second act is very moving: it was an imaginative stroke to have Foscari's romanza in prison interrupted by the gondoliers. But will it be effective? I am sorry you have omitted the departure of Jacopo and his death. If I were you I would put it near the start of the third act.

I would start with the scene representing the piazzetta of St Mark's with a chorus of men and women. Mingled with this chorus there could be a gondolier singing an octave of Tasso from the lagoon in the distance. Then let Jacopo come in accompanied by Marina to create a beautiful duet etc. ... After that it can stand as it is, but make it short ...[4]

Equally brimming over with suggestions was the next letter, written on 22 May:

I have sent the sketch to Rome and hope that they will approve it; nevertheless you can suspend your work for the time being because I have plenty to be getting on with. Think about it carefully and try to continue as you have begun: so far everything works splendidly except for one small thing. I see that so far there has been no hint of the crime for which Foscari was condemned: it seems to me that this must be mentioned.

In the tenor's cavatina there are two things that don't work well: the first is that when the cavatina is finished Jacopo still remains on stage, and that always has a poor effect; the second is that there is no contrast of thought between the *adagio* and the cabaletta: this is something that may work very well in poetry, but it is very bad in music. After the *adagio* write a short dialogue between the officer and Jacopo, then an official should say 'Bring in the prisoner', then a cabaletta; but make it a forceful one ...

The soprano's cavatina works excellently: I think that now you should write a very short recitative, then a solo for the Doge and a grand duet. Make this duet really beautiful because it is the finale. Get yourself in an emotional state and write some beautiful poetry ... Do the third act as we have already agreed and try to graft the gondolier's song on to a chorus of the people. Wouldn't it be possible to have this happening towards evening so as to include a sunset, which is such a beautiful effect?[5]

Compared with Rossini or Donizetti, Verdi was a slow and painstaking composer, at least until it came to the more mechanical business of orchestrating his short score. The composition of *I Due Foscari*, an exceptionally short opera, was begun in the latter part of May and must have occupied the best part of the next four months.

Until the end of June things were going swimmingly. Emmanuele Muzio, another young musician from Busseto, who had just become a private pupil and general assistant of Verdi's, recorded his first impressions of the work in a letter to Antonio Barezzi on 29 May:

... We are getting up early now to compose *I Due Foscari*. The introductory chorus, which is an assembly of the Ten, is magnificent and terrible. In the music one can sense the mysterious atmosphere of those terrible gatherings that had authority over life and death: you can imagine whether the 'father of the chorus', as the Milanese call him, will have composed it well!! ...[6]

A fortnight later, 'the signor maestro is composing flat out and doesn't leave the house until evening at dinner time'.[7] But Verdi's growing reputation brought distractions too:

On Saturday a singer came who wanted the signor maestro to write a contralto part for her in the opera he is composing for Rome. He said the libretto was already finished and he couldn't. 'That doesn't matter,' said the lady, 'just one scene, a *sortita*, a cabaletta ...' It was funny, he could not dissuade her from her purpose; afterwards she wanted him to promise at least to write a part for her in the opera for Carnival. The signor Maestro, who was losing patience, said: 'no, no' and so she went away ...

A composer, I don't remember his name, has written a letter to the signor maestro, in which he prays and beseeches him not to set to music *I Due*

Foscari, because he too has composed it, and he fears that the same will happen to his opera as happened to Mazzucato's *Ernani*; the signor maestro has replied that he is already engaged on the work and cannot comply with this ardent request . . .[8]

By 30 June, according to Muzio's weekly epistle to Barezzi, the first act was virtually finished.

Towards the end of July the Milan press announced that the new opera was practically ready. But this was clearly untrue. In August Verdi betook himself to Busseto, to stay with Barezzi; and in his house enough of the opera was composed to entitle Barezzi, in later years, to talk to his guests of 'the room in which Verdi wrote *I Due Foscari*'.[9] Yet at the end of the month much still remained to be written.

Just a couple of words to tell you that I shall be in Milan very very soon . . . My native air does not suit me. Oh, this is an accursed spot! It really is completely off the map . . .

. . . I am wild because I am not getting anything done, and if you knew how much of the *Foscari* I still have to do! . . . Poor me! . . .[10]

The only surviving letter from Verdi to his impresario Lanari is also from these summer months, a businesslike account of some details of the production arrangements:

Concerning the opera *Due Foscari*, I see from your various letters that it has now been confirmed that the opera will be produced about 22 October. I shall employ three principals: Signora Barbieri, Roppa, De Bassini, and three supporting singers, a *basso profondo*, a tenor and a soprano.

Moreover I shall employ a female chorus, I shall make some use of the *banda*, and a harp. The librettist will come to produce for a payment of 40 *scudi* . . .

With this then we have come to a complete understanding, and it only remains for me to urge upon you the importance of the production.

It is a subject which is worth taking trouble over and which is immensely effective . . .[11]

Despite the eagerness to get back to Milan which Verdi expressed in his letter to Countess Appiani, he was still in Busseto on 9 September when he wrote to Piave to request some further modifications in the libretto. At the same time he asked him to clarify some production points: as librettist and producer Piave was of course responsible for deciding exactly what groups of singers should be on stage at any given time.

. . . Let me know at once . . . whether or not you want the choruses to take part in the aria (following the barcarole) in which Jacopo dies. Notice that I have used men and women in the barcarole – and let me know too if you want Pisana and the female chorus in the last *finale della campana*.

... If you have not already done so, send the libretto to Ricordi to get it approved. I need one last favour, and that is to change the cabaletta of the tenor's first aria. These words: 'Io so ben ...', which he repeats twice over, put me in mind of a comic aria by Donizetti: and I can't do anything with them ...[12]

Piave was in fact sending the libretto to Ricordi the very day that Verdi wrote: the covering note records another of the impositions of contemporary censorship:

There exists in the Austrian Empire a law which forbids subjects of His Majesty the Emperor of Austria to publish abroad any writings until they have been examined and permission given by a state censor. I have particular reasons not to wish to present I Due Foscari to the censor here. And so at the suggestion of our dear Verdi I am sending it to you, for you to submit to the Milanese censor. I beg you, as soon as the requested permission is granted, to let me know by letter to Rome, at Sig. Lanari's, as I shall be leaving in a few days for that address.[13]

By the end of September the composition of the opera was at last finished, and Verdi too left for Rome where, as he informed Ricordi, he arrived on 3 October:

I have been in Rome since the day before yesterday, and although the sea was rough between Livorno and Civitavecchia I wasn't ill.

I have given out the parts and we shall be starting in a few days. Piave tells me that you are to send him a letter assuring him that permission has been obtained from the censor.

... I am strolling around Rome and am flabbergasted. Sanchioli is having a success in Norma. Very soon Bonifazio [dei Geremei, by Poniatowski] will be produced and then mine. After that I shall come straight back to Milan. Early next month I shall be there ...[14]

There seem to be no surviving documents to describe for us the weeks of rehearsal on the opera. All we know is that when it was first produced on 3 November, Verdi felt that it was a failure. Historians have claimed that one of the reasons for the failure was that Lanari had put up ticket prices by an amount that the Roman audiences felt to be exorbitant, though Verdi makes no reference to this in his account of the première to Toccagni.

If I Due Foscari was not a complete failure, it almost was – whether because the singers were very much out of tune, or because expectations were raised too high, etc., the fact is that the opera was a mezzo-fiasco. I had a great liking for this opera: perhaps I deceived myself, but before changing my mind I want another opinion ...
(Postscript by Piave):
The very expectations of the audience caused them to be rather cool, and this was then increased by out-of-tune singing etc., etc. Verdi, however, was called quite twelve times to the stage, but that which would be for others a triumph is nothing to him. The music of I Due Foscari is divine and I do not

doubt that this evening, tomorrow and subsequently it will be appreciated more and more . . .[15]

Probably Piave was right in averring that Verdi exaggerated the coolness of the reception, and he was certainly right in predicting a better success at the subsequent performances. Muzio's next letter to Barezzi includes an illuminating extract from one of the first reviews:

You will know that the opera has created a great furore. On the first evening the singers, chorus and orchestra so disfigured and distorted it that on the second the Romans said he had changed everything. I transcribe herewith the article from the *Rivista di Roma*.

'. . . Maestro Verdi had one of the most signal triumphs yesterday evening . . . at the second performance of his excellent opera *I Due Foscari*. The singers, having overcome their nerves, abandoned the shouting which had caused such displeasure the previous evening and, having penetrated better into their characters, sang powerfully and masterfully. The public was also better disposed. They had rid themselves of that party which regularly intervenes at all *premières* with the firm intention of turning everything topsy-turvy, and applauded every piece thunderously. The composer appeared on stage at least twenty times amid the enthusiastic cheers of a packed house.[16]

A few days later Verdi was guest of honour at a celebratory banquet given by Prince Torlonia, lessor of the theatre. The occasion was celebrated with an ode, 'Verdi, alla stanca mia povera argilla', which Jacopo Ferretti, the well-known Roman librettist, declaimed to the assembled company. Later the poet sent Verdi a copy of his verses. The composer's letter of acknowledgement may close the story of his Roman début:

A thousand, thousand thanks for your letter and your *ottave*. I have been back in Milan for some days, after a long and tedious journey. Piave was in a very melancholy humour and we parted at Bologna almost without a word.

I have received the medal from the Cardinal Treasurer. I am most grateful for it and will make it my duty to thank him for it and pay my homage to him when I come to Rome next summer, on my way back from Naples . . .[17]

Giovanna d'Arco

I have already cited Verdi's letter to Ignazio Marini in which he mentioned the 'generous offers' made by Merelli after the success of *I Lombardi* (cf. p. 113 above); probably the impresario wanted to make of Verdi a kind of composer-in-residence, such as Rossini had been in Naples thirty years earlier. Though Merelli could not dissuade him from going off to Venice to try his luck there, he did manage, just before Verdi's departure, to engage him to compose again for La Scala for the Carnival season 1844–5. So much we know from a note Verdi sent from Padua to the theatrical journalist Regli of *Il Pirata*: 'If you like you can announce that I shall be composing the opera for La Scala next carnival season for Signora Frezzolini and Rizzi.'[18]

At La Scala it was the impresario's responsibility, not the composer's, to engage the librettist for a new opera. However there was nothing to stop a composer from indicating his preferences, and at this stage of his career both personal affection and artistic conviction made Solera the librettist of Verdi's choice. So, on 12 January, he included in a letter to Pasetti a request to 'remember me to Merelli, and tell him that he should find a couple of minutes to think about who is going to be my librettist for next year: tell him to write to Solera'.[19]

How much Verdi had to do with the choice of the subject we do not know. It seems curious that it should have been announced by *Il Pirata* and the *Gazzetta Musicale* at the beginning of September,[20] a time when Verdi was still 'off the map' in Busseto. Perhaps *Giovanna d'Arco* was the libretto which Solera had announced to Ricordi in the spring of 1843 (cf. p. 115 above). For all we know, Verdi may have reverted to his old habit of accepting a ready-made libretto from him. Certainly if *Giovanna d'Arco* had originated in a literary enthusiasm of Verdi's own, the letter to Ricordi in which Solera avouched the 'originality' of his libretto would have been a piece of humbug extravagant even for him:

I don't know the French drama of which you speak. I assure you categorically that my *Giovanna d'Arco* is a wholly original Italian drama; I merely wanted, like Schiller, to introduce Giovanna's father as the accuser; in everything else I did not wish to allow myself to be imposed upon either by the authority of Schiller or by that of Shakespeare, both of whom make Giovanna fall basely in love with the foreigner Lionel.

My drama is original; indeed I beg you to have it announced in your journal that, although some people have predicted that I should borrow the outline from Schiller, I have taken care to create an entirely original drama . . .[21]

Though information about the terms of the contract and the origin of the libretto is virtually non-existent, we do have an unusually full account of the progress of Verdi's composition of the music. It is provided by the letters written by Muzio to Barezzi during the winter months of 1844–5, commencing on 9 December:

If Giovanna had not eternalized herself by her own deeds, the signor maestro's music would have rendered her immortal. No Giovanna has ever had music more philosophical and beautiful. The awesome introduction (an inspiration that came to him, as you know, amid the mountain crags) and the magnificent piece 'Maledetti cui spinse rea voglia' are things that will astound every poor mortal. The demons' choruses are original, popular, truly Italian; the first ('Tu sei bella') is a most graceful waltz, full of seductive ideas that can be sung straightaway after a couple of hearings, the second ('Vittoria vittoria, s'applauda a Satana') is music of diabolical exaltation, music that makes you shudder and tremble; in short, they are divine things; in that opera there will be every type of music: dramatic, religious, military etc. Everything I have heard pleases me enormously . . .[22]

The comments about the inspiration for the introduction coming to Verdi 'amid the mountain crags' is generally assumed to mean in the Appennines on the return journey from Rome. So far as I know, it is the only explicit evidence we have of such 'romantic' origins for Verdi's music; and presumably if his travelling companion, Piave, had been less taciturn it might never have occurred.

Muzio's report on the progress of the composition is continued on 22 December:

. . . This morning the signor maestro wrote the march for *Giovanna*. How beautiful it is! . . .[23]

on 29 December:

Yesterday I heard the grand duet from *Giovanna* between her and Carlo, when they fall in love; this is the grandest and most magnificent piece in the opera; I have heard the third-act finale where there is the most beautiful melody that has ever been heard. I don't know when it will be produced.[24]

on 6 January:

You should hear the music of *Giovanna*: you would gape with amazement. What marvels! You should hear how the duet between Giovanna and Carlo, when they fall in love, is conceived; the angels' terrible words 'Guai se terreno affetto accoglierai nel petto' make you tremble, and poor Giovanna, who alone hears them, breaks into a song that is all desperation for her lost virtue. Then in the cabaletta from time to time one hears the demons singing 'Vittoria, vittoria' and here Giovanna's song becomes continually louder and more agitated; then at the great final cadenza there burst out the infernal choirs, the *banda* and orchestra singing 'Vittoria, vittoria plaudiam' etc.: the whole chorus is the equal of the sublime one in Meyerbeer's *Robert le Diable*. There are so many beautiful things that one would need a whole day to describe them. Carlo's romanza; the coronation Te Deum; then when Tebaldo accuses his daughter, etc.; they are all gems . . .[25]

The next week Muzio could report that 'the signor maestro has begun the orchestration of *Giovanna*, the mighty opera that will dumbfound all the Milanese'.[26]

So far in the history of Verdi's early career, La Scala has been the principal scene of activity, and its impresario Bartolomeo Merelli has played an extraordinarily honourable role. He had been quick to perceive Verdi's gifts, steadfast in his faith in them, wise in his encouragement and advice. It is saddening to see that the Carnival season 1844–5 marks the breakdown of this amiable and fruitful relationship, both with Merelli and with La Scala, which after *Giovanna d'Arco* in February 1845 had to wait thirty-six years before it could boast another Verdi *première*.

The trouble apparently began over the rehearsals of *I Lombardi*, which was to be revived as the first opera of the season. Merelli had cast the opera badly and provided an inadequate orchestra, with the result that Verdi was obliged to expend energies and emotion here that could have been better spared for the composition of *Giovanna*. Muzio describes the scene vividly:

I go to the rehearsals with the signor maestro and it makes me sorry to see him tiring himself out; he shouts as if in desperation, he stamps his feet so much that he seems to be playing an organ with pedals; he sweats so much that drops fall on the score ... At his glance, at a sign from him, the singers, chorus and orchestra seem to be touched by an electric spark.[27]

But despite Verdi's galvanizing presence, the cast of *I Lombardi*, which was also to be that of *Giovanna* a month later, must have been a dismal crew:

Frezzolini is not singing with her old force and energy; she is mortified at being less applauded than she wished, and then she weeps because her voice is not what it was in former years. Poggi is not liked. Yesterday in his cavatina he fluffed his high notes and the audience began to hiss and grow restless. Colini's singing is too honeyed; and in the ensembles he can't be heard since he is a baritone and the part is written for a *basso profondo* ...[28]

The atmosphere cannot have been helped by the breakdown of the Poggi/Frezzolini marriage. Poggi had recently become the lover of the scandalous Countess Samoyloff, and was afraid that, quite apart from his fluffed notes, he would be roughly handled by La Scala audiences because of her vaunted pro-Austrian sympathies.[29] So heavy did the air become, and so wide-eyed were the accounts that Muzio was sending back to Busseto, that Verdi's compatriots seem genuinely to have believed that their local hero was in danger of being poisoned. Not that Verdi was himself subject to any such dark imaginings; he rebuffed Demaldè's expressions of concern in no uncertain terms:

But what the devil are you thinking of with this talk of poisons ... For heaven's sake, what century is this!! ... Believe me, they are not used any more, these days. Bellini died of consumption, of nothing else but consumption.

I am better now; the mountain air, and even more the rest, did me good; I fear I shall become unwell again when I resume work. Ah, these three years will pass quickly, I hope . . .[30]

But the kind of anxieties and the kind of personal tensions so far described were certainly not unique to Merelli's La Scala. In themselves they could not have sufficed to drive Verdi out of that particular theatre for half a lifetime, and to have destroyed a personal relationship to which, as he can hardly have failed to recognize, he did owe a genuine debt. The real problem was that Merelli's impulsiveness and generosity were inclined, in artistic matters, to degenerate into happy-to-lucky slovenliness, and slovenliness into the crassest disregard for artistic standards. In the mid-1840s this was exactly what was happening at La Scala.

We do not know how badly *Giovanna d'Arco* was produced. Neither Verdi's surviving letters nor the critics have anything to say on the matter. According to 'R', reporting for the Bologna *Cenni Storici intorno . . . agli Spettacoli Teatrali*, the performance of the singers was excellent: 'not only did they provide a feast of pure song, but, with uncommon zeal and devotion, they paid attention, too, to everything concerning the dramatic action'. Nevertheless by the start of the autumn season 1845 Verdi's relationship with Merelli had deteriorated gravely. The composer refused to lift a finger to help with a new production of *I Due Foscari*.[31] Later in the season, during a visit to Milan of the Tsar Nicholas I, Merelli confirmed all Verdi's worst opinions of him by putting on a performance of the same opera in which the third act preceded the second.[32]

A year later feelings were yet more embittered. Muzio reported to Barezzi:

Merelli was summoned by the directors of the theatre, who wanted to make him give *Attila*, and this shameless fellow said in public session that *Attila* is a rotten opera, not in the least beautiful; however, in spite of his words, the directors compelled him to put it on to begin the Carnival season. Now, in hope of gain, he is doing all he can to get the signor maestro to rehearse it; but he does well not to accept and to make them pay heavily for it; after the signor maestro learned what Merelli said to the directors, he sent for Lucca, the proprietor of the score, and asked him as a favour to make Merelli pay 3000 francs for *Attila*. In no theatre has so much ever been paid for any score; not for a simple hire, for just one season.[33]

On 27 December, having reported a tremendous triumph for Verdi and enthused over the excellence of the singing, Muzio continued his indictment of Merelli:

The *mise-en-scène* was wretched. The sun rose before the music indicated it. The sea, instead of being stormy and tempestuous, was calm and without a ripple. There were hermits without any huts; there were priests without an altar; in the banquet scene Attila gave a banquet without any lights or fires, and when the stormy tempest came the sky remained serene and limpid as on the most beautiful spring day. Everyone (aloud and in their hearts) cursed Merelli for having treated *Attila* so badly ...[34]

Two days later Verdi wrote to Ricordi a letter which could be said formally to sever his associations with Italy's premier opera house:

I approve the contract you have made for my new opera *Macbeth*, which is to be produced next Lent in Florence. I give my assent for you to make use of it, on the condition, however, that you should not permit the production of the said *Macbeth* at ... La Scala.

I have examples enough to persuade me that here they cannot or will not mount operas properly, especially mine. I cannot forget the deplorable way in which *I Lombardi, Ernani, Due Foscari* ... etc., were produced. I have another example before my eyes in *Attila!* ... I ask you yourself whether, despite the good cast, this opera could be worse staged ...

So, I repeat, I cannot and must not permit the performance of *Macbeth* at La Scala, at least not until things have changed for the better ...[35]

The opportunism and cynicism of Merelli's La Scala productions at this period perhaps contributed to the bouts of disillusion and the weary melancholias to which Verdi was now becoming increasingly prone. It does seem extraordinary that a vigorous and idealistic man, hardly over thirty, should already be contemplating retirement. Yet this was the situation. 'Ah, these three years will pass quickly, I hope,' he had written to 'Finola' (i.e. Demaldè) early in 1845. A few months later, in the course of another letter to the same old friend, he elaborated a little: 'I can't wait for these three years to pass. I have to write six operas and then farewell to everything.'[36]

Whatever the deficiencies may have been in the first performances of *Giovanna d'Arco* there is no doubt that it was one of Verdi's most clamorous popular successes. Muzio wrote:

The opera becomes ever more popular. On Saturday and Sunday they wanted the signor maestro and shouted 'Out you come, maestro!' But he wasn't in the theatre. On Wednesday, Thursday, Saturday and Sunday it is always *Giovanna*; and on those days the theatre is absolutely packed as at a première, and (apart from the subscribers) they have sold a thousand or more tickets for the stalls, and 500 or even 600 for the gallery.[37]

By April, bands were playing appropriate extracts at serenades at the viceroy's palace, while in the streets of the city barrel-organs were grinding the hit numbers to an appreciative populace.[38]

A few weeks earlier the Carnival/Lent season had concluded with a Verdi evening of the most animated kind, delightfully described by Muzio:

On Saturday evening the season ended with the last two acts of *Ernani* and the last two acts of *Giovanna d'Arco* . . . I have never in my life seen so many flowers and wreaths; it is said that la Samoyloff has spent 3,000 francs on flowers, and I assure you that she and her friends went on throwing flowers and garlands for a good half-hour . . . They threw many to la Elssler, but more to la Frezzolini, to whom there appeared, after her death scene in the finale of *Giovanna d'Arco*, about twenty girls, all dressed in white, with bouquets of various kinds in their hands; one of these I call a Monster Bouquet; it was so enormous it took two theatre attendants to carry it. The final terzetto of *Ernani* was repeated, and then came sonnets dedicated to la Gabussi and De Bassini. Poggi was received with hisses, and after his *romanza* various pieces of paper were seen flying through the air; everyone believed they were sonnets in his praise, and he even thanked the audience for its courtesy, with a smile on his lips and a number of bows; but there was surprise and a burst of laughter on seeing that instead of sonnets they were what the Milanese call *guzzinate*, i.e. songs the populace sings about a husband who beats his wife, a miser, a drunkard, a guzzler, etc., and I can tell you that all the Milanese are still laughing about it.[39]

Alzira

Verdi's contract with Vincenzo Flauto to compose an opera for production at the San Carlo theatre in Naples was one of a positive flurry of such negotiations in which he found himself involved after the Venetian *première* of *Ernani* in March 1843. In fact the letter in which he states the conditions under which he would be prepared to enter into a formal contractual arrangement with Flauto is the very first to be entered into the *Copialettere*:

It is true: the advantage of composing an opera on a libretto by the distinguished poet Sig. Cammarano, with those performers, and the reputation which the Teatro Massimo bestows on any deserving composer make me accept without the slightest hesitation the offer you make me, on the following conditions:
1st. The management will pay me 550 (five hundred and fifty) golden napoleons of twenty francs, payable in three equal parts: the first on my arrival in Naples; the second at the first orchestral rehearsal; and the third the day after the first performance.
2nd. The management must send Sig. Cammarano's libretto to me in Milan at the end of the current year 1844.
3rd. I shall not be obliged to go into production before the end of June.
4th. The singers to be selected by me from the roster of the company, always provided that Signora Tadolini, Fraschini and Coletti should be included on this roster . . .[40]

Despite Verdi's eagerness, it was some months before a contract satisfactory to both parties was drawn up. The Neapolitan management proved quibbling bargainers, and when Verdi heard that Giovanni Ricordi was going to be visiting Naples in the near future he asked him to act on his behalf, clarifying and finalizing the details of the contract. Even after Ricordi had done his best Verdi was not entirely satisfied, as the following letter to Ricordi shows:

Examining the Naples contract carefully I find that I simply cannot accept it as it is. You know that the management there invited me to compose one opera, for which I asked 550 golden napoleons: as you were going to Naples I entrusted you with the job of sorting things out, always provided that the sum should not be reduced to less than 12,000 Austrian *lire*. The amount I am now offered is still less than 12,000. But I don't want to spoil all your good work, and I agree to compose one opera for 1845. I can't do another, nor would it suit me to.

I am new to Naples, so you won't be surprised if I am a little bit fussy over some clauses, which will have to be changed.

Here Verdi reiterates in slightly different words the conditions laid down in his original letter of 21 March. The only material alteration is in clause 2, which now reads: 'Sig. Cammarano's verses must be delivered by the management to Maestro Verdi in Milan four months before the production.'

Verdi concluded:

If the contract is corrected in the ways indicated during this month of July I am ready to accept it. After the end of this month I shall consider myself free from any obligation whatever.[41]

Clearly the contract was emended to Verdi's satisfaction, and his engagement to compose for Naples stood. But in the immediate future there was the composition of *I Due Foscari* for Rome and of *Giovanna d'Arco* for Milan to be attended to. Nothing further is heard of *Alzira* until March 1845.

In due course Verdi and Cammarano were to develop a working relationship as interesting as any enjoyed by Verdi during his early years in the theatre. It began slowly, however, even inauspiciously. Verdi was inhibited by his preconceptions about Cammarano's talent; he was reluctant to instruct or bully a man of the theatre with more experience – that quality by which he set so much store – than himself. Unlike Piave, Cammarano was a 'riputato poeta', a man it behoved Verdi to approach with deference, a man in whom he believed he could have absolute confidence. As a result the composer's own idealism and his quest for originality – those factors that so often prompted the finest features of his early operas – were never really engaged in *Alzira*.

The history of the first stages of work on *Alzira* has been confused by the misdating of two letters in the *Copialettere*. The first, in which Verdi acknowledges the receipt of the synopsis of the libretto, cannot, for several reasons, be from May 1844. In the first place it refers to the terms of a contract which, as we have seen, was not drawn up until July 1844. Secondly it is clear that, as well as the synopsis, some of the verses had also been sent, and all the evidence suggests that the versification of the libretto was done in the spring of 1845. Finally, the problems over Tadolini were due, it transpires in subsequent letters, to her pregnancy: a child due to be born in April 1845 can hardly be held responsible for contractual problems in May 1844. March 1845 seems a likely date for this letter.

I have received the synopsis of *Alzira*. I am very happy with it from every point of view. I have read Voltaire's tragedy, which in the hands of a Cammarano will make an excellent melodrama. I am accused of being excessively fond of noise, and of treating the singers badly: don't take any notice of that; put plenty of passion into it, and you will see that I can write tolerably. I am surprised that Tadolini is not singing: I would remind you that according to the terms of my contract there is the following article 3: 'The company to be engaged to perform the opera to be composed by Signor Verdi will be chosen by him from those the management has under contract.' So, if Tadolini is under contract, Tadolini will have to sing, because I certainly shall not give up my rights for anything in the world.

For the time being I should like this to be kept quiet; indeed I should be most grateful if you would give me some enlightenment about the matter, and furthermore let me know something about Signora Bishop's style of singing.

To return to *Alzira*, I beg you to send me quickly some more verses. I don't need to tell you to keep things short. You know the theatre better than I do ...[42]

The next letter to Cammarano must also be from March 1845, not May, for it was written from Venice, where Verdi was spending a few weeks supervising a revival of *I Due Foscari*. Moreover, according to the postmark it arrived in Naples on (?) 2 April 1845.

I received your very dear letter a little late because it was forwarded to me here from Milan. These verses for the cavatina of *Alzira* are extraordinarily beautiful, especially in the recitative and *primo tempo*. Be so kind in your next letter as to indicate the characters and how many acts you are going to divide the drama into. It is unnecessary for me to urge you to be brief and to provide a fine role for Coletti.

The management tells me that until July they have no other soprano except Bishop. If Tadolini is not singing, it is useless to discuss the matter; but if Tadolini is on the roster of the company then without doubt I shall choose her ...

P.S. Excuse one observation: don't you think three cavatinas in succession too many? ... Please excuse me.[43]

But hardly was Verdi back in Milan hoping to get started on the composition of the opera than he became ill. On 10 April Muzio informed Barezzi that

The signor maestro has a rotten stomach-ache. I think we shall be going to Lake Como for a while, so that the signor maestro can recover and start composing; because so far he hasn't written a note of the opera for Naples.[44]

Medical bulletins fill Muzio's letters for some time:

... he cannot compose because they have bled him, but today he is better, and let's hope to goodness he will continue to get better ... For the opera at Naples there are only two months left; he will have a doctor's certificate made out and send it, and then go there a month later.[45]

... His health is much improved, but his stomach pains continue and now they are making him take pills. The doctors will make out the certificate to send to Naples, and so he will write the opera when he can ...[46]

Not only was Verdi ill: Cammarano was being culpably tardy in supplying the verses. According to the terms of the contract the libretto should have been delivered to Verdi in February, four months before the production. Yet even in April it was still far from complete.

I have been in bed for a couple of days with stomach trouble ... I am better now, but I still can't work.

I have received the finale, which is stupendous: I await (as you promised me) some clarifications, and at least the synopsis of the final act.

It will be absolutely essential to get the management to delay the production of the opera for at least a month, because even when I can work again I shall have to take things easy ...[47]

Verdi's letter must have crossed with one of Cammarano's, for while Verdi was urging Cammarano to get the opera postponed, Cammarano was apparently urging the same on Verdi. We learn of Cammarano's letter, and the reason for it, from Muzio:

The opera for Naples will not be produced until July or perhaps more likely August; and so Tadolini will sing in it, and not Bisoph [Anna Bishop] (unless however the former loses her voice in childbirth; and there is some fear of that, for she is over forty).

All the Neapolitans want the signor maestro to compose for Tadolini, and Cammarano, not knowing that the signor maestro was ill, wrote asking him to find some excuse to delay the production until the time I told you; now the signor maestro has made me reply that he has no need of excuses or pretexts, because he really is ill (then not now) and will send the certificates; and so he will get what he wants and have a good protagonist. The opera will be composed of only thirteen or fourteen pieces. The poetry is very beautiful ...[48]

On 25 April Muzio reported that he was

going round getting the signor maestro's certificates stamped and all the signatures authenticated; the only one still missing is that of the Governor, Count Spaur. If the Neapolitans accept and believe him he will write the opera later; if they don't believe him he won't do the opera at all, for the very good reason that he doesn't wish to kill himself for other people. La Tadolini has already had her baby and as soon as she has got over her confinement she will resume her place at the San Carlo theatre at Naples . . .[49]

The same day, Verdi himself wrote to Flauto:

I am sorry to have to tell you that I shall not be able to give the opera at the time arranged, because the doctors insist that I rest for at least a month and so it could not be produced before the end of July or the beginning of August. I shall be forwarding the certificates in a few days so as to put things in order.

I repeat I very much regret this inconvenience, and assure you that as soon as I am able to work I shall do so with all zeal.

Cammarano is perfectly in order, and I have received all the prologue and the whole of the first act, and am assured of the second act in a matter of days. I am very pleased with this libretto, which is very well written, and of an ever-growing interest . . .[50]

When, next day, the medical certificates were sent off to Naples with a covering letter,[51] Verdi must have imagined that things were settled. Everything had been done thoroughly and stylishly as Muzio explained:

They haven't replied yet from Naples; the certificates will already have reached their destination; so that they should arrive safely and quickly at Naples he made me frank them and then have a receipt for the letter made out by the Post Office Director, so that they can't say they haven't received them and so that they don't get lost, and thus reach the hands of Signor Flauto, who is obliged to give a receipt to the Post Office Director at Naples, and then the latter sends the receipt to the Director at Milan, and he gives it to the Signor Maestro.[52]

Despite the elaboration of these ceremonies it was some time before Flauto replied. In the meantime Verdi had received another instalment of Cammarano's verses.

I have received the second-act duet and aria. How beautiful they are! Your poetry succeeds excellently. I wonder how I shall do with my music? . . . I beg you to be indulgent towards my notes. I shall do what I can. My health is better, but I cannot work as hard as I used to.

I await with impatience the impresario's reply to the letter in which the medical certificates were enclosed. Farewell, my dear friend; wish me well, and believe me one of your great admirers.

P.S. Do the final scene at your earliest convenience, or wait until I get to Naples as you wish. But make it moving.[53]

On 14 May Flauto's reply was at last received. It was a missive of truly preposterous impertinence:

We are immensely sorry to learn from your letters of the 23rd and 26th of last month that you are indisposed. The illness from which you are suffering is however a trifling affair and needs no other remedies than those of tincture of wormwood and a prompt expedition to Naples. I assure you that the air here and the excitability of our Vesuvius will get all your functions working again, above all your appetite. Determine then to come at once, abandoning that troop of doctors who can only aggravate the indisposition from which you are suffering. You will owe your cure to the air of Naples and to the advice which I shall give you when you are here, for I too have been a doctor, and now have abandoned such impostures . . .[54]

The enraged composer replied at once:

I am immensely sorry to have to inform you that my illness is not a trifling matter, as you judge, and that 'tincture of wormwood' is useless in my case.

As for the excitability of Vesuvius, I assure you that that is not what is wanted to get my functions working again: I need peace and quiet.

I cannot leave at once for Naples, as you suggest, because, had I been able to do so, I should not have sent a medical certificate. I advise you of all that so that you can take the appropriate measures while I think seriously about getting myself fit again.[55]

The same day Verdi also wrote to Cammarano:

Today I have received a very curious letter from Sig. Flauto. He makes no reply to my request, supported by a medical certificate, to postpone the production for a month, but simply invites me to come to Naples immediately. Moreover this letter is written in a tone which I find offensive. I have replied in the same way, saying that for the time being I cannot come to Naples.

I should like the management to be reasonable about this, and to believe that I am accustomed to carry out my duties scrupulously and have never yet failed in them; that if a very serious stomach upset had not prevented and did not still prevent me from working, I should, to my advantage, have finished the opera by now, and be in Naples; and if it had not been for the pleasure of composing one of your librettos and of writing for that theatre, I should have followed the advice of the doctors who told me to rest for the whole summer. If you think it would be any use to speak to the directors I should be most grateful to you, for in a word, I cannot come now, nor can I be ready for production in June . . .[56]

Also on 14 May, Muzio wrote to Barezzi, transcribing for his benefit both Flauto's letter, which 'infuriated the signor maestro' and Verdi's reply. He also told Barezzi that Verdi was 'not doing anything yet.'[57] Apparently the composer could not or would not proceed with the composition of Alzira as long as he felt under improper pressure from Flauto. Even on 26 May Muzio still had not heard a note of the opera, though by then 'it seems that he is about to start composing'.[58]

One would be glad to leave this protracted debate about Verdi's state of health for matters of more obviously artistic concern. But there is an element of extravagance not to say absurdity, about all Verdi's dealings with Naples, from the time of *Alzira* to the time of the String Quartet, and it cannot be savoured if the story is left half told. Despite medical certificates, and despite Verdi's last letter and Cammarano's intercessions, Flauto was still refusing the requested postponement, suspecting the medical certificates to be fraudulent, emphasizing the artistic obligations he owed to the Neapolitan government. Verdi tried again:

The medical certificate was made out in good faith and my illnesses are neither imaginary nor pretended. For what reason? For almost two months I have been incapable of working, and even now I can compose only in short stretches. So it is impossible for the opera to be finished before the end of July.

I have never questioned the good faith of anyone in the world, nor do I wish to with you. So let us try to be reasonable and do me, as you put it, the 'small service' of postponing the opera for a month, or longer if you wish. – You refer to your obligations to the government; but if consideration is shown to sick prisoners, why is it not shown to me?

Believe me, if I only had my health to think about, I should rest for the whole of this year; but I shall make every effort; I shall write the opera; do you, I pray, grant me the time . . .[59]

Verdi was by now so exasperated that he decided to have recourse to a method that one cannot on the whole feel to be typical of him – the intercession of an influential acquaintance. Moving in the more rarefied strata of Milanese society for the past two or three years, Verdi had come to know the Duke of San Teodoro. He, in turn, was a friend of Marquess Imperiale di Francavilla, *Maggiordomo di settimana* to the King of the Two Sicilies, and superintendent of the theatres of Naples. San Teodoro seems to have advised Verdi to write directly to the Marquess Imperiale, and himself to have added a commendatory note, as Verdi explained to Cammarano:

We artists are never allowed to be ill. It is not enough always to have behaved honourably. The impresarios believe, or don't believe, whatever is most in their interest. I cannot be satisfied with the way in which Sig. Flauto has written to me. Even in the conversation he had with you, he continues to doubt my illness and my certificates.

I have made the acquaintance here of the Duke of San Teodoro who is adding a few lines to a letter which I am writing to Sig. Marchese Imperiale di [Francavilla] as you will see. In this letter I ask him to help me obtain from the directors the months' postponement requested. As soon as the postponement has been obtained I shall set out at once for Naples . . .[60]

The letter to the Marquess Imperiale, sent the same day, reads:

I beg you to excuse me if I write to Your Excellency without knowing you.

The kindness of the Duke of San Teodoro, whom I have the good fortune to know here, gives me the courage to do this.

You will know that I am under contract to the directors of the theatre in Naples to compose an opera, which should be now in production. A far from trifling illness has prevented me from working for almost two months: for that reason I sent on 26 April a medical certificate (which has been received by the management), and requested that the production be delayed for a month. The directors answered without either granting or denying the postponement.

Now I have recourse to Your Excellency, requesting that you should have the goodness to obtain for me, through the appropriate channels, the postponement I requested, and assuring you that, as soon as it is obtained, I shall set out immediately for Naples, to carry out my obligations scrupulously ...[61]

Flauto equivocated as long as he could. Muzio reported to Barezzi that

Signor Flauto has promised Cammarano and Fraschini that he will concede the requested postponement and give him Tadolini. But the signor maestro doesn't want words, he wants it in writing; and when Cammarano went to get that from the said Signor Flauto, he didn't want to give it. What a scoundrel!

... Some of the signor maestro's friends who are in Naples have written to tell him not to leave Milan, because once he is there Flauto is capable of playing him some dirty tricks.

Tadolini begins to sing on 20 July, and the signor maestro will go into production on the 27th of the month, exactly a month after the date originally fixed ...[62]

But eventually even Flauto had to capitulate. Verdi left Milan on 20 June. According to Muzio he had done

everything except the last finale; because he did not have the poetry.

He hadn't orchestrated anything, but hoped to do it all in six days ...[63]

His reception in Naples was described by the correspondent of the *Rivista di Roma*:

When the news spread through the city, not only that he had arrived, but that on the same evening he would certainly be present at the San Carlo theatre for the performance of *I Due Foscari*, the public, moved by legitimate curiosity, gathered in crowds at the theatre to see the famous composer in person. The galleries and the vast hall of San Carlo, packed with spectators, presented a brilliant scene. The performers, inspired by Verdi's presence as if by a charge of electricity, surpassed themselves, so that the opera, although heard an infinite number of times in the past two seasons, seemed, judging by the effect produced in the auditorium on that evening, quite new. All the singers were warmly applauded, but the enthusiastic audience wished to demonstrate its admiration for the composer of *I Due Foscari*. Being called for repeatedly and vociferously, he appeared twice on the stage amid the most cordial, loud and unanimous applause.[64]

The Neapolitan determination to make Verdi into a 'public figure' probably retarded work on the last stages of the composition. It was not until 10 July that he could write to Muzio and other friends informing them that the composition (except for the orchestration) was finished. And the orchestration, far from being tossed off in six days as he had hoped, was to occupy him for the best part of three weeks further. A letter from these weeks to his Roman friend Ferretti introduces a new theme: the tiresomeness of the clan of journalists: 'Here everything is going well. With the exception of the journalists, I enjoy wholehearted public favour; and there seems no need to fear fatal cabals or intrigues on the night as I had imagined ...'[65]

Neapolitan journalists rapidly became a real bugbear. He complained of them again in a letter to Piave: 'I don't have enemies in Naples (and to tell you the truth I am sorry for it). The journalists are not my enemies but the enemies of my purse, or at least they would like to be. Whatever may be the success of my music, don't frighten yourself by reading newspapers. They will say all the bad things imaginable. I'm certain of it ...'[66] And the day before, writing to Antonio Tosi, editor of the *Rivista di Roma*, he had explicitly charged them with corruption: 'I believe the newspapers will say every possible bad thing about it, all the more as la Bishop has now increased her monthly payments to those gentlemen, because I don't want her in my opera.'[67]

It was not only, perhaps not primarily, their ill will towards his music that Verdi found objectionable. It was also, as he put it to Flauto on another occasion, 'the endless trivial gossiping which had nothing to do with an opera. Why I had been shopping or why I went to a café, or why I was on Tadolini's balcony, or why I had brown shoes instead of black ones, and a thousand other footling little things certainly worthy neither of a serious public nor of a great city ...'[68]

Verdi had more to say about the pecularities of the Neapolitans in a letter to Andrea Maffei, the chief news of which was, however, that the opera was absolutely ready:

I have finished the opera and the instrumentation. I don't think I could express any opinion about this opera of mine, because I wrote it almost without noticing and with no trouble at all: so that even if it were to fail I shouldn't be particularly upset ... The Neapolitans are curious, some of them are so coarse, so impolite that one has to beat them before one is respected; others overwhelm you with a tempest of courtesies, enough to make you die of asphyxiation. For myself, to tell the truth, I cannot but be satisfied with things, because even the directors (and that is all that counts) are kind to me ...[69]

In fact, though, Verdi had not finished the opera. When the directors received his score, they judged the precipitate setting of Cammarano's text an inadequate evening's entertainment, and offered him an additional 200 ducats for the composition of an extended *sinfonia* to preface the work.[70] Verdi must have tossed this off pretty casually, adding an irreverent 'Amen' after the final cadences, but it proved to be one of the more successful movements of the opera. The start of rehearsals was delayed because of the indisposition of Coletti, and as late as 16 July Verdi could report to Piave that he was spending quite a lot of time sight-seeing. [71] But by the end of the month things seemed to be going really well: 'the singers enjoy singing it,' he told Maffei, 'and some parts of it must be tolerable'. [72] On 13 August Muzio sent Barezzi the news that 'he began the orchestral rehearsals on the 2nd ... *Alzira* won't be produced until the 12th, because the painters have not yet finished the scenery.'[73] Muzio's next letter describes what was to prove to be the zenith of *Alzira*'s career: 'At the dress rehearsal there was so much enthusiasm that the professors of the orchestra all got together to accompany him home with applause and cheers.'[74]

There survive no fewer than four of Verdi's notes to friends informing them of the success of the first night: to Toccagni, to Clarina Maffei, to Piave and to Giuseppina Appiani. That to Piave is the most interesting:

My *premières* are not performances but battles: one needs to fight factions, prejudices, and the devil knows what else besides. *Alzira* pleased as much as *Ernani* in Venice on the first evening. With that I have said everything. I hope that subsequently it will please more and have a place in the repertory for who knows how long. It will also (if I am not mistaken) go on tour as usual, and promptly too because it seems to me more completely effective than the *Foscari* ...[75]

But Verdi was too optimistic. It rapidly became clear that *Alzira* was not going to be a lasting success. Verdi himself, a day or two after the *première*, had to admit to Giovannina Lucca that '*Alzira* was a modest success on the first night and less on the second.'[76] Writing in the *Omnibus* Vincenzo Torelli recorded the waning enthusiasm with which the opera's brief run was greeted.[77]

Verdi soon came to view *Alzira* with a distaste surpassing that of the most censorious Neapolitan journalist. When Ferretti sent him a report on the Roman performance in the autumn, he replied:

I am very grateful to you for your news of that unfortunate *Alzira*, and even more for the suggestions you are kind enough to make. Even at Naples before it was produced I saw these defects, and you cannot imagine the trouble I took over them! The trouble is in the opera's guts and tinkering about with it would only make it worse ... I had hoped that the *sinfonia* and the last finale would compensate in large measure for the defects of the rest of the opera, and I see that in Rome they let me down ...; but they shouldn't have done! ...[78]

His final judgement on the opera is well known: '*Alzira?* Quella è proprio brutta.'[79]

Attila

There can be no doubt that, when Verdi first appeared in Venice in December 1843, both he and his music made an immediate impression on the Fenice authorities. Very soon the president of the theatre, Count Mocenigo, seems to have raised with Verdi the question of how soon he could come back to compose another opera for Venice. At the time the rehearsals for *I Lombardi* were going 'not badly'[80] and Verdi seems to have been not displeased with the idea. On 24 December he wrote to Mocenigo:

In reply to your verbal enquiry as to whether I could compose for La Fenice in the Carnival season 1844–5, I can now say that, as my engagement with La Scala will terminate in January, I could very well compose an opera for this theatre to be performed either on the last Saturday of February or the first of March 1845.

I beg you for a prompt reply, of whatever sort, since I must reply to offers which have been made me by other theatres ...[81]

In the event plans for a second opera for La Fenice were put off by a year, and arrangements were eventually made through the impresario Alessandro Lanari. In May 1845 Verdi told Piave that he had 'contracted with Lanari to write for Venice in the Carnival season '45–'46 always provided that Lanari has the theatre: if not I shall write under the same terms for Florence'.[82] An announcement in the Milanese theatrical journals in August confirmed that the destination of the new opera was to be Florence. In November, however, it transpired that Lanari had somehow persuaded Verdi to write not one but two operas. While the Florence contract still stood and was to result in *Macbeth*, another contract with La Fenice for Carnival 1845–6 was officially announced in *Il Pirata*.[83]

A few months later Lanari, who had made the contract, decided to sell his rights in it to Francesco Lucca, the publisher. Muzio wrote to Barezzi: 'The publisher Lucca has at last acquired the ownership of one of the signor maestro's operas, and it will be the one he is writing for Venice next Carnival season. He has acquired it from Lanari for thirteen thousand Austrian *lire* ...'[84]

Two overcrowded years

The history of *Attila* really begins in February 1845, immediately after the production of *Giovanna d'Arco*. Verdi was proposing to go to Venice for a few weeks in March to supervise a revival of *I Due Foscari*, and naturally enough proposed to take the opportunity to discuss with Piave the plans for their next opera:

It is time we spoke of the opera for the next Carnival season. I need a subject with four strong and beautiful characters, a fair share for everyone. Primadonna Signora Loewe, Guasco, Costantini, Marini. They all have to be treated well with equal parts. Prepare the subject and send it me at once, or else have it ready for me when I arrive in Venice.[85]

During this visit to Venice Verdi persuaded Piave that they should do *Attila*. As the poet did not know the work Verdi apparently undertook to send him a synopsis and a copy of the original on his return to Milan. An undated letter cited by Abbiati clearly belongs at this point in the story.

I am back in Milan. The journey was good, my house is good, my bed is good, and I hope I shall find supper good too.

I have seen Maffei and Solera and others, but Toccagni is ill in Brescia. I very nearly feel like coming back. Maffei will do the sketch of *Attila* for me, and I will send you the German play, and the ballet, by Viganò, I believe.[86]

Maffei went to work with commendable expedition. On 12 April Verdi was able to forward it to Piave, providing in his accompanying letter a detailed commentary:

Here is the sketch of Werner's tragedy. There are some magnificent and very effective things in it. Do read Madame de Staël's *Allemagna*.

In my opinion there should be a prologue and three acts. The curtain must go up to reveal Aquileia in flames, with a chorus of people, and a chorus of Huns. The people pray, the Huns threaten, etc. Then the *sortita* of Ildegonda, then of Attila etc., and the prologue ends.

The first act should open in Rome, and instead of the banquet being on stage, let it be off stage, while on stage the pensive Azzio meditates on the events, etc, etc. The first act should end when Ildegonda reveals to Attila that the cup is poisoned, so that Attila imagines Ildegonda has revealed this out of love for him, whereas in fact it is only to save for herself the pleasure of avenging the death of her father and brothers etc.

In the third act the whole of the scene with Leo on the Aventine hills and the battle below should be magnificent: perhaps they won't permit it, but we shall have to be careful to disguise it in such a way that they will permit it without the character of the scene being altered.

I don't like the Act IV finale, but with a little thought something good could be found. Do the best you can do and I shall do the same.

Meanwhile there are three stupendous characters – Attila, who defies the mutability of fortune – Ildegonda, at once a lovely and a proud character, who broods over the vengeance for her father, her brothers and her lover. Azio is likewise a fine character and I do like it in the duet with Attila when he proposes to portion out the world etc., etc. . . .

I think a good piece can be made of this, and if you really study it seriously you will produce your best libretto ... I will send you Werner's original in a few days, and you must get it translated, because it has some passages of very powerful poetry. In short, make use of everything, but make a fine job of it. Above all, read Madame de Staël's *Allemagna*, which you will find very illuminating ...

I recommend you to study this subject hard, and to keep everything clearly in mind; the period, the characters etc. etc. Then do the synopsis, but in detail, scene by scene with all the characters; in short, do it in such a way that there only remains the versification; in that way you will give yourself less trouble. Read Werner's choruses especially, they are stupendous.[87]

Soon, however, for reasons that are no longer clear, there was a change of plan. On 24 June *Il Pirata* announced: 'Fr. M. Piave will write for Maestro Verdi the librettos for the Spring and Carnival seasons 1846 instead of Signor Solera. In exchange he is ceding to Solera the libretto that is to be set by the same maestro for the next Carnival season in Venice.'[88]

As a matter of fact, Piave's next two Verdi operas, *Macbeth* and *Il Corsaro*, were delayed much longer than could have been foreseen at this stage. What concerns us here, though, is the fact that *Attila* was now in the hands of the man who by virtue of his strident muse should have been able to make the most of it.

Whether or not Solera, like Piave, was enjoined to 'study' the subject we do not know. But there was a delay of some weeks before, in mid-August, during Verdi's Naples sojourn, the poet suddenly burst forth in verse. Two letters from Muzio to Barezzi describe the situation at this time.

13 August 1845

... The signor maestro has written to Solera that he is coming to Milan expressly to collect the libretto of *Attila*, out of which he wants to make his most beautiful opera: but that lazy hound of a poet hasn't done a thing. I have told Cavaliere Maffei and Toccagni and they will make him do some work; and he has promised that he will keep at it day and night and finish it before the signor maestro arrives. This morning at eleven o'clock he was still in bed, so it seems that he is not working ...[89]

18 August 1845

... Solera has almost finished the libretto and by Thursday morning he will have prepared a fair copy; he is very pleased and has told me that it is beautiful, and that those who have heard it like it very much indeed. And that's good news.[90]

Verdi too was impressed. In a letter to the French publisher Escudier he was already dreaming of a glorious future for the opera, although he had as yet composed nothing of it:

... In a few days I shall begin *Attila* for Venice; it is a stupendous subject. The poetry is by Solera, and I am pleased with it ... How fine *Attila* would be in the Grand Opéra in Paris! One would only need to make a few additions, and all the rest would go well. On other occasions you have written to me about translating either *I Lombardi* or *Ernani* this year; tell me now if it would not be possible to do *Attila* in about two years ...[91]

During September and the early part of October Verdi was in Busseto, where he hoped to begin composition in earnest. On 12 September he was able to report to Maffei that he had begun the opera on the previous day; but in the torpid rural surroundings he seems to have been unable to recapture the zest that Solera's words had aroused at a first reading in Milan: 'from now on I shall sleep only twenty-four hours a day instead of twenty-five' was his own estimate of the opera's leisurely progress.[92]

Throughout the autumn the composition proceeded erratically, desultorily – proceeded in fact in a manner that matched exactly the extraordinarily volatile moods to which Verdi was prone at the time. On 5 November, for example, he wrote two letters to friends in Rome who had sent him news of the *Alzira* performances there. One, to Masi, reads:

Thanks for the news of *Alzira*, but more for remembering your friend, condemned continually to scribble notes. God save the ears of every good Christian from having to listen to them! Accursed notes! How am I, physically and spiritually? Physically I am well, but my mind is black, always black, and will be so until I have finished with this career that I abhor. And afterwards? It's useless to delude oneself. It will always be black. Happiness does not exist for me.[93]

The other, to Ferretti, reads:

I am most grateful to you for the news you give me of the unfortunate *Alzira*, and especially for the suggestions you are kind enough to make ...

I am very busy with *Attila!* Oh, what a fine subject! and the critics may say what they like, but I say: Oh what a beautiful libretto for music![94]

It would be naive to attribute these vacillations between morosity and elation to the way work on *Attila* was progressing. But we may conjecture that his considered reflections on the new opera were at least a contributory factor. Though Verdi had rejoiced in the flair of Solera's libretto, certain passages left him dissatisfied, and the final act was not yet completed. Worse still, Solera had gone to Spain, and was inaccessible or deaf to Verdi's repeated pleas for completion and emendation. The prospect of seeing an opera of which he entertained the highest hopes founder because of idleness and lack of interest on the librettist's part must surely have contributed to

Verdi's extreme nervous irritability at this time. On 1 November he had made one last attempt to get Solera to co-operate. The baritone Antonio Superchi was at the time engaged to sing in Barcelona – in the same company as Solera's wife – and unwittingly had sent Verdi some news calculated to provoke the maestro's most wrathful irony. In replying Verdi tried to use Superchi as an intermediary:

I hear with pleasure that Solera has written a hymn. What do you say? Has he sent me a copy of it? Just think! he doesn't even send me what he ought to send me for *Attila*, so you can imagine whether he would wish to send me one of his hymns!* Indeed (as I know you see him often), I would beg you to goad him on a little to finish once and for all this little matter of *Attila*. I shall be most grateful if you would employ all your eloquence (since mine is of no avail) and do so with all speed . . .[95]

But neither was Superchi's eloquence of any avail. By the end of the month Verdi still had nothing more tangible than an invitation to make use of the talents of some other librettist. So he turned once more to Piave, who readily assumed the humble task of completing Solera's work. A long and informative letter of about the end of November is the first document describing the resumption of work.

The last thing I want is to go into production as the second opera. I know that Lanari has arranged it this way, but I am not of his opinion, because I still have a lot to write, and because it is a good thing neither for me nor for the management to give two operas in succession by the same composer . . .

I know that the Kinschi band is an excellent band as I heard it last year; but I am tired of these on-stage bands. Besides the subject does not permit it; there is no place for it: unless we had a march for the arrival of Attila which would slow down the action to no purpose.

And then these bands no longer have the prestige of novelty, they are always nonsensical, and make such a din; besides I have written my marches: one warlike one in *Nabucco*, and another solemn and slow in *Giovanna* which I shall not be able to improve upon. And what is that about not being able to write a grand opera without the din of the band? . . . Are *Guglielmo Tell*, and *Roberto il Diavolo* not grand? . . . And they don't have bands! By now the band is a piece of provincialism not to be used any more in the big cities . . .

Then a finale *alla Foscari*! Accursed *alla* . . . I should prefer to say *alla* nothing at all; like the trio in Ernani which is like *nothing* else. Look at it carefully and try to arrange everything without incongruities: I want a fine part for Odabella and for Guasco: but not a duet because they have already had one! . . .

See that I find everything ready when I arrive. Instead of the evening of the fourth [December] be in Padua on the evening of the fifth . . .

The room will be booked already; tell Lanari that the pianoforte should be

---

* It is possible that Verdi was doing Solera an injustice. The hymn may have been the proposed finale of *Attila*. Cf. Solera's letter of 12 January 1846, below.

a good one with English stringing because I cannot get on with those which are most often used; tell him to book it and to have it tuned but not delivered, because as soon as we arrive we shall go and try it out together.

Verdi then asks Piave to arrange French tuition for him, and he concludes:

I am in bed with a heavy cold! I haven't slept for two nights: I have decided to stay put until I am better though I ought to be on my way, that is why I have delayed my departure which had been fixed for Monday. Don't forget anything . . . have a good room prepared, a good fire, and a good meal.[96]

There is a certain ominousness in this casual remark about his health. Although temporarily Verdi recovered, the dank atmosphere of hiemal Venice was hardly calculated to invigorate the convalescent. The production of *Attila* was to be delayed for the best part of two months while he struggled with rheumatism and gastric fevers that made it impossible for him to concentrate on the final stages of composition.

For the time being, though, things were going well. Verdi presumably did arrive in Venice on about 6 December, and presumably did find Piave's libretto ready. On 22 December he sent Giuseppina Appiani an encouraging progress report:

I am extremely busy finishing *Attila*, because I should like to put it on about 28th January; I have also had to write a cavatina for la Loewe, which is her own property and which she will use for her entry in *Giovanna d'Arco*. I have not taken, nor am I taking, the rehearsals for this opera, which I yet love very much, but I should not have been able to stand up to the work and it would have been so many hours lost to *Attila*. I am very pleased with the latter and unless the devil brings us bad luck it should turn out well . . .[97]

Indeed by Christmas Day 'nothing was left to do but the recitatives and the orchestration'. We have this from a letter addressed, rather unexpectedly, to Solera. Despite his intolerable conduct, Solera had not yet been irrevocably abandoned. Verdi's conviction that he was potentially 'the first librettist of the age'[98] was already formed, and he still hoped for his advice, perhaps even for a few Soleran touches in the scenes that Piave had completed.

I waited until the middle of the month to see if I received from you the alterations to the fourth act, which I asked for in my last letter from Milan. Seeing that you never sent them I got Piave to do them, as you authorized me in your last letter. I have copied them out for you so that you can make any observations you think fit and send them to me as quickly as possible, because we must go into production about 20 January . . .

Verdi then lists the modifications, from Foresto's 'Che non avrebbe il misero' through to the end of the opera. He continues:

It seems to me that it would do like this, and that it could be effective; there may be some lines you don't like, but you can change them and make them beautiful like all the others in this libretto. I warn you though that I have already written all the music, especially in the important parts, because I couldn't wait for your reply: so be sure that any modifications you want to send me are done immediately, since, I repeat, we are in production about the 20th, so I should have to have your letter about 12 January.[99]

But Verdi wrote in vain. Solera had not received his letter soon enough to react positively to it, even had he wished. He replied simply to record his sorrow and indignation at the ineptness of Piave's endeavours:

Only today, 12 January, have I received a letter from you dated 25 December; how can my answer arrive in time?

My Verdi, your letter was a thunderbolt for me; I cannot deny my indescribable sorrow at seeing a work on which I had dared to compliment myself end in parody. How was it that the solemnity of a hymn could not succeed in inspiring you, when it offered the possibility of providing your imagination with something new? In the conclusion that you send me I find only a parody: Attila pursuing Odabella – Odabella fleeing from a bridal bed in which she had placed all her hopes of revenge, etc., these seem to me things which ruin everything which I thought I had instilled in my characters.

Fiat voluntas tua: the cup which you make me drink is too grievous; only you could have made me understand so well that libretto-writing is no more a profession for me.

I very much hope that you will send me your news quickly, and about the opera as soon as it is staged. Meanwhile I beg you at least to change some of the lines that are not mine, so that the pill tastes less bitter to me. I send you your own copy, so that you can see the corrections better.[100]

Altogether January and February 1846 were dismal months for the composer. Tantalizingly close to completion as it was, *Attila* was probably not finished before the beginning of March. The greater part of January – 'twenty days which seemed like twenty centuries'[101] – was spent in bed with gastric fever, and even when he did get up he was in no state to drive himself to complete the opera. A business letter to Lucca, written on 25 January, concludes: 'My health is improving, but very slowly, and I have no strength to work: besides the doctor said to me yesterday: what a good thing if you could take a rest for at least six months!'[102]

It seems to have been well into February before he again found the energy to occupy himself with matters operatic. On 11 February he wrote a letter to Luccardi in Rome, particularly interesting as an example of that concern for historicism in theatrical production which in the next years was to develop into something of a passion.

... I need a great favour! I know that in the Vatican either in the tapestries or in Raphael's frescoes there should be the meeting of Attila with St Leo. I need a pattern for Attila: so will you make me a quick sketch and then explain in words and numbers the colours of the costume: I need the head-dress in particular. If you do me this favour I will give you my holy benediction ...[103]

By 15 February, when he wrote to Pillet, manager of the Paris Opéra, refusing a contract, he was once more in bed with a 'touch of fever'.[104] And towards the end of the month, whether he is writing to business acquaintances like Giovannina Lucca or to dear friends like the Maffeis, the idea that *Attila* might not get finished at all becomes a recurring theme in the correspondence: the enthusiasm of December has quite withered away, its place taken by a sickly lassitude. To Clarina Maffei he writes:

I can tell you nothing of the pleasures of Venice because I have been perpetually condemned to stay at home, for nearly two months now, and I am bored to death, also because I can't work much. I know that Elssler is working her usual miracles, though rather less than last year in Milan ...

Tell Andrea that *Attila*, even if I am able to finish it, won't be staged until the last three or four evenings [of the season].[105]

Andrea Maffei was obviously planning to come to Venice for the production.

Attila was finished, probably in the early days of March. But by this stage Verdi can have felt little of elation or satisfaction. In later years he looked back on these winter months in Venice as among the wretchedest of his career: he recalls how he had to 'force himself to finish *Attila* in a deplorable state of health',[106] and again 'how, having given his word to finish *Attila*, he did finish it, albeit virtually on his death-bed'.[107]

It was 17 March when *Attila* was at last heard. To Gina Somaglia Verdi reported on the *première* thus:

Attila enjoyed a very good success. There were calls after every piece, but it was the whole of the first act that was applauded with the greatest enthusiasm. I had high hopes of the second- and third-act finales, but, either I was mistaken or the public did not understand, because they were less warmly applauded.

Perhaps this evening it will be better performed by the singers too, because although they performed it with the greatest care, the effect did not match their good intentions. My friends try to tell me that this is the best of my operas, the public disputes it: I believe it is inferior to none of my other operas: Time will decide.[108]

The *Gazzetta Privilegiata di Venezia* for 17 March confirms Verdi's report with a profusion of the kind of circumstantial detail in which nineteenth-century critics revelled. Most of this we can spare, but the critics' explanation of the coolness of the reception of the second and third acts is illuminating:

Justice demands however that we should state that not all the songs were savoured in their perfection; in the grand finale, for example, someone was in too great haste to enter, and so spoiled the ensemble and the beauty; Costantini had contracted a fever, and Guasco did not seem in good voice, for which reasons we may entertain greater hopes for the subsequent performances. In this respect the third act can hardly be said to have been heard at all, and indeed ended in the most embarrassing silence ...[109]

It is difficult to know really how enthusiastically *Attila* was received. The voice of the sceptical critic of *Il Gondoliere*,[110] who speaks of 'instead of true inspiration only a noble artistic attempt at inspiration', might not in itself be considered to carry much weight. It is striking however, that although *Attila* had been squeezed in at the end of the season, and with a maximum run of six performances hardly had time to succeed artistically or commercially, it was never revived in Venice.

But whether *Attila* was a moderate success or a furore, Verdi was in no state to savour it. He returned to Milan on 22 March still chronically ill, and was ordered by his doctors to take a six months' rest-cure. A mere two years after the *première* of *Ernani* Verdi had learnt that he had neither the facility nor the stamina to sustain a career in the Donizetti mould. For two years he had driven himself relentlessly to produce operas more rapidly in cities more distant. His talent had coarsened; success had become a shade more elusive; his health was in ruins. His breakdown in the spring of 1846 was in fact a blessing in disguise. It provided him with the repose to recover that idealism which, in the grim and remorseless routine of the past two years, he had been in danger of losing.

Verdi the idealist – the Florence *Macbeth*

We have already seen that, like so many of Verdi's projects in the 1840s, *Macbeth* originated in the spring of 1844. On 22 May, in one of the letters to Piave about the libretto of *I Due Foscari*, he observes:

By all means agree to write for Pacini, but try not to do *Lorenzino* because we shall do that together another time . . . I have contracted with Lanari to write for Venice in the Carnival season '45–'46, always provided that Lanari has the theatre: if not I shall write under the same terms for Florence . . .[1]

In the event Verdi was to compose operas for both Florence and Venice, that for Florence being delayed by a year, until the Carnival/ Lent season 1847. And it is only in May 1846 that the surviving documents take up the story again. On 17 May, Verdi wrote to Lanari from Milan:

Now that we are in complete agreement about the fantastic character of the opera which I am to write for Florence, it will be necessary for you to let me know the cast as quickly as you can: for I have in mind two subjects, both of them fantastic and very beautiful, and I shall choose that which is best suited to the cast . . . As far as production in Lent is concerned, there are really various things that would make that difficult for me, but we will try to get round them, especially with a helping hand from you . . .[2]

We are now, of course, in the middle of the period of rest that followed the production of *Attila*, that 'strange interlude in these "years in the galleys"' when 'for precisely six months, obeying his doctor's orders as scrupulously as he was accustomed to fulfil the terms of his business engagements, Verdi did absolutely nothing'.[3] One might well choose to see the hand of providence in the fact that at precisely the same time, one of Verdi's closest friends, Andrea Maffei, was no less in need of spiritual refreshment. His marriage with the Countess Clarina Maffei finally broke down in June 1846, and the two friends were together even more than usual in the weeks that followed. Verdi, together with Giulio Carcano, was one of the witnesses to the legal act of separation, and once this had been completed he and Maffei went off together to take the waters at Recoaro, leaving Milan on 3 July.[4] During a period when, for the first time for years, Verdi had leisure to think and to dream – not just, as he sometimes cynically professed, about making his fortune and retiring, but also about his ambitions as an artist, about what he had achieved, and what he still aspired to achieve – he thus found himself in company with one of the best-read men of the day, a translator of Shakespeare, Milton and Byron, of Goethe, Heine and Grillparzer, and especially of Schiller. Despite the emphasis which both Muzio and Verdi lay upon the fact that the 'signor maestro' was leading a life of complete indolence – as Verdi put it in a letter to 'Finola', 'sleeping, eating, excursions into the country, carriage-rides, theatres, etc. etc.'[5] – this summer of 1846 proves to be one of the turning-points of Verdi's career, one of his most decisive cultural awakenings. Stimulated by Maffei, and very likely by Carcano too, who, according to Abbiati, was working on his *Macbeth* translation at precisely this time, Verdi was discovering themes which were really worthy of him and which, by virtue of the sublimity of their ideas and the majesty of their language, acted as a welcome antidote to his youthful zest for Byron and his abiding enthusiasm for the French Romantics. Certainly it is not difficult to see the fruit of companionship with Maffei in the news which Muzio conveyed to Barezzi on 13 August:

The signor maestro is thinking about the libretto for Florence; there are three subjects: *L'Avola* [Grillparzer's *Die Ahnfrau*], *I Masnadieri* [Schiller's *Die Räuber*] and *Macbeth*. If he can have Fraschini he will do the *Avola*, but if instead of Fraschini they give him Moriani, as seems likely, then he will do *Macbeth*, where he doesn't need a very powerful tenor . . .[6]

A few days later Verdi wrote to Lanari:

Time is pressing and something must be decided upon: the months left are barely sufficient for creating a work of any importance. Well then, if you have fixed and confirmed the contract with Fraschini, nothing could be better . . . in the event of Fraschini not being engaged, I do not want to take risks with other tenors: . . . so I propose to work a subject in which we could do without the tenor. In that case it would be absolutely necessary to have the two artists I hereby name: *Signora Loewe and Varesi.*

Varesi is the only artist in Italy at the present time who, by virtue of his style of singing, his sensibility and his actual appearance, could do the role I have in mind. All the other artists, even the best of them, could not do this part for me the way I want. I don't deny the merits of Ferri, who has a more handsome presence and a more beautiful voice, and, if you like, sings better too; but not even he could create the effect in this role that Varesi would. So try to arrange an exchange, ceding Ferri, and everything will then be fixed. The subject is neither political nor religious: it is fantastic. So make up your mind: either take Fraschini (and then Signora Barbieri would suit me better), or, if you cannot manage to get Fraschini, do your utmost to get Varesi. If you like, I will try to arrange the affair with Varesi myself, provided you give me the authorization. The rest of the company must be composed of good supporting singers, but I shall need a good chorus ...; but we can discuss this later. Reply at once, by return of post, and see that all the care I have taken and all the work I have put into these damned subjects aren't in vain.[7]

Verdi presumably received from Lanari the requested authorization, for a few days later he wrote to Varesi:

Do you want to come to Florence for the Lent season, then? If so, I will write *Macbeth* for you! ... Few words, and a very quick reply. Tell me when you would be in Florence, when you would be ready for production, and remember that you would be required not to sing in anything except the opera I write expressly for you. Let me know briefly your conditions and financial requirements, and I beg you to restrict them as much as you can, because as you know Lanari has got Ferri and certainly won't want to make great sacrifices. Reply by return of post and don't forget anything.

P.S. Keep things absolutely secret because, believe me, it is not going to be easy to arrange ...[8]

Varesi's reply must have been enthusiastic. But there was one difficulty, namely that he did not think he would be able to stay in Florence long enough to sing in more than three performances. Despite this drawback, Verdi remained optimistic:

I have received your very dear letter. As far as money is concerned, I shall do my best to see that, if we can arrange this affair, you are properly paid. Perhaps there will be a difficulty over the three performances, and I think it would really be essential to do four, etc. ... When you come to Milan let me know as soon as you arrive where I can find you, because by then I shall perhaps have had a definite answer from Lanari.

P.S. I beg you still to keep things secret and also let me know if there would be any way of staying on at Florence after 18 March. It is true that he has got other basses, but if we are launching the opera with you we ought to continue with you.[9]

Varesi's interest really decided the matter as far as Verdi was concerned. On 25 August, at the end of an acidulous letter to Piave about the *Corsaro* libretto, he had remarked: '... there is no news. I am well; I am not working because I want to get myself really fit. The company for Florence still isn't decided, so I am not thinking about that at the moment ...'[10]

But within days of hearing from Varesi, and despite the fact that Lanari had still not written, Verdi had the synopsis of *Macbeth* ready for dispatch to Piave.[11] A few weeks later we learn from Muzio that Verdi had not been above a bit of underhand manoeuvring to ensure he got the cast he wanted:

The signor maestro is writing *Macbeth* for Florence. The performers will be Signora Loewe and Varesi, not Ferri, because the signor maestro did not want him. Ferri doesn't know that Varesi has been engaged, nor that he won't be singing in the new operas. It will be kept secret until the Lent season, and then he will be told that Varesi is to sing in *Macbeth*. Varesi's contract is not to be announced in any newspapers so that Ferri doesn't get to know about it.[12]

Piave's role in *Macbeth* was again that of a mere versifier. Verdi himself, probably with the advice and assistance of Maffei and Carcano, had spent part of his recuperative summer preparing the synopsis – as he explained years later to Tito Ricordi:

It is ten years ago now that I had the idea of writing *Macbeth*: I made the synopsis myself; indeed I did more than the synopsis, I wrote a full prose version of the drama, showing the distribution of the acts, the scenes, the musical numbers etc. . . . then I gave it to Piave to versify . . .[13]

In the letter to Piave which Verdi enclosed with this sketch we sense his eager desire to make a new start, to escape from the suffocating routine of the preceding years, to create something different from and better than what he had achieved in the past:

Here is the sketch of *Macbeth*. This tragedy is one of mankind's grandest creations! . . . If we cannot make something great out of it, let us try to do something that is at least out of the ordinary. The sketch is clear, unconventional, without superfluities and short. I beg you to keep your verses short too: the shorter they are, the more effective they will be. It is only the first act that is a bit long, but it will be up to us to keep the pieces short. Do remember that there must not be a single superfluous word in the verses: everything must tell. You will need to adopt an elevated style of writing except for the choruses of witches: these must be trivial, but extravagant and original.

When you have completed the introduction please send me it: it consists of four short scenes and can be done in a few lines. Once this introduction is finished, I shall leave you all the time you like because I know the general character and colour as well as if the libretto were already completed. Oh, I urge you not to fail me with this *Macbeth*, I beg you on my knees, if only for my sake, and the sake of my health, which at the moment is very good, but which will become very bad again at once if you give me cause for disquiet . . . Brevity and sublimity . . .[14]

But, as Abbiati observes, Piave was neither brief nor sublime, neither extravagant nor original. No doubt he was sufficiently awed by the tone of Verdi's letter to do his best, and some of the remarks made during work on the opera suggest that he was dimly aware of its importance; but even if his potential as an artist had been greater, he had not had the benefit of such a six-month period of quiet reflection as Verdi had had. Piave never escaped from his galley years, and although, because of his amenability and because of the personal friendship between them, Verdi long continued to work with him, it was the collaboration on *Macbeth* that first betrayed the

[handwritten margin note: crappy words by Piave]

fact that a cultural gulf was opening up between them. We do not know exactly what the verses were like which Piave sent Verdi in mid-September 1846, but they clearly showed all the flabbiness of diction, all that deficiency in colour and character that Verdi most abhorred. Rarely was he more insulting than in the letter acknowledging the receipt of a second instalment of verses, those of Lady Macbeth's *aria di sortita*:

I have received the cavatina, which is an improvement on the Introduction. Nevertheless how long-winded you are!! For example, the letter which Lady reads is really just words arranged in lines: there is little energy in the rest of the recitative – and very little in the first quatrain of the *adagio* – the line 'vieni su questo core!' is so commonplace that it deprives the verse of all its energy: the cabaletta works well; so in this piece correct the letter; it can be shortened without omitting anything; you have taken too many words to say 'Ma tu abbastanza non sarai malvaggio' and too many words again at 'Chi a congiurarsi non si sente forte e vi si addentra infamia aspetti e morte.' The same things could be said in a more elevated style in half the words! Change the first quatrain of the *adagio* for me too, etc.

In the Introduction many things have to be done. To have any character the first verses of the witches must be more strange: I can't tell you how to achieve this, but I know that they are not good as they are: everything might perhaps be better if you had written in short lines. In short, you will have to experiment and find how best to write bizarre poetry, at least in the first verse. The last short verse could work well with just one quatrain. (ALWAYS REMEMBER TO USE FEW WORDS ... FEW WORDS ... VERY FEW, BUT THEY MUST MEAN SOMETHING.) Afterwards you can shorten the *tempo di mezzo* as much as possible and change the three salutations of the witches into hendecasyllabic verses. Then shorten the duet between Macbeth and Banquo to six lines apiece and cut all those rotten lines which I indicated in my last letter. (I REPEAT, FEW WORDS.) If I were to cut out all the words which say nothing and which have only been included for the sake of the rhyme or the metre I should have to cut out a good third: so you can see whether the style is as concise as it should be.

Before going any further please correct these two pieces for me, and do it so that I don't have to think it has been thrown off in a hurry to get finished, which is the impression I get so far ... So get to work on correcting and completing these pieces before going any further, so that I can start composing ... A CONCISE STYLE ... FEW WORDS ... Do you understand? ... On second thoughts it seems to me that to write the first chorus entirely in lines ending on accented syllables would give it a strange sound that would be characteristic. Take care too over the choice of words ...

Good-bye ...[15]

Presumably Verdi remained dissatisfied with Piave's efforts at improvement: presumably he felt that the poet did not share his own high seriousness, his sense of mission, in embarking on this first Shakespearian opera. For before the end of the month he decided that rude letters alone were not going to do the trick, and summoned Piave to Como to talk over the opera with him.[16]

The topics they discussed will surely have included the production, the style of the costumes, stage designs and so forth, for which, as librettist, Piave was strictly responsible. But before Piave really got to work on this, Verdi was himself in touch with Lanari, softening him up a little, and seeking to give him a proper sense of occasion:

Here is the sketch of *Macbeth*, so that you can see what it's about. You see that I shall need an excellent chorus: the chorus of women in particular has to be very good, because there are two choruses of witches of the greatest importance. Look to the stage machinery too. In fact the things in this opera which need particular care are: *Chorus and Stage Machinery*.

For the rest, I am convinced that you will stage everything with that lavishness for which you are so distinguished and that you will not be influenced by considerations of economy. Notice too that I shall also need the ballerinas to do a short elegant dance at the end of the third act. I repeat, don't worry about expense, because you will, I hope, gain your reward. Besides I shall bless you a thousand times a day, and you know my benedictions are worth almost as much as the Pope's . . .[17]

Ten days later, 25 October, he wrote to Piave, giving him the cue to get to work on production matters:

Get in touch with Lanari at once about the production of *Macbeth*. Write to him quickly and describe the ordinances [*ordinanze*, i.e. production notes], properties, designs, stage sets, costumes, 'supers' etc., etc. . . . Don't forget anything and do everything with devotion if you don't want me to fly into a rage. Lanari is disposed to do everything that is necessary. Think it out carefully, and write the ordinances precisely: nothing more and nothing less than is necessary . . .[18]

For the next month, as well as wrestling with the intractable problems of the libretto, the harassed Piave was engaged in a somewhat inadequate correspondence with Lanari about the production. At first, having nothing really to say, he attempted to fob off the impresario with echoes of Verdi's own enthusiasm.

Our friend Verdi writes to say that I should get in touch with you and send you the notes about the production of *Macbeth*. I will do this as soon as possible, but at the moment I can't, for I need to do some further study and I want to do everything exactly right so that there is no need for regret later. Dear Lanari, this *Macbeth* is going to be something really great; I am full of enthusiasm about it. The role for Signora Loewe in particular will be the most sublime role ever to have appeared on the operatic stage in Italy, and so will that of the baritone. I think that if this opera is a success, it will give our music new tendencies and open up new paths for composers present and future; and you will be the first to have given Italy such a work. You deserve it . . .[19]

Lanari replied:

It is my wish too that when you send me the notes about the production of *Macbeth* they should be precise. Nevertheless, please hurry up with them, because the more time we have, the better things can be done. I am very glad that so much is to be hoped for from this subject, and had already seen myself that it is very impressive and of an extraordinary nature.[20]

But as the days passed Lanari became more importunate: letters from Piave on 7 and 17 November still gave no real satisfaction, despite the 'precise and clear' production notes enclosed in the latter. At last, on 23 November, Lanari made it quite clear that Piave had really got to get down to some hard work:

Concerning the ordinances for *Macbeth* which you have forwarded to me, they are too brief, and it is essential that you should give the respective numbers of the groups of supers, how you wish to group them, whether they are pages etc. ... work on the basis of a stage the size of La Fenice. You say that the synopsis you had sent and the notes you now provide will be enough for Romani, but without the definitive libretto he cannot know at which points in the action people appear, what their movements are and how the action develops, and as everything else depends upon this, upon the machinery etc., ... it is essential to be clear about it, before timing it, if we are going to achieve an accurate performance ... I notify you too that the aerial spirits, which you say *must dance*, will have to be cut, as I have already told Verdi, since, during Lent, dances of all kinds are prohibited and cannot be included. So while there is time, you will have to think of some other idea at that point so as not to have to mutilate things later ... Verdi himself will be writing to tell you to send me a copy of the libretto, so don't keep me waiting: if you want an accurate *mise-en-scène*, you must make your ordinances fuller, as I said, and send me the costume designs if you can. You will see yourself that there is nothing irregular about sending a copy of the libretto to the impresario for whom the new opera is being written and who has got to arrange the staging ...[21]

Nor did Piave get much chance, as he 'studied' the subject and thought about problems of production, to rest on his laurels as a versifier. Right through to January of the following year Verdi was sending him letters in which words of approval or encouragement were conspicuously rare. Every instalment of Piave's verses seems to have prompted criticism of some kind; savage, ironic, didactic, dogmatic.

25 October 1846

... at the start of the second act, in the soliloquy, don't have Lady writing a letter to Macbeth about the murder of Banquo – I don't like having her writing a letter in an entrance-hall, and besides in a few words one could do just as well without a letter.

'Banco, e suo figlio vivono ... ma la natura non li creò immortali ... Oh Macbet ... Un nuovo delitto! ... Le imprese cominciate etc., etc. ...'[22]

29 October 1846

... You are already talking about the third act? And is the second act finished? Why don't you send it? ... You are going too fast and I foresee trouble! Enough! How can one possibly write an act of such sublimity as the second act of *Macbeth* in so short a time?

P.S. In Lady's first scene in the second act don't give her anything to say except one simple phrase referring to the murder of Banquo ... 'Oh Macbet è necessario un'altro delitto!'

P.S. Why the devil don't you know what to give the witches to say when Macbeth has fainted? Is it not in Shakespeare? ... Oh poor me! ...[23]

3 December 1846

The more one thinks about this *Macbeth* the more one finds that needs improving. There is an awkward spot at the start of the second act, and that is that Lady ponders and then decides upon the murder of Banquo, and hardly has she left the stage when the assassins come on to carry out Lady's orders. It is true that by changing the scene for the chorus of assassins one could suppose that a little time has elapsed, but in any case it is not very satisfactory and would be much better rearranged as follows: [here Verdi provides a prose version of Act II, scenes 1 and 2 up to and including Lady Macbeth's aria text].

I don't need to tell you that the whole scene between Macbeth and Lady should be in recitative and that the lines should be powerful and short, in the manner of Alfieri, especially towards the end of the recitative. When Lady is left alone two quatrains are wanted, but the old ones cannot stand. The first one particularly needs changing, and then instead of an *adagio* I shall write an *allegro* which will be even better.

The chorus of assassins follows, and here the action has to move on to prepare for the banquet scene. Lanari is moaning about you because you have sent him a synopsis which is quite unintelligible (I believe it) and I am moaning too because you don't send me this blessed third-act chorus. You have taken on too much work and now I am the one who has to put up with it.

Meanwhile do the enclosed scene for me, which won't take you very long, and send it to me as quickly as possible; send the rest quickly too ...

Take care that everything is properly linked together, and that there are none of the usual muddles. And hurry up if you don't want me to fly into a rage.[24]

10 December 1846

From henceforth we shall always admit that you, Signor Poet, are always right: yes, yes, *you are right, you are right, you are right*, always, always ...

However, I don't in the least like this chorus of witches, although I laughed heartily reading the heading of the scene ... 'Witches in ceremonial costume' ... Witches in ceremonial costume? ... Is that Shakespeare's intention? Have you really grasped what *Shakespeare* is wanting to do with these witches? ...[25]

By this time Piave had clearly broached the question of the dancing witches in the third act, and Lanari's urgent desire to have a copy of the libretto. Indeed – remembering Lanari's letter of 23 November – Verdi must already have heard directly about these things from the impresario. But in his present severe and uncompromising mood he preferred to turn them into another cause of vexation with Piave. And when Shakespeare was at stake Lenten observance was not going to inhibit him, nor pressure from impresarios hurry him:

Why are you making these difficulties about the aerial spirits not being able to dance? Just do them as I indicated. The poem and the music have to be like that, so that is how you must do them. Notice that while the spirits dance around the swooning Macbeth, the witches must sing two verses . . . As far as Lanari and Ricordi are concerned, leave me to worry about them. You cannot and must not send anything to anyone without my authority.

I wish you could make me understand the last act properly. I would like the scene to start with an imposing, pathetic chorus describing the wretched state of Scotland under Macbeth's rule. The chorus should be made up of Scotch refugees in England, whether ordinary people, or thanes, or both doesn't matter: do as you think best. In this chorus I should like a characteristic, sublime and pathetic picture of the wretchedness of Scotland (such as Shakespeare draws in a dialogue between Ross and Macduff). The scene must be in England but on the borders of Scotland. In short, I am telling you what I would like, but if you can think of a way of doing it better, do it. What is absolutely necessary for the drama is that there should be a description of one kind or another of Macbeth's tyranny and thus of Scotland's misery. Here is the synopsis . . .[26]

The synopsis that Verdi sends Piave – it is printed in full by Abbiati – is clearly a revised version of an earlier synopsis that had proved to be inadequate. Thus, at one point Verdi remarks 'The sleepwalking scene is quite all right in the synopsis which you have, though one small change will have to be made . . .' Throughout the synopsis Verdi adds brief remarks to guide Piave. Of the opening chorus: 'The poetry should be beautiful and pathetic, in any metre you like except decasyllabic'; of the sleepwalking scene: 'it would be excellent if you could write this whole scene in octosyllabic lines, because when she repeats in her sleep ideas already mentioned in the drama, I would do the same with the music'; of the death of Macbeth: 'Write two verses. Try to give them something of a pathetic character, but don't forget the character of Macbeth.' The letter ends: 'Get to work quickly and try to do better than you did in this chorus of witches. Send me the third act at once, and then try to get everything finished before the end of the year. Good-bye, good-bye.'[27]

A final set of instructions was sent off to Piave on 22 December:

Please hurry up with the last act; incidentally, when I was trying to compose the first chorus I couldn't think of anything sufficiently grand because the metre is too short. So be so kind as to write four verses in octosyllabic lines.

I would like to write a chorus as important as that in *Nabucco*, but I don't want to adopt the same type of movement and that is why I ask for octosyllabic lines. Don't let this moment be a lost opportunity, because it is the only pathetic one in all the opera. So do it with passion, and let there be (I would even say) more thoughts than words.

Remember in the tenor's aria too to make the *adagio* really pathetic. The cabaletta should be a *tutti* for everyone, but not in hendecasyllabic verses. Try to do it quickly. Good-bye. Do take particular care with the sleepwalking scene. Keep close to the last synopsis.

Another idea; after Macbeth's aria in the last act 'un cadavere armato almen cadrà ...' I should like Macbeth to take flight with the chorus and for the scene to change; a vast plain, and in the background one can see all the soldiers (who are supers) carrying branches of trees in front of them: they should be well back and move gradually to the sound of the *banda*. Macduff should say:

'Ecco il castello: Corraggio: la fortuna ti secondi: suonino le trombe foriere della battaglia!' All of them depart and leave the stage empty for a moment, while the noise of a battle is heard off stage. Then comes the scene between Macbeth and Macduff etc. In that way it would be better motivated and have a better theatrical effect.[28]

The composition of the opera only gradually gathered momentum. On 22 October Muzio reported that 'the signor maestro is composing very very slowly and is well'.[29] And a remark in a letter to Escudier a fortnight later suggests that even then he had still scarcely begun to compose: 'I shall be writing *Macbeth* for Florence, and you know what an important subject that is and how much study it requires.'[30] It was mid-December before Muzio began to provide progress reports for Barezzi:

Today I shall take almost a whole act of *Macbeth* to the copyist's. You can't imagine the originality and beauty of this music; when the signor maestro lets me hear it I can't write for two or three hours, it fills me with such enthusiasm. The Florentines are very lucky to be the first to enjoy it.[31]

19 December 1846

Macbeth gets better and better: what sublime music! I can tell you there are things in it to make your hair stand on end! It costs him enormous effort to write this music, but he succeeds marvellously. The first two acts are almost finished, and apart from the arias the rest is already at the copyist's and will be sent next week to the respective singers.

Varesi, when he left for Rome, took with him the scene of the Banquet and the Vision, and he created quite a stir in all Milan saying that that was Verdi's most beautiful and most dramatic music. At Piacenza he said even more. In all the towns he passed through – Parma, Bologna, Florence – he shouted like a madman to everyone that he had with him Verdi's most sublime music.[32]

[handwritten margin note: Verdi worried about Piave's nephew]

The pace was now obviously hotting up. On 12 January 1847, in the course of another letter to Escudier, Verdi observed that '*Macbeth* will be finished very, very soon.'[33] But this can only mean that Verdi felt that it was going well, for at the time, as Muzio's letters make clear, he was still in the middle of the third act. The opera was finished in fact at the end of January. Muzio's letter to Barezzi on the 28th announced.

On Sunday the signor maestro will have finished the whole opera and on Monday he will begin to orchestrate it. When that is finished he will go to Florence.

The music of *Macbeth* is immensely beautiful. There is not one poor number; all are beautiful. The *tempi di mezzo*, even the minor parts, have turned out really beautiful. I don't believe that anyone could compose music more beautiful than this *Macbeth*. If the effect of the *mise-en-scène* is good, it is certain that no modern opera provides so grand and solemn a spectacle.

Throughout the weeks of composition Verdi's harrying of the unfortunate Piave had continued unabated. But by mid-January he had become so exasperated with the ineptness of his librettist's offerings that he requested Maffei's assistance with the final stages of the work. At the same time, presumably because Verdi felt that he showed insufficient understanding of the subject, Piave appears to have been relieved of the responsibility for producing the opera. Indeed he never travelled to Florence to stage or even to see the *première*. His temporary disgrace was sealed in a withering letter:

Indeed you have done nothing wrong, except to have neglected these last two acts in a quite incredible manner. Patience! Sant'Andrea [Maffei] has come to your assistance and to mine; to mine even more, because, if I must speak frankly, I could not have set them to music, so you see what a difficult position I would have been in. Now everything has been put right, by rewriting almost everything. I shall send the libretto to Lanari, and there is now no need for your ordinances ...[34]

A cooler and probably juster estimate of Maffei's role in the preparation of the libretto comes in the letter, already cited, to Tito Ricordi of April 1857:

... As I found things to criticize in the versification, I asked Maffei, with the consent of Piave himself, to revise these lines, and completely rewrite the chorus of witches in Act III and the sleepwalking scene. Well, would you believe it? Although the libretto did not bear the poet's name, it was believed to be by Piave; and the chorus I mentioned and the sleepwalking scene were the most criticized and even ridiculed! Perhaps it would be possible to improve on these pieces, but, such as they are, they are wholly the work of Maffei, and the chorus in particular has a lot of character ...[35]

Apart from Piave's failure to rise to the occasion there were remarkably few upsets for Verdi during his work on the new opera. One matter did cause some distress though. On 2 November Muzio had informed Barezzi that

Signora Loewe is retiring from the stage. She appeared at Florence in *Ernani* and had a fiasco. She was pregnant and wanted an abortion, saying that this was the reason she had virtually lost her voice . . . The signor maestro is very sorry about it, because there is no soprano around at present who could create the same effect as Lady in *Macbeth* that Signora Loewe could. Signora Barbieri will sing instead.[36]

But Verdi took the disappointment in his stride: 'I don't think about it,' he had written to Piave a few days earlier; 'What will be will be! I am so used to these difficulties that they cease to surprise me. Forget about it and get writing.'[37]

Macbeth appears to establish a new routine in Verdi's habits of composition: a routine that may have been partly anticipated by the special circumstances of *Nabucco*, and that was to become absolutely typical of him in later years. The actual detailed work of composition was preceded by a long period of thought about and absorption in the selected theme – the summer months of 1846. This in turn was followed in the autumn by the fashioning of the libretto and the sketching of musical numbers. As far as one can see, the working out of the composition in full was completed in the period from mid or late November to the end of January. It was the comparative leisureliness of the earlier stages that distinguishes the composition of *Macbeth* from that of the immediately preceding galley operas. Even so, by the New Year drudgery had set in once more. Muzio quotes Verdi's own description of his way of life at that time: '. . . They enjoy themselves: I work from eight o'clock in the morning until twelve o'clock at night, and kill myself with work. What a perfidious destiny mine is!'[38]

For all that, there was never a moment when Verdi relaxed or sacrificed anything of the uncompromising idealism with which *Macbeth* had fired him. We can see this quality in the letter he wrote to Ricordi on 29 December.

I approve the contract which you have made for my new opera *Macbeth*, which is to be performed next Lent season in Florence, and I give my consent for you to make use of it, on condition, however, that you do not permit the performance of the said *Macbeth* at La Scala.

I have examples enough to persuade me that they either cannot or will not produce operas properly here, particularly mine. I cannot forget the dreadful way in which *I Lombardi, Ernani, Due Foscari* etc. were staged. I have another example in front of my eyes with *Attila*! . . . I ask you yourself whether, despite a good cast, it would be possible to produce this opera worse? ...

So, I repeat, I cannot and will not permit the performance of *Macbeth* at La Scala, at least not until things have changed for the better. And I feel bound to observe, for your guidance, that this condition which I now make for *Macbeth* will in future be made for all my operas.[39]

And we see it again in the unprecedented interest which he took in the details of the staging.

It was towards the end of the correspondence between Lanari and Piave, on 22 December 1846, that Verdi himself started to take over as the authority on matter of production. In the form of a postscript to a note to the effect that Signora Barbieri would have to wait a little longer for her music, he observes:

Notice that Banquo's ghost must disappear underground: he must be the same actor who played Banquo in the first act; he must have an ash-coloured veil, but one so thin and fine that it is scarcely visible, and Banquo must have dishevelled hair and several wounds visible on his face. All these ideas I have from London, where this tragedy has been performed continuously for two hundred years and more.[40]

During the next weeks he apparently discussed his ideas for *Macbeth* with several Milanese theatre and history authorities. On 21 January he sent Lanari a letter almost wholly concerned with production questions:

In fact I haven't written to you because I have been excessively busy. Doubtless I shall write to Romani very soon, asking him rather to take over the *mise-en-scène*; but as I don't wish to see the poet pulling faces, I will wait a few days yet – I must tell you as well that when I was talking to Sanquirico about *Macbeth* a few days ago, and expressed my desire to see the apparition in the third act really well staged, he suggested various things to me, but the best is certainly the phantasmagoria. He assured me that it would be something very fine and most appropriate; and he took it upon himself to speak to the optician Duroni about preparing the machinery.

You know what a phantasmogoria is, and I don't need to describe it to you. By God, if the thing worked well, the way Sanquirico described, it would be an amazing affair and masses of people would come running along simply to see it. He assures me that it would be little more expensive than any sort of machine ... What do you say to it? ...

Within a week you will have all the third act, the beginning of the fourth, a complete libretto and I hope the figurines too. I want the figurines to be well made; you can be sure that they will be done well, because I have sent to have some delivered from London, I have sought the advice of first-rate scholars about the period and the costume, and then they will be made by Hayez and the other members of the Commission etc. etc.

You will see, when you get the music, that there are two choruses of the greatest importance: don't economize over the chorus members and you will be pleased with the result. Notice that the witches must always be divided into three groups, and it would be best if they were 6.6.6, 18 in all ... Take care over the tenor who is to do Macduff, and make sure that all the secondary roles are well taken, because the ensembles need good performers. And I am very attached to these ensembles.

I cannot tell you exactly when I shall be in Florence, because I want to finish the opera in peace here. But be assured that I shall be there in time. Hand out the parts for chorus and soloists as soon as they are ready, so that when I arrive we can start with the orchestra after two or three rehearsals, because it will be necessary to have many orchestral and stage rehearsals.

I am sorry that the person playing Banquo doesn't want to play the Ghost! And why not? ... Singers ought to be engaged to sing and to act: moreover it's time these old habits were abandoned. It would be monstrous if someone else played the Ghost, because Banquo must retain his appearance exactly, even when he is a ghost ...[41]

A few days later he was on to Lanari again, emphasizing once more the importance of Macduff and pointing out that neither silk nor velvet should be used in the costumes.[42] This is presumably a deduction from the historical researches which he had been conducting and which, for the benefit of the designer Perrone, he retailed to Tito Ricordi:

Do me the favour of letting Perrone know that the period of *Macbeth* is much later than Ossian and the Roman Empire.

Macbeth assassinated Duncan in 1040, and he was then killed in 1057.

In England in 1039 Harold, called King of Hares [actually Harefoot] was reigning, a king of Danish extraction. He was succeeded in the same year by Hardicanute, half-brother of Edward the Confessor ...

Don't fail to give Perrone this information promptly, because I think he has mistaken ideas about the period.[43]

But perhaps the most interesting of the documents testifying to Verdi's unrelenting high seriousness are the three letters written to Varesi about the interpretation of his role.

7 January 1847

... I have been a bit late sending you music, because I was needing a bit of a rest. Now here are a duettino, a grand duet and a finale for you. I shall never stop urging you to study carefully the context and the words: the music comes by itself.

In short I would like you to serve the *poet*, better than the *composer*. You will be able to create a really powerful impression with the first duettino (more than if it were a cavatina). Notice the position carefully: it comes when he meets the witches, who predict that he will have the throne. At this news you remain astounded and terrified; but at the same time the ambition to come to the throne is born. For that reason you must sing the start of the duettino *sotto voce* and make sure you give significance to the lines: 'Ma perché sento rizzarsi il crine?' Pay close attention to the markings, the accents, the *pp* and *f* ... given in the music ...

In the grand duet the first lines of the recitative, when he gives the order to the servant, are said with no great emphasis. But when he is alone he is gradually transported and imagines that he sees a dagger in his hands, which shows him the way to kill Duncan. This is a very beautiful point, dramatically and poetically, and you must take great care with it!

Notice that it is night: everyone is asleep: the whole of this duet must be sung *sotto voce*, but with a dark voice that inspires terror. Macbeth alone (as if in a moment of transport) must sing a few phrases with a strong, open tone; but you will find all this indicated in the part. So that you understand my ideas fully, I would add that in the whole of this recitative and duet, the instrumentation is for muted strings, two bassoons, two horns and a kettle-drum. You see that the orchestra will sound extremely soft, and you two must sing with your mutes on too. Please bring out clearly the following poetical ideas, which are extremely beautiful: '– Ah! questa mano! ... Non potrebbe l'Oceano queste mani a me lavar!' And the other: 'Vendetta tuonarmi come angeli d'ira Udrò di Duncano le sante virtù!'

The first section of the duet goes rather fast. The second is an *andantino mosso*. The last section goes very fast, *sotto voce*, and at the end one should hardly hear the word 'Lady' which is sung as if in a trance. The first finale is clear enough. Just notice that after the first bars there is a section for solo voices, and you and Signora Barbieri will have to be really secure to support the others. Excuse all this chatter; I will send you the rest soon.

[Undated]

... Here is the third act, which, as you will see, has turned out less arduous than I expected. The scene represents a cavern where the witches are performing their spells in chorus; then you enter and question them in a brief recitative. Then come the apparitions, during which you only have a few words; but, as an actor, you must accompany it all with by-play. Then you have the cantabile when the eight kings are presented to you: to begin with it is broken up to accompany the apparitions; but then there is a cantabile *sui generis* in which you should be able to create a great effect: I don't need to tell you that there is one kind of effect on the words 'Morrai fatal progenie', and then another at the end, on the words 'Ah, che non hai tu vita.' This section is in two different styles: do it as you think best, and then write and tell me how I should orchestrate it.

I would ask you to take particular care with the cabaletta: it doesn't have the usual form, because after all that has gone before, a cabaletta in the usual form with the usual ritornellos would sound trivial. I had composed another one, which I liked when I tried it by itself, but when I joined it up with what had gone before, the effect was intolerable. I think this one works well and I hope you will think so too ...

I hope you have received the first act too ... I am sure the tessitura will suit you well; but in case there should be any awkward notes and phrases, let me know before I start the orchestration. Now there is only the last scene to come, which, as far as you are concerned, consists of a quiet *adagio cantabile*, and a very short death scene: but it won't be one of the usual oversweet death scenes. You will see quite clearly that Macbeth cannot die as Edgardo and the rest of them do ...

4 February 1847

Here now is the last piece, which you will have to get a copyist to make a fair copy of, so that you can study it; with that you will have the complete role. Please learn it thoroughly before coming to Florence, so that you can start production rehearsals at once. This last scene is in your hands. It is an *adagio* in D^b, which must be performed with great refinement, *cantabile ed affettuoso*. In the transition I would ask you to pronounce the words 'La vita! . . . che importa! E il racconto di un povero idiota. Vento e suono che nulla dinota . . .' with all the irony and all the contempt possible.

With the death scene you will be able to create a great effect if your singing is combined with well-thought-out acting . . . Let it be pathetic; but more than pathetic, terrible. The whole scene *sotto voce* with the exception of the last two lines; and here too you must match your singing with action, breaking out with full force on the words 'Vil corona' and 'sol per te'. You are (of course) on the ground but in this last line you must raise yourself almost erect and create the greatest possible effect. Be in Florence in good time with the part memorized.[44]

Before his own departure for Florence on 15 February Verdi was in touch with Lanari again:

I hope you will have received my last letter in which I thanked you for the kind offer you made to accommodate me in your house: I am in company and cannot take advantage of it, but be assured I am none the less grateful.

I shall come and see you later; but if in the mean time you could send one of your people to me, I should be obliged, because I am in need of instructions of various kinds: which hotel it would be best to stay at and which would be convenient for the theatre too . . .[45]

Verdi apparently took with him to Florence a letter of introduction to Giuseppe Giusti which Clarina Maffei had procured from Manzoni. Soon he must have felt as much at home in the artistic circles of Florence as in those of Milan. In a letter to Barezzi on 25 February Muzio reports:

Signora Barbieri arrived yesterday evening. Today rehearsals for *Attila* which will be staged on Sunday. The maestro doesn't wish to attend any rehearsals and instead has given the job to me. Then on Saturday the first piano rehearsals of *Macbeth* will begin. Next week I shall perhaps be able to tell you the exact date of the production. Remember that we are expecting you and Giovannino, who is asked after by some of his acquaintances. We are staying at the Pensione Svizzero, where we have magnificent rooms, heavenly air, and *dine like kings*; and the maestro is proposing to pay for it all . . . that is, the impresario is.

If I tell you that the maestro is idolized, visited and revisited by everyone it will only be what you will have expected. The most distinguished men have wanted to make his acquaintance: Niccolini, Giusti, Bartolini, Dupré etc; and even the grand duke . . . sent to invite him to call upon him, and yesterday evening, somewhat unwillingly, he went. The grand duke could tell him his whole life story. Even that he wasn't wanted in Busseto. In fact he knew everything ...[46]

It was not to be expected that the strenuous demands made on everyone by Verdi during the genesis of the opera would be relaxed at the rehearsal stage. His letters to Varesi, already quoted, show that he was counting on having plenty of time to rehearse really thoroughly. And the rigorousness with which he directed these rehearsals was something unprecedented in the Italian theatre, as the memoirs of Marianna Barbieri-Nini, his Lady Macbeth, vividly recall:

The piano and orchestra rehearsals amounted to more than a hundred, as Verdi was never satisfied with the performance and required a better rendering by the artists. They, for their part, partly because of these exaggerated demands of his, partly because of his peculiarly reserved and taciturn character, entertained no particular sympathy for him. Morning and evening, in the rehearsal room and on the stage, all eyes were on the maestro the moment he appeared, so as to see, from the expression of his face, if anything new was coming. If he came in smiling, it was as good as certain that he would be requiring an additional rehearsal today. I remember that there were two climactic moments in the opera, the sleepwalking scene and my duet with the baritone. It sounds hardly credible, but it is a fact, that the sleepwalking scene alone demanded three months of study. For three months, morning and evening, I attempted to impersonate someone who speaks in her sleep, who (as the maestro put it) utters words, as it were, without moving her lips, the rest of the face motionless, the eyes shut ... It was enough to drive anyone mad! ... And the duet with the baritone was rehearsed, incredible as it may sound, one hundred and fifty times, so that, as Verdi said, it should succeed in sounding *more spoken than sung*. Well now, that was all past. On the evening of the final rehearsal, when the theatre was full, Verdi insisted in addition that the artists should wear their costumes; [Footnote: Artists have never observed this sensible custom in Italy; it has several times been attempted to introduce it, but in vain.] and when he made up his mind about anything, there was no contradicting! At last we were all dressed and ready, the orchestra was in place and everything on stage, when Verdi, having beckoned to me and Varesi, called us behind the scenery and requested us to do him the favour of going with him into the rehearsal room, to rehearse this accursed duet once again. 'Maestro, how can we,' I said, shocked, 'we all have our costumes on already.' – 'Put a coat over you.' But Varesi, unwilling to comply with the strange request, could not refrain from exclaiming: 'But, for heaven's sake, we have already rehearsed it a hundred and fifty times!' 'You won't say that in half an hour, because by then it will be a hundred and fifty-one times!' We had, perforce, to obey the tyrant. I still remember the furious look with which Varesi followed Verdi as he went into the rehearsal room. With his hand on his dagger he looked as if he was going to strike down Verdi as he had to King Duncan a little later. However, he finally resigned himself as well and the hundred and fifty-first rehearsal took place while the public milled about impatiently in the auditorium.[47]

Despite the novelty of its subject and treatment *Macbeth* enjoyed a handsome success at its *première* on 14 March. Abramo Basevi, author of the earliest critical study of Verdi's music, who was present, suggests that it was really a *succès d'estime*. 'Well received; but more out of respect for the composer, who was present, than because of the music, which was only half appreciated.'[48] But if so, the Florentines expressed their respect uncommonly effusively. To Clarina Maffei the composer reported: 'There are many people to whom I have no consolation to offer ... The opera was not a fiasco – I cannot tell you all the details because, to tell the truth, the Florentines did more than they should have done. The demonstrations of approval were enormous, and I will tell you about them in person.'[49] To Piave, enclosing the rest of his payment for the libretto, Verdi confided one of the particulars: 'As you know, the reviews of *Macbeth* have been tremendous ... they have presented me with a golden crown worth 200 *zecchini*, the beautiful Barbieri presented it to me at the third performance: THE FLORENTINES TO G. VERDI. Amen ...'[50]

Signora Barbieri herself records the most intimate particulars of the evening:

I shall never forget how, on the evening of the first performance, before the sleepwalking scene, Verdi walked restlessly round and round me without saying a word. One saw clearly that the success of the opera, which was already great, would seem definitive to him only after this scene. So I crossed myself (a custom that survives on the stage even today in moments of difficulty) and went on stage ... The journals of the time can say whether I interpreted the great composer's dramatic and musical thoughts aright. I knew only one thing: before the waves of applause had fully died down, still trembling and incapable of saying a word, I had gone to my dressing-room; the door opened – I was already half undressed – and I saw Verdi come in, gesticulating with his hands and moving his lips as if he wanted to speak: but he was unable to get a single word out. I laughed and cried and likewise couldn't speak a word, but looking at the composer I saw that he too had red eyes. We pressed one another's hands firmly and warmly, and then he bolted out. This scene of sincere emotion amply compensated me for so many months of perpetual work and continuous agitation.[51]

The fullest account of the *première* was Antonio Barezzi's, which he dictated to Muzio to send to his family in Busseto.

... Yesterday evening was the great day of the production of *Macbeth*, which, as usual with Verdi's operas, provoked immense enthusiasm: he had to appear on stage thirty-eight times during the performance, and I can assure you that *Macbeth* is a grand opera, extremely grand and magnificent.

The Florence *Macbeth*

When I came out of the theatre with Verdi we were surrounded by a huge throng of people who accompanied us shouting and cheering to our hotel, a distance of about a mile from the theatre. From time to time Verdi had to stop to thank the Florentine public, which was composed of young people of the very first rank.

I forgot to tell you that on the first evening there was a terrible crowd; the theatre opened at four o'clock, a few minutes later it was full; I already had to take the seats reserved for myself and for Giovannino, which cost a *pisis* [a small Tuscan coin originally minted at Pisa] for each reserved place in addition to the cost of the ticket.

The opera began at eight o'clock exactly and the introduction was at once applauded and the maestro called for; then the chorus of witches was repeated and again the maestro was called for with frenzied enthusiasm, the duet for Signora Barbieri and Varesi was likewise repeated, and so were two other choruses, and in the whole course of the opera the maestro was called for twenty-seven times.

This is the simple truth about the first night. I will tell you the little anecdotes in person, as I will also tell you what happens tomorrow evening, the last with Verdi in attendance, because today is the rest-day and consequently free for diversion. At the moment I am waiting for Baron Ricasoli's carriage to go out for the day viewing these truly heavenly sights ... I cannot describe the sensations aroused in me by Florence! From the descriptions I had had before I believed it would be beautiful, but not so beautiful as I find it really is ...[52]

One of the clearest indications that we have come to a new period of Verdi's works with *Macbeth* is the fact that, until the thorough-going revision made for Paris in 1865, the Florence score remained definitive. No longer was the composer prepared to write additional or alternative arias to suit a particular singer for a particular revival, as he had done with most of his earlier works. But this does not mean that the story of the Florentine *Macbeth* is finished with its *première*: on the contrary, the 'follow-through' of the opera was as uniquely interesting as the story of its composition.

To begin with it prompted a memorable exchange of letters with Giuseppe Giusti, in which two of the major artists of *risorgimento* Italy make a mutual confession on the topic of Italian art. Giusti wrote from Pescia:

... I was sorry not to find you at home last Monday, because as I had to be away from Florence for a few days, I would have liked to see you before leaving.

Your opera will be understood and appreciated more the more it is performed, because the merits of some things are not obvious at once. Continue in your path and you cannot fail to win a great name. But if you will heed a well-wisher of art and of yourself, do not miss the opportunity to express in your music that sweet sadness of which you have shown that you have the command. You know that the chord of sorrow is that which echoes most strongly in our hearts, but sorrow assumes a different character according to the period and temperament and condition of this or that nation. The type of sorrow that now fills the hearts of us Italians is the sorrow of a people who feel the need of a better destiny; it is the sorrow of one who has fallen and desires to rise again; it is the sorrow of one who repents and awaits and longs for regeneration. My Verdi, accompany with your noble harmonies this lofty and solemn sorrow, do what you can to nourish it, to strengthen it, to direct it towards its goal. Music is a language understood by everyone, and there is no great effect which music is not able to produce. The fantastic is something which puts the imagination to the test; the true puts both the imagination and the heart to the test. I wish that the imaginations of the Italians would all join in a strong and wholehearted union with Italian art, and abstain from the exotic charms of foreign liaisons. I mention these things to you in this vague and sketchy way, because I feel them deeply but hardly know how to express them, and because when one has a good listener a few words are sufficient.

I shall be returning to Florence on Monday or Tuesday at the latest, and want to embrace you before your return to Milan; but in case I don't find you there any longer, be assured that you have left there another friend, one who hitherto has been a great well-wisher of your work and who is now a well-wisher of your work and of yourself.[53]

Verdi replied from Milan:

Thanks, a thousand thanks for your very dear letter; you have recompensed me in part for the disappointment at not having been able to embrace you before leaving Florence.

Yes: you put it very well: 'the chord of sorrow is that which echoes most strongly in our hearts'. You speak of art like the great man you are and I shall certainly follow your suggestions, for I understand what you mean to say.

Oh, if we only had a poet who knew how to devise the kind of drama you have in mind! But unfortunately (you will admit it yourself), if we want something at all effective we have, to our shame, to resort to foreign things. How many subjects there are in our own history! . . .[54]

Another habit broken with *Macbeth* was that of dedicating an opera to a person distinguished by social rank or influence in the theatrical world. The opera into which Verdi felt that he had put the best of himself was dedicated to Barezzi. On 25 March Verdi wrote to him:

For a long time I have been intending to dedicate an opera to you, who have been a father, a benefactor and a friend to me. It was a duty which I should have fulfilled before now, and I would have done so had not compelling circumstances prevented it. – Now, here is my *Macbeth* which I love more than my other operas and which I therefore deem the more worthy of being presented to you. The heart offers it; may the heart accept it, and may it be a testimony to the everlasting remembrance, to the gratitude and love of your most affectionate

G. Verdi.[55]

Finally we must cite as an unprecedented phenomenon the

interest which Verdi continued to take in productions of *Macbeth* for
several years after its Florentine *première*. Towards the end of 1848
when he was working on *La Battaglia di Legnano*, neither *I Masnadieri* nor *Jérusalem* nor *Il Corsaro*, nor indeed *La Battaglia di
Legnano* itself had dislodged *Macbeth* from the special place it held
in his affections. And when he heard about a proposed revival in
Naples with a cast that seemed less than ideal he at once pricked up
his ears. From Paris, on 23 November, he wrote two letters, one to
Flauto, the other to Cammarano. Flauto as impresario was simply
urged 'to supervise the rehearsals' and to see that it was not treated
like any old repertory piece.[56] But to Cammarano, who would have
been responsible for the production, Verdi wrote more fully:

I know that you are at present rehearsing *Macbeth*, and as it is an opera in
which I take a keener interest than I do in the others, permit me to say a few
words about it. The role of Lady Macbeth has been given to Signora
Tadolini, and I am surprised that she has agreed to do this role. You know
how I esteem Tadolini, and she knows it herself; but in our common interest
I think it is necessary to make a few observations. Signora Tadolini has too
great qualities to do this role! You will perhaps think this an absurd thing to
say!! ... Tadolini is a fine-looking woman, and I should like Lady Macbeth
to look ugly and evil. Tadolini sings to perfection; and I should like *Lady* not
to sing at all. Tadolini has a marvellous voice, clear, limpid and powerful;
and I should like Lady's voice to be harsh, choked and hollow. Tadolini's
voice has something angelic about it, and I should like Lady's voice to have
something diabolical. Submit these reflections to the management, to
Maestro Mercadante, who more than anyone will appreciate these views of
mine, to Tadolini herself, and then do what in your wisdom you judge best.
   Notice that the two most important pieces in the opera are the duet
between Lady and her husband and the sleepwalking scene: if these pieces
fail, the opera falls flat: and these pieces absolutely must not be sung:
      They must be acted, and declaimed
      in a hollow, veiled
      voice: without that they
      cannot be effective.
      The orchestra with *mutes*.
The scene is very dark. – In the third act the apparitions of the kings (I
have seen it in London) must come from a trapdoor in the stage, behind a
fine, ash-coloured veil. The kings must not be puppets, but eight men of
flesh and blood: the ground over which they pass must be like a small hill,
so that one can see them ascending and descending. The stage must be
completely dark, especially when the cauldron disappears, and only lit up
where the kings are passing over. The instruments under the stage must (for
the large San Carlo Theatre) be augmented, but take care that no trumpets or
trombones are used. The sound must seem distant and muted, and so only
bass clarinets, bassoons, and double-bassoons should be used, nothing else
...[57]

Opera as a business

The long period of imposed quiet during which *Macbeth* could be pondered, and the sublimity of the subject itself, had combined to draw from Verdi the most considered and idealistic score he had yet written. Of course, even in the composition of *Macbeth* he did not neglect to 'look after his interests'; nor would one wish to imply that there would have been anything artistically or morally commendable about it if he had. But the priorities strike us as right: Verdi acquired an advantageous contract, and when that was done, he emptied his mind of all considerations save that of doing the best of which he was capable as an artist. But *Macbeth* did not mark quite the turning point in Verdi's career that one might have expected. The surviving documents give us a rather different impression of the next twelve months. Contracts with London and Paris, at that time the two most ostentatiously wealthy cities in Europe, and business with the publisher Lucca, a far less sympathetic and cultivated man than Ricordi, were things calculated to bring out the worst in Verdi. The exalted passion that fires the letters on *Macbeth* burns fitfully; the rapid accumulation of wealth and a materialistic rigour in claiming his 'rights' have become the leading themes. And *I Masnadieri*, *Jérusalem* and *Il Corsaro* are the inglorious harvest. Surely it was primarily of this phase of Verdi's career that Giuseppina Strepponi was thinking when she wrote five years later: 'Sometimes I fear that your love of money will reawake and condemn you again to many years of toil!'[1]

I Masnadieri

The idea of composing an opera for London first arose in the autumn of 1845, when the director of Her Majesty's Theatre in the Haymarket, Benjamin Lumley, came to call upon Verdi in Milan. On 27 October Muzio informed Barezzi that

as soon as he learned of the success of *Nabucco* [in Paris] Lumley came from London together with Escudier to engage the signor maestro for next spring.

Not finding him at Milan, they went to Clusone, where he was; but while they were going there, he came back here, so they were chasing after him for some time until they found him . . . It is very likely that he will make a contract for London with a fee a third larger than when he composes in Italy, plus lodging, because over there they want twenty francs a day for two small rooms.[2]

Two days later Muzio announced:

Yesterday morning the signor maestro was formally contracted to compose for London. They wanted to engage him for ten years! ! ! to give one opera a year.[3]

At this time Verdi had just entered into a contract with Lucca, Ricordi's chief rival in music publishing in Italy. It will be recalled that in January 1845 Lucca had bought the rights in *Attila* from Lanari; now he succeeded in breaching Ricordi's Verdi-monopoly a little further by contracting directly with the composer. The terms are recorded in a letter of 16 October:

I undertake to compose for you an opera to be performed in a leading Italian theatre by a first-rate company during the Carnival season 1848, provided that I do not have to write an opera for a theatre outside Italy for the same Carnival season: in that case I should compose your opera for a different season, to be agreed upon with you, within the year 1849. For this you will pay me 1200 (one thousand two hundred) golden napoleons of 20 francs in four equal instalments: the first on 1 November 1847, the second on 1 December 1847, the third on 1 January 1848, the fourth on 1 February 1848. If these conditions are acceptable to you, I will hold myself engaged for five months, provided that *Attila* has been produced by that time.[4]

In some way which is no longer quite clear Lucca also got himself involved with the London business. Indeed arrangements for the London opera were finally made in the form of another contract between Verdi and Lucca. Clearly it would be useful for Verdi to have someone easily accessible in Milan who could act as intermediary between himself and Lumley in London; and in this capacity Lucca busied himself more or less ineptly throughout the winter months. The kind of responsibility he assumed may be deduced from a letter written by the composer on 25 January 1846:

. . . I remind you of what I told your wife when I spoke to her:
(1) to sort out the muddle with Maggioni, since I cannot set to music his *Corsaro*, as I am already under the obligation to get Piave to write this libretto.*
(2) to let me know if you will come to London with me (always supposing that I am able to go).

* Manfredo Maggioni, an Italian poet resident in London, clearly had either prepared or been asked by Lucca to prepare a *Corsaro* libretto.

(3) If Piave is left behind, whether Maggioni would be willing to make such small modifications as may be necessary.

(4) to write to Lumley to delay the production by one month, and my arrival in London, both because of the time of year and because living in London is very different from living in Milan . . .

Verdi's first thought had been that his London début offered the ideal opportunity to realize one of his keenest and most long-cherished aspirations. Towards the end of November, in a letter to Piave about *Attila*, he had remarked: 'I am busy with *Lear*, studying it carefully. I will bring a sketch of it with me which you can elaborate into a fuller synopsis to be offered to London.'[6]

Lumley's own memoirs confirm that the original plan had been for 'an opera, founded on *King Lear*, the principal part in which was destined for Lablache'.[7] But soon after Verdi's arrival in Venice to prepare for the production of *Attila* he and Piave had decided to abandon this ambitious project and to adapt Byron's *The Corsair* for London instead.

During the weeks of illness that delayed the completion of *Attila*, Verdi must have found the energy to talk over the *Corsaro* project with Piave. Soon he was sending off to Lucca a synopsis of the libretto: 'I enclose the synopsis of *Il Corsaro*, so that you can do me the favour of sending it to Lumley. If there should be any difficulties I beg you to overcome them since I could not find nor imagine a subject more beautiful, more passionate or more apt for music – as you will see, as far as one can judge from a synopsis.'[8]

One might have expected the publisher to warm to Verdi's enthusiasm for his Byronic theme; but in all his dealings with Verdi Lucca displayed an amazing obtuseness. Having once blundered by attempting to foist on to the composer Maggioni's version of the story, Lucca now compounded his error by raising objections to *Il Corsaro* in any form. His letter seems to be lost, but Verdi's impatient retort indicates its character sufficiently:

You may have all the reasons in the world, and I may be completely and utterly deceived, but either I do *Il Corsaro* or I do nothing. *Ginevra?* . . . It may be beautiful (as you claim), but I like things which others don't like. In fact *Nabucco* had been refused, *I Lombardi* was a bad libretto, *Ernani* couldn't be set to music, etc.[9]

The complete physical and mental breakdown that Verdi suffered during the composition of *Attila* made it necessary for his visit to London to be cancelled. Dr Giacinto Namias, who had attended him in Venice, and Dr Gasparo Belcredi, who examined him on his return to Milan, both provided medical certificates to the effect that a long period of complete rest was absolutely essential and that, in the words of the latter, 'he could *not* undertake a long journey, still less involve himself in the composition of musical works, without putting at grave risk his health and perhaps even his very life . . .'[10]

Verdi himself wrote to Lumley:

I know that the news I have for you will not be unexpected: it is that, because of the illness from which I suffered in Venice, I am in no condition to come to London, far less to compose the opera. This very day Signor Lucca will be sending you two medical certificates which I handed over to him, which will verify this matter. You cannot imagine how much I regret having to renounce the honour of composing for London. My health is improving so slowly that I am incapable of even the slightest exertion, and I am compelled to stay here, resting and undergoing scrupulously a medical cure, until it is time to go to Recoaro to take the waters etc.

I hope that this misfortune will not harm our relationship, and would ask you to write me a few lines in acknowledgement . . .[11]

The effusive and insensitive breeziness of Lumley's acknowledgement (written in French) was worthy of Flauto.

It was with keen regret that I learned of your illness at a time when I was counting on the pleasure of seeing you again here almost immediately. I can well imagine that you are suffering from the cares to which the so sensitive organism of a creative genius such as yourself is prone. Pray accept the expression of my wholehearted sympathy. I dare to hope that in a few days you will be better, and that travelling in short stages you will arrive here in good health, at a time of year when we enjoy the fairest weather, with a sky less blue, but an air less stimulating than that of Italy.

It only remains to request you to give me your news as quickly and as often as you can . . .

P.S. I am sure that the change of scene and a visit to London during so fair a time of year and so successful a season (I have never known anything more brilliant than our theatre) will do you more good than all the cures imaginable.[12]

A month later Lumley followed up with an account of the 'succès de vrai enthousiasme' enjoyed by his London revival of *I Lombardi* and expressed the hope that 'this news will act as an efficacious antidote to your indisposition, and that you will come here to take a stronger dose of applause . . .'[13] But Verdi put a decisive end to such vain imaginings:

I see with surprise that you are expecting letters from me, but I frankly admit that I was not thinking about writing to you over a matter which I consider legally closed, as I wrote to you in a letter of 9 April last, to which I have not received a reply. Furthermore, having consigned the medical certificates to Signor Lucca in good time and having had a proper receipt for them, I have done all that the circumstances require.

My natural curiosity to see a city so extraordinary as London, my self-esteem and my self-interest were reasons enough for not delaying in fulfilling my contract with Signor Lucca. But my health prevented it, and I need absolute rest.

I rejoice that *I Lombardi* has appealed to the taste of the English, and thank you sincerely for having given me such gratifying particulars about it . . .[14]

The imposed delay should have been a good thing for Lucca and Lumley, for instead of Verdi's London opera being a product of the darkest 'galley-years' it thus became a work composed after the Recoaro summer. Indeed its relationship to the experiences of that summer was even more intimate than was the case with *Macbeth*. One of the consequences of those weeks was that Maffei himself agreed to write a libretto for Verdi. For his theme he proposed to go to that literary hero whom he knew best, to Schiller, and of his works to select *Die Räuber,* 'of all his literary works that which offers the situations best fitted for musical treatment'.[15] The news that the convalescent comrades were contemplating writing an opera together is first given by Verdi in a letter to Clarina Maffei on 3 August: '. . . Maffei is well: it is very likely that he will write a libretto for me, *I Masnadieri*.'[16]

Originally of course, *I Masnadieri* had nothing to do with the London engagement; it was one of the contending subjects for Verdi's Florence contract. Muzio's letter of 13 August to Barezzi has been quoted in the previous chapter (see above, p. 170). By 3 September he could report a simplification of the problem: 'everything will be finalized for Florence within the next week. Either there will be Fraschini, in which case he will do *I Masnadieri*, or there won't, and then he will do *Macbeth* with Varesi, which would be better, because it is a subject which everyone knows.'[17]

As soon as *Macbeth* was decided upon, Verdi began to wonder whether *I Masnadieri* might not be a better choice of subject than *Il Corsaro* for the London opera he was still eager to write. This idea rapidly hardened into a conviction, and when he reopened negotiations with Lucca and Lumley later in the year, their readiness to accept *I Masnadieri* was to become a condition of his resuming the contract. On 24 September Muzio wrote to Barezzi: '. . . Lumley is expected any day; if he forms the company which the signor maestro wants he will go to London in the spring. He would like Signora Hayez or Signora Barbieri, Fraschini, Varesi and the elder Lablache, and then he would write *I Masnadieri*'[18]

In fact Lumley did not arrive until the end of October or even November.[19] Meanwhile Verdi had decided on his own conditions: '1. to compose *I Masnadieri*, of which two acts are virtually ready, 2.

to have the singers he wants, 3. as much money as possible'.[20]

Before Verdi's London visit could be replanned, however, it was necessary for him to get a Naples engagement postponed,* as he explained in letters to Lucca on 9 November and, more interestingly, to Lumley (who was now in Milan) on 11 November:

If the Naples management will allow me to postpone until the autumn the opera which I have contracted to write for June next, 1847, I should, for my part, be disposed to compose an opera for Her Majesty's Theatre, London, to be produced towards the end of June. I should have the right to choose the artists for the cast, among whom must be Signora Lind, and Fraschini. You know furthermore that the opera I compose will belong to the publisher Francesco Lucca, with whom it will be necessary for you to come to an agreement over all particulars . . .[21]

The Neapolitan disengagement was accomplished later in the month, and on 2 December Verdi offered to re-enter into the contract with Lucca:

I inform you that the opera that I was engaged to write for the next Spring season 1847 in Naples has been postponed, and that I can therefore write for you the opera that is to be performed in Signor Lumley's theatre in London at the end of June 1847. Signor Lumley must, however, leave to me the choice of the singers from his company, among whom must be included the names which I indicated to him in a letter of 11 November last, when he was in Milan.

I can now accept the offers which you have kindly made me so many times, and shall be grateful if you will pay me on the first day of 1847 the first instalment for the opera which I am to write for you next spring . . .[22]

Lucca seems to have been an amazingly obtuse and undiplomatic man. He must have known about Verdi's change of mind over the subject, either from conversation with him or from letters now lost. But no sooner did he receive Verdi's letter than he attempted to pressurize him into going back to *Il Corsaro*. Verdi bristled:

. . . As far as the subject is concerned, you know that I have changed my mind about *Il Corsaro* and have had a new libretto written: *I Masnadieri*, of which I have written about a third of the music. You know this very well, and I am perfectly amazed that you talk about such matters. These then are the accepted conditions: that I am to write *I Masnadieri* and that Lumley guarantees to give me the two promised singers on the roster of the company.[23]

This letter to Lucca gives the impression that Verdi was leaving it to him to make arrangements for a new contract with Lumley. Having slept on it, though, Verdi decided that it would be better to approach Lumley direct:

* On this Naples engagement see below, pp. 220f.

The opera which I was engaged to write for Naples in the spring of 1847 has been postponed until another season, and so I should be at liberty to compose for London in June unless some real obstacle should arise.

Last year I had chosen *Il Corsaro* for a subject, but after it had been versified I found it cold and theatrically ineffective, so I changed my mind and, although it involved me in twice the expense, decided to have another libretto written, based on Schiller's *I Masnadieri*. My illness had annulled the contract of last year and I was fully within my rights to choose now another subject, especially as this was known to Signor Lucca. He knew furthermore that I had composed about half of *I Masnadieri* because it is more effective, and because it suits the company better.

I repeat that I stand under no obligation to anyone to compose one subject rather than another, and that if I am to compose for London I certainly have time to finish *I Masnadieri*, but not to compose the whole of *Il Corsaro*.

If *I Masnadieri* is acceptable to you, I shall undertake . . . to compose it for London, always provided that you undertake, by letter addressed to me personally, to leave me the right to choose the singers from the roster of your company, on which roster must be included the names of Signora Lind and of Fraschini, as we agreed in Milan . . .[24]

With these proposals Lumley was 'obliged to close'.[25] Various remarks in the letters already quoted in this chapter show that *I Masnadieri* was the first music Verdi started composing after his six-month convalescence – we read of 'two acts virtually ready', of the opera being 'almost half composed', well before anything of *Macbeth* had been written. It would seem that Maffei's libretto, at least in part, was done during August; and that Verdi began to compose it while working on the early stages of the *Macbeth* libretto with Piave. *I Masnadieri* would have been abandoned probably in November, when Verdi began to apply himself unremittingly to *Macbeth*. For four months thereafter the only reference to the London opera is in a letter to Escudier:

. . . Very soon *Macbeth* will be finished, and so I shall have one opera less on my shoulders – for London I have arranged to do *I Masnadieri*, the libretto of which is already finished. It seems to me very successful as far as the dramatic situations are concerned, and certainly has been excellently versified by one of the most distinguished Italian poets. – So we shall be seeing one another soon, on my way to London, and I cannot wait to see with my own eyes a production at the Opéra . . .[26]

No sooner had Verdi resumed work on *I Masnadieri* after the completion of *Macbeth* than he found that certain parts of the second act needed rewriting. In the same letter to Maffei in which he requests these modifications, he thanks him for the revisions made to Piave's *Macbeth* verses in January; and remarks on the question of payment for the libretto of *I Masnadieri*, which suggests that it had been completed only comparatively recently.

Please accept as a keepsake this trifle [a gift of a gold watch and chain]: it is very little in comparison with what you have done for me, but let it serve at least to show that I would like to and will express my gratitude to you. You will be receiving also 50 golden napoleons for *I Masnadieri*, in exchange for which it will be necessary for you to write to me ceding the libretto, so that I can cede it to my impresario. I would only ask that you should revise some things in the second act, which is theatrically very ineffective; and if you are as anxious as I am that this libretto should create a good effect, you must make this last sacrifice.[27]

This letter is undated. But that the revisions in the *Masnadieri* libretto postdate the production of *Macbeth* on 14 March is clear from Maffei's letter of acknowledgement, in which he alludes to one of the reviews of that opera.

When you gave me the commission to write *I Masnadieri* for you it was a blessed hour for me, and but for the fear that you would withdraw it, I should never, never have consented to accept payment for it. Now the thousand francs which you send me exceed – at least I think so – the sum agreed between us, which was that which you have always given to Piave and to Solera; the excess amount absolutely must be restored to you. But why do you add to that the magnificent gift of the gold watch and chain? Do you perhaps want to pay me for the miserable scraps which I added to Piave's libretto? Ask the *Rivista Fiorentina* how much they are worth. Your heart, which ought to know me, cannot have intended that, which would make me die of shame. Should I send back your gift? But how could I do it without offending you?

And I would wish to attach myself to you as to the dearest, noblest, and most glorious of my friends . . . My dear Verdi, I am not an easy person, the solitude in which I find myself would be welcome to an egoist, but not to me who have need of friendship, especially of yours; you could not take it away from me without tearing my heart. Do not speak of sacrifices when you want anything from me. My pen and my poor talents have for a long time been yours to command.[28]

Probably Maffei's revisions were written in the early part of April. By 14 April Verdi was 'working hard'.[29] He continued to work hard throughout the month, and on 17 May Muzio could tell Barezzi, 'I think he only has a little more to do to have the opera completely finished.'[30]

At about this time Verdi learned that Fraschini would not after all be singing in London. Lumley had tempered the news with the remark that he was not liked in London anyway, and that Italo Gardoni, the new principal tenor, was generally more popular.[31] Verdi made no difficulties about this. But earlier in the year something had made him suspicious about whether Jenny Lind would be available, and on this matter he had been uncompromising. On 27 March, acknowledging an advance part-payment for *I Masnadieri*, he wrote to Lucca:

I acknowledge the receipt of two hundred and fifty golden napoleons of 20 francs, being the first quarter-payment for the opera ... it is of course understood that in the said opera, apart from the other artists, Signora Lind must sing, as has already been arranged with the impresario Lumley. In the event of Signora Lind not going to London, this quarter-payment will be restored to you, or some other arrangement will be made.[32]

Even after receiving reassurances that Lind would be in London Verdi remained mistrustful: to Lucca he wrote again on 10 April:

I am glad to hear that Signora Lind will be going to London: but it looks to me as if she is going very late and I wouldn't want the season to become too prolonged for the sake of my opera.

Rest assured that I will not tolerate that, and that I am not disposed to tolerate the least shortcoming. I have been treated shabbily in this whole affair, so if my opera is not put on at the proper time and in the proper manner, I tell you quite frankly I will not have it performed.[33]

The irascible, sometimes unreasonable frame of mind in which. Verdi approached his London début contrasts strangely with the firm but warm-hearted idealism he had shown over *Macbeth*. One wonders how he had been 'treated shabbily'. The editors of the *Copialettere* speak of a request for a postponement of the opera which Verdi had made in February and which was refused. But neither they nor, to the best of my knowledge, anyone else has produced the document in question. Budden on the other hand wonders if it was not the result of working with a man so crudely materialistic as Lucca. That this gentleman still had not learnt that it was unwise to adopt bludgeoning tactics when Verdi's affairs were at stake is clear from a letter which the Escudiers got Giuseppina Strepponi to write from Paris to her old friend Giovannina Lucca:

... The Escudiers are still gazing open-mouthed and with telescopes glued to their eyes, wondering whether they are reading aright the figure you demand for *I Masnadieri* (ten thousand francs!). They are particularly amazed at this demand because none of Verdi's operas which they have bought from Ricordi's have exceeded the sum of three thousand francs each, not excepting *Macbeth*, which will probably be a great success in Italy and is one of the subjects best fitted for the French stage.

Today they have had another letter from your husband in which he urges them to reply 'without the least delay, yes or no!' ... It is impossible for them to reply before tomorrow, and I read the letter by chance, having gone to their office for some pieces of music. I am sorry to see them out of sorts and ill-disposed towards your husband. I confess that *quite apart from your bad and hostile treatment of Escudier*, I cannot see that it is in your interest to dismember Verdi's operas, which up to now have all (with the exception of *Nabucco*) passed through the hands of this firm, by giving them to someone else, who until now has perhaps been a bitter enemy of this composer and will only pay a lot of money for one of his scores out of pique and personal dislike.

You mustn't think of the momentary advantage of a few thousand francs, but of the consequences. The Escudiers have always fought vigorously against all Verdi's enemies, of whom there are *not a few*, and it is not right to make them pay such a sum for an opera which, for Paris, has two great disadvantages: *the subject and the fact that it has been written for London*. But despite such disadvantages, they want to have it, because they have all the other operas, and because they want to be the sole editors in France of Verdi's music as Troupenas was of Rossini's, and as every great composer has his particular one.

I would add that, if the score belongs to them, they would be prepared to go to London and do everything possible to ensure a brilliant success. However beautiful the music may be which Verdi writes, it would certainly be no bad thing on such an occasion (with Meyerbeer etc.) for someone to take a keen interest in him, especially someone who knows the country. If the score doesn't belong to them, it won't be surprising if they take things very calmly and stay quietly in Paris . . .[34]

It was the Escudiers who sent Verdi, some time in May, the first news of the sensational triumphs Jenny Lind was enjoying in London. Verdi's letter of thanks, written on 23 May, dates for us his departure from Milan, and also gives the first intimation of his intention of settling in Paris for a brief period on his return from London,

. . . I have received your last letter in which you so considerately give me the news of Signora Lind's success. I am very glad (since I am obliged to compose for her) that she has had such a success, and I shall be setting out from here in two or three days on the journey to London. It is probable that I shall go there direct without passing through Paris because time is short. Nevertheless we shall see one another on my return, and then I shall really stop in Paris for a few months in order to see your city and also to rest myself from the continual fatigue of these last few years. For once in my life I should like to find out for myself if a gentleman's life is a fine thing . . .[35]

Most of the initiatives taken by Lucca during his association with Verdi were to prove inept or abortive. But a fortnight before Verdi's departure for London he did have one genuinely happy inspiration. Verdi was fussing about his health again, and wondering whether he should undertake so arduous a journey, when Lucca made a proposal: in Muzio's words, 'if the signor maestro is willing to go to London, [Lucca] will send me with him and give me 2000 francs, so that I can help him, and be near him, and so that for any eventuality he has with him someone in whom he can have confidence'.[36]

Thanks to the presence of Muzio we have a fuller account of the last stages in the preparation of *I Masnadieri* than of any other of

Verdi's early operas. On 1 June he describes their journey as far as Paris.

On Wednesday we left Milan in a suffocating heat; once we were at Como we did not feel it so much, because we kept always to the shore of the lake, and being in the middle of the mountains, there was a bit of wind. At four o'clock on Thursday we arrived at Flüelen in Switzerland, and went on the lake in a steamboat which carried us to Lucerne.

From Lucerne we went in a diligence to Basle. From Basle on the railway we went to Strasbourg. When we got to Strasbourg we couldn't find the diligence which left at once for Paris; and the maestro, not wanting to wait, suddenly had the whim of going to Paris by way of Brussels; and instead of continuing through France we crossed the river Rhine and entered the Grand Duchy of Baden-Baden. Here an omnibus took us from the river to Kehl; from Kehl we went by steam, on terra firma, to Karlsruhe; from Karlsruhe to Mannheim, from Mannheim to Mainz, from Mainz to Koblenz, from Koblenz to Bonn, from Bonn to Cologne, from Cologne to Brussels, from Brussels to Paris.[37]

On this last stage they crossed 'the plain of Waterloo, where Napoleon was defeated, and saw with great displeasure the monument erected by the English . . . in memory of that victory . . .' In Paris Verdi heard yet another rumour that Jenny Lind was not after all going to sing in his opera. In his present tense and nervous condition, which cannot have been improved by the grotesque itinerary he had just subjected himself to, he was not disposed to shrug this off, and simply refused to cross the Channel until the rumour was authoritatively denied. Muzio was sent on ahead to London to see what was really happening. On 4 June he reported on his mission to Barezzi:

I have been in London since yesterday. I am here alone without the maestro, who is still in Paris and will be coming tomorrow evening. He sent me on ahead, because they told him in Paris that Signora Lind didn't want to sing any new operas. If this had been true, since it stands in the contract that Signora Lind must sing in his operas, he would have protested to the management and not come to London and I should have returned to Paris in ten hours the way I came.

As soon as I got to London I went to Lumley with a letter from Verdi, and he assured me that the rumour was untrue, that Signora Lind couldn't wait to get her part to learn it, and that she was very distressed that Verdi was not yet in London. So I wrote at once to inform the maestro, who is in Boulogne-sur-Mer, and so he will continue his journey tomorrow and be in London at six o'clock in the evening.

. . . What a *chaos* London is! What confusion! Paris is nothing in comparison. People shouting, poor folk weeping, steam engines flying along, men on horseback, in carriages, on foot, and everyone howling like the damned. Dear Signor Antonio, I cannot give you the least idea of it . . .[38]

Opera as a business

Verdi's own first impressions of London come in a letter to Clarina Maffei, postmarked 9 June:

I have been in London just two days. It was a disgusting journey, but I quite enjoyed myself. When I arrived in Strasbourg the mail coach had already left and rather than wait twenty-four hours I went by way of the Rhine: and so it was not too tiring. I have seen some delightful spots, I stopped in Mainz, in Cologne, in Brussels and two days in Paris and now here I am in London. In Paris I went to the Opéra. I have never heard worse singers and more mediocre choruses. Even the orchestra (with the permission of all our *Lions*) is little better than mediocre. I liked what I saw of Paris very much, and liked particularly the free and easy life that one can lead there. Of London I can't say anything because yesterday was Sunday and I didn't see a soul. But I find the smoke and the smell of coal horrible: it is like being forever in a steamship. In a few minutes I shall be going to the theatre to get things sorted out. Emanuele, whom I sent on in advance, found me accommodation so homeopathic that I cannot move. However, it is very clean, like all the houses in London.

Signora Lind has created an indescribable enthusiasm: at the moment they are already selling boxes and seats for tomorrow evening. I don't know when I shall have a chance of hearing her. I am very fit. The journey didn't tire me much, because I took it in easy stages. It is true that I arrived late and the impresario could complain: but if he says one word that doesn't suit me I shall say ten to him, and go straight back to Paris, and he can do what he likes.[39]

From London Muzio provided Barezzi with a steady stream of social gossip and priceless descriptions of the English and their way of life. These letters have been delectably anthologized by Frank Walker, and here we must confine ourselves to what Muzio has to say about the progress of the opera. Despite the fact that in mid-May Verdi had given the impression that *I Masnadieri* was all but finished, it is clear that much remained to be done even a week after their arrival in London:

...Without my saying so, you can imagine that we are working from morning to night. We get up at five in the morning and work until six in the evening (dinner time); then we go to the theatre for a little and return home at eleven, and go to bed so as to be up in good time in the morning. The opera is progressing; two acts are already at the copyist's and perhaps by next Monday it will be entirely finished; then there remains the orchestration. I am of the opinion – mark my words – that after *Ernani* this is the most popular opera that Verdi has written, and the opera which will have the widest circulation.

It has a simplicity, a clarity, a melodiousness so beautiful and graceful that it catches the ear at once, and anyone with a bit of an ear for music can appreciate it at the first hearing . . .[40]

Muzio also conveys his first impressions of Jenny Lind, which we can safely assume were also those of Verdi:

I have heard Lind in *La Figlia del Reggimento*, in *La Sonnambula* and in *Robert le Diable*, and can tell you that she is an artist in the full sense of the word. She is magnificent in all three operas. In *Robert le Diable* she is incomparable. Her voice is slightly harsh at the top, and weak at the bottom, but by hard work she has succeeded in making it flexible enough in the upper register to execute the most formidably difficult passages. Her trill is incomparable; she has an unsurpassable agility, and to show off her virtuosity she is inclined to err in using excessive fioritura, turns and trills, things which pleased in the last century, but not in 1847 . . .[41]

There is more about the progress of the work and about Lind's qualities in Muzio's letter to Barezzi on 29 June:

. . . this humid, heavy air reacts strongly on his nervous system and makes him more lunatic and melancholy than usual; it is now three weeks and more since he started to make a fair copy of the opera, and he still hasn't finished, and he also still has to do the orchestration. Everything is arranged to start the piano rehearsals tomorrow with all the singers . . . I have already been to some of them to give them their parts.

I have been to Signora Lind's more often than to the others, not so much because of the difficulty of the music, but because of the words, as she is not very good at Italian. I found Lind good and kind, well-educated and courteous. She is a consummate and profound musician, she reads absolutely any song at sight . . . She leads a very retired life . . . She tells me that she hates the theatre and the stage; she says she is unhappy and that she will only be happy and start to enjoy herself when she does not need to have anything to do with theatre people, or with the theatre itself. On this point she is very much in agreement with the views of the maestro; he too hates the theatre and cannot wait to retire.[42]

Muzio was learning to know the Jenny Lind so memorably depicted in Lumley's *Reminiscences*:

But amid all the honours they lavished upon her, the shy *prima donna* invariably preferred the intimacy of her choice private circle, and was glad to flee the flattering incense sought to be bestowed upon her, by escaping to the country house of the kind friend who had first welcomed her to London. There she would heartily enjoy a ride, or rural ramble; and anon, seated among wild ferns and shaded by ancient beech-trees, she would study her new parts, the score laid open upon her lap.[43]

Muzio's long letter continues with an account of how Verdi's 'affairs' were flourishing:

Lumley has tried to engage the maestro for next year; but he doesn't want to enter into any contract before having seen the outcome of *I Masnadieri*. The maestro still has an opera to write for Lucca and he would transfer this opera to London next year; in that way he would be able to rest all the winter. This is what the payment would be: Lucca is to pay him 24,000 francs; Lumley will pay him £1000 sterling (25,000 francs or more); which would make fifty thousand francs; whereas if he composes in Italy he would not get more than 24,000. Furthermore he will put in the contract provision for lodgings in the London area for a month, and the carriage . . .

. . . at the Opéra they would like to produce *Macbeth*, and if the maestro wants to prepare a French version, they would grant him author's rights, which could bring him twenty thousand francs; and he could make this money without exerting himself . . .[44]

Muzio also tells us that Verdi was leading 'the most retired life you could imagine; he doesn't go to academies or concerts or dinners'. Nor does he seem to have had much inclination to write letters. Only very few survive from the weeks spent in London, expressing, if with less engaging naivety than Muzio, the amazement the city inspired in him, and explaining how difficult he found it to work. To Giuseppina Appiani, for example, he wrote:

Long live our sun which I used to love so much, but which now I adore, being among these fogs and this smoke which suffocates me and oppresses my spirits! But on the other hand, what a magnificent city! there are things that are enough to turn you to stone . . . but this climate paralyses every beauty. Oh, if there were only the sky of Naples here, I think one wouldn't need to wish for Paradise. I haven't started the rehearsals for my new opera because I haven't got the energy for anything . . .

The theatres are very crowded and the English enjoy the performances . . . And they pay so much money!! Oh, if I could stay here a couple of years, I should like to carry off a sackful of this *blessed* money. But it is no use thinking of such lovely things, because I could not tolerate the climate. I can't wait to go to Paris, not that it has any particular attraction for me, but it is bound to suit me very well because there one can lead the sort of life one likes. And what a pleasure it is to be able to do as one likes!! When I think that I shall be several weeks in Paris without being involved in musical affairs, without hearing people talk about music (because I shall show all publishers and impresarios the door), I swoon with pleasure . . .[45]

Three weeks later he wrote to Clarina Maffei:

You will be amazed to hear that I am still in London and have not yet gone into production! It is the fault of the smoke and fog and this devil of a climate which deprives me of all will to work. Now at last everything or almost everything is finished, and on Thursday 22nd for certain will be the *première*. I have had two orchestral rehearsals and if I were in Italy could give you a cool assessment of the opera, but here I don't understand anything. It's the fault of the climate . . . the fault of the climate! . . . You can imagine that I shall be leaving London very soon and I shall stay a month in Paris if I like it, so in future you can address your letters to Paris *poste restante*. For the rest, I am not at all displeased with the state of my health, but if I can drag myself away from London this time it is unlikely that I shall return, despite the fact that I like the city extraordinarily well.

It is true that they have offered me 40 thousand francs for an opera and that I have not accepted. But don't be amazed, because it is not an excessive sum and if I was to come back I should want much more.[46]

The same day Muzio provided Barezzi with further details:

There have already been two orchestral rehearsals, and the effect produced by the music is immense, *I Masnadieri* is the topic of all talk and all discussion. Signora Lind sings like an angel and all the others too sing with great care. If you could see this old fellow Lablache with his mountain of a belly, you would be amazed; he still has the most beautiful voice that could be imagined. The other day he went to see the Queen, who conveyed her regards to the maestro, and wanted to meet him; but he doesn't want to go. The Queen herself has given instructions that the opera should be produced on the day of the closing of parliament, which is said to be one of the greatest state occasions in England; it is something which happens only every seven years. She will be present at the performance in gala, and all the advertisements have already announced it; with the Queen going to the theatre in gala, Lumley will make 50 thousand francs extra . . .[47]

Apparently Muzio was instrumental in persuading Verdi to conduct his new opera. Exceptionally, this responsibility cannot have formed part of the original contract. 'Everyong is trying to persuade him to conduct the opera himself, but he doesn't want to hear of it. However I am still hopeful, and yesterday I spoke with the Russian ambassador, who will have an official letter written and signed by some lords, and then he won't refuse. At least that is what I am hoping . . .[48]

Muzio's final preview came on 19 July:

This morning I saw Signora Lind again and she told me that she had never heard music more beautiful than that of *I Masnadieri*, and that she had never had a part which suited her better, or was better adapted to her voice. Gardoni, too, who has the most important part, has learnt it well and performs very well. Coletti is very pleased, too, and the maestro has written a magnificent part for him. Lablache is great in this opera, 'greater than his belly' . . . The orchestra and the chorus have rehearsed with the greatest care; everything promises a complete success.

This morning's rehearsal . . . attracted a large number of people, all lords and dukes, who applauded frantically. Tomorrow, Tuesday, there will be a stage rehearsal; Wednesday, at noon, a final dress rehearsal, and Thursday, at eight o'clock in the evening, *The performance of 'I Masnadieri', by command of the Queen.*[49]

The opening night was obviously as brilliant an occasion as had been anticipated:

The opera has created a furore. From the prelude to the last finale there was nothing but applause, evvivas, calls and encores. The maestro himself conducted the orchestra seated on a chair higher than the rest and with a baton in his hand. As soon as he appeared in the orchestra there was applause which lasted for a quarter of an hour. They hadn't yet finished applauding when the Queen arrived with her consort Prince Albert, the Queen Mother and the Duke of Cambridge, uncle of the Queen, the Prince of Wales, the Queen's son, and all the royal family, and a crowd of lords and

dukes which never came to an end. Suffice it to say that the boxes were full
of ladies in *grande toilette* amd the pit so crowded that I don't remember
ever having seen such a throng. The doors were opened at half past four and
the people poured into the theatre with a fury never seen before. It was a
new spectacle for London and Lumley made them pay well for it.

The takings amounted to £6000 and surpassed what they took on the
grand gala night attended by the Queen. The maestro was cheered, called on
to the stage alone and with the singers, flowers were thrown at him, and
nothing was to be heard except *viva Verdi! bietifol.*

. . . The performance was good; the orchestra marvellous: it couldn't be
otherwise when Verdi was conducting. The singers all did well, but they
were very nervous. Signora Lind and Gardoni had never sung in new operas
and this was the first time it had happened to them. Lablache was
marvellous and so was Coletti. The maestro was very satisfied; the management was so satisfied that they have offered him through me a contract for as
many years as he wants at 60,000 francs an opera, and this is the best test of
whether an opera has succeeded or not.

The papers, *The Times*, the *Morning Post*, the *Morning Chronicle* etc. are
all very complimentary, both about the music and the libretto which was
also well liked.[50]

But *I Masnadieri*, like *Alzira*, was one of those Verdi operas whose
star waned rapidly. The excitement had quietened down considerably even by the second night. Muzio's final assessment of the
London audiences is altogether more measured:

Verdi created a decided furore in London, but the English *are matter-of-fact
and thoughtful people* and don't get carried away with enthusiasm like the
Italians, partly because they don't understand too well, and partly because
they say educated people shouldn't make a row. The English go to the
theatre to show off their riches and luxury; when an opera is performed
which is already published they have the score in their hand and follow
with their eyes what the singer does and if, according to their ideas, the
singer does well, they applaud and call for an encore; but they never insist as
our people do . . .[51]

Even this account seems over-enthusiastic, though. Despite the
prolongation of the season to 21 August, only four performances of *I
Masnadieri* were given, two under Verdi's direction, two under that
of Balfe. It looks more like a total failure than a resounding success,
as if the incomparable Chorley had put his finger on it again, when
he wrote:

I Masnadieri . . . must increase Signor Verdi's discredit with everyone who
has an ear. We take it to be the worst opera which has been given in our time
at Her Majesty's theatre . . . the field is left open for an Italian composer . . .[52]

Lumley, too, despite what he admitted to have been the 'brilliant
success' of the first night, was disappointed with the work:

The libretto was even worse constructed than is usually the case with adaptations of foreign dramas to the purposes of Italian opera. To Her Majesty's Theatre the work was singularly ill-suited. The interest which ought to have been centred in Mademoiselle Lind was centred in Gardoni; whilst Lablache, as the imprisoned father, had to do about the only thing he could not do to perfection – having to represent a man nearly starved to death.[53]

Verdi waited until he reached Paris before writing to his friends in Milan. His summing-up of impressions of London makes poignant reading for a loyal subject of the 1970s.

Despite the fact that I found the London climate horrific I liked the city extremely well; it is not a city, it is a world: there is nothing to compare with its grandeur, its wealth, the beauty of its streets, the cleanliness of its houses, and one is stunned and humbled when among so many magnificent things, one examines the Bank and the Docks. Who can stand up to this nation? The surroundings and the countryside near to London are stupendous. I don't much care for English manners, or to be more precise, they don't suit us Italians. How absurd some of the aping of English ways in Italy are!

I Masnadieri, without having created a furore, was a success, and I should have returned to London next year to write another opera if the publisher Lucca would have accepted ten thousand francs to release me from the contract which I have with him. As it is I shan't be able to go back until two years from now. I am sorry about it; but I cannot break my contract with Lucca . . .[54]

Despite the forbidding prospect of being condemned to endure a climate that made him 'more lunatic and melancholy even than usual', the money that was to be made in London obviously did tempt Verdi to take up a long-term contract with Lumley. Indeed it was Lumley, observing the waning fortunes of I Masnadieri, who eventually prevaricated and procrastinated over confirming a contract he had at first been so eager to make. Verdi wrote to him from Paris on 2 August:

I have delayed in replying to the proposal you made me before my departure from London, because when it is a matter of entering into such a long-term contract of such importance, I wanted to reflect calmly before committing myself to a definite decision.

I cannot conceal from you the fact that assuming the musical direction of a whole season is something which doesn't much appeal to me, because it would perhaps be too much of a burden to me, and because I should have to limit myself to writing one opera a year, which might be disadvantageous for me. Nevertheless I could accept the contract which you proposed to me and undertake to compose one opera a year for the three consecutive years 1849, '50, '51 and at the same time conduct all the other operas of the season, extending from the middle of February to the middle of August approximately, if you would pay me an inclusive sum of 90,000, ninety thousand, francs for each season: that is 60 thousand for the new opera and 30 thousand for the direction of all the other operas to be given during the season. Additionally I should require a house in the country and a carriage. – The librettos would have to be written by a distinguished poet at your expense, as we agreed verbally. If you are disposed to grant me this, we can discuss in another letter the way in which the payments are to be made, and the manner in which I would wish to have the orchestra arranged and the spectacles staged.

May I take this opportunity to express my gratitude for the courteous and generous manner in which you treated me during my stay in London: whether or not what you have suggested can be arranged, I hope that you will not disdain my friendship, and will put it to the test in any circumstances where I can be of service to you . . .[55]

This, for Verdi, was unusually effusive. Lumley replied evasively on 7 August:

I am delighted that you have arrived safe and sound, and thank you for your courteous letter which I have just received.

Since your departure from London circumstances have arisen which make it desirable, in your interest and in mine, to defer for the moment the conclusion of our affairs until my approaching visit to Italy, when we can discuss things thoroughly, conveniently and effectively . . .[56]

Jérusalem

It will be recalled that one of the pleasures that Verdi anticipated in Paris was that of not having to become involved in musical affairs, of being able to live 'without hearing people even talk about music (because I shall show all publishers and impresarios the door)'. But he was a man who found it almost impossible to resist a real bargain, and hardly had a week elapsed when Muzio, on the point of setting out on the next stage of the journey home, was announcing to Barezzi a new contract. Verdi was staying on in Paris, because he was

contracted with the Paris Opéra to adapt the music of *I Lombardi* to a new libretto, and to compose additional music. The opera will be produced early in November. They are giving him all an author's rights as if it was a new opera.

The performers will be Signora *Julian, Duprez, Alizard*; and for the dances Signora *Rosati-Galetti*.

The impresarios have put all the resources of the theatre at his disposal. They have already ordered the costumes. The libretto is being shifted to the period of Guascone, but keeps the same character; so that instead of it being the Italians who go on the Crusade it will be the French.

The authors of the libretto are *Scribe, Royer* and *Vaëz*. All the main newspapers have already announced it . . .[57]

In fact the possibility of making a French adaptation of *I Lombardi* had apparently been in Verdi's mind for a couple of years. On 19 November 1845 Muzio had mooted it in a letter to Barezzi: 'I think it is very likely that the Paris Opéra will do *I Lombardi* in French for the Carnival season '46/'47. But the signor maestro will write some additional music, some ballets and other things. This is an opera well-suited to that stage . . .'[58]

Nothing had come of that original, more modest scheme. Now, quite apart from the new music, 'the distribution of the pieces [was] to be quite different from what it is at present'.[59]

With Muzio out of the way, we have lost a precious witness. Verdi himself provides us with little material to illuminate the history of the opera, the reason obviously being that, as was the case with the early Milan operas, everyone was on the spot and could be met with in person to discuss such problems as arose during the course of work. Only the most impressionistic hints of its progress are to be found in letters to his Milanese friends. To Giuseppina Appiani, for example, he confided the amused exasperation he felt at the Parisian fashion of dividing all responsibilities between two people: 'Just imagine spending one's whole day in the middle of two poets, two impresarios and two music publishers (here they always go two by two), trying to engage a prima donna, to arrange a subject for a libretto etc., and say yourself if it is not enough to drive one mad . . .'[60] And from a couple of weeks later we have a letter to Clarina Maffei:

One thing I like about Paris is that in the middle of so much din I seem to be in a desert. No one bothers about me, no one points at me, I see no one except my poets who are two splendid fellows in the full sense of the word . . . Yesterday evening I was at the Opéra: I was very bored, but at the same time amazed by the *mise-en-scène*: it was *La Juive* by Halévy.
I am composing desperately and shall certainly go into production in November . . .[61]

Despite the combined skills of MM. Royer and Vaëz, the libretto with which they presented Verdi proved to have an ineptly managed second act. Verdi explained the problem to Escudier, in a letter which, though undated, can be assumed to be from late August or September, and which is really the only evidence we have that Verdi's dramatic imagination was seriously engaged in the work of adaptation.

I've examined the second act over and over again and find two faults which are absolutely basic. The first is that the pilgrims' chorus will fall quite flat if it follows straight after Roger's aria because it has the same character and it will seem too long; the other fault is that Hélène's aria has no dramatic interest, nothing to set it off and is utterly useless where it stands. For myself, I'm quite convinced that at that moment Hélène must have had a surprise. Something unexpected and pleasurable must have happened to her to make her break out in a cabaletta full of enthusiasm. It seems to me, the only way to set this right is to put Hélène's aria immediately after Roger's and it doesn't matter if that means two arias one after another because one of them is solemn and the other very brilliant so that the musical effect is of one aria in two contrasted movements. Please pass all this on to Royer and Vaëz. As you know, in this opera – no matter whether it's performed well or badly – the pieces which never fail to come off are this aria, the chorus and the trio. If we leave the scheme as it is we run the risk of letting two of them go for nothing.[62]

Escudier proved to be an obliging servant to Verdi throughout the weeks of work on *Jérusalem*, to some extent taking over duties for which Muzio was no longer available. The archives of the Opéra contain a series of short notes, undated and hand-delivered, but obviously stretching over a period of several weeks in September and October, which show the kind of relationship it was:

Do me the favour of taking the final hymn to the copyist's and urge them to get the chorus parts and all the solo parts copied and delivered quickly to the singers, so that we can rehearse tomorrow afternoon.

I am not feeling too well and shan't come out at two o'clock: the band can very well rehearse by itself: besides it is probable that Giraud will be in the theatre and could be so kind as to keep an eye on them.

I hear that Caraffa's band cannot manage it . . . I think that at the moment the best thing would be to go to *Saxe* and ask him if he would undertake to provide the band . . .

Would you be so kind as to take this music to the copyist's as quickly as possible? . . . Tomorrow the opera will be finished, in very good time, so your brother will no longer have grounds for saying (as he did to the directors the other day) that 'if the opera is delayed it will be my fault'. Admittedly, the way they are performing at the moment it is unlikely that I will permit the performance. I hope everything will work out, but I must admit I foresee great difficulties.

M. Adolphe Saxe did come to the rescue with a band, entering into a contract to 'keep at the disposal of MM. Duponchel and Roqueplan additional musicians to the number of twenty to be employed in the new opera by M. Verdi, entitled *Jérusalem*'.[63]

As was customary at the Opéra, no less than two full months were allowed for rehearsals, twice as long as Verdi had required even for *Macbeth*. On 22 September he reported to Giuseppina Appiani that he had begun the rehearsals of my opera, which is *I Lombardi* transformed out of all recognition. Everyone appears to be satisfied and I certainly am. We shall be going into production in November for certain, because I am hurrying things along.

The *mise-en-scène* will be absolutely stupendous, because here no expense is spared; then the new directors are taking exceptional care, not because it is my opera, but because it is the first opera under their direction and they want the public to appreciate that they wish to raise up the Opéra again from its present deplorable condition.[64]

One wonders if it was a surfeit of rehearsal that caused the 'boredom and distaste' with which Verdi speaks of the work in his only surviving letter from the period immediately after the *première*. Written only a week after what should have been the thrill of the first night, this letter to Clarina Maffei, of 3 December, begins:

it is ages since I wrote to you and you will be furious, especially as I have given you no news of my opera: now it is too late to speak about it, and besides I am so weary of having this word 'Jérusalem' in my ears, that I wouldn't like you to share my boredom and distaste.[65]

Verdi goes on to complain that it was now only with great difficulty that he could continue to enjoy 'the life of delicious anonymity that I have led for four months'. Whatever the defects of *Jérusalem*, it had clearly made its composer a celebrated figure in Parisian society.

From the contemporary reviews I quote two paragraphs of Théophile Gautier which confirm that the *mise-en-scène* was indeed stupendous, and show that the newly composed scene for Duprez, which Verdi had promised Muzio would be 'the principal number in the opera',[66] did not fail of its effect:

. . . when we speak of an army of crusaders, do not imagine one of those armies which could be hidden behind a bush and which consists of half a dozen extras.

The army of the Opéra is as numerous, for certain, as the contingent of the most powerful baron of the Middle Ages. There are crossbowmen, archers, pikemen, knights covered in mail from head to foot; real armour, real cuirasses, and above all real horses . . . But to provide an army is not enough, it needs baggage, pack-mules and chariots for the provisions. – Nothing is missing from the retinue. One had even spoken of those fine Homeric chariots drawn by oxen, which are so popular in the Orient, but it was feared that inopportune lowings might be added to the basses at some moment of pathos . . .

. . . This scene [the new scene for Duprez] . . . is certainly the finest in the score. Duprez was admirable in it. Each time the herald of arms, in his monotonous voice, pronounced the formula for the delivery of a piece of the panoply to the executioner: 'Ceci est le heaume d'un traitre! Ceci est l'épée d'un félon! . . .' Duprez, with a cry impossible to describe, replied 'Tu mens! tu mens!' which is the supreme and sublime appeal of innocence revolted by injustice. One would need ten columns to tell of the ideas and sensations evoked by this simple monosyllable, howled out by the great artist. Every time it recurred a shudder of admiration ran through the auditorium: the dull thud of the weight of the executioner's arms as they fell on the helmet, on the cuirass, which rang as they were being crushed, and the sound of the tam-tam, brought to its highest point the terror inspired by this lugubrious scene . . .[67]

Verdi had been a successful and prosperous composer from the time of *Nabucco*. But there is no doubt that that side of his character which, for whatever reason, tended to lust for gold had been indulged in an unprecedented manner in London and Paris. When Ricordi, hearing that a new opera was in the making, sought to buy the Italian rights, Verdi seems to have seen the chance for starting money-making on an Anglo-French scale even in Italy. The letter of 15 October 1847 with which he resumed contact with an old and intimate friend seems almost brutally materialistic:

I won't make preambles or excuses about not having written before because I don't have much time, but will come straight to the point, that is the opera *Jérusalem*, which you ask for and which is to be produced at the Académie Royale probably before 15 November.

I cede the aforementioned score to you for all the musical world except England and France. You will pay me for the printed material *8 thousand francs* in 400 golden napoleons to be paid either in Paris or Milan, whichever I shall advise, in the following manner: 100 golden napoleons on 1 December 1847; 100 on 1 January; 100 on 1 February, and the last 100 on 1 March 1848.

As to the hire charges, you will share them with me for ten years in the following manner: for the first five years you will pay me 500 francs for each hire; for the remaining five years 200 francs for each hire . . .

But Verdi continues in a way which shows that, even when he was most preoccupied with making a lot of money as fast as possible, that keener sense of the dignity of the artist and the inviolability of the work of art which he had acquired while working on *Macbeth* would no longer leave him.

If I can find an Italian poet here I will see to the Italian version myself; if not, I will send you the French score, on condition however that you get *Emanuele Muzio* to do the underlaying of the text.

It remains forbidden to make any additions to or deletions from the score (except for the ballet, which may be omitted) under the penalty of a fine of a thousand francs which I shall require from you every time this score is performed in theatres of the top rank. In theatres of the second rank the clause remains equally in force and you will be obliged to study all possible means of exacting the fine in the case of contravention: however, if you cannot exact it, you will not be obliged to pay it me . . .[68]

That Ricordi protested or at least expressed unease over the terms proposed by Verdi is clear from another letter written from Paris a few weeks later. Verdi remained adamant.

You speak of being hard up? . . . You, Signor Ricordi? Of being hard up to a *maestro di musica?* Let me not hear you talking like that again, because then I should have to choke. As far as a reduction of prices is concerned we will not speak of it: you know that things will go all right as they are, and then you know that I am not in the habit of making claims: as to the payment, you will make them in four equal instalments beginning on 1 December next . . . I am hunting over land and sea for a tolerable poet who knows a bit about music to make the adaptation; it is not an easy matter. If I don't find him we shall have to be patient and you can get it done yourself . . . [69]

Verdi's search for an Italian poet proved fruitless. Some time in December he sent off the score, still untranslated, to Ricordi in Milan, who in turn made Verdi the first payment, actually on the 20th December rather than the 1st of December. On the 21st Verdi acknowledged 'the receipt of a cheque for two thousand francs paid me yesterday by Signor Fould'. He concluded his letter: 'I hope that you will by now have received the score of *Gerusalemme*. Have it translated as well as possible, and see that nothing is left out except the ballet music'.[70]

Verdi had, however, pressed both his bargaining and his idealism too hard. Each in turn had to be compromised in the face of the realities of Italian musical life. By the end of February 1848 Ricordi had persuaded Verdi that the idea of fining heavily anyone who dared to tamper with the score of *Gerusalemme* was simply not practicable. Some time in March Verdi wrote:

What you tell me about *Gerusalemme* in your letter of 22 February is enough to fill me with compassion. I put a fine of 1000 francs on this opera not out of greed for profit, but to put a curb on the insolent licenses taken by *maestri* and singers. How hard our condition is! How can an opera ever stand up to the ignorance and vanity of these people, who under the pretext of adapting it to the exigencies of their respective publics take the liberty of making any alterations they please without ever understanding, not even accidentally, the composer's intentions. Well then, if you like, I will release you from this 1000-francs fine which you have in the contract for *Gerusalemme*, but I beg you to make your contracts with the impresarios in such a way that the operas are harmed as little as possible . . .[71]

Within a couple of years the need to change the financial arrangements for the opera had also become abundantly clear. On 26 January 1850 Ricordi wrote Verdi a vastly long and infinitely patient letter, explaining the situation. I cite just a few of its paragraphs:

Opera as a business

How sorry I am to have to bore you with a long letter, but what can you expect? If you were here, an hour or two of conversation would be enough, but with you far away many pages are needed . . .

Listen, my dear friend, I have no secrets from you, nor do I from Muzio who is your other self, and I have shown to Muzio all my letters, the replies received, and my registers, as I would have done with you, if you were here, to persuade you that this alteration is necessary in the interests of both of us. Your friend should have convinced himself that no hires of *Gerusalemme* are being made because, as the hire charges include a quota in your favour of 500 francs together with the part owed to me who have to bear the expenses, the total demand comes always to at least 1000 francs. All the impresarios run away from this, especially on the pretext that, after all, *Gerusalemme* contains all the music of *I Lombardi*, except for a few new pieces and some changes of orchestration, and when *I Lombardi* was a new piece they never paid heavy hire charges for it. The proof of all this is in the contracts with Rome, Florence and other places, which have come to nothing. And so *Gerusalemme* remains still *unperformed in Italy*, and abroad, except for France . . .

. . . I mention these circumstances to show you that . . . by charging a standard fixed sum it becomes impossible either to sell or to hire the two aforementioned operas, with the result that . . . 1. You receive nothing. 2. And I receive nothing either on sales or on hire charges. Besides that, I suffer the very grave damage, which I have to bear alone, of the much smaller use of my editions, which in general are only in request in the places where your operas are appreciated, that is to say enjoyed, applauded and consequently purchased as printed scores . . .

The burden of predetermined quotas to be paid to you on every hire or sale leads inevitably to prices having to be constantly maintained at a certain level, a level that small theatres with limited means cannot meet. And yet they have the right not to be excluded by reason of their lack of money from sharing the most acclaimed operas of the day such as yours . . . I would add that the resultant high prices also favour piracy, from which the small theatres get their scores on very low terms . . .

The problem is then . . . to reduce the payment owing to you on a proportional basis dependent upon the sums we really can get from sales and hires, sums more equitable, and not predetermined and unalterable so that, as I have shown, they restrict and in most cases prevent contracts altogether. In sum I would propose that we arrange between ourselves a system like that of the authors' rights in France which is based on the proportional sharing of *receipts*.

I therefore suggest that, instead of predetermined amounts, we fix your portion of the payment up to the end of the agreed ten years at *30 per cent* of the receipts for every hire which I make of the two aforementioned scores [*Jérusalem* and *La Battaglia di Legnano*] and at *40 per cent* of the receipts for every sale of the same, the same to apply for all countries . . .

Ricordi ends by warning Verdi, in the most polite way imaginable, that he will be more careful about adapted French operas in future:

The same can be said of any other opera that you may compose in future, and for example, also for the opera which Muzio tells me you may perhaps be writing for Paris. With the condition, however, that in the case of non-Italian operas, you will have to arrange and adapt them for the Italian theatre on an original Italian libretto, which you will find reasonable enough and in the interests of both of us; for experience shows that, quite regardless of their intrinsic merit, French operas, or French operas simply translated and retaining their French characteristics, have always had little luck in Italy and have made very little money . . .[72]

Verdi replied on 31 January:

I cast no doubt on what you tell me in your letter of 26th inst. I know perfectly well that times are critical: that you have enormous expenses to support, that you have lawyers all over the place (though not only for my scores), but you know too that I have ten years in front of me and in this time theatrical conditions can improve . . . But I don't want to weary you with thousands and thousands of arguments which I might produce to my own advantage, and I am only surprised that, although Emanuele had written to me that you had agreed on 50 per cent, you now lower my share to 30. It is too much! ! Nevertheless I don't wish to be stubborn and I will accept your proposals . . . henceforth you will keep the contracts for every hire and sale which you make, to be inspected by me or by a person I shall delegate, twice a year. You will pay the money owed me at the end of June and the end of December. This arrangement will begin from today, and my rights will last for ten years beginning on the day on which these operas have their first performance.[73]

At the end of the year the Italian *prémiere* of *Gerusalemme* realized all the fears that had caused Verdi to impose the original conditions. He wrote to Ricordi:

I hear with displeasure that they want to give *Stiffelio* at La Scala, because normally the operas that are not composed expressly for this theatre are carelessly done. *Gerusalemme* provides another proof. Why was the Duettino at the start cut? Why was the Ave Maria omitted? (Quite apart from the washed-our performance on the part of the chorus and orchestra.) When scores don't suit it is better not to perform them . . .[74]

Il Corsaro

The origins of this least-esteemed of Verdi's operas lie back in 1843–4, the composer's Byronic period, which had produced *I Due Foscari* and plans for a *Bride of Abydos* and a *Cain*. *Il Corsaro* was indeed, as far as the evidence shows, one of the very first dramatic themes chosen by Verdi himself when he had outgrown the habit of accepting ready-written librettos from established poets. Early in the negotiations with Venice over the opera which was eventually to become *Ernani*, he had written to Mocenigo: 'I shall let the Presidency know as quickly as possible the subject of the opera, which will depend upon the cast I have. For example, if I had an artist of the calibre of Ronconi, I should choose either *King Lear* or *The Corsair*.[75]

As an artist of the calibre of Ronconi was not forthcoming, nothing came of *The Corsair* for the time being. But the subject was by no means forgotten, and when the London contract was arranged in the autumn of 1845, Verdi returned to it with more positive results. As we have seen in the early part of this chapter, *Il Corsaro* rapidly became the favoured subject for Verdi's London opera, and during the months spent in Venice in the winter of 1845–6 he and Piave completed the greater part of the work on the libretto. But for the breakdown of Verdi's health in the spring of 1846 there can be little doubt that *Il Corsaro* would have been the opera with which he introduced himself to London.

The most significant outcome of the period of rest and reflection that followed was *Macbeth*, a work in which Verdi decisively and deliberately moves away from the habits of his early years. But not everything at this critical stage of Verdi's career is so clear-cut as this. Interests, predilections, plans from pre-*Attila* days were not simply put out of mind. The commitment to write a work for London still stood; the interest in *Il Corsaro* had if anything intensified during the months in Venice and could not simply be suppressed.

During the early months of Verdi's convalescence Piave continued to work on the libretto, completing it presumably in the early summer. And although none of Verdi's criticisms of it has been preserved, there is no reason to doubt that the talents of both men were fully engaged in the work. When in August Piave tried to persuade Verdi to let him use the libretto for a commission he had received from some other composer, Verdi expressed his abiding enthusiasm for the subject in vigorous terms:

What? Are you quite mad or just on the way! I make over *Il Corsaro* to you? This *Corsaro* which I have cherished so, which so much occupies my thoughts, and which you have versified yourself with more than your usual care? And you don't even say for where or for whom? It is true that it had been fixed for London, but although the London affair has come to nothing I have been writing this *Corsaro*, and have sketched out some of the bits that I found most attractive, the duet in the prison and the final trio . . . And you want me to make it over to you? . . . Go on, go to hospital and get your brain looked at . . .[76]

It was only after Verdi had been immersing himself for some weeks in *Die Räuber* and *Macbeth* that the Byronic magic began to fade, and the 'cherished' subject so carefully versified by Piave to appear 'cold and theatrically ineffective'.*

Full details of the switching of Verdi's thoughts from *Il Corsaro* to *I Masnadieri* have been given earlier in this chapter and need not be repeated here. We may resume the story of *Il Corsaro* by returning to the already-quoted letter to Emilia Morosini, written from Paris on 30 July 1847:

> . . . *I Masnadieri*, without having created a furore, was a success and I should have returned to London next year to write another opera, if the publisher Lucca would have accepted ten thousand francs to release me from the contract which I have with him. As it is I shan't be able to return until two years from now. I am sorry about it, but I cannot break my contract with Lucca.[77]

Lucca's refusal to release Verdi from his contract was the issue which was to lead to the total breakdown of the already strained relationship between the two men. Nevertheless, Verdi initially accepted the situation with a good grace, addressing himself to the fulfilment of his contract with courtesy, even with eagerness:

> I believe I owe you a reminder that, according to the terms of the contract between us made by letter on 16 October 1845, I shall compose the opera for one of the principal Italian theatres during the Carnival season 1848.
> So far I have in mind one of the following subjects: *Il Corsaro* or *L'Avola* (a fantasic German Drama) or *Medea*, making use of Romani's old libretto. If you have anything better to propose to me, feel at liberty to do so, as long as it is within the current month of August . . .[78]

It is noteworthy that *Il Corsaro*, though it had temporarily been ousted from its place in Verdi's affections, was still at the top of his list of operatic projects. All other things being equal it seems likely that Verdi would have gone to work on it now with a will, extracting from Piave those alterations necessary to make the libretto more passionate and effective, and making of it an opera worthy of its place in the succession from *Macbeth* to *Luisa Miller*. But other commissions continued to arrive: one, to adapt *I Lombardi* for the Paris Opéra, which in view of that theatre's status could not but seem more important than the contract for the as yet indestinate *Corsaro*, others which despite their attractiveness Verdi was unable to accept because of this contract. *Il Corsaro* was probably already beginning to lose its pristine allure, when Lucca blundered again, and manifested again his deficient sense of timing, tact and taste. He

---

* Cf. the letter to Lumley of 4 December 1846, above, pp. 195–6.

sent Verdi, some time in September, a libretto which he hoped would be set instead of *Il Corsaro*, and persuaded an old Milanese friend of Verdi's, Giuseppina Appiani, to write an accompanying letter. Verdi's reply is the first in which all pretence at politeness with respect to Lucca is abandoned:

I have received your very dear letter accompanying Signor Giacchetti's work. I don't know whether I shall write an opera for Italy this Carnival season, because my contract with Lucca does not absolutely oblige me to do so. In any case I shall never compose an opera of much importance for this most odious and indelicate gentleman Lucca, and I am astounded that he should have the courage to urge Signor Giacchetti to send me a subject like this *Giuditta*. Signor Lucca is always up to something: last Sunday he sent me a draft for a thousand francs! . . . What does he think he is doing? . . . Does he want to buy me? . . . The imbecile!!

Nevertheless thank Signor Giacchetti, but tell him that I cannot undertake to set his *Giuditta*.[79]

Nor did the autumnal months bring any mellowing of Verdi's sentiments. To Clarina Maffei on 3 December he remarked: 'I shall stay here for some time yet to put some matters in order, and also to be far away from Signor Lucca, from this most tiresome and ungrateful man, who has deprived me of one contract worth *sixty thousand* francs and of another which would have made my fortune, without Signor Lucca suffering any disadvantage . . .'[80]

How much of *Il Corsaro* had been composed before the winter of 1847–8 seems impossible to establish. It is surely improbable, though, that Verdi had not, after almost two years of intermittent occupation with the work, a profusion of musical ideas on which to draw when he sat down to work at it steadily. *Jérusalem* had its Parisian *première* on 26 November 1847, and probably the greater part of *Il Corsaro* was composed between then and the following February. Nor despite his expressed intention of 'writing nothing of importance' for Lucca, can one hope to find any real evidence that he composed with distaste or lack of conscientiousness. Whatever his feelings about Lucca, when it came to music, he composed in the manner demanded by the confrontation of a dramatic subject and his own genius. There is certainly no suggestion that *Il Corsaro* was a uniquely wearisome project in the letter to Luigi Toccagni written on 24 January 1848 when the opera must have been nearing completion: 'I enjoy good health; I write a lot; my affairs go well; everything goes well except my head, which I always hope will change, and which never does change.'[81] Nor in that to Luccardi on 17th February: 'I have written an opera for the publisher Lucca of Milan, and I was counting on taking it to Italy myself, but I decided to send it because

I didn't feel fit to undertake the long and tiring journey at this time of year.'[82]

Apparently Verdi's decision not to go to Italy to deliver *Il Corsaro* came as a surprise to those closest to him. From Milan on 17 February, Muzio wrote to Barezzi;

All my hopes and yours too of seeing the maestro are disappointed. This morning, instead of Verdi, I find a letter of his, dated the 12th, and explaining that the day before he was to set out he caught a feverish chill, and that he didn't want to travel for fear of getting worse . . . Tomorrow I am expecting another letter and the libretto of the opera, together with his instructions for the musical interpretation, and (if Lucca pays me well) I shall go to produce it . . .[83]

Verdi's letter reads:

I authorize you to collect from Signor Francesco Lucca, music publisher in Milan, the sum of 1200 golden Napoleons of twenty francs, owed to me for a score expressly composed by me and already posted to you from Paris on 12th inst. When the payment has been made, deliver the said score together with its libretto to Signor Lucca, and additionally a certificate in which I recognize Sig. Francesco Lucca the sole proprietor of the said opera.[84]

Reading the certificate enclosed for Lucca one again finds oneself wondering how much *Il Corsaro* did mean to Verdi. Did he ever dispose of another opera quite so recklessly as this? Having described it as an opera 'which I have composed expressly to satisfy the obligation I had assumed in the contract dated 16 October 1845', he continues: 'I repeat that Signor Lucca can make whatever use he pleases of the poetry and the music of *Il Corsaro* both in Italy and in all other countries, whether it be to publish this opera in all possible reductions for any instrument whatever, or whether to hire it to all theatres.'[85]

From this point, one is obliged to admit, Verdi showed absolutely no further interest in *Il Corsaro*. In the event neither he nor Muzio supervised the preparation of the opera. Verdi remained in Paris; and Muzio, as a result of the political turmoil in the latter part of 1848, had to take flight to Switzerland. The Trieste *première* enjoyed the benefit of no assistance, or advice from, or any kind of direct association with the composer whatever.

Concerning the *première*, we know only the cast, and what the local press tells us about the reception of the work. *Il Corsaro* was a failure bordering on a fiasco, and was withdrawn after three performances. Verdi seems to have offered no comment, no 'tempo deciderà': indeed only once thereafter does he seem to have mentioned the opera at all and that was to concur with the Trieste verdict. On 6 July 1854, when the opera was being revived in Naples, he remarked in the course of a letter to De Sanctis: 'I hear that *Il Corsaro* is being given at the San Carlo! It is not a happy inspiration: especially for the San Carlo.'[86]

10

Collaboration with Cammarano

La Battaglia di Legnano

Of all Verdi's contracts the most inexplicable is surely that which he announced to Antonio Barezzi in June 1845: 'You know that in '47 I have to write two operas, for Naples and for the publisher Lucca.'[1] That Verdi should choose to enter into another engagement with Naples in the midst of all the haggling over whether or not he was fit to go and stage *Alzira*, and before the success of that work was assured, is singular indeed. Yet, in the event, out of this contract came not one but two operas, *La Battaglia di Legnano* and *Luisa Miller*.

It would be wearisome to pursue the vicissitudes of this contract in full detail – they occupy the larger part of pp. 23–40 of the *Copialettere* – but some description of them must be given to counter the misleading impression given by Budden that Verdi, after having entered into the contract in June 1845, 'spent the next three years trying to withdraw from it on one pretext or another'.[2]

From a letter which Verdi wrote to Flauto on 31 August 1846 we learn that the original intention was that the opera should be written for June 1847.[3] It was Flauto himself who proposed changing this plan, suggesting a number of alternatives which were to be the source of much of the confusion of the next few years. He wrote to Verdi:

Having had no news of you for some time, I cordially enquire with my present letter to know the state of your health. At the same time I judge that it will not be superfluous to reveal to you that the management which I administer has been prolonged up to and including Passion Sunday 1852, under the obligation of opening the San Carlo theatre for the Autumn and Carnival seasons only.

If therefore you wish yourself to put on the opera which you are to write next year, it will be necessary for you to determine to come here in the autumn. If on the other hand you would like to leave to me the responsibility for mounting it, you could send me the score. Signora Barbieri-Nini is the prima donna, Fraschini the tenor, and Balzar the bass. But if, after all that, you would prefer to postpone the production of your opera, giving it not next year but rather in the autumn of 1848, I would be agreeable to that if that would be in your interests . . .[4]

Of the alternatives that Flauto suggested, Verdi accepted the second, that of sending a complete score in the autumn of 1847 and leaving Flauto the responsibility for staging it.[5] Flauto however soon changed his mind, deciding that the presence of Verdi in Naples would be essential after all. But Verdi in turn, because of his slowly forming plans for the conquest of Paris and London, now found this impossible. He remained accommodating, however, writing to Flauto on 21 September:

. . . In the autumns of 1847 and 1848 I shall be abroad and if I had to come to Naples (which I should have to do in great haste) it would involve rushing about in a way which my health could not possibly stand. The best arrangement seems to me to be for you to accept the score without my coming to Naples, and instead of paying me 3000 ducats to pay me 2500 on the delivery of the said score to Naples.

Send me by return of post a small contract from the management, undertaking additionally to send me Cammarano's libretto four months before the production, choosing either the autumn of 1847 or that of 1848, whatever suits you better . . .[6]

It seems likely that Flauto's change of mind and his dithering about in the next few months were partly due to pressure from Ricordi. At the time the rival publishing house of Lucca appeared to be taking an ever fuller share in the publication of Verdi's music, and Ricordi had an understandable commercial interest in seeing an opera that he was to publish properly launched by Verdi himself; or, if Verdi was not going to be present, he required his share of the financial compensation. Unknown to Verdi, however, Ricordi's contract with Flauto expired on Passion Sunday 1848; and so the composer was, one imagines, an innocent party to the stroke with which Flauto, by proposing that the opera be postponed until the autumn of 1848, effectively cut off Ricordi from any further say in the matter. It was when Ricordi protested to Verdi about this in April 1847 that we come to the point where the history of *La Battaglia di Legnano* can really be said to begin.

In two letters of 20 May and 24 June, Verdi offered to compensate Ricordi for his losing the right to publish the Naples opera by composing a new opera specifically for him 'to be performed by a first-class company in one of the leading theatres of Italy (with the exception of La Scala)'.[7] The contract is of particular interest in that it is the first in which Verdi imposed those conditions which we have already met with in the previous chapter for fining theatres which tamper with an opera. But the contract with Ricordi was, Verdi made quite clear, only to be entered into the event of his being released from the Naples contract.

Really there was no reason to suppose that Verdi would be so released. On 25 December Flauto wrote to him, suggesting a subject, enclosing some notes from Cammarano, and emphasizing his continuing zeal in the Verdian cause.

It is true that in the artistic and literary world I am a person of no importance,* but I am second to none among those who esteem Verdi. I have always regarded you as the greatest of the *maestri* of the *true Italian* school . . . Pray send me the librettos of *I Masnadieri* and of *Gerusalemme* because, as I have gone to much trouble to put on performances of *Ernani* and *Attila*, I shall put on the others, less in the interest of your self-esteem than to calm the baffled ears of my fellow-citizens.

Meanwhile I must talk about the new opera which you are to compose. Read the enclosed notes and you will see what Cammarano proposes. I had suggested doing *Cora*. But Cammarano declares himself in favour of the subject I hereby enclose: he says that *Cora* has a happy ending and that what the public wants are catastrophes, people dead, dying and weeping, not people who are happy. That may be so, but I declare that it is better to be happy than to weep, a truth to which my poor nerves can testify. But in the end you must decide whether to work Cammarano's subject or that which I prefer.

Cora or *La Vergine del Sole* you will remember. It is spectacular and original because it departs from the usual style of daggers, poisons, and old Italian costumes . . .[8]

But the early months of 1848 were no time to be working on such escapist exotics as Flauto proposed. The political developments of that period have been described in an earlier chapter. Particularly important among them for our present purposes was the granting of a constitution to the Kingdom of Naples in February. Verdi's view of the problems normally posed by Neapolitan censorship is shown in a remark made to Count Arrivabene that it was 'too strict to permit interesting subjects'.[9] Now he had every reason to hope that it might be possible to be bolder, as Muzio explained to Barezzi: 'For the Naples opera he will take the subject *Cola di Rienzi*; now the Neapolitan constitution is expected he can compose absolutely any subject.'[10] Cammarano was not however a man to be pushed into working a subject he could not see a way of doing effectively. Eventually, with the time running out for the dispatch of the libretto to Verdi, he wrote to say that he had spent much time on *Cola di Rienzi*, 'but I fear in vain', and to propose some alternatives: the

* 'I am like the letter H' – that is, the existence of the letter H is barely recognized in Italian.

Collaboration with Cammarano

Congiura di Fieschi, or the *Vespro Siciliano*, or *Virginia*, or best of all *La Battaglia di Legnano*:

> if there burns in you as in me the desire to evoke the most glorious episode of Italian history, that of the Lombard League . . . by heavens, a subject of that kind must stir every man with an Italian soul in his bosom . . . Farewell, illustrious maestro, wave these pages to the breezes, they contain my kisses for undefeated and heroic Milan.[11]

Though no letters on this matter survive, Verdi obviously warmed to Cammarano's suggestion and urged him to get to work. But at this crucial point all on the Naples front fell silent. According to the terms of the contract, Verdi was to receive the libretto four months before he was due to dispatch the completed score to Naples, that is to say at the end of April 1848. But April and May passed; Verdi received neither a libretto nor any kind of communication from Naples and was beginning to imagine that the turbulent political situation had caused Flauto to abandon his plans for the autumn season. Technically speaking he was now no longer bound by his Naples contract, and might well have taken the opportunity to confirm the contract hypothetically drawn up with Ricordi a year before. But in fact Verdi did not leap at the first opportunity to escape from his Naples contract. On 31 May he wrote to Cammarano:

> I have left for Paris and have stopped for half an hour in Como to write to you. I was hoping for a letter from you containing some poetry for the new drama; but perhaps the grave events in your area have distracted you, perhaps even doubts about producing the opera in Naples. If that is the case, I beg and beseech you to continue your work and to finish it as quickly as possible, because even if they will not or cannot perform it in Naples, I will keep the drama for my own use and Ricordi is obliged to pay you what you think reasonable and just. So carry on your work with as much speed as possible and, as soon as you can, send the prose synopsis and the first movements to me in Paris.[12]

It was not until the end of August that Verdi heard anything from the Naples management. By this time he had presumably confirmed the contract with Ricordi, and felt perfectly entitled, as indeed he was, to decline to have anything further to do with Naples. He wrote to Sig. Guillaume, a colleague of Flauto's.

> After an absence of about a month I have returned to Paris and found . . . your letter of 29th ult. This will explain and excuse my silence.
>
> Political developments have been rapid and violent and have done great damage and caused disarray also in theatrical affairs. I imagined that you were in some such critical situation when I saw the whole of April and the whole of May pass, not only without your sending me the libretto, according to the terms of our contract, but without your so much as writing me a line.

I said to myself: only the sheer impossibility of doing so would have prevented the Naples management from fulfilling its obligations. In these difficult times one must be resigned and I do not want to aggravate the difficulties of the management by writing and complaining. So I decided to accept new contracts and wrote to Cammarano at the end of May asking him to write the libretto for me in any case. So I regard your letter as a courtesy, an effort not to let your contractual obligations go completely by default. For this courtesy and effort I thank you, and I reply declaring you released from each and every obligation you assumed toward me, and I am ready to return your signature to you as soon as you return mine. However, since I did not receive the libretto at the proper time and did not make any protest, the contract was automatically null and void . . .[13]

But though Verdi was now determined that *La Battaglia di Legnano* should be written for Ricordi, he could make little progress on the composition of the opera, for the simple reason that Cammarano was not sending him the verses. He may have received one or two instalments during the summer months, but by mid-September he had become so exasperated with the delays that he wrote to the librettist to express his 'surprise and mortification at not receiving either letters or any further verses so that I can continue with the opera'.[14] The impossibility of getting on with the composition of *La Battaglia di Legnano* was the more distressing because of the eagerness which Verdi felt to make some artistic contribution to the cause of the Italian revolutions of this year. In July, he was even moved to write to Piave to suggest starting work on another opera on a patriotic theme. Piave could be got to work at whatever pace Verdi chose. The letter may be quoted in full as it provides a good example of that intertwining of artistic and political concerns that was so typical of Verdi at this period.

I don't know whether you know that I have been in Paris for more than a month, and I don't know how long I shall be staying in this chaos. Have you heard of this latest revolution? What horrors, my dear Piave! God grant this may be the end of it! And Italy? Poor country!!! I read and re-read the papers always hoping for some good news, but . . . And why do you never write? It seems to me that these are just the times when friends should remember one another.

In the midst of these world-wide convulsions I have neither the head nor the will to occupy myself with my own affairs (it seems really ridiculous to occupy myself with . . . music), but I have to think about it and think about it seriously. So tell me, if I asked you to write a libretto for me, would you do it?

The subject would have to be Italian and free, and if you can't find anything better, I suggest *Ferruccio*, a colossal character, one of the greatest martyrs of Italian freedom; Guerrazzi's *Assedio di Firenze* could provide you with some grand scenes, but I would like you to stick to history. It seems to me that the principal characters could be: Ferruccio, Lodovico Martello, Maria Benintendi, Bandini Giovanni.

These would have to be the principal roles, but you could add as many secondary roles as you liked to make a lofty and impressive theme. You could add the traitor Malatesta (in fact he would be essential), Dante da Castiglione etc. I should want the priors to appear on stage, or the Florentine Senate, and I should like Clement VII to be given a drubbing, without him appearing however. What do you think? If you find this a good subject, make a synopsis and send me it. But remember that I like a really comprehensive synopsis, because I need to make my own observations; not because I think I am capable of criticizing such work, but because it is impossible for me to compose good music if I haven't understood the drama throroughly and am not convinced by it. Be careful to avoid monotony. In subjects that are naturally sad one ends up if one is not very careful with a funeral, as for example I Due Foscari, which has too uniform an atmosphere and colour from beginning to end.

Farewell, farewell! Let's hope for happier times. But I am terrified when I glance first at France and then at Italy ... Then Russia is advancing towards Constantinople. If we let the Russians take possession of Constantinople we shall all become cossacks in a few years ... Christ!![15]

In supposing his Naples contract dissolved, Verdi had reckoned without the unscrupulous resourcefulness of Signor Flauto. That preposterous gentleman had popped up again at the end of August. Blithely disregarding the fact that he had failed to abide by the terms of the contract, he now informed Verdi of what modifications in the arrangements he expected for the future:

I am busy reorganizing the theatre and see that it will be impossible to give your opera this year. You did not know the company and I am convinced that you would not have composed. I shall be talking to Cammarano at once to make the necessary arrangements, but must inform you that the government here require that Verdi should come in person ...

So let me know what your ideas are and be assured that everything is quite different here. My new colleagues or, to be more precise, the new management is of a quite different sort from the old ...[16]

Verdi's 'ideas' were quite clear: namely that

after such a prolonged silence, after such a total failure to fulfil the terms of the contract, I was no longer under any obligation to keep myself at the disposal of the management. I accepted new contracts and consider that I behaved delicately in not demanding the fulfilment of the contract as I was entitled to ...[17]

But in the meantime Flauto had been putting pressure on Cammarano – presumably on the grounds that he had not sent Verdi a completed libretto when he should have done – and made it clear to him that if he did not help persuade Verdi to take up his Naples contract again the consequences would be very unpleasant. Quite how unpleasant Cammarano did not at first explain; he simply seems to have written to Verdi, claiming that the original contract still stood, and suggesting that instead of *La Battaglia di Legnano*, which was now Ricordi's, they should start thinking about other possible subjects without delay. Verdi replied on 18 September:

I cannot believe that your letter of the 9th was written seriously! What! I am 'still under an obligation to compose and deliver the music four months after receiving the libretto'? So, if the Naples management takes the fancy to give my opera in a year's time, or two, or three, or ten, I am still obliged to be the management's most humble and submissive servant. And I should have to abandon every other project until such time as the management deign to send me a libretto? Oh, admit it yourself, you are not serious! Do you know what the first article of my contract says? 'The music is to be performed in October 1848; Signor Verdi will deliver the complete score by the end of August, having received the complete libretto four months previously.' – And then you speak of litigation . . . of going to law? . . . So be it: I cannot take fright at these threats.

In view of my friendship for you I am sincerely sorry that you should have to suffer, and I assure you that so far as it is in my power, I will do my best to get you out of this mess. On the other hand though, I am in a worse mess than you are. – You know that I have disposed of this opera on the grounds of its not being given at the proper time in Naples. – I have taken on other engagements here at the Opéra which it is impossible to defer for an hour. If you hadn't left me with nothing to do for two months by not sending me a word of poetry I should have finished this opera by now. Finding myself now in a position where it is virtually impossible to fulfil this obligation, I find it the more difficult to accept the proposal you make. For all that, I shall do all I can to arrange things amicably, but it is essential that you should send me the next lot of poetry, without delay . . .[18]

By this time it was clear that *La Battaglia di Legnano* could not in any case be ready for the Autumn season, and in writing to Ricordi to defer the date for the opera to the Carnival season, Verdi did raise the possibility of dissolving the contract altogether, presumably so that *La Battaglia di Legnano* could go to Naples after all.[19] Ricordi was understandably not interested in this, so Verdi found himself in a real dilemma when a day or two later he received another letter from a by now quite desperate Cammarano. The librettist had been threatened by the Naples management with claims for damages, and with imprisonment in the event of his being unable to pay. Cammarano besought Verdi to 'stretch out a hand to an artist, to the father of a family . . . With a heart full of tears and on my knees, as if before the Giver of all good things, I and my children wait for this grace.'[20]

On 24 September Verdi replied in two separate letters. The first reads:

The Naples management is trying to obtain by illegitimate and inhumane means the things which it ought to achieve only by carrying out the responsibilities it has contracted.

You, an honest man, father of a family, a distinguished artist, would be the victim of all these ignoble intrigues.

I, by virtue of my contract, could treat the threats of the management with contempt and leave it at that; but for your sake, *for your sake alone*, I will write the opera for Naples next near: it will rob me of two hours of peace every day, and of my health.

I cannot at present be precise about the period in which I shall give the Naples opera (that will depend on the way in which I can defer or dissolve other engagements), but you can assure the said management that it will be some time next year, as they themselves requested, on condition that you have nothing to suffer, because it is for you alone that I am making this sacrifice. If that condition is not observed, this letter is not binding.

I will close this letter by saying that from a man with Signor Flauto's intelligence and his understanding of business, and I would add from the bad way he has behaved previously, I would have expected a different sort of procedure.

Farewell, my dear Cammarano, send me some more poetry as quickly as possible.[21]

The second:

In case you should have come to some agreement with the management in the meantime, I beseech you, in the name of friendship, not to make use of my letter, because it will be extremely difficult for me to find the time to do this opera.

If you cannot do without it and I am obliged to compose, at least bear in mind that I need a short drama of great interest, with plenty of action, and a great deal of passion, if I am to succeed in composing it easily. I beg you meanwhile to continue to send me the drama already started, and tell me: in case the censor should not permit it, do you think it would be possible, changing the title and the locality etc., to keep all or virtually all the verses? At the moment we must press on and fix it like that.

Allow me to beg of you one favour in the last act: at the start, before the church of Sant'Ambrogio I should like to combine together two or three different cantilenas: I would like, for example, the *priests* inside, and the people outside, to have a metre to themselves, and Lida a cantabile in a different metre: leave me the problem of combining them. You could also (if you think it a good idea) put in some Latin verses for the priests ... do what you think best, but take care that this part must be effective.[22]

With it now being agreed that Verdi should write another opera for Naples in the following year, there is no need to follow the negotiations further: they belong to the history of *Luisa Miller* and will be discussed in the next section. What we must examine now is the relationship between Verdi and Cammarano, who, having made his peace with Flauto and with mind at rest, could put his back into the completion of the libretto for *La Battaglia di Legnano*.

What we know of the history of *Alzira* suggests that at that time

Verdi's respect for 'experience' had made him excessively deferential towards his collaborator. There was no danger of that by 1848. Albeit in a very different tone from that he used to Piave, Verdi was now requiring the librettist to provide exactly the kind of libretto he felt he needed. On the other hand Cammarano was no mere hack, submissively manufacturing verses for the composer. He had his own ideas about how scenes needed to be composed to be really effective, and felt it to be one of his responsibilities as a dramatist to suggest these ideas to Verdi. It is an approach to the librettists's task that in its modest way resembles that of the great Metastasio himself.

On 9 October Cammarano sent Verdi Act III of the libretto, probably the first section to be completed since his rescue from the threat of a debtor's prison.

I am convinced that when the curtain goes up, you will introduce the chorus with a grave ritornello, this being really required by virtue of the solemnity of the place and the occasion. As far as Rolando's aria is concerned, the section between the cantabile and the cabaletta could perhaps appear rather long, but if one considers the intensification of the drama that arises from this, that will not be a defect, especially if the letter is not read in prose, nor against a violin tremolo, but set with musical phrases denoting the tempest by which Rolando's soul is agitated ...

In the section of poetry with which the [third] act ends you will see at a glance that the real effect is to be hoped for in the line 'Un infame un vile egli è', and especially on the 'No' which follows. It would be a good thing to repeat it in the excess of his wild desperation, and to say the whole phrase twice, for example:

ARRIGO:	Teme il ferro dei nemici,
	Un infame, un vile egli è!
	No ... no ... no ...
LIDA:	Eterno Iddio! ...
ARRIGO:	O furor! ...
LIDA:	Piu non reggo! ...
ARRIGO:	Ov'è Arrigo (*sclameranno*)
	Un infame, un vile egli è! ...
	No ... no ... no ...

Forgive me if in my zeal I have gone into these particulars, and take as much notice of them as you think. In the fourth act I shall do all the things you suggest: as far as the three cantilenas are concerned, it is a curious thing to know that I had been thinking in exactly the same way. I think that if we avoid insults to the enemies of Italy, there should not be any obstacle to the performance of this drama ...[23]

A similar profusion of suggestions accompanied Act IV, which was dispatched from Naples on 29 October:

Here is the last act. In my opinion the off-stage chorus should be in Latin verse: but we can save ourselves that in the libretto, and I think in No. XIII of the Psalms of David there are some analogous verses, but I don't have a Latin version at hand just now. The four lines of recitative between Lida and Iginia – as you see, it is essential that they should be clearly heard – are spoken rapidly *parlato*, over the ritornello which precedes the off-stage chorus, and which I imagine will be on the organ, in such a way that the musical phrase is not in any way protracted. I would say that they should be regarded as virtually non-existent as far as the harmonic form is concerned.

That part of the chorus which has sung off-stage will come on stage with the second consul, so as to have all voices at the lines 'Dall'Alpi a Cariddi' etc., and those few who have to intone the Te Deum will enter the cathedral after the verses indicated I would urge however that everything should go very rapidly from the first shout of victory right up to the explosion of popular rejoicing, that this shout be repeated, and come nearer (it is sung by the chorus who sings the psalm); I think the clangour of the bells and trumpets should really be heard, and that the *banda* should not be planted on stage, but cross over the stage at the head of the soldiery; perhaps it should be divided into two parts for the repetition of that phrase. Lida will sing together with all the others: I have added two solo lines for her, because in some corner of the portico her voice could be heard alone, or could very briefly take a dominating part, without ever depriving the piece of the appearance of an ensemble, and so sacrificing situations and good sense to a maladroit convention.

Once the effect of this outburst of universal enthusiasm has been achieved, I think that the mournful scene that follows should have a pathetic effect by virtue of its colouring. At the verse 'Per la salvata Italia' etc., after a sustained cantabile, and a kind of breakdown on reaching the words (saria) ... (mentir) ... (spirando), I would like Arrigo, as if he were gathering his last strength, to say

> Chi muore per la Patria,
> Alma sì rea non ha!

with energetic impetus, which could then be repeated by the three voices together. Arrigo should revive once more at the intoning of the Te Deum, and having declared enthusiastically 'E salva Italia!', say the other words 'Io spiro ... e benedico ... il ciel ...' with a failing voice, broken by the gasps of death. The Te Deum should continue until the lowering of the curtain. It only remains for me to ask you to change every heading of 'Atto' to 'Parte', and in the second scene of the third act to change the line reading 'Cader fra l'armi giuriamo estinti' to 'Cader giuriamo nel campo estinti'.[24]

The not inconsiderable part that Verdi played in giving the libretto its final shape may be judged from a letter written to Cammarano on 23 November after the completed libretto had been delivered:

I am still waiting for a reply to my letter in which I acknowledge the receipt of the third act, and futhermore asked you to add a scene for the prima donna. I still hope that out of friendship you will do this favour for me. – In case you haven't received my letter I will repeat what I had in mind. As it seems to me that the prima donna's role doesn't equal that of the other two in importance I would like you to add after the chorus of death a grand, very agitated recitative in which is expressed love, the despair at knowing that Arrigo is consecrated to death, the fear of being discovered etc. After a beautiful recitative bring in the husband and write a beautiful, pathetic duettino ... make the father bless his son or something else of the kind ... etc.

I would ask a last favour of you, a very small one. At the end of the second act I would like four lines for Arrigo and Rolando (together) before

Infamati e maledetti
Voi sarete in ogni età.

I would like to give some importance to this section before the finale and I wouldn't like at this point to repeat words. I want these lines to be strong and energetic; I would like them to embody this idea:

'A time will come in which your descendants will be horrified to bear your name' etc., etc. then 'Infamati e maledetti', etc.

If you could write them and send me them at once you would be doing me a great favour, because I have no time to lose.

Tell me, too (don't be alarmed!): in the concerted movement of the introduction I need another voice, a tenor; would it be possible to add for example, a *shield-bearer* for Arrigo? I think the same shield-bearer could also be added to the last finale! ... he could support Arrigo when he is wounded. – Reply on this point too ...[25]

One can see that with Cammarano Verdi was developing a real artistic relationship, and it shows in the ever-growing mastery of the works they wrote together. Verdi had got the best out of Solera the first time with *Nabucco*, and the rest is a decline. With Piave it was a matter of hit and miss, largely dependent upon the literary source chosen. With Cammarano the matter is quite different. No other librettist ever provided him with a subject quite so ill-suited to his musical character as *Alzira*, and never again did Verdi as a composer fall so low. Thereafter the relationship becomes steadily more fruitful, more genuinely co-operative, as Verdi became less deferential and Cammarano extended and exerted himself to provide the kind of libretto that Verdi intuitively knew he needed. From the dismal *Alzira* the pair progressed to the *succès d'occasion*, *La Battaglia di Legnano*. Their next collaboration a year hence would result in a near-masterpiece, *Luisa Miller*, and their last in *Il Trovatore*.

It would be mistaken however to give the impression that the collaboration on *La Battaglia di Legnano* was entirely happy and unproblematic. Even after the scandalous affair between Flauto and Cammarano had been cleared up, there was the librettist's notorious indolence to be coped with. And there was also, given the turbulent political and social conditions in 1848, the problem of postal communication between Paris and Naples. We have seen that Cammarano sent Verdi Act III of the libretto on 9 October. It was the 23rd or 24th before Verdi received it, and in the meantime he had fired off an impatient protest:

I have written you three letters without having a line in answer, and they were certainly very pressing . . . I simply cannot understand your silence. I have had absolutely nothing to do for a fortnight now, and if you go on like this I certainly shall not be able to finish this opera, and I see that I shall not be able to fulfil the obligations which I have in Italy and here. If you delay any longer it will be necessary for me to take some kind of action so as not to be subjected to protests on all sides. If you cannot write it, tell me frankly, but don't leave me in a ruinous dilemma – So send me some poetry, whether an act or a scene, or else write to help me decide what action I should take.[26]

Presumably it was during this fortnight in which Verdi had 'absolutely nothing to do' on *La Battaglia di Legnano* that he wrote the setting of Mameli's 'Suona la tromba' that had been requested of him by Mazzini. He dispatched it to Mazzini on 18 October, accompanied by the following letter:

I send you the hymn, and although a little late, I hope it will arrive soon enough. I have tried to be as popular and simple as possible. Make what use of it you think fit, and burn it if you think it unworthy. If you publish it, get the poet to change a few words at the start of the second and third verses, where it would be a good thing to write a phrase of five syllables which made sense by itself, as in all the other verses. 'Noi lo giuriamo . . . Suona la tromba etc. . . .

May this hymn soon be sung amid the music of the cannon on the Lombardy plains.[27]

As was the case with *Il Corsaro, La Battaglia di Legnano* was composed in fulfilment of a contract with a publisher, not with a theatre, and Verdi was therefore under no obligation to assume responsibility for staging the opera. In the event he did go to Rome to supervise the rehearsals and the first performance, but the terms of the arrangement were vague and at first looked like creating a lot of bad feeling. The full story is far from clear, but in the latter part of November Verdi wrote two letters, one to Colini, the other to Luccardi, which show him reacting touchily to the tone of some of the news he had had from Rome. The less opaque of the two is that written to Luccardi:

After almost a year I have at last received a letter from you, and you can imagine with what pleasure, since you speak of a matter which, because of the way in which it has been handled, displeases me greatly. You tell me that the Senate has *accepted* my score. *Accepted?* . . . but who has offered it? . . . I should be doing a manifest injustice to the many managements to whom I have refused contracts, if I were to submit myself to endure the *opposition of some members* of your Assembly. No, no: I cannot and must not so submit myself.

By virtue of an old contract I owe Ricordi a score: once it is written my obligations are fulfilled. At his request I consented to come to Rome, which will be a sacrifice on my part because the thousand francs which I asked for won't suffice for the journey from Paris to Rome, and from Rome to Paris . . .

I didn't want anyone to be under an obligation to me; and I don't want to be under an obligation to anyone. I thought that this would be mutually agreeable, but I would never have thought that they wanted to do me a *favour*. I am much obliged for the good intentions of all my friends, but I cannot willingly subject myself to this favour, to this condescension which they wish to show me in *accepting* a score of mine.

Despite my liking for Rome, the desire to see my friends, the superior and *charmante* society, it is very likely that I shall stay in Paris. It is true that I did promise by letter to come to Rome, but the answers have not yet come and perhaps it is now too late.

But let us leave these miserable trifles!! Why don't you say a word about yourself? About your friends? . . . About your work? . . . About the political situation in Rome? . . . All that would have interested me a thousand times more than speaking to me about operas, and music. It is true I am an artist, at least by virtue of my passion if not of my talent, but as you know, I abhor everything that is mere professional drudgery! Art is beautiful but it is no good thing to have to do it! What do you say? You who are an artist just as I am? . . . Another time when you write don't talk about music!! Talk of yourself; of your friends . . . and tell me (it is now four years since I have been in Rome), do the few I got to know still remember me?

I don't know what to say about myself: I am writing a bit of music, and read a lot, books and newspapers because I am anxious and very interested in the state of affairs in Europe . . . but oh dear! . . . I find nothing to comfort me! . . . And our poor Italy? . . .[28]

Any ill-feeling toward the Roman management was dispelled when Ottavio Scaramucci, the Conservatore, or Magistrate, wrote formally to invite Verdi to come to Rome to supervise the preparations for the opera, with a view to staging it in mid-January 1849. Scaramucci confirmed that he would be paid 'the modest fee of 1000 francs.'[29]

As usual Verdi was working on the composition of the opera right up to the last minute. Indeed he seems not to have received the words of the 'beautiful, pathetic duettino' he had requested from Cammarano until early in January when he was already in Rome. Even then he was still wanting improvements made:

I have received the scene and it seems to me to work very well not only from the musical point of view but also from the dramatic, except for the eight lines at the end of the duettino which after the two sestinas seem to me to cool the piece down: I think that if after the sestinas you had made the son kneel down and had given Rolando two lines to accompany the action and two more to Lida, the situation would have been more interesting. If you agree to this write these four lines, two for Rolando, two for Lida, as quickly as possible; if you don't agree then I will finish the duet with the two sestinas leaving out the last eight lines . . . 'Cessa ti calma' etc.

Let me know as soon as possible if the Naples management is going to pay you for the libretto you have written: If not, write to tell me what you require so that I can pay you while I am here or give instructions to Ricordi ...[30]

The last-minute additions and alterations must have been very vexing for Ricordi, who, since the opera was primarily his and only secondarily Rome's, will have been eager to get the score published promptly. It cannot have been many days before the *première* that Verdi sent him the Act III scena and duettino covered by the following note: 'I send you the scena and the new duet which I have composed. I send you besides some passages which I have added to various movements. Please see that all these changes are made in the printed score. I should be very vexed if you had already had the opera printed. Farewell, farewell. The *première* is on Saturday the 27th.'[31]

Considering the flagrant way in which Cammarano and Verdi flaunted their political commitment in *La Battaglia di Legnano*, and the unique interest that therefore attaches to the first performances of it, we know disappointingly little either about the period of rehearsal or about the performances. A note sent off to Cammarano on 18 January includes the information, 'I shall be leaving Rome immediately after the first performance of the opera, and that will be soon because today I start the orchestra rehearsals, and I shall have two of them.'[32] But with Muzio not on the scene, and with Verdi rushing off apparently before having time to send his usual first-night reports, the picture is speculative indeed. However, in the letter sent by Muzio to Barezzi on 4 February there is a secondhand account of the dress rehearsal.

Yesterday I had reports of the dress rehearsal of the opera: I am still waiting for that of the first performance. At the dress rehearsal the people wanted to force their way in to see the performance and burst into the theatre, filling it *as full as an egg* as we would say. The maestro had twenty curtain calls. On the next day there was neither a box, nor a ticket nor a libretto of the opera to be found: everything was sold out![33]

During the period of reaction that followed the suppression of the revolutionary and patriotic movements of 1848–9 it was inevitable that *La Battaglia di Legnano* should be a proscribed work in its original form. Before it could win even a modest currency, its flamingly and explicitly nationalistic tone had to be rendered harmless by translation into foreign climes. Though Verdi himself gave permissions for its transmogrification into *L'Assedio di Arlem*, he cannot have been pleased that an opera of which he was genuinely proud, and which had been composed specifically as a contribution to the revolutionary movements of 1848, should need to slink about the country in sober Flemish disguise. In 1854 he decided that it would be worth while to attempt to make a kind of *rifacimento* of it, as he had done with *I Lombardi*, and as he was in the process of doing with *Stiffelio*. Through his Neapolitan friend Cesare De Sanctis, he approached Bardare, the poet who had put the finishing touches to the libretto of *Il Trovatore*, explaining that

I don't want a mere change of names and title with a few lines and words here and there; I want an entirely new subject, of the same character and no less exciting. As regards plot and action this shouldn't be too difficult, but as regards *colorito* it will be very difficult indeed. To retain all the enthusiasm for fatherland and freedom without actually mentioning either will be a hard task, but we can try . . .[34]

This letter was written in July 1854. For the best part of two years Bardare and Verdi, all the time with De Sanctis as mediator, picked away at it, without really achieving anything. In May 1856 Verdi offered to pay off Bardare for the fruitless work he had done, but even there the matter did not rest. Verdi raised the possibility one last time with the Naples impresario Torelli during the early stages of the negotiations about *Un Ballo in Maschera*. He suggested 'abandoning the idea of writing a completely new opera for this year, and substituting for it *La Battaglia di Legnano*, adapting it to another subject, and adding such new pieces as are necessary as I did with *Aroldo*'.[35] Torelli manifested no interest in the proposal, and *La Battaglia di Legnano* remains in its pristine form as 'the opera of the revolution'.

Luisa Miller

The extraordinary and scandalous circumstances which prompted Verdi to engage at once in another collaboration with Cammarano have already been examined in the previous section. The history of *Luisa Miller* can best be traced from that September day in 1848 when the composer, despite his outrage at Flauto's conduct, consented, 'for Cammarano's sake alone', to write an opera for production in Naples the following year. At the same time, it will be recalled, he observed that it would be essential for the new opera to be 'a short drama of great interest, with plenty of action and a great deal of passion'.[36] Arrangements were informally sealed with a blithe letter from the incorrigible Flauto on 14 October:

A line in haste, which I have not been able to write before as I was suffering exceedingly from my nerves.

I have the pleasure of informing you that, released from the avidity of

my old colleagues, I have been able to mount a spectacle of the greatest
splendour at the San Carlo, And this was *I Lombardi*. Sig. Gazzaniga,
Bonnardi (a new but good tenor) and Rodas were the principals – a chorus
of seventy, etc. The production enjoyed a brilliant success: Verdi is desired
here and everyone hopes that, with my mediation, they will see you.

And so, how relieved I was when Cammarano told me this morning that
all differences are resolved, and that you will be composing next year.

In about twenty days I shall tell you who is to be in the company, and we
can get to work at once ... You will believe me when I say that my only
desire is to show you how much I esteem you, and am your respectful and
affectionate friend. I am grateful to you for having got the good Cammarano
out of a scrape, a gesture that does great honour to the qualities of Italy's
leading maestro ...[37]

The idea of composing an opera based on Schiller's *Kabale und
Liebe* had originally been Verdi's own. His enthusiasm for the
subject went back, as one might expect, to the Recoaro summer with
Andrea Maffei: the scheme was of the same vintage as that for a *Die
Räuber* opera. Probably on 31 August 1846 he had written to
Cammarano about the play.

It is a magnificent drama, passionate and very effective theatrically, but it
would need two women principals. If Signora Bucini is there she would be
excellent.

Discuss this with Flauto, and if the company is right, it seems to me that
one couldn't find anything better.[38]

But it was not until late in 1848, after Cammarano had completed
the libretto of *La Battaglia di Legnano*, that the question needed to be
taken up again. Cammarano wrote to Verdi in Paris suggesting as
possible subjects for his next Naples opera

... *Kabale und Liebe, Niccolò di Lapi, Ettore Fieramosca*. There would still
be *Fedra* and *Saul*, but as Mercadante is to compose a *Virginia* it would be
better, by way of contrast, to keep to a mediaeval subject: and I would be for
Fieramosca, which has never been well done in music ...[39]

However, as we have already seen, Verdi had, during the summer,
become engrossed in Guerrazzi's *L'Assedio di Firenze*. After writing
to Piave to see if he was interested in the project, he had begun to
work out a *scenario* for such an opera, the surviving portion of
which is reprinted in Luzio's essay 'Il Ferruccio di Verdi';[40] and
when he replied to Cammarano this was the subject in which he
tried to interest him:

... Now let's come to the opera I have to write. We won't think about
subjects taken from antiquity then. Certainly *Fieramosca* recalls one of our
great eras, and is a fine subject. But I don't much like subjects that have
already been worked. Besides, do you think the characters are sufficiently
well delineated, that there is enough passion, action, deep pathos, and above

all that it would be sufficiently imposing and spectacular? Because without that I don't think it would be a success in a large theatre.

I think that in a huge theatre like the San Carlo a work that isn't somehow imposing and spectacular lacks something. Besides I can do that sort of thing better, and I do prefer subjects which offer me something really big and really impressive. If you think *Fieramosca* has all these things, then do it; if not, I suggest *L'Assedio di Firenze*, or *Ferruccio*.

To me Ferruccio seems a giant, a colossus of greatness and patriotism ... And then if one wants to keep close to Guerrazzi's novel there are the characters already drawn, all of them splendid. Ferruccio, Lodovico Martelli, Maria Benintendi and Bandino ... and then there are so many subsidiary roles to choose from, Dante da Castiglione, the Prince of Orange, Malatesta etc. etc. Then the Gonfalonier, the Three Hundred etc. etc., and then above all bringing Clement VII on to the stage in a great procession. Think about it: then decide yourself on one or other of them ...[41]

Cammarano was a difficult man to goad into activity, however. From Rome, where he had gone for the rehearsals of *La Battaglia di Legnano*, Verdi wrote on 6 January 1849 begging the librettist 'to send as quickly as possible the synopsis of the new opera'.[42] But twelve days later he had still heard nothing. Seeing that Verdi had agreed to compose the opera only for Cammarano's sake, the librettist's inertia must have been more than usually exasperating. He tried again: 'If you could send me, before I leave, the synopsis of the opera I shall be writing for Naples, I shall be obliged. Do remember that my only obligation is to compose this opera with you, so if you do not want me to compose it I shan't.[43]

Eventually Cammarano did agree to Verdi's suggestion to work Guerrazzi's *L'Assedio di Firenze*. Nothing is known of the early stages of work on the libretto, not even whether Verdi offered Cammarano his own *scenario* of the work; but on 14 February he did write to suggest that Cammarano should 'incorporate in the introduction of *L'Assedio di Firenze* the sermon of the friar of Foiano as described in chapter 10 of the novel'.[44] And the active role which Verdi played in the preparation of the libretto is still more clearly shown in a long letter of 24 March in which he details for the librettist 'all the mad ideas which came into my head about our drama'.[45] But the grandiose patriotic sequel to *La Battaglia di Legnano* was not to be. On 14 April, Cammarano reported:

It is with the deepest regret that I have to inform you of an unlucky occurrence: the Authority that supervises the theatres here has demanded to see the Sketch of *Maria de' Ricci* [*L'Assedio di Firenze*] and has officially rejected it in the following terms: 'It should be returned to the management because of the inopportuneness of the subject, given the present situation in Italy, and especially in Florence', and the attempts of the management itself to get the veto revoked proved vain. Being put in such a difficult spot I cannot think of anything better than to return to a subject which you yourself suggested on another occasion, Schiller's *Kabale und Liebe*, and while I await your reply I will draw up a synopsis so as to save time. That does not mean that, if there is another subject which you would favour, you should not indicate it; indeed I should be more zealous than ever in your support, and should have no regret over the waste of a second synopsis if we achieved what we wanted with the third. I would only ask you not to exceed a comparable periphery, so as not to stumble upon new obstacles. If you are not averse to working an incident from ancient history, take a look at Gerardini's *Cleopatra*, published in Paris; there's lots of spectacle in it; otherwise I leave it entirely to you. I shall certainly redouble my zeal and my good will to ensure that your opera may have that happy success of which, whether one considers the loftiness of your genius or the sympathy which your classic compositions have won with the Neapolitan public, one cannot really be in doubt . . .[46]

If the closing phrases of Cammarano's letter seem imbued with a Flauto-like tone, it may have been because they were written under the eye of that impresario.* Indeed Flauto added an endorsing postscript. And before proceeding to discuss the work on *Luisa Miller* it will be opportune briefly to describe several other exchanges between Flauto and Verdi during the winter of 1848–9.

Flauto's assertion, back in October, that 'Verdi is desired here' had rather caused the composer to wince than flattered him. He would probably have preferred to send his opera to Naples and entrust the staging of the work to Flauto rather than undertake the responsibility himself: Flauto himself had once made that proposal.† It was in reply to Flauto's October letter that Verdi wrote the indictment of the Neapolitan character already quoted in connection with *Alzira*.‡ But he continued in a more conciliatory tone, 'I want to convince you that if I do not come to Naples it is not because I don't want to: I should sincerely like to be able to show the Neapolitans that I can write something not unworthy of their theatre. But listen and say yourself whether I could assume any more obligations . . .'[48] And Verdi went on to point out that his commitments in Paris made it impossible for the time being to enter into any further arrangements with Naples.

Flauto replied eloquently on behalf of his fellow-citizens.

Let us then agree that your opera will be produced next autumn, as you

---

* In his letter of 9 October 1848 Cammarano had explained to Verdi that he was sometimes made to write things he did not wish to, and that to make it quite clear which letters were really his he would henceforth inscribe them 'Amico sempre a me caro'.[47] This letter of 14 April is addressed 'Maestro pregiatissimo'.
† Cf. the letter of 4 July 1846, cited above, p. 220.
‡ Letter of 23 November 1848, cited above, p. 158.

wrote to me. I hope you will be satisfied with the company when I tell you that you can count upon Signora Gazzaniga, Bassini and Bettini ...

But now about your reluctance to come to Naples; permit me to say that I do not agree with you. Intrigue has a short life. If there was some about when you were in Naples, it is dead now. Allow me to make here the apology of the Neapolitans who all have good hearts and esteem superior genius. All the most distinguished talents have been honoured here; and one must take no notice of the odd little contretemps. I have too much esteem for you – too much regard – to offer prophetic counsel. I hope you will be able to find a month's time and come yourself to produce your opera. If Naples does not pay you the homage you merit, as one of the common fatherland, you may complain bitterly to me. In my judgement the success of an opera depends primarily upon the presence of the composer, of a composer such as yourself ...[49]

Cammarano's dilatoriness in getting on with the libretto of *L'Assedio di Firenze* may have contributed to a restless uncertainty about the Naples project to which the *précis* letters at the start of the *Seconda Copialettere* bear witness.[50] On 13 February Verdi wrote to Giovanni Ricordi to request advice.

... I am still in a state of expectancy, of great expectancy, about the Naples business. If I were not bound by this contract I should already have agreed to write another opera here for next year with a libretto by Scribe. What should I do? Something has got to be decided. It would be a shame to give up the opera, but on the other hand the Opéra urgently needs another work if Meyerbeer decides not to do *Le Prophète*. Tell me, what ought I to do? Do you think I should write to Flauto myself? Perhaps I could get a postponement if you made no objection ...[51]

The next day Verdi did indeed write to Flauto, proposing that the production of the new opera should be postponed for one year. By way of bait, Verdi added that he would be willing to compose a further opera for Naples, and would undertake the responsibility for staging the first of them.[52] But Flauto was unable to oblige him:

Concerning the idea of postponing your opera until next year, I have to tell you that the suggestion reached me too late. I have entered into an agreement with the government, according to which I am committed to give your work next year. As a result of this agreement the San Carlo theatre will open at Easter and close on Passion Saturday, in other words there will be theatre all the year round. The artists will be supplemented in the Autumn and Carnival seasons, but there will be a complete company in the Spring and Summer seasons too. If this agreement, which has already been approved by the king, should by any chance come to be suspended, then I could agree to your proposition and would write to you at once; but if you do not receive another letter you may assume that no modification has been possible. And then there is always that fellow Ricordi fussing about getting your score quickly.[53]

Clearly the Naples opera was not to be deferred any longer; the hopes of writing another piece for Paris would have to wait; Verdi and Cammarano must get down to work. On 26 April Verdi accepted the proposal to work *Kabale und Liebe*,[54] and with this the preliminary negotiations were concluded.

Cammarano worked out his synopsis of *Kabale und Liebe* and dispatched it to Verdi on 3 May.[55] It is a typically assured and efficient piece of operatic adaptation which Verdi was unable to modify in any fundamental way at all. Indeed Cammarano's synopsis would still serve very well for reprinting in programme notes to productions of *Luisa Miller*: the only detail missing is the brief scene between Rodolfo and Wurm after 'Quando la sera placida'. Verdi's reaction to it was not entirely passive, however. Respectful as ever of Cammarano's experience and expertise, he nevertheless attempted, in that way that was so typical of him, to keep his colleague as close to his literary source as possible – to persuade him that there were contexts where the uniquely Schillerian would be stronger, more vivid, more convincing, than the conventionally melodramatic.

I have just received your synopsis and have to admit that I would have preferred two leading ladies, and that I would like the prince's favourite fully rounded out as a character, exactly as Schiller has done. There would have been a contrast between her and Eloisa, and the love of Rodolfo for Eloisa would have been more beautiful; but, after all, I know that one cannot do everything as one would like to, and it will be all right as it is. But I do think that the whole of that infernal intrigue between Walter and Wurm, which dominates the drama like fate, doesn't have all the colour and all the force here which there is in Schiller. Perhaps when you have done the verses it will be a different matter, but in any case see for yourself whether I am right or wrong. And I do think that when Eloisa is forced by Wurm to write the letter it would seem to me to carry more weight and be more natural and credible if, instead of saying that she was the lover of Wurm, she declared that she was in love with someone else.

Take such notice of these observations as you think fit, but what I must tell you is that in the first finale I don't want a *stretta* or a cabaletta finale. The situation does not demand it, and a *stretta* would destroy its whole effect. You can start the piece and do the concerted section as you please; but at the end you must do it exactly like [Schiller].

[Here Verdi transcribes the crucial lines from the end of Schiller's II.7.]

You can make this finale as extended as you like; since one is not obliged to repeat the piece (indeed one must not), it will not become too long.

In the second act do take care with the duet between Wurm and Eloisa. The terror and desperation of Eloisa will make a good contrast with the infernal coldness of Wurm. I even thought that if you give the character of Wurm a touch of comedy, the situation would become still more terrible. After the other duet, between Walter and Wurm, will you write a quartet? I was wondering if one could not write one for unaccompanied voices.

I think you will be writing an aria for Rodolfo's scena. That will be all right for the first part of the piece, but I think it will make an ineffective close. Bringing down the curtain on just two characters after having had a grand finale in the first act! Think about it. I think we shall have to find something here.

The third act is very beautiful. Develop fully the duet between the father and daughter: make it a duet to draw tears. The duet that follows is very beautiful and powerful, and I think it will also be necessary to finish with a trio including the father.

When Walter enters, write as few lines as possible! But if you need to extend the two pieces to develop them more fully, do so. As far as the three basses are concerned, I think the principal role is that of Eloisa's father. So make that a fine part, then Walter, and lastly Wurm. Don't forget to keep a suggestion of comedy in Wurm's whole role, so as to give greater emphasis to his cunning and villainy . . .[56]

Such were the vagaries of the post in the confused political circumstances of 1849 that it was more than a fortnight before Cammarano received Verdi's letter. Indeed the whole course of this particular collaboration was bedevilled by wretched postal communications. Cammarano had sent Verdi the synopsis before actually receiving Verdi's letter of 26 April, which must have included some indications of the style in which he would like the subject treated. Now he received Verdi's criticism of his synopsis only after a month's work versifying and filling out the details of his scheme, and with several scenes already finished and in the post for Paris. Under the circumstances it is hardly surprising that rather few of Verdi's suggestions could be adopted. It had been only on 15 May that Cammarano and Flauto had answered Verdi's letter of 26 April.

By now the synopsis of Eloisa Miller must have arrived; I have done what I could to give the chorus some scope and to introduce a bit of spectacle. As far as the character of the other woman is concerned, it was an act of prudence to change it, and it seems that if necessary a supporting artist would do, so as to avoid foundering on the conventions associated with two leading ladies, especially as it would be impossible to make the role of the rival as important (at least dramatically) as that of Eloisa. We have Signora Salandri (contralto) here, or, if you would prefer a soprano, the management would consider providing one. If on the other hand you persist in the idea of having two leading ladies, we have Signora Albertini and Signora Maray for Federica; Signora Gazzaniga, as you said yourself, would be absolutely ideal for Eloisa. – While we await your reply a start can be made with the verses for the first pieces in which Federica has no part . . .[57]

And it was only on 4 June, when he was already well advanced with the versification of scenes 1 and 3 of the first act, that Cammarano could answer Verdi's letter of 17 May.

Here is the finale of Act I. There is a lacuna between this and Miller's aria for reasons which I explained in my last letter: you will soon get the part that is missing. Your letter of 17 May reached me in time, and you will see that the enclosed poetry does incorporate the proposals you made on the subject. I shall subject all your other suggestions to mature reflection: I cannot now depart essentially from the drama, for fear of delaying these verses.

The idea that Miller should have served in the wars as a young man is not a bad one: it elevates his character, gives him a certain energetic dash, and forms a dramatic contrast with that pathetic element which is so beautiful a part of his character. But I do urge you to mark well the strong words when he turns threateningly to Walter. – However you are going to compose the concerted sections, I am of the opinion that towards the end the tempo should accelerate, and that it should have a very animated close: I think that otherwise (in view of the fact that there is no *stretta*) the piece could relapse into inertia. – The basses of the chorus will be the archers; the tenors and the women the villagers . . .[58]

The mature reflection which Cammarano promised Verdi's other suggestions bore fruit a week later. His letter of 11 June is one of the most interesting documents of the whole Verdi–Cammarano correspondence, an intelligent if somewhat routineer appraisal of how the politics and decorum of the *ottocento* opera house tended to impose a certain conformity upon the way in which any dramatic theme was handled.

I wrote to you last week, but fearing that my letter did not take an absolutely sure route, I think it prudent to repeat it here. At the same time you will find enclosed the first duet of Act II. I shouldn't have to make any observation at all about this scene, which is absolutely clear, but as, in such cases, it is no bad thing to say too much, I beg you to leave the two verses:

> LUISA: La tomba è un letto . . .
> MILLER: Di rughe il volto . . .

as they are, separated from one another and forming two solos, and not to weave them together in the manner of an *adagio*, which would spoil the following dialogue. [At this point Cammarano repeats the letter of 4 June. He then continues:]

Did I not fear the imputation of being an Utopian, I should be tempted to say that to achieve the highest degree of perfection in an opera it would be necessary for both the words and the music to be the product of one and the same mind: and from this ideal follows my firm opinion that, when it has two authors, they must at least be like brothers, and that if Poetry should not be the servant of Music, still less should it tyrannize over her. Convinced of the truth of this maxim, I have always worked in accordance with it, and the composers with whom I have collaborated have always been consulted on these matters. I have therefore carefully examined your letter of 17 May, and this is my reply.

The dramatic conception of Schiller in the role of Lady Milford is sublime: I have been able to make only feeble amends for the suppression of it, but one has to submit to inexorable necessity: besides, if she had remained as the favourite, and the number of her pieces increased, there is not one leading lady (among singers) who would have taken on the role; since whatever trouble we took we could not have compensated in the operatic balance for the fact that Luisa's role is the predominant one. – That the infernal intrigue should lose something of its harshness is the inevitable consequence of the suppression of the favourite, because of whom the ambitious Walter went so far as to wish to sacrifice even the honour of his own son. But I do not find that Luisa's letter, originally directed to the court chamberlain, and now to Wurm, is any less credible. Wurm had already, on another occasion, requested Luisa's hand, and this circumstance must have a strong influence on Rodolfo's blind jealousy: and one should recall that to find another suitable person is a tough proposition now that the action has been transported to a village; a fact which has been a great help in a subject where, at first sight, the intervention of the chorus seems not so much difficult as impossible. All the same I will think about it again.

We are of one mind about the first finale, and that movement has already been sent you. In the third act too our ideas are in agreement. There only remains the second, and particularly the distribution of the pieces which this act is to consist of: in my plan it comprises an aria for Luisa, a quartet, and an aria for Rodolfo. You think it should comprise a duet for Luisa and Wurm, another for Wurm and Walter, the quartet, the aria for Rodolfo and then something else better suited to the end of an act. Many objections arise. The opera is getting rather long; three basses are involved (we have De Bassini, Selva and Arati here, but what about other places? . . .); the role of Wurm is concentrated just in the second act, with three pieces one following the other; the unlikelihood of Selva undertaking Walter or Wurm; the impossibility of adding anything after Rodolfo's aria which would not be superfluous and therefore ineffective. It might be possible to reverse the order of the quartet and the aria and finish with the quartet, but the placing of the aria seems to me more effective; you might add that if the scene in which Luisa writes the letter remains an aria, we should have two of them, one after the other. A more sensible plan would be to bring in the chorus together with Rodolfo, and to finish the act as in the synopsis. – But your letter of 17 May left you before my distribution of movements had arrived: having had that, are you still of your original opinion, or have you come round to mine? For me a resolution of this doubt is absolutely essential, and so I shall hope for a very prompt reply, in which, I am sure, you will take into account the points made in this letter. Meanwhile, so as not to lose time, I will press on with Act III. – In Act I only Federica's scene is missing; but the début of Signora Salandri has been delayed here, and I must hear her before I settle on what to do . . .[59]

At the same time as hammering out the details of the libretto with Cammarano, Verdi was corresponding with Flauto on a more mundane level.

. . . I think it is too early to decide on the singers already, especially as there could be some alterations to be made. Nevertheless you can be virtually certain that it would be best to have Signora Gazzaniga as leading lady, and *Bettini* for the tenor.

As far as composing another opera and coming to Naples are concerned, I cannot at the moment say more than I said before. My affairs do not permit me to make any decision yet . . . In case you should have the idea of doing *Gerusalemme* with Bettini, I certainly could not discourage it, because Bettini is doing this opera in Lyons at the moment with great success, but I would rather you did it after the production of the new opera. *Gerusalemme* calls for so much splendour in the production; and neither you nor I would profit by following it with an opera with much simpler costumes . . .[60]

In the middle of June Verdi became involved in a dispute that had arisen between Flauto and the deputies of the Royal Supervisory Committee of the Theatres of Naples. Perhaps because of Verdi's inability to commit himself to coming to Naples to direct his new opera, Flauto was refusing to reveal to the committee the full details of the contract between himself and the composer. One of the deputies, the *cavaliere* Colle, was instructed to write direct to Verdi in the hope of getting some information out of him. Verdi however was unco-operative:

Although I do not have the honour of knowing you, and there is no official heading on your letter such as is normal in such correspondence, I nevertheless believe that it comes from the Supervisory Committee of Theatres, and I therefore make it my duty to reply at once.

I do not know the reasons for which Signor Flauto is refusing to inform you of the conditions existing between us relative to the opera which I am to compose: but I am sorry to say that I do not feel free to reveal that which Signor Flauto thinks it proper to conceal, as this is a matter which is almost exclusively his concern . . . I can do nothing more than assure the committee and the management itself that I shall scrupulously carry out all the obligations I have assumed.[61]

On the same day, Verdi wrote to Cammarano, explaining what he had done and probably asking him to get Flauto to clear the matter up.[62] The impresario wrote to express his gratitude for the composer's discretion on 7 July: still, however, the real cause of the dispute is not exactly clear.

I thank you for the way in which you have replied [to Colle]; but tomorrow I will explain to those gentlemen of the Supervisory Committee everything relating to your contract. Their excessive zeal to have you here and the fear that your music might not materialize make them suspicious and nervous. I shall faithfully show them what has passed between us: your cordiality and friendship for me make me confident not only that you will write the music, but also that, if you can, you will come to direct it.[63]

Once Flauto had assembled his company for the season the details of the casting became less his affair than the affair of Cammarano, the librettist and producer. It was with Cammarano that Verdi took up once again the question of the cast:

For many reasons which it would take too long to explain in a letter, I think it will be best to keep to Selva for the part of Walter, so there is no need to do a duet for the first act, though I would ask you to ensure that Walter's role should be a principal one. Arati will do Wurm. You can arrange things over Federica. You only need to tell me the voice-range of the woman who is to sing Federica, and of the second woman who is to do Laura as well. I have received Luisa's aria which is very beautiful – To save writing another letter would you do me the favour of telling Flauto all this. Tell him, too, that I have seen in a French paper an article reprinted from *Il Pirata*, according to which Gazzaniga is marrying a Count Malaspina: as a count is involved, might there be any danger of her dissolving her contract with Naples? If that should be the case, I hope Flauto will let me know, and that some agreement can be reached about finding a substitute, always provided that among those at Naples we had one who could do the ingenious and extremely dramatic role of Luisa.[64]

Again Verdi's letter crossed with one from Cammarano at least partly concerned with the same questions. But more interesting are Cammarano's further thoughts on the Act II finale.

The Gazzaniga affair was a false alarm: we can count on her; although she is married she is coming. You will be receiving from Flauto Rodolfo's aria, which is the Act II finale. Still missing however is the concerted piece that precedes it, and the other piece from Act I, which I have left writing until it has been definitely decided which artist you are choosing to do the part of Walter. I have thought carefully about the end of Act II, and certainly not out of obstinacy but rather through reasoning have returned to my original idea. This aria is (I hope I am not deceiving myself) very effectively, very dramatically, placed; it is to be performed by one of our principal artists; it is to be composed by Verdi: given these factors one can count on a good success, and it is always good to bring the curtain down on applause. The concerted piece is a necessary link in the chain of events, but its position, though not without interest, comprises simulation on one hand and suppressed grief on the other, and that deprives it of that explosiveness of passion and that seething energy which usually prove such effective aids in finales. The arrival of Rodolfo with the letter could supply this defect, but this incident, while theatrical and effective in itself, would have a bad effect on the third act which would have had to be rearranged, something which I would not willingly have done for anything. Add to that the fact that an identical scene is to be found in my drama *Elena de Feltre* which has been performed in the San Carlo. Having produced these reasons, and flattering myself that you will agree with my judgement, it only remains to urge upon you that the *tempo di mezzo* of the aria in question [that is, from the appearance of the chorus and of Walter] should have a rapid, urgent tempo. That will have two good effects: it will better express the impetuosity of Rodolfo's passion, leaving him no room for reflection, or for any suspicions concerning Walter, and it will dispel the feeling that this particular scene is too long-drawn-out.[65]

These first stages of the work on *Luisa Miller* were completed in the first half of August: at that time the final decisions on the casting were made, and Cammarano completed the libretto. Forwarding an instalment of verses to Verdi on 6 August, Flauto wrote:

Here is some more poetry. We hope that the final instalment will soon follow. Cammarano has given me your letter to read, and here I am with all the news.

Although I am proposing to let Selva go, he is still here at the moment, and long experience has shown me that making a contract with someone goes quickly whereas dissolving one is a long business: so it is very probable that he will stay. So write for him. You can take Signora Salandri, a good contralto, for Federica. I have no good supporting artist to offer you; but if you would prefer a soprano, you could use Signora Riva-Giunti, who will perhaps be known to you.

For the second woman you will have Signora Salvetti, an excellent second soprano.

Signora Gazzaniga has made no mention of matrimony, let alone of dissolving her contract. And so I think there will be no problem about her coming to fulfil the contract. – But if there should be any news, you do me great wrong to suppose that I might conceal it from you. You will know all.

Yesterday evening *Ernani* with Signora Tadolini, de Bassini, Malvezzi and Arati aroused fanatical enthusiasm. What beautiful music! Though I have heard this music so many times I continue to admire it. You are a great composer; I will say it, though I am but a nonentity.[66]

Cammarano sent Verdi the completed libretto a week later:

Here is the complete libretto. You will find that I have put Walter's cantabile, which was in the second act, into the first; I did this for reasons which I hope will seem good ones to you too. Without this change Walter would have nothing but recitatives in the first scenes, and these, with no cantabile to break them up, would become tedious. Finally, as there are three pieces in a row for Walter in the second act, it seems a good idea to remove one of them. If the recitative in the second act which precedes the cantabile in question should now be a nuisance, we could, if you wish, cut it down a little.

Farewell, dear maestro ... your work is awaited here with the keenest interest ...[67]

Doubtless a certain amount of composition had already been done by the time Verdi received the complete libretto. But by far the greater part of the music must have been written between mid-August and 3 October, when Verdi, in company with Barezzi, set out from Busseto on the first stage of the journey to Naples.[68] His absorption in *Luisa Miller* was total, and only once, as far as we know, did he take up his pen to discuss other matters. This was on 7 September when he wrote to Flauto to confirm his willingness to enter into another contract with Naples (cf. below, p. 281. He added just a few details about *Luisa Miller*:

As far as the opera I am writing now is concerned, I shall be in Naples about 8 or 10 October, so as to go into production at the end of the same month.

Arrange things so that I can start rehearsals the day after my arrival, as I shall bring the score with me complete except for the orchestration. On the matter of payment for this opera you will refer to the very first contract of all.[69]

In the turbulent political conditions of Italy in the autumn of 1849 a journey through half the length of the land was no trifling undertaking. Though Verdi and Barezzi had left Busseto in good time, it took them more than three weeks to reach Naples. To begin with they went across the Appennines to Genoa, proposing to embark there and make the rest of the journey by sea. But in Genoa they found themselves stuck, as Verdi explained to Escudier in a letter of 6 October:

I have been in Genoa for two days without being able to leave for Naples. Today I have decided to go by land, so who knows when I shall be in Naples! And what are you doing? Have you had my letters? Have you written me any? How is your brother? ... And then there is so much other news, political and unpolitical, which I must know! Is the theatre still closed? So write me a long letter to Naples and let me know all the thousands and thousands of things you have to say.

I shan't tell you anything of our country. It is a pitiful business! It will be enough to say that the place one lives least badly is Piedmont! All this time I have been living in a country district far from all human intercourse, without hearing any news, without reading newspapers etc. It is a life to bring you down to the level of beasts, but at least it is peaceful ... I shall be leaving any minute for Pisa ...[70]

From Pisa, Verdi and Barezzi went on to Rome where they arrived on 13 October. Here misfortune struck once more, for a cholera epidemic held them in quarantine for two weeks. Presumably Verdi made some progress on the orchestration of *Luisa Miller* during this period, but his exasperation at the unforeseen delay is clear from his attempt to get Flauto to use his influence in Naples to circumvent the quarantine regulations. But this was a hopeless undertaking, even for Flauto.

You can very well imagine with what regret I received your letter with the announcement that you are having to remain in quarantine; and what is worse is that it is impossible to be of any help. How can you hope to be given permission to come to Naples, when not even the king can possibly infringe this sanitary law? One must be patient! Meanwhile all is ready here. Your accommodation is fixed too at the Hotel de Rome as you desired ...[71]

Flauto further urged Verdi to forward his score, so that parts could be copied and rehearsals begun. Verdi's unwillingness to do this was doubtless due to several factors – unwillingness to entrust something so precious to the post, or the need to continue work on the orchestration; but a major consideration must have been a disconcerting letter he had just received from Cammarano.

A very serious problem has arisen: Bettini has not won the public's favour in Naples. I decided that I would advise you, as soon as you arrive here, to hear Malvezzi and Bouccardé before casting the part of Rodolfo. You know Bettini, but you do not know what an unfavourable impression he has made on the audience. I am deeply distressed to have to say it, but I would not, I am profoundly convinced, take Bettini, although I do not share the general opinion, which rates him much lower than I do. However, your most fervent admirers have pressed me to convey to you this advice which I have been brooding over in my mind: Mercadante himself, who wanted to cast Bettini in his opera (from a friend like you I have no secrets), has given up the idea.

To ignore two artists who have deservedly pleased in order to hold on to one who has been unsuccessful would certainly not be a good policy; I would be inclined to prefer Malvezzi, who is at least the equal of Bouccardé in artistic merit, and surpasses him in docility, in good will and in the care he takes in learning the music. All the same, don't think I have anything against Bouccardé. Meanwhile it is a difficult decision to give a part to someone one doesn't know, especially a part that is essential, even decisive to the opera. In your position I should send on those pieces in which the tenor is not involved (it is always a time-saving, if only to copy the parts) and wait until your arrival in Naples, when everything has been explained, before coming to a decision.

If I did not think I should be doing wrong to both, I would remind you, to exonerate myself from any charge of partiality over the casting of Rodolfo, that I have never mentioned the matter, because I was quite confident that Bettini would be a success; but this proved to be disastrously wrong. I will not leave this matter before telling you that the management has already brought an (unjust) lawsuit against Bettini, so as to dissolve the contract. Pending judgement they cannot give him any roles, and that is another obstacle. But I sincerely avow that I have given you this news not to persuade you of my opinion, but so that you do not confuse my interests and those of the management. Theirs are sordid, the outcome of bad faith; mine are artistic, and arise, as I have said, from profound conviction and from the instinct to protect an opera in which I have a part. I would do the same if it was yours alone, out of feelings of friendship.

I have one other note to sound and then I shall finish. Although I have reason to think that they will make an exception for you, nevertheless I will not conceal from you the fact that the affairs of the management are in a bad way; so I warn you to take the strictest precautions.[72]

Cammarano was speaking from bitter experience. In 'Gli anni del Rigoletto'[73] Gustavo Marchesi has published a number of letters written by the librettist to Flauto during September and October. They provide a painful illustration of the near-bankruptcy, moral and financial, of Italy's second theatre at the time. One letter, written on 11 September, will suffice to indicate their character. At the time Cammarano had still not received his salary for July.

I am truly what is called a wretched man. Seeing that your promise was not being put into effect, I sent to the administration to get accounts settled, but was told that no provision whatever had been made for me. I am sorry to have to trouble you, but since the first of this month my difficulties increase from day to day, and now I am completely at a loss, so that, without your immediate help I see I shall be ruined. In the direst need, therefore, I implore your assistance, and trusting in your goodness, I remain ...[74]

Verdi was not a man to neglect such a warning as Cammarano's. He arrived in Naples, after his fortnight's quarantine in Rome, on 27 October; and apparently the first instalment of the fee was not ready for him as, according to the terms of the contract, it should have been. Seeing this confirmation of Cammarano's report, Verdi took steps. On 1 November he wrote to Flauto:

It has come to my knowledge that the affairs of the management have not taken a turn for the better, and I have therefore resolved to come to some decision, although not without notifying, through you, the management with which I have entered into the contract. You know the sacrifices I have made, and the losses I have suffered; you know my obligations; you know that I came to Naples to comply with your entreaties, and to do Cammarano a small service; you know that I could have taken advantage of the offers which you have made me a thousand times, and have not done so; and finally you know that I don't compose operas for 3000 ducats any more and that it would have been within my rights to refuse to write this one. I have nevertheless submitted myself willingly to these sacrifices, but now I should like to be sure that I did not have to suffer anything in the future. – I know that the management finds itself in critical circumstances, and if it proves difficult to pay me the first instalment, it will be still more difficult to meet the two subsequent ones, especially if the hopes entertained of a great success for my opera are not realized. Great successes are difficult in Naples, and above all for me. Now, to arrange things as best we can, there seem to me to be only these two means, namely: either to deposit the three thousand ducats owed me with a person who enjoys my confidence, or to dissolve my contract.

You see that I cannot be more reasonable: discuss it with the management or with the Supervisory Committee, so that everyone involved can come to a decision. I am going to the rehearsal again today, but I do not know that I shall do as much tomorrow. If you think that the contents of this letter should be a secret between me, you, the management and the Supervisory Committee, I give you my word that for my part it will be one ...[75]

The reaction of the Neapolitan authorities to this blunt message was characteristically melodramatic. At least, the story is told that one member of the Supervisory Committee, the Duke of Ventignano, threatened Verdi with the invocation of a law that could have held him in Naples at the committee's pleasure, and that Verdi did contemplate seeking asylum aboard a French warship anchored in the bay.[76] But otherwise the documentary history of *Luisa Miller* rather fizzles out at this point. There seems to be no record of how, after amity had been restored, the rehearsals progressed, nor even of what Verdi thought about the first performance on 8 December. We know only that, perhaps because of the enforced stay in Rome, and the possibility of getting on with the orchestration there, Verdi had more time than usual to see the sights, accompanying Barezzi on donkey rides, railway excursions and steamer cruises to beautiful and curious resorts in the vicinity.[77] The best, albeit indirect, reflection of Verdi's feelings during these weeks is perhaps that found in a letter from Muzio to Barezzi, written from Milan on 22 November.

In a letter of the maestro's dated 15th inst, I read that you left Naples the day before aboard the *Capri*, bound for Genoa, And in a letter from my mother I hear of your arrival home.

You went to Naples to enjoy yourself and instead you will have had uneasiness and will have suffered, because the maestro had such irritations. How many things occur that cannot be foreseen! . . .

A poet says that Naples is an earthly paradise inhabited by demons; and I think he is right. A treacherous, infamous people, rogues every one of them! From the first to the last! Bad seed can only give bad fruit! Bad institutions, and bad governments only give perverse subjects . . .[78]

King Lear

It will be recalled that Verdi had first considered composing a *King Lear* opera for Venice in 1843. 'If I had an artist of the calibre of Ronconi', he had written to Mocenigo, 'I would choose either *King Lear* or *The Corsair*.' *King Lear* appears in a place of honour at the top of the memorandum 'Argomenti d'opere' jotted down early in 1844, and in the autumn of 1845 Verdi was wondering whether it might not make an appropriate theme for his London début. Writing to Piave in November about *Attila* and his forthcoming visit to Venice he observes, 'I am busying myself with *Lear* and studying it carefully; I will bring a sketch with me which you can develop into a full synopsis to be offered to London . . .'[79]

But it was only during the most intensive period of Verdi's collaboration with Cammarano that he got properly to grips with Shakespeare's most awe-inspiring tragedy. The two men must have discussed the project of a *Lear* opera during the weeks Verdi spent in Naples preparing the production of *Luisa Miller*. At least, it seems reasonable to assume that *Lear* is the work referred to in two letters written after Verdi's return to Busseto. On 28 December in the course of a letter to De Sanctis he remarks,

I am glad Cammarano has finished *Virginia*, because now he can apply himself to the work we have to write together. I hope he will do me something worthy of himself and of the subject we are working; something with a lot of sense, a rare commodity in the theatre, and especially something worthy of treatment by conscientious artists such as Cammarano and myself . . .

Greet Cammarano and tell him to send me the synopsis when it is done.[80]

Further details emerge from a letter to Ricordi:

As for the other opera which I was to write for Naples, I dissolved the contract, because I was disgusted with the disgraceful way the management and directors carried on. Nevertheless, as the subject is already fixed with Cammarano, I am writing it all the same and it should be finished, I hope, in four or five months . . .[81]

Unfortunately no records survive of the preliminary discussions between Verdi and Cammarano. The tone of the letter to De Sanctis, however, suggests that Verdi was the senior partner in this enterprise. His knowledge of Shakespeare was surpassed by few men in the Italian theatre; he felt no compunction about impressing upon the librettist the onerousness and magnitude of the task they were setting themselves; and when Cammarano dragged his heels a bit, it was Verdi who took the initiative, countering Cammarano's objections and himself preparing the scenario. He sent if off to Naples on 28 February, accompanied by an encouraging, exhortatory letter:

At first sight, King Lear appears to be so vast, so complex, that it seems impossible to derive an opera from it: and yet, considering the matter carefully, it seems to me that the problems, though no doubt great, are not insuperable. You know we should not have to make King Lear into a drama in the traditional form, but treat it in an entirely novel manner, on a vast scale, and without regard to conventions of any kind. The roles, it seems to me, can be reduced to five principals: Lear, Cordelia, Fool, Edmund, Edgar. Two female supporting roles: Regan and Goneril (perhaps we should have to make the latter into another prima donna). Two bass supporting roles (as in Luisa), Kent and Gloucester, the rest minor roles.

Would you say the pretext for disinheriting Cordelia is a bit infantile for our times? Some scenes will absolutely have to be omitted, such as that in which Gloucester is blinded, that in which the two sisters are brought on to the stage etc. etc., and many, many others which you know better than I. The number of scenes can be reduced to eight or nine, and I would point out that there are eleven scenes in I Lombardi, and that was never an obstacle to productions.[82]

Curiously enough, at precisely the time Verdi was pondering King Lear, his Parisan friend and publisher Marie Escudier wrote to him to suggest that he might like to compose The Tempest for production in London at Covent Garden. Verdi declined, but in the course of his letter confessed that

I do plan to compose *The Tempest*, indeed I plan to do the same with all the major plays of the great tragedian, and whether Halévy treats the same themes before or afterwards is quite unimportant . . .

What you propose is impossible. We are virtually in the middle of March, and two or even three months would not suffice to treat so vast a subject . . .[83]

Nor, it soon became clear, would four or five months suffice to complete the work on *Lear* in a worthy manner. In any case, since the dissolving of the contract with Naples there was not the same urgency about this project.

Stiffelio and *Rigoletto*, themes chosen for engagements that really were pressing, began to preoccupy him. Under the circumstances it seemed best to let Cammarano go on mulling over *King Lear*, and take all the time needed to handle such a vast theme really well. Some time in the spring or early summer Verdi must have written to Cammarano suggesting that *King Lear* be temporarily shelved. A little later he wrote again. What exactly this second letter contained is far from clear; but it certainly led to the abandoning of the project. 'Your last letter has cast me upon a sea of confusion,' Cammarano answered. 'I waited in vain for further post, hoping that you would have written again. Really since you suggested suspending work on *King Lear* I have nothing to reproach myself with, for I have worked the best I could, as the poetry enclosed . . . will testify . . .'[84]

The Tempest rejected in February, *King Lear* temporarily laid aside in the spring or early summer; by a strange coincidence a third abortive Shakespearian project was proposed at about the same time. One of Verdi's oldest and dearest Milanese friends, Giulio Carcano, suggested that they should collaborate on a *Hamlet*. Verdi replied on 17 June,

My very dear Carcano,
How many sad and sweet memories are contained in the few lines you sent me! Dear Carcano! It is impossible to forget the past; the future? . . . I don't know what that will bring.

It would have been a great pleasure for me to associated my name with yours, because I am convinced that if you make the suggestion of setting *Hamlet* to music, it would have to be an arrangement worthy of you. Unfortunately these great themes require too much time and for the time being I have had to renounce the idea even of doing *King Lear*, leaving Cammarano with the commission to adapt the play for another more convenient time. Now if *King Lear* is difficult *Hamlet* is even more so; and constrained as I am by two contracts, I have had to choose shorter and simpler subjects to be able to fulfil my obligations. But I do not abandon the hope of one day being able to discuss with you whether it might not be possible to work together on this masterpiece of the English theatre. I should be proud to adorn your verses with my notes, and so to enrich the music theatre with a fine, poetic work.[85]

But this chapter must end with Verdi's last letter to Cammarano, which, sadly, Cammarano did not live to receive. It was written in the first instance to acknowledge the receipt of the completed libretto of *Il Trovatore*, but in it Verdi returns briefly to the *King Lear* that was never to be; he also expresses with a rare if somewhat gruff heartiness something of the warmth he had come to feel for his unhappy Neapolitan librettist and friend.

I have received the rest of *Il Trovatore*. I read and re-read it with increasing pleasure. These verses of yours are full of originality, of life, of passion. Courage, my dear Cammarano – we must do *King Lear*, which will be our masterpiece. I hope that with the aid of your doctors and your friends you will soon leave that bed of pain, to resume your business, and console all your well-wishers, among whom, I hope, you would wish to count me, for I love and esteem you immensely. To get well quickly one has to banish black humours and say to yourself: 'I must and will get well quickly.' Morale does more than doctors or medicines. You must take heart; so I will expect a letter from De Sanctis very shortly, to tell me that you are fully convalescent. On that day I shall celebrate at home, then I shall celebrate again with you when I have satisfaction of embracing you. Perhaps at Rome, this winter. Farewell, my very dear Cammarano! Courage, courage! Think of me always as your passionate admirer, and very sincere friend.[86]

Bouts with the censor

Stiffelio

After the *première* of *Luisa Miller* Verdi left Naples without regret. He had atoned for *Alzira* with the loveliest of his operas to date, and it seems to have enjoyed a good success; he had prepared the ground with Cammarano for embarking on the grandest of all his operatic projects, a *King Lear*. But further acquaintance with the Neapolitans had not mellowed his opinion of them, as we see from a letter to De Sanctis, written from Busseto soon after his return:

The Gazzaniga affair didn't surprise me; certainly it's an ugly business, very ugly, but you know the gentlemen attached to your Royal Theatre don't hesitate to do such things and worse, if it is necessary. Let's draw a veil over these sordid matters, I am thankful to have got out of it fairly well myself . . .

Someone in Naples has written to tell me that all sorts of intrigues are being plotted to make *Luisa Miller* flop . . . and that some of the artists in the opera are, for reasons of politics, taking part in the intrigues . . . I am inclined not to believe any of this, but even if it were true, so much the worse for them; it doesn't matter much to me. Imbeciles, the lot of them!!!) Do they suppose that these disgusting intrigues can prevent the opera going round the musical world, if it is a good one? . . .[1]

According to the terms of the arrangement made with Flauto in September, *King Lear*, the opera on which Verdi and Cammarano were now collaborating, was to be performed in Naples about Easter 1850. But the more Verdi pondered this, the less he liked it, and at some stage during these winter weeks in Busseto he wrote to dissolve the contract. He explains this in the course of a letter to Ricordi on 31 January 1850.

. . . As far as the other opera I was to write for Naples is concerned, I dissolved the contract, disgusted with the undignified way the management and directors go about their affairs. Nevertheless as the subject has already been fixed with Cammarano, I shall write it all the same, and it will be finished, I hope, in four or five months. I make it over willingly to you, leaving you the responsibility of getting it performed some time during November of the present year 1850 in one of the leading theatres of Italy (excepting La Scala in Milan) by a company of the first rank, undertaking myself to be present at the rehearsals. In return you will pay me 16,000 (sixteen thousand) francs, in 800 golden napoleons of twenty francs either on the day of the production, or in monthly instalments to be fixed by mutual consent if you accept the principal conditions. Furthermore you will give me 30 per cent of all the hire charges, and 40 per cent of all sales in all countries for ten years after the day of the first performance of the said opera . . .[2]

Some weeks later, in March, Verdi accepted an invitation from Venice to compose a new opera for La Fenice in collaboration with Piave; so that his obligations now were, as he explained to his Roman friend Borsi, 'to write an opera for Ricordi in the autumn, and another for Venice'.[3] Still the assumption was that the opera for Ricordi was to be *King Lear*. The search for something suitable for Venice was well under way by April when both composer and librettist were splashing about in an ocean of predominantly French Romantic literature. *Le Roi s'amuse*, *Manon Lescaut* and *Kean* were among Verdi's suggestions, *Conte Herman*, *Ruy Blas* and a certain *Stiffelius* by Émile Souvestre and Bourgeois, among Piave's.[4] It was towards the end of April that the search really began to narrow. Verdi wrote to Piave,

. . . *Stradella* is passionate, but it is a paltry piece and all the situations are old-fashioned and commonplace. A poor artist who falls in love with the daughter of a patrician, seduces her, and is pursued by the father are the sort of things which offer nothing imposing, nothing original.

I don't know *Stiffelius*, send me a synopsis of it.

I do know Dumas's *Conte Herman*: it won't do.

As far as the genre is concerned, it doesn't matter to me whether it is grandiose, or passionate, or fantastic, as long as it is beautiful. All the same the passionate style is the safest. The characters should be exactly what the subject requires . . . I doubt if we shall find anything better than *Gusmano il Buono*, though I would have another subject which, if the police were prepared to allow it, would be one of the greatest creations of the modern theatre. Who knows! They permitted *Ernani* and might permit this too, and there would be no conspiracies in this one.

. . . The subject is *Le Roi s'amuse* . . .[5]

Piave forwarded the requested synopsis of *Stiffelius* with commendable promptitude, but, though mildly interested, Verdi was obviously becoming more and more obsessed with *Le Roi s'amuse*. He wrote on 8 May:

Stiffelius is good and interesting. It wouldn't be difficult to involve the chorus, but the costumes . . . would always be dreary. Transpose the action wherever you like, there will always have to be a Lutheran and the leader of a sect. Besides, is this Stiffelius a historical figure? I don't remember this name in any of the history that I have read.

Oh, *Le Roi s'amuse* is the greatest subject and perhaps the greatest drama of modern times. Tribolet is a creation worthy of Shakespeare! ! . . . You

know, six years ago when Mocenigo suggested *Ernani* to me, I exclaimed:
'Yes, by God . . . that would be a winner.' Now I was going over several
subjects again when *Le Roi* came into my mind like a flash of lightning, an
inspiration, and I said the same thing . . . 'Yes, by God, that would be a
winner . . .'[6]

As long as the *King Lear* enterprise progressed, Piave's *Stiffelius*
was going to have to yield to Verdi's *Roi s'amuse*. But as the weeks
passed it became clear that *King Lear* could not be ready in time, and
by June Verdi had resigned himself to a further postponement of this
dearest and boldest of projects. Once *King Lear* had been abandoned,
Stiffelius and *Le Roi s'amuse* were no longer contending dramas:
they could both be used, the one for Ricordi, the other, granted the
censor's approval, for Venice. By 25 June Verdi was prepared to have
Stiffelio officially announced, together with the fact that it was to be
produced in Trieste. He confirmed with Ricordi: 'Let the autumn
opera be for Trieste then . . . It will suit Trieste well. Personally I
wouldn't like the contract to be published, but if you and Ronzani
want to, you can, and you can also announce that the subject is
Stiffelio.'[7]

Stiffelio was now the more pressing obligation, and progress on it
was rapid and, as far as one can tell, unproblematic. But during the
summer months of 1850 he continued to ponder *Le Roi s'amuse*.
Indeed by 24 August he could aver to Marzari that he had been
'studying the subject, thinking deeply about it, and the basic
conception, the musical colour is already clear in my mind. I could
say that the larger part of the work is already done.'[8] Nothing in the
few surviving reports on the composition of *Stiffelio* suggests that
Verdi experienced the music with anything of the intensity occasioned by *Rigoletto* or dedicated to it a comparable study. The
documentary history of this opera must limit itself to such everyday
practical questions as the printing of the libretto, the casting, the
supervision of rehearsals, and above all censorship.

Some weeks of the summer Piave probably spent with Verdi in
Busseto working with him on the libretto. In the letters written earlier
in the year, Verdi had several times urged him to come, 'but . . . after
we have chosen a subject'.[9] By the middle of July Piave's work was
virtually ready, albeit a day or two later than Verdi and Ricordi had
hoped, and Muzio was given the job of delivering the text to the
hands of the publisher, as we learn from a letter of his to Ricordi
written on 13 July: 'Verdi received your letter yesterday and told me
to write to tell you that as Piave has not yet finished the drama he
cannot post it to you in time for the 15th as he wrote previously.

Instead I shall bring it to Milan myself when I next come, three days earlier than planned, that is I shall be in Milan on the 21st.'[10]

Just a week later Verdi himself wrote to Ricordi, to give his views on the casting of the opera and an encouraging report on its progress.

The company as a whole would suit the opera, although Colini would not be entirely right for the role of the father. Stiffelius would be perfect for Fraschini. We shall make of Raffaele a tenor in the style of Arvino in *I Lombardi*. Signora Gazzaniga will, I hope, be better than she was in Naples . . . As far as accommodation is concerned, I am very grateful for the kindness which people wish to show me, but I like my freedom and shall stay in a hotel for the few days I am in Trieste . . . We should be able to go into production by 10 November . . . I hope to have it finished in fifteen or twenty days from now . . .[11]

Muzio, writing to Ricordi again on 26 July, confirmed that 'Stiffelio is advancing in giant strides, and Verdi is working passionately on this subject, so beautiful and congenial.'[12]

By the end of September, when Verdi was due to go to Bologna to supervise a production of *Macbeth*, *Stiffelio* must have been virtually finished except for the instrumentation. He took the music to Bologna with him, hoping to get much of the scoring done between *Macbeth* rehearsals, for to keep up to schedule he would need to leave again for Trieste soon after he had got back to Busseto. On 13 October, however, he reported to Ricordi that things were not going quite to plan:

I am at last back in Busseto with a badly upset stomach; it's exhaustion from the rehearsals in Bologna. I could not go to Trieste immediately, unless I wanted to risk being ill there. But I don't want to delay the production of *Stiffelio* because of that, so some charitable soul would have to begin the piano rehearsals about the 18th of this month, even without me. If Ricci would do me this favour, I should be much obliged to him.

You will have received with the mail-coach from Parma the introduction to *Stiffelio*; as soon as possible I will send you the finale, so everyone but the principals will have all their parts. It is strange that in fifteen days I should only have been able to orchestrate one piece, but the rehearsals in Bologna were horribly fatiguing. It is an excellent idea to send Grolli to Trieste: I will write to tell you when you should send him. So do what you can to see that the rehearsals start promptly: I shall be there very soon, and my delay will do the score no damage at all. Keep calm, all of you, and don't be despondent.[13]

Verdi eventually announced his departure to Piave on 22 October: 'Are you coming to Trieste? I shall be in Venice on Monday or Tuesday.'[14]

The apparently calm and uneventful genesis of *Stiffelio* was rudely interrupted during the last days of rehearsal. So far in his career Verdi had been lucky with the censors, and though sometimes he had been put off a particular subject, as with *Catherine Howard* in 1843 or *L'Assedio di Firenze* in 1849, his operas, once completed, had had to suffer only very minor adjustments. Now, quite without preliminary warning, Verdi was to see *Stiffelio* subjected to censorial expurgation on a scale which for him was unprecedented. A lively account of the incident appeared in the Trieste paper *La Favilla* on Sunday 17 November:

Early on Thursday morning a dull noise, a sepulchral whisper, spread though Trieste: ladies not yet fully awake started up in their soft beds at the sound; gallants trembled at it; it murmured in gossipy coffee shops; it filled warehouses, shops, and offices, and wherever people met on the street they asked one another with corrugated brow and staring eyes: 'However could it happen?' Do you know, gentle readers, the cause of such a stir? Oh! it wasn't some troublesome, mysterious drop in the public funds, it wasn't the news of a bloody engagement with those obstinate Prussian fellows, it wasn't that the sails of Palmerston's fleet had appeared in the Adriatic, it wasn't even the fall of that Bonapartist ultrarepublic that had occasioned such surprise, that had aroused such consternation. Quite the contrary: it was the report, half true and half false, that *Stiffelio* was not after all going to be produced. And indeed it was on the very point of being cancelled; and if it was not to be cancelled, it would have to come to terms with a terrible enemy, and to avoid a worse fate submit itself to a cruel transaction, do you know with whom? . . . with our Reverend Signor Lugnani . . .

You know how a long time ago the management of our Teatro Grande announced in all corners of the city, in sesquipedalian letters, the opera *Stiffelio*, poetry by Signor Piave, composed expressly for our theatre by the illustrious Verdi. But you must also know that our aforesaid management first presented it (as is usual with operas) to the Imperial and Royal Directorate of Police, who having pondered the matter with the acumen proper to a Directorate of Police accorded it an *admittitur*.

Meanwhile, by a singular coincidence, the Rossi–Leigheb company have themselves presented, this time to Signor Lugnani, the drama of the same name, but which the censor had already flayed and mutilated, and which was given by the same company last time they performed in the Teatro Filodrammatico. And Signor Lugnani granted it his *placet*. With the *admittitur* of the Imperial and Royal Directorate of Police on the one hand, and the *placet* of the Reverend Signor on the other, one could hope, indeed one had the right to hope, that no further obstacle would arise to prompt tergiversation on the performances so desired, so longed for, by the public. But, gentlemen, no; unhappily Lugnani opened his eyes wider and, in the guise of Jove *omnia supercilio moventis*, suddenly unleashed a terrible tempest against the unfortunate opera *Stiffelio*.

. . . Signor Lugnani, either after reading Piave's libretto or attending the first rehearsals of the opera, felt the twinges of his most catholic bowels; he felt his senses reel, and phantasms Lutheran, heretical, republican and red crowded around him as the evil spirits did around Saint Anthony, and filled his devout soul with pious horror. Afterwards he was seen running in much agitation through the S. Nicolò quarter to the house of His Highness the Director, where he must have spoken in a manner that would have put the most expert missionary to shame; so that His Highness the Director himself finally had to agree that the Imperial and Royal Directorate of Police had made a colossal blunder, and that *Stiffelio* could not be produced in its present form without danger to public morality and to Roman Catholic Apostolic doctrine.

Meanwhile, you can imagine, gentle readers, the perplexity of the directors, the despair of the impresario, the oaths of the poet, the scorn of the composer. To avoid total ruin, to fulfil at least something of the undertaking given to the public, and guaranteed by public authority, to avoid making the scandal still more clamorous, it was unavoidably necessary to offer Signor Lugnani at least one hecatomb; and do you know what the victim was? The poet's verses. His unfortunate libretto! What expurgations, what manglings, what ignominies it had to undergo! Signor Piave very nearly died of a broken heart, but what is the life of a poet to the Reverend Signor Lugnani? . . .[15]

The basic alteration on which Lugnani insisted was the elimination from the final scene of the reading of the Biblical story of the woman taken in adultery. In its place a mere moral was proclaimed: 'Al suo nemico Chi pace dà, clemente avrà il Signore.'

Despite this fatuity, which had deplorably obscured and weakened the dramatic climax of the opera, *Stiffelio* was cordially, even warmly received at its *première* on 16 November. The newspaper reviews are unanimous in affirming this even when the reviewers themselves disliked the opera.[16] Some could not refrain from irony, however, over the fact that the hapless Piave ventured to take a bow. The generally derogatory account in *Il Diavoletto* for 19 November, for example, having praised the performances despite the fact that 'the music is anything but designed to make the singers shine', concluded:

The composer was honoured by being called to the proscenium repeatedly, and in the finale of the second act, which is marvellously contrived, there were sonnets and a crown of laurel: it seems that the sight of the laurel so enraptured the poet, that although no one was dreaming of him, nevertheless the public had the pleasure of seeing him at Verdi's side.[17]

A subsequent issue of the same paper is one of several to confirm that during the course of the season the opera 'became progressively better liked, as is proved by the tumultuous and repeated applause received by the admirable performers'.[18]

But *Il Diavoletto* was mistaken in predicting that '*Stiffelio*, if it is lucky enough to have such a cast in the future, will be able to, indeed must, hold its place in the repertory.'[19] Censorship, which had so ineptly intervened at the time of the Trieste *première*, continued to bedevil the opera. At first Verdi himself hoped to be able to patch up the opera to everyone's satisfaction as we see from a letter written to Marzari of La Fenice at a time when *Rigoletto* looked like being unconditionally forbidden:

... However, to show all my good will, I offer you the only thing I can. *Stiffelio* is an opera new to Venice. I suggest that, and I would come myself to produce it at whatever time during the Carnival season 1850–1 the Presidenza thinks fit. There is in this opera one very serious problem (this too is occasioned by the censor) and that is the final scene. It simply cannot be done as it stands; if, however, permission cannot be obtained from Vienna to perform it as I originally conceived it, then I would be willing to change the dénouement, which would be a novelty for Venice ...[20]

But the more accommodating attitude taken by the Venetian censors later in the month made this unnecessary. With work on *Rigoletto* now going ahead, Verdi had no time for tampering with *Stiffelio* and struck a more intransigent attitude on the censorship issue. To Ricordi, on 5 January 1851, he wrote:

I hear with displeasure that they want to perform *Stiffelio* at La Scala, because normally the operas which are not written expressly for that theatre are too negligently done ... If they are quite certain they want to do *Stiffelio*, the first essential is that the censor should be persuaded that there is nothing in the libretto either against politics or against religion, and that the original libretto should be left with all the words and the appropriate *mise-en-scène*; and that it should be performed without any alterations or castration and with the greatest care on everyone's part. Notice carefully that in the last scene the whole effect is dependent upon the way in which the crowds are grouped on the stage, and don't just have one technical rehearsal, as usual, but ten or twenty if they are necessary.
   Without these conditions I cannot permit *Stiffelio* to be given at La Scala, and notice that, if the effect should be spoiled by inadequate performances, I shall hold you, Signor Giovanni Ricordi, responsible for any damage that may result ...
   ... If the censor does not permit the original libretto, including the words 'Ministro confessatemi ... Ah Stiffelio io sono!', it cannot be effective, and in that event it is better to wait until I have time to rewrite the last scene without the church. Then I shall go and produce it myself in a theatre and with a company that suit me ...[21]

By February, when the opera reached Rome, it had suffered the same fate as *La Battaglia di Legnano* and *Giovanna d'Arco*. With its subject transferred in time and place, it became *Guglielmo Wellingrode*, and in this form enjoyed a modest success for some years.

Soon it was clear to Verdi that he could not hope for *Stiffelio* in its original form to be so much as performed, let alone successful. Its reworking into *Aroldo* came only in 1857, but the principle behind the reworking he had stated quite clearly to De Sanctis on 6 July

1854: 'That the new subject should be permitted by all the censors goes without saying: *that is the motive for changing it.*'[22]

Rigoletto

Stiffelio's viability as an opera was destroyed by the unforeseeable intervention of the censor just a few days before the *première*: on that occasion Verdi had suffered an artistic humiliation largely because there was neither the time nor the resources to resist or outwit Signor Lugnani. In the case of *Rigoletto* censorship troubles were foreseen almost from the start, and the 'absolute ban' was received two months or more before the proposed *première*. This time Verdi and his friends in Venice had just time to join battle with the censor and, by dint of patience, cunning and determination, to win a famous victory.

Victor Hugo's *Le Roi s'amuse* had been on the short list of Verdi's proposed operatic projects since he returned to Milan from Venice in the spring of 1844. But the first really positive reference to it comes only in September 1849, at the time when Verdi was proposing to write a second opera with Cammarano for Naples to follow up *Luisa Miller*. He suggested it to Cammarano via Flauto, describing the play as a 'fine drama with stupendous situations' and with 'two magnificent roles in it for Signora Frezzolini and De Bassini'.[23] During the winter months of 1849–50 however, the still more exciting possibility of a *King Lear* opera caused *Le Roi s'amuse* to be temporarily forgotten, until one day in April 1850, as Verdi was thinking over some possible themes, it came back to him 'like a flash of lightning, like an inspiration'.[24]

Something of the contractual background to *Rigoletto* has already been described. The story appears to begin on 9 March 1850 when Marzari, the president of La Fenice, wrote to Verdi inviting him to compose a new opera for Venice.

Desirous of giving the Venetian public the opportunity to admire a new product of your outstanding musical genius, I invite you to inform me whether you have any engagements for the coming Carnival/Lent season 1850–1. If not, be so kind as to tell me whether you would undertake to write a serious opera for this theatre, and on what conditions.

The Presidenza would prefer to leave to you the ownership of the actual opera, paying an agreed sum as a hire charge for the first performance in this theatre.

If however the question of ownership should be an obstacle to the conclusion of the contract, we will hold it for ourselves or for the impresario; only, in seeking to know what you would claim, we would ask you to keep in mind that the vicissitudes suffered [in the wars of 1848–9] have considerably reduced the resources of Venice and consequently of this theatre, which can no longer take upon itself the charges which it granted in other times . . .[25]

However, letters written to Piave in February and early March[26] show that Verdi had been anticipating this invitation for some time. Perhaps he had informally approached Venice himself, as an alternative to the Naples contract he was so eager to dissolve.

On 14 March, he outlined his requirements:

Highly flattered by the request you make, I reply with all promptitude, especially as I don't have much time to spend on contracts. Indeed I beg you to do what you can to let me have a reply before Easter. – These are the conditions . . .

1. The score will remain my property, though of course the Presidenza of La Fenice will have the right to perform it in the Teatro La Fenice alone during Lent 1851.
2. The libretto will be charged to me.
3. The opera will be produced in the first days of Lent, I undertaking to be in the city twenty days before the production.
4. Dress rehearsal, with décor and costumes as at the *première* (with or without an audience as the Presidenza pleases.)
5. For this the Presidenza will pay me the sum of 6000 (Six thousand) Austrian *lire*: half at my arrival in the city, half on the day of the dress rehearsal.

I repeat the request that you should favour me with as prompt a reply as possible, reserving only the right not to sign a definite contract until I know the names of the principal singers.[27]

A period of tenacious contractual haggling now ensued. Not being disposed to meet Verdi's demands in full, Marzari made, seemingly through Piave, counter-proposals which put the composer in a state of some dudgeon. He replied on 24 March:

According to what you write the Venetian business has started badly! If they offer me 4000 Austrian *lire*, all negotiations will be broken off. More than once a hire charge of 3000 and 4000 Austrian *lire* has been paid. Just ask the Presidenza what they paid for *Macbeth* a year after it had been performed in Florence. Add that this would be an expressly composed opera.

And the cost of the libretto? And my expenses, and the trouble it will cause me? The great Teatro della Fenice would seem to want to rank below the San Benedetto, which paid me 80 golden napoleons in cash to produce the *Foscari*, which had already been performed in ten or twenty theatres? No, no: I am not making contracts like this! After due consideration I asked for a very modest sum. If it doesn't suit the Presidenza no harm is done. Do you want to know the calculation I made?

Hire charge for a specially written opera	3000 Austrian *lire*
Cost of libretto	1000
My expenses, troubles & miscellaneous extras	2000
Total	6000

Please urge the Presidenza to make some reply. I have no time to lose.[28]

Further correspondence followed. Verdi wrote formally to the president, Marzari; with cordial urgency to the secretary, Brenna; irascibly to Piave. But he yielded no ground, and eventually Marzari conceded the greater part of his case:

. . . For the pleasure of acquiring for Venice the *première* of a new opera by the leading Italian composer of the day, I leap with both feet over all considerations of economy and grant you the requested 6000 = six thousand Austrian *lire* . . .

In recompense, I hope that you will agree to grant:
1. that the production should be fixed for about the middle of February, in view of the fact that, as the season ends about 20 March, a heavy weight of responsibility would fall upon me if the new opera, which will certainly become the Achilles of the season, should be given on too few evenings.
2. that this theatre should be entitled to the exclusive right to perform the work for the following successive season(s): a right which the Presidenza has normally reserved for every expressly composed score. – It is a right moreover which cannot harm your interests, as it is very rarely that the theatre avails itself of it, and one could say that the case of *Ernani* was virtually unique, the opera being written in the Carnival and Lent season 1843–4 and repeated in the same season 1845–6.

I hope that you will be so kind as to agree to these two modifications in the terms you proposed. It is not in my power to depart from them, without exposing myself to the censure of the society I represent.[29]

At the same time Brenna wrote more informally, providing, losses on the terms of Marzari's letter, and then going on to the question of the singers:

Concerning the cast, tell me in confidence which artist you would like engaged, and I will do all I can to help you. Only Mirate is definitely engaged. Contracts have been sent to Varesi and Signora Sanchioli, but not yet accepted. And as there are some differences about their demands it could be that arrangements won't be finalized. – I believe the Presidenza wants you to write an alto part, which would be sung by Signora Casaloni. She is engaged, because perhaps your *Luisa Miller* will be given as the first opera, in which Count Mocenigo claims that you have written a part for contralto. They say many handsome things about this singer, so we shall see . . .[30]

On 18 April Verdi decided to accept the terms and wrote separately to both Marzari and Brenna to that effect. In his letter to the former he requests some slight rephrasing of the terms:

. . . it only remains to have the contract completed, and I would ask that the article concerning the production should be couched approximately in these terms: 'Maestro Verdi undertakes to be in the city at the end of January so as to start rehearsals on 1 February 1851 and go into production as quickly as possible. At that date the Presidenza must put at Maestro Verdi's disposal all the artists who are to take part in the opera'. I don't waste much time in scoring and rehearsing, so the Presidenza can be sure that if things run smoothly we can go into production on 20 February . . .[31]

In the letter to Brenna he turns to the questions of casting and subject.

. . . Take good care in engaging the company. I say this in my interests and in the interests of the theatre alike. Mirate will be fine. As far as the women are concerned, since Signora Frezzolini and Signora Barbieri are not free, why not try to get Signora De Giuli?

There is a part for contralto in *Luisa Miller*, but a very small one. I can neither promise nor refuse to write for a contralto. It will depend on the circumstances and on the subject we have to choose.

. . . Tell Piave, to save time, that if he hasn't found the Spanish play I mentioned, I suggest *Kean*, which is one of Dumas's best plays. One could do so many fine things in this drama without wasting time. I could get down to work in a month from now . . .[32]

Despite all this preliminary debate, when the contract was finally drawn up in due form on 23 April, it was still not to Verdi's complete satisfaction. On 28 April he wrote to Marzari again:

The few modifications which I am obliged to make will not, I think, materially alter our contract. The first concerns not me, but the poet: it is very difficult to choose the subject and to write the libretto in two months; nevertheless if the poet can do it, so much the better . . . The second concerns the singers more particularly: suppose that any difficulty in learning should be found. For the rest be assured that, for my part, we can go into production by 20 February and perhaps even sooner . . .[33]

The same day, Verdi also wrote to Piave. *Kean* had been objected to, and Piave had made a number of alternative proposals, *Stiffelius* among them (cf. above, p. 254). In his reply Verdi made a counter-proposal. He returned to the idea of *Le Roi s'amuse*, wrapping up the suggestion with a deal of mystifying and furtive preamble which, as Budden justly observes, 'shows that he was well aware of the risks involved'.[34]

I doubt if we shall find anything better than *Gusmano il Buono*, though I would have another subject which, if the police were prepared to allow it, would be one of the greatest creations of the modern theatre. Who knows! They permitted *Ernani* and might permit this too, and there would be no conspiracies in this one.

Do try! The subject is grand, immense, and there is a character in it who is one of the greatest creations that the theatre in any country or any period could boast. The subject is *Le Roi s'amuse*, and the character I'm speaking about would be Tribolet; and if Varesi is engaged nothing could be better for him and for us.

P.S. As soon as you get this letter, get moving: run round all the city, and find some influential person who could obtain permission for us to do *Le Roi s'amuse*. Don't fall asleep: bestir yourself: and be quick about it. I expect you at Busseto, but not yet: after the subject has been chosen.[35]

As the prospects for *King Lear* faded, Verdi's enthusiasm for *Le Roi s'amuse* correspondingly intensified. On 8 May, writing again to Piave, he exclaimed,

Oh, *Le Roi s'amuse* is the greatest subject and perhaps the greatest drama of modern times. Tribolet is a creation worthy of Shakespeare! ! Even more than *Ernani*! ! it is a subject which cannot fail. You know, six years ago, When Mocenigo suggested *Ernani* to me, I exclaimed: 'Yes, by God . . . that would be a winner.' Now I was going over several subjects again when *Le Roi* came into my mind like a flash of lightning, an inspiration, and I said the same thing: 'Yes, by God, that would be a winner.' So then, get the Presidenza interested, turn Venice upside down and get the censor to permit this subject. What does it matter if it doesn't suit Signora Sanchioli? If we had to take any notice of that no more operas would get written. Besides, with everyone's leave, who is reliable among today's singers? What happened on the first night of *Ernani* with the best tenor of the day? What happened on the first night of the *Foscari* with one of the best companies of the day? Singers who can by themselves ensure a success . . . like Malibran, Rubini, Lablache etc. etc., don't exist any longer . . .

P.S. If we are doing *Le Roi* and this woman Berduzzi is really talented why doesn't La Fenice engage her? Certainly Signora Sanchioli, with what she calls her Michelangelesque poses, would be quite unsuitable for Bianca, and, believe me, it would be difficult to find a part for her.[36]

Piave's reply apparently raised a few half-hearted objections to Verdi's choice of subject. But these were swept aside:

I have received you letter of 14 May. At last! . . .

There will be no difficulty over dividing up the scene, nor over the sack. Keep close to the French and you can't go wrong.

As to the title, if we can't keep *Le Roi s'amuse*, which would be good . . . the title would necessarily have to be *La Maledizione di Vallier*, or, to be briefer, *La Maledizione*. The whole drama is in that curse, which turns out to be the moral, too. An unhappy father who laments his daughter's lost honour, is mocked by a court jester whom the father curses; and this curse hits the jester in an appalling manner. It seems to me both moral and as grand as grand can be. Take care that La Vallier should only appear twice (as in the French) and say a very few emphatic words.

. . . Come to Busseto and we shall work out everything . . .[37]

Piave did go to Busseto for part of the summer, and no doubt for this reason there are no further documents relating to the opera until 5 August, when Piave, from Busseto, forwarded a synopsis of the libretto to Marzari. He assured Marzari that the libretto would be finished in good time, and continued:

Verdi is not happy about Signora Sanchioli. He says it will be impossible to get anything out of her in this role, and that because of her the opera will fail! He added besides that he would never have accepted the Venice contract if he had thought that it meant having Signora Sanchioli, who has never done a complete season at a major theatre. He urges you, in the common interest, to give serious thought to this matter.

The title of the opera has yet to be decided upon and I have left it blank. It is taken from the celebrated drama by Victor Hugo and I have been verbally assured that no difficulty will arise over permission to perform it in the theatre. Verdi would like to call it *La Maledizione*, but I confess I'm reluctant and would prefer some other. But we have time to think about that, and it will soon be decided . . .[38]

But verbal assurances from Piave that he had had verbal assurances from someone else that *Le Roi s'amuse* would be an acceptable subject left Verdi unsatisfied. Later in August, presumably as a result of Marzari's letter of the 10th,[39] his unease increased and on the 24th he sent Piave back to Venice to clarify the situation. Piave took with him a letter to Marzari:

I have myself urged Piave to return to Venice with the sole object of delivering this letter to you personally, and explaining in full what I can only outline in writing.

The doubt that *Le Roi s'amuse* might not be permitted puts me in serious embarassment. I was assured by Piave that there was no obstacle to this subject, and, trusting in his word, I got down to studying and thinking deeply about it, and the basic conception, the musical colouring were worked out in my mind. I can say that the main work, and the most difficult, was done. If I should now be obliged to take up another subject, there would not be time to make such a study, and I could not write an opera with which my conscience would be content. It might be added that, as Piave wrote to you, I am unconvinced about Signora Sanchioli, and if I could have imagined that the Presidenza would engage such a singer, I would not have accepted the contract. It is in my interest and I think that of the theatre to make the success of the opera as sure as possible, and therefore, Signor Presidente, it is essential that you should find ways to overcome these two obstacles, to obtain permission for *Le Roi s'amuse*, and to find a prima donna (whether of the first rank or not) who suits me. If these obstacles cannot be overcome I think it would be in the common interest to dissolve my contract . . .[40]

Although the *Copialettere* dates it 27 September, Brenna's note assuring Verdi that 'the authorities will put no obstacles in the way of the production of the subject you have chosen to set'[41] must have been written in response to this, and should presumably be dated 27 August. Verdi wrote again on the 30th:

I am glad that the difficulties over the subject are removed; and I wish the difficulties on the *second subject* could be removed likewise. I believed that, having proposed Signora De Giuli, I had made myself sufficiently clear, and I did not think that an artist who had never done a season at the San Carlo or

La Scala would be engaged for La Fenice. How, you ask, can she be excluded from *Luisa Miller* and from the *opera d'obbligo*?! Let her do Luisa ... But what claims can she have on the new opera? Put another soprano on your roster, even a beginner, provided she satisfies me, and you will see whether I can exclude the *primissima*. For the rest I don't wish to dispute the merits of Signora Sanchioli: I am inclined to accord her all the merit that the rest of the world does: I only say that she cannot do my new opera well ... [42]

During the autumn months *Stiffelio* was a more pressing matter than *Rigoletto*; and though one presumes that Piave was sending the occasional instalment of verse, such of Verdi's letters as survive deal only with the question of casting. One from Bologna, written on 5 October to Brenna, finds him in his most ironic form:

I can't say anything about Signora Cruvelli as I've never heard her. The general opinion is that she is a good singer and a madwoman. I tell you frankly that I don't like these caricatures of Malibran, who have only her eccentricities and nothing of her genius. The idea of composing an opera for such maggot-brained creatures is terrifying. They are quite capable of neglecting anything they don't understand, and ruining the opera.

I remember another German woman who is now a princess, and who didn't like the final trio of *Ernani*: perhaps she wanted a rondo, and meanwhile poor *Ernani* was horribly treated on the first night. However, as you find yourselves in the virtual certainty of not having a woman who satisfies the requirements of your great theatre, I don't want it to be said that I am opposed to the engaging of Cruvelli.

As to the other two, you know Teresina Brambilla and can say better than I can whether she would be suitable for your great theatre. But of the two you suggested to me, Brambilla sings better and has more talent ... [43]

A fortnight later he still remained sceptical of the qualities of the artists offered him:

Piave hasn't understood the least thing of what I wrote about Signora Boccabadati. I wrote that the lady was available, and that enquiries might be made: I did not say that I was satisfied with her, nor that I preferred her to Brambilla. I am satisfied neither with the one nor the other: only the result will be able to reconcile me with whichever of them you should engage.

I would add that Lasina's observations on Boccabadati's voice could be right, because I have also had very bad reports from Milan ... I have never heard her myself ... [44]

Verdi received the completed libretto from Piave just before setting out for Trieste. He acknowledged it on 22 October, but only gave a few hints about the alterations he would require, as he knew he would soon be seeing Piave anyway:

I have received the rest of *La Maledizione*; and I have written to Ricordi to send you the 500 Austrian *lire*, being half the payment for the aforesaid libretto.

That it is fifty-four lines longer or shorter than *Stiffelio* doesn't matter:

sometimes twenty lines are long, while on other occasions 100 aren't long: in the theatre verses are long if they can be spared: an idea expressed in two lines is long if it could have been expressed in just one: for example Tribolet's six lines after the quartet 'Riedi m'odi, a casa ritorna' etc. are far too long, because this idea could be expressed in a few words; if the rhyme embarrasses you, then do it in recitative, but let it be brief and as fast as possible ... It seems to me that it would be a good thing to change Francesco's verse 'Bella figlia a che giova' etc. because it is too reminiscent of other things.

There are a lot of things to cut and to tighten up which I will tell you in person; the 'file' is needed here even more than in *Stiffelio*, but there is no need to wait to do it until the music is written ...[45]

At this point the censorship issue – which, as far as the actual choice of subject was concerned, Verdi had presumed closed in August – was reopened. Quietly but ominously Marzari reported that

The local Imperial Central Directorate for Public Order ... demands that you submit to them the libretto which you are composing for this theatre.

This demand is provoked by the rumour that Victor Hugo's play *Le Roi s'amuse*, from which Signor Piave has taken his new work, has had an unfavourable reception both in Paris and in Germany because of the licentiousness with which it is so replete.

Nevertheless the said Central Directorate trusts that, considering the good character of the poet and the discretion of the composer, the plot will be developed in a fitting manner, and it is only to assure themselves of this that they require to see it.

However, in requesting you to hasten the production of the libretto itself, I remind you that, while last August the Presidenza and the *podestà* gave their approval to the subject you suggested, Brenna, the secretary, acting on behalf of the Presidenza, informed you that the poet, Signor Piave himself, was personally given the job of obtaining the permission of the Authority for Public Order ...

This is for your information, and in the hope that Signor Piave did overcome the difficulties which I predicted in my letter of 10 August ...[46]

Verdi, who was in Trieste at the time for the production of *Stiffelio*, apparently saw no immediate cause for alarm. He worked out a quick and effective way of getting through what he supposed to be a mere formality, and then, on 15 November, wrote to Brenna:

The Presidenza requests me to submit the libretto which I am to compose for the Carnival season for Venice. I notify you that it will be forwarded to the Presidenza on the steamboat on the 17th. As I shall be with Piave in Venice on Wednesday the 20th at midday, I would beg you to take particular care to obtain the formal political approval by that date, as I shall not be reckoning on staying in Venice more than two or three hours. You know I have no time to lose and so it is indispensable that you should exert yourself vigorously for me ...[47]

The next day he sent notes both to Brenna and Marzari, confirming that the libretto had been delivered to the steamboat as planned.[48] But when he and Piave arrived back in Venice on the 20th, Brenna had failed to expedite the procedures of the Central Directorate for Public Order, and Verdi was obliged to return to Busseto with formal authorization still unobtained. By the end of the month he was becoming gravely concerned, and was toying with the kind of hypothetical concessions that might prove necessary:

I have waited in vain for a letter from the Presidenza bringing me the political authorization for *Le Roi s'amuse*. I am not wasting time, and continue composing, but I am concerned. So urge the Presidenza to write to me as quickly as possible. Don't take things in your usual phlegmatic way because this is a serious matter, a very serious one.

Take care not to allow yourself to be persuaded to do anything which will result in altering the characters, the subject, or the situations: if it is a question of the words then you can do it, and if it is a question of changing the situation in which Francesco gets into Bianca's room with the key you can do that too; indeed I think (as I told you in my last letter) that we shall need to find something better: but take care to leave intact the situation in which Francesco goes to Saltabadil's house, without which the drama ceases to exist; it is also necessary to leave the business with the sack: that is of no concern to the police; it is not their business to wonder whether something is going to be effective.

Farewell. Write to me more often: it seems to me that we shouldn't let this affair drag on too long, and *if I were the librettist* I would go to a great deal of trouble, especially as you would have a heavy responsibility in the event of this drama not being permitted . . .[49]

But while Verdi was musing over such compromises, the censor, uncompromisingly, had already struck. On 1 December Marzari delivered the grim message that

. . . despite all the efforts of the Presidenza and the poet, the subject has been absolutely forbidden, it is even prohibited to propose any amendments whatever.

Piave hopes that, by substituting for the King of France a contemporary feudatory and removing some of the obscenities with which it is indeed crammed, virtually the whole canvas can be resubmitted. But the Presidenza, after the efforts that have been made, cannot be confident of success . . .

Marzari sent Verdi a copy of the censor's report at the same time.

His Excellency the Military Governor Cavalier de Gorzkowski . . . has commanded me to inform the Noble Presidenza that he regrets that the poet Piave and the celebrated Maestro Verdi have not been able to choose some other theme on which to exhibit their talents than one of such repellent immorality and obscene triviality as the subject of the libretto entitled *La Maledizione* . . .

His Excellency has therefore determined absolutely to forbid the performance, and wishes me, at the same time, to admonish the Presidenza to refrain from all further representations on this matter . . .[50]

The letter was signed by one Martello. Verdi was devastated by the blow. Coming so soon after the 'castration' of *Stiffelio* it seems to have deprived him, momentarily, of all determination and resource. Had things depended on him at this juncture, it looks as if *Rigoletto* would have got no further:

The letter that has arrived with the decree absolutely forbidding *La Maledizione* has taken me so by surprise that I have almost lost my head. In this matter, Piave is much to blame: entirely to blame! He has assured me in several letters, written to me since May, that he had obtained approval. Apart from this, I composed a good part of the drama and was working most assiduously to finish it at the appropriate time. The decree banning it reduces me to desperation, because it is too late now to choose another libretto, and so it would be impossible for me, *absolutely impossible*, to compose for this winter. It was the third time which I have had the honour of composing for Venice and the Presidenza knows how scrupulously I have always carried out my obligations. You know that although virtually on my death-bed I promised to finish *Attila*, and finish it I did. Now, on my word of honour, I repeat that it is impossible for me to compose a new libretto, even if I wanted to work so hard as to ruin my health. However to show all my good will I offer you the only thing I can. *Stiffelio* is an opera new to Venice: I propose that . . . The hurt and displeasure which this prohibition occasions me are so great that I do not have words to describe them.[51]

While Verdi was thus lamenting Gorzkowski's ban, Piave had been goaded into activity; moreover he had managed to find an unlikely ally in that very Martello who had signed it. Despite the terms of the decree, and despite the pessimism of the Presidenza, Piave did make the kind of transpositions that Marzari had outlined on 1 December and did, thanks to the efforts of police official Martello, succeed in getting it approved. When the proposed emendations were submitted to Verdi, however, he was unimpressed:

I have not had much time to examine the new libretto: but I have seen enough to understand that, changed in this way, it lacks character and significance, and that the dramatic situations have lost all their effect. If it was necessary to change the names, then the locality had to be changed too, and a Duke or a Prince of somewhere else introduced, for example a Pier Luigi Farnese; or the action could be put back to the time before Louis XI when France was not a united kingdom, and a Duke of Burgundy or of Normandy could be made of him, in any case an absolute ruler . . .
In the fifth scene of Act I all the anger of the courtiers against Triboletto is meaningless. The old man's curse, so terrible and sublime in the original, becomes ridiculous here, because the motive which drives him to curse him

no longer has the same importance and because it is no longer a subject speaking so boldly to his king. Without this curse what point, what significance does the drama have?

The Duke is a nonentity: the Duke absolutely must be a libertine; without that there is no justification for Triboletto's fear that his daughter might come out of her hiding-place: and so the drama is impossible. In the last act, why ever should the Duke go alone to a remote tavern, without an invitation, and without an appointment?

I don't understand why the sack should be taken out? What concern of the police is the sack? Are they afraid it might be ineffective? But might I be permitted to ask why they suppose that they are better judges in this matter than I? Who can do the composer's work for him? Who can say this will be effective, that won't? Ernani's horn was a difficulty of that kind: well, who laughed at the sound of that horn? And if you take out the sack it is unlikely that Triboletto would talk to a corpse for half an hour before a flash of lightning reveals that it is the corpse of his daughter.

I observe finally that we are to avoid making Triboletto ugly and hunch-backed! ! A hunch-back who sings? why not! . . . Will it be effective? I don't know; but if I don't know, I repeat, neither does the person who proposes this change know. Putting on the stage a character grossly deformed and absurd, but inwardly passionate and full of love, is precisely what I find the beautiful thing. I chose this subject precisely for these qualities, these original traits, and if they are taken away, I can no longer write music for it. If you tell me that my music can stay the same even with this drama, I reply that I don't understand such reasoning, and I say frankly that whether my music is beautiful or ugly I don't write it by chance, but always try to give it a definite character.

In short, out of a drama which was powerful and original has been made something utterly commonplace and ineffective. I am very grieved that the Presidenza has not replied to my last letter. I can only repeat what I said in that, and urge you to do that, because I cannot conscientiously compose this libretto.[52]

Piave, who had attempted to atone for earlier negligence not only with this revised libretto but also by doing a few errands for the composer, received an implacable rebuff at the same time.

I thank you for the powder and the wafer biscuits which you can send me a bill for. Don't bother to take the fish because I could not have it fetched from Cremona.

I am writing to the Presidenza about the new libretto. I am not sending you the 200 Austrian lire, because for one thing I shall not be writing the opera for Venice, and for another I commissioned Le Roi s'amuse on condition that you should obtain the permission of the police. As they are not permitting it (to my great loss) our contract is of course dissolved . . .[53]

Though Piave's first attempt at refashioning the libretto must have been a piece of abject botching, it had at least served to reopen communications between the theatre management and the censor. In the debate that followed, Verdi's letter of 1 December, even if it was written in a mood of contemptuous disinterest, proved eloquent and persuasive. By 23 December Marzari was able to report censorial concessions:

While your letter of 14th inst. plunged me into grave difficulties, I could not but acknowledge that some of your observations were irrefutable. I therefore made these the subject of renewed representations to the Authority for Public Order and have finally agreed with the General Director of Public Order himself that, if it is seriously intended, as you yourself agreed, to change the place and time of the action, the libretto may conserve the colours and the original characters which you desire.

The character substituted for Francesco, who could be either a Pier Luigi Farnese or perhaps better a Medici or a Duke of Burgundy or Normandy, as you please, can be a libertine and the absolute ruler of his state. The jester can be deformed, as you desire. There will be no obstacle to the sack, and it will only be necessary to give to the abduction of the jester's daughter a colour which conserves the decency proper to the stage . . .

Despite these very substantial concessions it was clear that a great deal remained to be done, and that it could be done best if Piave and Verdi got together again, especially with someone like Brenna on the scene too, to keep them under control. Marzari's letter continued:

To get all the appropriate agreements the Secretary of the Presidenza, Guglielmo Brenna, will be coming to Busseto together with the poet Piave; they were both present at the discussion held between me and the General Director of Public Order.

They will leave here with the first train on Saturday, as the Presidenza cannot do without the secretary before the first production of the season which, as usual, will take place on the 26th. But meanwhile I think it as well to tell you about this so that you can continue your work in peace . . .[54]

A pleasingly intimate account of the arrangements Verdi made for his Venetian visitors is provided by the note he sent Piave on 29 December:

I am sending my small carriage to bring you and Brenna to Busseto. The servant (Giacomo) will be on this side of the Pò because he doesn't have a passport. So don't be annoyed at having to walk these few paces, crossing the Pò by way of La Croce, where Giacomo will be on the bank. He will wait for you until ten o'clock tomorrow morning (Monday), so make sure you leave Cremona about eight o'clock.

You know my house, and now as my mother is living in your room I don't have two more free. If you can put up with two beds in one room they will be ready; and if not, the inn is only a couple of paces away as you know.[55]

Presumably, then, Piave and Brenna arrived at Busseto late in the morning of 30 December. They got to work with the urgency the situation demanded and later the same day sent off their proposals to Marzari:

The Secretary of the Presidenza invited Maestro Verdi to outline the changes to which he would consent to subject the libretto submitted under the name of *La Maledizione* . . .

With the co-operation of the poet Francesca Maria Piave, it was agreed as follows:

1. The action will be removed from the French court to that of one of the independent Duchies of Burgundy, of Normandy, or of one of the petty absolute princes of the Italian states, probably to the court of Pier Luigi Farnese and to the period which would be most appropriate from the point of view of *décor* and scenic effectiveness.

2. The original character types of Victor Hugo's play *Le Roi s'amuse* will be preserved, the names of the characters being changed according to the situation and the period which is chosen.

3. The scene in which Francesco declares himself determined to make use of the key he possesses to let himself into the room of the abducted Bianca will be avoided altogether. Another scene will be subsituted for this, one which preserves the necessary decency without depriving the drama of interest.

4. The King or Duke will be invited to the amorous rendezvous in Magellona's tavern by a deception practised by the character who is to take the place of Triboletto.

5. As far as the sack containing the body of Triboletto's daughter is concerned, Maestro Verdi reserves making such modifications as may be deemed necessary until he has tried the effect in practice.

6. As the changes mentioned above will require more time, Maestro Verdi declares that he will not be ready to stage his new opera before 28 February or 1 March . . .[56]

The document was signed by Verdi, Piave and Brenna. In his letter of acknowledgement Marzari urged Verdi

and the poet Piave, in particular, to avoid in his new work everything that could affront stage decency, so as to have no further obstacles from the side of the Authority for Public Order.

I rather regret the need to delay the production of the opera. Nevertheless I am convinced that the difficulties that arose through the censor make postponement unavoidable, so as to make up for the time lost. However I count on your kindness to limit the delay to the shortest possible time, and although you are authorized to delay the staging of the opera as far as 1 March next, I do not doubt that you will not wish to delay your arrival in Venice beyond 3 or 4 February.[57]

Marzari wrote to Verdi again on 14 January to report that

Signor Piave submitted on Saturday the 11th the new libretto which you have undertaken to compose; having been approved by the Presidenza and the *podestà* it will be submitted tomorrow for the approval of the Authority for Public Order. As it conforms with the information previously received I hope that it will not encounter any obstacles, and I shall do all I can to speed up a definite certificate of approval.

Meanwhile, in reply to the memoranda which you submitted to Piave, I advise you that you are free to write the part of Maddalena for contralto, as Signora Casaloni has indicated her willingness to take on the role even if it has no real solo piece.

As far as the secondary roles are concerned, you have at your disposal the baritone Damini, engaged as understudy to Varesi, who sang in that capacity in this theatre last year too and gave pleasure for the way in which he willingly performed on various evenings in place of the *primo baritono assoluto*. If you should need to use him in your opera, the task of understudying will be given to the other baritone Signor De-Kunert. The second bass, Andrea Bellini, also a baritone, and the second tenor Zuliani Angelo, who have been engaged at this theatre for some years, enjoy the favour of the public. The second woman is Signora Luigia Morselli, who has a strong voice, but is a mezzo-soprano. These are in addition to the first *basso profondo* Signor Feliciano Ponz, who has a strong voice and is a convincing artist.

Maestro Malipiero's opera will be produced not later than 1 February, which means that you should be in Venice by 4 or 5 February at the latest.[58]

If Piave supposed that with his rewritten libretto now submitted to the censor his task was done, he deceived himself. Verdi, loyally aided by his librettist, by Marzari, Brenna and apparently Martello, had won a notable victory, but now he could settle down to his usual way of working, ruthlessly rooting out every weakness and longueur in the librettist's verses, checking over and over again that not one dramatic opportunity was wasted. The process, already familiar from *Ernani* and *Macbeth* and *Luisa Miller*, begins in earnest with this letter of 14 January:

... Meanwhile this infernal *Rigoletto* – between one oath and another – progresses. The Duke's aria is done too, and it was difficult enough because ... I must make a few observations: the two following verses

> Poiché la festa cessò di corte
> Moviamo uniti prima del dì

cannot stay as they are because after the feast Triboletto changes his clothes, *sings a duet with a ruffian*, an interminable scene *with Gilda*, a duet *with the Duke*, an *aria* and finally this abduction.

All that cannot happen in just one night, since if the feast finishes at daybreak, Triboletto cannot meet the ruffian in the *evening*; besides it is unlikely that Bianca would stay up all night ... So these two lines must be changed.

I would like that blessed aria of the Duke's filed down a little, which is your job: for myself, at the end of the recitative after the line 'Ella mi fu rapita', I need another hendecasyllable ('Chi fu l'iniquo? Ma ne troverò vendetta!'), then a last tender line, but I don't like the one which stands because 'Ah senza Lei languir sento la vita' doesn't mean anything.

I should like the second verse of the *adagio* to be more beautiful than the first, and here it isn't: after the two lines 'Ed ... io potei ... soccorrerti Cara fanciulla amata', you will need to rewrite the four that follow and find some

beautiful idea, well-arranged and affecting, and abandon the idea of 'Vendi-
cato sarò . . .'

Finally the cabaletta must be naturally accentuated because (and you
poets really must pay attention to this) I cannot set

>Corrò
>
>Volò
>
>Quandò etc.

So change it to make the accent fall on the second syllable. I need these
alterations quickly . . .[59]

Verdi continued in this vein on the 20th:

I have had a letter from the Presidenza in which he says that he hopes the
libretto will be approved, but meanwhile approval is not certain. In the
meantime I am composing and the second act too is almost finished: I say
almost because the *stretta* of the duet finale is ineffective as a result of the
words which Gilda says aside. I find it ineffective to have two characters
singing about their affairs one on one side, the other on the other, especially
in *quick movements*. So I have decided to rewrite this *stretta*, but I need you
to help and I suggest a *decasyllabic* metre which is easy for you to do
quickly . . . do it as you please but take care that there should be some
dialogue.

Verdi then sketches out quite fully the sort of cabaletta text he
requires. He continues:

You see then that there are six lines each (decasyllabic): the last two of Gilda
can be delivered aside: but the other four should be addressed to her father.
Take care to write six fine lines which express the joy of revenge. I could
then write a *splendid* cabaletta, really effective, which I cannot do with the
verses that are here now. I should like the second line in particular, both
Rigoletto's and Gilda's, to be expansive . . .

I hear that Malipiero is going into production on 1 February! . . . is it
possible?! The Presidenza therefore asks us to be in Venice on the 4th or 5th.
I hope and desire that Malipiero will be a little later, in which case I should
be in Venice two days after Malipiero's *première*. Arrange this business
yourself, and do it so that I can stay as long as possible in Busseto . . .[60]

The days passed, and neither the approval of the police authorities
nor the requested verses from Piave were forthcoming. Impatient
and exasperated, Verdi eventually exploded:

Well then?! Am I to come to Venice or to stay in Busseto? I'm not joking! I
see that you continue to take this business very casually but I repeat, I am
not joking, and I take it very seriously. It is enough for me to do to stay here
day and night tearing my guts out with this damned opera, and I have no
desire to come to Venice to do battle with the censor. If the police have
approved the new libretto than I will come to Venice as I fixed with you, that
is after Malipiero's opera; if the formal approval of the police is not granted
it is pointless for me to make the journey, and I shall stay here. Reply at
once.

P.S. Granted that the police have approved the libretto, do please get the

Presidenza to let me stay in Busseto as long as possible. I am waiting for the verses I asked you for.[61]

Meanwhile the worthy librettist was in fact 'hammering his brains' and invoking Minerva in readiness for renewed labours on the libretto. He had written to Verdi on 20 January:

It is only today that I answer your dear letter of the 14th, because I was hoping to be able to inform you of the definite approval of the libretto; but yesterday evening one of these colonels told me that we shouldn't get it for a couple of days still. But be assured that both I and the Presidenza are doing all we can, and in my view you can be sure there will be no obstacles.

Another reason for my delay was that I have not yet been able to change those verses which you asked me for, however much I hammer my brains. Verses I have written, but none that could satisfy you, so I don't think it is any use sending you them. I shall not fail to send them as soon as I have had some success.

. . . Malipiero's rehearsals started eight days ago, but I think the production will be delayed because the music has got no rhythm and the singers are in a sweat and finding it hard to learn. God knows then what sort of pandemonium they will find in the orchestra. . . . Mirate is happy and dreams only of your opera, which is looked forward to here as a redemption for this theatre.

I again ask your pardon if I have not sent any verses because, I repeat, I don't find them worthy of your inspection, and I hope to do some better ones which I shall not fail to send you as quickly as possible. Oh! this *Rigoletto* will be an epoch-making event in my life! Do believe that I am neither indolent nor unwilling, but that, *invita Minerva*, no man can do anything worthwhile . . .[62]

Next day Minerva was more gracious:

Here at last are the variants which I was not able to send you yesterday . . . You will see I have done the two last lines of the *largo* of the aria in various ways: choose those that suit you best. With regard to the cabaletta it seems to me that this will do.

I can't give you any news except that today there was a rehearsal for all the understudies, and they tell me it will be a bad look-out for Signora Brambilla if her understudy has to sing even once: they might perhaps find that her voice is better than that of the woman she is understudying. I haven't heard her, but *relata refero*. Tomorrow I shall be knocking at the door again for this blessed licence, but you can be sure that you are needed too badly for them to risk annoying you again. So you can and must regard the affair as finished . . .

I have already given all the instructions for the stage sets, which will be magnificent, and young Caprara is wanting to try his hand on the practicables . . .[63]

At last on 24 January formal approval was granted.

GOOD NEWS! Malipiero's rehearsals are suspended, as the music presents the performers with too many difficulties; *Allano** limps along; you need time, so it is proposed to give *Lucia* as a stop-gap, and it will go into production on Tuesday 28th. This will push back Malipiero's production to at least the middle of February, which gives you time to breathe.

Today I have at last received the signature of the Director General of Public Order for *Rigoletto*, without any lines being changed at all. I have just had to change the name of Castiglione to Monterone and that of Cepriano to Ceprano because there are families of that name. It was also necessary to omit the name of Gonzaga, and say in the list of characters simply: The Duke of Mantua. This can't matter much to us, because everyone knows who reigned at that period. For the last five days I have been running around like the devil from the government to the police, to the Comando di Piazzo, to the Presidenza, I assure you that by the time this is over I shall be a real athlete. The colonel tells me that tomorrow without fail he will get me the signature of the governor, and so there is no need to talk about it any more.

At the time of writing it is four o'clock and I have been on the go since nine, because Signor Martello had taken it into his head to change the period and the place as well as the characters. Finally I succeeded, partly with *charm*, partly with *desperation*, and partly by saying 'I couldn't' etc. in this vital transaction, and I swear it seems almost like a dream. Cheer up then. The wind has turned, and our ship is heading for a safe harbour.

Here is the new cabaletta which I hope will work all right . . .[64]

The epic engagement with the Venetian censors was finally concluded the next day. On 26 January Piave sent Verdi the glad news:

TE DEUM LAUDAMUS!
GLORIA IN EXCELSIS DEO!
ALLELUJA ALLELUJA!

Finally yesterday at three o'clock in the afternoon our *Rigoletto* returned to the Presidenza safe and sound without fractures or amputations. I still seem to be dreaming. You will have to laugh when I tell you the story of my last battle! . . . But to return to us. Instead of Tuesday 28th, *Lucia* will go on on Wednesday 29th, so we shall have gained one day by the postponement of Malipiero's rehearsals. I assure you that Mirate in *Lucia* is a young Moriani. Stupendous![65]

Verdi wrote first to Marzari, expressing his satisfaction at the news and reporting his own progress and plans:

I am delighted that the police have finally granted approval to this blessed *Rigoletto*. For myself it only remains to compose the last duet, and that too would have been finished had I not been suffering from a bad stomach these last few days.

I shall be in Venice two days after Malipiero's opera is staged and I shall be there early in the morning so that I can attend the rehearsal too. In case Malipiero's opera should have to be delayed a few days I would beg you to let me know through Piave and leave me in peace here. I repeat I shall be in

---

* *Allan Cameron*, Pacini's setting of the libretto originally written for Verdi in 1843.

Venice on the morning of the second day after Malipiero's production, specifically to take the rehearsal on that day; for which reason I also hope to send the parts some days before my arrival. Once the last duet is done I have only five or six days' work on the orchestration to do . . .[66]

On 5 February Verdi resumed correspondence with Piave. The time that had seemed so short a few days before was now dragging, and he was eager to get arrangements for rehearsing and copying fixed:

I am sorry that Malipiero is going to be so late. I could go into production in a few days from now because I have just today finished the opera. I only need to make a fair copy of the second act and the last piece. So as not to lose time I am sending you meanwhile all the rest of the opera. So go straight to the diligence from Cremona where you will find addressed to you two-thirds of the opera, that is numbers 2, 3, 4, 5, 6, 7 and 11, 12, 13. You will consign these nine pieces of music to Gallo in my name. Get Gallo to have the singing parts copied from them, and you will then consign them as follows: Gilda, Brambilla; Duca, Mirate; Rigoletto, Varesi; Maddalena, Casaloni; Sparafucile, Pons; Castiglione, the company's best baritone; there is not much urgency about the rest.

I shall bring the rest of the opera with me and while we are rehearsing I shall do the orchestration. Take note that I shall start to rehearse the day after Malipiero's opera; to save time get everything ready for the secondary roles at least, as they have a lot to do in the ball scene; and we shall get into production quicker. I shall be in Venice on the morning of the day after Malipiero's opera, and see that a rehearsal is arranged for that day. If they like, Brambilla, Varesi, Mirate and Casaloni can stay at home for the first rehearsal.

P.S. I repeat that you should deliver the opera to Gallo in my name (despite the fact that Ricordi engaged him) because as a result of the uncertainties with the censor I dissolved the arrangements with Ricordi . . . and the conditions are still not properly fixed. But Gallo should just get copying and keep calm! . . . Get the *banda* part of the ball copied; it is important and difficult . . .

Giuseppina added a postscript:

Dear Signor Piave, called The Gracious!
I very much suspect that Verdi *always* leaves in his pen my good wishes to you, despite the fact that I *always* beg him to convey to you a thousand cordial greetings. This time, to be on the safe side, I will send my own good wishes, past, present and future. Allow me too to express my sense of that *graciousness* which makes you celebrated *throughout the Universe and in other places!* I beg you to be generous in the education of Verdi, so that he may return to Busseto a little less bear-like! ! ! ! !

Joking apart, don't forget that at Busseto both Bears and Graces will always be delighted to see you whenever you can make the sacrifice of leaving Venice to come and bury yourself in this wash-tub. Verdi is bellowing that he wants the letter, so I have only time to shake your hand . . .[67]

Piave replied, on 8 February:

... Gallo had already had from Ricordi the express commission to get the parts copied and he authorized him to get the work done by the theatre copyists; but now the look of things has changed, and Gallo, being given charge of the music by you, will tomorrow begin to get it copied in *his house* and under his direct supervision and responsibility.

... When the copies are made I shall have the parts distributed as you told me, except for that of Monterone (quondam Castiglione and late Saint-Vallier), since you must choose the better of the two baritones yourself: so Marzari tells me. But I warn you there is a baritone here who is doing or undoing the part of Wurm in *Luisa*, and who is now singing second tenor in *Lucia*. As this baritone is patronized by Varesi it could be that you will be pressed by him to give him the part; but apart from the fact that his voice is completely colourless, he is regarded with contempt by the public; and so it is the opinion of our friend Marzari too that it will be enough to give him a subsidiary role, or, if possible, no role at all. But that must remain a confidence between you, Marzari and me. This canorous hero, master of a bunch of keys [clefs], namely *basso profondo*, baritone, tenor, soprano and contralto, is called Kunnerth. By God, he is a greater man than St Peter who always had only two!

I am touched by the courteous Signora Peppina's gracious letter, which I shall endeavour to answer as soon as my emotion has subsided. It rather increased reading the superscription of your own letter: *To the gracious Signor F.M.* etc.[68]

More information followed next day.

There were performances here on Thursday and Friday because we have had the forty-eight Maids of Vienna. Today, Saturday, we shall at last be having an orchestral session on Malipiero's opera, and they say that the first performance will be given on the 15th, but I don't believe it. However I will write *poste restante* to Cremona on the 13th to give all the exact details, so you can make your arrangements with confidence. So on Saturday morning send the consul Cincinnatus (of this Age of Folly) trotting to the Pò, and there will be the despatches.

The two best rooms of the Albergo dell'Europa are at your disposal from the 16th, and for only 4 Austrian *lire* a day. You will find them warm and with Clampoy's best piano, which I got *maestrino* Bozzoni to select.

No more music has arrived yet and Mares, who greets you, would like to have at least the greater part of it in good time. Marzari tells me that he will be writing to you today or tomorrow: let him go whistle and set out when I tell you in my letter of the 13th.[69]

There seem to have been no reports on the progress of rehearsals during the latter part of February and early March. We may deduce that they went smoothly and happily enough from an allusion in a letter Verdi wrote to Marzari a year later. He speaks of his 'lively memory of the kindness shown me by the Presidenza last year, and the zeal and exceptional conscientiousness which I found in all performers in *Rigoletto*'.[70] One anecdote relating to the *première* on 11 March was preserved in the Varesi family. The great baritone's daughter Giulia Cora Varesi recalled:

Bouts with the censor

How many times I have heard tell of the emotions of that Venetian première. My father, ashamed and timid in his ridiculous buffoon's costume, did not know how to pluck up courage to appear before the public, for he feared their derision; and at the very last moment, it was Verdi himself who, giving him a shove to get him on stage, made him stumble over the planks behind the scenes and flung him out on to the stage, staggering all over the place. The audience thought this an inspiration for a buffoon's entry and were enraptured . . .[71]

Despite the fact that *Rigoletto* was 'a somewhat revolutionary opera'[72] it was from the start one of Verdi's most brilliant popular successes – though some of the critics made heavy weather of it. The *Gazzetta di Venezia* provides probably the most interesting of the reviews:

. . . An opera like this cannot be judged in one evening – Yesterday we were almost overwhelmed by its originality; originality or rather strangeness in the choice of subject; originality in the music, in the style, even in the form of the pieces; and we did not comprehend it in its entirety. Nevertheless the opera had the most complete success and the composer was applauded, called for and acclaimed at almost every piece; two of them had to be repeated. And in truth, the skill of the orchestration is stupendous, wonderful: the orchestra speaks to you, weeps for you, transfuses passion. Never was the eloquence of sound more powerful.

The vocal part was less splendid, or so it seemed at a first hearing. It is quite distinct from the style previously employed, since large ensembles are wanting, and a quartet and trio in the last act in which the musical thought was not even perfectly grasped scarcely gained our attention.[73]

A week later it reported that '*Rigoletto* is gaining every evening in the public favour. Never was Verdi's inspiration happier, never did he strike a more fruitful vein.'[74]

We may fittingly end this chapter with one of Verdi's best-known expostulations on the subject of censorship, for it was prompted by a season at the Teatro Argentino in Rome later in the year, when were performed both *Stiffelio*, transformed into the abhorred *Guglielmo Wellingrode*, and *Rigoletto*, transformed into the not less abhorred *Viscardello*. The letter was written to the sculptor Luccardi on 1 December 1851.

. . . I know that not only *Stiffelio* but also *Rigoletto* have been ruined at Rome. These impresarios have not yet understood that when operas cannot be given in their integrity, as conceived by the composer, it is better not to give them; they do not realize that the transposition of a movement or a scene is almost always the cause of the failure of an opera. Imagine what it means to change the subject!! It is much as if I have not made a public declaration to the effect that *Stiffelio* and *Rigoletto*, as performed in Rome, are not my operas!

What would you say if someone tied a black ribbon on the nose of one of your beautiful statues?[75]

Giuseppina's operas – *Il Trovatore* and *La Traviata*

Giuseppina Strepponi, the friend and counsellor of Verdi's earliest years in the theatre, from 1847 his mistress, and finally from 1859 his second wife, had an intimate and special association with several of his operas. She had been instrumental in persuading Merelli to stage *Nabucco* during the Carnival/Lent season 1841–2, and between then and her retirement from the stage in 1846 had been a celebrated interpreter of the role of Abigaille. Her relationship with *Jérusalem* was of a more intimate kind. Apparently by the autumn of 1847 when Verdi was making this adaptation of *I Lombardi* she had become a familiar of his study. She lent her hand to Verdi's autograph full score, copying part of the text of the Act II due in her own purple ink to turn it into a declaration of love.

In *Il Trovatore* and *La Traviata*, the first operas written after Verdi and Giuseppina had withdrawn from Busseto and set up home at Sant'Agata, the association seems if anything still more intimate. There are good reasons for regarding *La Traviata* as being, at least in part, an artistic reflection of the relationship between the lovers;* while in the case of *Il Trovatore*, Giuseppina claimed a modest role as assistant author. I cite two details from letters written by her to Verdi while he was at Rome to produce the opera: in the first Giuseppina urges Verdi to 'write me a nice letter and hurry up and give *OUR Trovatore*';[1] while in the second she gives some homely particulars to substantiate her claim to a kind of co-authorship: '... and you haven't written anything yet? You see! You haven't got your poor Nuisance in a corner of the room, curled up, in an armchair, to say: "that's beautiful, mage, that's not – Stop – Repeat that: it's original".'[2]

Il Trovatore

The history of *Il Trovatore* really begins in February 1849, when

---

* Cf. below, pp. 647–9.

Verdi, still resident in Paris, was engaged in negotiations with Flauto and Cammarano over the opera that was eventually to become *Luisa Miller*. In that month he wrote to Flauto proposing that the opera he had contracted to compose for Naples should be postponed until the following year, and, presumably by way of compensation for this inconvenience, offering to compose a second opera for Naples straightway thereafter.[3] Although unable to consent to the first part of Verdi's proposal, the impresario was not likely to forget the second: throughout the early part of the correspondence concerning *Luisa Miller*, he attempted to persuade Verdi to commit himself to the composition of another opera for Naples. Flauto's zeal was doubtless the greater in that, although Verdi had become disaffected with La Scala, and had still failed to find a second operatic home, Naples – with only *Alzira* to its credit – had done less well out of the peripatetic maestro than any other major operatic centre in Italy. Verdi for a time remained non-committal. But that his thoughts were sometimes on this question is proved by the survival of a memorandum made sometime in June 1849: 'for the opera I shall be composing after Easter 1850'.[4] Eventually, a few days before his departure from Paris for Busseto, he wrote to Flauto:

If you still want me to come to Naples to produce this opera [*Luisa Miller*] and to compose another new one, there is, if not absolute certainty, at least every likelihood that this too can be arranged. I should have to write this new opera in the coming Carnival season for production in about the middle of February 1850 . . . leaving to you the ownership of poetry and music for all places within the Kingdom of Naples, and keeping for myself ownership of the poetry and music in all other parts of the world, you will pay me for such ownership, *one thousand five hundred* ducats payable in three equal instalments in a manner to be agreed upon mutually.

As I said before, this proposal is only a probability, but if it suits you reply at once . . .[5]

That this proposal, with some very slight modifications, would suit Flauto was to be anticipated, and by 7 September, Verdi was, as it seemed, already concluding the preliminary stages of negotiation for his next Neapolitan opera:

I have little time for writing a long letter and will only say that I shall do as you suggest and compose, after this *Eloisa*, another opera to be produced the day after Easter 1850. So send me the contract in accordance with the proposals made in my last letter [26 July] . . .

We must now think seriously about the libretto for the opera to be produced the day after Easter, because in order to do things properly Cammarano will have to have made the synopsis and have delivered the first pieces to me by the end of October, when *Eloisa* is produced. I shall be leaving Naples for some time then, so I should like to have with me some verses to set. For a subject, suggest to Cammarano *Le Roi s'amuse* by Victor Hugo. A fine drama with stupendous situations, and there are two magnificent roles in it for Signora Frezzolini and De Bassini . . .[6]

However, after the vexatious if faintly farcical experiences that awaited Verdi in Naples at the time of the *première* of *Luisa Miller*, it was hardly to be expected that he would contemplate with equanimity the prospect of composing another opera for the city in the immediate future. When exactly he released himself from the contract to write this second opera is not quite clear, but it was certainly by the end of January 1850, when he proposed to make it over to Ricordi instead.*

It was some time before anything further came of this next collaboration with Cammarano. During the weeks spent in Naples at the time of the *première* of *Luisa Miller*, thoughts of *Le Roi s'amuse* were apparently abandoned because of the still more haunting prospect of doing a *King Lear*. In the spring of 1850, however, *Le Roi s'amuse* returned to favour, but was made over to Piave, as it was intended for production in Venice. Work on *King Lear* was 'temporarily' suspended.

It was not until after the production of *Stiffelio* that Verdi resumed negotiations with Cammarano. And it was presumably at this time that he discovered García Gutiérrez's *El Trovador*. Those authors who have claimed that Verdi had already been pondering this subject for a year appear to have been deceived by a letter cited by Monaldi and almost certainly misdated by him. On 19 December 1850 Cammarano had written to Verdi about their next opera.

. . . I have thought several times about *King Lear*, but, in all conscience and considering the haste that is going to be necessary, I should prefer another subject, as you propose; but to avoid putting myself in the wrong, I cannot promise a synopsis before 15 February nor any verses before the end of that month. However, I do not ask for more than a very brief respite of fifteen days, hoping that this proposal will not inconvenience you. We can do *King Lear* later . . . Send me at once the subject you promised.[7]

The letter cited by Monaldi was surely written in response to this, and should accordingly be dated 2 January 1851:

. . . The subject I should like, and which I now propose, is *El Trovador*, a Spanish drama by Gutiérrez. This seems to me very beautiful, imaginative and full of strong situations. I should like to have two female roles: the principal one is the gipsy, a woman of very special character . . . So to work, little man, and make haste. It will probably not be difficult to find the Spanish drama.[8]

---

* Cf. letter of 31 January 1850 to Ricordi, cited above, p. 253.

For some weeks Verdi was in Venice, fully absorbed in *Rigoletto* and not unduly put out by Cammarano's silence. After his return to Busseto, however, he began to grow impatient. The only news to have come from Naples was from De Sanctis, who seems to have expressed some reservations – whether his own or Cammarano's is not clear – about the bizarre romanticism of García Gutiérrez's play. Verdi swept aside his friend's doubts, and suggested that he might help stir Cammarano to some activity.

I am extremely angry with Cammarano. He has absolutely no regard for time, which for me is a very precious thing. He has not written one word to me about this *Trovatore*: does he like it or doesn't he? I don't understand what you mean when you talk about difficulties for *common sense* as well as for the theatre!!

However, the more Cammarano provides me with originality and freedom of form, the better I shall be able to do. Let him do anything he likes: the bolder he is, the better I shall be pleased. Only don't let him lose sight of the public's preference for brevity. You are his friend, so it's up to you: urge him not to lose a moment. Although I am angry, give Cammarano a kiss for me ...[9]

As a matter of fact Cammarano had not been quite as idle as Verdi supposed. Indeed, he had already written a letter which must have crossed with Verdi's to De Sanctis, explaining his first thoughts on the problems of turning *El Trovador* into a libretto. Clearly he had found certain details in the story offensive or implausible: and he may have proposed a bowdlerized version of it. Verdi sought to set his mind at rest:

I have received your very dear letter of 27 March, and I see what you propose to do. A word about your objections.

The scene of the taking of the veil must be left in (it is a thing too original for me to be able to forgo) and indeed we must derive from it every advantage, all the effects possible. If you don't want the nun to flee voluntarily, let the troubadour (with many followers) carry her off after she has fainted. It is true that the 'gipsy does say that Manrique is not her son', but they are words that escape her during her narrative and which she withdraws again so quickly that the troubadour, far from thinking anything of the kind, cannot believe they are true. The gipsy does not save herself and Manrique because at the stake her mother had cried out 'Avenge me'. In another place she says 'Stretching out its arms towards me, the fierce apparition shrieked: Avenge me! ... And it hurtled through the clouds in the air repeating Avenge me!' ... The last word of the drama is 'You are avenged.'

You don't say a word about whether you like this play. I suggested it because it seemed to me to offer some fine theatrical moments, and above all a quality at once singular and original. If you were not of my opinion, why haven't you suggested some other subject? In this sort of thing it is as well if the poet and composer feel in agreement.

As far as the distribution of the pieces is concerned let me say that when I am given verses that can be set to music, every form, every distribution is good; indeed the more novel and bizarre they are, the more I am pleased with them. If in operas there were neither cavatinas, nor duets, nor trios, nor choruses, nor finales etc. etc. and if the whole opera were (if I might express it this way) one single piece, I should find it more reasonable and proper. For this reason let me say that if it is possible to avoid a chorus at the beginning of the opera (all operas begin with a chorus) and Leonora's cavatina, and simply to begin with the troubadour's song, and to make one single act of the first two, that would be a good thing. These isolated pieces with changes of scene after each one always seem to me more like concert pieces than opera. If you *can*, do that. Also I don't very much like it that Manrique should be wounded in the duet. For the rest do what you think fit. When one has a Cammarano, things cannot but go well.

P.S. I don't have a noose round my neck to write this opera, but all the same I want to get started. So I await your scenario, and then as soon as possible the verses . . .'[10]

Cammarano had already completed his scenario for *Il Trovatore* before he could have received Verdi's letter with its incitements to boldness and formal freedom and bizarrerie. Very probably he had already sent it off to Verdi, and again the letters to and from Naples crossed in the post. It is not surprising, then, that when Verdi read Cammarano's sketch he found it disappointingly tame and conventional. On 9 April he sent another lengthy epistle to his librettist.

I have read your scenario, and you, a man of talent and of so superior a character, will not be offended if I, the meanest of creatures, take the liberty of saying that if we cannot retain all the novel and bizarre characteristics of the Spanish play in our version it is better to give it up.

If I am not mistaken, some scenes do not have the power and originality they had before, and Azucena especially does not retain her strange and novel character: it seems to me that the two great passions of this woman, *filial love* and *maternal love*, are no longer present in all their force. For instance I shouldn't like the troubadour to be wounded in the duel. This poor troubadour has so little to call his own that if we took away his valour what would be left for him? How could he interest a lady of such high rank as Leonora? I shouldn't like Azucena to tell her story to the gypsies . . . and finally I don't want her to be mad in the final scene. I should like you to leave out the big aria!! Eleonora has no part in the song of the dead and the troubadour's canzone, and this seems to me one of the best positions for an aria. If you are afraid of giving Eleonora too large a part, leave out the cavatina . . .

In order better to explain his ideas, Verdi then offers his own scenario. He concludes:

Please excuse my boldness: no doubt I am wrong, but the least I could do was to tell you everything I feel. However, my first suspicion that you wouldn't like this drama is perhaps true. If that is the case, we should still be in time to put matters right, rather than do something which doesn't suit you. I have another subject here, simple, tender, and one could say, virtually ready: if you like I will send you it, and we will think no more of *Il Trovatore*.

Drop me a line about this matter. And if you yourself have a subject, let me know ...[11]

These letters are particularly valuable in revealing to us the state of mind in which Verdi began work on *Il Trovatore*. Clearly they disqualify Toye's rather appealing notion that Verdi assumed the comparatively conventional style of *Il Trovatore* as a kind of reward to a public which had remained faithful to him despite the revolutionary boldness and novelty of *Rigoletto*. It is apparent that Verdi began work on *Il Trovatore* more than ever eager for originality and freedom from the formal and stylistic conventions of Italian opera, more than ever disposed to esteem the fantastic and the bizarre above the heroic. Certain words recur over and over again as he discusses the Spanish play – 'nuovo' and 'originale', 'strano' and 'bizzarro' – and these concepts are surely the cause of his infatuation with it. Similarly, 'novità' and 'libertà' are to be the hallmarks of the manner adopted by Cammarano and Verdi in making their operatic version. Nowhere is there any suggestion of that stylistic retrospection discerned in *Il Trovatore* by many critics.

From this time for more than a year work on *Il Trovatore* progressed erratically. Cammarano may have been more than usually lethargic in providing the verses – by the end of June 1851 nothing more than the introduction seems to have been ready[12] – and for Verdi himself it was a difficult and distracted period. The death of his mother in June 1851, the mounting tension between Verdi and the people of Busseto occasioned by his living with Giuseppina Strepponi, the problems of settling in at Sant'Agata, whither they had moved in May: all these things made concentration on the new opera unusually difficult. As Verdi explained to Cammarano in a letter of 9 September, 'An accumulation of misfortunes, serious ones! have so far distracted me from serious thought about *Il Trovatore*. Now that I begin to recover my breath, I ought to be busying myself with my art and my affairs ...'[13]

And as he did begin to busy himself once more with *Il Trovatore* he rapidly became aware of other problems. The more the opera crystallized in his imagination the more apparent it became that it would make unprecedented demands on the performers, especially on Azucena and Manrico. Although impresarios from all over Europe were fluttering eagerly about him, it was far from clear where he would find a company likely to render the work in proper style. In this same letter to Cammarano he explained the problem fully:

Rome and Venice have asked me for an opera. For singers Rome offers me Signora De Giuli, Fraschini and Colini; Venice, Signora Frezzolini and Coletti. The Roman company is more suitable for *Il Trovatore*, but they don't have the actress for Azucena, for this Azucena whom I care about so much. It seems to me that Signora Gabussi would do this part very well, but I don't know whether she is under contract or free, either in Naples or anywhere else. If she were free, I could perhaps get her to sign a contract for Rome; if she is under contract for the San Carlo with other really fine artists, I should almost be inclined to renew the contract I broke off this winter, when I was so irritated by the condescending manner they adopted in offering me the contract.

Similarly, in a letter to the Venetian impresario Gallo, Verdi gave as one of the reasons for his unwillingness to commit himself to a contract the fact that 'for the subject I am working on (to which I am very attached) the company, although most excellent, would not be suitable. First of all, and above all, I need a most uncommon tenor, and so far you do not even have a common one'.[14] Understandably, after his recent experiences, censorship was another cause of concern to Verdi. He assured Gallo that he was determined 'not to sign any contract without first presenting the libretto to the censor in whatever state it is where I am to produce the opera. This is so as to avoid the immense bother I suffered over *Stiffelio* and *Rigoletto*.'

The idea of taking up a contract with Naples once more fell through when Cammarano sent his report on Signora Gabussi:

Signora Gabussi is not contracted with Naples, nor am I as poet, and for us to involve ourselves in negotiations about an opera would have had the air of an intrigue: besides the prospectus of contracts is already published with a large company and an undertaking for a new composition by Pacini. Perhaps the desire for a new work from you could have induced the administrators (I say perhaps) to release itself from this undertaking, but that would have been not only an offence, but an insult to your dignity as man and artist, so it did not even enter my head to do anything so base. I have spoken to Signora Gabussi about Rome, about the role of Azucena, about your concern; she was pleased and would accept readily, on the condition that she should be granted the choice of one other opera during the course of the season. But she has been requested in Spain (which certainly is not very convenient for her) and for another theatre in Rome itself. For this reason you must reply by return of post, not indeed to press for a contract, which would have to depend on an impresario, but because with a letter of yours she would have some tangible sign of regularization, and could disengage herself from other responsibilities, or temporize . . . I would add that you could not hope to do better for Azucena, and that I know of no artist better suited than Signora Gabussi to perform the role well.[15]

Verdi replied:

God preserve me not only from plotting intrigues, but from taking even the smallest step that might have the faintest resemblance of an intrigue (I would rather die of hunger). Since Signora Gabussi is not at Naples, it is a matter of no concern to me whether I compose for one theatre rather than another. As yet, while I was waiting for your reply, I didn't want to sign any contract, indeed the negotiations with Rome are virtually broken off. So tell Signora Gabussi quite frankly to arrange her affairs where and how is most convenient for her.[16]

Negotiations with Rome did in fact drag on for a few weeks more. In October or November Cammarano submitted to the impresario Jacovacci the synopsis of the libretto, to see whether there was any chance that Il Trovatore might be permitted in Rome. Jacovacci, after having consulted the Papal authorities, replied in the following cheerfully dispiriting manner:

In my opinion, the modifications cannot substantially injure the action. As you will see, instead of witches they are called gipsies. Outlaws and partisans of factions are cut out, as such things may not be mentioned. Instead of burning at the stake, which could be supposed due to condemnation by the Holy Office of that period, it will simply be called sentence of death ...

Leonora must not let the audience see that she takes poison, because suicide is not permitted, so that can be altered.

Such types of music as off-stage choruses can, as you wish and as was done in Stiffelio, be accompanied by a large accordion, which has the same tone as an organ; but there must be neither sacred nor immoral words in any part.

Leonora must approach the convent through a vestibule. Church, convent and vows are not to be mentioned. You, who (without making idle compliments) are the leading opera poet of the day, can imply these things like the others, without meeting any opposition from the censor.[17]

Doubtless it was this report of Jacovacci's that prompted Verdi to abandon all thought of producing Il Trovatore in Rome or anywhere else that winter. He reported to his Bologna friend, the theatrical agent Mauro Corticelli, 'I must first of all tell you that I have broken off negotiations with Rome. That will be the fifth contract I have refused for this Carnival season, but the circumstances are such as to make it impossible for a good Christian to compose conscientiously ...'[18]

The winter of 1851–2 was spent by Verdi and Giuseppina in Paris. February brought them from Naples the news that Cammarano was ill, so again work on Il Trovatore was hindered if not altogether suspended. But the same month apparently brought a compensation too, in the form of Dumas's newly dramatized version of *La Dame aux Camélias.*

From now on, as far as one can see, work on the long-pondered *Il Trovatore* and the freshly recollected *Dame aux Camélias* proceeded simultaneously. Which would first be completed and produced would depend more on Piave and Cammarano, on the ability of an impresario to get together a suitable company, and on the indulgence of the censors than on any preference of Verdi's. In the event the contract for the *Dame aux Camélias (La Traviata)* was signed early in May, a month earlier than that for *Il Trovatore.*

The history of *Il Trovatore* passes into another critical phase in the summer of 1852. In May Verdi had received a letter from De Sanctis in which his Neapolitan friend attempted yet again to persuade him to offer *Il Trovatore* to the San Carlo. Verdi indicated the conditions on which he would be prepared to do this and urged De Sanctis to hurry the Neapolitan management along, but it is clear that he was sceptical about the chances. Nothing came of this initiative and finally, despite the forbidding prospect of dealing with the Papal censors, Verdi decided to place the opera at Rome. In June, he sent Jacovacci a draft contract the form of which shows that long months of frustration had not lessened his determination to insist upon an uncensored and properly acted performance:

I shall come to compose an opera for next Carnival season in Rome, to be produced on about 15 January 1853, on the following conditions:
1st. If I have reports that satisfy me of the merits of Signora Penco [who was to sing Leonora].
2nd. If you find another dramatic prima donna to take the part of the gipsy in the drama which I have conceived.
3rd. If the censor approves Cammarano's libretto *Il Trovatore.*
The ownership of the libretto and score will remain wholly mine. You will have the right to perform it at the Apollo theatre only during the Carnival season 1852–3. I shall be in Rome on 20 December 1852 to attend to all the rehearsals of the opera. For this you will pay me six thousand francs, in three hundred golden napoleons of 20 francs, in two equal instalments: the first on the day of my arrival in Rome, the second the day on which the dress rehearsal of the said opera is held ...[19]

Eager to make sure of the opera that had slipped from his grasp the previous winter, Jacovacci promptly made his way to Busseto to talk things over with the composer. Meanwhile Verdi himself was seeking informed opinion on Signora Penco – from Cammarano, from De Sanctis, and from Luccardi to whom he wrote, 'Jacovacci is here. Perhaps I shall be coming to Rome for the Carnival season. Don't say anything to anyone for the time being. Do you know

Signora Penco? What do they say about her in Rome? How did she get engaged? Tell me quickly all you can ...'[20]

Regarding the proposed Azucena, too, Signora Goggi, he sounded out his acquaintances. To Prince Poniatowski in Florence he wrote:

Thank you for having given me the information about the talents and voice of Signora Goggi. I see there are some difficulties, but that doesn't frighten me. With talent and good will one can succeed. The role I intend for her is strange, original: difficult if not impossible for someone with no talent, but easy for anyone who understands. And since you have been so kind as to write to me a first time, I hope it won't be too much trouble to write again, sending me a musical scale covering the whole range of her voice, and writing under each note, *good, bad, weak, strong* etc. If that is too much trouble, Signora Goggi can do it herself without fear of confessing her sins: it will be under the seal of confession, and a great help both to her and to me ...[21]

Though much of the opera must have been composed by this time, it was certainly not finished. Indeed Verdi had not yet received all of Cammarano's libretto. As far back as 1 October 1851 he had been 'urging [Cammarano] with all [his] heart to finish this *Trovatore* as soon as possible'.[22] But the usual hazards of working with Cammarano – his desultoriness, and the excessive number of his commitments – were exacerbated in this instance, partly because, with no firm commitment to stage the opera, the pressure was taken off him, partly because from January onwards he was genuinely and, as it proved, gravely ill. In May, Verdi made another attempt to hurry Cammarano along. In the course of a letter to De Sanctis he writes: 'You haven't written anything more about Cammarano. So I suppose he is quite recovered. Urge him to send me the rest of the libretto as quickly as possible, and tell him that, if he would like to write another one when this is finished I should be delighted.'[23] Two months later when Jacovacci visited him to discuss the contract Verdi had still received nothing more. On 3 July he wrote to Cammarano:

I shall write *Il Trovatore* for Rome, if I have good reports of Signora Penco, if they find me another prima donna, and if the censors permit the libretto. I entreat you therefore to finish it at once and send the rest of it to me. Also to give a copy of it to Jacovacci, who will be calling upon you soon, so that he can submit it to the censor's office. It is understood that if they only require a few phrases to be changed, I think we shall have to do it, but not to the extent of spoiling the libretto.

All this should be kept secret, and send me detailed accounts of Signora Penco at once ...[24]

What Verdi cannot have known was that Cammarano was by now

virtually on his death-bed. The librettist probably did know, however, and receiving Verdi's letter he made a last supreme effort to get
the rest of *Il Trovatore* written. He finished it on about 9 July and had
it despatched to Busseto a week before he died on 17 July. Sadly, he
never received Verdi's enthusiastic acknowledgement: 'I have received the rest of *Il Trovatore*. I read and re-read it with increasing
pleasure. These verses of yours are full of originality, of life, of
passion.'[25] Verdi had had a preliminary warning of the gravity of
Cammarano's condition from De Sanctis, but knew nothing more
until he read of his death in a theatrical journal. His distress and the
confusion occasioned by such a loss at such a time are apparent in a
letter written to De Sanctis on 5 August:

I was thunderstruck by the sad news of our friend Cammarano. It is
impossible to describe to you my deep grief! I read of his death not in a kind
letter, but in a stupid theatrical journal!!! You, who loved him as I did, will
understand all the things I cannot say. Poor Cammarano!! What a loss!! How
ever was it that you did not receive a letter I wrote on the 19th of last month?
How ever was it that a promissory note sent in my name, by Ricordi, to our
poor friend was not found in the post? But on your return to Naples you will
find everything and reply to me.

As you know, if the censor will permit it, *Il Trovatore* is to be given in
Rome. My head is so confused that I cannot explain in detail but, as you will
see in my last letter, this *Trovatore* seems to me rather too long; and tell me:
what if there were need for some judicious cutting? What if the censor
should require some small change? What if I myself needed some small
matter modified or changed? (Note that all these things must in no way be
allowed to affect the work of our poor friend, whose memory I more than
anyone wish to respect.) In such a case, to whom should I look? Did this man
Bardare have Cammarano's confidence? Is he able? Write to me at once, for
there is no time to lose.

It will be a good thing to guard the verses of *Il Trovatore* jealously, and for
the heir or heirs, in making a receipt for the promissory note, to transfer to
me the possession of *Il Trovatore*.[26]

De Sanctis' account of the abilities of the above-mentioned Leone
Emanuele Bardare satisfied Verdi. Some weeks later when he had
decided exactly what modifications were required in Cammarano's
libretto, he wrote to De Sanctis again, asking him to commission
Bardare to do the job.

I am in agreement with you that the changes in *Il Trovatore* should be made
by the young poet friend of poor Cammarano. This is what it entails:

First, in Part Two I should like a characteristic canzone for Azucena
(which I could make play with, musically speaking, at different points in the
drama) Instead of the two verses 'stride la vampa' etc. etc., on which it
would be difficult to make a popular theme, I should like two verses of six
lines each, as for example (You can laugh!!)

Stride la vampa, la folle indomita
Urli di gioia al cielo innalza.
Cinta di sgherri giunge la vittima
Bianco vestita, discinta e scalza . . .
Sorride, scherza, la folle indomita
Urli di gioia innalza al ciel . . .

. . . This would have to be the form and the metre. The poet can modify and do as he thinks best.

Secondly, in the finale (the old one) of Part Two I should like to write an aria for the Count, and so remove the romanza from Part Three, as was agreed with Cammarano. It will need an adagio cantabile of eight or ten lines after the line 'novello e più possente ella ne appresta' etc. or where he thinks best. Then when he says to his followers 'di quei faggi all'ombra celatevi' I should like the chorus, as it departs, to sing a verse (in septenarii) in a fragmented, *sotto voce* style, which I should play off against the following cabaletta, which would perhaps be quite effective.

Thirdly. A cantabile is missing in Eleonora's grand aria in Part Four. The very beautiful verses 'Quel suon, quelle preci' etc. only lend themselves to a declamatory *lento*. So it will be necessary to add eight or ten passionate and beautiful lines after the recitative 'Arreca i miei sospiri' . . .[27]

On 23 October De Sanctis replied:

The young poet is beside himself with joy at having worked for Verdi: his feelings you will find expressed in a letter from him which I enclose. The verses seem to me quite good. Knowing your heart and the needs of the poet, I will tell you his hopes. He would wish, I believe, for just a little something for the time he has spent on this work, having for a time abandoned some other operatic pieces . . . Urge the most diligent Ricordi to print the original libretto and not the mutilated Roman version.

. . . Signora Penco under your direction will be able to please you: she has some defects, but many good qualities. I find that she makes a mistake in always singing in a piercing style. She is not a perfect soprano. I should tell you, attentive maestro, that she is very pretty, I warn you, however, that she is a devil! She will certainly beat the other prima donna . . . They tell me that Goggi is an old singer, but you will rejuvenate her with the magic of your music.

Maestro, we all await a masterpiece in *Il Trovatore*. Verdi with his music must immortalize Cammarano's last work. Remember that the last piece, written eight days before his death, was the tenor aria! . . .[28]

It was about this time that the final details of the contract were being sorted out with Jacovacci. Verdi sent off the final form of the contract to him in November. In the way that had become typical of him he glosses his businesslike note about the contract with artistic exhortations:

I warn you that for Ferrando's part a bass tending to baritone will be required. He certainly need not be an absolutely first-rate singer, but not one of the usual second-rate ones either. Think about this in good time, because I am very attached to the introduction, which depends entirely on Ferrando . . .

For this same introduction a large bell will be needed to ring the full peal of *midnight*.[29]

Even after Bardare's efforts in October, the libretto had not yet assumed its final form. Right up to the last minute Verdi was compressing, and deleting, and altering, in his search for maximum dramatic intensity. On 14 December he wrote to De Sanctis once more:

Il Trovatore is finished, and on the 25th I shall be in Rome. I must trouble you once gain to consult the poet Bardare. In the second-act finale ... I have, almost without noticing it, made the *primo tempo* not an *adagio* of the kind that is always employed, but a more animated, lively section.

If I am not mistaken it has come out well; at least I have done it the way I feel it. I should have found a *largo* impossible. After that I thought of suppressing the *stretta*, especially as it doesn't seem to me necessary for the drama, and perhaps Cammarano only wrote it to follow custom.

This is what I have done, then: please submit it to the judgement of Signore Bardare, and if he doesn't approve we can print the libretto with the *stretta* in inverted commas (a thing which I shouldn't like).

Verdi then transcribes the text as he has set it. He continues:

In this way it turns out more original in form, perhaps more effective, and above all short (which is not bad thing especially in this libretto, which is rather long).

Verdi had similarly abbreviated the end of the fourth act:

I have also curtailed Leonora's last words, and instead of setting twelve lines, which in that position would have had an absolutely frigid effect, I have set just five in recitative, making use of almost all Cammarano's words.

Again the passage in question is transcribed. Verdi concludes:

Let Bardare alter any words he thinks necessary. And if he thinks it best to leave them as Cammarano had them I should not object. But it does seem to me that these are things that would do no harm to the libretto and which are of great benefit to the theatrical effect ...[30]

It was New Years's Day 1853 before Verdi, already in Rome to prepare *Il Trovatore* for production, was able to tell De Sanctis of his final decisions on the form of the opera. At the same time he offers a few thoughts on opera librettos in general, which show that his passion for imaginative daring was as unimpaired as ever:

We are agreed then about the Act II finale which I shall have printed as I transcribed it for you, and of course with the stage directions ...

The last finale puts me in some confusion, because I have had to write the music without awaiting your reply, and the musical layout is such that it would be impossible for me to set the lines you mention. For my part I maintain that five lines of recitative would not spoil the effect, at least not as much as six rhymed lines would ... To say 'sei vendicata o madre' and to say 'tarda vendetta! . . . ma quanto fiera avesti o madre' is the same thing as far as the drama is concerned. Except that the former is shorter and more suitable. However, if you don't think so, we will print all the lines Cammarano wrote, adding a note in the libretto: 'the following lines have been changed for the sake of brevity . . .'

. . . I should like nothing better than to find a good libretto and hence a good poet (we have so much need of one), but I cannot conceal from you that I read the librettos that are sent me very reluctantly: it is impossible, or virtually impossible, that another person should divine what I want: I want subjects that are *original, grand, beautiful, varied, bold* . . ., and bold to the last degree, with *original forms* etc. etc. and at the same time capable of being set to music . . . When they say to me: I have done it this way because that is what Romani, Cammarano etc. have done, then we don't understand one another any more: precisely because these great men have done it this way, I should like it to be done differently . . .[31]

The surviving letters tell us next to nothing about the rehearsals for *Il Trovatore*. We know simply that the rapid approach of the date for the production of *La Traviata*, and very probably too the melancholy, adoring letters of Giuseppina, made Verdi less eager than ever to linger in Rome any longer than absolutely necessary. The opera undoubtedly enjoyed a tremendous success, but there are no personal accounts of the *première*, of public acclamations or of celebratory banquets, such as Muzio used to provide in former years. To De Sanctis, Verdi simply reported in one laconic phrase '*Il Trovatore* didn't go badly',[32] and hastened back to his 'desert'.

La Traviata

From mid-December 1851 to mid-March 1852 Verdi and Giuseppina were living in Paris, and it is plausibly assumed that the composer's interest in Dumas the younger's *La Dame aux Camélias* dates from that time. For it was during this period – on 2 February, to be precise – that the play received its *première*, and nothing seems more likely than that Verdi, who may well already have been familiar with the subject in its novel form, and who was certainly an enthusiastic admirer of the elder Dumas's *Kean*, should have seen the play at some stage during the next few weeks.

It was also during this second Parisian sojourn that preliminary negotiations over the contract began. Eager to follow up the success of *Rigoletto*, Marzari had written from Venice on 24 January to propose a new engagement with La Fenice. Verdi replied:

Nothing could be more gratifying and courteous than your letter of 24 January last. I cannot at present give you a definite reply, but if I am to compose in Italy, I desire nothing better than to do it at Venice, being still mindful of the courtesy shown me last year by the presidenza, and of the enthusiasm and exceptional conscientiousness I found in all the performers in *Rigoletto*: this was more precious to me even than the very gratifying success of the opera itself. In view of that, Signor President, you will understand that I cannot sign a contract without knowing the company. Among the prima donnas of the present time Signora Albertini is distinguished; I have never heard her, but she has enjoyed such successes as guarantee a good result. I think that she would be not displeased at the idea of my writing for her, but no time must be lost in engaging her. For myself the conditions would be more or less the same as last year except for some increase in the payment.[33]

Verdi's determination to be satisfied of the calibre of his leading lady is sometimes taken to suggest that he had already set his heart on a working of *La Dame aux Camélias*. But he had not been lucky with his sopranos in recent years. Probably he thought that the Italian theatre had hit a thin patch as far as sopranos were concerned, and that as a result, singers with insufficient experience or talent were being entrusted with roles far too taxing for them. At any rate the question of the prima donna seems to have been the main issue of debate during the exchanges that led to the drafting of the contract. Still in Paris, Verdi wrote to Marzari again on 20 February:

I reply at once to your letter of 12th inst even without first having spoken to Signora Cruvelli. Certainly it would be a great stroke of fortune to be able to have her at La Fenice, and assuming ... that we were to come to some arrangement, with such a singer (excuse my boldness) I should dare virtually to guarantee the success of my score. But she is engaged for three years with Lumley for London and Paris, and it is impossible to have her in Italy.

Signora Medori has been successful in St Petersburg, and they say very nice things about her to me. You should not be afraid, Signor President, to make her an offer as soon as possible. If Medori cannot do it, I think Signora Barbieri is still free, but I should not think much of Signora Gazzaniga (between ourselves).

I have written two very important roles expressly for her in *Luisa Miller* and in *Stiffelio*, and wasn't satisfied with her. Moreover *Rigoletto* has been an appalling fiasco in Bergamo, for which Signora Gazzaniga was very largely responsible, at least according to what our friend Piave tells me.

Try then, Signor President, to get the company formed as quickly as possible, and as far as I am concerned we can arrange things in a couple of words ...[34]

Despite all Marzari's efforts Verdi remained dissatisfied. Nearly two months later he was writing from Busseto:

With regard to the women, I tell you frankly that I have very little confidence in the three you mentioned to me. I know the many difficulties involved in finding an excellent prima donna these days, but you, Signor President, must do your best to find one who together with the tenor and baritone would complete the Triad, and satisfy the high demands of the Fenice theatre.[35]

At this stage Marzari decided to see whether a personal visit from Brenna might help to get Verdi to commit himself.[36] Brenna performed his mission well, as he had done sixteen months earlier with the *Rigoletto* libretto; and though 'Verdi would have infinitely preferred that the prima donna should be La Alaymo rather than La Salvini-Donatelli'[37] he returned to Venice with all the information needed for drawing up a contract. When Verdi received this, his reply could, thanks to Brenna's preliminary work, be quite unprecedented: 'I have nothing to say about the contract sent me, and therefore return it signed.'[38]

One clause in the contract does however provide a remarkable demonstration of Verdi's continuing concern over the prima-donna question.

... 3. The artists who are to perform it will be selected by Maestro Verdi from the company engaged for the said season ... Concerning the prima donna Fanny Salvini-Donatelli engaged by the said theatre, Maestro Verdi reserves until after the opera in which she is to make her début the right to decide whether or not she is to perform in the opera which he today undertakes to compose. In the event of his not finding her suitable, he will declare this not later than 15 January 1853, and the management will be obliged to engage as substitute for the Lent season 1853 an artist satisfactory to the composer ...[39]

For several months Verdi seems to have done next to nothing to advance the progress of his Venetian opera. Such composing as he did was devoted to *Il Trovatore*, and he even displayed an unusual lethargy in looking for a theme. But in the next surviving letter to Marzari, written on 26 July, there is a hint that there was one subject, dependent upon the availability of an excellent soprano, which Verdi was pondering and perhaps 'studying deeply' in his usual way. Was this *La Dame aux Camélias*?

I must thank you for having of your own accord offered me twenty days longer for the submission of the libretto; but this, I must regretfully inform you, will still be insuffficient. Piave has not yet presented me with one of those original and pungent subjects on the choice of which success largely depends. So we must search and search again. I must say, though, that the choice is proving very difficult, because, apart from the fact that I don't want those commonplace subjects which are to be found by the hundred, there is the difficulty of the censor, and still more the mediocrity of the company. If there was a really first-class soprano at Venice, I would have a subject ready, and certain to be effective; but things being as they are, we shall have to look for something suitable, adapted to the circumstances, and so we need time. Grant me then a further extension of a month at the most, that is to the end of

September. You can do this with an easy mind, because it is absolutely certain that the opera will materialize and that the theatre will have nothing to lose on my account . . .[40]

The unusually passive role which Verdi was taking in the business of finding a subject emerges still more clearly in a letter written to Piave some weeks later. The librettist was obviously finding the responsibility which Verdi had placed on him vexatious and depressing, for nothing he offered met with approval; he presented his latest proposal in near despair. 'L'Ebrea: if this suggestion is no good either, I should not know where to put my head.'

Allons donc! [replied Verdi] you must not say such things, even in jest. You must not refuse to write this libretto. You have got to do it; happen what may, it must be done. Certainly you have started work a bit late, but that doesn't matter: *it has to be done!* You understand.

When one says firmly, with a fixed idea, with obstinate determination *I want to*, one always succeeds. Look! If I didn't have other things to do, I'm sure I should find a fine subject, a great subject. It is difficult to find anything in the jumble of French dramas, because the best ones are all known.

It has to be done, I repeat for the twentieth time; if you can't find it anywhere else, search in your own head, but . . . *it has to be done*.

P.S. Has Emanuele sent you a play called *Matilda?*[41]

The wretched Piave seems even to have pressed Varesi to join the search, to judge from another letter written by Verdi to the singer at about the same time:

. . . As to telling you what the subject is to be for Venice, I cannot for the simple reason that it hasn't yet been found . . .

As far as *Jone* is concerned I must say I didn't like this play. Once upon a time I might have been able to set it, but after having read it attentively, and after having seen it performed several times in Paris, I am more than ever convinced that although some magnificent pieces of music could be made out of it, an opera never could. At least I should not be capable of it . . .[42]

What the subject was that Verdi and Piave eventually agreed upon we do not know. But following the practice employed with *Rigoletto*, Piave came to Sant'Agata, to work on it with the composer during the autumn. What happened then is best told in Piave's words – a letter to Brenna who, one imagines, had suggested that it was quite time the poet was back in Venice with something to show for his trip to the country.

You know the topography of Sant'Agata, and can imagine whether one would stay here for pleasure. It rains and rains and I fear we shall all be transformed into frogs . . . As for Verdi, it's the *Ernani* business all over again. The libretto was nicely finished off, and I was on the point of departing, when the maestro took fire from another subject. In five days I had to toss off a scenario which I have just this minute finished and which he will send of to La Fenice tomorrow for approval. I think Verdi will write a fine opera because I can see that he is very excited. As for me, I don't see the moment to say *Amen*![43]

This last-minute change of plan had almost certainly been prompted by the receipt late in October of a copy of *La Dame aux Camélias* sent him by Marie Escudier from Paris. On the 29th Giuseppina wrote to Léon Escudier at Verdi's dictation – he was himself indisposed at the time – asking him to 'greet Marie and thank him for *La Dame aux Camélias*, which I received some time ago'.[44] This, it may be supposed, gave substance and conviction to a half-formed determination to set the subject which as yet he knew only from stage performances and perhaps from the novel, and whose allure had made him so desultory in the pursuit of other themes. If he had indeed been musing over this theme during all those summer weeks when Piave was trying in vain to get him excited over something else, then probably just as with *Rigoletto* the 'idea, la tinta musicale' were clear in his mind well before the libretto was completed, and this would help explain the otherwise unprecedented rapidity with which the opera was composed in January and February 1835. The probability that, again like *Rigoletto*, *La Traviata* was an opera born of total absorption in a single mood might also explain the difficulty Verdi experienced in trying to get some of the music composed while he was in Rome in December and January for the production of *Il Trovatore*: whatever muse was proper to *La Dame aux Camélias* would have been invoked in vain while Luna and Azucena were in the company.

In mid-December Verdi wrote to Luccardi: 'I shall be in Rome on the 25th ... Would you go to Jacovacci who will give you a piano, and get it put in my study, so that as soon as I arrive I can write the opera for Venice without losing a moment ... See that the piano is a good one! Either a good one, or none at all! ...'[45] But the music simply would not come. Theoretically he was still full of the subject, as his New Year's Day letter to De Sanctis shows: 'For Venice I am doing *La Dame aux Camélias* which will perhaps be given the title *Traviata*. It is a contemporary subject. Another person might not have done it because of the morals or because of the period and for a thousand other silly scruples ... I am doing it with great pleasure. . .'[46]

To Giuseppina, however, he had to confess that he was not doing it at all. We deduce this from that fascinating paragraph already quoted earlier in this chapter (above, p. 280) in the letter she wrote him from Leghorn on 3 January: 'And you haven't written anything yet?' etc. A fortnight later Giuseppina was 'very sorry about what you tell me concerning the opera for Venice. I hope however that the siuation is not quite so black as you paint it, and that on your arrival at Leghorn you will have several finished pieces in your trunk . . .'[47]

How much Verdi did get composed in Rome we do not know. But it was not until he was back in Sant'Agata that he was able to apply his mind sufficiently to appreciate that much in Piave's libretto was unsatisfactory and that another conference was therefore desirable. Moreover he had heard worrying accounts of the Venetian prima donna Salvini-Donatelli, and though the time limit had expired, attempted to call into force the remarkable clause 3 of his contract. He wrote to Marzari:

The reports I receive from Venice, especially after *Ernani*, are so depressing that I am obliged to declare that I shall certainly not give the role of *La Traviata* to Signora Salvini! I believe it is in my interest and the theatre's to engage another prima donna immediately. I know it is very difficult to find an artist who can satisfy the requirements of the theatre, but circumstances demand that some attempt be made.

The only women who would seem suitable to me are: 1st, Signora Penco, who is singing at Rome; 2nd, Signora Boccabadati, who is singing in *Rigoletto* at Bologna; and finally, Signora Piccolomini, who is now singing at Pisa. Penco (the only one of these I know) would be the best, I think. She has a good figure, plenty of spirit and a good stage presence; excellent qualities for *La Traviata*. She is at Rome and you could engage her at the moment. It would be necessary to make the condition that she does not sing before *La Traviata*.

I still have something wrong with my arm; I desire and hope that it may be a passing affliction. I shall keep the Presidenza informed and if by some misfortune I should be unable to fulfil my obligations, I should send the medical certificates necessary for the guaranty of myself and the Presidenza. For this reason too Signora Penco would be more suitable than the others, beause in the event of my not being able to come to Venice, she could do *Il Trovatore*.

Piave has not yet finished polishing *La Traviata*; and even in the things he has finished there are some longueurs that would put the public to sleep, especially towards the end, which has to move rapidly, if it is to be effective. I would therefore request the esteemed Presidenza to let Piave have a few days free to come here and arrange these small matters with me. There is not a minute to lose . . .[48]

Piave was released at once and sent off to Sant'Agata, obviously not simply to tidy up the libretto to Verdi's satisfaction. As far as the Venetian management was concerned, an equal part of his mission was to reconcile the composer to the Fenice company, Signora Salvini-Donatelli included. Initially Verdi was adamant, insisting that *La Traviata* required a singer 'with an elegant figure, who is young and sings passionately'.[49] But by 4 February Piave was able to report a measure of success:

My persistence in a long conversation yesterday evening has succeeded in obtaining from our friend Verdi the following avowal, which I repeat to you word for word.

The Presidenza, he says, is legally right, I admit, but artistically wrong, because not only Signora Salvini, but the entire company is unworthy of the great Fenice theatre; I do not know whether my indisposition will allow me to finish the opera, and in this state of uncertainty it would be pointless for the management to engage other artists, so let it be Salvini and company. But I declare that, in the event of the opera being given, I have no hope of it being a success; indeed I expect it to be a complete fiasco, and so they will have sacrificed the interests of the management (which moreover could be blamed on me), my reputation, and a large sum of the proprietor of the opera. Amen . . .

P.S. I wrote all that in Verdi's name, but now I must add on my own behalf that he is in an infernal bad temper, perhaps because of his indisposition, but still more because he has no faith in the company. I have myself read letters sent him in Rome which analyse and pulverize not only Signora Salvini, but 'Varesi's exhaustion' and Graziani's 'marmoreal' and 'monotonous' singing (they are the epithets I read!). I have had my share of the reproaches too for having concealed from him the 'chronic condition' (as he calls it) of the company. He adds too that it was perhaps improvident counsel to give Il Corsaro, because he says that the opera will have the same fortune as the others. It can easily be imagined how I had to discuss things over and over again, but I am satisfied because if, as I hope, he remains in good health, the opera will be finished, for it is well advanced. I have even heard the first act, which I think is marvellously effective and original. I feel a new man today because the most excellent Salvini is thus to be saved . . .[50]

Only one letter survives from the weeks between Piave's visit to Sant'Agata and the opera's première on 6 March. It accompanied an instalment of music which Verdi forwarded to Piave on 16 February:

Here are two more pieces, a tenor aria and a bass aria, and so the second act is finished. In the cabaletta of the tenor's aria you will have to rewrite the third and seventh lines to get the stress right. In the scene in which Giuseppe comes to say that Violetta has left, Annina cannot have returned, so Violetta and Annina could not leave together. I have patched it up, so as to compose it, but you must write some better lines.

I received the tenor's cabaletta today. It says nothing at all. I shall be in Venice on Monday evening; have my usual apartment prepared at the Europa with a good, well-tuned piano. I would also like you to find, either from a joiner or by borrowing it, a writing-desk so that I can stand up and write. Please see that everything is ready because I am counting on starting the orchestration the evening I arrive.

I have received an anonymous letter from Venice telling me that if I don't get the soprano and bass changed I shall have a complete fiasco. I know, I know . . .[51]

Verdi seems to have been quite determined that *La Traviata* could not be a success. Nor were his expectations disappointed. It was – as he reported with a certain grim satisfaction to Muzio, to Ricordi, to Luccardi and to Mariani – a fiasco, a decisive fiasco. The most interesting of these notes is that to Mariani: 'La Traviata was a grand fiasco, and what is worse, they laughed. However I'm not disturbed about it. Am I wrong, or are they wrong? I believe myself that the last word on *La Traviata* is not that of last night. They will see it again and we shall see! Meanwhile, dear Mariani, register the fiasco.'[52]

Budden has commented on the various false traditions that grew up around this fiasco.[53] The documentary evidence suggests that the root of the problem was that alienation between the composer and his singers of which we have already seen the omens. More than with any other of his operas, Verdi was blithely disregardful of the qualities and capabilities of his cast when he composed *La Traviata*; as a consequence they proved incapable of realizing it convincingly. The reviews of the opera laid the blame for the failure squarely on the singers. The *Italia Musicale* remarked that 'both Varesi and Graziani were so exhausted by the rehearsals that they scarcely had the breath to keep going to the end of the opera'.[54] Ironically enough, only the unwanted Salvini-Donatelli escaped the general censure. She was said to have sung the

florid passages, which the composer wrote for her in large quantities, with an indescribable accomplishment and perfection: she ravished the house which, quite literally, overwhelmed her with applause. This act gained the greatest success for the composer; to begin with he was called for even before the curtain went up for a most sweet harmony of violins forming the prelude to the score; then at the brindisi, then at the duet, then I don't know how many times more, both alone and with the prima donna at the end of the act.

In the second act, alas, the fortune changed. Three things are wanted in the art of music: voice, voice, voice. And truly, a composer has done his work in vain if he does not have people with the understanding and skill to perform what he creates. Yesterday evening Verdi met with the misfortune of not finding the above-mentioned three things, except on one side; and so all the pieces which were not performed by Signora Salvini-Donatelli went literally flying. None of the other singers was in the best of voice ...

While granting that the music was magnificently played by the orchestra, we must therefore, to avoid taking a false step, reserve judgement on the rest of the opera, until it is better sung ...[55]

One of the singers reviled, the great Varesi himself, was sufficiently incensed to write to Lucca, the publisher, who was a close friend of his, about the possibility of making some appropriate reply. This letter, dated 10 March, is quite the most fascinating document in the whole history of *La Traviata*, sad though it is to see the alienation between the composer and the man he had once consulted over the scoring of *Macbeth*.

... I take advantage of the courteous invitation you made me during your brief stay in Venice and in giving you the news about Verdi's opera *La Traviata* beg you to take up my defence against the imprudent article in the *Gazzeta di Venezia*, which has provoked the indignation even of Verdi's idolaters.

I will refer you to reliable Milanese witnesses, including Arioli, Giulini, and Vittadini who are here now . . ., and who will tell you how I sang in *La Traviata*, and whether I was in good voice: besides, the most convincing proof is that when the third performance was cancelled because of Graziani's illness and *Il Corsaro* performed instead, I created such an effect and was so applauded that the public said that I wasn't recognizable between one opera and the other. I don't intend to set myself up as judge of the musical merits of *La Traviata*, but I do certainly maintain that Verdi didn't succeed in making use of the qualities of the artists he had at his disposal. In the whole of Salvini's part only the cavatina suited her really well. In Graziani's little or nothing. In mine the *adagio* of an aria; and this caused much strong feeling among the Venetian public, because they were expecting me to have something that suited me really well, as Verdi had already created the colossal roles of Macbeth and Rigoletto for me with such success, and especially because before the production it was known that the composer was very satisfied with me.

Here is the story of yesterday evening, the third performance, a performance for the benefit of the poor: an absolutely wretched house. Some applause for the brindisi and a lot for Donatelli's cavatina, and two calls. In the grand duet between Salvini and me, some applause for the *adagio* and for the cabaletta. Applause for the second finale and two calls for the composer and for the singers. In the third act no applause, and one call to say goodbye to the composer who was known to be leaving the next day.

I shall be very grateful to you if you would make some mention of this to vindicate my self-respect, which was so offended by the article in the *Gazzetta*. That would put the weight of responsibility for the public's displeasure on my shoulders, but if that was the case, they wouldn't have applauded me in the few passages that were suited to my abilities . . .[56]

A last document relating to the *première* confirms the *Gazzetta*'s admiring words for the orchestra. On 9 March Verdi wrote to Mares, the first violinist and director of the Fenice orchestra: 'As I cannot myself, I request you in my name kindly to convey my warmest compliments to the professors of the orchestra for the devotion and precision with which they performed this poor *Traviata*.'[57]

Exceptionally, we must pursue the history of *La Traviata* beyond its unhappy *première*: for after due reflection Verdi decided that, even if the performance was largely responsible for the débacle, his own part in the work was not above reproach. Before it next appeared before the public, he was to submit the much-criticized second and third acts to a thorough process of revision. *La Traviata rivendicata*, the *Traviata* we know today, appeared only in May 1854.

In September 1853 Mariani had been the first to express eagerness for *La Traviata* 'to rise again on the stage of the Carlo Felice' (in Genoa). He observed that 'Salvini-Donatelli and Graziani, for whom you wrote that opera, are already engaged for the Carnival season.'[58] But that was, of course, a singularly unfortunate line of approach. Verdi, too, in letters to Vigna in December and De Sanctis in February, wrote of his desire to 'restore her to a position of honour in the world'.[59] It was not until March 1854, however, that the process leading to the reparation of the opera began.

Antonio Gallo, who ran the little San Benedetto theatre in Venice, had been pestering Ricordi for some time with requests to perform the opera. Ricordi may be presumed to have been enthusiastic, but before Verdi was prepared to give his assent he wanted to know who was to be in the cast, and he wanted to revise the music. Tito Ricordi, who, since his father's death just a year earlier, was now head of the firm, wrote to Verdi on 18 March 1854.

I wrote yesterday to tell you that, as far as Gallo's *Traviata* is concerned, I had done what you had suggested. Today I received a reply from Gallo showing that he has engaged Landi, Signora Spezia, Coletti and the *comprimario* Luigia Morselli, who was so enthusiastically applauded at Venice both last year and this . . . Dr Grawil will be the same Andrea Bellini as last year. Galletti will be the Viscount. The second woman will be quite different and better than the one last year. As to the *comprimario* baritone and second bass, he would like the best, but is waiting to arrange the question of hire charges before engaging them, because he would not need them for the other operas. Bosoni will be musical director, Piave will do the staging, the costumes will be the same as last year, but touched up: the stage painter, Bertoja: and as to rehearsals, Gallo . . . proposes that there should be as many and of whatever kind Maestro Verdi desires . . .

. . . You will have received the original pieces from *La Traviata* which you requested with your letter of the 10th, and today I have forwarded the last finale.[60]

Verdi's revisions would have been made during the next two or three weeks. Ricordi wrote again on 9 April reporting that 'Gallo was very eager to have the music of *La Traviata*, the performance of which will, I think, take place.' He therefore urged Verdi to send him the five movements in question 'as quickly as possible'. [61] On 13 April he acknowledged their receipt:

I have received the five movements of La Traviata ... Grolli is dealing with them at present with the utmost diligence, and on Saturday (the day after tomorrow) they will be sent off to Gallo. Muzio will then make the piano reductions and correct the printed pieces very carefully ...

My dear friend, I couldn't do anything other than send Gallo the Venice copy of the score, because no others had been made after you had told me to hold up everything until such time as you could perform the opera under your supervision. But don't worry: Gallo, who is very concerned about all this, has the most precise instructions to start rehearsing all the rest of the opera, leaving out the five original movements, until he has the new ones. Besides, my instructions and my agreement with Gallo over the performance of this opera are positive and explicit, and he gives me the clearest undertakings every day. He realizes too that his whole fortune as an impresario is dependent upon the success of this opera. So let us hope for the best, especially with the assistance of Bosoni and Piave. With regard to Signora Spezia's voice, I telegraphed, wishing to make sure that she was a soprano, and then he confirmed this by letter, declaring that one who had sung in Rigoletto, Nabucco, Lombardi, Foscari could not be a mezzo-soprano.[62]

As well as supervising the revival, Ricordi took it upon himself to keep Verdi informed of how things were developing. On 6 May he reported:

This evening La Traviata goes on in Venice, and as you will see from the enclosed letters and from the notices I have had from Piave, from Coletti and from Vigna too, not to mention Gallo's journals, one may count on the most complete success. From certain information which I had had about Signora Spezia's health, which looked as if it would make it impossible for her to sing, I had been very apprehensive, and had not failed to make a formal protest to Gallo; but now I am calmer, Gallo will give me the news by telegraph after midnight. If it is as is to be expected, Cerri will communicate it to you tomorrow, as I can't, having to leave at once. I would have acceded to Gallo's request that I should go to the first performance, but after what I had been told I didn't have the courage. Now it is too late. If the success is up to everyone's expectations, I shall go there during next week.[63]

The success was indeed complete. The letter sent Verdi by Ricordi's secretary Cerri rounds off the story well:

I enclose a letter received late yesterday from Gallo. Today there were more of them, both from him and from Vigna, which speak of the indescribable enthusiasm with which La Traviata was received, still greater, if that is possible, than on the first night. It is an unexampled triumph. You were speaking prophetically when you said: 'La Traviata failed; whose fault is it? Mine or the singers'? I don't know. Time will decide.' And time has decided, and in the same city and with the same spectators who had at first condemned it. While now, as Vigna writes, everyone claims to have judged it a very beautiful opera ever since last year![64]

PART III

The development of Verdi's musical language

13

The first operas – *Oberto* and *Un Giorno di Regno*

Some preliminaries

Many critics have detected in *Oberto* the sound of a new voice in Italian music: and it is commonly agreed that this newness is most clearly manifested in the forcefulness, the sheer physical energy, by which each scene in the opera is propelled. Already Verdi's musical style is vehement and precipitate, able to make audible the fiercest and above all the most compulsive passions. Already one can discern those characteristics which, with the maturing of Verdi's mind and the refining of his craftsmanship, were to make him the superlative artist of the inevitable, the inexorable, the fated.

The earliest operas – particularly *Oberto*, for *Un Giorno di Regno* is in most respects an untypical and irrelevant production – exhibit this distinctively Verdian character in music that is often slovenly or drab. Nevertheless the artistry of which the young Verdi was capable, and the validity of the style within which this artistry was achieved, need to be insisted upon. His immense development as a musician began from, and remained for ever rooted in, a complete understanding of and acquiescence in the Italian operatic idiom of the 1830s. This idiom we may justifiably describe as simple and over-formal: but we shall mistake the simplicity and over-formalism for imaginative poverty or deficient sensibility only if we attempt to judge by totally irrelevant criteria – the expressiveness of the harmony, for example, or the subtlety of the orchestration.

Fundamentally the principles of the style derive from the fact that the protagonists, the singers, are regarded as in every way pre-eminent among the forces that realize the drama. Opera is song – dramatic, lyrical, declamatory, virtuoso, as varied and as resourceful as may be, but always song – and the pre-eminent musical values are therefore those that can be most fully expressed in this one-dimensional medium. The elements of melody and rhythm are of more significance that those of harmony, counterpoint and colour.

Moreover, the greater emphasis placed upon these elements of style dictates a manner of treating the harmony and orchestration that is difficult to reconcile with more Romantic and modern practice.

In the Italian idiom of this period, the melodic and rhythmic elements cannot be disengaged from one another: the subtlety and richness of a melody can be seen best in its rhythmic formation. It is by the rhythmic development of a melody out of regular, clearly defined phrases into flowing asymmetric climaxes that the young Verdi achieves a sense of movement and of growth, as, for example, in the *largo* of the 'rondo finale' of *Oberto* beginning at 'Ad ucciderlo qui venni', where the music gathers strength and impetus through the scheme of rhythmic development shown in Ex. 1.

Ex. 1

Similarly, where a German composer might achieve the heightening of expression during an aria by harmonic means, the Italian is likely to employ rhythmic elaboration. The basic rhythmic patterns of an aria are subject to continued embellishment; the symmetries and reprises in its melodic structure are likely to be intensified by progressively more complex arabesque. Ex. 2 is from the cantabile 'Oh chi torna' (*Oberto*, Act II).

Ex. 2

At this period Verdi's harmony is clearly subordinate to the sovereign melodic/rhythmic dimension. It is not the function of harmony to be expressive or even colourful: its role is physical, rather than expressive or sensuous. It is used to clarify form, and to underline the chief rhythmic and dynamic events of the movement.

For this reason the harmony is entirely without feature in those places where a composer who understands harmony as an expressive resource would demand its fullest contribution – where the mood of an aria is being defined, where the singing voice is in full melodic flow. Here, unless some chromatic inflection in the voice demands a temporary touching upon alien harmonies, the accompanying chords will retain a completely impassive neutrality; none but the most fundamental and commonplace harmonies within the tonality will be employed. Such arresting juxtapositions of harmony, such arresting chromatic alterations as are to be found in the idiom serve a different purpose. Most often they are associated with cadence, with the delimiting of structure: hence the apparent paradox that it is only when the lyrical and expressive interest of a movement has been exhausted, only when we move from the aria into its *stretta*, only when the contents of the song are forgotten and the composer is wrapping it up for presentation to the public, that we find a high incidence of chromatically altered harmony. The treatment of such harmony is always strictly formal, calculated to give to the passage in question a rigorous and decisive finality, and its physically aggressive nature is frequently emphasized by a sprinkling of marks of accentuation.

The young Verdi's understanding of the purposes of modulation is equally dependent upon the desire to serve melody and to articulate structure. Modulation is rarely used with a view to elaborating the musical architecture. Generally its purpose is to enable the preeminent musical dimension – the melody – to employ a wider variety of cadences and of vocal colour. And because Verdi frequently does not modulate back to the tonic, but simply and promptly steps back, the juxtaposition of contrasting tonalities gives vivid definition to the phrase structure of the song. In those rare instances in which a contrasting tonality is retained for any length of time, it will almost always be found to mark a parenthesis or episode in the structure, and most often, as in 'Gia parmi udir' (*Oberto*, Act I), the contrasting key is not arrived at by modulation: it is simply stated in formal juxtaposition.

Vivid orchestral colouring plays as small a part in Verdi's early style as intrinsically interesting harmony. It too is a resource strictly subordinated to the requirements of the singing voices. Within the lyrical movements its essential task is to furnish a vibrant and elastic continuum with the aid of which the song propels itself. Just occasionally, in more introspective movements, such as 'Sciagurata, a questo lido' (*Oberto*, Act II), it is deprived of any distinctiveness of feature and becomes a mere sonority, a harmonic immanence within which the voice rhapsodizes.

The definition of the more usual pulsing accompaniment figurations is almost always entrusted to the strings. In the most vigorous movements they are supported by the horns, and in exceptional cases by the full lower brass and bassoons. As yet the woodwind instruments are treated with absolutely no distinctiveness of character: each and every one of them aspires perpetually to the condition of song. It is the woodwinds to whom introductory statements of thematic material are given, and who double or thicken out in thirds or sixths the occasional phrase of vocal melody. Their most individual role is that of imparting a richer colour to the ends of vocal phrases. Frequently the bars in which the voice embarks on its song are supported by nothing but a string figuration: just as frequently when it turns back towards the cadence a glow of woodwinds is perceptible behind the continuing string figuration.

Within the lyrical movements one curious feature of orchestral style remains to be noted. Possibly because at this period the leader of the orchestra was still responsible for setting tempo and securing unanimity of ensemble, the composer frequently avoided using the first violins in the opening bars of an accompaniment: the texture and rhythm were defined by second violins and lower strings. The characteristic occupation of the first violins therefore became not accompanying but colouring the vocal melody. Ex. 3 (*Oberto*, Act II)

Ex. 3

is typical, intensifying by the addition of string tone those notes that are expressively or rhythmically most significant.

In the freer sections of the opera, the introductions and the recitatives, the treatment of the orchestra is generally more interesting. Here the orchestra is able to play a significant part in the depiction of the scene and the definition of mood. Thus in the opening chorus of *Oberto*, before the formal musical design commences at bar 9, Verdi uses the orchestra like a 'tone-painter', evoking the luminousness of the dawn by the exclusive use of woodwind and horns. Or in the introduction leading into Riccardo's romanza (*Oberto*, Act II), the desolation that succeeds the frenzy is vividly portrayed in the two sustained chords for horns and bassoons, following more than twenty bars of syncopated and tremolo writing for strings. As yet, however, even such simple strokes as these are deemed superfluous whenever song is in progress.

Arias

Notwithstanding their dissimilarity of style, both cantabiles and cabalettas generally employ a similar formal pattern. We may describe it as comprising an orchestral introduction, a thematic exposition, an episode, a partial reprise, and a coda; and though there is rarely any marked contrast in the material used, each of these members does have a typical style. In the cantabiles, though not the cabalettas, the orchestral introduction is more often than not omitted altogether (in two cases out of five in *Oberto*, and four out of five in *Un Giorno di Regno*). But where it does appear, it is almost invariably as an anticipation of the principal theme. The only exception in these operas is in 'Grave a core innamorato' (*Un Giorno di Regno*, Act I) where the introduction is in fact less an introduction than a transition suggesting in the most economical way imaginable the change of mood from eager plotting to tender musing.

Of all the sections of the aria it is the thematic exposition that has the greatest breadth. It normally consists of four phrases of which the first and third match one another either exactly or in the relationship of theme and variant, while the second and fourth differ: an ABAC scheme. Frequently either phrase B or phrase C will modulate momentarily. But it is the third section of the aria, the episode, that with few exceptions regularly provides this element of tonal contrast. In addition it is more tightly symmetrical than the exposition, being composed normally as a single repeated or varied or sequential phrase. The most interesting exception to this rule, the cantabile 'O chi torna' (*Oberto*, Act II), will be discussed more fully in due course.

It is in the final stages of the aria that cantabile and cabaletta practices tend to diverge. In the cantabile the reprise is normally just half the length of the exposition, and normally consists of the third and fourth phrases of the exposition in a more or less ornamented and intensified form. The three cantabiles in *Un Giorno di Regno* where the final phrase of the exposition has been modulatory ('Grave a core innamorato' in Act I, and 'Pietoso al lungo pianto' and 'Si mostri a chi l'adora' in Act II) develop the principal themes in a new manner at this point in order to stay in the tonic key.

After the reprise the coda theme brings about a surge of movement into the closing cadenza. Formally the coda most often consists of a single repeated phrase, the repetition being protracted or dissolving into the cadenza. Within these repeated phrases the vocal line tends to become rhythmically more hectic, with more verbal reiteration; the orchestral textures will be broken into shorter note values, and there will be both an acceleration in the rate of harmonic change and an enlarging of the vocabulary of chords. The function of the coda is by means of this *accelerando* of incident to break away from the severe formalism of the aria design. Only in 'Si mostri a chi l'adora' (*Un Giorno di Regno*, Act II) does Verdi abandon this coda scheme. Here the refashioning of the reprise becomes so comprehensive, prompts such magniloquent expansiveness, that the one huge musical sentence serves as reprise, culmination, and dissolution.

The cabalettas sometimes employ a scheme of reprise and coda similar to that described above. But equally often the more dynamic character of the cabaletta, and probably the fact that it is to be repeated, prompts Verdi to attempt various types of short-cut. Thus in both the Act I cabalettas in *Oberto*, the element of reprise is wholly lacking: Verdi moves directly from the episode into a new climactic phrase, incorporating a modest amount of coda-like repetition. Apparently unconvinced by these, he reverses the process in Act II; both Cuniza's 'Più che i vezzi' and Oberto's 'Ma tu superbo giovane' recapitulate the main theme, but by omitting the element of repetition from the coda theme both fail to achieve that breadth that is typical of cantabiles at this point. The most interesting solution to this particular problem of cabaletta design comes in 'Si, scordar saprò l'infido' (*Un Giorno di Regno*, Act II), where Verdi introduces a new theme in place of the reprise, repeating it for amplitude, and gets the characteristic coda-surge by developing a short figure out of this new theme.

Notwithstanding the exceptions among the cabalettas, the dominant aria form of the period may be represented diagrammatically as follows:

introduction	thematic exposition	episode	reprise	coda
AB	ABAC	DD	AC	EE

It can rarely be claimed that these formal patterns are a necessary or even natural consequence of the texts that Verdi was setting. The form described above was adopted so regularly because, in the eyes of composers of the period, it had an ideal propriety: it was concise, it was fastidiously formal, and yet a certain dynamism, so essential in a dramatic genre, also made itself felt.

Leonora's cantabile 'Sotto il paterno tetto' (*Oberto*, Act I) illustrates particularly well the concern of the young Verdi to comprehend the mood of the poem within a poised form, rather than to express the text in detail. Its formal design is precisely that I have described – ABAC, DD', AC, EE – and a comparison of this with the contents of the verse at once shows how architectural considerations have outweighed expressive considerations in its choice. Thus phrase A is used for 'Sotto il paterno tetto' and 'radiante nell'aspetto' in the exposition, but for 'mi tradì l'ingrato' in the reprise. It is certainly true that in setting this last line Verdi achieves more than the perfecting of the form: the melodic recapitulation is intensified and the emotional momentum sustained by the continuation into the reprise of the cello figuration from the central episode. Clearly, however, the lyrical unity of the cantabile is of greater moment to Verdi than the representation of the conflicting ideas the librettist has suggested within it.

Within the exposition it may be observed how every detail is calculated to enhance the formal perfection. In the phrases which launch the melody – the A phrases – the harmonic and orchestral styles are wholly without distinctive features, but both the form-giving phrases B and C are coloured by the addition of clarinet and bassoon to the string texture, and ornamented by the rapturous cadencing of the singing voice. It is the simplicity of the cantabile as a whole that enables the coda to achieve a real amplitude by the most modest means: by taking the climactic rhythm from the cadence phrase C, by fashioning a new melodic contour for it above more urgent and more richly coloured harmonies, and by extending it through six-bar phrases without interior cadence.

The intensification of repetitions or reprises achieved in this aria by means of the orchestral texture is more often achieved by melodic ornamentation: an excellent example, Cuniza's 'Oh chi torna'

(*Oberto*, Act II), has already been mentioned. The same cantabile provides a rare example of the use of the orchestra in a more than subsidiary role. For the climactic phrases, which here coincide with the episode, Solera provided the splendid text:

> Un suo sguardo, un dolce suo sorriso
> M'eran vita, gioir, paradiso,

and the way in which he has achieved this rapturous note by the piling up of short fragments of text stimulated Verdi to an essay in antiphony, in which the short fragments of vocal melody interchange with a melodious and euphonious ornamental figuration in the woodwinds. The effectiveness of the pattern is enhanced by a decisive modulation to the dominant, by an acceleration in the rate of the antiphony at the point of the modulation, and by the characteristically refined rhythmic shape Verdi gives to the vocal melody.

Clearly the departure of this splendid passage from the norm is prompted by the text. But its originality and boldness affect only a single part of the aria design; the relationship of the parts to the whole, the symmetry of the proportions is immaculate as ever.

It is in such transient details that Verdi first manifests his sensitivity to the text. An example of a different kind is found in 'Grave a core innamorato'. Here the change in lyrical style and the syncopated accompaniment at the cadence of the exposition and in the coda are obviously designed as a musical image of the 'palpito', which strikingly foreshadows Gilda's 'Caro nome'. But there is no hint of any balladesque nervousness in word-setting, no threat to Verdi's instinctive and trained preference for severe architectural formalism. Nowhere does he yet show anything of Bellini's freedom and inventiveness in handling the conventional structures.

That Verdi at first regarded the form and habits of *ottocento* opera as binding, that he had little ambition to vary or distort or bend them to serve the demands of character or situation, is most clear from the cabalettas. It is understandable that the basic rituals of the cabaletta should be complied with; but not even in the details of the structure does one find any suggestion of that alertness to the sense of the words commented on in connection with the cantabiles. The cabaletta was not merely a form, it was a manner; a manner that depended less on the dramatic meaning of the text than on its placing as the virtuoso climax of the solo scena. And so, for example, although in 'Oh potessi nel mio core' (*Oberto*, Act I) Leonora is contrasting her former dreams of love with the present reality of tears and sighs, the music really develops in a contrary sense, beginning with what it might be possible to interpret as strutting, suppressed desperation, but evolving into manifestly exuberant coloratura. By the time it reaches the cadence phrase, the irrelevance of the music to the sense of the text is truly astonishing (Ex. 4).

Ex. 4

At this period in Verdi's career the overall treatment of the solo scena was absolutely stereotyped. It was drastically rethought only under the most exceptional circumstances, in death scenes or mad scenes, which consequently derived no small measure of their eloquence from their derangement of the formalities that surround them. The one scene of this kind in these earliest operas is Leonora's 'rondo finale' at the end of *Oberto*. In the cantabile 'Sciagurata! a questo lido', the inspiration is manifestly that of Bellini: Verdi has made a valiant attempt to emulate his 'melodie lunghe lunghe lunghe'. Within the span of this melody only one internal cadence is found – that in the tonic after the first sentence – and as the melody evolves, the absence of formalizing features becomes progressively more striking. Here, for once, there is no melodic repetition, no over-emphasis of the musical form. In its place we find an ever-changing melodic continuum, moulded at every point round the meaning and emphasis of the text. The climax of the cantabile is marked by a disruption of the melodic line and a resumption at a faster tempo in a major key, with a fuller accompanying texture, and the splendidly accruing rhythms typical of this phase of Verdi's work.

Having dared so much, Verdi checks himself. To the overwrought despair of Leonora:

> Ad ucciderlo qui venni
> Colla man del seduttor.

the chorus replies:

> Calma, calma il tuo dolore,
> Stai nel seno all'amistà,

but expressive truth has yielded to formalism: the closing phrase of the cantabile is simply reiterated in choral form.

Nevertheless this major-key conclusion, together with another one in the cabaletta, is the earliest example of what was to become one of the hallmarks of Verdi's mature style: an enrichment of the formal musical structure by a progressive substitution of new melodies for old. Always the new melodies that carry forward and crown the musical design are stimulated by details of imagery or sentiment in the text, but always too they are reconciled with a fastidious concern for form.

Most operas of the period include one or two solo movements in more concise and freer forms. Two are found in Act II of *Oberto*, Riccardo's romanza 'Ciel, che feci' and Cuniza's *adagio* 'Vieni, o misera'. Their architectural slightness is a symptom of the density of dramatic incident at this point in the opera, not of the insignificance or decorativeness of the moods that inspire them. Indeed these movements, more clearly than any others in the opera, embody the tragic passions of remorse and pity begotten by the dramatic catastrophe, Riccardo's killing of Oberto.

Cuniza's *adagio* is strangled to death by Verdi's youthful preoccupation with formalism: within so brief a movement the result is a gross superfluity of simple repetitions and cadence formulas. 'Ciel, che feci', on the other hand, is one of the triumphs of the score. Certainly there are primitive features even in this: the attempt to find a harmonic analogy for the anguished exclamation 'Ah no!' at the central climax of the aria is embarrassingly crude, and the orchestral peroration is an irrelevant and absurd soliciting for applause; but overall, in conception and execution, it remains one of the opera's most happy attempts to give voice to violent passions within a coherent musical design.

For the success of the romanza credit must first be given to the librettist, who, in three quatrains and an epilogue, has provided Verdi with a psychologically convincing sketch of Riccardo's state of

316

mind. Initiated in a mood of remorse, coming to a climax of disintegrative horror as the last groans of the dying man are heard from within the forest, closing in a prayerful search for peace of mind, Solera's verse finally motivates Riccardo's flight by depicting the haunting return of shame and remorse. This motivation Verdi rather inhibits, by treating the two lines of the epilogue:

> Oh rimorso! del morente
> L'ombra ognor m'inseguirà

as a passing shadow of horror. Characteristically he prefers to perfect the form and stabilize Riccardo's state of mind by recapitulating the prayerfulness of Solera's third quatrain.

Apart from this conflict between musician and dramatist, the most notable feature of Verdi's setting is the disintegration of the lyricism that marks the second section: 'Ah, si fugga! . . . Oh Dio! . . . chi piange? . . .' This is finely conceived, an absolutely convincing musical equivalent of the obtrusion of the outer world – Oberto's groans, the sighing of the wind – upon Riccardo's consciousness. Without destroying the overall flow of the composition, these features are transmuted in the orchestral accompaniment to Riccardo's exclamations. The climaxing of this unusually detailed phrase in the absolutely austere cantabile of 'L'ultimo lamento' etc. is one of Verdi's most imaginative strokes (Ex. 5).

Un Giorno di Regno has no such movements as these. It departs only once from the classic double-aria pattern, and that is to provide Belfiore's Act I aria with a second movement more in the manner of a buffo ensemble. The wholesale repetition of the movement is certainly cabaletta-like, but the details of the organization are quite different: the solo exposition being followed by a choral repetition, the place of the episode being filled by a Rossini crescendo for the orchestra while soloists and chorus patter and plod, and this in turn being succeeded by tutti cadences. In the repetition these are extended with all the lunatic persistence proper to the buffo genre.

Elsewhere buffo effects are scarcely perceptible in the solo music. They have left their traces only in three orchestral passages: the link between the two statements of the cabaletta 'See dee cader la vedova' (Act I), and the transition into, and stretta following, 'Si scordar saprò' (Act II), all of which pay tribute to the Rossini crescendo. But it is noticeable that Verdi is too impatient an artist to carry it off with real style, and cannot bring himself to indulge in more than two statements of the phrase.

Ex. 5

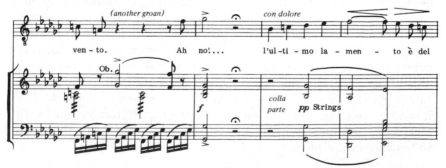

mi - se - ro   che   muor, _____ è del   mi - se - ro   che _____ (muor)

Ensembles

The duet, being at this period primarily a lyrical rather than dramatic ensemble, generally assumes the same overall musical design as the solo aria; often the cantabile is preceded by a third organized *allegro* movement, the '*primo tempo*'. The basic principle of the duet, whether in *primo tempo*, cantabile or cabaletta, is that it should begin with two short solos in which the sentiments of the protagonists are clearly defined, and conclude with an extended section of genuine duet writing in which they are harmoniously combined. Straightforward enough in *primo tempo* and cantabile, this principle does present problems within the repetitive form of the cabaletta, where the meaningful involvement of both voices is by no means easily achieved. Traditionally a duet cabaletta was set out in the following pattern: (1) solo cabaletta in short form for the first singer, (2) solo cabaletta in short form for the second singer, (3) duet cabaletta in full. The most artistic way in which to shorten the cabaletta for the solo sections is certainly by omitting the cadence phrases, as in the Riccardo/Cuniza cabaletta (*Oberto*, Act I). But Verdi is far from sure of this solution. In the Leonora/Oberto cabaletta (*Oberto*, Act I), for example, the cadence phrases are retained, while the wider tonal range and the melodic growth normally found in the episode of an aria are altogether wanting. Elsewhere, in the Edoardo/Belfiore cabaletta (*Un Giorno di Regno*, Act I), Verdi avoids the problem altogether by writing in parallel thirds throughout.

It was to be typical of Verdi's music for many years that the most masterly duetting should be found in the cantabile rather than the cabaletta. The cantabile of the Leonora/Oberto duet (Act I) provides an early example. What distinguishes it is the subtlety of the

319

relationship between the two solos. Leonora's uses an absolutely regular ABAC design, each of the constituent phrases being of two bars. In Oberto's answer, his character and the nature of his entreaty to the heavens prompt Verdi to transform rather than simply to restate. Phrase A is distorted and irregularly extended, giving a bolder emphasis to the rhythm ♩ ♫; B is virtually identical but in the dominant key; a new third phrase replaces the reprise of A, but at the cadence Oberto's solo is 'rhymed' with Leonora's by means of a simply rhythmic variant of her phrase C. Moreover, the whole of this transformed melodic sentence is propelled by more animated accompaniment figurations and more eventful harmonies.

Already in this fine differentiation between the two styles of song in the duet, Verdi is aspiring to a type of psychological counterpoint that in due course was to become a permanent ingredient of his operatic style. It continues more explicitly in the latter part of the duet. Leonora repeats the whole of her melody, while Oberto sings only those fragments of his that distinguish him most clearly from her – 'Io venni vindice dell'onor'. The orchestra too blends Leonora's pleading lyricism with Oberto's pulsing ardour.

In the coda, typically highlighted by richer harmony and fuller orchestration, we perceive that the perfecting of the form remains Verdi's ideal even when he has taken some pains to emphasize the alienation between its constituent elements. The distinctiveness of the singers' rhythms becomes less obtrusive; they echo one another and blend together.

Curiously enough Verdi makes no use in *Oberto* of that kind of duet that sets the singers against one another with distinctly contrasting types of theme. In this respect he may be described as a follower of Bellini, rather than of Donizetti and Mercadante.

It is in the duets and ensembles that the distinctness of the heroic and comic traditions becomes clear. Only the first of the *Un Giorno di Regno* duets is strictly comparable with those in *Oberto*, and even here, in the cantabile, the juxtaposition and later counterpointing of the sentimental and the comic manners is the most apparent feature. Verdi is essaying a type of which Donizetti was the master and of which his 'Ai perigli della guerra' (*L'Elisir d'Amore*, Act II) and 'Sogno soave e casto' (*Don Pasquale*, Act I) are the classics. In the other duets of the opera the *buffo* manner dominates completely; *allegro* and *vivace* movements are ubiquitous; the setting of the text typically progresses from declamation through lyrical song into syllabic patter. The patter is perhaps comparable with the accelerating coda sections in the heroic style, but the structure in these comic pieces is really based on a different principle altogether – not on the symmetrical rounding-out of the lyricism, but on hyperbole of repetition. The dynamic of the comic forms is not passion but clockwork.

Nevertheless the *buffo* style does permit a composer to play with the words in a way the heroic style does not. The *parlando* interruptions in 'Diletto genero' (Act I) and the *a piacere* phrases in 'Ch'io non possa' (Act II) are quite conventional; so is the more fundamental irregularity in 'Giurai seguirla' where the lyrical style of the opening never recurs after Giulietta has begun to sing, because the concern for formal song is superseded by a concern to match the music to an animated encounter. But such things did not occur in *Oberto*. The experience of working in the comic genre can only have sharpened Verdi's awareness of the details of an aria text.

In these earliest operas even the more complex and dramatic ensembles tend to assume structures basically dependent upon the cantabile and cabaletta framework. Indeed, in the Act I finales of both operas, in the quartet in *Oberto* and the terzet in *Un Giorno di Regno*, these forms are just as clear as in the duets. But features are found in these fuller ensembles that distinguish them from the purely lyrical solo or duet scena. There is, for example, a tendency for the lyrical music to overflow the boundaries of the formal slow and fast movements. These remain lyrically the most sustained and structurally the most secure, but the freer music introducing them and linking them may well incorporate quite extensive lyrical sections. Conversely, in *Un Giorno di Regno* we sometimes find Verdi beginning the cantabile with differentiated declamatory phrases that underline the antithesis of the stage situation before the cantabile proper is launched. A good example is provided by the opening bars of the *adagio* in the Act I finale. Moreover, whereas in the duets Verdi seems to have been inhibited by attempting to accommodate the fuller resources within the normal cantabile–cabaletta time-scale, in these pieces he makes no such attempt and suffers from no such inhibition. On the contrary, the richer musical resources prompt him to some pleasingly imaginative variations and elaborations of the standard scheme.

Of the dramatic ensembles, the Act I terzet in *Oberto* may be singled out as the most complex and interesting, particularly because of the expressive flexibility of the *primo tempo*, where the *agitato* exclamations of Cuniza are nicely differentiated from the more passionate, almost cabaletta-like sentences of Oberto and Leonora. The cantabile is provided in this instance by a canonic trio.

Verdi's earliest operatic essay at a form which he seems to have studied *ad nauseam* under Lavigna is less than successful, mainly because of the immensely long theme, the second sentence of which does not furnish sufficient variety of style and harmony to animate the vastnesses that ensue. In the *andante mosso* of the Act I finale, too, Verdi uses contrapuntal elaboration to achieve maximum sonority. The type of movement which was still immensely attractive to Bellini, Verdi was rapidly to tire of. It belonged perhaps to a more leisurely era than his.

The resourcefulness of the cabaletta movements is very unequal, comparisons generally being much to the disadvantage of the comic work. While such a movement as the *Oberto* terzet shows a keen concern for varying the vocal texture, that in *Un Giorno di Regno* is in a strident unison throughout. The cabaletta movements of the Act I finales show the same kind of thing on a more elaborate scale, that in *Oberto* exploiting the resources, albeit modestly, and embodying the stage situation with some vividness, that in *Un Giorno di Regno* – once the preliminaries are over – setting the sentimentalists in unison and using the rest of the ensemble simply to harmonize their song.

Choral and orchestral movements

Within five years of the first performances of *Oberto*, Verdi had apparently been graced by the Milanese with the sobriquet 'Father of the Chorus'. This was a popular acknowledgement of a gift which Verdi developed only under the stimulus of those librettos by Solera in which the chorus was placed at the centre of the dramatic action: *Nabucco* and *I Lombardi*. It certainly was not that Verdi had any spontaneous or absolute predilection for the choral medium.

Because of the dramatic style of *Oberto* Solera had been obliged to retain a purely decorative function for the chorus, such as one presumes was found in Piazza's original. In composing these pieces and the choruses in *Un Giorno di Regno* Verdi perpetrated a substantial proportion of this most entirely uninteresting music. The decorative quality of the choruses, their status as music incidental to the drawing of the new stage tableau at the beginning of each of the scenes in which they appear, is most clearly demonstrated by the fact that in many of them the opening choral sentence is simply wrapped around a repetition of the orchestral introduction like so much wadding. And the total lack of procreative passion in these choral openings is manifested in their failure to beget anything more fruitful than repetitions, transitions and cadences.

The only substantial pieces of instrumental music are the introductory sinfonias. As in the choruses, here too, away from the dramatic core of his operas, the young Verdi seems a singularly unpromising artist. Despite the enthusiasm of Soffredini, who deemed the *Oberto* sinfonia 'brillantissima', and whose account claimed an immediate and lasting triumph for it, it is difficult today to propose any criteria by which it might seem anything more than a depressing potpourri of several of the least interesting themes of the opera, all presented within a stultifyingly narrow tonal range. It is a piquant experience to set beside it an early overture of Rossini – say, *La Cambiale di Matrimonio* – which already shows as total a mastery of symphony as his arias do of song.

The themes Verdi strings together are: for his first subject, the wedding chorus 'Fidanzata avventurosa' (Act I); for his second, the introduction to Oberto's scena 'Ei tarda ancor' (Act II); for his third, the march from the conclusion of Riccardo's 'Gia parmi udire il fremito' (Act I), and for the *stretta*, cadences from the quartet (Act II). It is symptomatic of Verdi's lack of interest in the sinfonia that none of these themes has dramatic or expressive value in the opera itself: they are all formal or decorative. And it was precisely at decorativeness that Verdi was least adept.

The sinfonia to *Un Giorno di Regno* is slightly more sophisticated in design, using a kind of abbreviated sonata form in which the modulating central episode leads straight into a reprise of the second theme: according to Julian Budden it was a pattern 'current in Mayr's day'. Again all the thematic material is taken from the body of the opera. In this case most is from the two finales, while the introductory theme, which recurs in the coda, is from the opening chorus. Thus the overture, together with the two finales, furnishes *Un Giorno di Regno* with the rudiments of an overall rondo form. The thematic recurrences clearly have nothing of the dramatic force they were to acquire in later works; they simply contribute an element of patterning to the work.

Musical continuity

This kind of thematic patterning is simply one of the variety of means used by Italian composers of the period to give a greater sense of unity and consistency to their operas. The characteristic structure of an opera, with its profusion of short discrete numbers, was, in many cases, tightened up by such a use of recurring themes. The type of recurring theme which Verdi ultimately came to prefer was the reminiscence theme; the theme which recalls, in order to enhance some dramatic point, an earlier context in the opera. But outside dreams and mad scenes such recurring themes were rare in the 1830s, and the only example in these operas comes at the start of Act II of *Oberto*. The chorus of damsels reflects sympathetically on the fate of the unhappy, betrayed Cuniza, and their words are set against an orchestral restatement, at a slower tempo and in a different key, of a theme from her Act I love duet with Riccardo.

More typical of this period is the purely formal use of recurring themes. An example is found in 'Si mostri a chi l'adora' (*Un Giorno di Regno*, Act II), where the music of the *tempo di mezzo* recurs, rhythmically transformed, in the interlude and postlude of the cabaletta. But Verdi is far less systematic than Bellini had been in his use of this device, and certainly does not attempt to apply it on the same kind of scale. There is, for example, nothing in Verdi to compare with the use Bellini makes of the priests' march in the opening scenes of *Norma*.

A more highly developed sense of musical continuity is the one respect in which *Un Giorno di Regno* might be regarded as a maturer work than *Oberto*. For one thing, thanks to Romani's libretto, it has one of those multi-movement introductions – comprising choruses, a duet and a *sortita* – which were common in the *buffo* genre. It was this kind of structure that marks the starting point for such triumphant achievements of musical and dramatic continuity as we find in the first acts of *Rigoletto* and *La Traviata*.

But to understand the most important lesson Verdi learned from the *opera buffa* we must examine the recitatives and transitions. The recitatives and transitions used by him and his contemporaries to link the arias and ensembles took as their point of departure the conversational and declamatory recitative styles of the eighteenth century. Indeed much of the recitative in *Un Giorno di Regno* is true *secco* recitative, scurrying in quavers and semiquavers, and accompanied by a pianoforte which played from a figured bass.

But this was something of an anachronism by 1840. The orchestrally accompanied recitative normal at this period and used throughout *Oberto* is more measured in its movement, tending at moments of expressive vehemence to fall into robust trochaic patterns. Inevitably, since its adoption as the standard type of recitative in heroic opera, it had acquired a whole range of habits that distinguished it from the *secco* recitative. Some, like the orchestral punctuation of the sung phrases, the conventional figurations – dotted rhythms, tremolos, symbolic figures – or the periodic recurrence of material from the introductory bars to bind together a scene, had been part of the *recitativo accompagnato* tradition for a century or more. Others were newer: Leonora's first recitative preceding 'Sotto il paterno tetto' shows some of them – an orchestral passage to suggest the manner of her movement on to the stage, the lyrical *adagio* phrase to point the words 'delle nozze il canto', the arioso 'Di qual duolo' which embodies the psychological core of the scene, the formal rhetorical gestures that precede the cantabile.

In transitions between cantabile and cabaletta, or within ensembles, the orchestra tends to play a fuller role so that the impetus of the scene can be maintained. A popular style in more vehement contexts is antiphony between voice and orchestra such as that in the Leonora/Oberto duet (*Oberto*, Act I). But in *Oberto* Verdi has not yet fashioned a recitative idiom that would enable him really to bring to life in music the dramatic encounters and psychological crises of the scena. This idiom he discovered in *opera buffa*, though Bellini and Donizetti applied it to serious opera years before; and it was surely the most precious asset gained from the experience of composing *Un Giorno di Regno*.

The resource in question is the so-called *parlante*. In the *parlante* the music acquires its coherence and continuity from the orchestra, which reiterates or develops a single rhythmic or melodic idea to form a sustained musical period. Against this the text is declaimed by the voices, which, thanks to the solid framework offered by the orchestra are at liberty to use any style appropriate, whether recitative, or naturalistic ejaculation, or song.

It would be vain to look for complete mastery of the *parlante* in *Un Giorno di Regno*. It was a resource of infinite flexibility whose full potential Verdi realized only after years of experience. In the opening bars of the Act I finale, there are some modest glimpses of what the medium was later to become: varied by a wide range of modulation, developed or broken down into new types of figuration, suspended altogether for dramatic or expressive emphasis, notably at the Marchesa's 'La vendetta più sicura è sposarla addiritura'. More typical of this opera, however, as of the masters from whom Verdi learned his craft, is a setting out of the orchestral music precisely in the manner of a formal aria, full of exact repetitions and imperturbable symmetries: a good example is the *tempo di mezzo* in the Act I terzet.

14

Italian grand opera – *Nabucco* and *I Lombardi alla Prima Crociata*

To the best of my knowledge Verdi never referred to *Nabucco* and *I Lombardi* explicitly in terms of Parisian grand opera. Nevertheless the kinship is clear. *Nabucco* reflects the influence of the revised, Parisian version of Rossini's *Mosè*; *I Lombardi* was seen as an opera 'well suited to the [Parisian] stage',[1] and was in due course reshaped into the genuine grand opera *Jérusalem*. Resemblances between this pair of operas and the classics of the Parisian repertory are numerous. They extend from the actual choice of subject – in both cases involving religious conflict within a clearly defined historical setting – through the manner in which the subject is treated – dependent less on continuously developing intrigue than on oratorio-like tableaux with unusually prominent roles for the chorus and orchestra – to the finer details of musical style – notably the resourceful symphonic development and *recherché* harmonic sallies found in certain movements of *I Lombardi*.

In one important respect however they differ markedly from the genuine Parisian article: in no sense can the entertainment they provide be described as escapist. On the contrary, *Nabucco* and *I Lombardi* are two of Verdi's most committed operas, two of the works in which his faith in the patriotic ideals of the *risorgimento* finds most aggressive expression.

Popular elements: marches and hymnody

As the dramatic substance of both operas is concerned more with communities than with individuals, their musical idiom is accordingly somewhat different from that of the main stream of *ottocento* opera. The virtuoso singer dominates the scene less; on the other hand the two great repertories of contemporary community music, the march and the hymn, occupy a central position. Marches are especially prominent in *Nabucco*, and much of the opera is pervaded by the timbre of the brass band. This brassiness manifests itself in a number of ways. Most obviously, there are four formal march movements in the opera, two of them – in the Act I finale and in the introduction chorus of Act III – employing the Babylonian march, and two of them recurrences of the funeral march for the procession to Fenena's execution, in which Verdi relies on the 'banda interna'. As usual the scoring of the music for this basically military band combination was left to assistants, though in the case of the *marcia funebre* in Act IV, Verdi does to some extent particularize, requesting 'soli istromenti di metallo senza gran cassa'. In many more movements, especially marches and choruses, Verdi's own scoring retains something of the flavour of the town band. Accompanying chords are thickened up by horns, bassoons and cimbasso; choral melodies are doubled by trumpets and trombones. Finally brass instruments are used to accompany Zaccaria's recitatives, and in religious contexts those of Nabucco too. Probably Verdi had in mind the brass- and woodwind-accompanied recitatives of Moses in Rossini's *Mosè in Egitto*. The effect is characteristically more blatant in Verdi's opera, and given the dramatic theme of the opera and the pervasive brassiness of its scoring, the result is that the music of holiness and the music of militarism appear to be brought into an unprecedentedly intimate association.*

It is in the *risorgimento*-tinted episodes of *I Lombardi* that the inheritance of *Nabucco* most obviously weighs upon Verdi, and that its undeserved reputation as a pallid imitation of the earlier work has been earned. Generally the marches quite fail to equal their *Nabucco* counterparts in vividness. According to Pougin, the score of *I Lombardi* includes reworkings of some of the music written for the Busseto Philharmonic in Verdi's earliest years. It is difficult to see what could come into this category if not the marches, and the very fact that in this idiom Verdi may already have been peering back into old portfolios is symptomatic. In this particular style he had already expressed himself fully, the capacity genuinely to experience such music was already a thing of the past. A few years later, at the time of working on *Attila*, he himself was to make the point quite explicitly: 'I have written my marches, a warlike one in *Nabucco*, another solemn and slow in *Giovanna*, which I shall not be able to improve upon.'[2]

Moreover it is where the opera most demands the successful exploitation of this idiom that Verdi fails; that is, in the march tune

---

* This question is discussed more fully below, pp. 455–9.

that he uses to accompany the crusaders as an identifying theme. The bludgeoning monotony of the harmonies, the ludicrously incongruous chromatic scale that terminates the opening sentence, the lyrical impotence of the 'big tune' are all factors that contribute to the dismal overall effect. But having said that, one must go on to remark that Verdi's operatic handling of this march and of the *banda* apparatus with which it is inextricably involved is of a sophistication unprecedented in the earlier opera.

The march is first heard in the Hermit's *gran scena* in Act II. Indeed its most effective use in the whole opera is this stealing upon the ear during the conversation between the hermit and Pirro, gradually to take full possession of the scene. In the early stages its over-heavy tread is deliciously suspended by echoes and by *arioso* declamation. Also the fragments of theme are played with that homorhythmic unanimity which had lent such ardour to the *Nabucco* marches, and which is lost when it relapses into a tune-with-accompaniment texture.

Verdi's most imaginative use of this material comes in the Act IV *battaglia*, an instrumental movement accompanying the decisive battle for Jerusalem. Here the crusaders' march is broken down into its several constituent phrases, which are always played by the orchestra. The Saracen march tunes from the chorus 'È dunque vero' in Act II are similarly treated, but played by the *banda*. The battle is thus represented by fragmented and overlapping march themes tossed about from orchestra to *banda*. A central climax breaks free from these thematic associations in a series of *tutti* ideas without any obvious conceptual meaning; then stylized trumpet calls lead into the final stage. The battle is over, lost and won, and the music fades away in a series of chromatically approached half-cadences to which the *banda* representing the Saracens contributes nothing but a series of languishing sigh-figures.

While the marches in *I Lombardi* seem but feeble imitations of those in *Nabucco*, the hymn comes into new prominence, with the claustral chorus in Act I and the pilgrims' choruses in Act IV, together with several solo or ensemble movements in which the idiom is much infected by hymnody. This may seem poor compensation for a modern audience, to whom few idioms can sound more disagreeably dated than those of nineteenth-century operatic hymnody, but in Verdi's time his use of this style was found deeply moving. It was not one of his blood-tingling military marches nor even one of his great romantic arias or duets that prompted the most eloquent homage to his art in contemporary Italian literature, but the idealized hymn tune 'O Signore, dal tetto natio' (*I Lombardi*, Act IV):

> ... Dalle trombe di guerra uscian le note
> Come di voce che si raccomanda,
> D'una gente che gema in duri stenti
> E d'perduti beni si rammenti.
> Era un coro di Verdi; il coro a Dio,
> Là de' Lombardi miseri assetati;
> Quello: *O Signore, dal tetto natio,*
> Che tanti petti ha scossi e inebriati ...[3]

Like the marches, the hymnic episodes of *I Lombardi* have their own distinctive tone-colouring, related more closely to the ethos of popular music than to that of opera. The claustral chorus in Act I is accompanied by 'Istromenti d'Armonia che dovrano immitare il suono del'organo'. As Verdi himself does not further specify the scoring, one imagines that the instruments were selected from the *banda* rather than the orchestra and that, as with the full *banda* music, the precise choice was left to the *banda*'s director. Similar wind-band scoring, enriched by two harps, is employed in the vision of celestial spirits in Act IV. And although in 'O signore, dal tetto natio' Verdi uses the pit orchestra and himself spells out the details of the scoring, the prominence of brass and woodwinds in the opening pages shows that he intended to sound the same ecclesiastical associations as in the 'istromenti d'armonia' episodes.

The characteristic features of Verdi's hymnic style at this period are a general rhythmic and textural lifelessness, and a total unconcern for relating the music either rhetorically or expressively to the text that ostensibly inspires it. The grotesque ineptitude of the rhythms in the claustral chorus and the arbitrary chromatic harmony that renders each phrase 'expressive' are typical. Despite the dramatic weight which the idiom has to bear in *I Lombardi*, Verdi treats it in the way the *ottocento* opera had traditionally done – as a touch of background colour, to which the syntax of the normal musical language scarcely applies (Ex. 1).

Tableau

In both *Nabucco* and *I Lombardi* the dramatic theme prompts Verdi to lay unusual emphasis on the chorus. Chorus movements are more numerous and of far greater dramatic significance than in the earlier operas; furthermore, on a number of occasions the chorus becomes involved with the solo music, to thrilling effect. Verdi has used this

Ex. 1

kind of mixing of media before. In Riccardo's 'Questi plausi' (*Oberto*, Act I) and in Giulietta's 'Non san quant'io' (*Un Giorno di Regno*, Act I) the brevity of the lyrics and the convenient presence of a chorus of sympathetic bystanders prompt him to give the episodes to the chorus. The effect is charmingly ornamental and inconsequential, showing not the faintest trace of awareness of the dramatic effects that might be gained from such a procedure.

By the time of *Nabucco*, however, Verdi has absorbed the lesson implicit in such works as Bellini's *La Sonnambula* – where the choral involvement in solo arias reflects the warm sense of community among the characters of the opera – or Donizetti's *Marin Faliero* – where it reflects the commitment of the chorus to the ideas expressed by the protagonists. In each of the arias of Zaccaria the chorus joins in. And in each case this formal device reflects the dramatic point that Zaccaria is the spiritual leader of the Hebrew people, and that they eagerly associate themselves with what he does and says.

The most brilliant exploitation of this kind of procedure is found not in Zaccaria's music, however, but in Nabucco's cabaletta 'O prodi miei' (Act IV). Here the chorus does not simply follow or join in with the soloist. Indeed the relationship between soloist and chorus is quite different from that in the Hebrew aria-with-chorus pieces. At the start, for four consecutive musical sentences, no attempt is made to sustain an organic musical progression. Each sentence is simply juxtaposed against its predecessor, a distinct block of music, contrasting in colour, mass, and thematic style. Uniquely for this opera, the orchestral introduction is no mere definition of tempo and texture, nor is it a mere partial anticipation of the aria broken off at the half-cadence. Instead, in shrill clarion colours Verdi presents a complete period of a march tune. The most extraordinary moment of all comes when, after this, not Nabucco but the unison chorus is heard striking in with a new theme in a new key, the subdominant. This sensational effect is almost repeated when Nabucco does at last sing, for he wrenches the music back into the tonic and returns to the principal theme heard in the introduction. Nabucco proceeds to use the chorus tunes for his second and final quatrain; and it is only at this late stage, when the text has already been exhausted, that the music begins to behave more like a normal cabaletta, with accelerating harmonies and a more rapid delivery of words urging the music toward the final cadences. A last felicitous touch comes with the orchestral postlude, where Verdi at one stroke returns to the massy block-like style of the opening, and underlines a dramatic point – the recovery of the glory of Babylon – by a statement of one full period of the march theme from the Act I finale.

The imposing, oratorio-like tone of substantial sections of *Nabucco* is not simply a matter of the choral resonance of so many passages. At a structural level, too, the succession of tableau-like scenes in Solera's libretto prompts Verdi to a new kind of formal emphasis. Many of his musical designs are of an aspect at once clearer in outline and more massive than usual.

One undeniably impressive example of such architectural forms is the opening chorus of Act I. It is without doubt a superb *coup de théâtre* on Solera's part, particularly telling in that, before particularizing feelings or taking action, the first *tutti* is devoted wholly to a description of the scene of woe. It is thus peculiarly apt for Verdi's favourite manner of choral opening, a chordal declamation superimposed upon a repetition of the orchestral introduction. The huge blocks of choral sound are relentlessly, and without regard to verbal rhythm or emphasis, hammered on to Solera's verses. Nor does the composition grow or develop in any way during the course of the verse: it simply stands four-square, a mass of grim sound, defining the atmosphere from which the rest of the chorus and thereafter the rest of the drama takes its tone.

Obviously, the extreme clarity and massiveness of the formal outlines of much of this music are interesting or meritorious only in so far as they harmonize with the dramatic or scenic sense of the opera: in such tableaux as the introductory chorus, in ritual movements, to gain such frankly sensational effects as those in Nabucco's cabaletta. Nevertheless there is at least one important respect in which the youthful Verdi's passion for such formalism, which reaches a climax in *Nabucco*, was to prove enduringly valuable to him as a composer of opera. I refer to his genius for analysing a confused or over-detailed dramatic situation, and reducing its complexity by just so much as is necessary to render it harmoniously and lucidly in operatic terms. Splendid examples of this are found in the *andante* sections of the Act I finale in *Nabucco* and of the *introduzione* to *I Lombardi*.

Perhaps what most impresses in this latter movement is the way in which Verdi cuts through the confusion of thought in Solera's libretto to form a tableau of absolute lucidity which is yet psychologically animated. In Solera, no one except Pagano and Pirro really seems certain how to respond to the scene of reconciliation. But Verdi relegates to an entirely subsidiary position the doubts in the minds of Giselda and Viclinda. Giselda sings her first two lines in an introductory manner; they act as a kind of hesitant preface, swept aside by the 'Gioia immensa' in bar 7 and never recurring: Viclinda never sings the complete text assigned to her. From the seventh bar, in fact, the sopranos sing of joy and nothing else, and in this, despite the sense of his words and notwithstanding a suggestion of doubt in his first solo phrases, Arvino joins. Thus the furtive plotting of Pirro and Pagano have an unmistakable impact, set off against the rapturous harmony of the higher voices.

Such a simplification is wholly characteristic of Verdi's art. It is in no way due to a simplicity of mind, to deficiency of psychological discrimination, or to the inadequacy of the tradition, but to a clear understanding of what is meaningful in theatrical terms. Arvino's music contradicts his words in order that the essential conflict within the tableau may be made clear. And even this essential conflict is not presented so realistically that there need be any sacrifice of that harmoniousness of sound and lucidity of form that was obligatory for Italian music at that time.

Within this general harmoniousness and lucidity Verdi's use of the chorus may be singled out as another masterly detail. Like everyone else on stage, the chorus has a quatrain to sing; theirs however, is held in reserve until the ensemble is well advanced. After the central D♭ major – F major section, during which the individualities of the protagonists have been dissolved into the torrent of song, the burden of the music is suddenly shifted, assumed by the anonymous choral forces at the back of the stage. We are restored to a new objectivity, in which we are able to discern the individuals of the ensemble once more, able to perceive once more the character of their thoughts: each is put across with perfect clarity against a kind of *cantus firmus* effect in the chorus.

Recitatives and transitions

But if the zeal for massive lucidity encouraged Verdi's mastery of ensemble writing, it was instrumental in impoverishing his recitative idiom. Particularly in those arias and ensembles that are built up out of several contrasting lyrical sections, Verdi's concern for the wholeness of the scene and his unwillingness to relax its momentum when once it has been established may lead to a negligence of declamatory nuance and rhetorical emphasis that alone give beauty to recitatives. For audiences who had been brought up on the still spacious recitative scenes of Rossini and Bellini, one of the most arresting features of the young Verdi's style must have been the impatience with which he dashed from one lyrical number to another. Characteristic of his scenes is a tendency to treat the recitative not as vivid, free declamation, but as composed transition. Zaccaria's recitative 'Sperate, o figli' leading into the cantabile 'D'Egitto là sui lidi' (*Nabucco*, Act I), or the transition from Pagano's 'Sciagurata, hai tu creduto' to the chorus 'Niun periglio' (*I Lombardi*, Act I), are typical of the melodic and rhythmic lifelessness of such passages. In the latter case, although the text is full of melodramatic details, Verdi's composition amounts to nothing more than a protracted series of half-cadences on A, the key of the ensuing chorus. By his exclusive preoccupation with the structural function of such recitatives, Verdi neglects precisely those features that might give them an intrinsic life and beauty. From every point of view, but especially from the point of view of rhythm, most of these transitional recitatives are among the poorest Verdi ever wrote.

Occasionally, in *I Lombardi* more than in *Nabucco*, one does find passages in which Verdi strives for real expressive intensity. But only one recitative episode, that introducing the Act III duet in *I*

Lombardi, compares with the finest pages of the arias and ensembles of this period. It is of remarkable formal fluidity, and prodigal of the kind of irruptions of lyrical ardour that one associates more readily with the middle-period operas. The scene commences with a solo recitative, as if preparatory to a Giselda cantabile. However, the musing on love comes not to a songful termination but to a theatrical one, the appearance of the beloved Oronte himself. From here the music assumes the form of a free dialogue – a remarkably vivid and ardent one – always ready to flame up into arioso, as at 'la fronte ch'io t'innondi' or at 'di vederti una volta e poi morir'.

It may appear somewhat paradoxical in view of the many oratorio-like details in these operas, but it is only now that Verdi achieves the complete blending of *seria* and *buffa* idioms that had long been practised by his predecessors. In some respects Verdi was the most primly formal of the masters of *ottocento* opera. It is in *Nabucco* and *I Lombardi* that we find him first applying to his serious operas such resources as the differentiation of character in duets and large scale ensemble, or – in both *primo tempo* and *tempo di mezzo* sections – the *parlante* technique.

The greater freedom with which *parlante* is already being treated is illustrated by the *primo tempo* of the duet 'Teco io fuggo', the continuation of the recitative scene just described (*I Lombardi*, Act III). Essentially the dialogue is articulated in three phases, each leading to some kind of cantabile climax. Thus the first, acidly orchestrated and in the minor key, leads to 'Infelice, un voto orrendo'; the second, more gaily orchestrated and now in the major key, to 'Oh mia gioia'; and the third, with fuller orchestration, more energetic figuration, and modulating harmonies, to the formal cantabile 'Oh bella, a questa misera'. Moreover, the *parlante* is abandoned entirely for a sustained cantabile solo at 'Per dirupie per foreste'.

Arias and ensembles

Those aspects of *Nabucco* and *I Lombardi* so far discussed have been those that gave these operas their tone, those that set them apart from the romantic Donizettian melodrama that formed the main stream of the Italian tradition in the early 1840s. Nevertheless Verdi's growing mastery of his *métier* is perhaps more apparent in the solo and ensemble music which does belong to this main stream.

On the other hand, it cannot be denied that in certain of the

cabalettas, in 'Come notte' (*Nabucco*, Act I) or in 'Salgo già' (Act II),
for example, with their very brief modulatory episodes, their melodic recapitulations, their harmonic accelerations into the cadences,
and their general carelessness in the handling of the text, the lasting
force of mere convention is clearly seen. A year later, in *I Lombardi*,
some cabalettas such as Pagano's 'O speranza' (Act I) or the original
version of 'Come poteva un angelo' (Act II) have already lapsed into
slovenliness: 'already' because it was this primitivism that was soon
to become typical of Verdi's cabalettas. By the time of *Attila* the
short-breathed repetitions and the crudely monotonous rhythms of
these pieces had become standard. From their intermingling in *I
Lombardi* with other cabalettas so resourceful in style and technique
it is clear that there was no question of Verdi not having fully
mastered this type. The choice of the more primitive design was a
symptom of his declining interest in the old-fashioned cabaletta, or
of his theatrical impatience over its elements of ritual.

The young Verdi's boldest and most imaginative reinterpretations
of the formal traditions of Italian opera are to be found in *I Lombardi*
rather than *Nabucco*. They are but one sign of the closer approach of
the later work to the manner of Parisian grand opera. In the hermit's
gran scena in Act II, for example, one finds an unprecedented
vividness of detail in the recitative, brought about very largely by the
dramatically motivated elaboration of accompanying figures and
textures in the orchestra. In such a movement as this, Verdi is
consciously cultivating that responsiveness to words that within a
few years would bear fruit in such things as Macbeth's *gran scena*
'Mi si affaccia il pugnal'. The duettino that follows discovers Verdi
experimenting in the lyrical organization of dramatic dialogue.
Again one's thoughts run ahead to the mastery achieved in such an
idiom in the scene for Sparafucile and Rigoletto. Neither *Macbeth*
nor *Luisa Miller* contains a cabaletta more imaginatively refashioned
than Giselda's 'No, giusta causa' in Act II, in which, moreover, the
refashioning is prompted by and in some measure expresses the
dramatic context. In the remarkably resourceful figure-develop-
ment in the *prestissimo* of the Act I finale, save for its
one-dimensionalness scarcely less Beethovenian than the familiar
episodes in *Falstaff*, and in the fastidious tonal layout of the *nuova
cabaletta* for Oronte's Act I aria, we find Verdi exploiting composi-
tional resources which had not loomed large in the operatic repertory on which he had been trained.

Between the radical boldness of such passages as these and the
stale conventionalism of the feebler cabalettas, there is a substantial

body of music which bears witness to Verdi's quietly maturing grasp of the musical language.

We have seen that in his earliest operas Verdi was equally at ease in two distinct types of lyrical composition. While the predominant type was formalized, symmetrical, and sprucely articulated, he commanded equally that type of melody, of which Bellini was the supreme master, which starts out from vivid fragments of declamation and gradually welds these into a continuously flowing melody, evolving without any kind of formal recapitulation. By the time of *Nabucco* and *I Lombardi*, Verdi is investigating the middle ground. In several of the most masterly movements he succeeds in combining what is most vital in both these types of song: from the one its flexibility of rhythm and its responsiveness to the verbal text, and from the other a well-balanced musical design. He does this by replacing the principles of repetition and symmetry by that of variation. In some movements these variation processes are still merely ornamental, as in 'Dio di Giuda' (*Nabucco*, Act IV), in others quite incidental, as in 'Tu sul labbro' (*Nabucco*, Act III), where the melody of 'E di canti a te sacrati', in an irregular diminution, provides the orchestral burden of the cadence phrases. But in the finest examples, such as 'Anch'io dischiuso' (*Nabucco*, Act II) or 'Se vano è il pregare' (*I Lombardi*, Act II), we seem to hear a new and more fastidious type of song.

'Anch'io dischiuso' is one of the most fragrant of the youthful Verdi's cantabiles. Much of its elegiac charm is to be savoured in the threefold statement of the principal theme at the start, first in the flute, then in the singing voice (Ex. 2a); for this theme is already adorned with all that mastery of old-fashioned fioritura variation which we have admired in *Oberto*. What more arrests the attention, though, is the resumption of this melody after the modulating episode. Here it is instantly transformed and intensified, first by harmonic side-steps and then by a multiplication of appoggiatura-figures in a towering, impassioned, climactic phrase which adumbrates the Verdi of *Il Trovatore* (Ex. 2b). It is characteristic of the young Verdi that, because this transformation of the principal melody has overbalanced the formal symmetry of the movement, he now seeks a new equilibrium, breaking off the cadence phrase to repeat the climactic transformation of the main theme, and following this with a new cadence theme in which he makes a return to the old-fashioned ornamenting idiom with which the aria began.

A more complex application of variation principles is found in *primo tempo* of the duet 'Donna, chi sei?' (*Nabucco*, Act III). Because

Ex. 2 (a)

Ex. 2 (b)

the detailed and lengthy dialogue defies lyrical stylization, Verdi employs the *parlante*. He uses the orchestra as the form-giving factor in the ensemble, composing for it a kind of aria; and with this aria the detached, conversational phrases of the singing voices have only the freest, most casual association. The orchestral aria contains quite a variety of figures, for to it must be matched a wide range of feelings, but the most interesting thing about it is that when it has run its course, and as the scene moves to its dramatic climax, the music is repeated in a fascinating and ingenious variation.

The dramatic exposition of the scene is set against the first, expository statement of the orchestral aria, which, for all its richness of detail, really falls into two parts. The first is, technically speaking, straight from the world of *opera buffa*, where this kind of strongly figured orchestral continuity is frequently found, giving coherence to the primarily verbal utterances of the singers (Ex. 3). In the second section, however, Verdi appears to be attempting some kind of alienation effect. The true 'meaning' of this music becomes clear in due course, especially at its recurrence in the cabaletta: here its *élan* simply gives the lie to Abigaille's solicitous words (Ex. 4).

Ex. 3

Ex. 4

For the second part of the dialogue, this scheme together with its concluding cadences is repeated in a varied form. Apart from the transposition of the opening theme to C♭, much of the music is identical. But within this section come two dramatic cruxes –

Ex. 5

340

Abigaille's persuading Nabucco to sign the execution warrant, and Nabucco's realization that he has condemned his own daughter – and it is in order to accommodate these that Verdi's repetition breaks away from mere symmetry. Suspending the lyrical flow of the music in harmonic parenthesis, and in the first case sustaining the tension of the crux by figural reiterations (Ex. 5), he shows a keen awareness of the greater dramatic flexibility the orchestrally based scena may enjoy.

Henceforth the symmetrical, dutifully recapitulating type of song plays no significant part in Verdi's work: it is ousted by such intensifying variation designs as these. On the other hand that type of aria in which symmetry and reprise are replaced by a dynamic lyrical momentum is well represented, particularly in I Lombardi.

The most striking examples are perhaps the Act I *preghiera* and the Act III *gran scena*. But it is a less ostentatiously original movement that evinces Verdi's real mastery of the style. Soffredini, whose ardour for Verdi's early works can sometimes be ludicrous, picked a winner when he wrote, of Oronte's cantabile 'La mia letizia' (Act II): 'in questa cavatina c'è il primo vero *slancio* di Verdi, lo slancio più sublime e che Verdi stesso non ha potuto più superare'. Verdi contrives a wonderfully true expression of the mounting enthusiasm of Oronte's passion by dispensing with all recapitulating schemes and composing one unbroken, unfolding melody. It remains a single, whole melody, rather than a chain of thematic fragments, by virtue of its beautifully calculated, mounting tessitura, and the various pervading rhythms, those that 'rhyme with' or adorn the rhythm of the opening phrase, and those employing the woodwind accompaniment figure from the 'tante armonie' episode to sustain the momentum of the song.

It is during this central episode that Verdi begins to depart from the more common and formal manner of aria construction. There is here a complete absence of repetition or variation, the whole phrase is composed through, to attain the return to the tonic key at 'seco al cielo' at a heightened pitch of intensity. This intensity is masterfully sustained – by phrase repetitions, by commencing these phrases on bars of dominant-seventh harmony which project them urgently forward, by the usual accelerating harmonies and mounting tessitura in the 'ir seco' phrase. In the final bars of the aria we get another of those rethinkings of convention, another of these anticipations of the fully mature Verdi, that so frequently surprise us in *I Lombardi*. A whole succession of *stretta*-like chromaticism is packed in the most nonchalant manner into the cadence phrase, becoming a source of delight in itself, without losing its form-making character. At the actual cadence, the adumbration of 'Celeste Aida' that results from the toying with these chromatic patterns is remarkable (Ex. 6).

As a final example of the manner in which Verdi, for all the novelty of certain aspects of *Nabucco* and *I Lombardi*, remained an artist not merely obligated to the conventions of Italian opera but keenly aware of the dramatic use to which they might be put, we may briefly consider one movement where he makes use of the conventions of the mad scene.

In Nabucco's *scena* at the start of Act IV, Verdi uses what we might call the *Lucia* stream of the mad-scene convention – that is to say, the convention according to which pathos is given a nostalgic bitter-sweetness by the use of thematic reminiscences drawn from

Ex. 6

more felicitous episodes in the character's history. It is to be doubted whether Nabucco is a character who would lend himself to this kind of pathos in its usual form – hitherto he has been a desecrator and blasphemer – his finest moments are still before him – and in any case there is already in the scene as a whole a strong and all-embracing formal design of funeral march, prayer, and battle-cry (recitative, cantabile, cabaletta) making the incorporation of that kind of rag-bag of reminiscences hardly feasible. Verdi has, though, the admirably ingenious idea of preluding the scena proper with a purely orchestral mad scene. Even more than in the acted mad scene, the themes are simply strung together, without elaboration or development or transition. The object is simply to sound in the mind of the audience associations of desecratory militarism and the putting down of pride, and to suggest that derangement in Nabucco's slumbers which otherwise would have remained a matter of sheer speculation.

The orchestra

Except for the new prominence accorded the *banda* the orchestral idiom of both operas is firmly rooted in the tradition described in chapter 13, and within that idiom most imaginative or innovatory strokes are quiet and unobtrusive. Certain chamber-music-like movements that from this time become a regular feature in Verdi's scores do haunt the memory, especially 'Su me ... morente' (*Nabucco*, Act IV), where a cor anglais duets with the voice, a harp defines the harmonies, and a solo cello figures them. Another detail that emerges with some effectiveness out of the standard orchestral usage is the employment of the solo flute – almost as if with an awareness of its ecclesiastical associations with the dove – as a symbol of grace. A conspicuous example is heard in this same finale, where at the words 'Ah! tu dicesti, o popolo: *Solleva Iddio l'afflitto*' the *obbligato* cor anglais withdraws and a flute takes its place. A flute cadenza follows Nabucco's 'Dio degli Ebrei perdona!', immediately before 'Dio di Giuda'; and in 'Salve Maria' (*I Lombardi*, Act I) flute arpeggios float upwards into the empyrean against a background of muted violins.

It is characteristic of Verdi that his most impressive effects should be gained within a narrowly circumscribed orchestral convention. What might, to the bleary eye of the seeker for novel orchestral effects, seem the most imaginative movement in *Nabucco*, Zaccaria's *preghiera* in Act II, which is scored almost exclusively for violoncellos divided into six parts, with only very modest support from violas and a solo double-bass, is in fact among the poorest. The remarkable scoring has in fact nothing whatever to do with a singularity of inspiration; rather it seems an attempt to cover up Verdi's unease in prayerfulness.

These two aspects of Verdi's originality as an orchestrator – the self-conscious straining for vividness on the one hand, and on the other an instinctive transformation of the standard accompaniment textures of the day – are epitomized in nine consecutive bars of the scene of the prophecy in *Nabucco*, those in which are set the words

> Fra la polve dall'aure commossa
> Un silenzio fatal regnerà!
> Solo il gufo suoi tristi lamenti
> Spiegherà quando viene la sera.

The first couplet is accompanied by an obtrusive and artificial attempt at pictorialism, which in terms of the ripening of Verdi's art was to lead nowhere, unless to some of the more superficial delights of *Falstaff*; but in the second, where a conventional figuration is made evocative and beautiful in its every detail, we have one of the most important sources of Verdi's development: a premonition of Lady Macbeth's sleepwalking scene, of Rigoletto's 'Cortigiani, vil razza dannata' and of all that was to develop out of such scenes.

When *I Lombardi* was first performed, the critic of the *Gazzetta Privilegiata* observed and deplored the fact that Verdi had broken with his earlier habit of preceding the opera with a sinfonia, and had provided merely 'a brief and simple prelude'. But if in terms of its own intrinsic merit the movement has little to offer it does have a modest functional interest. Verdi's intention appears to be to intimate to the audience the fact that this is a solemn opera, notwithstanding the raucous revelry with which the action begins. This orchestral premonition of the drama's real character long before the stage action confirms it was to become a standard feature in Verdi's idiom: *Rigoletto* and *La Traviata* provide the quintessential examples.

15

The early 'galley' operas – *Ernani* to *Attila*

The *anni di galera* began after the production of *I Lombardi* in 1843.
The expression was Verdi's own, used to evoke the sense of
relentless, grinding toil to which he chose to subject himself for a
period of years in order to consolidate his position as the most
successful maestro of his generation. Probably the foremost objective
of this phase of Verdi's career was to become independent, financially and artistically, as quickly as possible. But there is no doubt that,
to bring about this state of affairs, Verdi had to deliver himself into a
kind of bondage, created out of contracts, dates of delivery, commitments to rehearse and produce in every major city of Italy. He
obliged himself to compose too much and therefore to compose too
quickly. With *Nabucco* and *I Lombardi* Verdi had already manifested an eloquence and skill surpassing that of any contemporary
Italian. He was already master of his chosen medium. The circumstances of the 'galley years', however, were calculated so to drain his
energies, in purely physical terms, that his eloquence and his skill
develop altogether less impressively than in previous years. He
tended to fall back again and again upon mere expertise, employing
the conventional formal patterns and musical idioms of the period
more regularly and more carelessly than before.

Arias

At this period Verdi's musical gifts are seen at their richest in the
cantabiles. These movements do not in any drastic way depart from
the patterns established in earlier operas. The relationship of voice
and orchestra remains unaltered; the various types of repetition and
symmetry that can be accommodated within the general scheme of
exposition, interlude, and reprise-with-intensification are still the
basis of the musical form. Nevertheless one or two new developments are unmistakable.

In the first place it is quite clear that the weight of the musical
structure is being moved decisively on to the closing section of the

cantabile. Minor-key arias, which are becoming more common, regularly close with a new theme in the major key. In those cantabiles that are in any case in the major, this effect of powerful culmination is achieved by some form of reduplication. Such arias as Elvira's 'Ernani, Ernani involami' (*Ernani*, Act I) or Ezio's 'Dagli immortali vertici' (*Attila*, Act II) show the process at its most naive. While the culminating phrases of both arias are impressive specimens of a skill long practised in Italian opera, that of combining a more intense lyrical exaltation with elements of reprise, the actual repetitions seem pointless, or at least ill-motivated. In other examples this formal looseness is skilfully avoided. In Odabella's 'Allor che i forti' (*Attila*, Prologue), Verdi has the splendid notion of allowing Attila to express his admiration for the warrior–maiden during the course of her song, not subsequently. His appreciation heightens our own, and if it does not exactly motivate, it certainly gives a new dimension – one might say an ensemble dimension – to the ensuing repetition of her phrases. Some of the best cantabiles of the period show this feature. For example, the culminating phrases of Lucrezia's 'Tu al cui sguardo onnipotente' (*I Due Foscari*, Act I) derive much of their eloquence and aptness from the fact that they adorn and intensify the opening phrases of the aria. But, on the other hand, it is the interpolation of the chorus that gives dramatic and psychological point to the repetition of this music in the closing bars of the cantabile. They encourage Lucrezia to dwell on the idea she has just formulated and to give voice to it once more in yet a further variation.

The extreme example of this growing tendency to place the weight of the musical design on the closing section is found in 'Sempre all'alba' (*Giovanna d'Arco*, Prologue). For eighteen bars this is laid out like a perfectly normal cantabile, making entirely characteristic use of such features as ornamentation and rescoring to intensify the repetitions and reprises of material. As in 'Dagli immortali vortici', a brief orchestral link leads into a repetition of the culminating phrase, 'Ah se un dì'. But at this point Verdi adds to the design a new expansive coda, more ornate in its melodic writing and more energetic in its orchestral texture, and this too is repeated in a profusely decorated form. Even after this the design does not really end: in a way that is more typical of Verdi's late style, one of the orchestral textures from the aria is developed to provide the background for the broken recitative phrases with which Giovanna's soliloquy closes.

Despite the fact that the shaping of the melodic line and the building of the aria form are still the first priorities, there are some signs that Verdi was slowly becoming more interested in the problem of reconciling this aria craftsmanship with a more detailed eloquence in the delivery of the words. In 'Allor che i forti', for example, it is clear that by the style of his lyrical writing, and by the shaping of his musical design, he is seeking to illuminate the contrast that Odabella is drawing between barbarian women and Italian women. The opening phrases, those describing the barbarians, acquire from the emphasis on the monotone a detached, narrative, third-personal quality; whereas those describing the Italians are of a vividly experienced, plunging and soaring immediacy. Similarly the Italian phrases are resolutely and immovably in the tonic key, while the barbarian phrases sink to a cadence in which the mediant minor is not at all formal, but deliberately lacrimose, an effect confirmed and intensified in the little interlude that precedes the repetition of the final phrases of the aria (Ex. 1).

Ex. 1

It is a common experience in the early 'galley' operas to feel disappointed, let down, by the cabaletta. In the cantabiles Verdi's art is ripening unmistakably, the material is becoming more intrinsically interesting and better adapted to the words, the musical forms are showing a more satisfying balance of organic growth and predetermined formalism. Too often the cabalettas show no such characteristics; they are built on what the critic of the *Gazzetta Privilegiata di Venezia*, speaking of Foresto's 'Cara patria' (*Attila*, Prologue), called 'rather facile and trivial figures', and the musical forms are at once more primitive and more ungainly.

Verdi still perseveres in the attempt to combine a rigorously formal design with a sense of growing excitement. But the faster tempo and more energetic style of the cabalettas result in an exaggeration of the formalism so that, generally speaking, there is rarely time for that variation and intensification through which repetitions and symmetries in cantabiles are made expressive and alive. Too often the cabaletta is first rounded off in the squarest, most primitive design, and then has tacked on to it an *animato* based on different material, used simply to whip up excitement for the final cadenza and orchestral *tutti*: 'È gettata la mia sorte' (*Attila*, Act II) provides a clear example of the process.

Only a tiny handful of these cabalettas are as interesting as the cantabiles, whether from the point of view of how the musical material is developed, or of how it matches the sense of the words. Within a typically trim design, 'So che per via di triboli' (*Giovanna d'Arco*, Act I) employs an unusually wide harmonic and tonal range, to underline such concepts as 'il fallo primo' and 'la paterna lagrima'. While two cabalettas from *Alzira*, Gusmano's 'Quanto un mortal' and Alzira's 'Nell'astro che più fulgente' (both Act I), exhibit a modest degree of rhythmic resourcefulness. In 'Quanto un mortal' Verdi gradually intensifies the syncopated figure from the episode 'Ma non s'appaga l'anima', first working it into the reprise of the main theme, and finally deriving from it the more animated coda theme (Ex. 2). 'Nell'astro che più fulgente' is a series of variations on

Ex. 2

a single rhythmic idea: the normal processes of recapitulation (at 'seco unirmi') and the principles of symmetry (in the repeated coda phrases, 'vita d'eterno amor') are all disguised by the new contours and the new harmonic colourings taken on by this single motif.

Odabella's 'Da te questo or m'è concesso' (*Attila*, Prologue) is one of the rare cabalettas of this period in which Verdi does combine melodic symmetry with a sense of expressive development in the manner typical of the cantabiles. The culminating phrases neither merely recapitulate nor recklessly break loose from the idioms established in the opening bars: instead, they raise up the basic idea to a new pitch of brilliance and intensity (Ex. 3). Indeed the whole

Ex. 3 (a)

aria is a *locus classicus* for ornamentation and variation used as a vehicle of the most vehement emotional expression.

In addition to a number of cantabiles without cabalettas, such as the *Ernani* arias 'Infelice! e tuo credevi' (Act I) and 'Oh de' verd'anni' (Act III), there are a handful of solo movements – romanzas and so forth – which have little to do with the normal double-aria form. A distinguished example is the romanza 'Oh nel fuggente nuvolo' (*Attila*, Act I), a movement which shows how the romanza may be not merely an unattached cantabile, but a piece that stands stylistically quite apart from the main aria tradition. First, the place of the usual figured introduction is taken by a beautifully fashioned orchestral melody complete with a chromatically intensified ornamentation of the opening phrase, a modulatory episode, and a very distinctive cadence. Only in a greatly enhanced sense is this the music to accompany Odabella's entry: rather, it is the song of her as yet unspoken wretchedness, as she makes clear at the climax of the recitative where part of it recurs, conceptualized by a text and sung as well as played. The recitative cadences lead not straight into the romanza, but into instrumental cadences for flute, cor anglais, cello solo and harp; these no less than the singer are the protagonists in the romanza that follows.

For Solera and Verdi are drawing on a long Italian tradition, deriving ultimately from the echo scenes of the pastoral convention.

In such a scene the singing character is no longer entirely self-centred and self-sufficient, a world of emotions unto herself. She is in communion with the physical world around her, and the sympathy of this world, no less than her own emotions, is the subject of the aria. For this reason the orchestral music does not relapse into an anonymous, figured background texture, subordinate to the singer. Its music is a portrait of that physical world, in this case of those streams and breezes to which Odabella appeals for sympathy. The entrusting of this orchestral music to solo instruments sharpens our apprehension of the fact that every trill, every flourish, every arpeggio of its texture has a graphic significance.

Ensembles

The characteristic features observed in the solo cantabiles and cabalettas inform the duets and ensembles to an even higher degree; in particular, the contrast between the subtlety of the one and the crudeness of the other often verges on the ludicrous. In the cantabiles, besides his customary fastidiousness in the shaping of the cantilena, Verdi shows himself keenly aware of the demands of characterization. The *Attila* duets 'Tardi per gl'anni' (Prologue) and 'Si, quello io son' (Act I) employ the typical duet pattern of solo verses, which define the moods of the participants, and a final duet passage in which character and situations are largely superseded by rapturous song and unsullied harmony. But what art and what insight Verdi shows in the solo verses! In the case of the prologue duet, Verdi reins in the eloquence of Ezio's verse until the final phrase where its lyrical climax is matched to Solera's classic lines: 'Avrai tu l'universo, Resti l'Italia a me'. Throughout the song Ezio's calculating, his waiting and watching are matched in every detail of the music – in the silence before he begins; in the cool, even tone of the opening phrases, unruffled by passion; and in the suggestion of nervousness in the orchestral texture. Attila's mood is more complex, modulating from a genuine grief at the moral bankruptcy of the 'last Roman' to an eager anticipation of the widening dominion of Wodan. So his verse, albeit for a different reason, is likewise evolutionary and dynamic rather than symmetrical. Indeed formally it matches Ezio's verse very closely; but stylistically the contrast is complete – the figuration less nervous, the instrumental identification with the vocal melody more complete. There is no real tonic key presumably because there is no singleness of mood.

Even more fascinating is the cantabile of the Odabella–Foresto duet in which again the singers are set against one another in contrasting minor and major verses. The intriguing facet of this piece is the fact that although apparently the characters are emotionally out of key with one another, Odabella's verse comes remarkably close to being a *maggiore* variation on Foresto's. Consciously or unconsciously (it hardly matters which), Verdi has composed into the music the underlying sympathy which is so much deeper than the ostensible alienation. Another detail that captures the attention is the use of variation in the repeated phrases, not simply to intensify the mood in a generalized sense, but to point the words specifically: the sarcastic emphasis at 'tazze e cantici', the F♮ at 'misera' (Ex. 4).

Ex. 4 (a)

The cabalettas are almost wholly innocent of any suggestion that the duet is a confrontation of character as well as a musical form, though a partial exception must be made for 'Colma di gioia' (*Alzira*, Act II). Parallel thirds and sixths, even continuous octaves, are their normal textural resources. Add to this the fact that the extra amount of repetition almost inevitable in the duet medium prompts Verdi to an even more drastic trimming of the musical design, and one has defined those elements that chiefly contribute to the aura of impatient primitivism with which the cabalettas of the period are redolent. Only in 'Oh t'innebria' (*Attila*, Act I) does Verdi circumvent this formal problem, by the drastic means of having both singers sing in unison throughout. Its conspicuous *slancio* is due partly to this, partly to the palpitating orchestral texture with its pizzicato strings and syncopated horns, and to the singular, veering dynamics.

It would probably be true to say that the duets in *Alzira* and *Attila* represent a decline, if not in skill, at least in fastidiousness and thoughtfulness, from those of a couple of years earlier. The ensembles of *Ernani* are not only more numerous, more essential to the character of the opera: they are worked out in more varied and unpredictable schemes, schemes that match their dramatic context more closely. Its *gran scena* and terzetto finale (Act IV) is probably the most impressive ensemble movement in this whole group of operas. The scena incorporates a veritable cornucopia of expressive detail: such things as the opening recitative, seeming almost to be taken by surprise by the arioso 'Ve' come gl'astri'; the growing rapturous floridity of Elvira's music after the horn of doom has already sounded; the awful stillness preceding 'Tutto ora tace'. Even ideas that Verdi seems about to develop – the quasi-*parlante* at 'Cielo che hai tu' and again at 'Se m'ami, va, t'affretta', or the aria-like 'Solingo errante e misero' – are broken off in full flight. In addition Verdi brings back the oath theme in the brass, and plants a new lyrical idea, 'Fino al sospiro estremo', which will come to fruition in the final passages.

This wealth of material, detailed in its expressiveness to the point of nervousness, sets off admirably the vast scale, the sweeping, unfussy grandeur of the trio proper. Though one of the young Verdi's most ambitious lyrical designs, it has in common with virtually all his ensemble movements the basic principle of resolving antitheses into an overall harmoniousness. The pattern is of alternate solos and trios, thus: (1) Elvira solo verse, (2) trio, (3) Ernani solo verse, (4) trio merging into coda; and there are strong thematic and formal links between these various sections. The two solo verses are structurally identical, like miniature cantabiles, both based on a clear pattern of exposition, episode, culmination, each with its own tonal centre; and the culminating theme is common to both verses. The first trio verse begins at 'È vano, o donna'. Unlike the solo verses it fluctuates tonally and texturally. Its chief function is to introduce the crucial theme of Silva's inexorability (Ex. 5), which, in the second trio verse and coda, becomes the principal lyrical idea of the ensemble, developed broadly and symmetrically, and (apart from the usual kind of chromatic enrichment) solidly in the tonic key.

After a further return of the oath music, where Silva makes clear his determination to exact retribution on the lovers, the scene ends remarkably. A kind of divided aria begins, of which the principal theme has some faint suggestion of familiarity. It proceeds through a symmetrical exposition, and thence directly into a culminating

353

Ex. 5

variation on the same theme. Here the suggestion of familiarity is clarified, for this form of the melody is identical with that sung at the beginning of the scene at 'Fino al sospiro estremo'.

Many of the large-scale finales of the operas of this period are in essence elaborations of the conventional cantabile–cabaletta scheme. The Act 1 finale of *Alzira* is a typical example. Both movements show Verdi's usual priorities in this kind of massive ensemble. Both contrive to blend the most precise delineation of individuals with the most lucidly ordered general harmony. The characters are differentiated, their states of mind vividly expressed in the early stages. Subsequently euphony of ensemble and lyrical impetus become the dominant considerations, and the individual voices are merged into these. Also typical is the way in which the earlier themes in the movement remain private and local whereas the later ones pervade whole tracts of the music and become common property. Thus in the cantabile the opening duet for Alvaro–Gusmano is expressive of this particular confrontation and of nothing else. But the expansive theme sung by Alzira, 'Ah il contento', is not only her song; it is also the principal theme of the whole finale, its texture elaborated by the other soloists and by the chorus to form the climax of the movement. Similarly in the cabaletta: the splendid vigour of the solo themes embodies the confrontation of Gusmano and the lovers. And while the *pianissimo staccato* theme at 'nel tremendo apparato' at first expresses the awe of the bystanders with equal vividness, it gradually becomes a massive structural theme, reiterated in more full-blooded forms, and losing its original expressive point.

Like the solo arias, the ensembles are likely to adopt for special purposes a shorter one-movement form, generally related more closely to a cantabile than to a cabaletta. The one-movement ensemble finale was to assume particular prominence in *Macbeth*, but leaving out of consideration movements that are essentially solo arias with chorus, such as the aria finale of *Alzira*, the earlier works do include some examples of genuine ensemble finales in one movement, generally comprising a scena and a cantabile – the Act III finale of *Giovanna d'Arco*, for example, and the Act I finale of *Attila*. This latter movement affords another fascinating study of the young composer's art of translating a dramatic situation or a dramatically haunting figure into a celebration in song. Here the vanquished Attila is the protagonist. At first he sings alone, and his song is, in the usual way for massive ensembles, divided into two parts, a *declamato* and a *canto spiegato*. In the first, the pauses never allow a propulsive rhythm to take hold of the music, the broken phrases never grow together into a genuine cantabile; consequently every word describing Attila's state of mind is perceived and comprehended. In the *canto spiegato*, which coincides with that point in the text where the expression of Attila's emotions supersedes the description of his plight, the rhythmic figures of the *declamato* are organized into a regularly pulsing accompaniment, and melody ousts declamation. Once the song has begun, Verdi's extraordinary care for formal lucidity can be observed in every detail. The full ensemble responds to Attila in a musical period of absolute clarity and single-mindedness, and only when this has been rounded off does the musical texture begin to take cognizance of the emotional complexity of the scene. The re-engagement of Attila in the ensemble with his characteristic ♫♫♫ rhythm is matched to the harmonic excursiveness of the transitional passage that follows. And as the fresco-like scope of the whole movement begins to be revealed, the trio episode affords us a closer glimpse of those characters who most interest us.

Musical continuity

Although there is little that is positively novel in the material or the form of the lyrical movement during this period, Verdi's handling of the conventional schemes does acquire a more assured character in one important particular. In the earlier operas the constituent parts of the dramatic scene have not always cohered especially well. Notwithstanding the immaculate pattern to which the several cantabiles and cabalettas have always conformed, a sense of the scene as a musical and dramatic whole was sometimes lacking. During the early 'galley years' this failing is corrected. Henceforth, virtually without fail, Verdi does make of the whole scene one musical continuum which gathers momentum progressively and without real respite.

The way in which he achieves this is essentially simple. To generalize, we may say that he learns to differentiate more decisively and with more absolute consistency between the style appropriate to the scena that precedes the cantabile and that appropriate to the *tempo di mezzo* that fills the space between cantabile and cabaletta. The first employs a recitative manner, the second a transitional manner. That is to say, before the cantabile the dominant elements in the composition are words and action: the music has no independent tempo, no purely musical features. Its function is to underline the expressive nuances in the words, or to suggest the way in which the characters move about the stage. Between cantabile and cabaletta, however, though the text may be quite as expressive, and though there may be quite as much stage action, a situation in which music simply reflects these things is no longer found. The cantabile has established a musical momentum, albeit a gentle one, and once this has happened Verdi will not relinquish it. In the transition all declamatory nuance, all physical action has to be accommodated to the tempo of the orchestra, the function of whose music is to bring about an inexorable speeding of the scene to its cabaletta climax.

This feature in the operas is chiefly interesting in showing Verdi's growing concern with the question of musical and dramatic continuity. It is perhaps an early manifestation of that aspiration to 'scrivere quasi d'un fiato'[1] and to make of the 'whole opera . . . one single piece'[2] with which he was soon to become so preoccupied. The nearest Verdi got to realizing this aspiration in these years is the third act of *Attila*, which, despite the misleading and unauthentic subdivisions in the published score, really does consist of one single dramatic and musical design. Clearly there is a striking crescendo of incidents here – romanza, trio, quartet, catastrophe – which could not fail to have a certain theatrical efficacy however they were held together. But it is precisely in the links between them that Verdi shows his determination, once he has captured the audience, never to let it go.

Before the romanza Foresto's recitative is leisurely, each verbal nuance is given time to tell. But once the romanza has set up a musical momentum every lurid detail in this incident-packed act has to submit to it. In the transition into the trio the clarification of the pact made between Ezio and Foresto is delivered in consort with orchestral music that stylistically and formally corresponds precisely with a standard cabaletta pattern. The chorus that adorns the nuptials of Attila and Odabella is not only a *coup de théâtre*, suspending and thereby intensifying the violence of this last act; its musical momentum is also used to help along, and its sonority to accompany, the continuing dialogue between Ezio and Foresto. When Odabella appears, she too sings not a vaguely measured arioso but a pulsing fragment of aria. Nothing in this act is allowed to escape Verdi's desire to draw the whole into one single surging yet lucid design, not even the tumultuous final pages. The bursting-in upon the scene of Roman soldiers, the killing of Attila, the shouts of triumph all have the same kind of ritual formality about them as the final stages of a bullfight, and now Verdi sets them in an appropriate way: they are all subsumed into the long-drawn-out B♭ cadence that emerges from the quartet.

But while Verdi's control of the dramatic momentum becomes more assured it is impossible not to feel that the sensitivity with which he handles recitative is becoming coarsened. I have already cited the scena preceding the trio finale in Act IV of *Ernani* as a passage in which almost every nuance in the text prompts some lyrical response from the composer: spontaneous outbursts of song or at least arioso are to be found on every page. And though this is an extreme example, it is not untypical of the opera as a whole. Thus in Act I every phrase of the recitatives preceding Ernani's or Elvira's cantabiles is eloquent, and scrupulously fashioned to the text. They seem permanently to be on the brink of song, and move expressively and naturally into the formal cantabiles. This is especially striking in Elvira's scena where the cadence phrase of the recitative is clearly a derivative of the instrumental cadence phrase, which in turn has evolved out of the opening instrumental prelude and which in due course will permeate the cadence phrases of the cantabile.

One of the unmistakable symptoms of the fatigue from which Verdi was suffering a couple of years later is the exceptional poverty of the recitative. It is here, for example, rather than in the arias and ensembles, that *Alzira*'s 'real ugliness' becomes apparent. Almost everywhere it is formed of the most commonplace clichés. Only with exceptional rarity do its climactic phrases rise to arioso-like eloquence. Only once – in the recitative preceding 'Da Gusman' (Act I) – does Verdi seem to have taken any trouble over the evocativeness of the punctuating or supporting textures. The few attempts at *parlante*, such as that linking cantabile and cabaletta in the Alzira–Gusmano duet, are based on thematically unfastidious material, and worked out with extraordinary inflexibility. Even the most ambitious example of this technique, that acting as the *primo tempo* to the duet 'Risorge ne' tuoi lumi' (Act I), shows these characteristics. The use of sequential modulation to intensify the excitement, and the *cantabile* climax at 'Io non resisto', are potentially impressive features, but their effectiveness is much diminished by the square, ternary design of the whole scene, and by Verdi's inability to create anything new out of the material.

The decline of the chorus

The first period of the 'galley years' likewise marks the decline of Verdi in his role as 'padre del coro'. The imposing and imaginative use of the choral medium that had been characteristic of *Nabucco* and *I Lombardi* becomes ever rarer, so that by the time of *Alzira* and *Attila* it bears the brunt only of the introductions. Otherwise it is largely confined to adorning certain of the more complex ensembles with atmospheric vignettes – the revelling Hun warriors and the dancing priestesses of *Attila*, for example. On the subject of this choral music it is difficult to find an appropriately sympathetic critical tone. The forms are indolently symmetrical; the *risorgimento* tints that still shine brightly in the *introduzione* of *Giovanna d'Arco* have become faded and drab by the time of the *introduzione* to *Alzira*, or 'Cara patria' in *Attila*. In *Alzira* even the potentially poignant juxtaposition of revelry and wretchedness in the introduction to Act II is abominably crude.

To find a really imaginative and ambitious choral movement in this group of 'galley' operas one has to go back to the first of them, to the conspiracy scene in Act III of *Ernani*. This indeed marks the absolute peak of the young Verdi's choral writing. Its climax is formed by one of the grandest and most blatantly nationalistic of his unison choruses, the only one perhaps to rival the original 'Va pensiero' in the blood-stirring directness of its eloquence. Like that piece it is laid out in the form of an expanded aria, and the return of its principal theme is accompanied by a thrilling change in the orchestral figuration. Where 'Si ridesti il Leon' surpasses 'Va pensiero' is in the magisterial control with which the scene progresses towards this climactic outburst, the inevitability which its rhythms assume as a result of the development in the earlier stages of the scene, the way the orchestral colours become gradually brighter and more strident.

This earlier part of the movement can best be described as a kind of choral *parlante*, a series of variations on a single march theme, laid out in a broad tonal plan, and in such a way that each verse or variation of the march is matched to a new stage in the development of the action. A simple diagrammatic representation will make the scheme clear:

Verse 1	B minor	(Assembling of the conspirators) The rhythmic impetus of the scene is still hesitant because of the silences that slow down the answering phrases.
Verse 2	D major to B minor	(Arrival of the protagonists) Compared with verse 1, the answering phrases have become more continuous and developmental. The unison phrase at the end of the verse is identical with that of verse 1.
	Transition	
Verse 3	G major	(Denunciation of Carlo) A continuous melody now evolves out of the pervading rhythms, and is laid out in a regular aria form. The rhythmic character of the earlier verses is strictly preserved in the accompanying figuration.
	Transition	
Verse 4	C major to E minor to G major	(Drawing of lots) Begins as a more obviously strict variation on the basic march material. The process is suspended as the conspirators await the outcome of the drawing of lots; then the verse closes like verse 3.
Verse 5	G major to dominant preparation	(Dispute of Silva and Ernani) Like verse 3 until the reprise within the aria form, when it moves round to the sustained dominant preparation preceding the chorus proper 'Si ridesti il Leon'.

Instrumental music

In most of the operas of the period the only substantial piece of instrumental music is the 'preludio' (*Ernani, I Due Foscari, Attila*) or the 'sinfonia' (*Giovanna d'Arco, Alzira*). The latter type, a more extended composition in several movements, is already becoming the rarer; even *Alzira*, it will be recalled, began life with a brief 'preludio'. Despite its scale, the *Alzira* sinfonia is hardly a major achievement of the symphonist's art – certainly not to be compared with the sinfonia of Verdi's next Neapolitan opera, *Luisa Miller*. Essentially it consists of a potpourri-like concoction of ever-worsening crassness. Though only one of its themes, the march that brings the *allegro brillante* to its climax, is out of the body of the opera – it is the theme of the *coro d'introduzione* to Act I – the three movements of the sinfonia suggest an attempt to evoke the moods of exoticism, savagery and militarism which are obviously dominant themes in the opera. But there is so little consistency in the working-out of these dramatic themes in the opera, and they are (with the exception of the nicely exotic scoring of the *andante*) so feebly developed in the sinfonia, that both on its intrinsic merits and in terms of its bearing upon the opera as a whole it must be accounted a comprehensive mishap. Verdi recorded his own irreverent judgement with the word 'Amen' written at the end of the sinfonia in his autograph score, and must have derived some wry amusement from the enthusiasm with which the piece was received at early performances.

The shorter 'preludes' are generally more successful in adumbrating the dramatic atmosphere of the opera by the telling citation of one or more of its principal themes, though here too Verdi's performance is erratic. The most successful is again the first of the type, the prelude to *Ernani*. In this movement, the most important of the opera's recurring themes, that associated with Ernani's oath, is used to introduce and later to cut off an aria-like elaboration of the *arioso* phrase 'Ve' come gl'astri stessi' from the *gran scena* in Act IV. Thus it suggests in a miscrocosm that juxtaposition of tender romantic love and tragic destiny which informs the action of the opera.

Besides its prelude *Attila* has two pictorial movements, the storm and sunrise which adorn Foresto's scena and aria in the prologue. The storm episode, disciplined and methodical as one would expect, is built on a series of excruciated approaches to a couple of G cadences, those struggling up to G in the bars before figure 31, and those folding in on G in the bars after figure 31. In the first section both the harmony, entirely built on various diminished-seventh chords – (to Italian ears, clearly, they had by no means yet lost their horrendous quality), and the orchestral texture, dominated by brass and woodwinds, are noteworthy. As in *Otello*, decades later, the general grimness of the sound is intensified by a throbbing pedal-note.

The sunrise music, which provoked such enthusiasm at the early performances and was extravagantly praised by the early critics, is a piece of an even more extraordinary simplicity. One rhythmic figure is reiterated, filled out harmonically, intensified, until with a solemn horn call (omitted from the vocal score) all is light, and C major blazes forth. But how symptomatic of the 1840s that nothing musically compulsive caps this C major: the *tutta forza* reiterations are just a signal that a process has been completed, and that the audience is expected to pass judgement on it.

Doubtless it takes its inspiration from the sunrise prelude to Part III of Félicien David's *Le Désert*, a work which was enjoying an immensely successful run of performances in Milan in June–July 1845. Possibly it was designed originally for the prologue to *Alzira*, and discarded when Verdi was requested to provide a full-scale sinfonia for that opera. In one of several letters to Barezzi in which the rapturous reception of David's ode is described Muzio observes: 'The signor maestro is also composing a sunrise in the introduction to *Alzira*, and told me a few moments before setting out [for Naples] that he had already thought out the way of doing it'[3] – which sounds altogether too portentous for the handful of trills and twiddles that actually do begin the *Alzira* introduction. But while the inspiration may have been *Le Désert*, Verdi's movement is quite different in character. Compared with David's sumptuous scoring and his slow progressions of harmonies firmly anchored within a tonic framework, Verdi's music has a more glistering colour, for the role of the strings is reduced and the rhythms of the woodwind figures sharpened, and above all it derives a certain tense dynamism from the fact that it is built entirely over a dominant pedal.

That Verdi never entirely forgot the art of fastidious orchestration is shown by several movements from this period – such things as Jacopo's arioso 'Brezza del mar natio' (*I Due Foscari*, Act I) or Odabella's romanza (*Attila*, Act I). And he continued to experiment with the dramatic possibilities of orchestral colour, as we hear throughout Carlo's scena in Act III of *Ernani*. But what is perhaps more characteristic of his orchestral practice at this period is a tendency to overdraw, to exaggerate the idiosyncrasies of his earlier style. We find, for example, and especially in *Ernani*, that the habit of colouring the cadence phrases of an aria with woodwind chords is frequently taken a stage further, involving the supporting instruments in the rhythmic movements of the voices, applying the woodwind colours so thickly that the music positively squelches. A rather distasteful feature that is becoming increasingly apparent in the orchestration of the cabalettas is a growing stridency, what Chorley described as an 'utterly disproportionate predominance of the brazen instruments'.

It is perhaps not surprising that of all Verdi's operas *Attila*, in many ways the most representative work of this phase, should be the one regarded with most distaste by fastidious contemporaries. A report in the *Allgemeine Musikalische Zeitung* in December 1848 is worth recording:

Signor Verdi will shortly have completed two scores – probably following his forty-trumpet system – one for St Petersburg, the other for Naples. It is well known that in St Petersburg Sarti introduced *obbligato* cannons into a Te Deum. If anything remains in Russia of the taste which those explosions were intended to satisfy, then more than other maestri, the composer of *Attila* can be sure of a great success, and of the field marshal's baton.

Considered as a group the early 'galley' operas – particularly *Giovanna d'Arco, Alzira* and *Attila* – suffer from unconscionably large doses of the humdrum and the crude. But in an Italian context, where opera was still an integral part of the everyday experience of ordinary people, this was not an irrevocable or even an unqualified deficiency. The stage we have now reached in Verdi's career and his next steps in it recall some perceptive words which Chorley wrote of Donizetti:

He is remarkable as an instance of freshness of fancy, brought on by incessant manufacture. Such a change is almost exclusively confined to Italian genius, in its workings. It learns, and grows, while creating. If it be moved by no deep purpose, it avails itself of self-correction; it strengthens its form on unconscious experience. – Whereas German after German has gone deeper and deeper into fog-land, when aspiring to produce what Music cannot give – Italian after Italian has not merely perfected his own peculiar style, but has enlarged his science and arrived at novelty, at a period of his career when it might have been fancied that nothing but truism remained to be given out.[4]

Macbeth and its satellites

Overall design

Macbeth is one of the turning-points of Verdi's career; the most original, inventive and idealistic score he had yet written. None of his operas before *Rigoletto* is so uninhibited by the conventions of *ottocento* opera, and when the conventions are used, they are used with an intelligence and a dramatic acumen unexampled in the earlier works.

A mere descriptive listing of the solo movements of the opera will suffice to establish *Macbeth*'s formal venturousness. In Act I there is, besides the *aria di sortita* for Lady Macbeth, which is essentially conventional in layout, a *gran scena* for Macbeth consisting entirely of arioso passages and incorporating no genuine cantabile or cabaletta. Both solo scenes in Act II are drastically compressed, Lady Macbeth's comprising a recitative and a cabaletta without cantabile, and Banco's a recitative and cantabile without cabaletta. At the far end of the spectrum from these is Macbeth's mighty scena in Act III. In fact Verdi distinguished two scenes here, a *gran scena delle apparizioni* and a *gran scena e finale terzo*, but the latter is really nothing more than the cabaletta to the former, separated from it by the ballet and chorus 'Ondine e silfide'. In Act IV, there are three solo scenes: that for Macduff, which employs the full recitative – cantabile – transition – cabaletta pattern, but develops first into a duet and then into a chorus in the cabaletta; Lady Macbeth's *gran scena del sonnambulismo*, which, though related to the cantabile, is quite *sui generis*; and lastly the two solo scenes for Macbeth, the *scena ed aria* 'Pietà, rispetto, amore' and the *scena e morte di Macbeth*, which, although they are separated by the battle scene and although the second bears not the least resemblance to a cabaletta, do together form some approximation to the standard double-aria scheme.

In sum, then, and as far as the solo movements are concerned, *Macbeth* has only two scenes – those of Lady Macbeth in Act I and of Macduff in Act IV – which largely conform to the standard pattern of the time; two others – both for Macbeth, in Act III and Act IV – in which the double-aria scheme has been at once immensely expanded and fractured into two separate scenes; and four more – Macbeth's in Act I, Lady Macbeth's and Banquo's in Act II, and Lady Macbeth's sleepwalking scene in Act IV – where only a single element of the standard scene pattern is present.

Macbeth is in this respect an opera that clearly anticipates Verdi's later practice. The traditional patterns of *ottocento* opera are adapted to match the needs of the dramatic theme instead of the dramatic theme being stretched out and lopped down to fit the Procrustean bed of *ottocento* opera's traditional patterning. The other operas of this period, *I Masnadieri* and *Il Corsaro*, do not, however, share this characteristic. The reasons are not far to seek: in all essentials the design of *Il Corsaro* belongs to an earlier period, before Verdi's breakdown in 1846; while *I Masnadieri* was a drama written by Andrea Maffei, a man of letters rather than a man of theatre, and a man of letters, moreover, who despite his authority as a Schiller scholar had an inordinate, almost Arcadian reverence for formal decorum.

Convention and originality in the double-aria scenes

But how conventional are even the double-aria scenes of Lady Macbeth and Macduff? Lady Macbeth's in fact begins with a series of shocks, or at least abnormalities. The first feature which impresses is the prolonged and strange character of the opening orchestral prelude. The stage appears to be empty until the final bars, so the prelude cannot be said to provide an accompaniment to, or commentary on, stage action or gesture. Its material is conspicuously anti-formal – committed to no key centre, frantically modulating, melodically and rhythmically amorphous, strangely veering in its dynamics – and yet despite all this, the phrase-repetitions, rising in minor thirds, render the whole thing almost absurdly formal in effect. As so often when Verdi is composing most experimentally, experimentation and formalism are held in an uneasy and even mutually destructive incongruity.

A second surprise awaits the audience when Lady Macbeth begins not to sing, but to speak. In itself this seems to be nothing more than a *coup de théâtre*. But the effect of these spoken words is to lend tremendous weight to what she first sings: 'Ambizioso spirto tu sei Macbetto ... alla grandezza aneli ... ma sarai tu malvagio?' There needs no harmonic or melodic inventiveness to drive home this key issue of the opera: the conflict of ambition and an overnice conscience. The word 'malvagio' acquires great emphasis and suddenly lends to a reminiscence of preludial material a distinct emotional character: chromaticism and tremolos and veering dynamics are 'malvagio'. Warming to her theme, Lady Macbeth next delivers her article of faith, 'Pien di misfatti è il calle della potenza', with an electrifying vehemence.

In other respects, this scene, which has started with such reckless disregard for the normal standards of the *aria di sortita*, is inhibited by the conventions. The melting transition into the cantabile seems emotionally misleading. For a moment we almost imagine that, like Abigaille, Lady Macbeth is about to tell us that once upon a time she too was an innocent romantic maiden. More serious is the emotional distortion brought about by the idiom of the cabaletta. It is true that its energy and virtuosic exuberance could be interpreted as expressive of the rapture with which Lady Macbeth commits herself to the powers of Hell. And it is true that Verdi has to some extent avoided the merely conventional by designing the cabaletta on the pattern of his evolving, non-recapitulatory cantabiles, and by prescribing wildly veering dynamics for its performance. Nevertheless the predominating impression is of a thrilling specimen of the typical heroic cabaletta. The ornamenting reduplications, the accelerating harmonies, the syncopations and cadenza-like vocalizations are carried off with magnificent aplomb; but of the dramatic meaning of these routines we are given no clue.

The cantabile 'Vieni t'affretta', on the other hand, is one of the young Verdi's most masterly compositions. By the time of *Macbeth* he has discarded almost entirely the rounded recapitulatory forms of his earliest period; but the evolving melodies of his maturing style are nevertheless equally perfectly fashioned. This aria shows a typical scheme. The opening, expository melodic sentence becomes increasingly ornate, complex and protracted, and moves to a central modulation. The narrative lines 'Di Scozia a te' are matched to an episode of comparative tranquillity. The culminating sentences, beginning in an advanced state of harmonic and rhythmic complexity, gradually achieve simplicity and formalized repose. Exposition and culmination are linked by a prevailing accompaniment figuration which had been stilled in the episode, and by a hint of a melodic cross-reference from 'io ti darò valore' to 'ascendivi a regnar' (Ex. 1).

Within the exposition a number of features arrest the attention: how by placing the apex of the melodic phrase on its first note Verdi achieves a striking immediacy and vehemence; how he prevents the cadences, even in this context, from sounding anticlimactic, by packing into them an unusual amount of harmonic activity. The culminating sentences beginning at 'Che tardi? Accetta il dono' are climactic not only in the formal musical sense, but also because they

Ex. 1 (a)

(b)

give the first absolutely unambiguous statement of Lady Macbeth's feelings. The dark, satanic character of her thoughts is marvellously suggested by the tonal sidestep and the *pp* dynamics. This is surely an early example of Verdi using tonal contrast for expressive rather than formal purposes, though characteristically it is prolonged to serve a formal function too. The mounting melodic phrases struggle through to D♭, only to relapse again *ppp* on to F at the cadence. The whole phrase is a splendid example of a 'coloured' mood – apparent exultation shot through with dark and sinister undertones. And their malign influence can still be heard in the very closing bars, where the chords leading into the cadenza sink into the minor mode. No wonder Giusti spoke of 'sublime harmonies'.

Nothing in the overall conception of the double-aria schemes in *Il Corsaro* or *I Masnadieri* can be compared with this scene for boldness. Where the conventional is sometimes discarded or super-

367

seded is in the finer working of small details of form or style, invariably in the cantabile. All three cantabiles of *Il Corsaro*, for example, show Verdi aiming for a smoother sense of continuity with the previous recitative. In each of them he uses the long-established practice of moving from the recitative into the aria by means of transitional woodwind harmonies. But whereas in Lady Macbeth's 'Vieni, t'affretta!' these harmonies still form a distinct episode between the dramatic events of the recitative and the musical events of the aria, in *Il Corsaro* they are more happily merged into their surroundings: Verdi sets the woodwind chords in the rhythms of the following cantabile, so that they act at once as transition and introduction.

The other noteworthy detail of the cantabiles is the growing range and resourcefulness with which Verdi develops the reprises. Two movements from *Il Corsaro*, 'Tutto parea sorridere' (Act I) and 'Cento leggiadre vergini' (Act III), experiment with a form which is most beautifully used in Macbeth's 'Pietà, rispetto, amore'. Instead of the simple kind of reduplication of theme that we have come across in such arias as 'Dagli immortali vertici' (*Attila*, Act II), all of these arias give a new dimension to the music by placing a reprise of the principal theme in the orchestra (Ex. 2). Expressively this marks a nice development of the cantabile – which so often deals with secret memories or private affections in an unduly extrovert manner – for in this form the song seems to sink into the subconscious, the singer to muse in *parlando* style over the emotions in his heart.

Separate cantabiles and cabalettas

One of the signs of the growing formal freedom of Verdi's operas at this period is the comparative frequency with which he makes use of single-movement arias – not just of romanzas and canzonas of the traditional kind, but of movements that can only be described as unattached cantabiles and cabalettas, such as 'Lo sguardo avea' (*I Masnadieri*, Act I) or 'Trionfai, securi al fine' (*Macbeth*, Act II). He employs such curtailed designs, especially in *Macbeth*, both for purposes of characterization (as he had already done in *I Due Foscari*) and to achieve maximum clarity of dramatic definition. The *arie di sortita* of Amalia (*I Masnadieri*) and Medora (*Il Corsaro*) are both single-movement arias. Amalia's 'Lo sguardo avea' is a dream-like love song that in some measure – its bright colours and its florid adornment of a primitive chain form, for example – foreshadows

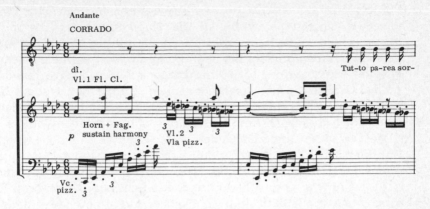

both Luisa's 'Lo vidi e'l primo palpito' and Gilda's 'Caro nome'. In Medora's *sortita*, actually headed 'romanza', the strophic form, the balladesque harp accompaniment, and the profusion of coloratura with which the theme is adorned are all designed to evoke as

369

precisely as possible the atmosphere of the equivalent scene of Byron's poem. In both cases, by suppressing the cabaletta Verdi aimed to suggest something of the languorous passivity of his heroines; and in both cases he was undermining one of the most pervasive conventions of the operatic form. With pardonable exaggeration Muzio wrote: 'No other composer would have dared to write a cavatina in one single movement. Until now cavatinas had their *adagio*, then their *tempo di mezzo*, and finally the cabaletta, but Verdi has escaped from these forms as from so many others.'[1]

Most of these single-movement arias show the same characteristics we have found in the double-aria scenes. Indeed, Banquo's 'Come dal ciel' (*Macbeth*, Act II) is the clearest example in this group of operas of what is now becoming the standard *cantabile* form. The form of the aria is built up from a succession of new ideas, each of which is presented in a balanced symmetrical unit: exposition, episode, culmination, coda. Within both the exposition and the episode, one is impressed by an almost graphic correspondence of words and music. Never had Verdi scored more gloomily than in the figurations that accompany the opening theme. Never had he allowed his lyricism to be so unpredictably shattered as at the outburst of fervour over the dead Duncan.

It comes as something of a shock when, at the climax of Banquo's expression of horror, the violins strike in and the music plunges into the major key. There seems a certain incongruity here, as if the determination to compose an aria that moves step by step to its emotional climax was more important to Verdi than the question of what motivated the climax. Only once, at the *tutti* outburst at figure 10, does the ardent music seem to take note of its subject matter. What this strange conclusion does undeniably do, however, is make it possible for Verdi once more to throw the music into darkness as an accompaniment to the murder of Banquo. The orchestral postlude is shot through with hints of darkness, with syncopations and minor-key notes: and at the words 'o tradimento' Verdi is able to plunge back into an *allegro*, minor-key *tutti* as a symbol of catastrophe.

The two single cabalettas in *Macbeth*, 'Trionfai, securi al fine' (Act II) and 'Vada in fiamme' (Act III), are probably the most commonplace of the solo movements in the whole score; certainly they were the only two discarded completely in the Paris revision of 1865. But there are imaginative, inventive touches even here: in the first, the squawking exclamation 'trionfai' before the cabaletta proper begins, the darkening flattened mediant harmonies in the episode, and the vivid psychological use of coloratura, almost as if Lady Macbeth were daring the heavenly powers to take action. Macbeth's cabaletta is more interesting at the formal level, noteworthy for the fact that, like several of the cantabiles, it culminates in a quite new melody in the major key, and that this *maggiore* section, in a texturally elaborated form, is the only part repeated after the intervening *tutti* cadences.

The scene *sui generis*

A number of scenes in these operas – Francesco's 'dream' in *I Masnadieri*, and the scene of the visions, Macbeth's death scene and the sleepwalking scene in *Macbeth* – are more complex and individual in structure. In some cases Verdi does not avoid an impression of diffuseness or fragmentariness. But the sleepwalking scene is one of the towering achievements of his early years and deserves a proper examination. Certain aspects of this movement will be discussed in chapter 23, in the course of a critical examination of the opera. In the present context I shall confine myself to the question of how Verdi succeeded in exercising such consummate craftsmanly control over an aria unexampled in scale and in imaginative boldness.

The first hallmark of his setting is that he uses the expressive potential of the orchestra to an unprecedented degree. The introduction becomes a veritable tone-poem, and after the entry of Lady Macbeth the accompaniment figurations are so rich in detail that they can carry the burden of expressiveness during her most inconsequential remarks, or provide a figured backcloth to her most sustained and impassioned *arioso*.

Maffei's text provides Verdi with six slightly dislocated quatrains, which he composes into one complex and continuous cantabile. It is in the opening two quatrains, as far as 'tanto sangue imaginar', that the orchestra is most centrally important. Although the audience knows what sort of world it is that Lady Macbeth inhabits, the dramatic tension chiefly depends on wondering when and how she will reveal it. In Shakespeare that tension is broken by the appalling 'Who would have thought . . .' The same sense of waiting, of terrible expectancy, is achieved in the opera by Verdi's throwing the whole weight of his conception on to the orchestral figurations. These are of an unprecedented tragic density, with throbs, creepings and sighs in almost every bar. The voice merely interjects against this sonorous void – there is no song, no expressiveness here until we come to 'chi poteva in quel vegliardo', when Lady Macbeth's tortured humanity and her suppressed sensibility flow out into a great lyrical phrase, underlined with more harmonic activity than has been heard in the whole movement so far.

A new style of figuration – again it is symbolic in every detail – is adopted for the opening of the following quatrain; but only for as long as the facts conveyed by the words are its most important element. At 'E mai pulire', pity and terror, and therefore song, resume their sway, and the original figurations recur. But as the mood of the scene intensifies, so the behaviour of these figurations changes. The music has more sweep now, no longer stopping harmonically in every bar; and it explores a wider range of harmonies, including a superb and manifestly expressive use of a flat submediant on the reduplication of 'e mai pulire' (Ex. 3).

A similar pattern recurs in the following section. Again an interlude-like passage shifts the key-centre, again a new thought prompts a new orchestral idiom, and again at the climax of the sentence that Shakespearean poetry through which we are made to feel Lady Macbeth's desolation is translated into Verdian song, suspended over a recurrence of the original figuration. Here, too, a key word – 'balsami' – is picked out harmonically, indeed picked out almost exactly as Othello's kiss was to be picked out forty years later (Ex. 4). Apparently this progression was a new discovery for Verdi at this time. He employs it again in the Act I finale of *I Masnadieri*, albeit rather formally, to mark the climax of passion and sonority in the coda.

The setting of the fifth quatrain of the sleepwalking scene is the freest of all. The impetus of the scene has become irresistible by now, well capable of taking in its stride the amorphous rhythms and obscured phraseology that mark the climax of this succession of revealed horrors. The final section, on the other hand, shows, albeit on a vast scale, all the characteristics of a cantabile coda: the major-key tonal clarification, the acceleration of the rate of harmonic change, the phrase repetitions.

Ensembles

It comes as something of a surprise to notice that there are in *Macbeth* only two ensemble movements (excluding the finales of Acts I and II): both of them are duets and both are in Act I. Of these, the first, for

Macbeth and its satellites

Ex. 3

373

Macbeth and Banquo, does not use the full two- or three-movement pattern of the conventional duet, but is an unattached cantabile. It amply compensates for its brevity, however, by its richness of style and beauty of detail. It is, for example, indubitably one of the early triumphs of Verdi's expanding harmonic imagination. One feature may be singled out: the use of the flattened submediant relationship, a relationship that recurs again and again in this opera. In the

Ex. 4

present instance, it is adumbrated in the dark harmonies of the
second bar, employed as a passing harmony at the end of a
sequential working-out of an interrupted cadence pattern, exploited
as a genuine tonal relationship in the second dialogue passage – 'Ma
perché sento rizzarsi' – and reiterated for a last time in the more
formal chromaticism of the coda section.

On quite a diffcrcnt scale is the great duet for Macbeth and Lady
Macbeth later in the act. Where the earlier duet is pared down to a
single cantabile, this one, under the pressure of Shakespeare's
stupendous poetry, expands and splits up into four movements –
allegro, andante, allegro, presto – and these individual sections are
packed with a wealth of contrasting expressive ideas.

The first *allegro* begins in a comparatively normal way, with a
repeated expositional phrase and a markedly episodic continuation;
but where this might be expected to lead to a culminating or
recapitulatory lyrical phrase, it leads in fact to a declamatory
outburst that stems the flow of the music and leads into material of a
strongly contrasting style, at 'Nel sonno udii'.

In the *andante* a formal cantabile grows imperceptibly out of a
dialogue in which Macbeth, quoting the mysterious voices he heard
while making his way to Duncan's chamber, adopts the idiom of
priestly ritual, and Lady Macbeth, beginning in urgent *parlando*,
moves into an aria-like idiom in which her scorn of Macbeth's
timidity is given sweetness and insinuation by the formality of its
setting. The regularly designed section of the movement, beginning
at 'Com'angeli d'ira', contrasts the protagonists with nice precision
in the opening phrases before drawing them together with a more
intensive working of the thematic figures in an episode and reprise.

Both the second *allegro* and the *presto* are of extreme brevity and
nervousness, the latter designed rather like a one-verse cabaletta.

Rather unusually, its exposition is developed out of a single thematic idea worked in sequence. It is followed by an absolutely symmetrical episode and a major-key culminating phrase, the contrasting styles here being used not only to give the evolving form Verdi now prefers, but also the underline the character contrast of the singers. The fade-away cadences at the end are a noteworthy feature.

In its nervousness and expressive volatility, freedom of form and absence of architectural restraints, this is the most advanced movement in the opera. It is therefore particularly interesting to observe that, although these were precisely the qualities that Verdi sought to give to other movements of the opera when he came to make the Paris revision in 1865, in the case of this particular duet he retracted to some extent. Here, uniquely, he reasserts his formalizing instincts in the revision by concluding the *presto* not with Macbeth's new major-key phrase, but with a reprise, rhythmically adapted, of the cadence phrases of the opening *allegro* (Ex. 5).

It is not only the formal freedom that distinguishes this movement among the ensembles of Verdi's early years. The imaginativeness and expressiveness of the orchestral texture and the dramatic use of the voices have few parallels in the music of the period. In the first *allegro*, for example, Verdi takes over from the preceding transition

Ex. 5 (a)

(b)

the wailing semitone Dᵇ–C, and works it into the string texture with admirable persistence and resource: and although the wonderful accompaniment texture to 'Sei vano o Macbetto' was finalized only in 1865, its origins are already to be found in the Florence version, where the conventional string accompaniment is elaborated with shivering turns in the *chalumeau* register of the clarinet (Ex. 6).

Ex. 6

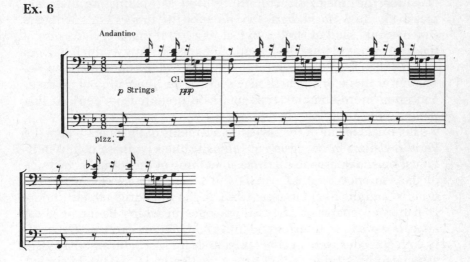

Throughout the duet it is by such touches of orchestral colour and texture that Verdi matches the vividness of the text. He also seeks to emphasize the stifling, horrific atmosphere by the unnaturally suppressed way in which the characters sing: 'Tutto questo duetto dovrà esser detto dai cantanti sotto voce, e cupa, ad eccezione di alcune frasi in cui vi sarà marcata *a voce spiegata*.' Eruptions of naturalistic declamation are rare, and much of the word setting, e.g. at 'Nel sonno udii', is as little concerned with speech-like verisimilitude as in his very earliest operas. On the other hand the dramatically essential idea of the growing alienation of Macbeth and his Lady is expressed with absolute clarity and precision. It begins to emerge towards the end of the first *allegro* as Lady Macbeth becomes increasingly impatient of Macbeth's fanciful narrative; it is preserved throughout the *andante* and the *presto*, far more clearly in fact than in the Paris version – in this respect too Verdi seems to have felt the need to give the material a firmer, more composed form when he revised it – and even in the transitional second *allegro*, the mere pacing of the orchestral music characterizes the eagerness of one character and the lethargy of the other. The whole movement is one of the opera's most astonishing achievements, as Verdi, his singers and his early audiences alike recognized.

Many of Verdi's finales have come to their emotional culmination in the slow cantabile sections. In *Macbeth*, however, the *adagios* dominate the finales to an even greater extent and, except for a few insignificant bars of *allegro* at the end of the Act I finale, now conclude the finales structurally as well as dominating them expressively. In *I Masnadieri*, too, none of the finales ends with the conventional kind of *stretta*. In fact, the Act II finale of *Il Corsaro* is the only example from this group of operas of a finale which mirrors or elaborates in ensemble form the structure of the double-aria scene. The Act II finale of *Macbeth* may serve as an illustration of the freer and often more complex type of finale preferred by Verdi at this period.

This finale is one of the several movements of the opera where the Paris revision, in its desire to intensify the vividness of the individual episodes, was to sacrifice something of the formal coherence of the Florence original. While the brash ceremonial music, the *brindisi* and the final *largo* cantabile retain their original, fastidiously patterned character, the two episodes in which Banquo's ghost appears were to be transformed into vivid, nervous ariosos. Originally both episodes were in effect brief arias for Macbeth, and they were associated musically, as they are dramatically, by the use of similar vocal rhythms and orchestral textures, and both culminate in an identical final phrase (Ex. 7). Of course the design of these movements is less strict than in a true aria: they evolve out of recitative-like declamation, they tend to be broken up by dialogue episodes, they lack thematic symmetries. Nevertheless, by 1865 Verdi obviously felt them to be too formalized to match the harrowing psychological crisis in which Macbeth finds himself.

Like so much else in this opera, the second finale finds Verdi using the orchestral and vocal textures with a new expressive power and technical confidence. In the opening festal music the woodwind instruments enjoy a degree of prominence which gives to the whole passage almost the sound of a stage *banda*, while, as always, Verdi is careful to compose into his music all the gestures and types of movement a producer could need: the text that accompanies the restatement of the opening orchestral music confirms that Verdi is thinking of one figure for the opening courtesies, another for the revelries that follow. In the *brindisi* we hear Verdi using the whole trilling, gracing, staccatoed paraphernalia of the *ottocento* prima

Ex. 7 (a)

Ex. 7 (b)

donna to evoke the mood of forced, garrulous gaiety; and in Macbeth's solos the accompaniment patterns are elaborated with semiquaver creepings and sighings in an absolutely typical manner.

Typical too is the final *largo*: the opening pages are taken up with vividly drawn characterizations of the protagonists. Macbeth's solo verse is especially admirable, the inward terror suggested by the orchestral figurations, the mystery of 'il velame del futuro' by the blanched chromaticism. And in the following section the grim simplicity of the chorus is nicely juxtaposed with Lady Macbeth's nervous, nagging insistence. In the standard manner, though, these distinctions are generally submerged in a grand harmony of rich textures and sweeping *cantabile* phrases.

Choruses

Frits Noske has analysed the distinctive character of the dramatic rituals to be found in operas at every stage of Verdi's career.[2] It is clear that in *Macbeth* such scenes play a prominent part. They present a confrontation of an individual with representatives of a superhuman power, engaged in a solemn ceremony of an almost arithmetical symmetry governed by the symbolism of the number three. Two choral movements, the introductions to Acts II and III, are structured largely on such threefold symmetries as Noske has discussed; and some of the recitative material in these scenes – for example, the greeting addressed to Macbeth and Banquo in I.2, or the opening stages of the apparition scene – incorporate similar triplicated patterns. Of these the most interesting is certainly the last, since here the formalism of the ritual is much distorted, partly owing to Macbeth's undisciplined conduct at the ceremony, but partly too because Verdi wanted to use more than a mere pattern to give cumulative power to the oracular utterances. Each of them as it sounds out, surpasses the previous one in forcefulness of rhythm and portentousness of harmony.

All the witches' choruses have protracted instrumental introductions that come close to being miniature tone-poems by virtue of the profusion of evocative and graphic figurations out of which they are built. The formal thematic anticipation of the chorus proper is becoming rarer, and where it is found, as in the Act III choruses, it follows a freely composed atmospheric introductory passage, rather than being stated with four-square obviousness at the start. The growing sense of continuity in Verdi's music depends as much on more subtle beginnings as on more subtle endings.

Such evocative introductions are equally prominent in the remaining choruses in *Macbeth* – that of assassins in Act II, and that of

Ex. 8

Scottish refugees in Act IV, the latter in particular being as rich in symbols of death, terror and sighing as the introduction of the sleepwalking scene. But in both, a formalism akin to that of the solo aria replaces that of ritual and dance to which the witches' choruses have conformed. The refugee chorus is a fine example of Verdi's *risorgimento* manner – though he deemed it insufficiently subtle for Paris in 1865 – texturally based on the choral unison, with a thickening-up and sweetening in the later stages, rather to wring the heart than to match any concept in the text in the way the 'tristissimo' unison of the Paris version does at 'd'orfanelli e di piangenti'.

The interest of the choral writing in *Il Corsaro* is negligible, but in *I Masnadieri* as in *Macbeth* the chorus resumes the central role which it had enjoyed in Verdi's earliest operas. Though there appears to be no documentary confirmation one has the impression that the composer knew he could rely on finding a large and able chorus in London. He makes conspicuous use of contrasts of colour and texture, dividing the chorus into as many as seven parts, making extensive use of various subdivisions within that ensemble, and devising unaccompanied or barely accompanied choral textures of rare freedom. From these points of view the most interesting movement is the Act II chorus 'Tutto quest'oggi'. The opening sections – for female and tenor voices only, divided *a 6* – has something of the character of a Beethoven scherzo and trio. A movement of conspicuous dynamic energy, in which the chorus is set in dialogue against an orchestral texture tightly packed with tiny rhythmic figures, is followed by a 'trio' of awe-inspiring stillness. Here the music is reduced to a long-drawn-out pattern of cadential harmonies, sustained by the sopranos and altos, to which the tenors contribute intermittent twitches of rhythmic life (Ex. 8).

Instrumental music

In this group of operas the prelude ousts the sinfonia entirely. As we have seen in earlier chapters Verdi's preludes are normally designed to adumbrate the mood of the opera, or perhaps even to give some intimation of its chief dramatic elements. They can do this, for an audience coming new to a work, only by the evocativeness of the musical material. But it is Verdi's custom also to provide for the habitual audience, creating definite dramatic associations for the prelude by drawing on the opera for its thematic materials.

None of these operas has a central dramatic motif like the oath in *Ernani* or the curse in *Rigoletto*. Consequently Verdi cannot use the preludes to plant in the mind the kind of terse, leitmotif-like figures that are used in his Hugo operas. In *Macbeth* three-quarters of the prelude is taken from the scene which Verdi seems to have regarded as the emotional climax of the opera, Lady Macbeth's sleepwalking scene. In *Il Corsaro*, on the other hand, he draws on two strongly contrasted episodes from the third act – the storm and Medora's death scene – to create an image of the juxtaposition of cosmic force and intimate emotion such as he had already attempted in the prelude to *I Due Foscari*. A comparable juxtaposition, but free from thematic associations with the main body of the opera, and with the weight of the design placed on the intimate mood, is found in *I Masnadieri*. Indeed this kind of prelude becomes almost a distinct genre in the 'outcast operas' of Verdi's early years.

17

Verdi à la parisienne – Jérusalem and La Battaglia di Legnano

It has already been observed that *Nabucco* and *I Lombardi* stand somewhat apart from the rest of Verdi's early operas, and show every sign of being an attempt to fashion an Italian equivalent to the Parisian grand opera of Meyerbeer. The resemblance is closer in *I Lombardi* than in *Nabucco*. The vast, pageant-like historical subject, a flexibility in the treatment of the musical forms with few parallels in the Italian repertory of the period, a sumptuousness of orchestration tending to bombast, a zest for recondite harmonic progressions of a rather obviously calculated kind: all these things suggest that Verdi took a creative interest in the traditions of Parisian opera several years before he had a chance to experience them in person. The kinship of *I Lombardi* with grand opera was acknowledged by Verdi in 1847 when, of all his works, he selected this as the one best suited to rewriting for the French stage.

This re-creative confrontation with what was in some ways the most ambitious of all his operas to date, together with the opportunity he now had for hearing and seeing Parisian opera at its source, paid handsome dividends when he came to compose *La Battaglia di Legnano* the following year. Here too the grandiose historical theme, the peculiar intertwining of personal and national destinies in the dramatic treatment, required a musical setting that emulated the Parisian, both in grandiloquence and in the flexibility and deftness of the lyrical forms. These qualities clearly differentiate this pair of operas both from the immediately preceding works and from the next group, *Luisa Miller* and *Stiffelio*, in which Verdi returns to the proper concerns and the traditional forms of Italian opera with a new refinement and confidence.

Arias

The majority of the solo cantabiles confirm the trend towards evolving rather than recapitulating melodies, and in most of them the orchestral textures are imaginatively fashioned to suggest some expressive emphasis, especially sighs. We see from such examples as Gaston's 'O mes amis' (Jérusalem, Act III) and Lida's 'Quante volte' (La Battaglia di Legnano, Act I) that Macbeth had far from exhausted Verdi's resourcefulness in the handling of this most fundamental of musical analogies. There is as yet no trace of that new simplicity of accompaniment that was to appear so strikingly in Rigoletto. But there is, as we see from comparing 'Oh, dans l'ombre' (Jérusalem, Act II) with the Lombardi original, 'Sciagurata! hai tu creduto', a revulsion from that type of overloaded figuration that imposes a mechanical impetus on the song, and gives the music scarcely time to breathe. The throbbing woodwind patterns in the middle of 'Je veux encore entendre' (Act II), compared with those in 'La mia letizia', have been reduced with a similar aim. And the concern for flexibility, articulation and a finer complementary relationship between the rhythms of song and accompaniment is apparent from the start in the textures devised for the arias of La Battaglia di Legnano.

Notable too in these *cantabiles* is the growing harmonic refinement. Verdi's harmonic sense is seen at its most subtle in 'La pia materna mano' (La Battaglia di Legnano, Act II), especially in the approach to the half-cadence at 'parea sepolto il cor', and in the delicious series of variations with which he replaces the traditional repetitions of the coda theme (Ex. 1). If 'Parisian' is the word for this, it is Parisian more in the manner of Chopin than of Meyerbeer, whose harmonic *trouvailles* are generally of a palpably cerebral character.

The same harmonic resource is apparent in the coda of 'O mes amis', which otherwise bears little resemblance to the normal type of cantabile. Indeed it provides a good example of how Verdi's interest in a wider range of lyrical forms was aroused by his experience of Parisian opera. The aria really consists of three contrasting lyrical themes, a B minor *andante*, an A major *più lento*, and a B major *più lento*, with linking passages less symmetrical in phrasing: each new theme has of course been fashioned to reflect a slight change in the mood of the words. The danger of diffuseness is countered by the rondo-like recurrence of the opening accompaniment figuration both after the A major section and in the coda.

The most distinctive feature of the solo cabalettas is the care which Verdi was now taking to avoid the curt reprises that had given an air of such slap-happy impatience to those of the pre-Macbeth period. Such a piece as 'A frenarti, o cor' (La Battaglia di Legnano,

Ex. 1

Act I) positively brims over with cadence themes. It may well have been this consideration that prompted the composition of 'Ah, viens, démon esprit' (*Jérusalem*, Act I) to replace 'O speranza di vendetta'. For while the style of the new cabaletta seems overshadowed by the *I Lombardi* piece in many ways – the key, the accompaniment figuration, the manner of the link into the reprise are all identical – Verdi completely alters the balance of the structure in the final section, treating the original thematic idea more freely and rounding off the design with a new coda theme.

Another feature of the cabalettas in these operas is probably directly attributable to the Parisian environment. In a well-known letter to his old master, Simone Mayr, Donizetti describes the changes necessary to adapt *Poliuto* for the French stage. One of the requirements was that 'between one statement of the cabaletta and the other, there is always poetry which intensifies the action'.[1] Only one of Verdi's Parisian cabalettas, 'Quelle ivresse' (*Jérusalem*, Act II), really seems to depart from Italian practice to that extent. But a purely musical concern that is related to this idea – a pleasantly tailored transition into the repeat of the cabaletta, in place of a succession of bludgeoning chords to announce its imminent approach – is found in several contexts: in 'A frenarti, o cor' (Ex. 2), in the duet 'T'amai, t'amai' (*La Battaglia di Legnano*, Act I), and even in such a fine point as the revising in a slightly more protracted form of the link back into 'Chrétien souviens-toi' (*Jérusalem*, Act I).

Ensembles

The structural variety typical of grand opera is if anything more apparent in the ensembles than in the solos. Examples of the standard type of ensemble scene with *parlante*, cantabile and cabaletta are rarer than the equivalent type of solo scene, and two of them, the sextet and chorus from Act I of *Jérusalem* and the duet 'O ciel, Gaston' from Act II, are taken over with only the most modest alterations of detail from *I Lombardi*. In the third example, the Act I finale of *La Battaglia di Legnano*, the traditional form is handled with a breadth and a symphonic resource that give it a grandeur unique among Verdi's ensembles of this period.

This splendidly conceived piece is based on a double set of verses of exactly the kind that might have been expected to prompt the usual kind of cantabile–cabaletta form. The scene does indeed end with an unusually grandiose cabaletta, 'T'amai, t'amai', but this is not really an independent movement at all: it is rather the culmination, and from the point of view of tonality and figuration one might say the recapitulation, of a scene composed as one vast single unit, in a manner partaking of cantabile, *parlante* and even sonata. The pair of verses with which Cammarano begins the scene, 'È ver, sei d'altri?' / 'Spento un fallace', are not composed into a duet at all. The first becomes a declamatory arioso, punctuated and later accompa-

Ex. 2

Ex. 3 (a)

(b)

(c)

(d)

nied by the ♫♫ ♫ rhythm which pervades the whole scene, including the cabaletta, and modulating to the dominant. In this key, Lida's
response, aria-like throughout, with all the characteristic harmonic
and modulatory touches, assumes almost the nature of a second
subject. That figuration which had gradually come to dominate
Arrigo's verse here takes a more subordinate position, and later it is
transformed into a sigh pattern (Ex. 3). Between this verse and the
cabaletta a widely modulating *tempo di mezzo* pervaded by the same
rhythmic figure behaves virtually like a symphonic development
section. In this duet, without sacrificing anything of the contrasts
and cumulative impetus of the standard scena, Verdi thus achieves a
quite new degree – an almost symphonic degree – of thematic
cohesion.

At the far extreme from this movement is the tiny duet in the
opening scene of *Jérusalem*, 'Non ce bruit ce n'est rien'. This must be
the slightest movement in all Verdi, really nothing more than a
single phrase with a coda. If anything could be said to be interesting
about it, it is the Meyerbeerian extravagance of the understatement.
Despite their different texts, the voices coo in sixths and thirds
throughout, thus reducing the movement to the smallest possible
scale, and the orchestral accompaniment is provided by a single
horn.

Although Verdi was prompted to ape this one tightrope trick of the
Parisian operatic circus, and although he certainly benefited from
the stimulus to provide a wider range of forms in his lyrical
movements, his ensemble idiom remains stoutly Italian. There is no
trace of that pecking kind of dialogue in which Meyerbeer likes to
engage his duettists, nor of those rondo-like forms in which whole
slabs of music recur in mechanical patterns of increasing complica-
tion. Verdi continues to compose his ensembles out of great arches of

song, and the music progresses slowly and inexorably to a single climax in which the identity of the individual voices is dissolved into perfect euphoniousness.

But by the time we reach *La Battaglia di Legnano* no two ensemble cantabiles exemplify these principles in the same way. The tendency for the ensemble forms to become more compact can be clearly seen in the trio 'Vendetta d'un momento' (Act III). Essentially this is a ternary design, the solo verse for Rolando being recapitulated in full in trio setting after a contrasting episode dominated by Arrigo. Notable in the verse is the fact that it settles into broad tonic harmony only for the cadence phrase. Up to this point the broken, snarling phrases had been expressively pointed by the wide ranging of the supporting harmony. The somewhat short-winded phrasing and square structure of the body of the trio are compensated for by the sweeping *cantabile* phrases of the coda.

Quite different again is the 'terzettino' in the last act, though it is typical of the opera in its vividly expressive accompaniment figurations and its vast harmonic range. In form it most resembles a slightly distended aria in which progressively larger forces become involved. After a perfectly regular solo exposition, the expansion of the form begins with the episode, which is elaborated almost to the extent of becoming a second exposition for the other two voices. Particularly remarkable is the tonal behaviour here which, by taking B^b major (the relative major) as a new tonic, succeeds in depositing the music in D^b major at the point where the transition into the G major culminating phrase 'Chi muore per la patria' is due. Inevitably this transition becomes one of Verdi's most abstruse harmonic sallies.

The small number of ensemble cabalettas is another symptom of the need in these chorus-based operas to pack the solo scenes into the most compact feasible design. Apart from the already-discussed 'T'amai, t'amai' and 'Chrétien souviens-toi', which is more like a finale *stretta* than an ensemble, and which in any case is taken over almost unaltered from *I Lombardi*, there are really only two such ensemble cabalettas. Both of them are drastically curtailed movements. 'Viens, viens, je t'aime' (*Jérusalem*, Act II), a reworking of 'Vieni, sol morte' in *I Lombardi*, is an attempt at a type of movement that will be perfected in *Rigoletto* with 'Addio addio, speranza ed anima'. The problem is the reconciling of the theatrical need to suggest precipitate haste and the musical need for a poised formal structure. In *I Lombardi* Verdi had cut down the lyricism to an almost naturalistic brevity and had had to reiterate cadential material rather absurdly to give the scene any measure of balance. In *Jérusalem*, more successfully, he does briefly repeat the principal theme, emphasizing the dominant passion and establishing the cabaletta form, and is able to prune down the cadential material accordingly.

Even more sketchy is the form of 'Ah, Rolando' (*La Battaglia di Legnano*, Act III), a quasi-cabaletta showing the most unusual feature of a complete breakdown of formal principles. The deranged character of the music is already suggested in the exposition, the two phrases of which are separated by a parenthesis of exclamatory cadence patterns, and followed by a development of a second cadence pattern to form a wholly unlyrical episode. The trumpet fanfare that drives home the dominant at this point leads, however, not into a reprise or culminatory phrase but to an off-stage statement of the 'Viva Italia' march tune in a new key. Thereafter the singers are engaged only in the merest exclamatory pandemonium.

There is little that is new in either of the grand finales of *Jérusalem*: a more nicely timed transition, the simplification of a too-breathless accompaniment figuration, the addition of a clattering Meyerbeerian bass line were the only kind of alteration Verdi needed to make to the prodigal score of *I Lombardi* to bring it up to standard for Paris.

The Act II finale of *La Battaglia di Legnano* interestingly enough marks a reversion of the older kind of grand finale with cantabile, transition and full-scale *stretta*, a form Verdi had rarely used since *I Lombardi*. Its most singular quality is the fact that it employs male voices only; and another colouristic eccentricity is the use of the French 'fanfares théâtrales' rather than the Italian *banda* for the martial music of Barbarossa's army. As a composition its most original feature is the splendidly menacing vigour of the instrumental figurations in the cabaletta. Verdi has not merely reverted to an old-fashioned form, he had brought to it the kind of figural virtuosity that he had been acquiring in the solo cantabiles and cabalettas of the galley years.

Choruses

The large number of choral movements in both these operas – seven in each – seems at first sight one of the most obvious signs of the influence of grand opera. It is also, of course, a kind of return to Verdi's own earlier 'grand operas', *Nabucco* and *I Lombardi*. In *La*

393

Battaglia di Legnano, no less than in them, the public voice is clamorous throughout. As in *Nabucco* and *I Lombardi*, one of the choruses belongs to a hostile group: in 'Udite? la grande, la forte Milano' (Act II), the unfortunate citizens of Como take on the unenviable role formerly assumed by the priests of Baal, or the Ambassadors to Antioch. Otherwise throughout the opera the chorus is the voice of patriotic, united Italy. Even the female chorus that adorns Lida's *aria di sortita*, usually the most footlingly decorative movement of an opera, reiterates the patriotic message: 'Plaude all'arrivo Milan dei forti'.

Perhaps it was precisely this all-pervasive patriotic tone, for which Verdi had in his earliest works cultivated an idiom starkly simple yet sensationally effective, that discouraged him from attempting more ambitious choral writing in these operas. Whereas in everything that pertained to the solo and ensemble movements, in everything that concerned his understanding of what the essence of opera was, Verdi had really very little to learn from the Parisians, here one feels an opportunity was lost. In all these fourteen choruses there is not a trace of that virtuosity in handling the medium, of those mercurially changing textures, those endlessly inventive rhythms that we find in the choral movements of *Les Huguenots*. Six of the choruses of *Jérusalem* are taken over from *I Lombardi*. Sometimes, as in the 'Choeur de la procession', they have been carefully reworked: but the reworking has nothing to do with the handling of the chorus as a medium. In all these pieces, as well as in the newly composed 'Le Seigneur nous promet' and the choruses in *La Battaglia di Legnano*, Verdi remains content with the choral unison and stolid block writing. The most that can be said is that in the *preghiera* of *La Battaglia di Legnano* his hymnic style has acquired a certain labile quality, both harmonically and rhythmically, which brings it almost as near to the sophisticated idiom of the *Quattri Pezzi Sacri* as it is to the soggy churchiness of the comparable movements in *I Lombardi* and *Jérusalem*.

The most impressive of the choral scenes is certainly the *introduzione, scena e giuramento* in Act III of *La Battaglia di Legnano*. It bears a marked resemblance to the conspiracy scene in *Ernani* and is really Verdi's first dramatically ambitious choral scene since that time. A particular interest attaches to the *giuramento* section, since it concludes, at 'siccome gl'uomini', with the last example in Verdi's work of that kind of major-key unison cantilena with which he had so often stirred the deepest patriotic sentiments in his audiences. Verdi's music in this vein no longer has quite the flagrant directness of 'Va pensiero' or 'Si ridesti il Leon'. Since *Giovanna d'Arco* he has preferred to reduce such outbursts to episodes within the composition, setting them off by more sombre and complex textures in the music that surrounds them. The orchestral figurations are indeed notable throughout this section, not least the way in which those at 'Giuriam d'Italia' evolve into those at 'siccome gl'uomini', so that this feature unifies the very different vocal textures (Ex. 4). In the coda the brassy two-part writing from the start of the *giuramento* and

Ex. 4 (a)

Ex. 4 (b)

the *maggiore* unison cantilena in which it culminated are brought into closer juxtaposition. The orchestral postlude continues with the work of consolidation by reintroducing rhythms and harmonies from the earlier part of the scene. It is in this kind of passage, with its wholehearted emphasis on evocative colour and thrilling harmony, that the Parisian influence seems clearest; by the time of the Sparafucile scene in *Rigoletto* Verdi will have learned to use it with an economy to match that of the rest of his style.

Instrumental music

Although in many ways *Jérusalem* and *La Battaglia di Legnano* are easily comparable works, they differ emphatically in the use they make of instrumental music. The genuinely Parisian piece contains a profusion of such music: not only a prelude and the four-movement ballet suite, but marches – crusaderly and funereal – and two descriptive pieces, a sunrise and a battle. *La Battaglia di Legnano*, on the other hand, has only its sinfonia, a movement which breaks with the trend of the previous six years during which Verdi had preferred the short dramatic prelude. His renewed interest in the full-scale sinfonia was to be carried over into the next group of operas.

Despite the reversion to a more formal, old-fashioned type of sinfonia, the movement nevertheless shows quite clearly Verdi's continuing desire to foreshadow the basic dramatic issues of the opera. Its principal theme is that of 'Viva Italia', the chorus which throughout the opera is used like a national hymn. In the opening pages of the sinfonia this theme is broken into rhythmic and harmonic fragments, nicely varied in tonal and colouristic layout; in fact it is handled in much the same way that the 'curse motif' of *Rigoletto* will be handled in the prelude to that opera. The same theme recurs in the extended *allegro* with which the sinfonia ends, in alternation and finally in combination with the descant-like theme that is associated with it in the victory scene at the end of the opera.

The slow movement of the sinfonia is based on a theme that plays a much less obviously significant part in the opera: it comes from that point in the scena and terzetto of Act III where Lida watches Arrigo writing to his mother. It seems in some ways a strangely elaborate working of such a subsidiary theme, but it is really the only one in the opera that suggests the sweet painfulness of the relationship between them. The form of this movement – increasingly rich variations with contrasting episodes – enhances the haunting obsessive quality of the theme itself, with its striking tonal ambiguity.

I Lombardi had been one of the very few Verdi operas in which the prelude gave no real intimation of what kind of drama was to follow. This prelude was one of the movements to be rejected as wholly inadequate when the opera was transformed into *Jérusalem*. Not that it was any easier to make a brief distillation of the dramatic essence of the new opera than it had been of the old: but Verdi could and did take two themes that reflect contrasting aspects of one dramatic crisis – the theme of accusation from the trial scene in Act

II and the theme of the condemned Gaston's longing for redemption from Act IV and develop them into a cogent musical form. Essentially this introduction becomes a series of meditations on the latter theme – fragmentarily presented in bar 7, developed canonically, extended as a cantilena, developed in tonal digressions – these various phases being articulated and framed by generally more fully scored statements of themes and rhythms from the trial scene.

All the instrumental movements except for the battle are new, composed specifically for the Parisian *Jérusalem*; but there is little to suggest that Verdi's mind was deeply engaged in them. Even when he rejected a *Lombardi* movement as inadequate, and composed a new one to supersede it – as with the new crusaders' march – he preserved the traditional Italian monotony of texture, and rhythmic stolidity. Here too a lesson that might have been learnt from Meyerbeer wasn't learnt.

Musical continuity

Because of the massive pageant-like structure of so much of these operas, the part played by recitative and other subordinate transitional idioms is much reduced. Hardly anywhere does one find the kind of sustained *parlante* idiom that Verdi had been developing in his earlier operas as a medium for dialogues and disputes. The most impressive feature of such recitative scenes as there are is the frequency with which they are brought into expressive focus by arioso phrases. Thus in Act II of *Jérusalem*, although each of the solos is an old piece from *I Lombardi*, the scenes in which they are placed have been expressively transformed by ariosos: Roger's 'à ce front pâle' is only a further poignant detail in an already complex scene, but both Hélène's 'O transport, il respire' and Gaston's 'Chère Hélène' bring about an intensification of the atmosphere of the scene, and thus a greater sense of ease and naturalness in the transition into the arias.

This profusion of arioso phrases is seen at its most extreme in the scena in *La Battaglia di Legnano* which precedes the Act III Duettino. Budden has described it well as 'a "mad scene" without an aria at its core'. Essentially it consists of a whole series of recitatives, each culminating in aria-like phrases that underline expressively the wildly contrasting moods, frenzy ('E il seno qual aspide'), remorse ('Ma Dio mi volle ad ogni costo rea'), sorrow ('Un forsennato s'avventa nella tomba'), and tenderness ('Questo foglio stornar potria'). Otherwise in *La Battaglia di Legnano* it is notable how often formal march music, especially the 'Viva Italia' chorus, acts as a background for scenes of dialogue and transition.

Jérusalem and La Battaglia di Legnano

Jérusalem includes one new scene that, developing from the pattern of the witch scenes in *Macbeth*, establishes Verdi's standard manner for the treatment of scenes of ritual. The scene is that of Gaston's condemnation, acting as a transition between his cantabile and cabaletta in Act III. Its elements are provided by the accusing voice of the Herald (recitative), the chorus of monks (unison pseudo-psalmody) and the emotional reactions of Gaston himself and the chorus of women (tenor and female chorus, richly harmonized). The piquant juxtapositions are transformed into a scene of ritual by the pattern of threefold repetition, each repetition being a semitone higher.

The grand opera panoply leaves little scope for the pervasive use of dramatically significant themes. In *Jérusalem* Verdi deletes from the score those recurring march tunes with which he had attempted, without much success, to bestow a measure of musical consistency on *I Lombardi*, and it thus becomes one of Verdi's very few operas to make no significant use of recurring themes.

La Battaglia di Legnano is another special case. Written to celebrate Italy resurgent and united, it begins with the chorus 'Viva Italia', in an idiom halfway between march and hymn, that could be said to serve as a kind of hypothetical national anthem. As it has already been made thoroughly familiar by the working in the overture, and as its associations are made quite clear in this opening scene, it can be used throughout the opera whenever it is desirable to stress the topic of Italy's glorious destiny. It is heard in Act II when Rolando and Arrigo come to parley with the Comaschi; at the culmination of Arrigo's would-be cabaletta at the end of Act III, as the Italians march off to do battle; and, in its fullest elaboration, at the return of the victorious troops in the last act.

The fact that these operas make an exhibition of harmonic erudition and orchestral finesse exceptional in Verdi's early operas has already been sufficiently emphasized. And that this is a major factor in their Parisian-ness is undeniable. It should perhaps be added however that this harmonic refinement and experimentation is almost always confined to those places where the Italian tradition itself had deemed it to be proper: in episodes, as in 'Quanto volte come un dono' (*La Battaglia di Legnano* Act I) and 'Udiste? la grande la forte Milano' (Act II), and in codas, and in 'Plaude all'arrivo Milan dei forti' (Act I) and 'Digli ch'è sangue italico' (Act III). Wide-ranging or expressive harmonies in the exposition, though they are certainly found now, as in 'Vendetta d'un momento', remain exceptional.

18

Luisa Miller and Stiffelio

When Verdi returned to the idiom of Italian melodrama he did not at once slip back into the routine of the early 'galley years'. But neither was he quite ready to bring the native form of opera to the degree of perfection it would attain in *Rigoletto*, *Il Trovatore* and *La Traviata*. One hesitates to use a word which may seem to belittle their own intrinsic interest, which is in fact exceptional, but *Luisa Miller* and *Stiffelio* are in a sense transitional works. Many features are still formal, even conventional; but the keener interest in expressive detail that Verdi had shown in *Macbeth*, the greater variety of structural resources and the pride in sophisticated musical craftsmanship in *Jérusalem* and *La Battaglia di Legnano* are beginning to be habitual. The Act I introductions in both operas surpass in scale and formal freedom anything he had hitherto attempted; even in the 'conventional' sections of the operas the craftsmanship, especially in joins and transitions, is finer than anything we have heard from him before. But the enlarging and the deepening of the expressive range of *ottocento* opera that Verdi was accomplishing at this period was not always carried out without cost. Sometimes, particularly in *Stiffelio*, the sheer density of material seems to clog up the musical momentum, or the growing sophistication in the harmonic and orchestral dimensions seems to inhibit the spontaneous flow of Verdian melody.

Arias

A growing freedom in the large-scale structure of the opera and an acuter attention to fine detail, then, are the hallmarks of this period. Nothing illustrates them better than the consistent inventiveness and beauty of the solo arias. Of the cantabile Verdi had been a consummate master years before; what we find now is that he rarely loses his grip on the rest of the scene – the cabalettas are equally resourceful formally and equally apt expressively.

In the cantabiles virtually all trace of the old recapitulatory designs has vanished. Instead Verdi regularly uses an evolving design which could best be described as consisting of an exposition, an interlude and a sublimation. This pattern can be seen most clearly where it parallels the text, for example in 'Sacra la scelta' (*Luisa Miller*, Act I), where the poet states the theme ('Sacra la scelta è d'un consorte'), moves briefly to a negative formulation of the same idea ('non son tiranno'), and concludes with idealization ('In terra un padre somiglia Iddio'). But such close parallelism of text and music is rare. The same scheme of non-repetitive lyrical unfolding, leading to a final climactic phrase, is found too in 'Quando le sere' (*Luisa Miller*, Act II). Here the only verbal clue for such a proceeding is the final line, 'Ah! mi tradia', which contrasts violently and tragically with the tender recollections in the earlier lines, and also forms the refrain in a second verse. These facts Verdi has in mind from the outset; the cool, almost negligent handling of the opening is all part of his mature conception of the aria: not so much the elaboration of an initial lyrical impulse as the dynamic progression towards a climactic outpouring.

Structurally the most remarkable aria scene of the period is 'Vidi dovunque gemere' (*Stiffelio*, Act I). Budden is probably technically correct to describe it as an 'aria con pertichini', but in effect it is a scene in which the cantabile has been suppressed in favour of a whole series of ariosos set off by Stiffelio's reactions to the reunion with Lina. The wide range of styles employed in these ariosos is notable. Some, like the angry 'Vidi dovunque gemere', are like short arias; others, 'ma ti rivedo' for example, are more like the conventional rapturous arioso outbursts; others again, like 'Ah no, il perdono', are given a somewhat recherché orchestral colouring which helps materially to suggest the uniqueness of the dramatic mood to which they are matched. What the scene lacks is the disciplining organization that one thinks of as typical of the composer. Only the little orchestral figure associated with Lina's sighing distress recurs and is developed.

In the cabalettas Verdi has apparently recovered from that impatience with the form that afflicted him in the mid-1840s. Still, with few exceptions, they employ a more symmetrical formal pattern than the cantabiles; but an examination of 'Oh gioia inesprimibile' (*Stiffelio*, Act III) will illustrate the new structural alertness sometimes to be found. The aria is given only a single statement, without the normal repeat, but, as if to compensate for this, is developed with unusual breadth and resource. The thematic exposition is already notably expensive, each phrase taking up two lines of text instead of one, and consequently occupying four bars of music instead of the customary two. And, though the layout of the material assumes the ABA'C pattern common at this juncture, A' involves not mere ornamentation or cadence adjustment, but a sequential extension of the material to create a six-bar phrase. The exceptional scale and elaboration of the exposition conditions the rest of the aria. Far more than usual, the episode has something of the air of a development – partly because its text consists simply of reiterations of the opening line of the lyric, partly because of the thematic use of sequential variants on the opening phrase A, partly because of the carefully calculated sense of harmonic progression resulting from the chromatically rising bass line. And while the culminating phrases first recapitulate the opening A with the kind of melodic and harmonic intensification that has by this stage become characteristic of the composer, they then draw out the climactic excitement further with ostinato-like reiterations over a dominant pedal.

The coda is particularly remarkable. It begins like a quiet *stretta*, with reiterated cadence phrases over a chromatic bass. But then follow first a distinctive, syncopated cadence theme and secondly a strange, exhausted-sounding fade-out – *diminuendo, perdendosi, morendo* – faintly reminiscent of the close of Florestan's aria. Finally there is a statement of the reprise-cum-culmination phrase, this time sung 'tutta forza'. For hitherto, rather like the grand duet in Act I of *Macbeth*, 'tutto questo pezzo ... deve eseguirsi estremamente piano'. The repeated final section which, as a largely formal device, we have met with as far back as *Nabucco*, and of which there are several further examples in this pair of operas, is here put to sensational dramatic effect as Stankar emerges from his self-induced trance to give explosive expression to his homicidal rapture.

There is absolutely nothing predictable about Verdi's handling of the text by this stage of his career. In some cases, he will manipulate verses to provide reprises and repetitions that were not part of the poet's conception. This happens in 'Ah! fu giusto', which he treats like a *da capo*, presumably finding the first quatrain more powerful than the second: in 'Tu puniscimi' (*Luisa Miller*, Act II) it is the single line 'Non mi lasci in abbandono' that he extracts from its position in the verse, and reiterates in a variety of contexts as the expression of the dominating passion of the aria. In 'Quando le sere' one finds a conception of word-setting wholly under the sway of a single musical principle, that of the climactic refrain. Thus, although in the second verse Verdi allows himself a fleeting moment of rhetoric – at the quoted words 'Amo te sol' – in principle the melodic contours and the rhythmic movement are calculated to bring out no individual details, to offer no particularizing nuances, but to direct the music to its final desperate refrain.

Together with the growing elaboration and beauty of the arias themselves goes a cutting away of those purely ritual elements in which they had for so long been embedded. Thematic introductions have by now been eliminated entirely, *strettas* and the other conventional rituals attendant on the cabaletta tend to become more lyrically saturated. Wurm's contributions to the link between the two statements of 'A brani' (*Luisa Miller*, Act II) are trembling on the verge of song. Walter's, at the same juncture in 'L'ara o l'avello', are genuine arioso.

One aria contradicts almost all the general observations so far made: Luisa's *aria di sortita* 'Lo vidi, e'l primo palpita'. Here, in one of the great traditional and ceremonial episodes of the opera, Verdi works out an aria scheme of immense breadth and a quite old-world formalism, making use of two full statements of the text. Every phrase of the aria is noteworthy from this point of view – the opera's solitary formal introduction; the expansion of the modulatory episode 'Quaggiù, si riconobbero' to a full eight bars, not simply providing harmonic contrast, but actually establishing a new key centre; the full recapitulations of the principal thematic section; the unusual amplitude of the closing section, which incorporates of course the common harmonic acceleration and repeated cadence phrases, and follows these with a postlude for orchestra in which Laura and the chorus join. How typical of this stage of Verdi's career that this old-fashioned and decorous movement should be followed by one of the opera's most imaginative transformations of tradition: a cabaletta that develops first into a duet and then into a huge ensemble.

Ensembles

Increasingly, at this stage of Verdi's career, it is in the ensembles that one finds the composer's psychological and expressive acumen at its keenest, and his structural inventiveness at its boldest. Generally however the cantabiles are conspicuously more apt and interesting than the cabalettas and *strettas*; these rarely exhibit the new poise and confidence evident in the solo cabalettas. As in the solo arias, symmetrical and recapitulatory forms have been largely ousted by various progressively evolving types of design. One striking example of such a design, indeed an altogether intriguing rethinking of the cantabile in response to an unusual dramatic burden, is 'Dall'aule raggianti' (*Luisa Miller*, Act I). Not only does the form evolve, it is open-ended, and is clearly dependent on a dramatic use of tonality. In the first section, as far as 'Le pene segrete', not only is there much repetition and symmetry, the tonality is unmoving, the chords and indeed the melodies and rhythms are of absolute stillness and simplicity, the very image of the idealized innocence of which Federica sings. For a long time Rodolfo cannot bring himself to break the spell; the orchestral textures become more detailed, more fanciful, more illusory, but no change effects the voices, which remain locked in a world of make-believe. Once Rodolfo has blurted out the truth, the original key can never return. The anguished exchanges that follow are based on the tonic minor and various related keys, and their idiom is on the very verge of recitative. The latter stages of the duet act as a transition into the cabaletta.

The expression of the dramatic tension of a scene again outweighs Verdi's usual search for an overall harmony in the quartet finale of *Stiffelio*, Act II. There is, needless to say, nothing *verismo*-like about the dramatic aptness in this movement, and the music remains carefully-patterned on the following scheme:

a. Solo – Stiffelio
b. Antiphony – Lina/Stankar (Raffaello)
c. Antiphony worked and extended into
d. Reprise of part of a, with accompanimental use of other voices
e. Coda

but the dramatic vividness which informs the whole of this pattern is remarkable.

Verdi had always tended to begin his ensemble cantabiles with a solo in which *parlando* only gradually gives way to *canto spiegato*, and rhythmic hesitancy only gradually to a slowly swinging momentum. In this movement one style never really ousts the other; declamation alternates with song, and it is not until the cadence phrase – 'È tolto il dubbio' – that Stiffelio launches the movement authoritatively.

Yet even here it falters again, for Verdi is as much interested in Lina as in Stiffelio, and her loneliness and fear call for as vivid a musical projection as his desperation. The musical imagery is drastic: the music turns from F major to F minor, and in place of the sharply profiled rhythms of the rest of the movement Lina sings a scurrying, unfocused string of semiquavers, so little under control that it actually overflows the metrical bounds of the music. These

Ex. 1

Ex. 1 cont.

bars are the more graphic for being presented in antiphony with the forceful and disciplined phrases in which Stankar comments on them (Ex. 1).

By this time the music has described a characteristic tonal arc: D minor – F major – F minor – A♭ major. The return to F major is the first 'worked' section of the ensemble, the first section in which craftsmanlike musical patterns take precedence over dramatic realization. In Stiffelio's reprise, on the other hand, the alienation between the characters is still carefully projected. For the voices do not, as is usual at this stage of a Verdian ensemble, fill out the pervading harmony on more or less equal terms; Stiffelio's song is the principal element, and the other voices merely punctuate and propel it. This dramatically motivated patterning is continued even into the coda, where the cadential harmonies of the other voices are punctuated in turn by Stiffelio's muttering monotone.

Such creative elaboration of the conventions of a form is rarer in the cabalettas. Often Verdi's aim seems to be to compress or abbreviate in some way the full duet–cabaletta form he had used in his earliest works. But such attempts meet with very unequal success. In 'O meco incolume' (*Luisa Miller*, Act II), for example, the episode is sung by the secondary character, Wurm, and the reprise that follows proves to be the second statement of the cabaletta. But the squareness and brevity of exposition and episodic phrases, and their refusal to budge tonally, deprive the movement of that élan and sweep that distinguish Verdi's best movements in this style.

Another of the cabalettas, 'T'amo d'amor' (*Luisa Miller*, Act I), is rather an expanded than an abbreviated design. Nothing is formally remarkable about the two solo verses beyond their dovetailing together: in the manner of many of Verdi's early cabaletta themes, they are concise, formal, square in phrasing. What is remarkable is the way in which the conventions of the form are subsequently used. Thus the interlude between the solo and duet statements of the theme, which, in the expected manner, is highly, if formally, chromatic and texturally agitated, is claimed by Miller as an expression of his own unease, without the pattern of the scene being disrupted. A little later the *stretta* following on the duet statement of the cabaletta is interrupted by the ringing of the church bell. This prompts the exit of most characters, during which they sing the cabaletta in abbreviated form a third time. But whereas it had once been a solo song, then a duet, harmonized and orchestrated by the chorus, Miller now has an important countermelody. Moreover, as he is left behind, the countermelody becomes progressively more audible, changing the mood of the scene from rapture to unease, and thus effecting a transition into the more sombre scene that follows.

The most radical break with the conventions of the *ottocento* ensemble is found in the *scena finale* of *Stiffelio*, as remarkable and original a passage as anything Verdi had hitherto composed. Its *andante* already grows out of the preceding *preghiera* in much the same way as, decades later, the brawl was to grow out of the *brindisi* in Act I of *Otello*. That is to say, it is a modulating 'development section', based here on the 'miserere' rhythm from the formal number before it. Above slowly moving harmonies this rhythm is reiterated over and over by a trumpet, 'appena sensibile'; from time to time the chorus punctuates the muttered dialogue of the soloists with a 'miserere' echo of their prayer. The fabric of the music is pulled even tighter by the addition of a second 'symphonic' figure – ♫♫ ♪—reiterated with the same obsessiveness.

Even when we reach the *grave* there is no relaxation into cantabile. The Bible-reading is also a passage of vocal *parlando*, sustained on a slow momentum established by orchestral figures, which are here stripped down to an absolute minimum, to create an atmosphere of hushed, breath-holding anticipation. 'Perdonata Iddio lo pronunziò', sung once by Stiffelio and once by the full ensemble, is really the only lyrical phrase in the entire scene, and it stands out electrifyingly from its austere context.

The whole scene is a splendid example of Verdi's growing fondness for placing the musical climax at the end of a movement.

Hitherto he had done this in aria and ensemble forms, or in the scena by soaring from recitative into arioso at the moment of deepest feeling. In *Stiffelio* we find the first example of the technique he was to perfect in the 'Amami Alfredo' scene of *La Traviata*. We are on the verge of what today is called 'music-theatre'; the music assumes no independent life of its own, but is limited to the strictly functional task of intensifying the effectiveness of a dramatic incident – here the public forgiveness of Lina's adultery. But though subordinated to a dramatic function, the music is not undercomposed as in a recitative; Verdi has turned quite decisively to a technique that may properly be described as symphonic.

The most elaborate ensemble movements in the operas are still the Act I finales. After an introductory chorus and some recitatives, *parlandos* and ariosos the core of the *Luisa Miller* finale comprises an *andantino* which, as usual, is fixed on the moment of maximum dramatic excruciation, and a very brief *allegro*.

In the *andantino* certain elements are well tried by now. Such is the full depiction of Miller's state of mind, half declamatory in idiom, half lyrical, with which the movement begins: this gambit goes back at least to *Nabucco*. But thereafter the formal pattern departs from that established in the early works. The expression of character, the embodying in tone of the stage picture, continues to be the chief concern in the antiphonal phrases sung by Walter and Rodolfo; but until Luisa begins to sing, nothing is heard that is vital to the lyrical organization of the movement: only a scalic accompaniment figuration (violas, clarinets and bassoons) which pervades much of it. We have a scheme – used again in the terzetto finale of Act III – in which the principal melodies only emerge after fairly long sections of freer declamatory or characterizing material. The melody is no longer the raw material out of which the movement is developed: it comes at the culminating moment, and the music evolves towards it, not out of it.

The *andantino* of the *Luisa Miller* finale is a characteristic product of these years; the equivalent movement in *Stiffelio*, an *adagio*, is more unusual in that it falls midway between the old Rossinian style of pseudo-canon and Verdi's own more dynamic type of ensemble. Its formal pecularities surely stem from the fact that Verdi has only one short quatrain of text to work with:

> Oh qual m'invade ed agita
> Terribile pensiero!
> Fatal, fatal mistero
> Tal libro svelerà!

The *minore* section with which it begins consists of a simple melody sung three times, by Stiffelio, Raffaele and Lina respectively. At its first appearance it seems a typical *adagio* solo, a broken declamatory *sotto voce*, punctuated by rapping chords. But instead of driving this material forward to a lyrical culmination as he usually does, Verdi simply sustains it, repeating it and elaborating it with vocal 'orchestrations' of increasing figural complexity. The development remains purely formal.

Even in the culminating *maggiore*, the music is statuesque to a remarkable degree (Verdi is still using the same text!). But while the *minore* had been melodically and tonally stationary, Verdi commences the *maggiore* with a phrase which, over chromatically shifting harmonies, mounts slowly from d″ to b″, before closing in a massive and ecstatic cadence. By virtue of this treatment, the G major cadence acquires immense force and finality, without the music having really 'been anywhere' at all. The final coda is typical of this period of Verdi's work, exceedingly rich in sensuous chord juxtapositions and ornamental chromaticism. But the extent to which the whole moment is, in dramatic and in musical terms, motionless is quite exceptional.

The growing richness of the musical language

It is of course not merely in the adroitness of his forms and in his manipulation of convention that Verdi's growing mastery as musician and dramatist is apparent. The sheer quality of his invention, melodically, orchestrally and harmonically, is of a new richness.

One feature of the melodic idiom that begins to be noticeable at this period is Verdi's search for a closer correspondence between text and music, without necessarily resorting to the *parlando* type of writing with its lyrical inhibitions. In certain particularly frenzied movements, such as 'Maledetto il dì' (*Luisa Miller*, Act III) or 'Chi ti salva' in the Act I finale of *Stiffelio*, the voice is launched at the peak of the phrase, rather than in the foothills of a gradually upsoaring melody. The effect may perhaps be seen as an aspect of Verdi's growing concern with theatrical verisimilitude, an attempt to suggest that, not merely in principle but in fact, song begins at the point where the passion has become uncontrollable, incapable of articulation in merely verbal form. Luisa's phrases in the cantabile 'Piangi, piangi', besides expressing her tenderness for Rodolfo, suggest almost graphically, in their contours and in the broken accompanying texture, the falling of his tears. Towards the close of 'Di qua varcando' (*Stiffelio*, Act I), the hitherto bland cantabile trembles naturalistically on the word 'spavento', and out of that rhythm develops an increasing agitation which culminates in an extraordinary 'madrigalian' (Budden) cadence phrase (Ex. 2). In 'T'amo d'amor'

Ex. 2

everything in the melody and in the accompaniment contributes to the movement's splendid *élan* – the melody with its breathless, detached quavers, the figuration of the accompaniment with its pulsing alternation of bass and chord. Not the least important contribution to the remarkable *slancio* is the harmonic scheme. The only contrasting tonality is the weak supertonic, and that primarily over its own dominant pedal. Thus the interlude never becomes a point of repose or cadence, the music is projected forward into the reprise, where the principal melody is quite transformed by the purposefully moving harmonies that underlie it, and by a towering melodic contour which no longer anheles or scurries.

Orchestrally, *Stiffelio* is the more original opera. Never before had Verdi made the horns – three of them in this case – the principal instruments within the accompaniment texture, as he does in 'Di qua varcando'; never before had the standard type of string-based aria accompaniment been elaborated in quite such detail as in 'Ah, dagli scanni eterei' in Act II where, reading from top to bottom of the score, we have: one solo first violin, one solo second violin, one solo viola; two first violins, two second violins; one first violin, one viola; first and second violins, violas, cellos and basses; one solo cello, one solo bass – all muted. Even when texture and scoring are generally conventional Verdi is always liable to surprise us by the details of his workmanship. In 'Ah! v'appare in fronte scritto', for example, the prevailing idea behind the musical texture is the discrepancy between Stiffelio's superficial self-control (the vocal melody) and the inner torment from which he actually suffers (the orchestral accompaniment); but the apparent schematicism of this texture is always being varied by illuminating smaller touches – syncopated sigh figures, chromatic scales in various forms.

Stiffelio is also an opera in which Verdi's harmonic imagination seems to be growing almost tangibly richer. Sometimes he sustains a veritable harmonic *tour de force*, as in the prelude to Act II, where the principal motif, reiterated obsessively above a more slowly moving chromatic bass, rambles through a tangle of chromatic counterpoint (Ex. 3). 'Lost in my labyrinth', we almost expect Lina to

Ex. 3

sing, as she begins her recitative. But above all it is at cadences and in codas that the harmony is most imaginative. That was always where Verdi's harmony had been most inventive, but it is not until the late 1840s that we find ourselves over and over again reminded of Chopin. His spirit certainly seems to hover about the chromatic cadence phrase of 'A te ascenda' (Act I), the enharmonic parentheses of the Lina/Stankar duet, and the syncopated displacements of harmony at the close of 'Lina, pensai che un angelo' (Act III).

As I suggested at the beginning of this chapter, there are passages in these operas where the richness of the invention, the very profusion of the material, seems almost to be an embarrassment. One such passage is the central section of the Act III duet in *Stiffelio*. This section, the section following the *primo tempo* 'Opposto è il calle', adumbrates such mature masterpieces as the Violetta/Germont duet in *La Traviata*, falling into a sequence of short episodes which make minimal use of formal patterns but reflect with maximum vividness the changing moods of the protagonists. And occasionally one does

411

tend to feel that the momentum of the whole is being sacrificed to the forcefulness of the details: the brassy diminished sevenths that accompany Lina's request for the marriage document flow none too easily into the palpitating syncopations of 'trama pensaste'; and an awkward hiatus impairs the dramatic impetus of the transition into Lina's main solo 'Non allo sposo' (Ex. 4(a)). It is notable that when

Ex. 4 (a)

(b)

Verdi came to revise this movement for inclusion in *Aroldo* the modifications he made were for the most part designed to increase the fluency, to simplify some over-contrived harmonic progressions, to make the joins more convincing (Ex. 4(b)). The *Stiffelio* duet is a movement in which Verdi's fertile and impassioned response to his theme has temporarily disturbed the skills of the musical craftsman.

Recitatives and transitions

The greater extent to which the idiom of recitative had depended upon cliché makes Verdi's concern to avoid the commonplace, the merely routine, even clearer in this medium than in the arias and ensembles. On innumerable occasions, the declamatory manner of the true recitative is interrupted by searing *arioso* phrases which serve to fix the audience's attention on the essential passions in the dramatic encounter. A particularly electrifying example of this comes in the Act I finale of *Luisa Miller* at 'Son io tuo sposo', where Verdi translates a tense dramatic moment into the operatic medium by a monumental slowing-down of the time-scale, by rewording the text ('sono tuo sposo' in the libretto), distending it almost grotesquely and fusing it into an already soaring and impassioned clarinet melody (Ex. 5).

Just as it is rare for the recitative declamation to persist through a whole scene, so too is it for the orchestra to supply nothing more than conventional accompaniments. More often the orchestral figurations are pointedly and specifically evocative. Typical are the recitatives preceding Stankar's aria (*Stiffelio*, Act III) or 'Piangi, piangi' in the third act of *Luisa Miller*, which are full of splendidly conceived figurations. Remarkable details in the latter are the shrill tremolo at 'Prega; ben di pregare è tempo!', the tragic vehemence of the *tutta forza* figures that follow, which for all their vehemence are hollowed out to open fifths and fourths at phrase ends, the writhing and shuddering string figurations at 'M'arde le vene', the leitmotif-like portentousness of melodic shape and orchestral colouring at the *largo*. And so the scene continues in an extraordinary succession of musical images, reflecting the passions in the protagonists' hearts and the rituals which they enact. In another fine passage, in the recitative preceding 'Tu puniscimi', Verdi establishes an alternating pattern of figurations – one of clockwork-like coldness, the other a broken *cantabile* – to embody in musical terms the dualism of deed and sentiment.

One of the most interesting of the developments in Verdi's style at this period is that of the *parlante* idiom. We may examine the *parlante* preceding the quartet in *Luisa Miller* as a good example of the growing flexibility and resourcefulness of his handling. Initially (from figure 26) the orchestra plays a quite formal melody of an AA'BAA' pattern, each element being of four bars. At its resumption (figure 30) the material has been intensified in a number of ways: by a faster tempo, by the upward shift of the tonality, and especially by

Ex. 5

the new phrase structure of this section, an AAA section in which each element is of only two bars, of which the first is a new accretion. The *parlante* is resumed a third time in a further intensified form, now a fivefold repetition of a one-bar phrase, compressed from the previous two-bar phrases, and modulating stepwise upwards. The final stage of this development at figure 32 is cadential, harmonically more static but with a new kind of intensity arising

415

from the *ostinato* melodic figure. Each stage of this *parlante* development is set apart from the next by freer passages in which more scrupulous attention can be paid to expressive details: the semitonal step up as Luisa brings herself to name Wurm, the arioso phrase at 'E non ottener mai d'amor lusinghe accenti da Luisa', serving as an ironic relish to Luisa's anguish, the superbly drawn-out cadence as Luisa comes so close to telling the truth.

As in the Parisian-style operas of the previous two or three years, the transitional passages between one number and another are as notable for the greater care Verdi shows in his craftsmanship as they are for the greater interest of their intrinsic material. Several numbers make use of the device I have already noted in the Act III finale of *Stiffelio*, where a musical figure taken from the body of the movement is used to sustain the momentum of the following transition. Verdi's newish delight in the arts of transition may be as apparent within the body of the movement; in the chorus 'A te Stiffelio' for example, where the restatement of the principal theme (abbreviated) is preceded not by mere padding, but by a genuinely development-like episode. The theme is given an anguished obsessiveness by Lina, smoothed out by Stiffelio, subjected to modulating sequence and figure development over a pedal as the re-establishment of the tonic key is approached.

Recurring themes

One notable aspect of the score of *Luisa Miller* is the extent to which Verdi makes use of recurring themes. Thus at the beginning of the Act II scena and duet for Walter and Wurm, Walter comes on stage accompanied not by a merely atmosphere-setting orchestral prelude, but by an orchestral reminiscence of his Act I aria, which suggests quite precisely the feelings of his heart:

> Il mio sangue, la vita darei
> Per vederlo felice, possente.

But the theme chiefly used is that first heard in the overture. Nowhere does it recur in a complete or literal form; but increasingly, as the love of Luisa and Rodolfo is menaced by fate, its gloomy, passionate character pervades the score. Sometimes, as in the accompaniment to the chorus 'Come in un giorno sole', the reminiscence is quite full; sometimes, as at figure 7 preceding 'La tomba è un letto', it is broken into a fragmentary figure and used as the basis of a tension-building development. More often the resemblance is vaguer: one of rhythm and tragic turbulence only, as in the two cognate themes in Rodolfo's Act II aria, one introducing the scene, the other providing the material for the transitional *parlante*. The introduction to Act III makes clear an association we might otherwise have missed, between these themes of doomed passion and that of rapturous passion in the opening scene, 'T'amo d'amor'.

It is the function of the overture to imprint this family of themes firmly on the audience's consciousness. To this end, Verdi fashions it as an elaborately worked-out monothematic sonata movement. There are certainly conventional Italian-overture features in this movement: for example, the *tutti* that marks the beginning of the transition, and the concluding *stretto*. But the intensity of the thematic workmanship and the harmonic and lyrical resourcefulness with which Verdi handles his single theme have few precedents in this repertory.

Choruses

The chorus built up around this theme, 'Ah come in un giorno solo', is the one that has least to do with the choral conventions of the time. Both the orchestral theme itself and the solo voice of Laura give it a pervading lyricism, which is emotionally committed, anything but formal or decorative. Mere clichés are conspicuously absent, even in the *stretta*, which is fused into the beginning of the following scene as if to by-pass applause, and to ensure that the following dialogues begin in the appropriate atmosphere of still intensity. Elsewhere in *Luisa Miller* and throughout *Stiffelio* the chorus performs its customary functions in the customary styles.

19

'The popular trilogy' – *Rigoletto, Il Trovatore, La Traviata*

I see no reason to dissent from the traditional wisdom that sees in these three operas the romantic Italian melodrama in its ripest and most perfect state. They are operas that are for the most part still conditioned by a profound faith in the formal aria, ensemble or chorus as a medium of emotional and dramatic expression, and by far the greater number of scenes are still dominated by those types of musical form whose development we have traced in the foregoing chapters. Neither the age-old primacy of the singer nor the preference for resolving dramatic tensions in lucid forms and harmonious patterns is threatened by the newer currents favouring 'realism' or the orchestra-based music drama. What distinguishes this latest group of operas is the fact that Verdi has acquired such a critical understanding of his medium, and has so refined his craftsman's hand, that he writes almost nothing that is not dramatically meaningful and musically beautiful in its every detail. The merely conventional has been stripped away; the recitative and arias and ensembles that remain have become more full of music, especially of song, than ever before. What used to be subordinate elements, the harmonic language and the orchestral colouring, have acquired a new finesse. Most impressive of all is the fact that, notwithstanding the increasing sophistication that almost every page of these scores shows, Verdi has become simpler in his utterance. Very rarely does one find that straining for vividness that so often shows through in the operas of the 1840s. He is now so much the master that he can express himself directly and without metaphor, confident that every phrase will tell and that in every phrase the tone of his voice will be unmistakable.

The transcending of convention

A signal feature in these operas is the ability to take a conventional pattern and to treat it in a manner that transforms it – enlarging its emotional range, or distorting the conventions slightly in the interests of dramatic or psychological vividness, or breaking down the purely formalistic barriers that isolate it from the rest of the drama. We can perhaps perceive this best if we examine two examples of scenes which had traditionally been among the most hidebound, those double-aria scenes for the prima donna.

The most electrifying of such elaborations is to be found in the so-called 'Miserere' scene from *Il Trovatore*: essentially a solo scena in which the cantabile is linked to the cabaletta not by a recitative or a conventional agitated *parlante* but by a whole series of distinctive musical vignettes evoking the dramatic situation with peculiar vividness: the austere and impersonal 'Miserere' chant of the monks, the terror-struck soliloquy of Leonora, 'Quel suon, quelle preci', the song sung by Manrico from his tower of imprisonment. But while this transition from cantabile to cabaletta is packed with such a profusion of musical details, Verdi does not lose control of it. It does not disintegrate into a sequence of picturesque fragments, because the composer remembers that it is really Leonora's scene and interprets it all through her sensibility. The 'Miserere' itself is austere and archaic, and in an opera that is so manifestly neither of these things, it might easily have remained alien and merely exotic. But it is at once reinterpreted through the medium of Leonora's imagination: in her mind the solemn, prayerful music is transmuted into a shuddering of terror which fills the whole atmosphere around her; having heard the music as it actually is, we hear it through Leonora's ears. Even during Manrico's song, Leonora is in a sense the central figure. The troubadour's verses are lamentably confused and non-committal, but Verdi composes them in a way that makes us hear him as Leonora hears him: ideally, almost celestially heroic, with harp and radiant tenor tones. Inspired by the picturesque and emotional richness of the scene, Verdi has elaborated the cantabile – cabaletta convention in an unprecedentedly grand manner. At the same time, it is thanks to the old discipline of the aria convention that he has acquired the capacity to visualize all the constituent elements through Leonora's unifying sensibility.

Even more brilliant in its adaptation of a conventional scheme to dramatic requirements is Violetta's Act I aria in *La Traviata*, which instead of preserving the self-sufficient independence usual in such movements is spiritually and thematically linked with the rest of the act. The cantabile 'Ah, fors'è lui' describes that yearning for true love which has tormented Violetta throughout the ostensibly carefree years she has spent as a 'kept woman'. Verdi composes it, as he composes most of his cantabiles at this period, as an open form, evolving from one theme to another in response to the text. But at the grand culminating moment it is not just any rapturous major-key outpouring that crowns the design; it is the theme already sung by Alfredo in the preceding duet, when he avowed just such a love as that which Violetta had always dreamt of. This mutual dependence of two separate lyrical movements affects the cabaletta even more remarkably. 'Sempre libera sarei', in which Violetta attempts to recover her professional attitude to love, is a model cabaletta – a quintessentially brilliant cabaletta. But just at the point where the hearer expects the conventional *tutti* cadences, the cabaletta is interrupted by the sound of Alfredo's song floating up to Violetta's room from the street below. This brilliant stroke does not just fill fuller with song one of the emptiest stretches of the traditional double-aria scheme: it also gives real psychological point to the second statement of the cabaletta, which now sounds more than ever forced, and on the brink of hysteria. In the *stretta* the theme is heard again, this time in the rhythm of Violetta's cabaletta, almost as if Alfredo's music were really sounding only in her own mind; and the counterpointing of it with her continuing roulades sums up the conflict of the whole scene (Ex. 1).

Nor should one forget Gilda in this context. She is wholly unlike the formidable *grandes dames* who had dominated Italian opera from time immemorial; the outrageously un-prima-donna-like character of her personality and behaviour prompts the most drastic rethinking of convention of them all. In *Rigoletto* the heroine's grand scena is suppressed altogether. Its associations were wrong for Gilda, and Verdi had to find other ways of expressing her character and her passions.

Arias

What holds for the scena as a whole also holds for its constituent parts. No new orthodoxy has come to exert its tyranny over cantabile and cabaletta in place of the earlier orthodoxy of symmetrical, rounded form. Nevertheless one can say that in the cantabiles the trend of the 1840s continues. Thematic reprises become rarer, and the ever-evolving type of melodic design, one that mounts irresistibly to a climactic phrase in which the pent-up passions of the singer are poured out, becomes the norm. The accumulation of intensity

Ex. 1

had generally been Verdi's aim in lyrical movements, but now it has become largely independent of the severe thematic rounding-off of his early style: What he once sought to achieve by ornamentation and rhythmic growth is now brought about purely by line and by harmonic control.

A new departure is marked by several cantabiles in strophic form: 'Tacea la notte', 'Ah, fors'è lui' and 'Di Provenza il mar'. The first two are both narrative pieces with necessarily long texts, pieces of the kind which Verdi had often struggled unavailingly with in the past, as for example in *Alzira*. It is salutary to observe that at precisely the moment in his career when he was turning his back for good on merely routine formalism, he was coming to the view that, even in opera, the specifically and undisguisedly formal strophic song was to be preferred to song that became rhapsodic or amorphous. 'Di Provenza il mar' is a rather special case, its strophic form exaggerated by the thematic and rhythmic repetitiveness within the verses, by the thematic instrumental introductions and by the tonal monotony. Clearly this is a question of dramatic characterization: rhetoric taking the place of passion, sermonizing and moralization taking the place of spontaneous self-expression, Germont living for the time being in another and alien world from that in which Alfredo and Violetta find themselves.

The new simplicity of idiom in *Rigoletto, Il Trovatore* and *La Traviata* is clearly seen in the absolute straightforwardness of the accompaniment figurations. There is no trace here of the complex and recondite textures found in some of the earlier operas. But the old-fashioned strumming and plucking shows the hand of the master in the richer harmonies and the smoother part-writing. Typical of this trend are the fuller integration of the episode into the aria structure, and the more varied harmonies that often mark this part of the aria, particularly in *La Traviata*. Thus in 'Ah, fors'è lui' the episode develops a rhythmic figure from the exposition through a sequentially shifting harmonic pattern, whereas in 'De' miei bollenti spiriti' the more widely ranging harmonies are supported by a strong linear movement in the bass, which flows through into the culminating phrase and recurs in a chromatic variant in the coda.

One apparently retrogressive feature is the carelessness about verbal values: the absense of declamatory or rhetorical nuance in most of the cantabiles, the tendency to let melody take over and impose its own rhythmic character on the text. We see this, for example, in the exposition of 'De' miei bollenti spiriti' (Ex. 2). But the impression is substantially mistaken. The fact of the matter is

Ex. 2

that by this stage Verdi has come to a clear understanding of what the function of words in opera really is. In ensembles, especially in duets, they play an active part in the dramatic dialectic, they embody the conflicts of viewpoint, they depict the shifts of emphasis or advantage within the scene, and they are generally set in an accordingly scrupulous manner. In a solo aria, where the expression of a single passion is the primary consideration, they can do little more than prompt the mood of the music. The music, however, is the medium through which the passions are expressed, and the processes by which it gains its eloquence take priority over any concern for verbal values.

The more square-cut designs of the solo cabalettas, with their symmetrical episodes, their thematic reprises and their more animated coda themes, has been standard for some years, and it must be said that one or two of the specimens from this group of operas would not be out of place in the crudest operas of the 1840s. Over and over again one gets the impression that Verdi had lost interest in the convention of the cabaletta, but had not yet seen any viable alternative to it. At least there is little sign of that growing richness and beauty which the cantabiles have shown right through his career. Rhythms of stultifying monotony and coarse, loud orchestration remain all too typical. Even such achievements as the widening of tonal range in the episode of 'Di quella pira' or the sense of genuine lyrical climax in the reprise of 'Tu vedrai' – the kinds of thing that one has taken for granted in the cantabiles for years – are exceptional among the cabalettas. 'No, non vedrai rimproveri' from *La Traviata* is interesting as being the single example of a curtailed form, with the second verse beginning only at the episode, and its *stretta* incorporates some unusually rich harmonic developments. But really only the brilliant use of the form in 'Sempre libera sarei', already commented upon in sufficient detail, shows Verdi's musical and dramatic imagination at full stretch in this medium.

The decline in the number of full-scale double-aria scenes is compensated for by the larger number of single-movement arias: four in *Rigoletto*, four in *Il Trovatore*, two in *La Traviata*. The *canzone* and romanza and *brindisi*, songs within the opera, all of which have strophic form and a balladic or popular style, need not detail us. More interesting are those strophic arias which Verdi used to express his characters in contexts where the full double-aria scheme would be cumbersome, the *ballata* 'Questa o quella' from *Rigoletto* and the aria 'Addio del passato' from *La Traviata*.

The former employs a standard aria structure with reprise, in two-verse form. It is a movement that might be taken as quintessential for these operas, with a tunefulness and catchiness worthy of folk music achieved by a previously unattained cunning in rhythm and harmony. What first beguiles is the rhythmic wizardry of the exposition, which fuses the phrases into a single melodic period that has little or nothing in common with Piave's sing-song verses. Equally impressive is the rapturous lyrical development of the episode idea, and the design is crowned by a reprise in which the final phrase of the exposition reappears transformed by harmonic parentheses and suspensions. One also notices with delight a single alteration in the harmonies of the second verse, so that the 'geloso furore' can be matched by a mockingly nonchalant diminished-seventh chord. The whole movement is nicely fused into its dramatic context by the dancing pedal notes that introduce it.

For all the dramatic and musical acumen with which they are elaborated, the arias so far described have been based on traditional forms of Italian aria. Perhaps still greater interest attaches to the two arias in *Rigoletto*, 'Caro nome' and 'Cortigiani vil razza dannata', and 'Condotta ell'era in ceppi' in *Il Trovatore*, where no such dependence is shown, and where the forms have in fact been devised specifically for the character and the context. The *Trovatore* aria is one of several which, because of the complexity of the plot of the opera, have to be used for narrative purposes. It gains its force from its juxtaposition with the preceding 'Stride la vampa' where the essentials of Azucena's narrative have just been told in a severely formalized, ballad-like song. Despite its faintly exotic flavour, this gave no clue to Azucena's character or to her degree of involvement with the events she described; but when alone with Manrico, she retells the story in her own words, and no trace of her former objectivity is retained. The music begins like a solo aria in the youthful Verdi's richest style: beautifully shaped as an artifact, quite dominated by the singing voice, yet with a figured, pulsing accompaniment which is itself full of expressive detail, the heavy thuds of cellos and basses, the strongly accented shudders of the inner strings, and the sigh figure of the oboe, resonating through the song like the 'eco eterna' of which Azucena speaks. One particularly noticeable feature is the strange and ominous veerings of dynamics, an early hint of the deranged convulsions which before long are to reduce Azucena to an incoherent frenzy.

After these opening aria-like phrases, the scene gradually undergoes a process of disintegration. The growing excitement Azucena feels prompts an acceleration, leading to a disintegration, of the musical elements so far employed. It is no longer possible for her to sustain her story-telling manner; she has become so involved in her narrative that she relives the experience and communicates it in a whole series of recitative and arioso passages. As Azucena mounts into delirium the tonality steps higher and higher at an ever more rapid pace; the orchestral texture accelerates into a tremolo; *pp* and *ff* are jabbed together in horrendous juxtapositions. The whole passage is clinched in a tremendous sustained cadential dissonance, which on resolution collapses through sinking chromatic harmonies. But only a psychological breakdown as drastic as this, only delirium or madness, are motives strong enough to warrant such wholesale distortions of the musical structure.

Ensembles

Verdi's abiding fondness for pattern-like forms, not only within single movements but over whole acts of operas, is shown clearly by the fact that, notwithstanding his growing interest in dramatic 'realism' and the incomparable precision and aptness his designs have now acquired, the ensemble scenes of his operas still continue to be laid out, in the great majority of cases, on the same long-established pattern of ensemble cantabile and ensemble cabaletta. These two movements are generally linked by a *parlante*, and often preceded by a third movement again in a *parlante* style. This deeply rooted pattern can be seen to underlie even a scene so extraordinarily original in many respects as that section of Act III of *Rigoletto* between 'La donna è mobile' and the Tempesta: the quartet provides the *parlante* and the cantabile, the trio provides the repeated cabaletta. The majority of exceptions to this general principle are variations on the scheme of the single-movement ensemble cantabile such as we find in the Act II finales of both *Rigoletto* and *La Traviata*.

The position held among the solo arias by the 'Miserere' scene is held among the ensembles by the *scena e duetto* from Act II of *La Traviata*. It shows a comparable phenomenon – the elaboration of the normal formal scheme until one almost ceases to be aware of its relevance. One may perhaps legitimately regard 'Morrò, la mia memoria' as the cabaletta, but this is preceded by not one cantabile but two – the first ('Bella voi siete') dominated by Germont, the other ('Dite alla giovine') by Violetta – and these in turn are preceded by two short arias, again one for each character. The scheme of the whole scene may be diagrammed thus:

i. Recitative	ii. Aria (Germont) 'Pura siccome un angelo'
iii. Transition	iv. Aria (Violetta) 'Non sapete'
v. Link	vi. Cantabile *a 2* 'Bella voi siete'
	vii. Cantabile *a 2* 'Dite alla giovine'
viii. Transition	ix. Cabaletta *a 2* 'Morrò, la mia memoria'

It is one of the supreme examples in Verdi's work of the new tendency, stemming from the Act I finale of *I Due Foscari* and the *gran duetto* in Act I of *Macbeth*, not to simplify the emotional tensions of the scene until they match the standard operatic pattern, but to enrich the pattern with a profusion of new lyrical growths until it is capable of reflecting every emotional fluctuation, no matter how fine, in such a dramatic encounter.

To illustrate the vast range which Verdi's ensemble scenes show, despite his basic adherence to the normal patterns, the *Traviata* duet may be set against the duet between Rigoletto and Sparafucile in Act I of *Rigoletto*. This is a *locus classicus* for a quite different kind of daring; for Verdi, recognizing that this type of scene is ill adapted to stylization as a cantabile, bases the structural organization wholly on the orchestra. After the dark and sinister introductory chords, and the formulation of the motif of the curse, the movement settles into the pattern of an orchestral aria, extended quite regularly as far as 'La vostra donna è là'. The tonal sequences that form the material of the subsequent episode suggest a new willingness to relax and digress within the closed form – they are not prompted by the text – just as the long dominant pedal with which the episode closes suggests a new sensitivity to the degree of firmness needed to hold such digressions in check. From 'Demonio!' onwards, there is an elaborated reprise of the principal orchestral theme, developing differently from 'Comprendo' onwards. Here, before the design is finally rounded off with the common type of flowing chromaticism, the tension is sustained by changing harmonies under a melodic *ostinato*, a characteristically impressive elaboration of a traditional feature (Ex. 3). Between the introductory bars and coda where the sombre harmonies give an awful emphasis to the words 'Sparafucil mi nomino', there is almost nothing in the music that could be said to point the sense of the words, and nowhere do the singers really take over the orchestral melody. The movement is a kind of operatic tone-poem, evoking the atmosphere in which the matter-of-fact conversation is held by the intriguing ambiguity of the harmonies and the 'sinister phosphorescence of the orchestration' (Budden).

Few operatic conventions are more ancient than that type of love
duet in which the supposedly perfect harmony of the loving couple
is reflected by the identity of the music which both sing. That Verdi
recognized that there was still a place for this type of duet is shown
by 'Parigi, o cara'; the kind of variation he was now capable of
playing on it, by 'È il sol dell'anima'.

This duet begins in a now slightly old-fashioned way, with a full

Ex. 3

Ex. 3 cont.

aria-like verse for the Duke. Clearly the point of this is that he is not really in dialogue with Gilda at all; he is apostrophizing the power of love. But this aria design is typical of the *Rigoletto* period in the single sweeping impetus of the episode (beginning at 'una pur avvenne') and the fusing of reprise, culmination and codetta-like harmonic acceleration in the final phrase: it is a perfect example of the mutual enrichment of the formal and the dynamic that is so essential in Verdi's art. Gilda has no solo verse, however. With unfailing dramatic understanding Verdi puts into her mouth a single phrase of the Duke's song, which she muses over, enraptured,

428

against a gently palpitating accompaniment. Then, as if the Duke fears she is indeed going into a trance, he brings her back to carnal reality, striking in with his most passionate phrase. In the long rapt coda, the Duke repeats the phrase Gilda had shown to be her favourite, and she continues merely to caress it, borrowing the palpitating semiquaver pattern that was originally in the orchestra. The stillness of this coda has one biting moment of ppp chromatics, and a really old-fashioned lovers' cadenza.

A love duet of a quite different kind is found in 'Sì, la stanchezza m'opprime' in Il Trovatore. Despite its apparent simplicity this is a beautiful example of the ever-renewed, ever-diversified type of melody worked out in ensemble form. Virtually a solo aria for Azucena with refrains for Manrico, its subtlety lies in the fact that it is these brief refrains that lull her into the state of tranquillity which prompts the changing lyrical idiom.

In Azucena's first verse one is impressed by the way in which a formal melody is made to embody a host of expressive or psychological details; the dragging rhythms, the lustreless colouring, the confined tessitura all contribute to that sense of unutterable weariness of which she speaks. The contrasting major key, B^b at first, becomes a symbol of 'quiete'. But bizarre accents and f irruptions betray the still-distraught condition of the singer. Manrico's refrain is laden with the warmth and tranquillity that he longs to bestow upon Azucena: flute and clarinet double it, strings tremolo on the sustaining harmony, the melody flows and aspires without any sense of weariness, uninhibited by, and independent of, any rhythmic characterization.

It has the required effect. Azucena's second verse is a different aria – indeed it has acquired an independent fame – linked with the preceding verse by a continuing rhythmic pulse, but now in Manrico's mood. She is day-dreaming of her homeland, in a beautiful incantatory melody that partly expresses her sleepiness, and partly guarantees that this feeling will lead a stage further, to sleep itself. 'In sonno placido io dormirò', it may be noticed, is not a surrender but an aspiration, and Verdi shapes the melody accordingly (Ex. 4). Even in the coda, it remains primarily Azucena's song: Manrico is not engaged in a dialogue with her, but is simply watching over her, providing a tender harmony for her cadences as if they were her dying days.

In cantabiles for larger-scale ensembles the processes, while of course more elaborate, rarely obscure the underlying formal pattern. It is, for example, quite clear that the *andante* of the *Rigoletto* quartet

Ex. 4

is a development of the type of form used in the duets. A freer
elaboration of the ensemble cantabile is provided by the Act III finale
of *La Traviata*, a movement preceded by a transitional accompanied
recitative and followed by a death-ritual slightly more drawn-out
than usual. The cantabile itself has a kind of preface, 'Prendi ...
quest'è l'immagine', in which Violetta sings a *parlando* premonitory
of her death, and on whose figuration – the elaboration of the
death-rhythm from *Semiramide* already perfected in the 'Miserere'
scene of *Il Trovatore* – the cantabile itself will draw. The most
extraordinary feature of this are the fact that it begins a third off key –
a reflection perhaps of the emotional sublimation Violetta is experiencing – and that, throughout the design, Verdi sustains the
tension between the disembodied, visionary quality of Violetta's
song and the grim reality of approaching death with which the
orchestra threatens it.

The ensemble cantabiles simply mark a further development of a
form on which Verdi had always lavished his most tender care. With
the ensemble cabalettas, however, we have reached a new stage. For
the first time we find that in these movements too Verdi never
forgets the cardinal principle that an ensemble is the musical
expression of a dramatic confrontation of some kind, and that
therefore the musical design must be built up by adding together the
characters and the moods of its various participants. No more will
the repetitive rituals and the indiscriminating vigorousness of the
cabaletta obliterate distinctions of character or defy dramatic sense.
Even those duet cabalettas in *Rigoletto* that appear to conform to the
old mechanical patterns prove to be dramatically right, for in 'Veglia,
o donna' and 'Si vendetta' Gilda is not emotionally autonomous; she

is feeling through Rigoletto, or gazing helplessly and reprovingly at the passion that consumes him. And even in those duet cabalettas in *Il Trovatore* where the rapturous impetus of the movement seems in danger of obliterating all memory of the moods that provoked it, Verdi is likely to be ready with some *coup* that will recall the movement's dramatic source. In the duet 'Perigliarti ancora languente' it is at the beginning of the coda that the conflict is suddenly brought graphically back to life: a rasping new string figuration and a rapid interchange of phrases

> Ferma, deh ferma! . . .
> Mi lascia, mi lascia! . . .
> M'odi, deh! m'odi! . . .

break into the lyrical stylization that had hitherto prevailed. A comparable stroke is found in the incorporation of the solemn

> Giurasti . . . pensaci!
> È sacra la mia fè

into the *stretta* of 'Vivrà! contende il giubilo'.

The two movements that best demonstrate the fact that the cabaletta has now acquired the same freedom to adapt its design to the dramatic context as the cantabile has long enjoyed are 'Addio, addio, speranza ed anima' in *Rigoletto* and 'Morrò! . . . la mia memoria' in *La Traviata*. In the former case, the headlong rush of the opening, with the answering phrase of the exposition already snatched by Gilda, and an episode in which the voices tumble over one another in canon, unmistakably reflect the urgent haste which the dramatic situation demands. But the vast extension of the culminating phase and the matching elaboration and repetitiveness of coda and cadences suggest with equal vividness that longing to 'say good-night till it be morrow', which is equally a part of the mood. The whole movement is also notable for the obsessiveness and the harmonic resource with which it elaborates the basic melodic and rhythmic figures.

The desire to tighten up the dialogue of the duet cabaletta and to make its intrinsic repetitiveness more dramatically congruous is equally clear in the *Traviata* duet. Again one has a design in which basically all the repetitions are accommodated within a single verse, except for a brief epilogue-like citation just before the end of the scene. A perfectly regular cabaletta-like exposition for Violetta is repeated at once by Germont, shifting the key to the relative major, where it thereafter remains. But it is the B♭ major theme that Violetta sings next that dominates the movement – the theme of her abiding love for Alfredo, not of grief for herself. After an episodic theme for Germont it recurs in duet, and it is this theme that is quoted in a quasi-recitative style in the epilogue.

One of the boldest formal innovations of *Rigoletto* is the fact that it includes no grand finale. *Il Trovatore* and *La Traviata* include one each, at the end of their second acts, and both of them continue with the trend observable throughout the 1840s to pack all the expressive tensions into a vast ensemble cantabile and either drastically to cut down (*Il Trovatore*) or totally to eliminate (*La Traviata*) the following *stretta*. Both movements, too, show in their later stages that kind of structural broadening-out and increasing richness of lyricism that we have come to regard as typical of Verdi's finales; but the *largo* of the *Traviata* finale is perhaps the one that gets further away from the habits of the smaller ensembles.

Initially the cantabile presents the confrontation of father and son in indignant and breathless *parlando*, which only at the end of Germont's verse hints at real lyrical force. Material from this verse – the cadence bars and the chromatically rising phrase that precedes it – is developed in a brief *tutti* to act as a transition into Violetta's verse. She in effect sings a complete aria, unusual only in the fact that the exposition is in the dominant key, and that episode and culmination have a certain amount of choral backing. Like so much of the lyrical material in these operas it is repetitive in small details of phraseology in the exposition, the effect being to consolidate the lyrical design at an early stage so that the later asymmetry never throws it off balance. But it also shows a cunning in rhythmic development more typical of the early works. Two details may be cited – the gradual elaboration and expansion of the triplet idea at phrase ends, and the growing expansiveness of the phrasing from 1+1+1+1 in the exposition, through 2+2 in the episode, to 4+2 in the culminating phrase (Ex. 5). The coda, a *tutti* virtually throughout, starts here. It has its own grand theme, distilled from material earlier in the movement, but still undergoing further development, variation and reharmonization, as one sees from the two answering phrases in bars 1–2 and 3–4. By such touches, without upsetting the grandiose swinging symmetry that he loved to sustain at this point in a finale, Verdi achieves a new richness of detail.

Both finales include one or more choral movements, and that to *Traviata parlante* movements besides. Indeed the application of *parlante* technique to ensembles on this scale seems to be an innovation in *La Traviata*. That section of the finale in *allegro agitato* which accompanies the gaming scene is particularly interesting.

432

Ex. 5

Largo

VIOLETTA *con voce debolissima e con passione*

Al–fre–do, Al–fre–do, di que–sto co–re non puoi com-

-pren-de-re tut-to l'a–mo–re... tu non co–no–sci che fi–no a

prez–zo del tuo di–sprez–zo pro–va–to io l'ho. Ma ver–rà

tem–po in che il sa–pra–i co–me t'a–mas–si con–fes–se-

–ra–i Dio dai ri–mor–si ti sal–vi al–lo–ra, dai ri–mor–si, dai ri-

–mor–si, Dio ti sal–vi, sal–vi al–lor..ah! io spen–ta an–co–ra t'a–me–rò t'a–merò...

The instrumental material around which this *parlante* is fashioned occupies the first eight bars (Ex. 6). It is characterized by repeated figures, but these are drawn out to form a large symmetrical design: A(8 bars) A(8) b′b″(8) A. Phase two of the *parlante* begins as a major-key variant with lighter, brighter scoring, but after the episodic phrase an extended transition brings the music back to the tonic: AAb′b″C. The third phase of the scheme assumes the pattern AA²C

Ex. 6

Allegro agitato

Cl. Strings

and the fourth Ab'b''a, where the 'a' represents a fade-away coda. The whole *parlante*, in short, is remarkable for its breadth and its regularity; it forms a musical analogy to the calmly proceeding salon-life in the background of the drama, less obtrusive, but almost as heedless of the foreground as a *banda* playing waltzes. But the wonderful feature of the scene has not yet been mentioned: it is the great lyrical phrase for Violetta that recurs between each phase of the *parlante*. This is in Verdi's richest style, cantabile at its smoothest and purest, unalloyed with fioritura or angularity or even rhythmic feature, its expressiveness consisting wholly in the tension between it and the bass and/or the harmony (Ex. 7). There is nothing in the

Ex. 7

libretto to suggest this poignant refrain, the text for which Verdi himself scrapes together from where he can. But it is absolutely typical that a scene that on the surface just seems full of time-passing incident should be given a 'heart' through which we can feel its underlying darkness and pathos.

Recitatives and transitions

The lyrical profusion so conspicuous in the works of this period frequently overflows the aria structures. *Arioso* passages become more conspicuous in the recitative, and almost all of them are of startling loveliness, serving to concentrate the listener's attention on a dramatic motive that is to be formally elaborated in the following aria or ensemble: thus in *Il Trovatore* alone 'Come d'aurato sogno . . .' precedes 'Tacea la notte', 'Di qual tetra luce' precedes 'Ah sì, ben mio', 'Gemente aura' precedes 'D'amor sull'ali'.

One relic of the old aria-based type of opera is by now in decline. The number of scenes which begin with a brief instrumental prelude on whose figuration Verdi subsequently draws to sustain the atmosphere or to maintain the momentum has become very small. Its flavour of formalized introspection is hostile to the unyielding dynamism with which he now prefers to invest whole acts of music. The few exceptions are either found in frankly conventional scenes like the Duke's 'Ella mi fu rapita' in *Rigoletto* or are used with a new sophistication, as is the case with Violetta's scena at the start of Act III of *La Traviata*. Here, the old-fashioned introduction is transformed into a veritable tone poem, growing out of the atmospheric chords of the opening into an aria-like design, albeit one of an unusually unsystematic and organic kind. Before the cadence and coda there is a marvellously protracted 'Neapolitan' parenthesis. Although it is largely the atmospheric chords that Verdi uses in the following scene to articulate the still, deathly recitative, he transforms the old convention by turning the 'Neapolitan' phrase into an arioso analogous to the spiritual refreshment that momentarily removes Violetta from her world of grief and pain.

Recitative deepened and illuminated by arioso, and an ever more flexible employment of the *parlante* idiom, remain the basic means by which Verdi sustains the impetus of his operas between the formal arias and ensembles. Occasionally, as in the Duke's scena and aria in *Rigoletto*, a formal chorus is still used to link up the constituent parts of the scene. A quite new degree of momentum and consistency is achieved in the opening scenes of *Rigoletto* and *La Traviata*, however, by setting them against an unbroken flow of instrumental music reflecting the social world in which these scenes play. One might associate this development with the older practice of setting dialogue against choruses or *banda* music, the sort of thing found in several scenes of *I Lombardi* or *La Battaglia di Legnano*. But Verdi is working on an unprecedented scale and with an unprecedented flexibility. We observe this flexibility in *Rigoletto* where the *banda* music is resumed a second time, after the *perigordino*, and is gradually developed into a *tutti* with a lyrical sweep and harmonic richness more typical of a grand finale than of either *banda* music or choral introductions. And we observe the immense scale of Verdi's design in *La Traviata* when after the duet the *stretta dell'introduzione* resumes the material of the *parlante* in a chorally distended form (Ex. 8).

Ex. 8 (a)

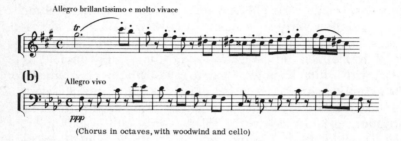

(Chorus in octaves, with woodwind and cello)

Two further scenes may be mentioned for the remarkable character of their overall design. One is the scene of the storm in *Rigoletto*, in which a generally conventional type of recitative is accompanied and punctuated by figurations that gradually congeal to form the central climax of trio and tempest, and are then resolved back into their original accompanying and punctuating forms as the storm fades into the distance. The essentially normal devices used here are given an unreal and ghastly air by the freakish figurations and sonorities, and by the explicit instructions to sing the recitative 'without the customary appoggiaturas'.

The other unexampled scene is Violetta's in Act II of *La Traviata*, not the least remarkable feature of which is the fact that it includes no formal song whatsoever. It begins with an aria-like sentence for solo clarinet, expressive of the innermost feelings of Violetta's heart, and this is followed by a brilliantly controlled passage of figure development, leading to the climactic lyrical epigram 'Amami Alfredo', the supreme early example of that characteristic which Grout has described as Verdi's ability 'to gather up the whole feeling of a scene in a pure and concentrated moment of expression'.[1] The power of this *cantabile* phrase is at least partly due to the double frustration of the growing excitement in the previous pages. An acceleration of figuration is once broken off at Alfredo's 'Oh quanto' and once suspended at 'sarò là'. Typical of the actual theme are the plunging line, the lack of rhythmic definition and the all-embracing harmonic tremolo.

This kind of theme is becoming a regular resource of Verdi's style at this period, the earliest example being at the end of the duet in Act III of *Luisa Miller*, though the *Traviata* example is rare in that it is not attached to a formal lyrical movement. It is only as Verdi's melody-writing becomes less rhythm-conscious, and as his use of harmony becomes less formal than it had originally been, that this kind of shaping of a melodic line within a harmonic immanence and without reference to other resources becomes a possibility. Such moments – 'Amami, Alfredo', or the final reprise of 'Al cor, al guardo estatico' in 'Tacea la notte' or of 'Sei tu dal ciel disceso' in the Act II finale of *Il Trovatore* – mark the very apotheosis of melody: rhythmic feature is dissolved into a tremolant timelessness, and the identity of every instrumental colour melts into a sonorous nirvana.

Chorus and orchestra

By the time of *Rigoletto* and *Il Trovatore*, Verdi's writing for chorus, which had once been one of the most admired aspects of his style, has become its most flagrant defect. Hardly a trace is observable of that ability to fashion every piece to its dramatic context which we admire in the solos and ensembles, or of that understanding of the need to subordinate the part to the whole. Choral movements remain block-like in design, repetitive and symmetrical in their thematic development. In the incomparably vivid and stylish drama of these operas they obtrude, either as flagrant set-pieces, such as the gipsies' and soldiers' choruses in *Il Trovatore*, or (still worse) as formal choruses masquerading as dramatic realism as in 'Zitti, zitti' in *Rigoletto*. It is typical of the greater perfection of *La Traviata* that here Verdi should have found a solution. It has nothing to do with the actual quality of music, merely with the fact that in this opera every one of the choruses is an entertainment of some kind, and the brightly coloured, formal patterns are thus entirely congruous.

Il Trovatore is unique among Verdi's earlier operas in beginning without so much as an orchestral prelude. As in his last operas, the music begins with the introductory bars of the first scene and the curtain goes up at once. In *Rigoletto* and *La Traviata*, the prelude remains as the one substantial piece of instrumental music in the opera. But they are preludes. The full-scale overtures that had introduced each of the previous group of operas from *La Battaglia di Legnano* to *Stiffelio* have been abandoned in favour of concise movements devoted to an anticipatory or atmospheric presentation of one of the chief dramatic motifs in the opera. In the case of *Rigoletto* it is a series of brassy meditations on the grim rhythms and sepulchral harmonies that are later associated with the curse by which Rigoletto is haunted; in *La Traviata*, a musical portrait of Violetta. The core of the latter piece is provided by a double statement of the 'Amami Alfredo' theme, the reprise being adorned with an almost chirpy counterpoint in the violins. It seems to suggest simultaneously the idealistic and the flirtatious aspects of Violetta's love, just as the introductory chords – those developed at greater length in the Act III prelude – suggest the sickly pathos of her destiny.

In addition to its prelude, *Rigoletto* has its tempest music, about which the most interesting thing is perhaps the fact that such a movement no longer has an independent formal life: the crescendo has been accomplished in the preceding scena and the instrumental movement simply represents the *tutti* and the diminuendo that follow from this.

The use of recurring themes remains, and will remain, unsystematic. Its range embraces the use of 'La donna è mobile' – it is not, as is often supposed, an aria expressive of the Duke's character, but his favourite song – in *Rigoletto* to act as an audible and operatic sign of the fact that he lives longer than he should, as well as the more long-range use of a theme associated with a particular dramatic event or emotional awakening. The best example of this is the theme 'Di quell'amor' in *La Traviata*, which, having appeared as the climax both of Alfredo's avowal of love in the Act I duet and of Violetta's solo cantabile, thereafter becomes a symbol of the love between them. Its recurrence in the 'cabaletta' of Violetta's aria has already been discussed. In the third act the theme recurs again in the solo strings as an accompaniment to the reading of the letter from Germont. Emotionally its function here is to symbolize the reconciliation of the lovers, of which the letter is the merest machinery, while the ominous chord that cuts it short makes it clear that a happy, fulfilling resolution is no longer to be looked for. The further recurrence of the theme at the end of the opera is more problematical. It is developed here, and finally dissolves in a *Liebestod*-like dizziness, apparently intended to suggest a glimpse of love continuing in a better world. Verdi rarely cared to treat this romantic–sentimental cliché with so little poise.

Perhaps most typical of Verdi's restraint with the recurring-theme device is the treatment of what is generally called the 'curse motif' in *Rigoletto*. It is scored into the listener's consciousness in the prelude, and its rhythm and harmonies inform the whole of Monterone's brief scene in Act I. Interestingly enough, though, it is not the Monterone scene in which it acquires its chilling authentic form. What Verdi was most interested in was the effect of the curse on Rigoletto's mind – that is the real psychological crux – so it is only as Rigoletto broods over the incident on his way home that the curse motif is actually formulated. During the scena with Sparafucile and the following 'Pari siamo' meditation it recurs three times, and again, with perhaps rather self-conscious irony, between 'Caro nome' and the finale. Its characteristic features are faintly suggested in the second scene with Monterone, and indeed at 'Ite di qua voi tutti', where Rigoletto addresses the courtiers with the same kind of quelling authoritativeness that Monterone had once turned on him. But in fact, once catastrophe has struck, the menace is no longer a dramatically efficacious thing, and the motif is simply abandoned. It does not even recur at the end of the opera, when the curse has been horribly fulfilled.

The simplicity and modesty of the orchestration is in keeping with that of the general style of these operas. It is notable that *Rigoletto* makes do without a harp – thus perhaps prompting the exquisitely rich but translucent scoring of the last pages of the final duet – and *Il Trovatore* without a *banda*. Generally a delicate scoring of simple textures prevails, particularly in the lyrical movements. Complex orchestral figurations such as those in 'Cortegiani, vil razza dannata' or 'Condotta ell'era in ceppi' and garish or brutal colouring such as that in 'Sì vendetta' or 'Oh mia infamia' are alike rare.

Nevertheless, despite the simplicity, Verdi was continuing to develop his feeling for orchestral colour as a dramatic resource. A fine example is provided by the second scene of Act I of *Rigoletto*. Here the ghastly colouring of low clarinets and bassoons, divided violas and cellos, and of the muted solo cello and solo double-bass that play the main theme, is not only vivid in itself: it provides a satanic point of reference against which the scoring for high woodwinds and violins associated with Gilda proves all the more telling. Again there is nothing systematic about this scoring, but the intent is unmistakable at 'Ma in altr'uomo qui mi cangio', or the prelude to 'Caro nome'. Similarly diaphonous scoring associated with Gilda is heard in the 'Lassù in ciel' section of the third-act finale, with its divided violins and arpeggiating or trilling flute. This too has been preceded by a long section of gloomy and freakish scoring in the storm scene, with low strings set against solitary high woodwind notes, and vocalizing tenor and bass chorus.

Growing harmonic refinement

Finally this group of operas shows a quite new grasp of harmonic resource, not in the sense that new chords or unprecedented juxtapositions are necessarily much exploited, but in the sense that the harmony now plays a vital part in the search for a type of musical movement that can be matched to the dramatic continuity. One finds that the *parlante* movements are laid out on an altogether broader tonal scheme than in earlier years (that in the second act finale of *La Traviata* serves as a good example); and one finds within the lyrical movements, especially in episodic and transitional phrases, a fluent pattern of modulation generally replacing the bald tonal juxtaposition of Verdi's earliest years. The 'Io son felice' passage in the Act I duet in *La Traviata*, and the transition into 'Non sapete' in the second act, match stepwise modulation to mounting excitement and carry it off with an almost Chopinesque refinement.

But nor by this time should one underestimate Verdi's capacity for imagining new chords, or at least new juxtapositions of chords. It is true that the boldest effects still tend to come in *strettas* in the old-fashioned way, as we see at the end of 'Non udrai rimproveri'. But increasingly what had once been arresting and emphatic is becoming exquisite, and is being pushed back into the lyrical part of the aria where it forms a delicious and effective parenthesis either in the cadence phase, as for example in the duet verse of 'Veglia, o donna' or in 'Caro nome', or even in the very heart of the song as in 'Questa e quella'. In such a scene as that between Rigoletto and Sparafucile we hear single chords or concentrated groups of chords lending an expressive intensity or rhetorical emphasis that Wagner himself could not surpass (Ex. 9). Another feature that is becoming almost a mannerism at this period is the use of changing chords under a repeated note or a brief melodic *ostinato*, again either to lend vehemence to the delivery of the text or as a means of controlling the impetus of the movement, holding it back perhaps that bit longer than anticipated. Good examples are found in 'Deh rallentate, o barbari', the cabaletta of the Act III trio of *Il Trovatore*, 'Addio, addio, speranza ed anima' or 'Non sapete'. All such passages are signs of the fact that operatic song is now a medium deficient in no dimension.

Ex. 9

The colour and texture of the accompaniment and the liveliness and variety of the harmonies will henceforth be matters of as much concern as are the shape and rhythms of the vocal melody that flows, flexes and dances above.

PART IV

The operas

20

Nabucco, a risorgimento opera

In November 1889, the month that marked the fiftieth anniversary of Verdi's operatic début, Giosuè Carducci wrote:

Giuseppe Verdi co' primi palpiti dell'arte giovane presentí ed annunciò la patria risorgente. Oh canti indimenticabili e sacri a chi nacque avanti il 1848! [With the first throbbings of his youthful art Giuseppe Verdi presaged and heralded the revival of the fatherland. Oh songs unforgettable and sacred to anyone born before the '48!]

But by 'the first throbbings of his youthful art', the poet would have understood not so much *Oberto* as *Nabucco*.

Of the crucial importance in Verdi's career of *Nabucco*, no one has ever been in doubt. Nor does there seem much doubt wherein its importance lay. *Nabucco* established Verdi in the front rank of Italian composers because in it he showed that his peculiar brand of vehemence and melancholy was ideally matched to expressing the dilemma of contemporary Italy in operatic terms. Solera had designed the drama in such a way as to offer the audience, among other things, a number of strong situations in which they could easily perceive a reflection of their own condition. When Verdi came to set it, the vividness of his realization of these allegorical episodes was such that every Italian who heard it was pierced to the heart by its psalmodizing melancholy and stirred to heroic aspiration by its pulsating march tunes. For Verdi's Italian contemporaries *Nabucco* became quite simply the most meaningful opera there was, the opera in which the moods of the *risorgimento* were voiced most authentically. At the same time it established a number of dramatic precedents to which Verdi returned again and again during the 1840s, the period during which, as an artist, he was most deeply engaged with the *risorgimento*.

Nabucco and the *risorgimento* operas that followed it in the next few years have a number of features in common which may be described in general terms before *Nabucco* itself is subjected to closer scrutiny. One such feature is the tendency to build up the dramatic theme not so much around a small group of strikingly idiosyncratic individuals as around a conflict on an international scale. The idiosyncratic individuals will probably be present, for drama is hard pressed to survive without them; but with their fates will inextricably be involved the fates of entire peoples. *Nabucco* is not just about Nabucco and Abigaille and Fenena; it involves a confrontation of Hebrews and Babylonians, as does *I Lombardi* one of Crusaders and Saracens, and *Alzira* one of Spaniards and Peruvians. The nation, and the historical and religious foundations on which the nation stands, are basic concerns in such operas, just as they are in other artistic media of the *risorgimento*.

Where the theatre differed from, say, the novel of the *risorgimento* was in the obligation to assume a disguise. Verdi and his librettists did not resort to Babylon or Peru in search of the exotic, as a French composer might have done, but because only in some such disguise was it possible for him to voice the true feelings of his compatriots. As we have seen, theatrical subjects taken from Italian history were among those to which censorship reacted most ruthlessly. The nationalist fervour aroused in one individual by a private reading of an historical novel by Guerrazzi or D'Azeglio was a minor worry. To allow such sentiments to be stirred simultaneously in hundreds of breasts in a public theatre would be asking for trouble on a far more threatening scale: hence the disguise. Only if the drama purported to be about some historically or geographically remote people could the protagonists express the real concerns of nineteenth-century Italy:

> Oh, mia patria sì bella è perduta!
> Oh, membranza sì cara e fatal!

That, ostensibly, is a chorus of Hebrews of the sixth century B.C. in *Nabucco*.

> Maledetti cui spinge rea voglia
> Fuor del cerchio che il Nume ha segnato!

And that anti-imperialist commination is ostensibly the sentiment of a group of fifteenth-century Frenchmen in *Giovanna d'Arco*. As Verdi himself put it, in the already-quoted letter to Giuseppe Giusti, 'Unfortunately ... if we want something at all effective, we have, to our shame, to resort to foreign things.'

It would be an oversimplification to suggest that in the operas of the 1840s Verdi was composing allegories commenting on the plight of contemporary Italy. Very rarely, if ever, can an entire opera be interpreted in such a way. Verdi's principal interests as a dramatic musician were bound to be with his characters, not with political ideology. And so it not infrequently happens that the tyrants – the

Nabucco, a risorgimento opera

Nabuccos and the Attilas – quite steal the show from those who represent the pan-Italian cause. Nowadays, when we expect a dramatic work to form a unified and morally coherent whole, this tends to cause dissatisfaction. It dismays us that, for example, in *Attila*, those characters who are at one moment expressing the loftiest patriotic ideals should at the next be engaged in cowardly intrigues. In the 1840s this perturbed no one. The circumstances of theatre life inevitably meant that opera was rarely listened to or criticized as a dramatic entity: audiences responded with singular abandon to the passions expressed in the individual arias and choruses, but they were less concerned than we are about the place of these pieces in the total dramatic conception. So instead of a fully worked-out *risorgimento* allegory, what we usually find is an opera which as a whole is ideologically untendentious, but which from time to time is punctuated with movements that are red-hot with the passions of the *risorgimento*.

But when all is said there is no doubt that, of these works, *Nabucco* sustains its *risorgimento* implications most consistently. In no other Verdi opera does the nation, as a political and religious institution, occupy the stage so continuously; in no other opera do the individual characters so regularly act as symbols of political and religious realities; in no other opera is the musical language so impregnated with the great popular repertories of march music and hymnody.

Possibly because of censorial scrupulousness, dramatic workings of Old Testament themes were something of a rarity in Restoration Italy, and before *Nabucco* only one Biblical opera, Rossini's *Mosè in Egitto*, had acquired the status of a repertory work. *Mosè* was certainly one of the musical and dramatic sources of *Nabucco*. In the present context, however, a more particular interest is to be found in two dramatic but non-operatic workings of the story of Nebuchadnezzar.

The first *Nabucco* had appeared in 1819, the work of the distinguished Florentine dramatist Giovanni Battista Niccolini. Those authors who have asserted that Niccolini's *Nabucco* has nothing to do with Verdi's are strictly speaking quite correct. Nevertheless the play does provide one of the most striking and meticulously worked-out examples of the tendency to analyse the political and religious concerns of the present by means of a story taken from a remote and exotic era. Indeed the printed edition of Niccolini's play includes a 'key for the understanding of *Nabucco*', in which the names of the characters are set out in two columns – on the left in their ancient

Babylonian forms, on the right in their modern European equivalents. For example, Assyria is the French Empire, Phoenicia is England, and Egypt Prussia. Nebuchadnezzar is in reality Napoleon, and his high priest Mitrane is Pius VII, that Pope who in turn crowned Napoleon, lost the Papal States to him, excommunicated him, was imprisoned by him, and survived to see the Papal States re-established after Napoleon's downfall. Niccolini, who wrote as an ardent republican and anticlericalist, was using the figure of Nebuchadnezzar to discuss such questions as the relationship of state and Church, and the putting-down of tyranny, just as Solera and Verdi were to do twenty-three years later.

But before this, another dramatic working of the Nebuchadnezzar story had appeared on the Italian stage, the historical ballet *Nabucodonosor*, by Antonio Cortesi, performed at La Scala during the Autumn season 1838. This, as the preface to the scenario-book makes clear, is not a wholly original working of the subject: it is based on a highly successful French play that had been performed in Paris two years earlier. The relationship between the play *Nabucodonosor*, by MM. Anicet-Bourgeois and Cornu, and Cortesi's ballet has been described in sufficient detail by Budden. For my purposes it is more important to examine the dramatic character of that ballet, because it was on this scenario that Solera appears to have based his libretto, and it was with its scenery and costumes that Merelli first staged Verdi's opera.

Cortesi's ballet was a full-length five-act piece which appears to have been written specifically for the Autumn season 1838. It was, that is to say, one of the major commissions for what one might call the Coronation season at La Scala, the season during which the Austrian Emperor Ferdinand was crowned King of Lombardy and Venetia in Milan Cathedral. This sumptuous occasion is generally seen by Italian historians as the proudest moment of the Restoration, the moment at which the Austrians in northern Italy reached the apogee of their power and prestige. The sacred symbolism of the coronation must have seemed finally to have extinguished all memories of the revolutionary period; the upheavals of the earlier years of the Restoration had apparently been stilled; Austrian rule of northern Italy was divinely authorized; the political power of the state and the spiritual power of the Church were once more in perfect harmony.

I do not believe that it is possible, without a positive perversity of cunning, to demonstrate that either Anicet-Bourgeois and Cornu or Cortesi designed their dramas as allegories on Restoration politics in the way that Niccolini had designed his as an allegory on Napoleonic politics. Nevertheless both works are apparently the products of a period of political and religious consolidation, and in the comparatively simplified action of the ballet it is even clearer than in the play that the pervading themes are the miraculous power of faith and the mutual dependence of Church and state.

The ballet has three principal characters, Nabucco and his two daughters Fenena and Abigaille, of whom the latter is – though the fact is kept secret – really the daughter of a slave; and two national and religious groups, the Jews, worshippers of Jehovah, and the Babylonians, worshippers of Baal. After Nabucco's destruction of Jerusalem and the exile of the Jews to Babylon, Fenena is sent back to rule as regent in Babylon pending her father's return. But during Nabucco's absence she becomes increasingly sympathetic to the Jews, and increasingly impressed by their religion. The priestly party in Babylon is thus driven to seek the support of Abigaille and, receiving it, to attempt to establish her as queen. When Nabucco returns to Babylon, basking in the glory he has won, and much displeased with the priests of Baal for their treason, he orders the abolition of the old gods: in future his own statue is to be worshipped in Babylon. But the superman who would be God is struck down by a divine thunderbolt. Enfeebled and imbecile, he can offer no opposition when Abigaille and the priests of Baal assume power. The plight of the Jews would now be desperate, but for the fact that Fenena has become a formal convert to their faith. Nabucco, moved by the faith of Fenena and her fellow Jews, steadfast even to martyrdom, himself cries out in prayer to the true God: his reason, his strength, and in due course his kingdom are restored. The ballet ends with Nabucco leading the Babylonians in worship of the God of Israel.

That Solera and Verdi should have created the quintessential *risorgimento* opera out of this monument of Restoration art is not without irony. It is the more remarkable in that the actual plot of the drama is scarcely altered; and of the alterations which Solera has made, only a minority can be attributed to the wish to politicize it in an Italian nationalist sense. Other alterations can probably best be attributed to the qualities of the company of singers for whom the work was originally designed. A strict operatic version of Cortesi's *scenario* would have required two prima donnas for the carefully balanced and juxtaposed roles of Abigaille and Fenena. In the opera, however, Fenena's role becomes a quite secondary one; neither her love affair with the young Israelite Ismaele nor her politico-religious confrontations with the Baalite faction in Babylon has such a central place in the opera as in the ballet.

Given the somewhat heavy, hierarchic flavour of the drama as a whole, it was a characteristic piece of Soleran flair to select the fanatical and vicious Amazonian Abigaille for his prima donna rather than the tender and womanly Fenena. Once he had made this selection, however, and reduced his protagonists to two, he could not fail to observe the need to expand the range of emotions experienced by Abigaille. He provides her with a romantic history that makes her a rival for Ismaele's love, and at the end of the opera smites her down – not dead, as Cortesi and his French models had done, but with one of those strictly theatrical madnesses that enable the heart to feel more tenderly and more morally. Granted that the actual dramatic mechanics by which these additional scenes are introduced are deplorably clumsy, the fact remains that thanks to such episodes of tenderness and pathos Abigaille's becomes a fully rounded characterization: the wild neurosis in which she storms through the greater part of the opera, and which Verdi rightly takes as the key of his musical realization, is more deeply motivated and leads to a more fitting tragic end.

It is on the roles of Nabucco, which Solera barely needed to touch, and Abigaille that *Nabucco* chiefly depends for its theatrical effectiveness. All its moments of high drama, the finales of Acts I and II, the great duet in Act III, derive their potency from the contributions of one or other or both of them. But all this has absolutely nothing to do with the *risorgimento*. To discover how Solera has sounded that note in his libretto one needs to look at his treatment of the national and religious groups, particularly his treatment of the Jews. To clarify this I transcribe from Cortesi's scenario all those passages in which the Jews as a national or religious group are directly involved.

Act I. The Hebrew people, in the midst of whom is Zaccaria, implore divine assistance. Ismaele, followed by a few warriors, brings the desolating news that Nabucco, having stormed the gates of the city, is approaching the temple, slaughtering everyone he encounters on the way. The Hebrews, who have in their power Fenena, Nabucco's daughter, wish to avenge themselves and kill her: she boldly offers her bosom, but is defended by Ismaele, who will not permit the crime. Meanwhile the arrival of Nabucco is announced. Zaccaria encourages the soldiers to defend the holy temple . . .
[Fenena] is close to death when Ismaele saves her a second time. General malediction of the degenerate Israelite, whose sword is broken by Zaccaria . . .

Act II. . . . Zaccaria presents the Hebrews to the regent [Fenena], but seeing Ismaele, they reproach him as the sole cause of their slavery. The despair of Ismaele is pitiable until Fenena declares that in saving her he has saved not a Babylonian, but a Hebrew. She prepares herself, under Zaccaria's instruction, to embrace the worship of the true God. She prostrates herself, and with her all the stupefied Hebrews, and Zaccaria, with the Levite who holds the book of the law, makes her repeat the formula of her conversion ...

Act III. ... Zaccaria ... urges Nabucco to destroy this presumptuous idol. The life of the priest is threatened, likewise the lives of all the Hebrews. Fenena implores mercy for them, and declares that she is a Hebrew herself ...

Act IV. None.

Act V. To the sound of a funeral march Fenena, Ismaele, Zaccaria and their Hebrew companions are led to death. The priest supports Nabucco's daughter, who kneels down before they mount the steps of the temple, and asks his blessing.

Nabucco goes to Zaccaria and unchains him, exclaiming – 'Hebrews, you are all free'; the chains fall from the hands of the captives. 'Babylonians,' the King continues, 'join with me in worshipping the God who has restored my daughter to me.' All prostrate themselves.

All this material is used by Solera. The two comparatively brief incidents of the cursing of Ismaele and Zaccaria's attempt to prevent Nabucco's blasphemy are treated as episodes in the first- and second-act finales respectively. Out of the rest he builds up a series of massive tableau-like scenes, one in each act: in Act I the introductory chorus and Zaccaria's cavatina; in Act II, Zaccaria's prayer and the chorus of Levites; in Act IV, the funeral march, Fenena's prayer and the last finale. In Act III, where Cortesi provides him with no suitable material for such a scene, he writes it himself – the chorus of Hebrew slaves and the prophecy. The latter seems to have been prompted by Verdi himself (see above, p. 106).

Nothing that Solera does in putting words to Cortesi's scenes affects their religious character: Verdi, we may recall, several times refers to the Biblical tone of the libretto. Indeed the four scenes in which the Hebrew people act as protagonist depict far more clearly than a ballet could the progress of a profound religious experience. In the opening scene, they do not merely 'implore divine assistance': they recognize the chastising hand of God in the conquests of Nabucco, they acknowledge their guilt, they repent.

> Ministro dell'ira del Nume sdegnato
> Il rege d'Assiria su noi già piombò ...
> ... Peccammo! ... ma in cielo le nostre preghiere
> Ottengan pietade, perdono al fallir ...

After the defeat and the exile to Babylon, we see the Israelites in spiritual disarray. In Act II they are no longer one people: they are divided into those who, like Zaccaria, remain steadfast in prayer and faith, and the greater number who seek only for a scapegoat on whom to lay the blame for their plight. The Act III scenes added by Solera juxtapose past and future: nostalgia for the Jerusalem that is lost, and a new-found confidence, inspired by Zaccaria's prophetic visions, in God's providential care. In this way they provide a natural transition towards the prayers of martyrdom and psalms of praise of the fourth act. Where then are the *risorgimento* overtones here?

They are to be found in the emphases, the choice of words with which Solera colours the given situations. In Act I, over and above the genuinely religious interpretation of their plight (already mentioned), the Hebrews have an ample capacity for hating and despising the 'foreigners' and the 'barbarians' who cause their sufferings.

> ... Di barbare schiere l'atroce ululato
> Nel santo delubro del Nume tuonò! ...
> ... Non far che i tuoi figli divengano preda
> D'un folle che sprezza l'eterno poter!
> Non far che sul trono davidico sieda
> Fra gl'idoli stolti l'assiro stranier!

Moreover, despite the emphasis on prayer and repentance and faith it is clear that, when it comes to the crunch, Jehovah is expected to be a God of military solutions:

> Tu d'Abramo Iddio possente,
> A pugnar con noi discendi;
> Ne' tuoi servi un soffio accendi
> Che dia morte allo stranier.

In the Act I finale and in Act II, two whole choruses are devoted to the anathema of Ismaele, who in being disloyal to his brothers in race and religion has committed the worst of all crimes.

> Dalle genti sii reietto
> Dei fratelli traditore!
> Il tuo nome maledetto
> Fia l'obbrobrio d'ogni età!
> Oh, fuggite il maledetto,
> Terra e cielo griderà.

Most eloquent of all is the *risorgimento* aspiration in the added scene in Act III, with its hymn to the fatherland,' Va, pensiero sull'ali dorate', and its vision of the end of oppression and servitude:

> Oh, sorgete, angosciati fratelli,
> Sul mio labbro favella il Signor.
> Del futuro nel buio discerno ...
> Ecco rotta l'indegna catena! ...

In 'Va, pensiero' itself, the nationalistic tone is most subdued, most inward, yet probably most deeply efficacious. With its emphasis on the natural beauties of the land, and on the decaying relics of former glory, its appositeness to the Italian condition was especially clear; and its elegiac melancholy surely stirred the hearts of many good Italians who found slogan-like proclamations of 'Death to the Foreigner' unappetizing, and exhortations to faith in God's providence nebulous. I have already quoted in an earlier chapter the words of the 'pale Italian' whom Heine met in Milan in 1828. Fourteen years before *Nabucco* was performed, he could almost be said to have predicted the sensational impact that such a piece might create:

Italy sits amid her ruins, dreaming elegiacally, and if sometimes, at the melody of some song, she awakens of a sudden and springs wildly up, this enthusiasm is not just for the song itself but rather for the old memories and emotions which the song awakened, which Italy always carries in her heart, and which now pour out in a torrent.[1]

For all the potency of the libretto, *Nabucco* achieved its status as the representative opera of the *risorgimento* largely because of its music, because of the eloquence with which Verdi's music matched the Biblical tone of the underlying theme, and the nationalistic and militaristic touches with which Solera had adorned it. Verdi's contribution was perhaps especially fateful in the militaristic episodes. As the libretto originally stood, the principal conflict at the national level would appear to have been between the militaristic Babylonians and the godly Hebrews. Nabucco conquers Jerusalem by armed might: even his priesthood seems to process in goose-step, to judge from 'Noi già sparso abbiamo fama' and 'È di Belo la vendetta'. Finally, however, by penitence, faith and prayer, the triumph is the Hebrews'.

But Verdi must have felt doubtful of his ability to inspire his audiences with operatic prayers, and must have suspected that his Babylonian march tunes would be more likely to send the blood coursing through Italian veins. Whether consciously or unconsciously, he determined to go much farther than Solera in militarizing the Hebrews. The opportunities offered him in the first scene are brilliantly exploited, especially in Zaccaria's cabaletta 'Come notte a sol fulgente'. Here, the whole chorus joins in the High Priest's song at the phrase 'Ne' tuoi servi un soffio accendi Che dia morte': but they break off before 'allo stranier' as if to check an impropriety – 'straniero' was after all a standard term for an Austrian – and thereby give the impropriety the greater emphasis. Where Solera had not provided such opportunities, Verdi created his own, notably in the

453

two episodes in which the Hebrews curse Ismaele, 'Dalle genti sii reietto' in the Act I finale, and 'Il maledetto non ha fratelli' in the Act II chorus of Levites. By the swing and *élan* with which he composes these anathematic incidents he transforms them into veritable recruiting marches in comparison with which the Babylonian march seems mere dulcet swaggering (Ex. 1). Moreover, Verdi imprinted these particular themes more deeply on the audience's consciousness by building the overture largely out of them.

Then, as a final touch, Verdi saw that if he was to sustain this interpretation of the Hebrews throughout the opera, he required something to counterbalance the exclusive emphasis on private

Ex. 1 (a)

(b)

prayer and community hymn-singing in the last acts, and demanded that Solera rewrite the end of Act III. As a result of this, a vision of the destruction of Babylon is offered to the enraptured Hebrews and they are (very properly) able to let fly yet again in the idiom of the military march.

A natural consequence of the prominence of marches and march-like movements in *Nabucco* is the conspicuous brassiness of the orchestral colouring, and especially the prominent place taken by the *banda*. The best-known and subtlest uses of the *banda* convention in Verdi come in the ballroom scenes of later operas like *Rigoletto* and *Un Ballo in Maschera*. In the early operas, too, Verdi may use the *banda* to evoke an atmosphere of courtly revelry, but equally often, and in *Nabucco* exclusively, he uses it in a quite different way, to lend a flavour of popular, indigenous music-making to the marches and processional scenes. Unlike the gorgeously scored operatic marches that Wagner was writing at about the same time, which were part of his Romantic vision of Germany's past, Verdi's bellicose and energetic marches, raucously and brassily scored, seem part of his vision of what was needed there and then, in the Italy of the 1840s.

Not surprisingly, in view of the mood of much of the music, this town-band sonority infects many of the fully orchestrated movements as well. Thus in 'È l'Assiria una regina', the strumming chords are not left to strings alone, but are doubled up by horns, bassoons and cimbasso, while the choral melody is reinforced by trumpets and trombones as well as the woodwinds. Again and again in the opera, in 'Lo vedeste?', in 'Noi già sparso abbiamo fama', even in the final stages of 'Va pensiero', the choral melodies are given this brassy

455

reduplication, this militaristic edge. Nor can one help suspecting that there was a touch of demagoguery in the use made of the brass instruments – with all the popularist and militaristic overtones acquired from town bands and military bands – as the instruments associated with the priesthood of the chosen people and particularly with Zaccaria. There was, of course, an unbroken operatic tradition to legitimize such an orchestral usage; but this does not in any way undermine their peculiarly ambiguous force. It may be noted too how the trumpet ushers in 'D'Egitto là', and punctuates 'Come notte', and flashes out again in the prophecy at 'del Leone di Giuda il furor'. At the very least we may say that it is extraordinarily difficult to disentangle the religious and military motives for the opera's distinctive timbre. And that the timbre was recognized in its own time as distinctive is demonstrated by that epigrammatist who greeted the work on its first appearance in Paris in 1845:

> Vraiment l'affiche est dans son tort,
> En faux on devrait la poursuivre,
> Pourquoi nous annoncer Nabucodonos-or
> Quand c'est Nabucodonos-cuivre?

The emphasis which Solera's libretto places on the nation necessarily prompts Verdi to lay unusual emphasis on the chorus in his composition. Indeed we learn from Muzio that on the strength of *Nabucco* and its sequel *I Lombardi* the Milanese dubbed Verdi 'il padre del coro', a sobriquet which may sound vaguely Handelian – until we recall the music. Then we perceive that the Milanese reverence for Verdi's choruses had very different grounds. He had realized that if the chorus is to stand for a whole people – not only the people involved in the world of illusion within the opera, but the people in the theatre audiences who are to be invited to read into the opera some commentary on their own condition – then the manner of its utterance must be as popularistic as possible. He achieves this ideal by writing for the chorus, whenever it is dramatically congruous to do so, in unison.

The unison chorus was not an unprecedented resource in Italian opera, but never before had it been used so extensively or with such a clear understanding of its demagogic possibilities. In *Nabucco* it is regularly used as an expression of national solidarity. In unison the Levites curse the traitor, Ismaele – 'Il maledetto non ha fratelli'; in unison the Babylonians acclaim Abigaille – 'È l'Assiria una regina'; and most memorably of all, in unison the Hebrews dream nostalgically of their lost homeland – 'Va, pensiero sull'ali dorate'. It is said that when Rossini heard this piece he observed that it was but an aria for chorus. No one has come closer to defining the secret of its magic. Apparently we all sit in an opera house dreaming or willing ourselves into a state of indentification with the serenading tenor, or the heroic baritone, or the lovelorn prima donna. In 'Va, pensiero' the dream has come true. The aria has become, one might say, absolutely democratic, and if the audience felt disposed to join in, no one could legitimately object.

These full-scale unison choruses are supplemented by several movements involving Zaccaria and the Hebrews in which the chorus joins with the solo singer. Zaccaria is nothing more than a Hebrew choragus, endowed certainly with a little more faith and a little more vision than the rest of his countrymen, but exercising no independent dramatic function. And so it is a matter of peculiar dramatic propriety that three times during the course of the opera – in both his cantabile and cabaletta in Act I, and in the scene of the prophecy in Act III – the chorus no longer remains formally in the background, to add strength and colour to transitional or *stretta* sections: it joins in the solo song itself, fully identifying the democratic voice with its sentiments. It is as if Zaccaria had found words that harmonize so precisely with the mood of the Hebrews that they are moved to say 'That is a sentiment we approve of; that is an expression of faith with which we wish to identify ourselves.'

The cantabile 'D'Egitto là sui lidi' provides, incidentally, a good example of that freedom in the handling of the text which Verdi always claimed as the composer's right. Solera's verse for this movement consists of two quatrains with an ABABCDCD rhyme scheme. In composing it, Verdi detached the first two lines –

> Freno al timor! V'affidi
> D'Iddio l'eterna aita

– to provide a kind of motto, and set them as a free recitative-cum-arioso, delivered with all the succulent rhetoric of a preacher announcing his text. On the other hand, the lines of text for the chorus which precede the aria, and which Solera no doubt expected to be composed once in the cadential approach to the cantabile and then forgotten, keep recurring in the later stages of the aria to show the extent to which the chorus is stirred and encouraged by Zaccaria's works. Indeed so prominent does the chorus become that it turns the cantabile into a two-verse movement. The texture of the second of these verses is altogether interesting. While the woodwind semiquaver patterns employ the conventional imagery for idealizing dreams, whether nostalgic or visionary – the figuration may be compared with that in the coda of 'Arch'io dischiuso', and in 'Va, pensiero' at 'O t'ispiri il Signore', to mention only comparable passages in *Nabucco* – the unison chorus doubled by the brass instruments gives the whole passage a popular anthem-like character.

In laying proper emphasis on the way in which Verdi has realized the popularistic and militaristic note in the libretto one should not fail to observe the care he has taken over the genuinely religious aspects of the drama. For example, although the opening chorus is to some extent a lament for the downfall of Israel, it is more important that the nation's plight should be seen as the result of a visitation from a wrathful God. The idiom is therefore based not on lugubrious cantilena, but on the instrumental evocation of tempest, with tremolos and chromatic scales and sudden streaks of high strings and flutes. That the latter idea is intended specifically as a musical symbol of the smiting hand of God is suggested by its still more emphatic employment in the accompaniment figuration of 'Come notte al sol fulgente', the cabaletta with which the scene ends (Ex. 2).

Ex. 2 (a)

(b)

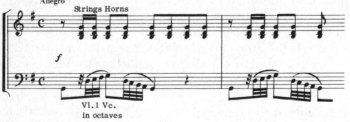

Altogether the religious symbolism in the music is as remarkable as the *risorgimento* symbolism. Divine grace hovers over the figure of the expiring Abigaille in the form of a florid flute obbligato; and lest its meaning should not be absolutely clear, it is spelt out by the chorus: 'Solleva Iddio l'afflitto'. Comparable flute figurations in the same key of E major accompany the prayer of the virgins in Act I, though here instead of hovering they float up, incense-like. The solitariness of Zaccaria in Israel's darkest hour, when his undiminished faith shines like the solitary lamp that illuminates the stage scene, is expressed with extraordinary vividness in a hymnic cantabile, 'Tu sul labbro dei veggenti', accompanied at first by a single cello.

Nabucco, then, while it depends as much as any other Verdi opera upon the passions and the wills of its individual characters for its theatrical excitement and vitality, has a further quality which surely accounts for its unique popularity in the 1840s. The nations and the faiths which have formed these individuals and which shape their destiny during the course of the drama are not, as is usually the case, relegated to a sketchy or misty background. They share the centre of the stage; they are given tangible substance, and they are lent eloquence by Solera's verses and especially by Verdi's music. The nation to which he owes his loyalty and the faith for which he is prepared to die are shown to be the most vital factors in the individual's experience of life. Albeit in a different medium from what Mazzini had anticipated, *Nabucco* surely satisfied the philosopher's quest for a type of drama which 'forms a brotherhood between earth and heaven ... and gives to human liberty the consecration of God'.

21

Verdi and French Romanticism – *Ernani*

The position which Verdi had won in the Italian theatre with *Nabucco* and its successor *I Lombardi alla Prima Crociata* was an illustrious one. But by the summer of 1843 he was already weary of the massive statuesque dramatic idiom of these operas, and looked forward to his Venetian commission as an opportunity to try something 'quite distinct from *Nabucco* and *Crociata* ... very fiery, packed with action, and concise'.[1]

Ernani does indeed mark a new departure for Verdi, a second turning-point in his operatic career. And in view of the extraordinary affection felt by Italians for *Nabucco*, in view of the incomparable way in which it voiced the aspirations and nostalgias of its period, it is perhaps understandable that this new departure was not universally welcomed. It was widely felt, reported the Venetian newspaper *Il Gondoliere* at the time of the production of *Attila*, that *Ernani* had marked 'the first phase of Verdi's decadence', from which there was as yet no sign of a recovery.[2] Alberto Mazzucato, a contemporary of Verdi's and one of his collaborators on the Requiem for Rossini, seems to have been expressing the same idea in his diary for 6 February 1871: '... Verdi awoke great surprise in me with his *Nabucco* and *I Lombardi*. I saw him then descend to popular passions in *Ernani*, *Il Trovatore*, etc. ...'[3]

If such reactions are hardly warranted by the music of the new opera, they are perhaps intelligible when we recall the dual nature of Italian Romanticism. For in *Ernani* Verdi was turning his back on the kind of theme preferred by so many of the choicest spirits of the *risorgimento*, in which the dramatic weight is placed on the collective and the national, on the institutions of state, both sacred and secular. His central concerns here are those matters which, he instinctively felt, were more genuinely and intrinsically theatrical – rapidity, violence and sensation in the action, and idiosyncratic extremes of passion in the characters. In a word, Verdi abandoned the distinctive Italian kind of Romanticism, the Romanticism of Church and state, in favour of a Romanticism more lurid in hue and more grotesque in form, a Romanticism fundamentally French. And it was this that, with some important exceptions like *Macbeth* and *Luisa Miller*, set the tone of his operas for the next ten years, up to and including *Il Trovatore*.

When a man is already devoted to Shakespeare, and when he is soon to learn to admire Schiller, his long obsession with the ridiculous and very dreadful plays of Victor Hugo and his imitators may at first sight seem inexplicable. There, are, however, two very good reasons for the fact that Verdi, like Bellini and Donizetti before him, felt a congeniality in the romantic dramas of early-nineteenth-century France so deep-rooted that not even experience of the immeasurably greater dramatic art of Shakespeare or Schiller could shake it.

One was what might be described as the habit of deference. For well over a hundred years Italy had been in the habit of looking to France as the source of all that was most vital in intellectual and cultural life. French thought and French taste had been exemplary for the Italians, and a habit that had been formed in the reign of Louis XIV and had not wanted for sustenance at any time up to the Napoleonic era was not to be quickly abandoned. The prestige of French civilization was undiminished, even at a time when the actuality on which that prestige was based had become a debased and tawdry thing.

No branch of French civilization enjoyed a more exaggerated esteem in Italy than the drama. After the Restoration the spoken theatre appears to have subsisted very largely on translations of French plays. It was in French adaptations that Shakespeare first became familiar to Italian audiences. And it was to French sources that librettists habitually turned in their search for subjects for new operas, even in the genres in which Italy had long been regarded as supreme. The pattern of such classical, Enlightenment tragedies as continued to be composed was no longer Metastasio but Voltaire, as in Rossini's *Semiramide*, or Bellini's *Zaira*. The presiding genius of the *opera buffa* and its sentimental sister the *opera semi-seria* was no longer Goldoni but Augustin-Eugène Scribe, whose unproblematic and not very funny 'well-made plays' were the source of such pieces as Donizetti's *L'Elisir d'Amore* or Bellini's *La Sonnambula*.

But the second reason for the Italian fondness for French drama is the more material one. The types of play most often appropriated by opera composers were, as a matter of fact, not the neo-classical tragedies, nor yet the light comedies. They were the melodramas of Guilbert de Pixérécourt and his imitators, and the Romantic dramas of Hugo and Dumas *père*, and they owed this fate to the fact that they were uniquely fitted for such adaptation: that they were, in Hanslick's words, 'less tragedies against which music would do violence, than librettos which have not yet been composed'.[4]

The melodrama was the most vital and widely enjoyed dramatic form in Napoleonic France. In the hands of Pixérécourt, 'le Corneille des boulevards', it rapidly became what Charles Nodier described as an 'honest picture of the world which society has created for us, and the only popular tragedy fitting for our era'. Pixérécourt's formula for success was to take a small group of sharply diversified figures, 'a hero, a heroine, a villain, a clown', and to weave round them a plot that was fast-moving, packed with violent, astonishing and farcical incidents, periodically wrought into situations of seat-gripping suspence, and liberally garnished with the horrific. As the century wore on and the technical resources of the theatres developed, a prominent part was found for the spectacular element: for stage designs and lighting effects increasingly sophisticated, surprising, and 'Romantic'.

Hugo's *Hernani*

It was this tradition that Hugo built on in attempting to establish a new tradition of Romantic verse drama. Though the times had become more settled and prosaic, his perfervid imagination was still obsessed with the violent, the picturesque, the contrary. Indeed passages of the famous preface to *Cromwell*, written in 1827, read almost like an intellectual's rationalization of the principles of Pixérécourt:

... What would the Romantic drama do? It would compress and mingle artistically together ... two types of pleasure. Every moment it would make the audience pass from seriousness to laughter, from farcical excitation to heart-rending emotions, *from the grave to the sweet, from the pleasant to the severe*. For ... drama is the grotesque together with the sublime, the soul within the body, it is a tragedy within a comedy. Can it not be seen that resting yourself thus from one impression by another, sharpening the tragic little by little on the comic, the gay on the terrible, even if necessary introducing the fascinations of the opera, these performances, while offering only one piece, would be worth all the others.

Unhappily Hugo's genius lacked the kinds of control that might have created a great dramatic art out of such a programme. He was incapable of devising stories that moved plausibly forward, without resorting to a great deal of meretricious machinery, disguises, improbable coincidences, shuffling of characters into and out of secret hiding-places and so on. Nor did he find it easy to sustain the tension of a dramatic encounter by the intrinsic quality of his dialogues. More often this dramatic essential is superimposed upon the scene from without, by, for example, planting a character to overhear the dialogue from a place of hiding, as Don Carlos overhears the lovers in Act I of *Hernani*, or the conspirators in Act IV, so that the dramatic excitement, such as it is, really consists in the audience's wondering whether and at what stage the concealed person is going to step out and confound those that he overhears. Finally, Hugo was quite incapable of the art of dramatic characterization. Though he understood that the gay and the terrible, the grotesque and the sublime might all be accommodated in a really vital kind of drama, his manner of doing this was scarcely more refined than it had been in the popular melodramas. He tended either to embody these different qualities in different characters, so that one is all unmitigated grotesque, another all uncompromising sublimity; or he created still more unlikely figures compounded of contrasting characteristics without troubling to demonstrate the relationship between them, or the relevance of one to the other. In the Don Carlos of Act IV of *Hernani*, who stands before the tomb of Charlemagne pondering the deepest questions of Empire and Papacy, we simply do not recognize the sardonic wit and unprincipled opportunist of the early acts of the play. As Rigoletto was to exclaim in Verdi's next Hugo opera, 'Ma in altro uomo qui mi cangio!'

With those qualities that have generally been regarded as crucial to good spoken drama – the ability to characterize, to devise plots that develop plausibly out of the interaction of character and situation, to lend the dialogues and soliloquies, however beautiful they may be, a certain tension or dynamic that bears upon the course of the drama – Hugo appears to have been quite unconcerned. His real interests were eloquence and spectacle, beautiful poetry and picturesque tableaux.

Indeed it is a general rule of Hugo's dramatic style, perhaps more strikingly exemplified in *Hernani* than anywhere, that the traditional relationship between poetry and drama is reversed. It is not the purpose of the poetry to develop or illuminate the dramatic issue; it is the purpose of the drama to contrive situations in which the characters can launch themselves into poetic speeches. Often these tirades are only tangentially relevant to the dramatic issue, and normally they are quite disproportionate to the dramatic purpose. But in them Hugo's breathtaking eloquence is brought to bear upon each of the themes which his plays touch upon: in *Hernani*, the emotional conditions of love, jealousy and hate, the moral issues attaching to the concept of honour, the philosophy of politics and society. The perplexing thing is that Hugo was manifestly aware of the awkwardness with which these effusions fit into the dramatic action. There is an ironic, sometimes even witty self-consciousness about the way in which he resumes the dramatic thread after the engulfing floods of his verse have at last subsided. In 1.3 Don Ruy Gomez discovers two men, Hernani and Don Carlos, in the room of his bride-to-be Doña Sol. Without so much as questioning anyone he breaks into a speech of some sixty lines, lamenting the decadence of the old ideal of honour:

> Des hommes chez ma nièce à cette heure de nuit!
> Venez tous! cela vaut la lumière et le bruit ...
> Quand nous avions le Cid et Bernard, ces géants
> De l'Espagne et du monde allaient par les Castilles
> Honorant les vieillards et protégeant les filles ...

to the inevitable conclusion –

> Écuyers! écuyers! à mon aide!
> Ma hache, mon poignard, ma dague de Tolède!
> Et suivez-moi tous deux!

Don Carlos replies,

> Duc, ce n'est pas d'abord
> De cela qu'il s'agit. Il s'agit de la mort
> De Maximilian, empereur d'Allemagne,

and the play creaks into motion once more.

The other cornerstone of Hugo's dramatic art is the tableau of confrontation, brought about not by an inevitable ravelling of the intrigue, nor by the momentum and impulse of character, but by *coups de théâtre* of the most palpably melodramatic kind. Act IV of *Hernani* is exemplary in this respect. Don Carlos, a favourite candidate for election as Holy Roman Emperor, has come to the vaults where Charlemagne is buried, in order to uncover a conspiracy against his candidature. Hidden in Charlemagne's tomb he watches the conspirators gather, and overhears their discussion. Then, as the threefold firing of cannon signals his election, he emerges from the tomb to denounce them. A moment later there is a brilliant transformation as the gates of the vault are thrown open, and torch-bearing soldiers pour in upon the gloomy scene. They are followed by the *cortèges* of the electors, come to acclaim

> Charles! roi des Romains,
> Majestée très sacrée, empereur! dans vos mains

Verdi and French Romanticism — *Ernani*

Le monde est maintenant, car vous avez l'Empire.

In such scenes as this one again senses a disharmony between Hugo's intention and the medium he has chosen to work in. For beautiful verse can no more match such crowd scenes, *coups de théâtre*, and sumptuous tableaux as these than it can supply the place of dramatically motivated dialogue in the more intimate scenes. In the one instance, mere verse lacks the grandiloquence to fill the theatrical frame; in the other it rather floods the theatrical frame with emotional or philosophical effusion. But it is precisely Hugo's bungling aspirations to a kind of *Gesamtkunstwerk* in which scenes of spectacle and the outpourings of emotion are strung out along and prompted by a chain of rapid, violent, and none-too-rational incidents that make such a play as *Hernani* so resemble a monstrously inflated opera libretto. It will be worth examining Act I of *Hernani* in some detail, even though it became fused together with Act II in Piave's libretto, to show how very closely it does approach an operatic pattern.

The play begins melodramatically enough when, to the consternation of the chambermaid, Don Carlos, heavily disguised, emerges from a secret door into Doña Sol's bedchamber. A very rapid staccato exchange of questions and answers, threats and submissions serves as a dramatic exposition, at the end of which Don Carlos is secreted in a cupboard to eavesdrop on the conversation of Doña Sol and her lover, the bandit Hernani, who now enter. The first of the lyrical 'numbers' follows, a love duet in verses:

> Doña Sol! Ah! c'est vous que je vous
> Enfin! et cette voix qui parle est votre voix!
> Pourquoi le sort mit-il mes jours si loins de vôtres?
> J'ai tant besoin de vous pour oublier les autres ...

Later the mood changes. Hernani expresses his contempt for the old uncle Don Ruy Gomez de Silva, to whom Doña Sol is betrothed, and his hatred for Don Carlos, son of the king who executed his father; and the scene ends with an evocation of the life of a bandit:

> Proscrits dont le bourreau sait d'avance les noms,
> Gens dont jamais le fer ni le coeur ne s'émousse,
> Ayant tous quelque sang à venger qui les pousse?

Each of the emotional states through which Hernani passes is the subject of a set-speech of generous proportions which acquires a certain theatrical sense of expectation only from the fact that we suppose that Don Carlos might at any moment step from his hiding-place. When at last he does, it is to good effect:

465

> Quand auriez-vous fini de conter votre histoire?
> Croyez-vous donc qu'on soit à l'aise en cette armoire?

He declares himself a rival for the love of Doña Sol, and despite the protests of the lady the two men prepare to fight a duel. It is at this point that Don Ruy Gomez returns and, discovering the men in Doña Sol's room, delivers his monologue on honour. As we have seen, Don Carlos deflates Gomez's passion as deliciously as he had Hernani's, and then, in the *coup de théâtre* that sets up the Act I tableau, reveals himself as the king. At this climactic moment, the king, the grandee, the bandit, and the woman loved by all three stand confronting one another. But it is perhaps an inevitable consequence of the disguises, the pretences and the surprises by which the confrontation has been brought about that they really have nothing to say to one another. Hugo's effect is a picturesque rather than a dramatic one, and he is incapable of continuing with it until he has broken it down into its constituent parts. Hernani and Doña Sol are mute for several minutes while Don Carlos and Don Ruy Gomez discuss the politics of the Holy Roman Empire. Then Don Carlos and Don Ruy Gomez are silent in turn while Doña Sol and Hernani plot their elopement. Well might Hugo later express envy at Verdi's ability to have all the characters in the *Rigoletto* quartet speaking at once. The act ends with a final solo scene in which Hernani dedicates himself to the task of hunting down and destroying Don Carlos:

> ... Va devant, je te suis. Ma vengeance qui veille
> Avec moi toujours marche et me parle à l'oreille.
> Va! je suis là, j'épie et j'écoute, et sans bruit
> Mon pas cherche ton pas et le presse et le suit!
> Le jour tu ne pourras, ô roi, tournez la tête
> Sans me voir immobile et sombre dans ta fête;
> La nuit tu ne pourras tourner les yeux, ô roi,
> Sans voir mes yeux ardents luire derrière toi!

The libretto

From the very nature of Hugo's play it followed that its adaptation as an opera was a relatively simple matter, attended by none of the problems with which Verdi had to wrestle when he attempted to work with real spoken dramas like *Macbeth* or *Kabale und Liebe*. The clarity with which, when Mocenigo first suggested the subject, Verdi apprehended the opera latent within it emerges from the letter he wrote on 5 September 1843:

... Oh! if we could only do *Hernani*, how marvellous that would be! ... Signor Piave has great facility in versifying, and in *Hernani* he would only need to condense and tighten up; the action is all ready-made ... Tomorrow I will write at length to Signor Piave setting out all the scenes of *Hernani* that seem to me suitable. I have already seen that all of Act I can be condensed into a magnificent introduction ... The second act could be made from the fourth act of the French play. And the third act finish with the magnificent terzetto in which Ernani dies.[5]

A few weeks later, when work on the libretto had already begun, he was impressing upon Piave the fact that 'in the last two [acts], the closer we keep to Hugo, the greater will be the effect ... Be brief and fiery.'[6] Verdi had perceived in *Hernani* the kind of libretto that he had not had the chance of setting since the days of the much-botched *Oberto*. It was a play of fast-moving, incident-packed 'recitatives', a play whose numerous soliloquies and incidental effusions of sentiment offered him the opportunity to deepen his skill of characterization, a play whose every act culminated in exactly the kind of confrontation that cried out to be translated into the language of the operatic ensemble.

Fast-moving, loaded with self-revelatory solos and tingling clashes of character, Piave's *Ernani* proved to be a libretto rather more typical of Italian opera of the 1830s and 1840s than either *Nabucco* or *I Lombardi* had been. No doubt Verdi's positive eagerness to compose something that was in a sense of reversion to type, a move back into the mainstream conventions of the period, was due precisely to the feeling that neither of his previous operas had really given him the chance to develop those skills that were fundamental for a composer of opera, the characterization of the individual, and the animated and yet harmonious fashioning of the dramatic ensemble. In *Nabucco*, only a small minority of the solo movements – Abigaille's 'Anch'io dischiuso' and perhaps Nabucco's 'Dio di Giuda' – had been primarily concerned with expressing unique and individual passions; and only the tiny terzettino had been an ensemble structure more elaborate than a duet and more fleet than a grand finale. In *Ernani* the vitality of the whole opera was going to depend upon Verdi's ability to compose such movements.

But this general rule must at once be qualified. For as in *Nabucco* and *I Lombardi* Verdi's characterizing skills and his feeling for ensemble had provided the idiom of '*risorgimento* opera' with movement and variety, so conversely in *Ernani* the hectic, egocentric passions of French Romanticism were sometimes to be

467

suspended to allow the contemplation of national, communal concerns. In this respect, too, *Ernani* set the pattern for the later operas of the 1840s. It is wholly characteristic of Verdi's dramatic style at this period that what one might call *risorgimento* episodes are let into the texture of subjects which really have no bearing on the *risorgimento* whatever.

In *Ernani* it is the third act that returns to the *Nabucco* manner: the act set in the vaults by Charlemagne's tomb. The plot and structure of this act stay very close to Hugo's original. It is easy to see in some of the music ideas that owe much to the play: the care Verdi takes to evoke atmosphere – particularly with the sepulchral solemnity of the prelude, and the furtive fragments of march music to which the conspirators assemble – the way in which his music momentarily becomes incidental, reduced to the merest symbols of astonishment and pageantry, during the spectacular *coup de théâtre* of Carlos's appearance and the entry of the electors. Nevertheless this is the one scene where Verdi and Piave have really enlarged the scope of the drama, and made it the vehicle of ideas that were no part of Hugo's purpose.

Gerhartz, whose comments on *Ernani* are as illuminating as anything in his book,[7] has written exhaustively on Hugo's inability to give plausible poetic form to this fourth act. One of Hugo's difficulties was to sustain the excitement of the gathering of the conspirators in IV.3 and to lead it to an appropriate climax at the end of the scene. In fact he could not do this in verse. Much of the most atmospheric material is visually conceived and can only be contained in the stage directions; and at the climax of the scene, the inadequacy of language to provide the kind of theatrical sensationalism that Hugo was seeking is all too apparent.

PREMIER CONJURÉ: ...Jurons
    De frapper tour à tour et sans nous y soustraire
    Carlos qui doit mourir.
TOUS (*tirant leurs épées*):   Jurons!
LE DUC DE GOTHA (*au premier conjuré*): Sur quoi mon frère?
DON RUY GOMEZ (*retourne son épée, la prend par la pointe et l'élève au-dessus de sa tête*): Jurons sur cette croix!
TOUS (*élevons leurs épées*): Qu'il meure impénitent!
    (*On entend un coup de canon éloigné. Tous s'arrêtent en silence. – La porte du tombeau s'entr'ouvre. Don Carlos paraît sur le seuil. Pâle, il écoute. – Un second coup. – Un troisième coup. – Il ouvre tout à fait la porte du tombeau, mais sans faire un pas, debout et immobile sur le seuil.*)

SCÈNE IV

DON CARLOS: Messieurs, allez plus loin! L'empereur vous entend.
(*Tous les flambeaux s'éteignent à la fois. – Profond silence. – Il fait un pas dans les ténèbres, si épaisses qu'on y distingue à peine les conjurés muets et immobiles.*)

Verdi's medium enabled him to do naturally what Hugo strove to do in vain, sustaining the impetus of the scene on slowly marching rhythms, building up its tension by the development of its rhythmic and melodic figures and by the thickening of the textures, and above all bringing it to a climax not in a nasty oath, but in a choral movement in which the common idealism of the conspirators is expressed.

There was little in Hugo's play on which to build such a movement, for there the discussion of the conspirators is innocent of either idealism or policy:

PREMIER CONJURÉ: Mort à lui!
LE DUC DE GOTHA: Qu'il meure!
TOUS: Qu'on l'immole!
DON JUAN DE HARO: Son père est allemand.
LE DUC DE LUTZELBOURG: Sa mère est espagnole.
LE DUC DE GOTHA: Il n'est plus espagnol et n'est pas allemand.
Mort! . . .
PREMIER CONJURÉ: S'il a le Saint-Empire, il devient, quel qu'il soit,
Très auguste, et Dieu seul peut le toucher du doigt!
LE DUC DE GOTHA: Le plus sûr, c'est qu'avant d'être auguste, il expire.

But neither were Piave or Verdi much interested in the psychological or philosophical motivation of the conspirators. At least Piave took very little care over the plausibility of his lines from that point of view. What is one to make of the 'Lion of Castile' as an heraldic emblem of patriotic Spain? Why should being 'all one single family' be an issue among the conspirators, who belong to an already united kingdom? Why should Piave have grubbed around in Spanish history books to discover that Don Carlos was at first resented by the Spaniards, because it was feared that he would impose on them an alien culture a fact quite irrelevant to the plot of play and opera alike? The answer to all these questions is that he has temporarily abandoned his central dramatic theme: that the chorus 'Si ridesti il Leon di Castiglia' has little or nothing to do with *Ernani*, but is a disguised *risorgimento* ode. By providing substitutions of the kind which *ottocento* audiences were so adept at, perhaps on the following lines –

Si ridesti il Leon di San Marco,
E d'Italia ogni monte, ogni lito

469

Eco formi al tremendo ruggito
Come un dì contro gli Unni oppressor etc. ....

– we can transform it into an Italian patriotic hymn, exalted and belligerent enough for Giuseppe Mameli to have been proud of. Verdi has set it in a manner obviously modelled on the patriotic choruses of *Nabucco*. The marching unison theme recalls the *profezia*, while the resplendent orchestral elaboration of the reprise, where the melody blazes out on trumpets and trombones, does homage to 'Va, pensiero sull'ali dorate'.

This episode apart, the dramatic and musical world of *Ernani* is far removed from that of *Nabucco*. Its impassioned individualism offered Verdi the opportunity to explore the expressive resources of his art with more finesse, to avail himself of shades of expressive differentiation that had not previously been required. Emotions stranger and more violent than those he had previously encountered filled the dramatic canvas more full.

That these passions never become anarchic, never undermine the firm structure of the plot, is due to the fact that they all centre upon Doña Sol – Elvira, as she becomes in the libretto. If, as seems probable, Verdi felt the need at this stage of his career to refine his art of characterization, it must have constituted a strong part of the appeal of Hugo's play that three men so different in character and background as Hernani, Don Carlos, and Don Ruy Gomez de Silva should all be in love with the same woman. It was no longer – as it had been with Ismaele and Fenena, or Oronte and Giselda – merely a matter of romantic love. In Hernani's case, romantic love was given a peculiar intensity and anguish and precariousness from the fact that he was an outlaw, forever obliged to retreat into a shadowy and disreputable background:

> Ange! ah! dans cet instant
> Où la mort vient peut-être, où s'approche dans l'ombre
> Un sombre dénoûement pour un destin bien sombre,
> Je le déclare, proscrit, traînant au flanc
> Un souci profond, né dans un berceau sanglant,
> Si noir que soit le deuil qui s'épand sur ma vie,
> Je suis un homme heureux, et je veux qu'on m'envie,
> Car vous m'avez aimé! car vous me l'avez dit!
> Car vous avez tout bas béni mon front maudit! (II.4)

With Don Carlos, on the other hand, a sardonic, opportunist, and wholly unsentimental absolute monarch, romantic love is not a noble passion, but a gratification he demands as by right:

> Eh bien, que vous m'aimiez ou non, cela n'importe!

> Vous viendrez, et ma main plus que la vôtre est forte.
> Vous viendrez! je vous veux! Pardieu, nous verrons bien
> Si je suis roi d'Espagne et des Indes pour rien! (II.2)

Silva's romantic love is different again, a kind of eroticized paternalism, severe and possessive, and unattractively mixed up with his addled nostalgia for honour and propriety.

> Hélas! quand un vieillard aime, il faut l'épargner.
> Le coeur est toujours jeune, et peut toujours saigner.
> Oh! mon amour n'est point comme un jouet de verre
> Qui brille et tremble; oh! non, c'est un amour sévère,
> Profond, solide, sûr, paternel, amical,
> De bois de chêne, ainsi que mon fauteuil ducal.

Fascinated as Verdi must have been by the scope which this triad of lovers offered, his collaborator Piave could not fail to observe that the unprincipled philandering of Don Carlos would be more than likely to provoke censorial wrath, and set about the task of 'writing the part ... in such a way as to cause no political affront, and yet preserve all its vigour and interest'.* Piave's execution of this task is in principle admirable, for he harmonizes and relates the two distinct functions which Don Carlos serves – as lover and as man of destiny – in a way which Hugo had not attempted. In the first two acts of the opera, Carlo, quite lacking in the self-dramatization and self-pity of Ernani and Silva, becomes the most tender of the lovers:

> Da quel dì che t'ho veduta
> Bella come un primo amore,
> La mia pace fu perduta,
> Tuo fu il palpito del core.
> Cedi, Elvira, a' voti miei;
> Puro amor, da te desio;
> Gioia e vita esser tu dêi
> Del tuo amante, del tuo re.

Even when, at the end of Act II, he takes away Elvira as a hostage against Silva's good faith, he is engrossed not in the lewd possibilities which the occasion affords –

> Par les saints! l'idée est triomphante!
> Il faudre bien enfin s'adoucir, mon infante!

but in lovingly and honourably putting her troubled mind at rest:

> Vieni meco, sol di rose
> Intrecciar ti vo' la vita;
> Vieni meco, ore penose
> Per te il tempo non avrà ...

---

* Cf. Mocenigo's letter to the censor, 23 October 1843: above, p. 126.

Well before the Aachen scene, then, we know that Don Carlo is a character of serious worth, even if Piave has not been able to mitigate the adventitiousness of the situations in which he is landed. The final admirable touch in the portrait is to make his Act III aria not merely an address to Charlemagne, or a disquisition on political philosophy unrelated to what has happened in the previous acts, but, before that, a renunciation of the fond passions of his youth:

> Oh de' verd'anni miei
> Sogni e bugiarde larve,
> Se troppo vi credei
> L'incanto ora disparve.
> S'ora chiamato sono
> Al più sublime trono
> Della virtù com'aquila
> Sui vanni m'alzerò
> E vincitor de' secoli
> Il nome mio farò.

The music

A discussion of the new musical resources which Verdi developed in composing *Ernani* cannot begin better than by citing Budden's words on the vocal typification.

This is the opera in which Verdi defines most clearly his male vocal archetypes: the granite-like, monochrome bass (Silva) older than the roots of his family pride; the heroic tenor, lyrical, ardent, despairing (Ernani); and partaking of both natures, now zephyr, now hurricane, the Verdi baritone (Carlo), the greatest vehicle of power in Italian opera.[8]

Nothing in the opera is more impressive than the way in which Verdi worked out the consequences of his discovery of these archetypes. And that it was a discovery, not a habit, is clear from the fact that Verdi apparently started work on the opera supposing that the cast would be as proposed by Brenna in September 1843 – Ernani, alto; Don Carlo, tenor; Don Rui de Silva, baritone; Don Riccardo, *basso profondo* (cf. above, p. 123). Only after weeks of thought and preparatory work did he come to the immovable certainty that, to make anything of the new opportunities for characterization which Hugo's play offered, he must avail himself of the inherent character, colour, agility and expressiveness of the three types of male voice.

Because of the change which Piave made in the role, a special interest attaches to the musical interpretation which Verdi gives

Carlo. And one does not need to read far through the score before perceiving that he has positively revelled in the opportunities he has been offered. The businesslike routine of a recitative scena is suspended by spasms of yearning tenderness whenever Carlo's thoughts turn to Elvira (Ex. 1) and the expression of love with which

Ex. 1

the Act I duet begins surpasses those of both his rivals in warmth and eloquence. The little flurries of words and the woodwind colouring added at the phrase-ends are not just the formal embellishments of key words, as they had been in Ernani's 'Come rugiada al cespite': they are part of a real, dramatically alive ceremony of love-making, rhetorically emphasizing Carlo's own 'palpito del cor', suggesting a caressing eagerness at 'puro amor da te desio'. Even the harmony contributes to the vividness of the song, marking a clear shift of stance at 'Cedi, Elvira', and chromatically intensifying the reprise.

Verdi follows Piave too in the Act III aria 'Oh de' verd'anni miei', linking the idealistic grandiloquence of the king with the private sorrows of the spurned lover by the idea of renunciation. As far as

473

the coda ('E vincitor de' secoli') the vocal melody proceeds like a normal cantabile, delicate and emotional in tone. Its mood of renunciation, the sense that those passions over which it muses are withering and falling away, derives from the accompaniment, a dryly scored, skeletal distortion of the kind of figuration that might have been expected to accompany such a theme. As Carlo raises himself above the turmoil of selfish passion in which his rivals are to perish, a new theme sounds, massively thickened up by the orchestra, and punctuated by imperious brass rhythms. There is no longer any tenderly floating coloratura, for Carlo has become a grave and formidable man. Even the conventional, indeed virtually obligatory, cadenza is discarded: instead we hear a succession of orchestral musings over the aspirational coda theme.

Not less admirable is the musical characterization of Silva. When we hear him first at the start of the Act I finale in a moment of deep grief we are most impressed by the dragging weariness of the music, and, frankly, by the suspicion that he suffers from a senile garrulousness that might well have been imitated from Hugo. But as the story progresses, as affronted pride, anger and hatred increasingly dominate his thoughts, his music becomes harder and more rigid in style. He tends to express himself within a narrow range of notes, in reiterated melodic and rhythmic formulae that are as stiffly obsessive as his sense of honour (Ex. 2).

Ex. 2

Verdi's fascination with this new expressive resource, his recognition that musical characterization was not just a formal duty of conscientiousness but an invaluable means of dramatic expression, is best shown in the *gran scena ed aria* of Don Carlo in Act II. Although this movement is strictly a solo for Carlo, Verdi gives it an extra, characterizing dimension by involving Silva in it. The cantabile is primarily concerned with expressing Carlo's anger at what he regards as Silva's dereliction of loyal duty; and the musical imagery is unmistakable. While Carlo outwardly sustains a magisterial dignity, the figuration of the accompanying strings evokes the agitation of rage by which he is really moved. But Silva too has his conception of honour and is not to be intimidated. Instead of waiting until Carlo's aria is over before expressing this, Verdi introduces Silva into the coda where the stiff and repetitive phrases that express his granite immobility act as a foil to Carlo's massive soaring lines.

The hero and heroine of a Romantic love story are by their very nature more stereotyped figures, and their music shows little sign of that singularity of conception found with Carlo's or Silva's. But what Verdi has very obviously done with Ernani and Elvira is to compose music for them which expresses an exceptional degree of sensibility, music more nervously and mercurially emotional than that he had written in his earlier operas. This quality is present from the start of Ernani's first recitative, where we hear a quite distinctive musical intensification of, in turn, his cordial regard for his companions – the courtesy flourish on 'a tanto amor mercé' – the cares that grieve him – in the throbbing chords at 'del mio cor gli affanni' – and the loneliness and desolation he fears – in the long, unaccompanied *adagio* phrase into the cadence. Indeed throughout the opera it is in the recitatives, the scenas and the transitions that this quality is most evident: in the transition into the duet 'Ah morir potessi adesso', for example, and most especially in the scena preceding the terzetto finale.

In this wonderful scene every thought, every mood taken over from Hugo's play is brought to a climacteric of vividness and beauty. If the agitated passages are in a fundamentally conventional style, and if much of the dramatic thrill is acquired by the device of the notes of the horn, drawing ever nearer to culminate in a restatement of the pledge motif from Act II, no admiration can be too high for the sensibility and resource which Verdi brings to the love music. It comprises not a formal duet but a series of exquisite fragments as fluctuating as Ernani's and Elvira's imaginings, and as evanescent as their happiness. Ernani's first arioso acquires a kind of portentous intensity from the fact that it, alone of all the vocal themes in the opera, has been played in an extended form in the prelude. But it has not progressed further than two phrases when Elvira floats deliciously in upon Ernani's reverie with a florid recitative, supported by richly remote harmonies. The first part of the scene culminates in an ecstatic unison cantabile in that idiom of 'total melody' – an idiom which was to become increasingly important in Verdi's later music – in which all subordinate elements are dissolved in a shimmering of harmony. But again after a single phrase the lyrical outpouring is cut short by the first sound of Silva's still-distant horn.

Even after the horn has been heard, Verdi continues to write music of a rare sensibility: Elvira, intoxicated with bliss, still muses ethereally; silence and stillness are magically conveyed in the barely accompanied phrases, suspended between recitative and song, and the delicate string harmonies of 'Tutto ora tace d'intorno' (Ex. 3).

This quality of intense sensibility is suggested in some of their formal lyrical music, too, particularly perhaps where one might least expect it – in the cabalettas of their *arie di sortita*. Ernani's makes use of an extraordinary throbbing syncopated accompaniment, perhaps inspired by the giddy figurations of Amina's closing cabaletta in *La Sonnambula* and later adapted for the love duet in Act I of *Luisa Miller*, and is tossed hither and thither by the profusion of *stentato* and *allargando* and *a tempo* and *brillante* markings. Elvira's is remarkable for the way in which suppressed emotions tend to burst forth. The energy of her detestation of Silva is held in check for several proudly tossing phrases, only to erupt in a sudden electrifying *forte* cadence: the swing of the music, gathering impetus with the brilliant coloratura of 'Vola, o tempo', is unpredictably suspended as she is overwhelmed by emotions of yearning. There is nothing in Piave's text to suggest this. It is simply a sign of the care Verdi was now taking to get inside his characters, of the quest to make richly emotional individuals of every one of them.

Given a dramatic theme in which scenes of confrontation play so prominent a role, and given Verdi's interest in exploring the art of musical characterization, a particular interest attaches to the ensemble movements of *Ernani*. There is no doubt that several of them reflect in an unusual way the impact of Hugo on Verdi's imagination. It is notable for example that in such a movement as the Carlo–Elvira duet in Act I the characters are so obsessed with their passions, so completely egocentric, that to combine them in a harmonious formal movement requires more cunning than Verdi yet has. As has already been suggested, Carlo's solo verse 'Da quel dì che t'ho veduta' is as beautiful and sincere a song as lover ever sang; but it receives scant reward from the lady to whom it is addressed. Elvira is the very embodiment of pride and scorn. The changes of key and orchestral texture shatter the mood Carlo had so lovingly created: where his phrases had reached up in gentle arches, hers sweep down in angrily shaking rhythms (Ex. 4). The extremity of the contrast makes the actual duet sections a problem: both singers are too committed to the irreconcilable for the coda really to work. What happens is that the accompaniment figuration compromises, and Elvira quite abandons the manner of her solo verse in order to be harmonized with what is

476

Ex. 3

left of the king's palpably hopeless ardour. Magnificent as its solo sections are, the duet is paradoxically a less accurate depiction of an emotional confrontation than is Carlo's Act II aria: it suffers from the Hugoesque shortcoming of two much speechification and too little mutual responsiveness.

In most cases, however, as we would expect bearing in mind the precedents in *Nabucco* and *I Lombardi*, Verdi showed an acute sense of the degree of stylization required in an ensemble. A drastic example of the kind of thing he would occasionally venture upon is provided by the trio 'Tu se' Ernani'. The expressive point here is the confrontation of two different kinds of hatred, the one cold and indignant, expressed by spitting declamation and gestic orchestral interjections; the other burning and impassioned, expressed by the headlong tempo, the syncopations, and especially the theatening rearing-up of the vocal phrases. As Piave was unable to find a useful role for Elvira, Verdi virtually ignores her, treating her as a four-foot stop to give edge and penetration to Ernani's melody, despite the fact

Ex. 4 (a)

(b)

that its style has nothing to do with the sense of her words. She plays a significant role only in the turmoil of the closing phrases, where she can appropriately observe 'No, quest'alma non conosce l'amante nè il re.' If Verdi's sense of stylization can sometimes lead to such a compacting of the constituent parts as this, it can also dissolve the effect of totality in an equally striking way; as, for example, towards the end of the *adagio* in the Act I finale, where, having built up the movement to a climax of dense undiscriminated harmony, he introduces a new thematic figure whose migrations serve to shift our attention from one group to another within the ensemble (Ex. 5).

It is in this *adagio* and the following *stretta* that we see the most curious reflection of Hugo's influence on the ensembles. Doubtless it was an old habit of Italian opera composers to conceive their ensembles, especially the finales, in strongly visual terms, as tableaux illuminated by sound, sometimes almost as sound-guides to spectacles of great magnificence; but in *Ernani* this habit comes to a climax. In no other opera of Verdi's do the ensembles so often suggest that they have been composed in response less to the words of the libretto than to an imagined picture of the scene.

In the *adagio* the assembled characters are largely occupied in expressing their surprise when the intruder into Silva's castle reveals himself to be the king: they are also amused to see Silva's transformation from fury to obsequiousness. While the greater part of the company continue to hold this pose, Ernani and Elvira detach themselves to arrange an elopement:

ERNANI: M'odi, Elvira, al nuovo sole
        Saprò torti a tanto affanno
        Ma resisti al tuo tiranno,
        Serba a Ernani la tua fè.
ELVIRA: Tua per sempre, o questo ferro
        Può salvarmi dai tiranni!
        M'è conforto negli affanni
        La costanza di mia fè.

Ex. 5

Elvira's words are spoken in answer to Ernani's, and by all rational literary criteria the two quatrains should be composed consecutively. But Verdi has imagined the scene visually, the two lovers whispering together apart from the main group of king, courtiers and nobles. Consequently he set it as a cantabile in which they sing simultaneously, contrasting strongly in colour and line from the unaccompanied declamatory music that had characterized the main group. A similar effect is found in the *stretta*, which is likewise composed around a picture of two quite separate groups of characters. One group – Carlo and Silva – is engrossed in a political discussion, but their words are never heard as a dialogue at all. They and their attendants are simply regarded as a homogeneous unit and given a unifying musical identity in the form of a fanatically hard-driven march tune, which obviously identifies their common interest well enough.

One last aspect of the music of *Ernani* deserves mention, its use of a recurring theme associated with the pledge

> Nel momento
> In che Ernani vorrai spento,
> Se un squillo intenderà
> Tosto Ernani morirà.

Ernani is the first of Verdi's operas in which the whole course of the drama is overshadowed by the sense of an inexorably pursuing nemesis. He was to return to this kind of theme frequently, in *Luisa Miller*, in *Rigoletto*, in *La Traviata*; and always the dramatic significance of the idea of nemesis, whether it is embodied in an intrigue or a curse or a disease, is marked by the use of a recurring theme. *Ernani*, where the nemesis comes about through a suicidal pledge from which, given the preposterous concept of honour on which the plot depends, there can be no escape, provides a demonstration of this hallmark of Verdi's style in its simplest form. It provides, too, yet another example of how much better Hugo's dramatic ideas fit the operatic medium than they do the medium of poetic drama.

Though Hugo's play makes a reference to Hernani's horn early in Act I – he uses it, apparently, to summon his horde of bandits – it obviously cannot play a significant part until Hernani makes the pledge at the end of Act III:

> Écoute. Prends ce cor. – Quoi qu'il puisse advenir,
> Quand tu voudras, seigneur, quel que soit le lieu, l'heure,
> S'il te passe à l'esprit qu'il est temps que je meure,
> Viens, sonne de ce cor, et ne prends d'autres soins.
> Tout sera fait!

The medium of the dramatic effect is hypothetically descriptive. When allusion is next made to the pledge, in the conspiracy scene of Act IV, it is for Silva to offer to release Hernani from it: a non-effect as far as the expressive symbolism is concerned. And in Act V, when he comes to claim the fulfilment of the pledge, the medium is different again, principally musical, notwithstanding all the poetic beauty in which Hugo embeds it:

> ... Car la musique est douce,
> Fair l'âme harmonieux, et, comme un divin choeur
> Éveille mille voix qui chantent dans le coeur!
> Ah, ce serait charmant!
> *(On entend le bruit lointain d'un cor dans l'ombre)*

When Silva reminds Hernani of his oath in the medium of spoken drama it impresses us less as a spine-chilling dramatic stroke than as an unnatural feat of memorization. Thereafter nothing more is made of the horn as a symbol of nemesis; Silva simply becomes an intolerably mean and vicious old man.

All these confusions of medium, all these half-effectual strokes cry out for the harmonizing and vitalizing touch of the opera composer. Set to music, the pledge becomes something dramatically three-dimensional: it still carries the conceptual force of Hugo's pledge, but is expressive and symbolic too. Our sense that it will have tragic consequences is intensified by the grim and solemn harmonies, and the brassy colouring of the chords makes of them a tonal symbol perfectly analogous to the visual symbol of the horn (Ex. 6).

Ex. 6

Although Verdi can do nothing with the non-effect in the conspiracy scene, the greater aptness of Hugo's device to the operatic medium becomes still more apparent in the last act. The off-stage monotone intonations that depict Silva's approach lead up with no sense of stylistic inconsequentiality to the full reprise of the pledge theme as Silva presents Ernani with the horn. What is more, after the long trio in which are embodied all the anguish, pleading, inexorability and resignation of this last of the drama's confrontation scenes, the theme is heard yet again to signal the moment of catastrophe. Finally, of course, Verdi could write the prelude, a movement in which the theme of the pledge overshadows an ardent romantic cantabile, like a malign presence in a summer garden. In Hugo the sense of implacable fatalism takes hold of the drama only from about the mid-point: Verdi, even before the curtain rises, can 'apprise the spectator of the nature of the action that is to be represented'.

22

Byronismo – I Due Foscari and Il Corsaro

Verdi and Byron

It is something, undoubtedly, to be put down to a man's credit [wrote Swinburne in 1884] that his work – if his work be other than poetic – should lose nothing by translation ... But what shall be said of a poet whose work not only does not lose, but gains, by translation into foreign prose? and gains so greatly and indefinitely by that process as to assume a virtue which it has not. On taking up a fairly good version of *Childe Harold's Pilgrimage* in French or Italian prose, a reader whose eyes and ears are not hopelessly sealed against all distinction of good from bad in rhythm or in style will infallibly be struck by the vast improvement which the text has undergone in the course of translation. The blundering, floundering, lumbering and stumbling stanzas, transmuted into prose and transfigured into grammar, reveal the real and latent force of rhetorical energy that is in them: the gasping, ranting, wheezing, broken-winded verse has been transformed into really effective and fluent oratory ... we are able to discern in the thick and troubled stream of his natural eloquence whatever of real value may be swept along in company with much drifting rubbish. It is impossible to express how much *Childe Harold* gains by being done out of wretchedly bad metre into decently good prose.[1]

One may feel that in turning against a former hero, Swinburne both overstates and trivializes the problem posed by Byron's continental reputation. His tumid denunciation does nevertheless highlight in memorable terms a very peculiar phenomenon: the fact that Byron enjoyed and continues to enjoy a vastly higher esteem among those for whom English is not a native language than among those for whom it is. Certainly Byron did for a brief period of time enjoy a popularity with the British public that was without precedent. But it is doubtful if anyone would have ventured to deem him England's greatest poet, as he evidently was for many foreigners; still less rank him with Goethe, as Mazzini did in 1839, as one of the 'two names that predominate, and, come what may, ever will predominate, over our every recollection of the fifty years that have passed away';[2] least of all concur with Goethe's own assessment of him as 'the greatest talent of the century'.[3]

In no country was Byron more extravagantly admired than in Italy.

485

The austere and idealistic philosopher Mazzini found implicit in his work epoch-making truths; leading figures of literary Romanticism like Guerrazzi, Niccolini, De Virgilii found an excitement, a dynamism, a richness of colour such as they had rarely experienced elsewhere. Guerrazzi admitted that he had not seen the Niagara Falls, nor the avalanches of the Alps, nor a volcano; but he 'could not imagine that they were remotely to be compared with the awe inspired in me by that immense spirit'.[4] The Italian enthusiasm for Byron penetrated to the simplest and most modestly educated classes of society. At Bologna, during the course of his Italian journey, Dickens ran into a headwaiter who was

a man of one idea in connexion with the English; and the subject of his harmless monomania, was Lord Byron . . . He knew all about him, he said. In proof of it, he connected him with every possible topic, from the Monte Pulciano wine at dinner (which was grown on an estate he had owned), to the big bed itself, which was the very model of his.[5]

To some extent this admiration may seem a natural reflection of Byron's own interest in Italy. He had lived there for several years, a brilliant and provocative figure, whose sympathy for the political plight of the country was apparent even from the company he kept. Moreover he wrote much and eloquently about Italy; not only, not even principally, about those beauties apostrophized by countless other poets, but rather about its miseries and humiliations. It was he, particularly in the fourth canto of *Childe Harold's Pilgrimage*, who helped his fellow-countrymen to a political awareness of those conditions with which the Italians themselves were most acutely concerned. Finally at Missolonghi he had died the kind of death to which the most heroic and idealistic young Italians of the time aspired, in the cause of the freedom of an oppressed people. The extent to which personal and political admiration for Byron mingled with the artistic judgement is eloquently shown by Mazzini:

Surrounded by slaves and their oppressors; a traveller in countries where even remembrance seemed extinct; never did he desert the cause of the peoples; never was he false to human sympathies. A witness of the progress of the Restoration, and the triumphs of the principles of the Holy Alliance, he never swerved from his courageous opposition; he preserved and publicly proclaimed his faith in the rights of the peoples and in the final triumph of liberty . . . I know no more beautiful symbol of the future destiny and mission of art than the death of Byron in Greece. The holy alliance of poetry with the cause of the peoples, the union – still so rare – of thought and action which alone completes the human Word, and is destined to emancipate the world; the grand solidarity of all nations in the conquest of the rights ordained by God for all his children . . .; all that is now the religion and hope of the party of progress throughout Europe, is gloriously typified in this image ...

Byron was, concluded Mazzini,

the poet beloved and admired by all the nations of Europe, and for whose death Greece and Italy wept as it had been that of the noblest of their own sons.[6]

It may seem curious, then, that of the operas composed by Verdi in the 1840s, *I Due Foscari* and *Il Corsaro* are among those in which the political note is most subdued. The other Byronic themes that he considered working, *The Bride of Abydos* and *Cain*, suggest equally that politics was hardly a factor in their appeal. Verdi's interest in Byron, like his contemporaneous interest in Hugo and Shakespeare, was surely due to the fact that he was looking for new types of character, types stranger, more original, more daring than those traditionally associated with the heroic humanism of Italian opera. And in this respect he was typical of his period. Italian readers were touched by Byron's sympathy for their country's political plight, they were stirred by his belief in what he called 'the very *poetry* of politics'; but by the defiant and lugubrious individualism of the Byronic hero they were spellbound, hypnotized, horribly fascinated. A few choice spirits, like Mazzini, saw beyond the extravagant world-weariness of his Harolds and Manfreds and Conrads, and perceived in their solitariness and their despair 'the last formula, effort and result of a society founded on the principle of Individuality ... The funeral hymn, the death-song, the epitaph of the aristocratic idea'. But almost certainly we must count Verdi among that larger number who were haunted by Byron's portrayals of 'outsiders' because of the arrogance of their sensibilities, the bizarreness of their passions. Verdi was momentarily succumbing to a fashionable ailment, which affected to see heroism only in defiance of God and contempt for the social order, and conceded sensibility only to those racked by the wildest passions, enduring infinitudes of anguish.

This kind of *Byronismo esagerato* was a motif in Italian cultural life from the 1830s through to the 1860s. It provoked the satirical protest of Giusti, who (as he explained to Manzoni) had written 'Il Giovinetto' in 1845 as 'a kind of scurvy elegy, in derision of the eighteen-year-old paralytics who are the scrofulous bane of the day'.[7] More pompous protest was voiced as late as 1865 by Prati who, in the preface of his *Armando*, and with reference to 'Byronism', commented, 'I observed a moral malady and I wrote a book.' Verdi's creative involvement with Byron, on the other hand, though not necessarily his admiration for him, was brief, four or five years at most; nor was it especially 'esagerato'. It was presumably stimulated by his friend Andrea Maffei, one of the busiest of the innumerable Italian translators of Byron, and it really had something to nourish itself on after the appearance in Padua in 1842 of the first complete Italian translation, the *Opere complete di Lord Byron, voltato dall'originale inglese in prosa italiana da Carlo Rusconi*. Despite its title, this was in fact a compilation including translations by many hands; of the works with which Verdi concerned himself, *The Bride of Abydos* and *The Corsair* had both been translated by Niccolini, *Cain* and *The Two Foscari* by De Virgilii.

There will be no need to recapitulate the story of Verdi's fleeting involvement with *Byronismo*; it has already been told in chapters 7 and 9. But the reader may be reminded that he was not long pleased with either of his Byronic operas. By 1848 he was describing *I Due Foscari* as 'a funeral ... [with] too uniform an atmosphere and colour from beginning to end'. And disillusion came even more promptly with *Il Corsaro*. As he put it in a letter to Benjamin Lumley: '... after it had been versified I found it cold and theatrically ineffective'.*

One 'cold and theatrically ineffective' work and one 'funeral' seem a disappointing legacy from the greatest Italian artist of the age of *Byronismo*. But even if we could take Verdi's judgements at their face value – and they are certainly over-harsh – there would be some interest in examining the way in which he attempted to re-create the Byronic flavour in these operas, and trying to understand what it was that caused his disenchantment.

The libretto of *I Due Foscari*

Byron's 'Historical Tragedy' *The Two Foscari* has two qualities which posed problems for Verdi and Piave when they decided to turn it into an opera, and which have left their mark even on the final form of the work. One of them, the tautness and continuity of the action, it owes to Byron's expressed desire of 'preserving ... a nearer approach to unity than the irregularity, which is the reproach of the English theatrical compositions, permits'.[8] The other, for which it is difficult to ascribe any ground other than the inadequacy of Byron's dramatic imagination, is the very odd nature of the characterization. One character, Jacopo Foscari's wife Marina – she becomes Lucrezia

---

* See above, p. 225 and note 15, p. 196 and note 24.

in the opera – seems really alive; a devoted wife and mother who has been turned into a veritable Fury by the oppressiveness and cruelty of Venetian governance. Whether exhorting her husband to be more spirited, or beseeching her father-in-law the Doge to listen to the promptings of a humane conscience, or confronting and denouncing Loredano and the representatives of 'The Ten', she expresses with rare eloquence all the best features of Byron's own libertarian and humanitarian beliefs, and all his hatred of the representatives of tyranny, of those 'old human friends' who

> counsel,
> Cabal, and put men's lives out, as if life
> Were no more than the feelings long extinguished
> In their accursed bosoms.

But the rest are mere 'masks', incarnations of a single fixation, to which they give voice whatever the circumstances in which they find themselves. Jacopo Foscari, whether tortured, imprisoned or exiled, whether solitary or surrounded by his devoted family, speaks only of his love for Venice, and in terms which become increasingly preposterous as the play proceeds. While we read with sympathy his apostrophe to the beauties of the city in Act I –

> My beautiful, my own,
> My only Venice – *this is breath!* Thy breeze
> Thine Adrian sea-breeze, how it fans my face!
> Thy very winds feel native to my veins,
> And cool them into calmness!

– by Act IV, where exile to Candia in company with his wife is deemed 'Double, Triple, and tenfold torture' in comparison with 'actual torture' in the Doge's palace, the hyperbole and monotony of his passion have become simply absurd. His father, the Doge, is the 'mask' of stoical submission to what he sees as his duty to the state, denying himself the right to personal feelings, and denying others, even Marina, the right of criticism. Loredano is the 'mask' of cold, inexorable hatred. It was precisely these idiosyncrasies – the 'mask'-like characterization, and the simple, undeviating and undecorated action – that Verdi and Piave became preoccupied with in their attempt to transform the play into an effective opera. We may examine Piave's treatment of the two Foscari, father and son, who illustrate the style of the revision at its most successful.

Piave found the adaptation easier with the Doge, and from the start his characterization impressed Verdi as 'noble, very beautiful and skilfully handled'. In a word, what Piave does with him is to remove him from the official political world in which Byron confines him virtually throughout, and to place him in more private and confidential contexts. For example, at the beginning of Byron's Act II there is a scene between the Doge and a senator about affairs of state. When the senator attempts to express sympathy with the Doge over the fate of his son, he is brusquely cut short: Byron's Doge can boast 'I have no repose, that is, none which shall cause the loss of an hour's time unto the state.' But this is not much use for opera. Although the political pressures need to be hinted at to motivate the development of the plot, Piave and Verdi are only really interested in the Doge when he has escaped momentarily from politics – 'Eccomi solo alfine' begins the equivalent scene of the opera – and can give expression to that grief which in public has to be suppressed.

The character of Jacopo gave Piave a tougher problem. In his attempt to remain faithful to the Byronic prototype, he at first presented Verdi with a character which the composer deplored as 'weak and making little theatrical impact'. What Piave had done was to reflect Jacopo's blind adoration of Venice, his passive submission to every kind of torment it heaped upon him, by writing in Act I not the usual kind of double-aria scene but a simple romanza, presumably the cantabile 'Dal più remoto esilio'. At Verdi's prompting this emphasis on elegiac lyricism was shifted. Jacopo does become a more rounded and convincing figure, following up the tender apostrophe to Venice with a spirited expression of defiance of the tyrants who exercise justice there:

> Odio solo, ed odio atroce
> In quell'anime si serra; ...
> ... Forza contro il lor rigore
> L'innocenza ti darà.

These ideas are certainly to be found in Byron, but they do not give the scene its tone, and nowhere are they expressed with the same sustained vehemence which Verdi's cabaletta brings to them.

This concern 'to make the character of Foscari more energetic' can be seen conditioning the adaptation of each of the scenes in which he is involved. Once, in the hallucinatory wrestling with the ghost of Carmagnola in the prison scene, the enlargement of the range of Foscari's passion is unconvincing, because the incident that prompts it is too palpably contrived. But generally, and especially when Byron is most implausible – in the scene of Foscari's departure from Venice (IV.99ff) – the modifications work well. By this time, in his despair at leaving Venice, Byron's hero has become grotesque, invoking the 'Adrian waves' and 'Auster, sovereign of the tempest' to

> dash me back on my own shore
> A broken corse upon the barren Lido,
> Where I may mingle with the sands which skirt
> The land I love . . .

No wonder that Marina, who is to accompany him, grows indignant, and urges him 'to master such useless passion'. Piave's Jacopo has better reason for these death-invoking rhapsodies, since he is going into exile alone, leaving wife and family in Venice. But the librettist finds room for some kind of manly firmness, too, providing a duet text in which Jacopo admonishes Lucrezia of those responsibilities which his exile will place upon her:

> All'infelice veglio
> Conforta tu il dolore,
> De' figli nostri in core
> Tu ispira la virtù . . .
> Di Contarini e Foscari
> Mostrati figlia e sposa!

By making these kinds of alteration, Piave has of course brought Jacopo more into line with the conventional type of operatic hero, and tends to undermine that distinctiveness, that extravagance, which presumably prompted the interest in Byron in the first place.

The alteration worked on the character of Loredano, on the other hand, is technical rather than psychological: he has been reduced to *comprimario* status, and thus the opera has no single formidable, hostile figure. In terms of psychology, Loredano had indeed little to lose; the calculating monotony of his hatred for the Foscari is exhausted of interest by the end of Byron's first act. But Marina's recognition of how much her family's sufferings are owing to his influence does prompt a couple of stirring confrontations – one in Act III in Jacopo's prison, the other at the end of Act IV over his dead body – which surpass in theatrical effectiveness almost everything else in the play. A brief extract from the first will sufficiently illustrate their character:

LOREDANO: Let her go on: it irks not me.
MARINA: That's false!
> You came here to enjoy a heartless triumph
> Of cold looks upon manifold griefs! You came
> To be sued to in vain – to mark our tears
> And hoard our groans – to gaze upon the wreck,
> Which you have made a prince's son – my husband;
> In short, to trample on the fallen – an office
> The hangman shrinks from, as all men from him!
> How have you sped? We are wretched, signor, as
> Your plots could make, and vengeance could desire us,

And how *feel* you?

LOREDANO: As rocks.
MARINA: By Thunder blasted.

Verdi's insistence that Piave should 'avoid long recitatives, especially for Loredano and Barbarigo', and his disdaining to set to music the one scene that Piave did provide for them reduce Loredano to a status hardly greater than that of a messenger; the hostility between him and the Foscari is consequently intelligible only in the light of Piave's preface to the libretto. Under these circumstances the splendid vituperations which reveal Marina's passions at their most distinctive have simply to be struck out.

The fact that in the opera Loredano has been reduced to such a skeletal figure, and indeed the fact that the Doge has been made more spontaneously human, make it the more important to find some other way of suggesting that secret, sombre and severe way of life which they represent in the play. And they are not its only representatives. The dark and repressive character of Venetian politics, the sense that 'men know as little Of the state's real acts as of the grave's Unfathom'd mysteries' is also emphasized by a number of short scenes between one Memmo and a senator. This note echoes through the whole play, and must be somehow recaptured in the opera if the drama is to make any kind of sense.

Piave and Verdi achieve a comparable effect in their medium by the unprecedentedly consistent and dramatically aware use of the chorus, which throughout the opera represents the voice of Venice. On two occasions, certainly, they seek to alleviate the relentlesssly gloomy character of the opera by evoking through the chorus a contrasting facet of the Venetian soul:

> Tace il vento, è queta l'onda;
> Mite un aura l'accarezza . . .
> Dêi mostrar la tua prodezza;
> Prendi il remo, o gondolier.

But even in one of these cases the effect is ironic, for the sounds of carnival are heard from within Jacopo's cell. Elsewhere the chorus is used to hymn the 'mystery', the 'justice', the 'rigour' which in Byron we perceive from the political dialogues of Memmo and his senator friends, from the suppression of instinctive feeling in the Doge, and from the denunciations of Marina. Thus the chorus sets the tone at the very beginning of the opera, with its incantatory refrain 'Silenzio . . . mistero', and thus even in a situation of maximum emotional excruciation such as the Act II finale they remain unmoved:

492

Son vane ora le lagrime;
Provato è già il delitto:
Non fia ch'esse cancellino
Quanto giustizia ha scritto;
Esempio sol dannabile
Sarebbe la pietà.

Byronismo in the music of *I Due Foscari*

All the commentators have observed that in *I Due Foscari* Verdi makes fuller and more systematic use of 'leading themes' than in any other of his operas, early or late. The implication seems to be that this feature of the score is a piece of somewhat arbitrary experimentation, promptly discarded again after *I Due Foscari* in favour of the restrained use of the traditional 'reminiscence theme', which, save for an occasional relapse, as in *Aida*, Verdi used with growing fastidiousness and subtlety to the end of his career.

Surely, though, the peculiar interest of the 'leading themes' in *I Due Foscari* is not that they were a mere device, expeditiously abandoned, but that they provide a close musical analogy to the unique type of characterization employed by Byron in his play. Verdi has observed that the obsessions of Jacopo and the Doge and Loredano are an essential quality of his literary model, and sets himself the task of finding some way of re-creating this feature in his score. No doubt his dramatic instinct told him that to attempt a literal transcription of Byron's mask-like characterization would be to suffocate every trace of vitality in the opera, to render each aria after the first act drearily tautologous, and to turn each ensemble – the form on which he was increasingly laying the weight of his dramas – into a deathly murmuration of robots. His chosen scheme has none of these drawbacks, for the 'leading themes' do not impinge upon the lyrical movements. They are used to characterize the obsessions in introductions and recitative scenes; after which their tone may be intensified, modified or altogether transformed, according to the circumstances out of which the freely composed arias and ensembles arise.

Each of the principal characters has such a theme – such a musical mask, we might almost call it, Jacopo's is a sorrowful cantilena for solo clarinet, first heard in the prelude, and given conceptual associations early in Act I as Jacopo is led out from the dungeon to face trial (Ex. 1). It recurs twice more: in the Act II finale, again as he

Ex. 1

is led from the dungeons, this time to listen to the reading of his sentence; and finally, preceding his Act III aria, as he is about to embark on his voyage into exile. The Doge's musical mask, which, because of Piave's shift of emphasis in the libretto, need not be an expressionless, public one, take the form of a sombre, dignified succession of triadic harmonies, listlessly adorned by viola figurations; it depicts him as a venerable, but weary and melancholy figure (Ex. 2). The music recurs in identical form to introduce his second scena in the last act. Lucrezia too has her characterizing theme, compounded of sorrow and energy, of weeping appoggiatura figures and surging *agitato* lines (Ex. 3). First heard at the start of her *aria di sortita*, it recurs when she confronts the Doge in the recitative preceding the Act I duet finale, as she makes her way into Jacopo's dungeon in Act II, and at her entrance in the Act III finale. This last instance is perhaps the one lazy use of a recurring theme in the opera; for there is no longer any dramatic point to Lucrezia's busy grief, and her part in this finale is negligible.

Of the mask-like characters in Byron's play, Loredano alone has no analogous musical theme, simply because in the opera his is no longer a major role. The Council of Ten, of which Loredano is a member, the *Giunta* and senators, on the other hand, do: for they assume that character – cruel, implacable, unchanging – which had been Loredano's in the play. Where Byron had kept Venetian politics and legalistic principles in a mysterious background, largely hidden from view, Verdi and Piave bring them into the light in a series of

Ex. 2

choral movements as dramatically conceived and thoughtfully organized as the music of the protagonists. The musical 'mask' of
political Venice is matched to the poetic leitmotif of Piave's introductory chorus – 'silenzio, mistero' – a cool, gravely elegant theme,
with a touch of sinister colour in the drummings and string grace-
notes, and a suggestion of chromaticism at the opening and in the
cadence phrase (Ex. 4). Three subsequent recurrences of the theme
in the introduction give the whole movement a clear rondo-like
structure. The 'Venice' theme, played in the orchestra, is used as a
framing ritornello for the later choruses in Acts I and II, and is heard
one last time at the start of the aria finale when the Council of Ten
come to urge the Doge to resign.

The systematic employment of such a group of characterizing
themes is a unique feature of *I Due Foscari*, a brilliant musical
analogy to the style of Byron's characterization. But Verdi knew that
he could not hope to sustain an opera on such stuff, that the
psychology of his characters needed to be more multi-faceted, that
they must be endowed with the capacity to sympathize with and

Ex. 3

respond to one another. In general, as we have seen, Piave was diligent in catering for this need, and the virtuosity with which Verdi seizes upon and brings to life his librettist's dramatic sketches is one of the most impressive features of the finished score.

The erstwhile limply doting Jacopo, 'weak and making little theatrical impact', has been most vigorously operaticized, particularly in his arias in Acts I and III. Of the former the real distinguishing feature – and it suits his character admirably – is the musical elaboration of Piave's apostrophe to Venice to form a sustained arioso, 'Brezza del suol natio'. Delicately pulsing and trilling, the music of this arioso haunts the whole scene: for the pattern of the string chords continues through into the recitative, and a comparable texture recurs, almost like an orchestral interlude, in the middle of 'Dal più remoto esilio'. While the poetry of Jacopo's character is thus beautifully reflected in the music, his Byronic lethargy is somewhat roughly remedied in the cabaletta. The arpeggio-like melodic figures, the fiercely impacted rhythms, the garish daubs of brass

Ex. 4

colouring, the screaming high notes – especially at the reprise – all suggest a very self-conscious attempt to endow him with vitality.

In the Act III aria, the transfiguring touch of a real dramatic imagination shows itself more subtly. It is the movement that really parallels Jacopo's death scene in Act IV of Byron's play; but the morbid raptures of the original provide material only for the recitative. The aria itself is new in tone, valedictory, exhortatory, and it is given a certain dramatic texture by the brief insets expressive of Lucrezia's despair and Loredano's hatred. In fact the whole scene provides an excellent example of the way in which, having set out from the mask patterns of the play, Verdi alleviates the Byronic monotony by giving a psychological dimension to his set-pieces. Here the Jacopo is altogether more vital and responsive than Byron's, waxing in serenity when he perceives the need to comfort Lucrezia, becoming more lofty and metaphysical in his disdain of Loredano. The aria thus moves through three stages, the first the 'mask' reaction to the given situation, the others born of an alert and feeling response to the intervention of the bystanders.

The operatic transformation of Jacopo is a matter of widening the range of his passions, lending him energy, resolution and a sensitivity to others. In the case of the Doge, it is not so much a matter of changing his character as giving him an opportunity to express himself. He is removed from the public world, his scenes placed in private or confidential environments. As a result of the style of Byron's play the psychological conflicts to which the Doge is subject have largely to be imagined by the reader: he provides the best example of what Byron was pleased to call the 'suppressed passions' around which he had built the drama. In such a movement as the Act I romanza, Piave, by setting the scene in Francesco's private apartments, gives Verdi the chance that Byron explicitly denies him, to express his sensibility. The frigid expostulation of the play is supplemented by a cantabile employing all the expressive resources of appoggiatura, of sigh-laden woodwind textures, and of juxtapositions of minor and major.

Though the opera gives eloquent voice to the suppressed emotions of Byron's Doge, it does not attempt to enlarge the range of his passions as it does in the case of Jacopo. The Doge is virtually comprehended by the tone of his musical mask, and from its mood of mournful, dignified resignation he never really escapes. A most striking demonstration of this is the fact that at no point in the opera does he summon sufficient energy to sing a cabaletta. Verdi in fact suppresses part of the normal design of the scene as a means of characterization. Either the Doge's scenes end with the cantabile, or the cabaletta is sung by another character, as Lucrezia sings 'Più non vive' in Act III. Even in the ensemble cabalettas he either takes no real part, as in the Act II quartet, or subdues the impetuosity of the music, as in the duet finale of Act I. Indeed by the time of the Act III finale his character has become markedly feebler than that of his Byronic prototype. 'Questa dunque e l'iniqua mercede', the cantabile with which this finale begins, pulsing with spirit and declamatory severity, has a grand dignity comparable with that of Byron's 'If I could have foreseen that my old age Was prejudicial to the state . . .'.

But where in the play Foscari resolves quickly on abdication, and then wins a psychological victory over the Council of Ten on the issue of doing things publicly, opera's need to simplify the plot and avoid explanatory elaboration results in compressions that leave the Doge only with the memories of loss. Stung by the chorus's implausibly tactless 'Pace piena godrai fra tuoi cari', he becomes more emotional, more lacrimose; the severe-visaged Doge is transmuted into the heartbroken father. And while this may lead more convincingly to his death, it does continue to limit him emotionally within the scope of his 'mask'. Even in the finale proper, 'Quel bronzo ferale', Francesco can summon neither spirit nor defiance: he simply strikes a funereal pose and warbles his own epitaph.

Lucrezia, like Abigaille, is one of the rare Verdian heroines for whom the cabaletta seems a more natural form of self-expression than the cantabile. In her *aria di sortita* the cantabile, though an exquisite movement, is transparently contrived, a pretext for varying the sombre and austere colours of the opera with a female chorus, and with the ethereal rippling of an *obbligato* harp. The cabaletta, on the other hand, is admirable and characteristic in every respect, particularly perhaps in the way it seems to emerge spontaneously out of the dialogue by way of a *minore* opening, and in the effect of almost deranged strenuousness which is brought about by the irregularity of the design, the widely modulating three-bar episode, and the curiously phrased coda theme.

It may be that occasionally in the later stages of the opera – in the aria 'Più non vive', for example – Verdi's characterization of Lucrezia becomes unduly obsessed with such Erinnic rhetoric. But the peculiar style of characterization in *I Due Foscari* does result in a number of real and curious triumphs, notably the duet finale of Act I. All its multitude of contrasting moods – its tears, its sorrowful reproach, its lilting tenderness, its resolution, its fleeting spasms of joy – are prompted by the dynamic Lucrezia. The Doge, save for a handful of allusions to the superior demands of duty, remains the weary melancholic of the preceding scene: only at the phrases of tenderness, 'senti il paterno amore', does he respond to and share in Lucrezia's music; elsewhere the grave, plangent cantabile of his romanza is preserved. And this surely accounts for the unusual formal character of the movement. For the shifts in Lucrezia's mood are expressed the more emphatically to compensate for the monotony of his: not only the cantabile but the cabaletta too is based on the principle of contrasting solo verses. Operatic characterization is also behind the fact that while the Doge is absolutely silent during

Lucrezia's verses, withdrawing again into his obsessional introspection, she is always ready to interrupt his, to attempt to manipulate his feelings or to react to his song.

Mention has already been made of the way in which Verdi's opera brings the severely impersonal world of Venetian politics into the centre of the drama by means of the male voices of the chorus, and distinguishes this facet of Venice with the same kind of musical 'mask' as Jacopo, Lucrezia and the Doge have. Unlike the individual protagonists of the opera, however, political Venice remains entirely mask-like. Not only are the first- and second-act choruses framed in the same ritornello; the idiom of the choruses thus framed remains unaffected by the developing dramatic situation. Indeed it looks as if Piave, with unusual acumen, may have designed the main part of the Act I chorus 'Al mondo sia noto' to go to the music of the introductory chorus: at least the metre is identical. But Verdi, having used his 'mask' theme as a ritornello to make the point, prefers to compose the chorus in a variety of idioms suggestive of massive, inflexible unanimity—unison declamation above a heavy texture of chords in pompous but regular rhythms, absolutely undecorated block-chord writing of great rapidity and force, and unison cantabile. Much the same is true of the chorus in Act II.

But Verdi does more than make the Byronic background of Venetian politics a protagonist in his opera. He evokes the unworldly beauty of the city by the pellucid and liquid textures of some of his orchestral accompaniments, notably those of 'Brezza del suol natio' and 'Speranza dolce ancora'; and he suggests something of its exuberant, carnival face in the off-stage chorus 'Tutta è calma la laguna' and in the Barcarola. This latter movement is nothing more than an episodic splash of colour, sonorous and visual, making tangible and present the nostalgic memories of Jacopo in Act I of the play:

> ... how often have they borne me
> Bounding o'er yon blue tide, as I have skimm'd
> The gondola along in childish race ...

But it is typical of the extreme consistency of style and atmosphere in *I Due Foscari* that thematically this movement is an elaborated recomposition of the music heard off-stage in the prison scene, and that despite the evocative detail of the text Verdi contented himself with the most massive and thickly daubed choral writing.

Finally it may be remarked that this 'Venetian' music is used with great skill as an impersonal foil to the personal dilemmas and crises of the Foscari family. The choral movements are aptly placed, their stony rigours juxtaposed with the idiosyncratic passions of Lucrezia's *aria di sortita* or the emotional turmoil of the Doge's farewell to his son in the prison scene. On a number of occasions such juxtapositions occur within the framework of a single lyrical movement. In the Act II duet, for example, while the imprisoned Jacopo and Lucrezia sing of the private griefs that Venice has occasioned them, chorus and orchestra evoke other facets of the city's life, the luminous delicacy of its scenery, its popular revelry. This quality seemed to Verdi so fundamental to the character of the opera that he built the prelude around just such a juxtaposition. The movement is focused on two solo woodwind themes: the clarinet theme that in the opera comes to be associated with Jacopo, and a flute theme later heard as Lucrezia's prayer, 'Tu al cui sguardo'. Surrounding these tokens of individualism and engulfing them, the *allegro agitato* is music of grim, featureless force.

Of Verdi's Byronic operas, *I Due Foscari* is certainly the more interesting. Few of his early works are so clearly affected by the attempt to adapt the *ottocento* operatic tradition in response to qualities in a literary original: the peculiar style of the characterization, symbolized in those recurring themes, the exceptionally consistent and serious use of the chorus, such formal peculiarities as the avoidance of cabalettas in the Doge's part, are all reflections of certain distinguishing features of Byron's play. The defects are Byronic too: a somewhat sepulchral monotony of tone in which such contrasts as Piave provided are rather palpably contrived; characters whose passions, despite Verdi's care, occasionally become too rigidly obsessive; a plot which, far from suffering from the usual superabundance of incident, rather runs out of steam, becoming limp and repetitive in the later stages. It was such factors as these that prompted Verdi's later dismissal of the opera as a 'funeral'; and in what looks like a kind of misconceived remorse he now embarked on a series of works in which crude, brash dynamism is the most distinguishing quality: *Giovanna d'Arco, Alzira, Attila, Il Corsaro*. Surprisingly, he seems not to have noticed the compensations which the leisurely and simple plot had afforded, the 'delicacy and pathos' which he had been able to take the time and trouble to re-create in this most indelicate of mediums, and the distinctive *colorito*, more consistent in *I Due Foscari* than in any other of his early scores.

The libretto of *Il Corsaro*

Il Corsaro was the first of Verdi's operas since *I Lombardi* to be based on a literary source in narrative rather than dramatic form. But although this meant that the work of adaptation needed to be much more fundamental than usual, *The Corsair* did in several ways provide a more congenial subject than *The Two Foscari*. The story certainly offers all that variety of colour and mood in which *The Two Foscari* had been so chronically deficient; the characters in the story, in intention at least, seem to have altogether more dramatic potential than the 'mask'-like figures in the play; and despite the narrative form, even the structure of the poem is in a sense more operatic. The play had progressed smoothly and inexorably from first to last; the design was kept taut by the interlocking transitions; every incident was prepared, worked out, and followed up. In *The Corsair* on the contrary, Byron employs an idiom in which the coherence and impressiveness of the whole are almost entirely dependent upon the set-piece, the purple passage. Most of the narrative is sketchy; sometimes it is barely intelligible; Byron wastes no time with links and transitions, with 'he said's and 'thus spoke's'; but when he comes to some incident, some scene, some thought, to which his poet's tongue can lend enchantment, he abandons the tale and writes himself out with bravura and intensity.

It does not of course follow that all, or even many, of Byron's set-pieces can provide material for the opera. Some of them are passages of evocative descriptive writing, of very little use to the librettist except to suggest stage sets or at best a few lines of chorus. Others are in fact virtuoso pieces of narrative writing, notably the description of the battle between the Corsairs and the Turks in Canto II, which Byron carries off with a Hollywood-like *élan*. For him, the sudden blaze of light, the terror of the Turks, Conrad's casting-off of his disguise, the appearance of his corsair crew, the cries of the harem women, the rescue of Gulnare, the cutting-off and defeat of the corsairs, are all matters worth lavishing his poetic exuberance upon. For Piave, however, they are nothing more than a series of moves, highly inconvenient because of their very number, necessary to get everyone positioned and conditioned for a tableau finale. On the other hand, Byron's tendency even to characterize his protagonists in set-piece analyses rather than in the way they speak or behave, though profoundly undramatic in the usual sense of the word, is not wholly unrelated to the kind of stylization required by Verdi in an opera. The fact that *The Corsair* is a narrative poem rather than a drama was really one of the more trivial problems; only in the Act II finale does one feel that this was the decisive factor in the unsatisfactory effect of the operatic scene.

Another problem for Piave which one need hardly be aware of in the opera was created by those disconcerting passages which foreshadow the ambiguous or abruptly veering tone of *Don Juan*, passages in which evocations or descriptions, apparently seriously intended, evaporate in mockery or cynicism. Generally this Byronic mannerism can be avoided altogether. But in one case Byron's urge to deflate does become a matter affecting the characterization of his story, and then Piave has to face up to it.

The character in question is Conrad's adversary, the Pacha Seyd, who, for no better reason than that he is a Turk, is presented in a paltry trivializing manner almost throughout. In the opening stanzas of Canto II he partakes of the general opprobrium which Byron heaps upon his countrymen, who bully the Greeks in a particularly nasty manner, shrink from the forthcoming battle, and yet because of their religious faith already feel entitled to celebrate a victory they have not earned. Byron flounders so confusedly in the sarcasm that his hatred for the Turks provokes that there is no trace of characterization in any serious sense, and unless Piave is prepared to present Seyd and the Turks in the guise of pantomime villains a drastic refashioning of the scene is imperative. In fact he does rather well, taking Byron's mocking line 'And less to conquest than to Korans trust' and subjecting this idea to a serious elaboration. The centrepiece of the scene becomes a hymn to Allah in which Seyd plays the role not of a superstitious ass, but of a high priest:

> Salve, Allah! tutta quanta la terra
> Del suo nome possente risuoni:
> Del Profeta ai credenti campioni
> Ei la spada invincibil farà.

And it is the religious fervour of this moment that justifies the braggadoccio of the chorus 'Sol girda di festa'.

The dignity which Seyd acquires in Piave's version survives the whole of the second act. But in Act III, when the time comes for his solo scena, Piave, with so little support from his literary source, falters miserably. The text of this double aria is based on Byron's line 'His thoughts on love and hate alternate dwell' – ideas which, with a relapse into the psychological conventions of Italian melodrama of a kind to which Piave was so prone and which here proves fatal, he links together by means of the passion of jealousy. In Byron's poem Seyd's jealousy develops not in his soliloquy, but during the ensuing dialogue between himself and Gulnare, and in so far as it is expressed, it is expressed in congruous terms:

> thy confession speaks,
> Already reddening on thy guilty cheeks;
> Then, lovely dame, bethink thee! and beware:

'Tis not *his* life alone may claim suçh care ...
Now 'tis thy lord that warns – deceitful thing!
Know'st thou that I can clip thy wanton wing?

In Piave, on the other hand, not only has there been nothing to provoke Seyd's jealousy, beyond the plea of the whole harem to show clemency to the man who rescued them from the flames, but the particular type of jealousy of which Seyd speaks is that of the romantic Western monogamist: 'oh quali orribil'ore tu prepari a colui che dubbia ed ama, che sospetta ed adora!' In its banal way it is the language of Renato and Ford. Indeed one wonders if the concept of the 'harem favourite' is not altogether a Western idea that makes it possible to treat a sensual relationship passionately and idealistically: at any rate the unique devotion to Gulnare, the disdain for all other beauties, which Piave's text emphasizes, certainly makes the whole idea of the harem a thoroughly wasteful investment. Once Seyd has sung 'Cento leggiadre vergini', everything that is terrible or exotic about him has vanished for good.

This mishap with the character of Seyd need, one feels, never have happened. It was due to the timidity of Piave's dramatic imagination, his unreadiness to dare to step beyond the bounds of conventional Italian melodrama. The case is different with Conrad, the Corsair himself. Here Piave had the task of bringing to dramatic life a quintessential Byronic hero, of making a convincing synthesis of Byron's descriptions and analyses and demonstrations of his character. The task was not only beyond Piave, it would have been beyond anyone; for Conrad, when thus given tangible form, proves to be fraudulent in almost every particular.

Byron's most extended analysis of Conrad's character comes quite early in the first canto, before we have really seen anything of him in action, or anything of the relationships he forms with other people. In the first verses we learn something of his salient characteristics, his solitariness, his gravity, his abstemiousness, his power of commanding fear and respect. But the more closely Byron invites us to examine Conrad, the more unlikely he becomes. He describes his unlovely physical appearance, especially his eyes, and the way they discomfited or terrified his adversaries; searching, sneering and hating are his chief faculties:

There was a laughing Devil in his sneer,
That raised emotions both of rage and fear;
And where his frown of hatred darkly fell,
Hope withering fled, and Mercy sigh'd farewell!

But, continues the poet, it is only if one can observe Conrad when one is oneself unobserved that it becomes possible to 'Behold his soul', to perceive how 'The scathing thought of execrated years ... sears ... that lone and blighted bosom'. The real psychological analysis comes in stanza 11, and very unconvincing it is. The crucial lines are these:

> Yet was not Conrad thus by Nature sent
> To lead the guilty – guilt's worse instrument –
> His soul was changed, before his deeds had driven
> Him forth to war with man and forfeit heaven.
> Warp'd by the world in Disappointment's school,
> In words too wise, in conduct *there* a fool;
> Too firm to yield, and far too proud to stoop,
> Doom'd by his very virtues for a dupe,
> He cursed those virtues as the cause of ill,
> And not the traitors who betray'd him still; ...

No clear moral line is perceptible in this welter of paradoxes, no real crisis is suggested, no 'bringing to the test'; all that Byron makes intelligible is the outcome, which is abundantly clear:

> Fear'd, shunn'd, belied, ere youth had lost her force,
> He hated man too much to feel remorse,
> And thought the voice of wrath a sacred call,
> To pay the injuries of some on all.
> He knew himself a villain – but he deem'd
> The rest no better than the thing he seem'd; ...
> He knew himself detested, but he knew
> The hearts that loath'd him, crouch'd and dreaded too.
> Lone, wild and strange, he stood alike exempt
> From all affection and from all contempt ...

Conrad has become a social rebel, affronting and assaulting a world he regards as contemptible and hypocritical. The bizarre, Byronic touch about this particular social rebel is the disgust he feels for himself, the pride he takes in being the most loathsome of the whole loathsome race. Stanza 12 reveals an unlikely redeeming virtue. Despite being a 'villain ... all other virtues gone', despite his coldness and callousness to the fair sex and his vicious cruelty to anyone else, he is a lover faithful with a more than Romeo-like fidelity:

> Yes – it was Love – if thoughts of tenderness
> Tried in temptation, strengthen'd by distress,
> Unmoved by absence, firm in every clime,
> And yet – oh more than all! untired by time;
> Which nor defeated hope, nor baffled wile,
> Could render sullen were she near to smile ...
> Which nought remov'd, nor menac'd to remove –
> If there be love in mortals – this was love!

So strenuously does Byron avouch the preposterous, that even these verses that merely analyse Conrad's character already present the librettist with formidable problems. What turns the formidable into the insuperable is the nature of the story in which Conrad subsequently becomes involved. For despite all the assertions to the contrary, this 'villain . . . all other virtues gone' proves to be in fact an exemplary Romantic hero, valiant, gallant, honourable and sensitive. Typical of the way in which Byron's perverse speculations are swept aside by a sane, even idealistic normality, when it comes to the crunch, is the reaction of Conrad to the cries of the women imprisoned in the burning harem at the height of the battle in Canto II:

> Oh! burst the Haram – wrong not on your lives
> One female form – remember – we have wives.
> On them such outrage Vengeance will repay;
> Man is our foe, and such 'tis ours to slay:
> But still we spared – must spare the weaker prey.

Similarly, in prison, the thoughts by which he is racked are profoundly and decently humane; and when it comes to leaving to Gulnare the killing of the man who on the morrow is going to torture him to death, Conrad's sensibility and sense of honour seem rather excessively than insufficiently fastidious.

Byron's tale, then, presents Piave with a protagonist who, despite all the misleading analyses to which he is subjected, is in most respects the very pattern of a Romantic hero; a great lover, a valiant leader, scrupulously honourable, exquisitely sensitive. He is an outsider in the sense that Robin Hood was, because he is too good for the world, not because he is a fiend. Only one of the mysterious, Byronic characteristics which are attributed to him stands up to examination, and proves useful to Piave: his taste for solitude, his taciturnity and melancholy; and even this had to be handled carefully to make sense in dramatic terms.

The way in which the traditional idealism of the Italian melodrama asserts itself and, in the case of Conrad, almost succeeds in making sense out of nonsense at the cost of diluting his Byronism, can be seen in the two scenes shared with his 'bird of beauty', Medora. The first of these is the Act I scene and duet, the operatic equivalent of Byron's Canto I stanza 14 beginning at line 363. Byron's verses must be briefly described.

They begin with Medora's evocation of the anguish of waiting and watching when Conrad is at sea, the emotions of her heart intermingling with the movements of wind and ocean:

Oh! many a night on this lone couch reclined,
My dreaming fear with storms hath wing'd the wind,
And deem'd the breath that faintly fann'd thy sail
The murmuring prelude of the ruder gale ...

Conrad breaks the news of his impending departure, prefacing it
with some retrospection and self-analysis which is clinched in the
grotesque line 'I cease to love thee when I love mankind'. Medora
attempts to delay him by describing the delights she has prepared for
him: they include allusions to some of the more improbable,
Bartholomew Roberts-like characteristics which have been ascribed
to him – abstemiousness, for example, and teetotalism – and to some
classical cases of desertion – Ariosto's Olimpia, Theseus and
Ariadne. Unmoved, unheeding, Conrad tears himself breathlessly
away, and the scene ends in a wildly desperate embrace:

Again – again – that form he madly press'd
Which mutely clasp'd imploringly caress'd!
And tottering to the couch his bride he bore ...

In the following stanza 15 Medora's weeping desolation is described.
Piave adapts the scene altogether convincingly. He ignores the
false and the irrelevant – Conrad's self-analysis, Medora's attempts
at culinary seduction – puts in the recitative such plot details as are
absolutely necessary, and builds up a duet on the principle of the
ideally matched romantic pair, making such use of Byronic colouring as remains appropriate. His most important modification is to
give to Byron's emotionally lifeless Conrad some kind of eloquence,
thereby transforming the scene into a genuine dialogue in place of
what had been virtually a monologue, unintelligible emotionally
because of the awful character of the hero. When Medora has sung
her agitated cantabile, based on the same intertwining of the
emotions of the heart with the moods of nature as Byron's 'Oh! many
a night on this lone couch reclined', Piave's Conrad finds words to
reply. Unlike Byron's hero, he has listened to her, and understood
her, and he finds appropriate words of consolation:

Oh così tetre immagini
Dal tuo pensier discaccia,
Tu mi vedrai dai vortici
Tornar fra le tue braccia,
E tergere quel ciglio
Mesto del mio periglio,
E le tue pene in subita
Gioia, amor mio, cangiar.

But Piave, though his plain common sense can sometimes check the follies of his-flying model, rarely sustains unaided a level of real excellence. For the cabaletta of this anguished scene of farewell, thrown entirely on to his own resources, he can find nothing more potent than a pat contradictory parallelism:

> Tornerai, ma forse spento
> Pria cadrà quest'infelice,
> Voce infausta al cor mi dice
> Che mai più ti rivedrò ...
>
> Vano è il duol che ti tormenta,
> Credi a me, sarai felice,
> Voce arcana mi predice
> Che tra poco tornerò ...

In some ways an even better example of Piave's instinct to normalize the Byronic is found in his treatment of the final scene of the opera, which he builds out of two separate sections of the poem; the beginning of Canto III, where the surviving corsairs report to Medora the failure of their mission and Conrad's capture, and the end of the same canto, where Conrad returns to his island and finds Medora dead. The crucial and (to Piave) wholly unacceptable thing about Byron's conclusion is its mysteriousness, the frustrations and uncertainties which it declines to resolve. Medora is dead before Conrad returns; it is not made clear why, but one supposes from shock and grief. The strange relationship torn asunder early in the poem can never now be resumed. Her dead body can only be described. What happens to Gulnare is even less clear. Once she has been given Conrad's kiss of reconciliation and allowed to sail with him to the corsair island she is mentioned no more. Conrad too simply disappears mysteriously; 'Nor trace, nor tidings of his doom declare Where lives his grief or perish'd his despair.'

Dead and vanished protagonists provide excellent material for the poet, affording infinite scope for pathos and evocative speculation, as Byron's closing stanzas demonstrate. But they are of little avail to the dramatist. The kinds of sentiment that Byron evokes with description and reflection have now to be evoked in action. The source of Piave's refashioning is perhaps to be seen at that point in the third canto where Conrad comes to accept and forgive the fact that Gulnare has murdered Seyd so that he might live, and seals his forgiveness with a kiss which says Byron, 'even Medora might forgive ... The first, the last that Frailty stole from Faith'. At any rate it is clearly not in the nature of Italian opera to conclude on Byron's note of alienation and uncertainty. Each relationship has to be led to an explicit finalization. Piave's slow cabaletta 'Per me infelice'

serves as a resolution of the curious triangle that has developed: love
is confessed, gratitude is expressed, death is looked in the face. From
here he proceeds to a cantabile finale which, though of course
concerned with squeezing the death scene for pathetic juices,
achieves harmony and rises to a pitch of heroic exultation, with
avowals of eternal love, and with a vision of prayers before the
throne of Heaven:

Oh mia diletta, guardami!	... più non ti veggo ... addio! ...
L'amante tuo son io ...	In cielo ... innanzi ... a Dio ...
Se a te serbommi un Dio	Volo ... per te ... a pregar!
Ah perchè mi vuol lasciar.	

Finally, there can be no mysterious timeless destiny for Conrad.
The medium demands an heroic gesture of despair: 'Spenta è
Medora! . . . i vortici m'inghiottano del mar (*si slancia in mare*)'.

The one Byronic character who is rendered less convincing by the
formal and psychological conventions of Italian opera is Gulnare.
The crux of the problem is that Byron's way of introducing her and
the way in which her love for Conrad is shown to grow out of the
developments of the story are simply incompatible with the dramatic decorum expected of a prima donna. In Byron, Gulnare appears
almost parenthetically at the height of the battle scene, carried out of
the burning harem in Conrad's arms, but a prima donna is expected
to make a formal and extended *sortita*; Gulnare is surprised, overcome almost unawares by her feelings of tenderness for Conrad, but
a prima donna is expected to know her heart; Gulnare finds herself
involuntarily thrust upon an already-formed Romantic relationship,
but a prima donna is expected to be the hero's heaven-ordained
bride.

Jacopo Ferretti had been exercised by these same problems when
he adapted *The Corsair* for Pacini in 1830, and the least that can be
said for Piave is that he improved upon the efforts of his predecessor.
In the traditional way of the prima donna Ferretti's Gulnare is in love
with Conrad before the opera begins: incredibly, she once caught
sight of him during a sea battle:

> Come obbliar quel dì
> Che per le vie del Mar
> Il Giovane Corsar
> Quest'alma mia rapì!
> La fiera sua beltà
> Fra l'arme a me brillò,
> Ma sparve, e s'involò
> La mia felicità.

And at the end of the opera, after Medora's death, Conrad renounces his freebooting way of life and sails off with Gulnare singing:

> (a mezza voce misteriosamente)
> Solcheremo ignoti mari
> Vesti, e nomi cangieremo
> Indivisi insieme andremo
> Aure nuove a respirar.

No wonder the preface to Ferretti's libretto exhorts the reader, 'Udite la musica'.

Of imbecility on quite this scale Piave was not guilty. But he too needs an *aria di sortita*, and though he is bold enough to begin Act II with an odalisques' chorus welcoming Gulnare to the delights of harem life, he seems to have quailed from the prospect of having a concubine for a prima donna. Gulnare might almost be the English lady out of an eighteenth-century Oriental Singspiel. At any rate she is a prisoner from a foreign land, with a different religion, homesick for her native skies, looking to Heaven to have mercy on her suffering; until Conrad appears, her dominant passion is a Constanze-like devotion to some distant and presumably imaginary Belmonte:

> Vola talor dal carcere
> Libero il pensier mio
> Al sospirato e limpido
> Aere del ciel natio:
>
> Ivi rapita l'anima
> Scorda le sue catene
> Oblia le antiche pene,
> Spazia in un ciel d'amor.

The rude bathos of Piave's final couplet, 'Ma di Seid nel talamo, Fugge il mio dolce error!', is omitted in Verdi's setting; so of Byron's 'Harem Queen' there is really no trace. Once the formal requirements of the *aria di sortita* have been satisfied, however, this virginal lady disappears and is replaced by a character quite different and altogether more formidable.

The music of *Il Corsaro*

By the time Verdi came to compose *Il Corsaro* there was not a great deal of the spirit of Byron left. Most of the passages of sustained eloquence had proved to be of little service in the dramatic medium;

the exoticism of his colouring had been sobered down; and, for better or for worse, his characters had been normalized by Piave's mediation. It is, then, rarely that one can point to a piece of music that is genuinely Byronic in its inspiration. The clearest example is perhaps Medora's romanza 'Non so le tetre immagini', which owes its strophic form and harp accompaniment to the fact that it is a song within the poem, and its tender and yet exotic style to Byron's characterization of it as 'wild and soft'. The next movement, the cantabile 'No, tu non sai comprendere', which matches Byron's 'Oh! many a night on this lone couch reclined ...', is a more detailed parallel: the interaction of Nature and the passions suggested in the poem is splendidly paraphrased in the tugging rhythms and surging figurations, the rearing and plunging of the melodic contour (Ex. 5).

Ex. 5

Moreover something of the nervous sensibility of the romanza is carried over into the florid cadences. But these, like the very much less successful attempt to match the poem's tumultuous description of the battle in the horrid veering modulations at the start of the Act

II finale, are the kinds of poetic/musical parallels that Verdi might have established with any writer.

Byronic in a more generalized sense is the instrumental *preludio*. For though a clear and specific dramatic intent certainly cannot be demonstrated, it does suggest an antithesis between cosmic grandeur and the most intimate sentiments of the heart, which could be said to be a concern of the poet's. Both themes are outside the usual scope of Verdi's sinfonias, though interestingly enough the *Corsaro* prelude shares them with that to *I Due Foscari*.

The very modest traces of Byronic inspiration so far described are rapidly cancelled out by the un-Byronic tone of so much else. Even the vivid, exotic colouring at the start of the second canto of the poem gets lost in the reworking of the scene in the second act of the opera. Because of the formal need to use the odalisques as choral attendants on the prima donna, the 'wild minstrelsy' with which they adorn the Pacha's feast in Byron is replaced by an effetely girlish song about the delights of harem life; the touches of modal and instrumental exoticism, far from giving it any suggestion of voluptuousness or abandon, merely emphasize its drivelling prettiness. With the odalisques put to this new purpose, the only theatrical demonstration of the splendid banquet described by Byron is the *coro ed inno* that follows Gulnare's aria. But this in turn is affected by Piave's and Verdi's desire to make a serious dramatic figure of Seid, and lusty, exotic colour is almost wholly suppressed in favour of a solemn, brassy cantabile more evocative of *Nabucco* than of Byron.

If it was indeed the magic of Byron's characters that aroused Verdi's interest, it should be in the musical treatment of them that one can most clearly see what has been gained by the experience of working with the poet. As we have seen, much of their original singularity has been reduced in Piave's libretto, but in the case of Conrad and the two women, at least, elements of strangeness have been preserved. The opening scene for Conrad probably provides the best example of a musical characterization genuinely Byronic in tone.

The first thing that strikes us is the simple yet effective way in which Conrad's spiritual loneliness is suggested. He enters on an empty stage, and the traditional opening chorus is removed into the distance, off-stage (despite the vocal score, both libretto and autograph score insist that the stage is empty). Consequently the description of the sea and the corsair way of life that forms the subject of this chorus acts as a background, not a diversion, and the loud, abrupt presentation of Conrad at 'Fero è il canto' suggests both his fierceness and his solitariness; he does not sit among his men like those other Verdian outlaws, Ernani and Manrico.

Thanks to Piave, Verdi is able to improve conspicuously on Byron in the portrayal of Conrad that follows in the scena proper. The crucial fact of alienation from the world is expressed in two ways: in terms of contempt in the savage and gloomy recitative, and in terms of regret in the cantabile. The emphases at once make of this outsider a sympathetic figure: his aspiration to a noble and useful life (the text should read 'Tutto parea sorridere al viver mio primiero'*) has inexplicably turned sour on him. As with Macbeth when his vision of a better might-have-been fades away to become hardly more than a subconscious memory, Conrad's song sinks into the orchestra (cf. p. 369, Ex. 2). Despite its inevitably more conventional form, the cabaletta admirably suggests those other aspects of Conrad's character, his abounding vitality and, by drawing the chorus into the aria, the hold he exerts over his men. Piave and Verdi have succeeded in evoking all the essential features of Byron's Conrad without being tempted into that hyperbole of rhetoric and fumbling moralization that make him totally incredible in the poem. Byron's contradictions are resolved in the depiction of one who scorns the world, yet regrets the beauty it might have had, and who in his chosen way of life is the very incarnation of valour. When in the duet with Medora he is shown to be a tender and considerate lover besides, he has acquired a range of faculties rare among Verdi's early heroes: Byronic, yet credibly Byronic.

The impressive excellence of these moments is not really matched by the scena and duet with Gulnare in Act III. Piave is insufficiently rigorous in his handling of the wealth of Byronic data, and the characterization of Conrad begins to show signs of authentic muddle. This unsatisfactory state of affairs is exacerbated by the need to compress the time-scale. Although the librettist based the text of the first part of this scena on the first of Byron's two prison scenes, Verdi's mood seems closer to the mood of the second. We hear very little that is expressive of 'chaos of the mind', much that is 'long, anxious, weary, still the same'. In place of the wild passions of the one Byronic scene and the grim thinking of the other, Verdi distils a single mood of unremitting melancholy.

Though the scene has its sad poetry, it does mark the beginning of

---

* Thus in the libretto printed for the first performance, and in Verdi's autograph score.

Conrad's decline into the world of incredible Byronism. At this point in the poem Conrad is becoming as lifeless, as lethargically enduring in the presence of Gulnare's love as earlier he had been with Medora. But this time Piave does not come to the rescue. He preserves Byron's fatalistic inertia, reducing the grand hero of Acts I and II to a nadir of implausibility, howling impotently at the thunderstorm, longing for a death that will end his hated life, yet a very stickler on the immaculateness of his honour. But where Byron does provide an idea worth dramatizing – for example, in the starkly contrasted visions that haunt Gulnare, the one of the scaffold, the other of love and freedom – Verdi is on to them in a flash, forming from them a cantabile, 'Non sai tu che sulla testa', of remarkable expressive freedom. Likewise inspired by the poem, by its sickening emptiness of atmosphere, its depiction of the cold despair of Gulnare after the murder of Seid, is the transition into the cabaletta. The mood of this admirably stark and creative writing is preserved in Gulnare's verse 'La terra, il ciel m'abborrino' with its thudding accompaniment and rearing melodic lines. But the self-reproach and the final reconciliation, which Byron stretches out over hours of narrated tension, here have to be encapsulated in a brief verse of cabaletta and a *stretta a2*. It is too formal, too dulcet, too easily flowing to capture much of the prolonged anguish of the Byronic mood.

Conrad then begins as a most excellently interesting hero, sufficiently singular for one to feel that the essay at Byronism was worthwhile. But an awful lot of Byronic pretence and confusion has had to be stripped away to achieve this success, and the more uncritical acceptances of Byronic raw material in the later stages of the drama prove to be rather a liability than an asset. The drawing of Medora begins equally well, the 'softness' and 'wildness' with which Byron endures her suggesting a magically unusual treatment of the *aria di sortita*. But the refashioning of the conclusion of the tale requires that at her second and last appearance Byron should be abandoned altogether, and that she should be drawn in the conventional language of the expiring soprano. There is perhaps a last suggestion of proper hectic in the cadence of her arioso 'Fra poco con lui sarò', but in her refrain 'Il mio Corrado' and in her final cantabile 'Oh mio Corrado appressati' she has become naturalized, singing with the direct, simple eloquence native to the Italian opera of the 1840s. Gulnare is likewise too much naturalized, by the prima-donna ritual of the *aria di sortita*, and by the easy harmoniousness into which she is finally resolved. As for Seid, the whole role needed to be rethought, and every ensemble situation in which he takes part reorientated, before he could appear as anything more than a pantomime demon king. And in this transformation his one Byronic asset, his garish Oriental colouring, has to be sacrificed.

Much of the Byronic magic, then, has proved to be false; much more either could not be re-created in the idiom of Verdian opera or was quite unusable in any dramatic form. Essentially Byron's inability to see his characters whole, the discrepancy between the sentiments he expresses and the realities he demonstrates, the fundamental inability to offer a coherent vision of life, even if it be a tragic one, make him a profoundly useless poet for Verdi's purposes. Despite the love which Byron's heroic devotion to national freedom inspired, despite the macabre allure which some of his characters were bound to have for a restless dramatic imagination, it is no wonder that Verdi turned his back so soon, and moved on to better things.

The impact of Shakespeare – the Florence *Macbeth*

Shakespeare in Italy

One of Shakespeare's most eloquent eighteenth-century apologists was an Italian: Dr Johnson's good friend Giuseppe Baretti, who had acquired the taste during his residence in London in the 1750s. When Johnson's Shakespeare edition appeared, Baretti, now back in Italy again, wrote to request a copy: he wished, he explained, 'to expound the great tragedian to the ladies of Italy'.[1] Baretti was as good as his word, writing in the literary magazine *Frusta* in January 1764 of this poet who 'in both the tragic and the comic styles stands quite alone, ahead of all the Corneilles, all the Racines, and all the Molières of Gaul'. It was Baretti, furthermore, who took up arms against Voltaire – whose prestige as a Shakespeare critic had hitherto been unquestioned in France and Italy – by publishing in 1777 his *Discours sur Shakespeare et sur monsieur de Voltaire*.

Nevertheless, how untypical Baretti was of eighteenth-century Italian men of letters; and how little impact his enthusiasm for Shakespeare really made in Italy! Italy's literary life, dominated throughout the century by the ideals of the Arcadians, with their pernickety absorption in matters of linguistic purity and formal propriety, afforded no facilities for cultivating such a taste. Only Italian authors who had the opportunity of savouring Shakespeare in the very different artistic atmosphere of London were really able to sense his greatness; men like Paolo Rolli, for example, for several years librettist to the Royal Academy in London, who in the preface to his translation of Milton's *Paradise Lost* (1729) wrote of the 'insuperabile sublimità' to which Shakespeare had raised the English theatre, and whose translation of Hamlet's 'To be or not to be' soliloquy (1739) is the earliest Italian version of any piece of Shakespeare; or like Alessandro Verri, who was so impressed by the Shakespeare productions he saw in London in 1767 that he made what can be described as the earliest genuine translations of complete Shakespeare plays into Italian. He selected *Hamlet* and *Othello*: but as neither was published their impact on Italian taste was nil.

When allowance has been made for such exceptions as Rolli, Baretti and Verri, one can say that Arcadian Italy was either totally ignorant of Shakespeare or professed a kind of condescending esteem for certain aspects of his work which Voltaire had indicated that it was proper to admire. None of Italy's literary or theatrical sages – not Metastasio nor Algarotti nor Quadrio – shows signs of any first-hand knowledge of his work, still less of any real understanding of its character. We may cite Quadrio's opinion, which was typical for the whole era.

This poet, despite the fact that he had a genius both fecund and powerful, and was gifted with a spirit which combined naturalness and sublimity, was wholly lacking, as M. de Voltaire writes, in any real understanding of the rules of art, nor is any glimmer of good taste to be perceived in his poetry. So instead of bringing benefits to the English theatre by correcting its defects, he led it to total ruin . . .[2]

Later in the eighteenth century, both Shakespeare's 'naturalness' and his 'sublimity' came to be more extravagantly admired; less emphasis was laid on his deficiency in taste. But the tone of Voltaire's criticism was still pervasive. Manzoni felt it still pertinent to make ironic use of Voltaire's phrase 'a barbarian not without genius' in *I Promessi Sposi* (1823), and in a letter written in January 1828 to his first English translator, the Rev. Charles Swan, complained about the 'strange way of praising [Shakespeare] by saying that in the middle of a series of extravagances, he comes out from time to time with wonderful flashes of genius . . .'

At once a cause and a consequence of the ignorance about Shakespeare in eighteenth-century Italy was the lack of translations. Until the very end of the eighteenth century only one work, *Julius Caesar* (Siena 1756), appeared in a complete Italian translation, and that under somewhat inauspicious circumstances. For the translator, Canon Domenico Valentini, as he candidly confessed, knew no English; however, he did have among his acquaintances 'several gentlemen from that illustrious nation who understand the Tuscan tongue perfectly [and who] have had the goodness and the patience to expound this tragedy to me'.[3] Nor did the situation much improve until after the Restoration of 1815. Up to that time only three other Shakespeare plays had been translated, *Othello*, *Macbeth* and *Coriolanus*, all of them by a Venetian noblewoman, Giustina Renier

Michiel, in the last years of the eighteenth century; a second version of *Julius Caesar*, by Michele Leoni, appeared in 1811.

Until the Restoration, then, only the comparatively small number of Italians who knew English could really get to know a representative repertory of Shakespeare's works. The rest of them were dependent upon the mediation of the French; upon Voltaire for their critical opinion, upon Laplace, Letourneur and Ducis for their translations. In some respects such dependency was worse than ignorance, for, with the honourable exception of Letourneur's, these French translations were very strange affairs. Laplace's work, issued from 1745 onwards, more resembled Sunday newspaper digests than real translation. His typical method was to translate the scenes that seemed to him most interesting and to provide a linking synopsis of the rest. And yet it was largely on Laplace's work that Jean-François Ducis, for many years the most influential of the French translators, relied in his versions of the plays; for Ducis himself, like Valentini, knew no English.

The crucial difference between Ducis's work and that of his predecessor Laplace and his contemporary Letourneur was that it was designed to be performed. And it was indeed thanks to Ducis that Shakespeare began to become popular in the theatres of France and of Italy. Several Italian pieces from the later eighteenth century that at first sight look like Shakespeare translations prove on closer examination to be Italian adaptations of Ducis's French versions. The trouble with this was that Ducis's versions were not really translations at all. Being a Frenchman, and having his eye on theatrical performance, he had the problem of 'making ... Shakespeare's plays fit into a dramatic system that was unquestionably the best, and please a taste that was no less unquestionably the most delicate in the world'.[4] Thus in *Hamlet* the number of characters is reduced from twenty-three to eight, the action of the play is carefully reorganized with a view to preserving the dramatic unities of time and place, and almost everything that a fastidious Frenchman might find tasteless or grotesque is either eliminated altogether – like Ophelia's madness – or rationalized – like the ghost, which becomes a dream. When one feels disposed to mock the stereotyped and timorous handling of the subject in the earliest Italian Shakespeare operas, one should perhaps recall that Ducis's versions were all that many Italians knew of him.

It was only when Italian authors and critics began to turn away from the ideals of the Arcadians, especially in the years immediately after 1815, that the appreciation of Shakespeare could enter upon a new phase. One of the specific ambitions of Italian Romanticism was to rejuvenate native literature by bringing it back into communion with developments in other parts of Europe (cf. above, pp. 10–11). Translation, especially from English and German authors, became a central preoccupation, and Shakespeare translations formed a not inconsiderable part of this activity. Michele Leoni, whose *Julius Caesar* had already appeared in 1811, and whose heroic endeavours as translator of Milton, Thomson, Pope, Ossian, Sheridan, Hume and Byron were to earn him the sobriquet 'this Hercules of translators', issued all Shakespeare's major tragedies between 1819 and 1822, each play being prefaced by Schlegel's introduction and provided with explanatory notes. Moreover the admiration of the new generation of writers, of Pellico, of Tommaseo, of Manzoni, was less often hedged about with qualifications, with complaints of Shakespeare's lack of taste or his ignorance of the rules of art. Rather was Shakespeare being used to show that the validity of some of these rules of art was due for reconsideration. As Pellico wrote in the *Conciliatore* in 1818, 'If Shakespeare's *Othello*, with its numerous characters and its disregard for the unities of place and time, nevertheless excites pity and terror, it is a true tragedy, an absolutely true tragedy, just as much as if it produced the same effects with three characters and in accordance with the precepts of the most venerable authorities.'[5]

The clearest indication of the fact that from the time of the Restoration Shakespeare began to be a real force in Italian cultural life is to be found in the writings of Manzoni. Manzoni was by no means an uncritical admirer – he could never reconcile himself to Shakespeare's mixing of comedy and tragedy, for example – but he did perceive in Shakespeare two qualities which he was disposed to regard as supremely important in themselves, and exemplary for his own work. One of these was Shakespeare's truthfulness and naturalness, and his consequent disregard for the rules and restraints by which French dramatists felt themselves bound.

In 1816 Manzoni touched on this question for the first time in a letter to his friend Fauriel:

After having read Shakespeare carefully, and some of the things recently written about the theatre, and after having thought them over, my ideas on some reputations have undergone a considerable change . . . What a lot of trouble people sometimes take to do badly! to avoid the beautiful and great things which present themselves naturally and whose only fault is that they do not conform to the author's narrow and artificial system. What hard work to make men speak neither as they do speak ordinarily, nor as they could speak, to shun prose and poetry and to substitute for them the coldest language of rhetoric, and the one most ill adapted to produce feelings of sympathy.

During the next few years Manzoni was much occupied with drama. His own poetic dramas *Il Conte di Carmagnola* and *Adelchi* appeared in 1820 and 1822 respectively, and in 1823 he summed up his reflections and experiences in this field in a long essay on 'The unity of time and place in tragedy'. In this essay he expounded more fully the contrast between Shakespeare and the French dramatists which he had alluded to in his letter to Fauriel, comparing for the purpose *Othello* and Voltaire's *Zaire*. In the one he finds a depiction of violent passion that is absolutely true and absolutely convincing: in the other, despite Voltaire's admirable talent, much that is contrived and factitious; this he has no hesitation in imputing largely to the artificial system to which Voltaire chose to bind himself.

The other quality in which Manzoni rated Shakespeare higher than the French dramatists was his morality: 'Shakespeare stands above all other artists, because he is the most moral.' In the preface to *Il Conte di Carmagnola* Manzoni had declared his intention of one day writing an essay refuting the claims of Nicole, Bossuet and Rousseau that drama is and must be immoral. Although he never carried out this undertaking, the 'pensieri e giudizi' in his notebooks do contain a précis of such a work, entitled 'Della moralità nelle opere tragiche'. Manzoni attributes the error of the philosopher–critics in question to their ignorance of English drama, to their supposition that there was not and could not be any other type of drama than that practised in France. And the deficiencies of the French dramas from the moral point of view was that French authors tended to concentrate on 'depicting characters bent on achieving some palpable aim'; they were too concerned with desires and strivings, too little with suffering.

Desire excites little sympathy, because to desire one must find oneself in particular circumstances, whereas to be moved and terrified one needs only to be a man. The representation of profound grief and insubstantial terrors is essentially moral because it leaves impressions that tend to virtue. When, in the imagination, a man leaves the battlefield of things known and of the mishaps with which he is accustomed to fight and finds himself in the boundless realm of possible evils, then he feels his weakness, the cheerful thoughts of strength and self-sufficiency abandon him, and he thinks that under such circumstances virtue alone, a clear conscience, and the aid of God can give any help to his mind. Let everyone ask himself after the reading of a Shakespeare tragedy whether he does not feel just such an effect in his mind.

The impact of Shakespeare

In emphasizing Shakespeare's naturalness and truthfulness, and in claiming for him a profound moral purpose, Manzoni was of course doing what all critics are inclined to do, finding in his work what he chose to find, using it to reflect his own preoccupations. The same is true to an even more marked degree of the other great Italian Shakespeare critic of the day, the philosopher Giuseppe Mazzini.

In 1830, Mazzini wrote two substantial and influential essays on drama, the 'Saggio sul dramma storico' and 'Della fatalità come elemento drammatico', in which Shakespeare plays a central role. There is, as far as I am able to perceive, but one fundamental tenet underlying all Mazzini's writings about literature and art: that the age of individualism is over and that the age of 'social humanity' is at hand; and this belief, whether Mazzini purports to be writing about Shakespeare or Goethe or Byron, is reiterated with all the droning relentlessness peculiar to political philosophers. When viewed from this point of view, Shakespeare, whom Mazzini regarded as the supreme exponent of the drama of individuality, was due to be superseded by a greater dramatic artist, one who would follow in the path blazed by Schiller. This new type of drama Mazzini calls 'the drama of providence'. In 'Della fatalità' he describes his ideal in these terms:

a drama which reflects an awareness of humanity; which, while it preserves a prominent place for the representation of the individual, finds a way of connecting the individual with the divine plan of which he is but one free agent . . . which seeks and teaches truth in reality, the principle in the fact, the universal law of the epoch in a particular selected action, and above all this, God, the initiator of all epochs, father of humanity . . . This social drama, profoundly religious, profoundly educative, which is as much vaster than the drama of Shakespeare in proportion and intention as the thought of humanity is vaster than the thought of the individual, will arise with the era to which we look forward, and should from henceforth be the goal to which all young talents desirous of new palms in the cause of Art direct themselves.

May the image of Schiller, the precursor of this kind of drama, watch over their writing desks and inspire their lucubrations . . .

But in the very act of demonstrating that, from a philosophical point of view, the Shakespearian type of drama is defunct, Mazzini praises certain of its artistic qualities in terms which, but for their long-windedness, might almost be Verdi's own:

Shakespeare's drama is the drama of the *individual*. For him the individual is everything, and in the art of creating a character in a few strokes perhaps only Dante, Tacitus and Michelangelo can rival him . . . Shakespeare's characters have life and movement as if they came from the hand of God . . .

521

they bring on to the stage life and being in the most real, the most true, the most perfect way that it has ever been granted a man to achieve . . .

While Manzoni and Mazzini both had their particular religious and philosophical axes to grind, their insights into the character of Shakespeare's art marked a new stage in Italian appreciation. Manzoni's comments on Shakespeare's unstylized, unsystematic manner, and Mazzini's on the truthfulness of his characterization carried conviction even with those who did not share their philosophical interests, and became part of the more rounded picture of Shakespeare that was gradually forming in Italy. We surely catch echoes of the Manzonian and Mazzinian comments in some of Verdi's own observations on Shakespeare. To Clarina Maffei, 20 October 1876:

> . . . To copy the truth may be a good thing, but *to invent the truth* is better, much better.
> There may seem to be a contradiction in these words: *to invent* the truth, but ask *il Papà*. One can perhaps grant that he, *il Papà* really did come across such a character as Falstaff, but hardly that he could have found a villain so villainous as Iago, and never, absolutely never, such angels as Cordelia, Imogen, Desdemona . . . and yet how true they are!
> To copy the truth is a fine thing, but it is photography, not art.[6]

To Giulio Ricordi, 20 November 1880:

> . . . Ah, progress, science, realism . . .! Alas, alas! You can have realism as long as you like, but . . . Shakespeare was a realist, but he didn't know it. He was a realist by inspiration; we are realists according to systems and calculations . . .[7]

Certain aspects of Shakespeare's works remained unappreciated. It was characteristic of the whole Italian Romantic movement, for example, that, unlike the Romantic movements in England, France and Germany it should be very little interested in the supernatural, or, to use the preferred term, 'the fantastic' (cf. above. p. 11). Nor does one feel that the sheer poetic calibre of Shakespeare's work was fully appreciated yet. Before this could happen more complete and better translations were required. Mazzini had called for a complete translation in his essay on historical drama in 1830; and that the need was generally felt is shown by the spate of translations that now began to appear. Between 1829 and 1834, at least six different authors produced Italian versions of at least eight Shakespeare plays. Then in 1839 appeared the first complete translation, the prose version by Carlo Rusconi, which Verdi seems to have used as the basis for his *Macbeth* libretto. Also in 1839 the young Milanese poet Giulio Carcano, who was soon to become one of Verdi's closest friends, published versions of some scenes from *King Lear*, which marked the beginning of a lifetime's devotion to Shakespeare translation. In 1843 Carcano issued his *Teatro scelto di Shakespeare*; and he continued to work on the project for the next forty years, the complete twelve-volume translation eventually appearing between 1875 and 1882.

Italian critics would not claim that Carcano's Shakespeare translation is quite to be compared with the German translations of Schlegel and Tieck as a literary achievement. But the level of soundness and eloquence is generally high. Thanks to him and to Rusconi, Shakespeare was no longer a remote and enigmatic figure; the whole vast scope of his imagination, his boldness, his inventiveness, the power and variety of his language had at last been made clear for all Italians to see.

Shakespeare operas in Italy before Verdi

A characteristic phenomenon of the operatic scene in Italy in the early nineteenth century, and especially after the Restoration, was the rapid abandoning of the Classical and mythological subjects that had for so long provided the matter for heroic opera, and their replacement by subjects borrowed from contemporary or at least fashionable literature from France and Britain, and to a lesser extent from Germany. It was one of opera's few concessions to the cosmopolitan tastes of Italian Romanticism that the novels of Scott and the verse narrative of Byron, the dramas of Schiller, of Scribe and later of Hugo should become favourite source-material for new librettos.

At first sight operas based on Shakespeare seem to play a quite prominent part in this movement. Most of the great tragedies – though not, as far as I know, *Macbeth* itself – had been given operatic settings of sorts well before Verdi. Rossini's *Otello* had been produced in Naples in 1816, Mercadante's *Amleto* in Milan in 1822. Also from Milan in 1817 had come Generali's *Rodrigo di Valenza*, a strange Iberian transmogrification of *King Lear* written by Romani. In addition to these one finds operatic versions of various of the Roman plays, such as Giuseppe Niccolini's *Coriolano* (Milan 1808), of the romances and of the histories; Luigi Caruso's *La Tempesta* (1799) and settings of *La Gioventù d'Enrico V* by Pacini (1820) and Mercadante (1834), for example. Of all Shakespearean themes quite the most popular, however, was *Romeo and Juliet*. Before Romani revised his version of the story for Bellini in 1830, it had been set at least twice, by Vaccai in 1825 and by Torriani in 1828. An earlier libretto on the same theme by Giuseppe Maria Foppa had been composed in 1784 by Luigi Monescalchi and, more famously, in 1796 by Zingarelli.

I do not doubt that with a little diligence this list could easily be extended; nor should one forget that there was a substantial number of Shakespearian ballets produced in Italian opera houses during the period. But what all these statistics are leading up to is not a claim that in the first forty years of the nineteenth century Italian opera was permeated by the spirit of Shakespeare, but rather a quite contrary one: namely that, notwithstanding a scattering of apparently Shakespearian operas produced all over the peninsula between the 1780s and the 1830s, Shakespeare's impact on the Italian theatre, his impact as a dramatic force, had as yet been virtually nil. Verdi's *Macbeth*, far from being just one example of a general trend, is absolutely the first Italian opera that is Shakespearian in any meaningful sense of the word. In all the other cases the resemblance of the opera to the corresponding play, in terms of plot and characterization and atmosphere, is tenuous in the extreme.

We can perhaps best perceive this if we consider briefly the various versions of the *Romeo and Juliet* theme. In the case of Foppa's libretto, set by Monescalchi and Zingarelli, there seems to be absolutely no direct association with Shakespeare. Foppa's source was apparently Gerolamo Della Corte's *Storie di Verona*, from whom he derived a smooth, streamlined version of the story from which both Mercutio and the nurse are omitted, and in which Tybalt and Paris are fused into one. That there should be parallels with Shakespeare is natural enough – in the opera as in the play, the most sustained expressive writing comes in a garden scene in which the lovers plight their troth and then are separated, and in the tomb scene – but they appear to be wholly coincidental. There are certainly no verbal parallels; for Foppa is an out-and-out Arcadian who seems to have known Calzabigi's *Orfeo* text rather well. Romeo and Juliet's love is expressed in such sub-Metastasian terms as these:

ROMEO:	Dunque mio bene,	Tu mia sarai
GIULIETTA:	Sì, cara speme,	Io tua sarò
ROMEO:	Il tuo bel core	
GIULIETTA:		Ti giura amore
ROMEO:	E la tua fede	
GIULIETTA:		Sempre tu avrai
ROMEO:	E m'amerai	
GIULIETTA:		Costante ognor

a2:   O cari palpiti   Soavi accenti
       Dolci momenti   Felice amor etc. etc.

Tybalt's fury in terms of 'le stigie Furie, le fiere Eumenidi', and so on. Romani referred to Foppa's libretto when he published his own version of the story in 1825, explaining that 'it was necessary to change the conduct and the situation of the drama as much as possible . . . and to avoid any ideas that too closely resembled those in the old libretto, so that no comparisons could be made between the new music and the old'.[8] Such narrative modifications as Romani made are largely to be found in the first act. Romeo is head of the Montagues and has killed Capulet's son; he and Juliet are in love before the drama opens; the conflict of the two families of Capulet and Montague is placed in a historical setting of the Guelph and Ghibelline struggle; Romeo openly proposes a marriage between himself and Juliet as a means of bringing an end to political strife in Verona. Romani claimed to have based his variants of the story on a sixteenth-century Italian source, presumably either on Bandello, who was in fact Shakespeare's own source for the play, or, as Leslie Orrey has suggested, on da Porto. But curiously enough his libretto resembles the stories of the *novellieri* rather less than does Foppa's; and it seems likely that at least as influential was the Shakespeare adaptation of Ducis. That there was a Shakespeare in the dim distance behind Ducis's travesty he seems either not to have known, or to have ignored. Nor do Bellini's surviving letters or recorded comments suggest that he had any inkling of the fact that he was composing a Shakespearian opera.

Some might argue that *Romeo and Juliet* is a special case. It was, after all, a familiar and well-loved Italian story; the Italian sources on which Shakespeare himself had drawn were still well known. Maybe one could not expect Italian dramatists to feel that they had much to learn from an ancient and idiosyncratic working of the subject by an Englishman. But the situation is not essentially different – that is to say, no more interest is shown in fidelity to Shakespeare's plot or the quality of his characterization – even in those subjects that must have been taken directly from a Shakespearian source.

As an example one might cite the five-act ballet *Macbeth* by Luigi Henry performed at La Scala in 1830. I quote from the scenario of Act I as a specimen of Henry's reworking:

Duncan, King of Scotland, is attending the warlike sports of his son [Malcolm], whose education is entrusted to the bards. The young prince is ignorant of his birth, and believes himself to be the son of a simple Scot. –

The witches, who have knowledge of the secret, wish to profit from their knowledge to obtain rich rewards, and offer gifts to Duncan. But he refuses to accept these. The presence of these Megaeras always bodes some disaster in the country. [Footnote: A Scottish superstition which is often mentioned by Walter Scott.] A distant sound of hunting is heard and Duncan with his attendants departs. The witches vow vengeance on the king. A terrible storm breaks, which they make use of to show themselves under a veil of mystery to Macbeth, who is taking part in the hunting sports ... Macbeth sees a vision of a crown and a dagger. – One of the witches tells him: 'You will be King' – and disappears, followed by her companions. Macbeth, terror-struck, follows them.

The discussion of the place of Shakespeare in the Italian musical theatre before Verdi would not be complete without a brief mention of the most famous of all the Shakespeare operas of the early *ottocento*, Rossini's *Otello*. *Otello* might reasonably have been expected to show a keener awareness of its Shakespearian source, for its author, Francesco Berio de Salsa, was no mere professional librettist but was (to quote Lady Morgan) 'A nobleman ... of very considerable literary talent and acquaintance, which extends itself to the utmost verge of the philosophy and belles-lettres of England, France, Germany, and his native country. He has read everything, and continues to read everything'.[9]

A large part of Shakespeare, as of Homer, Sophocles, Terence and Corneille, the Marchese Berio was reputed to know by heart. Nevertheless the quality of his *Otello* libretto, that is to say the degree of its fidelity to Shakespeare, is notorious. Berio was felt to have been bold to the point of outrage in retaining the killing of Desdemona by Othello, but by knowledgeable Shakespearians like Stendhal and Byron his work was from the start denounced as a travesty. Byron's report from Venice in 1818 is well known: 'They have been crucifying *Othello* into an opera ... the music good, but lugubrious, but as for the words, all the real scenes with Iago cut out, and the greatest nonsense inserted; the handkerchief turned into a *billet-doux*, and the first singer would not *black* his face, for some exquisite reasons assigned in the preface'.[10] Nor did Rossini manifest any interest in the fact that he was working a Shakespearian subject. His only recorded comments on the literary pedigree of the libretto are concerned with those lines from Dante sung off-stage by a gondolier at the start of Act III, which he himself insisted on including despite Berio's pedantic objection that 'gondoliers never sing Dante, and but rarely Tasso'.[11]

Given the character of Berio's libretto it is clearly impossible that Rossini's music should be marked by any genuinely Shakespearian inspirations. Of course Rossini writes a willow song for Desdemona in Act III, though its resemblance in diction and tone to Shakespeare's is negligible, and there are even examples of more unexpected parallels with the play – such as Iago's patter of counterpoint in the *andante* of the *introduzione* to Act I, which is a tolerably close analogy to the remark he makes in Shakespeare: 'O, you are well-tuned now! But I'll set down the pegs that make this music, As honest as I am' (II.1, 198–200). In general, however, one can claim no more for *Otello* than for the other supposedly Shakespearian operas of the period. Berio and Rossini turned to Shakespeare not in the spirit of idolization that Verdi was to feel, not because they believed that Italian opera might be dramatically and psychologically rejuvenated by the experience, but simply, one feels, because Shakespeare was becoming fashionable in cultivated circles, and because he no less than the next fashionable author could be looked to to provide the occasional subject for a Romantic melodrama. But the nature of these librettos, their handling of plot, their disregard for the finer points of characterization, their total failure to match any of the qualities of language in the original, meant that their composers never really came into contact with Shakespeare at all. Nowhere does one find a musical form, or a counterpointing of characters in an ensemble, or a piece of musical imagery which one could reasonably attribute to the impact of Shakespeare on the dramatic imagination of the composer.

But these are precisely the kinds of things one does find in profusion in Verdi's *Macbeth*. As well as being a landmark in Verdi's own career, *Macbeth* marks a quite new departure in the adaptation of Shakespeare for the Italian operatic stage.

The libretto

There can be no doubt that of all the operas which Verdi composed during the 1840s, *Macbeth* was that into which he felt he had put the best of himself. It was a work which, to quote his letter of dedication to Barezzi, he 'loved more than his other operas'; it was a work for whose sake he made unprecedented demands on the talents and the conscientiousness of his performers. No other score before *Rigoletto* is so consistently inventive, or so imaginative and resourceful in its adaptation of the habits of *ottocento* melodrama to a dramatic purpose. Moreover, there is a sense in which *Macbeth* was Verdi's own opera more completely, more unconditionally than any other he had composed in the past or would compose in the future. For in everything except the actual craft of versification the libretto was his, too. 'I made the synopsis myself; indeed I did more than the synopsis, I wrote a full prose version of the drama, showing the distribution of the acts, the scenes, the musical numbers &c . . . then I gave it to Piave to versify.'

For many parts of the libretto Verdi provided Piave with even more specific details than this, indicating the number of lines he required for a particular cantabile, or the number of syllables to the line for a particular chorus. When we talk of the libretto of *Macbeth* we are, then, talking about something whose dramatic character and whose form, down to the finest details, were dictated by Verdi himself.*

The basic principle underlying Verdi's conception – and this is where he parts company with the composers of the earlier Shakespeare operas – was that of fidelity to the Shakespearian original. It is true that whether an opera was modelled on Hugo or Byron or Schiller, Verdi tended to lay strong emphasis on the 'authenticity' of his adaptation. But nowhere else does he so insist that what he is attempting to do is not to transform a dramatic and literary masterpiece into a typical Italian opera, but to transform Italian opera into a medium flexible and eloquent enough to be a vehicle for such characters and such passions as those in a literary masterpiece like *Macbeth*. Throughout the months of work on the opera, Shakespearian authenticity remained the principle according to which all questions of poetic emphasis or scenic interpretation were to be decided.†

In his quest for authenticity Verdi did not of course go so far as to imagine that his opera must attempt to recreate everything in Shakespeare's play. For all the tautness and economy of *Macbeth*, there was a whole range of aspects that had to be or could be dispensed with. The various *bonnes bouches* for James VI were obviously quite irrelevant to Verdi's purposes. Considerations of length and theatrical practicability led likewise to the suppression of all those scenes treating the political background, the rebellions and wars in which Macbeth had won so much esteem, and later the organizing of an opposition among his oppressed and embittered subjects. Nor on the other hand did Verdi hesitate to handle certain episodes more fully or emphatically than Shakespeare had done.

---

* This matter is fully documented in chapter 8 above, pp. 172–9.
† Cf. (e.g.) letters of 29 October 1846 to Piave, and 22 December 1846 to Lanari; quoted above, pp. 176 and 181.

The banquet scene matches the operatic medium better than the medium of spoken drama, and is accordingly treated altogether more splendiferously by Verdi than by Shakespeare. The plight of Scotland under Macbeth's tyrannical rule, evoked indirectly by the speeches of Macduff and Ross in Shakespeare, IV.3 – 'each new morn New widows howl', and 'Alas, poor country, Almost afraid to know itself' – can be given a more direct and tangible expressiveness in opera thanks to the chorus.

This chorus, 'Patria oppressa', and the scene that follows it might nevertheless be regarded as a partial exception to the rule of Shakespearian authenticity. When Verdi sent Piave a revised synopsis of the fourth act he emphasized that 'what is absolutely necessary for the drama is that there should be a description of one kind or another of Macbeth's tyranny and thus of Scotland's misery'.* But he went further than this; for he could not fail to observe that such a gambit as

> Alas, poor country,
> Almost afraid to know itself! It cannot
> Be called our mother, but our grave . . .

offered the perfect cue for the incorporation into the dramatic scheme of one of those *risorgimento* episodes by which he set such store in the 1840s. Macduff and Malcolm can hardly be said to exist as independent characters at all; they are simply representative types of the suffering and freedom-thirsty nation. As the scene proceeds their music merges into that of the chorus; the authentically Shakespearian diction of 'Patria oppressa' gives way to the typical *risorgimento* diction of

> La patria tradita,
> Piangendo ne invita.
> Fratelli! gli oppressi
> Corriamo a salvar.

For the rest, though, *Macbeth* was anything but typical. Out of the magic of Shakespeare, lovingly and faithfully adapted, Verdi was determined to create such characters as had never before been seen or heard on the operatic stages of Italy. We can already sense this ambition in a passage from a letter Verdi wrote to Lanari before actually starting work on the opera: 'Varesi is the only artist in Italy at the present time who could do the role I have in mind . . . All the other artists, even the best of them, could not do this part for me the way I want.' We catch echoes of it in Piave's observation to Lanari

* Cf. letter of 10 December 1846, quoted above, p. 177.

that 'the role for Signora Loewe in particular will be the most sublime role ever to have appeared on the operatic stage in Italy, and so will that of the baritone. I think that, if this opera is a success, it will give our music new tendencies and open up new paths for composers present and future.' And the ambition appears to be fulfilled in the light of the observations made by Verdi to Cammarano at the time of the Naples revival of the opera in 1848.* In drawing upon Shakespeare Verdi clearly believed that he could substitute for the over-standardized heroes and villains of Italian romantic melodrama characters who were absolutely unique in their sublimity and terribleness.

Hand in hand with this quest for the unique in terms of characterization went a desire to renew the actual language of the operatic libretto; to substitute for the standard dulcet clichés in which the standard romantic passions were expressed a language that had something of the 'sublimity', 'extravagance' and 'originality' of Shakespeare's play. In the synopsis which Verdi sent Piave to act as the blueprint for the libretto it is clear that he kept as close as he could to the sequence of ideas, the imagery, the very vocabulary of the play. And even after Piave's work on the versification had been completed there was scarcely a phrase in the libretto that did not have a close parallel in the equivalent scene of the play. The consequences of such minute fidelity to the original are most apparent in the verses for cantabiles and cabalettas; for here instead of the usual eight lines or so expressing such passions as love or wrath or remorse, in Arcadian abstractions, we tend to find verses packed as densely with ideas and imagery as a Shakespearian soliloquy. A Piavean arioso and cantabile may be quoted alongside the Shakespearian originals to show the degree of correspondence between them:

Piave I.11	Shakespeare II.1
Mi si affaccia un pugnal?! L'elsa a me volta?	Is this a dagger which I see before me,
Se larva non sei tu, ch'io ti brand-isca . . .	The handle toward my hand? Come, let me clutch thee:
Mi sfuggi . . . eppur ti veggo! A me precorri	I have thee not, and yet I see thee still . . .
Sul confuso cammin, che nella mente	Thou marshall'st me the way that I was going,
Di seguir disegnava! . . . Orrenda imago!	And such an instrument I was to use! . . . I see thee still;

* Cf. letter of 25 November 1848, quoted above, p. 189.

Solco sanguigno la tua lama irriga! . . .	And on thy blade and dudgeon gouts of blood,
Ma nulla esiste ancor. Il sol cruento	. . . There's no such thing:
Mio pensier la dà forma, e come vera	It is the bloody business which informs
Mi presenta allo sguardo una chimera.	Thus to mine eyes . . .
Sulla metà del mondo	Now o'er the one half-world
Or morta è la natura; or l' assassino	Nature seems dead . . . Witchcraft celebrates
Come fantasma per l'ombre si striscia,	Pale Hecate's off'rings; and wither'ed Murder
Or consuman le streghe i lor misteri.	. . . towards his design
Immobil terra! a' passi miei sta muta . . .	Moves like a ghost. Thou sure and firm-set earth.
(*Odesi un tocco di campana*)	Hear not my steps . . . (*a bell rings*)
E deciso . . . quel bronzo, ecco, m'invita!	I go, and it is done: the bell invites me.
Non udirlo, Duncano! è squillo eterno	Hear it not, Duncan, for it is a knell
Che nel cielo ti chiama o nell' inferno.	That summons thee to heaven, or to hell.

In this text Piave has even preserved the contrast between blank verse and rhyming couplet.

Piave IV.5	Shakespeare V.3
. . . Eppur la vita	. . . my way of life
Sento nelle mie fibre inaridita!	Is fall'n into the sere, the yellow leaf,
Pietà, rispetto, amore,	And that which should accompany old age,
Conforto ai dì cadenti,	As honour, love, obedience, troops of friends,
Non spargeran d'un fiore	I must not look to have; but, in their stead,
La tua canuta età.	Curses, not loud but deep . . .
Né sul tuo regio sasso	
Sperar soavi accenti:	
Sol la bestemmia, ahi lasso!	
La nenia tua sarà!	

And here the single line which has no direct Shakespearian parallel, 'Non spargeran d'un fiore . . .', is based on the authentic vegetable imagery of the original.

A particularly interesting demonstration of Verdi's quest for authenticity is provided by the struggle to give satisfactory shape to the opening scene of Act II. No other scene in the opera seems to have given rise to quite such heart-searching as this, and even in the Paris version a fully satisfactory solution was never found. Presumably for reasons of textural and tonal variety, Verdi had intended to begin the second act with a solo scena for Lady Macbeth. The original form of the scene still survives in his fair copy of the libretto. It consists of a brief recitative which summarizes the most important narrative details of Shakespeare's III.1 – that, following Duncan's assassination, Macbeth has been crowned king, and that Malcolm has fled to England and is suspected of parricide – and which also reviews those factors that make Banquo a threat to the Macbeths' peace of mind; and a cantabile 'Pria che il tetro augel notturno', expressing the determination to have Banquo murdered. The language of the cantabile is closely comparable to that used by Macbeth in Shakespeare:

> Light thickens, and the crow
> Makes wing to the rooky wood . . .
> Whiles night's black agents to their preys do rouse . . .
> Things bad begun make strong themselves by ill . . . (III.3)

This scene falsifies Shakespeare in two ways. For one thing, it makes Lady Macbeth the instigator of Banquo's murder when it is fundamental to Shakespeare's play that, once Macbeth has embarked on a path of assassination, his erstwhile scrupulousness gives way to a positive zest for obliterating all those who can be suspected of opposing him or who can be felt to menace him in any way. For another, it puts into the mouth of Lady Macbeth the kind of richly imaged language which Shakespeare is careful to reserve for her husband. While Macbeth ponders the threat posed by Banquo in majestic blank verse:

> To be thus is nothing;
> But to be safely thus. Our fear in Banquo
> Stick deep, and in his royalty of nature
> Reigns that which would be fear'd . . .   (III.1)

Lady Macbeth employs the slick staccato of the calculating politician,

> Nought's had, all's spent,
> Where our desire is got without content:
> 'Tis safer to be that which we destroy
> Than by destruction dwell in doubtful joy.   (III.2)

What prompted the rejection of this version of the scene was, however, purely a matter of theatrical plausibility, or so it appears. On 3 December 1846 Verdi wrote to Piave, 'The more one thinks about this *Macbeth* the more one finds that needs improving. There is an awkward spot at the start of the second act, and that is that Lady ponders and then decides upon the murder of Banquo, and hardly has she left the stage when the assassins come on to carry out Lady's orders.'* As an alternative, Verdi provided the synopsis for a dialogue scene between Macbeth and Lady Macbeth, at the end of which he goes off to arrange the murder of Duncan while she remains to sing her aria.[12] In solving a problem of mere scenic manipulation Verdi also made an adjustment in the characterization, taking away from Lady Macbeth the Macbethian 'Pria che il tetro augel notturno', an *adagio*, and asking Piave to provide the text for an *allegro* based on the idea of her heart 'swelling with the hope that now at last they would be able to reign securely on their throne'. But the scene is not yet faithful to that in the play, because still Lady Macbeth is the leading partner in plotting the murder: it is she who lures Macbeth forward at every stage, pointing out that Banquo is not immortal ... that another crime is necessary ... immediately. Gradually, however, in the process of a further two rewritings by Piave, the balance was rectified. Macbeth did become the instigator of the next murder, and in terms of characterization, this rewriting, together with the new aria text, 'Trionfai securi alfine', has come back much closer to the Shakespearian source. But it was at the expense of the poetry. For while the tone of Shakespeare's scene is determined by the nocturnal ghastliness of Macbeth's speeches, that of Verdi's is determined by the icy virtuosity of Lady Macbeth's cabaletta. It was the tone of the scene that Verdi concentrated on remedying in the final Paris revision, sending Piave back to the 'Light thickens' speech for the aria text, and once again, as he had in his very first synopsis, attributing a Macbeth-like sensibility to the 'fiend-like queen'.

Before leaving the question of Verdi's fidelity to Shakespeare a brief word must be said about those several movements which are generally regarded as more or less legitimate embellishments, the choruses of witches 'E voi spirti' and 'Ondine e Silfidi', and Macbeth's death scene. These movements, it must be conceded, are in no literal sense Shakespearian: but at the same time, I think it quite likely that Verdi believed they were, or at least that he associated them with the living tradition of English Shakespeare performance. What has to be remembered is that at the time when Verdi was working on *Macbeth* the authentic Shakespearian text was only slowly winning its way back into the theatre even in England. Since the Restoration the *divertissements* of singing, dancing and flying witches which Davenant had concocted in 1671 had formed a standard part of *Macbeth* productions. Other interpolated speeches,

---

* See above, p. 176 and note 24.

songs and dances had an even longer history, going back to Middleton's productions of *Macbeth* in around 1610, and some of these, in the Hecate scenes, remain part of the established text of *Macbeth* even now. It was not until Samuel Phelps's production of *Macbeth* in 1847 that these Davenant and Middleton *divertissements* were completely suppressed; and at the time of the great spate of Shakespeare translations between about 1830 and 1850, at least one of them, Middleton's 'charm-song' in IV.1, still enjoyed an almost *Urtext*-like status:

> Black spirits and white, red spirits and gray,
> Mingle, mingle, mingle, you that mingle may!

In modern editions of *Macbeth* this is simply cued in in a stage direction; Piave's libretto at this point, however, is nothing more or less than a complete translation of Middleton's song:

> E voi, Spirti
> Negri e candidi,
> Rossi e ceruli,
> Rimescete!
> Voi che mescere
> Ben sapete,
> Rimescete!
> Rimescete!

The case of Macbeth's death scene is comparable. The various Restoration versions of *Macbeth*, besides turning the work into a semi-opera, strove also to make the verse more elegant and edifying. A characteristic touch in a 1674 revision, attributed again to Davenant, is the replacement of the lines

> The devil damn thee black, thou cream-faced loon!
> Where got'st thou that goose look?

by

> Now Friend, what means thy change of countenance?

A few minutes later Macbeth 'decorously expires . . . with a moral on his lips',[13] the metre broadening for the occasion into an Alexandrine:

> Farewell, vain world, and what's most vain in it, ambition.

When Garrick first performed *Macbeth* in London in 1744, the revival was advertised as being 'as written by Shakespeare'. It is true that most of the Davenant 'improvements' were abandoned in favour of a text substantially more authentic, but at the point of Macbeth's death Garrick chose rather to outdo Davenant than to undo him. The speech which he delivered at this point in the play likewise became a hallowed item of the English performing tradition, retained well into the nineteenth century by Kemble. Though there are no close verbal parallels it seems possible that Garrick's speech served as the model for Verdi's closing scene.

> 'Tis done – The scene of life will quickly close,
> Ambition's vain delusive dreams are fled,
> And now I wake to darkness, guilt and horror –
> I cannot bear it – Let me shake if off –
> It wo'not be – My soul is clog'd with blood,
> And cannot rise – I dare not ask for mercy! –
> It is too late – Hell drags me down – I sink –
> I sink – Oh! my soul's lost for ever.   (Dies)

When all due emphasis has been laid on the conscientiousness with which Verdi strove to preserve the Shakespearian character of *Macbeth*, it cannot be denied that the mere act of adapting the drama from one medium to another has substantially altered its nature in countless ways, shifting its points of focus, and in particular imposing a quite different kind of dramatic movement. The art of opera, especially as understood in nineteenth-century Italy, imposed some of its own conditions, even on Shakespeare.

One of these was the condition of what one might call company economics: the need to write an opera in such a way that it matched the capabilities of the singers assembled by an impresario for the season of opera in question. For English-speaking readers much light has been shed by Julian Budden's book on the actual tactics employed in fashioning an opera around such a small group of principals, sub-principals and supporting artists. And as Budden has suggested, there is no doubt that these tactics were in Verdi's mind in making his operatic adaptation of *Macbeth*, particularly with regard to the characters of Duncan and Banquo. In Verdi's opera, the overall plan of the drama can be seen to fall into three quite distinct phases. In Act I the ambition to be king is born, and the assassination of Duncan, which makes the realization of this ambition possible, is plotted and carried out. Act II is the Banquo act. Banquo, the incorruptible, the soothsaid progenitor of a line of kings, is feared as a rival, a threat to Macbeth's peace of mind. He too is assassinated, but returns as a ghost to haunt Macbeth. Acts III and IV embody Macbeth's downfall, firstly supernaturally predicted, then, by human agents, inexorably fulfilled.

Given the theatrical economics of the time, principal artists simply could not be engaged for the roles of characters such as

Banquo who disappears halfway through the opera, still less for Duncan, who disappears in the first act. The emphasis of the drama was bound to shift even more emphatically to the protagonists, Macbeth and Lady Macbeth: their world of feeling, a world of corruption, evil, madness and melancholy, was bound to over-shadow – more even than in the play – the old world order of valour and courtesy which they have destroyed.

Under the circumstances, Verdi decided to treat Duncan in a quite *ad hoc* manner, a manner that has a touch of genius about it, not reducing him to sub-principal status, still less to supporting-artist status – which would have been to rank him with assassins and apparitions – but to make his single appearance a symbolic dumb-show, a pantomime evocation of that chivalrous world which there is neither time nor money to evoke in more conventionally operatic terms. One cannot help thinking that Verdi had the play scene in *Hamlet* in mind when he conceived it. Like Hamlet's father, Duncan appears as a figure in a dumb-show, received with a great display of courtesy by those who are intent on murdering him.

Duncan is the light extinguished by Macbeth at the first step in his tragic career; Malcolm, aided by Macduff, is the sun whose rising puts an end to that career. Of the intervening reign of darkness Banquo is the chief victim. Indeed his principal operatic function is that of expressing a sense of awe and horror as the earth becomes covered with darkness. It is he who in the Act I finale describes the ghastly phenomena that portend Duncan's assassination, taking over for the purpose a speech that Shakespeare had given to Lennox, 'The night has been unruly'. And in the scene of his murder in Act II Verdi does not content himself with anything remotely resembling Shakespeare's quasi-realistic lightning incident. He uses his sub-principal, in what was no doubt a diplomatically expedient way, but for all that a thoroughly artistic way too, to evoke a musical image of that 'seeling night' and its 'black agents' which, in the first scene of the act, had had to be dispensed with in the interests of the characterization of Lady Macbeth. Banquo thus finds a new role in the opera, one more readily realizable in operatic terms – in sub-principal terms – than the ambiguous and multi-purpose figure of Shakespeare's play.

A second aspect of the work of adaptation that was bound materially to affect the character of the drama was the need for a more formalized type of dramatic movement. Verdi was as enterprising a composer as any when it was a matter of adapting the traditional lyrical forms of opera to a dramatic purpose, but he was not so mad as to wish to abandon them altogether. The work of turning *Macbeth* into an opera entailed the imposition of a much more obvious pattern of action and reflection than the unremitting impulse of the play readily allowed.

A good example is to be found in the Act I finale of the opera following the discovery of Duncan's assassination. Shakespeare puts the most pungent statement of what has befallen almost at the start:

> Most sacrilegious murder hath broke ope
> The Lord's anointed temple, and stole thence
> The life o'th' building. (II.3)

and then in the turmoil that follows, he demonstrates in brief the triumph of 'confusion', and sets in train a whole series of new dramatic developments. The opera on the other hand swirls momentarily in a state of frenzied excitement until Banquo's cry 'È morto assassinato il re Duncano' brings it back into focus and suspends the action. In place of all the realistic touches that follow in Shakespeare – Macbeth's explanation of how he has killed the grooms, Lady Macbeth's faint, Banquo's eagerness to get dressed, Malcolm's and Donalbain's decision to flee – Piave holds the action in suspense with an uncharacterized *tutti* in which the whole cast expresses its horror and offers its prayers for justice.

This kind of formalization, the need periodically to hold the action in suspense, is intrinsic to the character of Italian opera in Verdi's time. Shakespeare with his almost entirely unstylized dramatic movement was a difficult proposition in this respect; and the opera is full of movements where one feels that the characteristics of the two media are resisting one another rather than collaborating.

A single example of a rather different kind may be cited from the last act of the opera. In Shakespeare's sleepwalking scene we witness the complete psychological breakdown of Lady Macbeth. Until the banquet scene the apparent mistress of every situation, she had eventually been defeated by a menace she could not comprehend; after the departure of the guests Shakespeare had depicted her as weary and demoralized. In the sleepwalking scene itself the final stages of her downfall are expressed not with the superhuman grandeur of language that Macbeth himself would use, but in broken, prosaic fragments, distorted memories of her brilliant past. The scene only acquires coherence by virtue of the reactions and commentaries of the doctor and the waiting gentlewoman, who, in terms of the number of words spoken, play a more prominent role in it than Lady Macbeth herself. But *ottocento* opera had no resources really to match such a scene, no genuine parallel to barely articulate prose, no forms in which a great prima donna and rudimentary supporting artists could be sustained on equal terms. Inevitably the *gran scena del sonnambulismo* becomes a vast solo aria: a solo aria of an extraordinary character certainly, but a solo aria none the less, in which the few brief interjections of the bystanders have scarcely any dramatic or expressive significance.

Such shifts of emphasis as this may somewhat impair the expressive range of Shakespeare's play, and may sometimes spoil a fine point of dramatic characterization, but they certainly do not undermine altogether the validity of attempting to make an opera, a truly Shakespearian opera, out of *Macbeth*. The fundamental problem – that problem on which, if we judge it by the highest standards, Verdi's most idealistic opera founders – lies in the very nature of this particular Shakespearian play. Because *Macbeth* is obviously not simply a chronicle of the deeds done and the emotions experienced by 'this ... butcher and his fiend-like queen'. It is equally concerned, indeed in the crucial expository acts of the play it is more concerned, with the processes by which Macbeth became a 'butcher' and his queen 'fiend-like'. It portrays a valiant gentleman who despite all the promptings of reason and conscience succumbs to the temptation to commit political assassination; and it does this necessarily by means of morally questioning soliloquies, and a rational or philosophical contemplation of the future – in such terms as

> This supernatural soliciting
> Cannot be ill, cannot be good. If ill,
> Why hath it given me earnest of success,
> Commencing in a truth? I am thane of Cawdor
> If good, why do I yield to that suggestion
> Whose horrid image doth unfix my hair,
> And make my seated heart knock at my ribs,
> Against the use of nature? (I.3)

and

> If it were done, when 'tis done, then 'twere well
> It were done quickly; if th'assassination
> Could trammel up the consequence, and catch,
> With his surcease, success; that but this blow
> Might be the be-all and the end-all ... here
> But here, upon this bank and shoal of time,
> We'ld jump the life to come ... (I.7)

But opera is no medium for the analysis of moral or philosophical problems: its proper concerns are the way the characters experience the present, or remember the past, or imagine the future. Much in the opening acts of *Macbeth* is, in these senses, simply not operatic. In particular the whole process of Macbeth's temptation and fall – which Shakespeare himself had already reduced from a more ample process to an absolute minimum in a rewriting of the play about 1606 – is reduced to a few strip-cartoon-like fundamentals, so that the weight of the dramatic design can be shifted from the moral process that leads to Duncan's murder to the emotional experiences that result from it. The murder, which, Dover Wilson conjectured, would have come in the third act of Shakespeare's Ur-*Macbeth*,[14] comes halfway through Act I of Verdi's opera.

Macbeth himself thus becomes a fundamentally different type of character from what he had been in Shakespeare's play. The emotional world to which he has condemned himself by his fall, a world of terror and hallucination, of rage and despair, is quite fully realized. But that he was once 'valour's minion', the 'noble Macbeth', his king's bravest, most loyal, and dearly loved servant is nowhere suggested.

Shakespeare's Lady Macbeth is a much more obviously operatic figure than Macbeth himself and certainly loses less in the adaptation. Even in the play her dramatic career begins with what is formally and psychologically very close to an *aria di sortita*, and ends with a mad scene. The Piave/Verdi version of the first of these sets the tone for the treatment of Lady Macbeth throughout the opera. Shakespeare's 'Glamis thou art, and Cawdor' speech is divided into a recitative and a cantabile, the former rather changing Shakespeare's emphasis. Where Shakespeare is still concerned with depicting the unfallen Macbeth – his public image had been proclaimed by Duncan, now his wife confirms a nature that is 'too full o'th' milk of human kindness', 'not without ambition, but without The illness should attend it' – Piave concentrates her whole expressive emphasis on the vigorous, remorseless prosecution of power. The actual cantabile has precisely the mood of

> Hie thee hither,
> That I may pour my spirits in thine ear,
> And chastise with the valour of my tongue
> All that impedes thee from the golden round ...   (1.5)

In the cabaletta that follows Shakespeare is admittedly unduly diluted. The 'ministri infernali', to judge from the mildness of what they are urged to do, are a mere rhetorical adornment; there is no suggestion that Lady Macbeth is literally offering her soul and body to the fiends of hell to batten upon and to use for their own purposes. But if Verdi's Lady Macbeth is less terrible than Shakespeare's, she is also less vulnerable. That remorseless will for power which she expresses in this opening scene sustains her without scruple or faintness through every appalling situation in which she finds herself. In her *gran scena* and duet with Macbeth in Act I there is no trace of those pangs of humanity which momentarily discomfit her in Shakespeare:

> Had he not resembled
> My father as he slept, I had done't.   (II.2)

And though there is something of Shakespeare's nervous disconnectedness in the early stages of the duet, Verdi's Lady Macbeth scorns her husband's fears altogether more wholeheartedly than Shakespeare's does. Piave even goes so far as to provide her with a parodizing retort to his tale of the voice that cried 'Sleep no more! Macbeth does murder sleep':

> Ma dimmi altra voce non parti d'udire?
> Sei vano, o Macbetto, ma privo d'ardire:
> Glamis, a mezz'opra vacilli, t'arresti,
> Fanciul vanitoso, Caudore, tu se'.

This icy, sometimes mocking mastery of situation remains the hallmark of Verdi's portrait throughout the opera. It informs the brilliant cabaletta 'Trionfai, securi alfine', which, though it may have horrified Verdi at the time of the Paris revision (as Budden suggests), is much more obviously a link in the sustained personification of a steely 'super-witch' than the great aria 'La luce langue' which was to supersede it; and it is the most obviously new note in the *tutti* ensemble at the end of the Act II finale. Shakespeare's Lady Macbeth, after her superhuman but vain effort to bring Macbeth's hallucinations under control, relapses into a weary lethargy in which traces of humanity at last begin to reappear:

> ... Did you send to him, sir? ...
> You lack the season of all natures, sleep ...

Verdi's remains a scathing realist, mocking Macbeth's 'spirto imbelle', and stating as a self-evident truth that 'chi mori tornar non può', a phrase which appears to be based on a terribly ironic line from Shakespeare's sleepwalking scene: 'Banquo's buried; he cannot come out on's grave.' The shift in emphasis in the sleepwalking scene itself, from a prosaic semi-coherence to a sustained outpouring of neurotic passion, has already been discussed.

What role, finally, do the witches play in Verdi's interpretation of the drama? That he had some clear conception of their function is suggested by the ironical impatience with which he greeted Piave's suggestion to dress them in ceremonial costume for the apparition scene in Act III. 'Witches in ceremonial costume? ... Is that Shakespeare's intention? Have you really grasped what *Shakespeare* is trying to do with these witches?' It is indeed a question that has exercised the best critical minds, even when it had been recognized that substantial sections of their third- and fourth-act scenes are inauthentic interpolations. Clearly Verdi was himself misled by spurious performing traditions still current in his time. But if we leave out the passages in which he fell victim to these traditions, I think we must concede that he took an otherwise quite coherent view of their dramatic function. In the opera no less than in the play they are presented not really as witches in the usual sixteenth-century understanding of the term – Shakespeare indeed never actually calls them witches – but as unique and ambiguous creatures 'too witch-like to be Norns, too Norn-like to be witches'.[15] On the one hand they are used to incarnate all that is foul, destructive, and chaotic in the universe; on the other hand they are represented as a kind of satanic priesthood, most typically going about their business in obscene and lying rituals. In so far as Verdi does depart from Shakespeare, it is in laying less emphasis on what is abysmally evil, on the note sounded in the very first scene of Shakespeare's play, with its miauling and croaking familiars, and more on the power which the witches exert in their capacity as a satanic priesthood. It is typical of this slight shift in emphasis that at the end of the opening scene of the libretto, which corresponds closely with the start of Shakespeare's I.3, Verdi should place not a mere incantatory round-dance –

> The Weïrd Sisters, hand in hand,
> Posters of the sea and land,
> Thus do go, about, about,
> Thrice to thine, and thrice to mine,
> And thrice again, to make up nine.
> Peace! the charm's wound up.

– but a boast of the power which the forces of evil exert over land and sea:

> Le sorelle vagabonde
> Van per l'aria, van sull'onde,
> Sanno un circolo intrecciar
> Che comprende e terra e mar.

and that the introduction should conclude with what is, despite a passing reference to 'meeting again, in thunder, lightning, or in rain', really a new scene emphasizing the witches' fatal presiding over Macbeth's destiny.

S'allontanarono, – fuggiam! . . . s'attenda
Le sorti a compiere – nella tregenda
Macbetto riedere – vedrem colà,
E il nostro oracolo – gli parlerà . . .

If the blood-curdling atmospherics of Shakespeare's witch scenes are less evident in the opera, Verdi does come close to realizing that idea with which his friend Carcano justified Shakespeare's use of 'the fantastic': that it represented the attempt to give tangible form to metaphysical problems, 'the expression of thought wrestling with the infinite'.[16]

Music and drama

Our last task is to attempt to understand what kind of impact Shakespeare had on Verdi's music; to see how far his concern for the uniqueness of the characterization and the richness and sublimity of the language are reflected in his score.

It follows inevitably from the already-discussed limitations of the libretto that the central character, Macbeth himself, cannot have quite the emotional and spiritual range of his Shakespearian prototype. Nevertheless, if we examine just a few of the movements in which he is involved in a principal role, the impressiveness of Verdi's achievement will rapidly become apparent.

The text of the 'duettino' 'Due vaticini compiuti or sono' is based on three ideas from Shakespeare's I.3:

> . . . Two truths are told,
> As happy prologues to the swelling act
> Of the imperial theme . . .
> . . . why do I yield to that suggestion
> Whose horrid image doth unfix my hair . . .
> If chance will have me king, why, chance may crown me,
> Without my stir.

But instead of treating them as the stages of a temptation, as in the play, Verdi's music suggests that they conflict and alternate in Macbeth's mind. The three ideas are masterfully analysed in the opening solo verse: the first phrase really does seem to suggest Shakespeare's 'swelling act'; the second, with its harrowing outbursts, shuddering rhythms and chromatic harmonics, the beginning of awful imaginings; the last a winning through to humanity and emotional normality. Each phase of this process is then composed in fuller detail. At no stage does the movement become a duet in the full sense of the word; always Macbeth is the predominant character. If Banquo appears on paper to be more conspicuous in the second stage of the duet it is because Macbeth is musing on what has happened, and the silences that suggest this are filled in by the characterless, time-marking music of Banquo. Only once is there a genuinely duet-like thrill of tension in the music, and that is at the modulation to C major where both singers are asserting different views of the sense of the witches' prophecies. The nightmare visions return with a plunge into D♭; the winning back of spiritual repose in a thematic and harmonic pattern parallel to that in the solo verse. In the coda the whole expressive range of the duet is summarized in a series of symmetrical epigrams. Where Shakespeare's scene is the exposition of a spiritual process, Verdi's duet is the analysis of a state of mind. And if, by itself, it can hardly evince the vast psychological and spiritual understanding of Shakespeare's expository acts, at least the nature of Macbeth's problems and the source of his undoing is vividly sketched. And it is typical of the whole opera that in composing this movement as an aria with an *obbligato* for the sub-principal Banquo, Verdi should be thinking back beyond the symmetry of Piave's verses to the original Shakespearian form of the scene.

Before murdering Duncan, Macbeth has one more solo scena, the arioso 'Mi si affaccia un pugnal', the closeness of whose text to Shakespeare has already been shown. In this movement and in the duet that follows, Verdi comes close to an authentic re-creation of one crucial aspect of Macbeth's character: the kind of imagination that fills the world about him with visions, the imagination of a man whose actions are prompted by wish-fulfilling hallucinations and followed by conscience-haunting spectres. This profoundly interesting movement is the kind of composition that no conventionally minded maestro would have attempted; the fundamental dramatic idea behind it is not that Macbeth is in the grip of this or that passion, but that his surrendering of conscience is prompted by visions. This being so, it is manifestly impossible to give the monologue a self-sufficient form dependent upon impassioned song. It becomes a kind of melodrama, in which the words are preeminent, while the orchestra reflects the impact of the hallucinations on Macbeth's sensibility.

The scene begins in the manner of a conventional accompanied recitative, when Macbeth 'sees' the dagger. He tells us what he sees in a hoarse whisper – in fact he whispers throughout the scene – but the shock and the thrill that it gives him are communicated to the

Ex. 1

audience by the conventional formulae for shock and excitement in the orchestra (Ex. 1). Recognizing the nature of this vision, Macbeth nevertheless succumbs to it – 'Thou marshall'st me the way that I was going'. Verdi finds a marvellous musical equivalent for this notion. Macbeth is rising for action at this point, and so a regular figuration strikes up to give a measured tread to the atmosphere. But Macbeth is not – as he would be in an aria – the dominant personality; he creeps in pursuit of an hallucination. And so the sinuous melody that winds chromatically upwards through this figuration is an instrumental one, to which Macbeth blindly attaches himself (Ex. 2). Macbeth has more than hallucinations to cope with; there is also his heightened sensitivity to the atmosphere of night, a

Ex. 2

night for 'wicked dreams . . . Witchcraft . . . and withered Murder'. Here the music performs a slightly different task, giving tangibility, sensuous form, to those horrors that Shakespeare evokes with his poet's tongue. When, after the ringing of the bell, Macbeth sings *a voce spiegata* for the first time, it provides a more than adequate musical equivalent to Shakespeare's jangling rhyme, 'Hear it not, Duncan, for it is a knell That summons thee to heaven, or to hell.'

The Act III finale, Macbeth's aria 'Vada in fiamma', was one of the movements totally rejected at the time of the 1864–5 revisions. But for all Verdi's later impatience one should not forget the terms in which he had once written of it to Varesi:

I would ask you to take particular care with the cabaletta: it doesn't have the usual form because after all that has gone before, a cabaletta in the usual form with the usual ritornellos would sound trivial. I had composed another one, which I liked when I tried it by itself, but when I joined it up with what had gone before, the effect was intolerable. I think this one works well and I hope you will think so too.

One of the things we may, I think, deduce from these remarks is what keen attention was attracted in 1847 by even comparatively modest departures from formal conventions, especially in cabalettas: for in its actual thematic and harmonic material there is little except the minor key to distinguish this movement from many another. Its original features are the wild return to the minor at the close of the first verse, and the breakdown of this material into a series of fragmented exclamations (Ex. 3), followed by an incomplete reprise. The whole movement is thus fused into a single unit lacking obtrusive recapitulatory features, and as a result has a suggestion of uncontrol, even of madness, about it. This impression is strengthened by the high *tessitura*, and by the fact that Macbeth sings almost without pause.

Still more evocative in its refashioning of the traditional aria patterns is the cantabile 'Pietà, respetto, amore', where the musical pecularities seem very precisely designed to match the poetic ideas of the play. For the principal melody becomes a kind of symbol of 'that which should accompany old age', and in the latter part of the song slips away from the singer into the orchestra, haunting Macbeth with the memory of what might have been, while his own words tell of the present reality of 'curses, not loud but deep'.

If the full process of Macbeth's tragic fall is not made manifest in Verdi's opera, we can, I think, claim that Verdi's achievement in evoking the violent and gloomy recesses of Macbeth's soul is an astonishing one. The spectre-haunted tyrant whose rages flare up into destructive insanity and whose sorrows plunge him into melancholic lethargy is given a majestic eloquence worthy of Shakespeare's own hero. What is more, this eloquence is often directly derived from Shakespeare, not only in terms of the language of the libretto, but in terms of the musical imagery and the musical forms too.

The musical language of Verdi's Lady Macbeth, like the poetic language of Shakespeare's, is altogether less rich and visionary, altogether harder, dryer, and more brilliant. Of the Florence version of the opera one could even say that the poetry goes out of her with her humanity, after she has delivered herself to the fiends of hell in her Act I scena. Verdi's setting of this scene must be examined in detail.

The music of the prelude, with its tremolos, its surging and

The impact of Shakespeare

Ex. 3 cont.

subsiding wails of chromatic harmony, is surely intended to suggest that the atmosphere created by the witches in the introduction is not yet to be dispelled. Rather has it become more obsessive and menacing. And the remoteness of this idiom from that usually employed in a prima donna's *sortita* is given further macabre emphasis when Lady Macbeth begins not to sing, but to speak. After a much-underplayed statement of Macbeth's 'human kindness', and a last inhalation of witching vapours, she launches into a tremendous rhetorical recitative which, by means of bold intervals, rich harmonies, stark antiphonies, gives immense emphasis to her creed of unscrupulous, conscience-free power politics.

If Verdi is guilty of a brief miscalculation in writing a melting string and woodwind transition into the cantabile, the aria itself is marvellously evocative of those concepts of power, ambition and darkness around which Shakespeare's own scene had been built. Power and ambitions can be heard in the strong, high-lying exhortation with which the aria starts, and in several passages in which the idea 'ascendivi a regnar' is almost graphically conveyed – at 'io ti darò valore', for example; darkness seems to pass over the music in the sudden enharmonic modulation at 'Che tardi, accetta il dono', and again in the coda, where the same words are linked to what Noske has called the 'musical figure of death', the ♩♩ rhythm.[17]

Despite its apparently conventional character a number of features show that the transition into the cabaletta has been no less deeply pondered. The messenger's music is one of several almost parodistic march-like episodes which I shall discuss more fully later; then in a single *cantabile* phrase, 'Trovi accoglienza quale un re si merta', is concentrated all the hypocritical effusiveness of that sunlit scene before the castle (Shakespeare, 1.6) where the Macbeths welcome their king. As Lady Macbeth muses on the approach of Duncan, the unresolved chords of the string tremolo, with the long silences that separate them, suggest that the world is holding its breath. Finally in the colossal *tutti* preceding the cabaletta we hear once more the music of the powers of darkness, its style resembling that of the introduction both to the scena and to the first witches' chorus.

The cabaletta is more problematical. At first sight one is tempted to think it one of the few movements in the work in which the rituals of *ottocento* opera get in the way of the dramatic expression. Certainly there is no trace here of Shakespeare's diabolism, and only the merest episodic hint of that 'thick night . . . pall[ed] . . . in the dunnest smoke of hell', which Lady Macbeth invokes in the play; and certainly the exuberant virtuosity of the later stages of the aria seem more in keeping with the vanity of a prima donna than with the pride of a 'super-witch'. But there is no question of Verdi's having adopted this style over-hastily, after an insufficiently rigorous pondering of the issues involved. The tone set by this cabaletta, one of hard, icy brilliance and unremitting energy, becomes the tone of his interpretation of Lady Macbeth throughout the opera.

We hear it a second time in the 'grand duet' later in Act I. What is un-Shakespearian, or at least what gives this movement a slightly different emphasis from the equivalent scene in the play, is the prominent part given to Lady Macbeth. While it may have been conventional formal requirements that dictated this greater measure of equality between the voices, Verdi uses the circumstance with the nicest dramatic skill. The poetry of the music, which derives from the poetry of the play, remains wholly Macbeth's. But against his haunted, tormented eloquence Verdi sets a Lady Macbeth who is never allowed to quail for a moment. Inspired perhaps by Shakespeare's line 'A foolish thought to say a sorry sight', he devises for her a phrase of darting mocking rhythms with which she scourges Macbeth throughout the movement (Ex. 4 – cf. Ex. 5 on p. 376 above). While he pours out an unending stream of *cantabile* phrases, her only *cantabile* is a taunting parody of his visionary fancies. Similarly, in the second act of the opera, the prospect of

Ex. 4

Banquo's murder prompts a hard, glittering rapture, the aria 'Trionfai, securi alfine'; and the flavour is no different in the *brindisi* of the banquet scene, which, at first designed to celebrate Macbeth's kingship, is characteristically used later in an attempt to drive away the hallucination by which that kingship is threatened.

If the sleepwalking scene seems quite remote in style from the first two acts of the opera, it is surely because it is a kind of mad scene: not a mad scene brought about by the intolerable harshness of fate, and expressed by a rag-bag of reminiscences from earlier days in the heroine's history – though this had apparently once been in Verdi's mind* – but a mad scene induced by the rebellion of human feelings long suppressed. Where Shakespeare brings out the pathos of the situation by a realistic presentation of complete mental breakdown, Verdi does it in a more stylized and elevated way – as opera demands – restoring Lady Macbeth's humanity by restoring, albeit in a broken and spasmodic form, her lyrical eloquence, giving her back a beauty and tenderness that we thought had been driven out utterly by her trafficking with Satan.

We have already examined the factors that made it inevitable that some of the witch music should have a spurious Sterndale-Bennett-like elfishness. The majority of it, however – the Act I *introduzione* and *stretta dell'introduzione*, the first part of the Act III *coro d'introduzione*, and the whole of the scene of the apparitions – does show Verdi attempting to find musical analogies for those qualities which Shakespeare had suggested in his witches. The music, like the poetry, depicts them as mysterious, cosmic forces, as obscene perverts, and above all as celebrants of satanic rituals.

Their association with vast supernatural forces is suggested only briefly in the music, in the instrumental introductions to the first and third acts, which serve a function analogous to the 'thunder and lightning' stage effects called for in the play. The first-act introduction is particularly interesting in that the usual operatic thunderstorm idiom, replete with streaking scale passages, whistling piccolo, colossal *tutti* explosions and diminished-seventh-based harmonies, is laid out in a formal pattern of threefold repetitions. These repetitions are in fact designed to accompany the appearances of the three covens of witches; but at the same time they foreshadow the threefold patterns of the ritual scenes that follow. Only once, in the *stretta* of the Act I Introduction, does Verdi succeed in imparting this quality of elemental grandeur to the music actually sung by the

* Cf. letter of 10 December 1846 to Piave, quoted above, p. 177.

witches. This is a pity, for it was an aspect that he and Piave had tended to emphasize in the libretto, and in an age when genuine witchery was in incredulous disrepute, to have made more of their supernatural Norn-like qualities and less of their subhuman grotes-queries might have been expected to recommend itself. This chorus, 'S'allontanarono', alone shows what Verdi might have achieved in this line. Its sombre fanfare-like theme is surely intended to mock and threaten the military hero Macbeth, who has just left the stage; and the grim elemental tone is sustained in the unison theme that follows. Certainly the chorus becomes more conventional as formal patterning takes over in the later stages, but even in the *maggiore*, apparently inspired by the idea of the *tregenda* – the Weberian *wilde Jagd* – the sing-song theme is propelled with splendid sinister ener-gy on the thudding *ostinato* bass.

Of the passages in the opera that are quite literally rituals of one kind or another – the witches' prophecies to Macbeth and Banquo in Act I, and the apparitions in Act III – little need be said. They employ an idiom which, as Noske has shown,[18] is standard to all such scenes at all stages of Verdi's career, with a formal pattern of threefold repetition, rising stepwise or by thirds at each repetition in the pattern. The only peculiarity of the *Macbeth* scenes is their orchestral colouring, a hollow, reedy variant on the traditional priestly brass scoring.

It is the music which Verdi writes to suggest the subhuman loathsomeness of the witches that makes it virtually impossible for us to credit them with any serious dramatic function. There is no question of being unfaithful to Shakespeare in these episodes, rather of being more narrowly and literally faithful than the difference in medium warrants. For like Shakespeare in the story of the 'master o' the Tiger', which is the basis of 'M'è frullata nel pensier', or in the potion-mixing scene with its 'Double, double toil and trouble' refrain, which is the basis of 'Tu, rospo venefico', Verdi chooses to work in the treacherous idiom of lyrical parody. Vulgar tunes rendered grotesque by unnatural articulation and verbal misaccen-tuations strut or prance above crudely thudding accompaniment figurations: both melodies and accompaniment textures are coarsely orchestrated. But while in the spoken play abstract considerations of style such as the sing-song rhythms, or the short lines with their smacking rhymes, recede into the background, and the imagination fastens on the images evoked by the verses – the 'Toad . . . under cold stone', the 'ravin'd salt-sea shark', the 'slips of yew Sliver'd in the moon's eclipse' and so on – in the music the style is everything;

it cannot be reedeemed nor we distracted by anything in the beyond of the imagination. Verdi's (probably unique) expression-marking 'Nè dimenticarsi che solo streghe che parlano' was, one must regretfully conclude, all too necessary.

Verdi's inability to bring about a convincing synthesis of the elemental and the grotesque, the awesome and the nymph-like, in the nature of the witches is the gravest blemish on his score, and one he proved incapable of remedying at the time of the Paris revision. A comparable incongruity is found in the chorus of assassins in Act II. This movement is an extreme example of that mutual contradiction of form and content to which Italian opera has often been prone. In this instance we might even go so far as to say that there is a whole facet of Shakespeare's play which defies the kind of stylization necessary in Verdi's time. For it is not simply a question of celebrating secret, surreptitious deeds in a medium which is essentially, to borrow a phrase of W. H. Auden's, 'a form of public outcry'. There is also the fact that the assassins embody those forces of destruction and chaos which Macbeth is letting loose in the world, and which to express in the symmetrical and repetitive designs of an operatic chorus marks an extreme in inherent preposterousness. For all the furtive atmospherics of the opening and the imaginativeness of the basic texture – a cappella male voices with timpani – the scene is the most monstrous example of a whole genre, including also Verdi's own 'Zitti, zitti' in Rigoletto and 'Andiamo celiamoci' in Il Trovatore, whose ripeness for parody was masterfully harvested in The Pirates of Penzance.

The instinctive preference of the Italian opera composer for lucid and symmetrical forms comes into conflict with Shakespeare's irregularity, his mysteriousness of atmosphere, his psychological naturalism, at several points in Macbeth. And just occasionally Verdi seems to get his priorities wrong, if nowhere else so disastrously as in the assassins' chorus. The most typical phenomenon is that of a movement which, although beginning in a manner beautifully matched to the dramatic atmosphere, slowly seems to disengage itself and to become wholly taken up with its own pattern-making processes. At the end of a scene where the action is in any case freezing into tableau this can work triumphantly; Verdi's immense skill in the art of composing all manner of contrasts and antitheses into a single overriding euphony can seem as proper to the art of opera as Veronese's is to the art of historical painting. A good example is found in the final largo of the act II finale, whose dramatic elements are Macbeth's gloomy, throbbing brooding, the suspicions of Macduff and the nobles – secretness is suggested both by the 'più piano possibile' dynamics and by putting the melody under the accompaniment – and Lady Macbeth's nagging contempt. But once these ideas have been expressed they become simply the elements of a formal composition. Then not only can Macduff and Macbeth sing in parallel thirds, they can actually make use of a rhythm previously associated with Lady Macbeth's scorn; and at the climax of the movement Lady Macbeth and Macduff can without any sense of incongruity be singing the great cantabile theme in unison.

The effect is less satisfactory, however, in those shorter formal movements that occur in mid-scene. One of several such pieces, showing an extraordinary sensitiveness to mood on the one hand and a crippling reverence for formal typification on the other, is Banquo's 'Come dal ciel precipita'. Few of Verdi's accompaniment figurations so clearly take their cue from a poetic atmosphere as the thick, black, choking chords with which this opens. Yet the aria ends with a blazing major-key cantilena that has nothing to do either with that atmosphere or with the 'larve e . . . terror' of which Banquo now speaks. It simply marks the final stage of the unfolding of a standard lyrical pattern.

Nevertheless, such occasional lapses into old habits seem insignificant when compared with the numerous scenes in which Verdi has been inspired by the extraordinary character of the dramatic situations or by the very poetry itself to fashion movements unexampled in their formal designs and in their expressive aptness. The fruitfulness of Shakespeare's influence on the music of *Macbeth* is most clearly seen in those two movements which Verdi himself described as 'the most important in the opera', the grand duet in Act I and the sleepwalking scene in Act IV. It is the latter that provides the best example of a unique musical form inspired by the unique dramatic character of the Shakespearian prototype. Some of the differences between Shakespeare's scene and Verdi's have already been discussed, notably Verdi's inability to match the disconnected, prosaic character of Lady Macbeth's words. Nevertheless, there is somewhere in every one of her 'speeches' a phrase of tremendous potency, either because of its intrinsic eloquence ('all the perfumes of Arabia will not sweeten this little hand'), or because of its startling realism ('Yet who would have thought the old man to have had so much blood in him?'), or because of the tragic–ironic way in which it distorts a remark made earlier in the play ('What! will these hands ne'er be clean?' – 'A little water clears us of this deed' in II.2). In the text which Verdi devised for this scene, now in collaboration with

Maffei, such phrases as these are always placed at the end of a unit of text, and in composing the scene Verdi highlights them with a shift from a *parlando* to a *cantabile* style of writing. Thus 'who would have thought the old man to have had so much blood in him', instead of being thrown off with a shudder of disgust, is drooled over in a Salome-like rapture. Otherwise each verse begins with the same kind of disconnected, apparently casual phrases as dominate Shakespeare's scene. These casual phrases are thrown into a highly charged atmosphere, however – an atmosphere highly charged not so much by the grave, whispered conversation of the doctor and gentlewoman as by the style of the orchestral accompaniment, by such things as the vibrant rhythm, the sighs, the stealthy chromatism of the prevailing figuration, or the lamenting chromatism in violins and cor anglais tugging against the beating chords of the inner strings at 'Ohimè . . . i panni indossa' (Ex. 5).

In the case of the Act I duet one feels it is the character of the Shakespearian poetry more than the dramatic circumstances of the scene that chiefly prompted its singularity. Up to a point the pattern

Ex. 5

of Shakespeare's scene is not so dissimilar to that of the standard Italian aria or duet of the period, being half taken up with emotional reflections on what is past – the murder of Duncan – and half with a consideration of what is to be done next – the incrimination of the grooms, washing, making ready for the new day that has been announced by the knocking at the gate. But Shakespeare's scene is quite exceptionally full of purple patches. Macbeth in particular unburdens his feelings in a whole series of images and imaginings of tremendous expressive power. There is the sound of the owl's scream and the crickets' cry, there is Macbeth's report of how he overheard two men saying their prayers – 'One cried "God bless us!" and "Amen" the other: As they had seen me with these hangman's hands . . .' Then there is the aural hallucination that visited him:

> Methought I heard a voice cry 'Sleep no more!
> Macbeth does murder sleep,' . . .

and later the appalling thought

> Will all great Neptune's ocean wash this blood
> Clean from my hand? No, this my hand will rather
> The multitudinous seas incarnardine,
> Making the green one red.

Far from being disposed to reduce the richness of Shakespeare's language to some abstract expression of terror and guilt, Verdi retained almost every idea, almost every image in the libretto. Indeed he added to them another, from one of the great soliloquies for which he had not been able to find a place in the opera: the vision of Duncan's virtues pleading 'like angels trumpet-tongu'd against The deep damnation of his taking-off'.

This close fidelity to the poetic qualities of Shakespeare's scene was not an act of sterile and meaningless piety. Verdi used them to bring about a renewal – one might almost say a transformation – of the Italian operatic duet. For every one of the notions he took from Shakespeare he fashioned a musical analogy. The screaming of the owl is evoked by a lamenting figure in clarinet and bassoon, which by way of a series of mournful variants gradually develops into a regular orchestral figuration in the opening section of the duet (Ex. 6). The account of the prayer of the courtiers prompts a quite new theme to which the wind-band-like scoring gives a faintly ecclesiastical touch. The voice which cried 'Macbeth does murder sleep . . .' is treated as a supernatural oracle, clearly differentiated from the wailing semitones that surround it by the addition of brass and drums to the scoring; the trumpet-tongued angelic pleading of

Duncan's virtues, on the other hand, is matched to a towering cantabile phrase. Later in the duet we hear further musical ideas analogous to the knocking at the gate, to the despairing eloquence of

Ex. 6 (a)

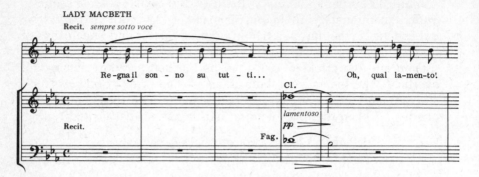

(b)

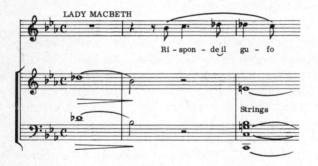

(c)

(d)

'Will all great Neptune's ocean wash this blood Clean from my hand?' and to 'Wake Duncan with thy knocking! I would thou couldst'. And all this is without considering the thematic ideas which Lady Macbeth initiates. With Verdi's mediation, the sheer pressure of Shakespeare's poetic imagination wreaks havoc on the self-contained formal units of nineteenth-century opera, with their repetitions and symmetries and fallow interludes. The operatic ensemble becomes as densely packed with the profusion of musical ideas as a Shakespearian dialogue is with poetry.

The originality of the musical forms and the sheer profusion of the invention are the qualities of the score in which Verdi's debt to Shakespeare is most obvious. Throughout the opera, though, one comes across instances of arresting ideas on a smaller scale which have their origin in some quality in the play. Sometimes it is a question of the musical articulation of a particular theatrical situation, as at the end of the first verse of Lady Macbeth's *brindisi* in the Act II finale, where Verdi composes into the music the two distinct dramatic levels suggested by Shakespeare: while Lady Macbeth continues to be 'large in mirth', Macbeth himself conducts a surreptitious conversation with the murderer (Ex. 7). Sometimes it is a formal quality in the verses that finds reflection in the music: it seems at least possible, for example, that Verdi's fondness for a pungent arioso phrase at the end of a section of recitative, a feature that had not been especially characteristic of his earlier works, was

557

Ex. 7

stimulated by the profusion of scene-clinching rhyming couplets in *Macbeth*. For both

> Hear it not, Duncan; for it is a knell
> That summons thee to heaven or to hell.

and

> It is concluded: Banquo, thy soul's flight,
> If it find heaven, must find it out to-night.

Verdi composes arioso phrases of tremendous portentous vehemence.

Another feature of the opera for which the play provided a model is the consistency of its tone and the use of pervading imagery. The parallel obviously cannot be a literal one, but the symbolism of night and day, and particularly the notion that the night of Macbeth's reign is filled with sighs and lamentations, is impressively matched.

Verdi's own comments on the interpretation of the opera are clear indications of how much store he set by its gloomy, sepulchral

colouring.* Banquo's music in the Act I finale and in Act II, the
scene of the apparitions, and Macbeth's death scene all share
something of this atmosphere of suffocating gloom, evoked by thick,
bottom-heavy scoring, with a prominent role for soft brass and low
woodwinds.

As Scotland under King Macbeth is full of 'sighs and groans and
shrieks that rent the air', so the orchestral texture of Verdi's opera is,
to an unprecedented degree, built around various musical styliza-
tions of the sigh. As I have already suggested, the first significant
appearance of this figure evolves out of the cry of the owl at the start
of the Act I duet. Thereafter it pervades both the accompaniment
texture and the theme of the 'L'ira tua formidabile' section of the Act
I finale, rings out at the start of the Act II prelude, and forms one of
the most significant ingredients both in the introduction to the
chorus of Scottish refugees and in the accompaniment of the
sleepwalking scene. When Verdi rewrote the chorus for Paris he
filled his orchestral textures no less full of sighing appoggiaturas:
indeed at 'd'orfanelli e di piangenti' he takes up in a much more
refined form the idea of double appoggiaturas in contrary motion on
which he had built the introduction to the chorus in its 1847 form
(Ex. 8).

Ex. 8

Altogether the richness of the musical imagery is remarkable
throughout *Macbeth*. There are even several passages in which Verdi
appears to be trying to put back into the drama some of the qualities
which in the libretto had necessarily been sacrificed. The most
remarkable instance of such a phenomenon comes in the opening
scenes. From the introduction as far as the *scena e marcia* to which
Duncan enters Macbeth's castle, the military-cum-political back-

---

* Cf. letters of 7 January 1847 to Varesi, and 23 November to Cammarano: quoted
  above, pp. 182–3 and 189.

ground to the drama is evoked in a series of martial epigrams. The approach of Macbeth is announced by the witches in drum and trumpet fanfares; Macbeth and Banquo enter the scene to the strains of a dignified march rhythm. But one has the impression that as the plot begins to develop, as forces of evil set about ensnaring Macbeth, as the world order represented by Duncan is threatened, these march-like fragments take on a parodistic tone. Both Macbeth's and Banquo's musings over the words of the witches in the introduction, and Lady Macbeth's cantabile, are interrupted by quick-march music in the most shockingly crass style. The last and fullest parodistic evocation of that world of valour and chivalry which is to be desecrated by Duncan's murder is formed by the march for the entry of the king. Its style is matched perfectly to the dumb-show medium. Duncan and his court are not expressing themselves in this music. Their pomps and rituals are seen from without, by those bent on smiting them down.

Verdi's *Macbeth* is an extraordinary achievement for a young composer in the 1840s. That there are numerous imperfections in the opera may be conceded; likewise that in many respects it falls short of the Shakespearian original. Nevertheless *Macbeth* is extraordinary precisely by virtue of Verdi's fidelity to Shakespeare. It is the Shakespearian characterization, the Shakespearian dramatic situations, the Shakespearian language that give him the courage and the authority to break with the old habits of Italian Romantic melodrama.

24

La Battaglia di Legnano – the opera of the revolution

The present chapter is really a pendant to the chapter on *Nabucco*. That early opera, the masterpiece on which the popular reputation of the young Verdi was based, had demonstrated the composer's adeptness at circumventing the problems posed by censorship and writing music which harmonized perfectly with his audience's political and patriotic aspirations. Though none of his subsequent operas assigns such a prominent part to aims of this kind, the *risorgimento* element is never entirely lacking. Even in such unlikely contexts as *Alzira* and *Macbeth* we find episodes in which the music is temporarily deflected away from the primary dramatic object towards the object of providing disguised *risorgimento* odes, of the kind described in the chapter on *Ernani*. No doubt it was because the nationalist tone of these episodes had to be disguised, because their real purport had to be a kind of open secret, that Verdi derived little satisfaction from them. In general he loathed repeating himself: yet such *risorgimento* episodes, modelled on those in *Nabucco*, are repeated from opera to opera throughout the 1840s. Because of the limitations imposed by censorship, Verdi was not able to work this vein explicitly, exhaustively and cathartically. The yearning to make an artist's contribution to the *risorgimento*, to the movement in which he so ardently believed, could not be appeased by such incidental, surreptitious gestures. The full-blooded Italian nationalist opera was still waiting to be written.

The successes won by the revolutionary movements that sprang up throughout Italy in the early months of 1848 signalized the fact that the time for such an opera was now come. Verdi was under contract with Naples at that time, and with the granting of a constitution in the city in February it seemed reasonable to expect that censorship would be far less restrictive than hitherto. Indeed, Muzio blissfully imagined that Verdi would now be able to compose 'absolutely any subject'.

The choice of *La Battaglia di Legnano* was perhaps prompted by another event of these perfervid months, the 'Five Days' in Milan in March. In his letter proposing the subject Cammarano concludes: 'wave these pages to the breezes, they contain my kisses for undefeated and heroic Milan'. The Battle of Legnano was an event that had come to acquire an exemplary educative significance for the Italian patriots. For it demonstrated how, by putting out of mind their petty squabbles and local jealousies and joining together in a bond of brotherhood, the North Italian communes had once been able to defeat the mighty Barbarossa himself, and drive the German Imperial forces from their land.

Cammarano and Verdi were absolutely at one in their desire to compose an opera that would celebrate Italian nationalism, that would draw its inspiration from the events of early 1848 and in turn provide the inspiration to follow those events through to the conclusion of a free and united Italy. Cammarano, as befitted a pupil of Gabriele Rossetti, had been an ardent patriot from his youth, but in his dramatic works he had hitherto had to disguise his nationalist aspirations – just as Verdi had – in such quasi-allegories as *L'Assedio di Calais*, composed by Donizetti in 1836. Now his dramatic imagination was ablaze with explicitly nationalistic motifs; there burned in him 'the desire to evoke the most glorious episode of Italian history, that of the Lombard League'. The new opera which he and Verdi were to write together would 'stir every man with an Italian soul in his bosom'. Though we do not know exactly how Verdi replied, it is not difficult to imagine. Throughout 1848, even when contact with Cammarano was temporarily lost and it looked as if the *Battaglia di Legnano* project would have to be abandoned, Verdi was inspired by the very ideals Cammarano had expressed: operatic subjects must be 'Italian and free'; the Mameli ode was composed to be 'sung amid the music of the cannon on the Lombardy plains'.*

La Battaglia di Legnano differs in the first place from all Verdi's earlier operas in that the nationalist note is flagrant and all-pervasive. There is no diffidence here, no indirectness or allegorization. The curtain rises on the first act to cries of 'Viva Italia', and it falls on the last act with the dying hero kissing the Italian standard, an act of homage to the flag whose mere colours had hitherto been banned from some Italian stages.

Throughout the opera there is scarcely a movement in which mention is not made of 'la sacra Italia', or in which characters are not

* Cf. above, p. 223 and note 11, p. 231 and note 27.

expressing their devotion to the Italian cause or being exhorted to take a pride in their history or their culture or, most often, in the mere fact of being Italian. Even in those scenes in which the passions of the protagonists are of greater dramatic moment than the political issues of nationhood, Cammarano rarely fails to supply some allusion to the patriotic occasion. Reproaching Lida for her infidelity to him, Arrigo modulates from the insults and despair and weariness with life that are proper to the hopeless lover, to a resolution inspired by a rather different set of values:

> T'amai, t'amai qual angelo,
> Or qual demon t'aborro!!
> Per me la vita è orribile ...
> Nel campo a morte io corro ...
> In tua difesa, o patria,
> Cadrò squarciato il seno ...
> Fia benedetto almeno
> Il sangue mio da te! (I.8)

Even in those scenes that form part of the conventional appurtenances of Romantic melodrama, the emotional flavour tends to be transformed by an element of patriotic exultation. The opera ends, as usual, with a death scene for the hero; in it, the dying Arrigo assures Rolando of Lida's purity and faithfulness, and so brings about a reconciliation between them. But in addition to the emotions of anguish and loss which we know from so many Verdian finales, this one is imbued with the spiritual values of a sublime and exhilarating patriotism. Arrigo swears 'per la salvata Italia' and by the blood he has spent for it; and at the end of the scene, as an expression of the reconciliation between the three protagonists Cammarano unites them with the refrain

> Chi muore per la patria
> Alma sì rea non ha. (IV.3)

Besides this all-pervasive appeal to the sentiment of pan-Italian nationalism, Cammarano, like Henry V before the Battle of Agincourt, is careful to pay his due to local patriotism. As Shakespeare had used the names of the great feudal lords of England, 'Bedford and Exeter, Warwick and Talbot, Salisbury and Gloucester', so Cammarano uses North Italian geographical names. The army that masses on stage at the start of the opera is not merely an Italian one, it is formed of units from Piacenza, Verona, Brescia, Novara, Vercelli. Over and over again in the recitatives the names of these old communes are sounded as if they were charms – 'Pavia ... Milano ... Como ... alla natia Verona ... tra le fiamme di Susa'.

It goes without saying that this profusion of references to Italy and to the Italians is made in no coolly objective spirit. Their emotive and demagogic power is enhanced by habitual idealizations, a trait shown most clearly in the second act when Rolando and Arrigo visit Como to attempt to persuade the Comaschi to break their treaty with Barbarossa and join the Milanese in the Lombard League. Italy is 'la sacra Italia'; the German Emperor's army, on the other hand, is an 'orda di barbari'. In appearance and in culture, Rolando continues, the men of Como are part of the chosen people, yet they behave no better than barbarians:

> Ben vi scorgo nel sembiante
> L'alto ausonico lignaggio
> Odo il numero sonante
> Dell'italico linguaggio,
> Ma nell'opre, nei pensieri
> Siete barbari stranieri!   (II.3)

In the finale of the same act the forthcoming battle is described as a conflict between hired assassins and a people rising up to liberty:

> Di tue masnade
> Le mercanarie spade
> Non vinceranno un popolo
> Che sorge a libertà.   (II.4)

The fact that *La Battaglia di Legnano* was designed more as a nationalist pageant than as a melodrama in the traditional sense of the word is reflected in several unusual features of the work. As in *Nabucco* and *I Lombardi*, the private world of the protagonists occupies a modest place in the dramatic scheme compared with the public world of treaties, battles, religious ceremonies and celebrations. Indeed, in the second act of the opera the domestic drama, the tragic triangle in which Rolando, Arrigo and Lida are caught, is not so much as mentioned. And, as we have seen, even in those scenes that are primarily concerned with the fates of the protagonists, Cammarano almost always contrives to beat the patriotic drum incidentally besides. The peculiar circumstances of the opera are reflected furthermore in the two 'giuramento' scenes, in the Act I *introduzione*, and in the scene of the *Cavalieri della Morte* in Act III, in which the oath to defend and to avenge, and the execration aimed at infamy, seem to represent a blending of the vows of medieval chivalry and those of the nineteenth-century secret society. There is perhaps a secret-society echo in Rolando's address to the Comaschi, too, with its allusion to their 'Ausonian features'. Ausonia was the kingdom which the Neapolitan *carbonari* aspired to establish, embracing all Italy from the Alps to Sicily. As a final instance of the desire to impart the thrill of *risorgimento* immediacy to the opera, one may mention those recitatives that sound rather like news bulletins or dispatches from the front line:

> Giunser dall'Alpi
> Esploratori: avanza
> D'imperiali esercito possente.
> Ad assembrar Duci e Senato un cenno
> De' consoli provvede. (I.8)

But over and above these merely opportunist and nationalist elements, Cammarano's libretto has another quality that raises it above mere tub-thumping demagoguery and ranks it with the most serious and characteristic manifestations of *risorgimento* culture. It aspires not merely to thrill and inspire, but to educate. There is scarcely a scene which does not in some way suggest the values, the ideals, the qualities of mind and heart on which the new, free and united Italy is to be built.

Some of the morals Cammarano draws, some of the lessons he inculcates, are casual or incidental. But two messages are intoned with unmistakable emphasis and solemnity. One is that for the Italian of the dawning new age there is a trinity of supreme values: God, Country and Family. They are most eloquently apostrophized in the duet which Cammarano added at Verdi's request in the third act. Rolando, recognizing the grave perils that face him in the forthcoming battle, bids his wife farewell:

> Pria di partir, te, donna, e il frutto
> Del nostro Imene a riveder mi trasse
> Amor! – (III.4)

If he should die in battle, she must instruct their infant son in virtue; and the burden of her teaching is to be this:

> Digli ch'è sangue italico,
> Digli ch'è sangue mio,
> Che dei mortali è giudice
> La terra no, ma Dio!
> E dopo Dio la patria
> Gli apprendi a rispettar.

Finally Rolando makes the child kneel, and raising his eyes to heaven, places his hand on his child's head:

> Deh! meco benedici
> Il figlio mio, Signor!

But Cammarano places most of his didactic emphasis where the recent history of Italy had shown it to be most necessary. The time has come to put away petty rivalries and ancient hostilities between one city and another: if Italy is to achieve anything, if it is to be anything, its people must with one accord bind themselves together in a spirit of comradeship and brotherhood. In the opening chorus of Act II Cammarano incorporates an analysis of the chronic, besetting ailment of Italy's political life: a civic rivalry nourished not on proper pride but on envy and the cherishing of grudges. Every unhappy memory in the relationship between city-states is to be warmed up again and again, and passed down as an inheritance:

> Scordò la superba [Milan]
> I danni mortali a Como recati!
> Ma qui la memoria ogni uomo ne serba!
> Ma l'odio qui vive ne' cori oltraggiati!
> Quest'odio col sangue ribolle confuso,
> Né volger di tempo scemarlo potrà!
> Dai padri, dagli avi in noi fu trasfuso!
> Ai figli, ai nepoti trasfuso verrà!

Rolando, the representative of the new Italy, counters by emphasizing the need for forgetting age-old enmities, for closing the ranks, for taking a pride in one's Italianness:

> Taccia
> Il reo livor antico
> Di Milano e di Como: un sol nemico,
> Solo una patria abbiamo,
> Il Teutono e l'Italia, in sua difesa
> Leviam tutti la spada. (II.3)

But if the Como scene is the one in which this message is presented in the most thorough and schoolmasterly way, it is from the opera's two 'hymns', strategically placed at the beginning and at the end of the opera, that is gathers its greatest emotive force. The hymn in the Act I *introduzione* is a kind of hypothetical national anthem, a microcosm of the aspirations of the whole *risorgimento*; unity, victory, regeneration:

> Viva Italia! sacro un patto
> Tutti stringe i figli suoi:
> Esso alfin di tanti ha fatto
> Un sol popolo d'eroi! – ...
> Viva Italia forte ed una
> Colla spada e col pensier!
> Questo suol che a noi fu cuna,
> Tomba sia dello stranier!

While that in the Act IV finale takes the geography-lesson form that may seem a little odd to nations who have no doubt where their boundaries lie, but which was common in nineteenth-century Italian patriotic poetry:

> Dall'Alpi a Cariddi
> Echeggi vittoria!
> Vittoria risponda
> L'Adriaco al Tirreno! ...   (IV.2)

The names of course have a certain evocative value, but primarily they are educative, and they make a political claim: that Italy is not merely a linguistic and cultural area but a tangible physical unity extending from the Alps to Sicily and from one ocean coast to the other.

Fraternity and loyalty to the pan-Italian cause thus become supreme virtues in *La Battaglia di Legnano* and the focuses of the opera's range of moods and passions. Conversely, the ideas of treachery or desertion become supremely appalling. Indeed infamy acquires an emotional force that may be well be compared with that carried by a curse, or a fatal oath in Verdi's more typically Romantic operas. This is shown in the Act III finale, after Rolando has found his wife hiding in Arrigo's room. Arrigo is not to be challenged, or thrashed, or killed, or any of the things that might be expected from a jealous husband: he is to be prevented from joining his companions in battle. The loss of honour, the ignominy of not being able to join his brother warriors: these prompt the opera's supreme expression of madness and despair. The emphasis which Cammarano sought to lay on the idea of 'infamia' is clear from his letter of 9 October 1848 (cf. above, p. 228), and he cannot have been disappointed with Verdi's setting, even if it does not accord exactly with his own suggestions: for with his trumpet fanfares, the rising chromatism, the *crescendo* up to the blazing, high-pitched triad for unaccompanied voices, he gives it exactly the kind of blood-curdling emphasis which in other contexts he gave to such exclamations as 'Sii maledico'.

Because *La Battaglia di Legnano* is not simply a drama in music, but a drama with a very specific missionary intent, it becomes a primary task for Verdi to set the text clearly and emphatically. Furthermore the remarks which Cammarano made when he sent Verdi Act IV of the libretto show that his verses were specifically designed to enable the composer to give maximum expressive force to key lines and phrases.

At the verse 'Per la salvata Italia' etc. after a sustained cantabile, and a kind of breakdown on reaching the words (saria) ... (mentir) ... (spirando), I would like Arrigo, as if he were gathering his last strength, to say

> Chi muore per la Patria
> Alma sì rea non ha!

with energetic impetus, which could then be repeated by the three voices together.

He tends to place such inflammatory lines either immediately before the formal lyrical movement, so that they can be delivered 'tutta forza' in a context of thundering *tutti* chords; or, more often, as the concluding line or couplet of a lyric, so that the impetus of the song and the mounting passion of the singer can combine to give it irresistible emotional eloquence. This is what we find in Rolando's romanza 'Ah m'abbraccia', in Arrigo's verse in the Act I duet, and most clearly in the Act III duettino 'Digli ch'è sangue italico'.

Verdi exploits these opportunities with much resource. In 'Ah, m'abbraccia' he makes the crucial line 'All'Italia un difensor' the climax of a contrasting middle section in a slower tempo. In 'Digli ch'è sangue italico' he sets the first part of Rolando's verse with sombre, rather short-breathed phrases in the minor key. Thereafter, for the climactic lines, the melody mounts to a flowing major-key culmination with a profusion of emphatic word-repetition (Ex. 1).

Ex. 1

The phrase recurs as a kind of under-descant at the close of Lida's verse. Finally – Verdi now taking a liberty with the libretto, which suggests nothing of the kind – the words are used again in the final cadenza; what is more, at this point Lida abandons her own text to exclaim *fortissimo* 'la patria!'. But the most elaborate exploitation of the possibilities Cammarano's text offers is to be found in the Act IV finale. As the librettist himself had suggested, Verdi sets the phrase 'Chi muore per la patria' 'with energetic impetus', and at once repeats it, giving it the effect of a refrain. By its style and by its placing, the theme acquires the character of a musical epigram, enshrining the whole heroic and reconciliatory philosophy of the opera. Though the words do not return, Verdi uses the theme once more at the curtain as Arrigo dies. Delivered with maximum force and sonorous richness, it expresses the community's proud homage to the hero.

Paradoxical as it may seem, it is when Verdi is most intent on composing nationalist opera that the influence of Parisian opera on his work is clearest. In *La Battaglia di Legnano* the shadow of grand opera falls even more heavily than it had in *Nabucco* or *I Lombardi*. We discern it in such obvious imitations as the Act I *giuramento* or the closing section of the Act III finale, modelled on the Act II finale of *Guillaume Tell* and the Act IV duet of *Les Huguenots* respectively; in such studied Meyerbeerian sophistications as the harmonies that introduce Act III, or the superimpositions of several independent strands of music in the Act IV *preghiera*. Especially perhaps we discern it in the curious style of the dramatic movement, which is more in the nature of pageant – a series of tableaux – than the usual continuous intrigue of Italian melodrama. The extreme example of this tendency is the second act, half of whose protagonists, the magistrates and captains of Como, and Federico Barbarossa himself, have not appeared in the opera before and will not appear again. They are marshalled before the spectators for the sake of the morals that can be drawn from their conduct; but then they are discarded, for they form no integral part of the dramatic action.

A comparable self-contained, statuesque quality is found in much of the music. An extreme example is provided by the Act I *intro-duzione*, a complex of movements laid out in a symmetrical architectural manner and marked by the characteristic French emphasis on instrumental music (especially marches) and choruses. Reprises both of the opening march and of the chorus 'Viva Italia', and the reduction of the solo arias to single movements, give the whole a very un-Italian cut, virtually eliminating the element of dramatic dynamism, but much enhancing the sense of pageant.

In addition to the predominantly formal matters so far considered, a large amount of the opera's expressive rhetoric and imagery is devoted to underlining its political message. As we would expect, the choral unison is used in both the *giuramento* scenes as a symbol of indissoluble unity; and fanfares of trumpets and the rattle of drums punctuate many a scene, both naturalistically, as for example at the end of Rolando's romanza, and to assist the expression of militarist sentiment, as in the *adagio* of the Act II finale. The idea of comradeship is suggested in the parallel thirds and sixths that characterize much of the music sung by Rolando and Arrigo, as in 'Ah, m'abbraccia', and especially the appeal to the Comaschi and the defiance of Barbarossa in Act II. But as in *Nabucco* and *I Lombardi* the all-pervasive musical image is that of the march: brisk, business-like marches in the French style, the funeral march, and, most characteristically, fervent hymnic marches that endow the Italian military scenes with the aura of the holy mission.

The most important of these marches is that sung at the beginning of the opera to those profoundly significant words 'Viva Italia!'. Appropriately enough this partakes of the nature of both march and hymn. Though it begins as an apparently naturalistic marching-song for male voices, and though it incorporates some measure of expressive detail in its middle section, the crucial thing about it is the combination of words and music in the principal section: a melody of archetypal simplicity in a fiercely martial rhythm, associated with the proclamation of a free and united Italy (Ex. 2). The process of transforming this music from a mere marching-song into a kind of national hymn begins at the end of the introductory chorus, when

Ex. 2

the women watching from the balconies add their voices to those of the soldiers below. And the transformation is completed when, after Arrigo's 'La pia materna mano', another group of soldiers enter singing the same music.

By the end of the *introduzione* the principal theme of 'Viva Italia' has become the musical emblem of the pan-Italian party. And because the aspirations of this party are really the idea that inspired the conception of *La Battaglia di Legnano*, Verdi subsequently uses the theme as a pervading motif. It accompanies Arrigo and Rolando when they arrive in Como to urge the Comaschi to join with the Lombard League. It recurs again at the end of Act III to bring to our mind's eyes the picture of Arrigo's comrades marching off to do battle with Barbarossa, and to act as a foil to the madness of his despair at not being able to join them. Finally, it is heard in the scena preceding the *Inno di Vittoria* in Act IV: this time its hymnic solemnity is transformed into a mood of exuberant revelry by the superimposition of a second, quick-march theme, a favourite resort of grand opera (Ex. 3). None of these recurrences of 'Viva Italia' owes

Ex. 3

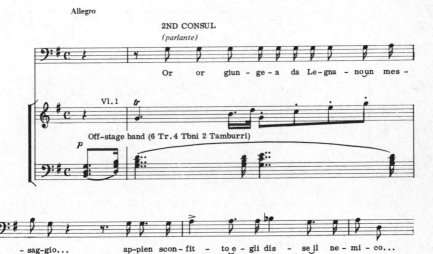

Ex. 4 (a)

(b)

anything to Cammarano's libretto; they are Verdi's own way of providing a musical analogy to the drama's pervading themes of sacred and valorous patriotism.

It is perhaps worth observing that one or two other political ideas in the drama are also treated to recurring themes, albeit in a much less systematic way. The chorus in which the Comaschi express their determination to continue harbouring their ancient grudges against Milan is transformed into an orchestral texture to underline their debate with Rolando (Ex. 4). More tenuously, perhaps even unintended by the composer, the grim ritornello that introduces the *Cavalieri della Morte* at the start of Act III is a sombre transformation of the cry 'Guerra adunque! ... terribile! ... a morte!' from the preceding finale (Ex. 5).

With *La Battaglia di Legnano* a phase of Verdi's career is closed; his political duty as an artist was done, and his patriotic passions

Ex. 5 (a)

(b)

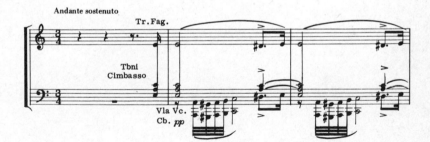

had at last been indulged without restraint. In the public world the *risorgimento* continued for twenty years or more, but Verdi as an artist was no longer interested. His next opera, *Luisa Miller*, marks a new departure: he begins to explore a world of psychological nuance and more refined sensibility, this time without distractions. Verdi the demagogue, who had reared up so erratically from the pages of *Nabucco, Giovanna d'Arco, Attila* and the other scores of the period, had had his fling and been laid to rest.

Essays with Schiller

The libretto of *I Masnadieri*

Of all the creative links which Verdi forged with great literary figures of the past, that with Schiller is perhaps the most difficult to describe. It was neither an ephemeral fancy, like his interest in Byron, nor a lifelong passion taken with the utmost seriousness from the very first, as was the case with Shakespeare. Out of his admiration for Schiller was eventually to be born *Don Carlos*, in some ways the richest and grandest of all his scores. Yet this relationship began, as far as one can see, accidentally, almost unconsciously; and it was only slowly that Verdi came to perceive how enriching for his own art Schiller might be.

To what extent *Giovanna d'Arco* can be described as a Schillerian opera is a moot point. When Solera averred that it was 'a wholly original Italian drama', that he 'did not wish to allow [himself] to be imposed upon ... by the authority of Schiller', and so forth (cf. above, p. 145), he was protesting too much. But one cannot fail to observe that Verdi's own list of operatic projects drawn up earlier in the same year betrayed no knowledge of or interest in Schiller at all, and that if he had felt for *Die Jungfrau von Orleans* any of that admiration for characterization and atmosphere, any of that desire to recreate its essential characteristics in his own operatic medium, which he felt for *I Due Foscari* or for *Macbeth*, he would surely have bullied Solera into producing something more authentic. On the whole we must admit that *Giovanna d'Arco* does not look like the result of a creative engagement with Schiller at all.

With *I Masnadieri* the case is very different. It may well be that the summer weeks spent with Andrea Maffei in Recoaro in 1846 mark the beginning of Verdi's acquaintance with Schiller, as they do of his serious involvement with Shakespeare. But as his first Shakespeare opera was composed in collaboration with Piave, whom he was in the habit of lecturing and bullying so that he produced exactly what was wanted, and who, as he lived in Venice, had to be communicated with by letter, the impact of Shakespeare on Verdi's dramatic imagination can be clearly seen from the surviving documents. The impact of Schiller, on the other hand, is all but invisible. Maffei was at hand; the problems and the principles of the adaptation could be discussed in private without leaving any obvious traces. And in any case it is likely that in this relationship Maffei was the senior partner. At very least, being the Italian translator of the complete works, he was the authority on Schiller. Verdi's own appreciation of Schiller is not documented in the literal sense until the correspondence with Cammarano over *Luisa Miller*.

It is well known that within a few years of the writing of *Die Räuber* Schiller himself had conceived a hearty detestation for the piece. He blamed his rigid and sheltered education for the fact that 'knowing nothing of mankind ... he had brought forth a monster the like of which is fortunately not to be found in the world'.[1] Maffei apparently alludes to this severe self-judgement when, in the preface to the libretto, he speaks of the play as a product of a period when 'maturity and the study of mankind had not yet tempered his too-ardent imagination'. But if *Die Räuber* contained much that was offensive to the critical judgement of Schiller's maturer years, there was no doubt that its torrential rhetoric and the blazing intensity of its passions had retained their potency as in few other monuments of the *Sturm und Drang* phase of German literature. Probably performances were no longer attended by such manifestations of hysteria as the 'rolling eyes, clenched fists, hoarse screeches'[2] that had accompanied the Mannheim *première* in 1782, but for Maffei it was precisely the explosiveness of the passions and the theatrical situations that made *Die Räuber* 'more suitable for operatic treatment than any other literary subject [he] could think of'.

The words of Maffei's preface should not necessarily be taken to mean that he was wholly responsible for suggesting *Die Räuber* as a worthwhile operatic theme. At least it is worth pondering what Verdi had said on the matter in the letter to Lumley of 4 December 1846: 'Last year I had chosen *Il Corsaro* for a subject, but after it had been versified I found it cold and theatrically ineffective, so I changed my mind and, although it involved me in twice the expense, decided to have another libretto written, based on Schiller's *I Masnadieri*.'[3]

In these years, in the later 1840s, when Verdi was seeking to enlarge the range of subjects for opera beyond the realms of the traditional heroic romance, three types of theme seem particularly to have fascinated him. One was the spectacle of moral corruption, which came to be exemplified in the figure of Macbeth; another, the mutually destructive antagonism of human passions and social order, bore fruit in *Luisa Miller* and later in *La Traviata*; the third, closely related to this latter type, was the psychological study of the outcast. Verdi at first thought he had found an ideal manifestation of this theme in Byron's *The Corsair*, only to be disappointed by the result when he read Piave's adaptation. Though the suggestion can only be hypothetical, it is at least possible that his first real confrontation with Schiller resulted from the search for a more convincing drama built round such an outcast as Byron's Conrad, and that Maffei knew where to find it.

Such a preoccupation with the tremendous figure of Karl Moor (Carlo) would perhaps explain Verdi's apparent obliviousness to some of the weaker links in the drama. Schiller himself, at the time of making the stage adaptation of *Die Räuber* in 1782, had commented on the feebleness and dramatic ineffectiveness of Amalia and Maximilian. Both are characterized by total passivity. Of Amalia he exclaimed, 'I have read more than half the play and still do not know what the girl wants, or what the poet wanted with her, and I cannot imagine anything that might conceivably happen to her.'⁴ And he found that Maximilian, instead of being 'tender and weak' as he should have been, was simply 'lachrymose and infantile', and that the veneration due to him was undermined by his intellectual feebleness. These defects Maffei could not really cure, though by omitting the first scene of the play, in which Maximilian is beguiled by Franz's far too palpable villainy, he at least plays down the father's lack of grasp. What made *I Masnadieri* such an unusual and interesting libretto, however, were the figures of the two brothers, Carlo and Francesco (Franz). As outcast and villain they far surpass Corrado and Seid in passion, originality and plausibility, and it seems strange that when faced with them Verdi did not rise higher above routine competence in his music.

The extent to which Maffei succeeds in preserving the character of Schiller's protagonist Karl can be judged from the opening scene of the opera, Act I, scenes 1–2. It forms the first of a parallel pair of scenes, marking that point in the emotional life of the brothers when, for very different reasons, they determine to let loose death and destruction on the world.

In Karl's case these destructive impulses are prompted by disillusionment. 'When I appealed to humanity, mankind hid humanity from me' are the words with which Schiller's hero rationalizes his decision. Karl's yearning not to be lost to humanity, the reluctance with which he assumes the role of outcast and rebel, is crucial to the dramatic theme; and it is good to see Maffei depicting the process of corruption more economically but no less conscientiously than Schiller himself had done. When the opera opens Carlo is revealed as a prodigal son awaiting reinstatement. He aspires to a life of heroic action in the service of liberty, such as that led by the great heroes of Classical times. As the scene continues it becomes clear that it is family, homeland, and the beloved that form the moral basis for these aspirations. This idea Maffei rightly concentrates in the cantabile 'O mio castel paterno', so that the first musical number in the opera takes the form of this vision of Carlo as he would wish to be. The letter of rejection, which he takes to be from his father, destroys the moral basis of his aspirations, and necessarily perverts his energy and his physical courage into viciousness. He seeks revenge on a mankind that has destroyed his dreams and poisoned his hopes; what could have been heroism in the cause of freedom is distorted into wanton terrorism. He becomes the leader of a gang of murderers and thieves, sworn to leaving a trail of slaughter and destruction across the land.

What raises Karl Moor above the level of an urban terrorist of the 1970s, what makes him so much more than a 'Jimmie Porter in Gothic script' – one must envy Budden his phrase[5] even while denying its validity – and makes of *Die Räuber*, despite its formal incoherence and its florid rantings, obviously the work of a great dramatic imagination and of a great man, is the fact that Karl's perception of the harmony and beauty of the world will not die, and his quest for a moral and metaphysical key to its meaning cannot be given up. Maffei does extraordinarily well in his attempt to capture something of these qualities in his libretto. Thus in the second scene in which Carlo appears (II.5–7) he wrestles philosophically and emotionally with the contrast presented by the sublime and exemplary beauty of the patterns of nature and the squalor of his own sinful deeds. He feels shut out from the world: its loveliness, far from bringing him joy, serves only to sharpen the misery of being

> Di ladroni attorniato
> Al delitto incatenato ...

When we next meet Carlo in the company of his brigand horde (III.4–6), the discovery of his father locked up by his brother Francesco to die of starvation prompts a terrible and delusory elation in his soul, which again Maffei has seen to be a crucial stage in the spiritual development of the drama. Carlo believes that at least he has the chance of creating harmony between the moral law and his own way of life: the wanton acts of terrorism with which he had insulted the pattern of the universe could now be transformed into a holy mission, could be redirected towards the task of exacting divine retribution; those energies that had become perverted by disappointed idealism could now be reconsecrated:

> E voi, Masnadieri, quest'oggi sarete
> Ministri dell'alta Giustizia divina!
> Piegate le fronti! nel fango cadete
> Dinanzi al Potente ch'a tal vi destina ...

Maffei came a long way towards making of Karl Moor a sketch for the most original and haunting protagonist in Verdi's early operas. What eventually defeated him the was fact that *Die Räuber* is more than a tragic action, packed with explosive passion: there is a pronounced element of moral discourse in it, and this cannot be concluded until the action is over and the passions are still. But Italian Romantic melodrama of the type which Verdi and Maffei were nourished on – whether out of mere habit or whether out of a convinced sense of dramatic form – found it difficult to escape from the view that the operatic design must cadence on the final cathartic or expiatory action. It is what one might call Schiller's moral epilogue, after the death of Amalia, that gives coherence to and makes sense of the whole hideous tale:

O über mich Narren, der ich wähnete, die Welt durch Greuel zu verschönern und die Gesetze durch Gesetzlosigkeit aufrecht zu halten ... o eitle Kinderei – da steh' ich am Rand eines entsetzlichen Lebens und erfahre nun mit Zähnklappern und Heulen, *dass zwei Menschen wie ich den ganzen Bau der sittlichen Welt zu Grund richten würden ...*   (v.2).

And this Maffei fails to provide. The character he develops so carefully is deprived of the one insight that alone can redeem him from appearing a mere maniac.

But though in the last analysis Maffei's Carlo falls short of Schiller's prototype, he is never conventionalized in the way that Byron's Foscari and Conrad or García Gutiérrez's Manrico are: he never begins remotely to resemble the conventional heroic tenors of *ottocento* melodrama. Maffei and Verdi were obviously of one mind on the issue of fidelity to the literary source. Verdi was not just interested in Hugo and Shakespeare and Schiller as sources of intrigues: he was interested in them as artists whose unique qualities of characterization and atmosphere and language should, as far as the medium allows, be retained in the operatic adaptation. Maffei shared this view – there can be little doubt that it was one of the issues he had often discussed with Verdi – as he makes clear in these sensible words in his preface:

Since the poet is confined to a very small space, he cannot give his thoughts the proportions or the psychological development the drama requires; he must work in broad strokes, providing the composer with little more than a skeleton which will receive form and passion and life rather from the notes than from the words.

In short he must reduce a vast conception to small dimensions without changing the original physiognomy, like a concave lens which reduces the size of objects while preserving their shape ...

Maffei lived up to these aspirations. *I Masnadieri* is an extraordinarily authentic libretto in the sense that it models the action and the characters closely on Schiller, and even succeeds in packing in a fair number of Schiller's philosophical and metaphysical ideas. In general the only things that are lost are those that are inconceivable or pointless in the operatic medium: the differentiation within the robber band of half a dozen highly idiosyncratic individuals; such literary graces as are provided by, for example, the Biblical overtones which Schiller gives the Karl/Maximilian relationship.

Only in one particular does Maffei take it upon himself materially to alter the conduct of the drama, and that is in the treatment of Amalia in the middle two acts. It will be recalled that the only criticism of the libretto voiced by Verdi during the composition of the opera was to the effect that in its original form the second act was ineffective (cf. above, p. 197). Whether its final slightly odd and inconsistent effect is because of Maffei's efforts to patch it up or in spite of them we do not know. But there is no doubt that he came close to bringing about an improvement in Amalia's role and that, whether in carelessness or haste, all he actually achieved was muddle.

At the start of Act II he has certainly scored over Schiller. In the equivalent scene of the play Amalia is alone in the garden singing of her love for the lost Karl. Franz enters and reproaches her for absenting herself from the feast that celebrates his entering into the Moor inheritance:

FRANZ: Schon wieder hier, eigensinnige Schwärmerin? Du hast dich vom
    frohen Mahle hinweggestohlen und den Gästen die Freude verdorben.
AMALIA: Schade für diese unschuldige Freuden! Das Totenlied muss noch in
    deinen Ohren murmeln, das deinem Vater zu Grabe hallte ... (III.1)

But Amalia's retort is hardly appropriate in view of the way she has been spending her own time. Maffei is much tighter, much more controlled, making of Amalia's song an elegy for the dead Maximilian, the poignancy of which is enhanced by the off-stage chorus of carousing and revelling.

AMALIA:	Dall'infame banchetto io m'involai,
	Padre, e qui mi rifuggo, all'obliato
	Sepolcro tuo che sola
	La furtiva mia lagrima consola
CORO INTERNO:	Godiam, ché fugaci
	Son l'ore del riso ...
	.... Dai calici ai baci
	Ne guidi il piacer.
AMALIA:	Tripudia, esulta, iniquo,
	Sull'ossa di tuo padre ...
	Tu del mio Carlo al seno
	Volasti, alma beata,
	E il tuo soffrir terreno
	Or si fa gioia in ciel ...

So far Maffei gives admirable scenic form to a situation only vaguely described by Schiller. But at this point he goes astray. It may have been that his instincts were too formal. Perhaps he felt that it was operatically imperative to build each unit of the action into a full-scale scena before proceeding further, that Amalia's cantabile must have its matching cabaletta. But perhaps Verdi's courage failed him too. After all, Amalia's *sortita* had already been handled in a somewhat free manner, as a single florid cantabile movement. To write a second cabaletta-less scena – and for Jenny Lind, of all people – might have seemed wantonly provocative even to him. The only thing to hand in the play that could motivate a cabaletta was Hermann's revelation (Arminio's in the opera) that, despite all appearances to the contrary, neither Karl nor Maximilian is really dead. To this news Amalia reacts in rapture:

> Carlo vive? ... O caro accento,
> Melodia di paradiso! ...

The fact that the scene thus concludes with this stalest of operatic clichés is not the worst thing about it. More serious is the fact that it weakens the dramatic tensions of the ensuing encounter with Francesco. In the equivalent scenes of the play Amalia is still prostrated by the deaths of Karl and Maximilian, and though she defies Franz, she does so in the knowledge that she is, in the long run, defenceless and hopeless. In the opera, on the other hand, she knows that Carlo and Massimilano live, she has re-celebrated her love in masterful song, so she can be neither tempted nor seriously menaced by the approaches of Francesco. On a more superficial level, it makes little sense for the cabaletta 'Carlo vive? ...' to be closely followed by Francesco' reproach, 'Vuoi piangerlo in eterno?' And a succession of four lyrical movements, solo cantabile and cabaletta, duet cantabile and cabaletta, in all of which Amalia is the protagonist, is a deplorable scheme.

There is no doubt that the way to tidy up this muddle is simply to cut the recitative and cabaletta. Such narrative details as they supply are either rendered superfluous or contradicted in the next scene in which Amalia appears, the love scene with Carlo in Act III. Here too there is no real equivalent in Schiller. The nearest thing he provides to a love scene is Act IV scene 4, an exceedingly bizarre episode in which Amalia, feeling a mysterious and what she takes to be guilty attraction to the visiting Graf von Brand, hymns the glorious qualities of her lost Karl. But Graf von Brand is in fact Karl in disguise, and he in turn hymns the glories of his lost love, who by chance is likewise called Amalia. Finally Amalia shows that she has recognized Karl by singing a verse of their favourite song; Karl acknowledges by taking up another, but then breaks off and flees. By withholding recognition in this way, Schiller builds into his love scene an extraordinary, and unresolved, emotional excruciation. Nothing of this quality is retained by Maffei, who writes a comparatively conventional and wholly harmonious love scene. Moreover he introduces it better than Schiller, for Amalia chances upon Carlo and his band while in flight from Francesco after he had 'minacciato la vita e l'onore'. These brutal and lewd threats we have witnessed both in the play and the opera: yet once they have been uttered they seem to constitute no more of a threat to Schiller's Amalia, who in her next scene is discovered, still in the Moor castle, serenely performing the duties of guide in the family portrait gallery.

Maffei's tendency to over-formalize the dramatic design of his libretto is perhaps the most obvious deficiency in his work. Further manifestations of the same habit of thought can be seen in the symmetry of the two scenes for Carlo and for Francesco in Act I, and in the duet for Francesco and Pastor Moser in Act IV, another of the weak links in the libretto. One feels that the structural weight of this scene should have been concentrated on the moments where Moser is speaking theological truth with awful severity and Franz ranting against it. The crucial speeches might be these:

MOSER: ... Meint Ihr dem Arm des Vergelters im öden Reich des Nichts zu entlaufen? und führet Ihr gen Himmel, so ist er da! und bettet Ihr euch in der Hölle, so ist er wieder da! und sprächet Ihr zu der Nacht: verhülle mich! und zu der Finsternis: birg mich! so muss die Finsternis leuchten um Euch, und um den Verdammten die Mitternacht tagen – aber Euer unsterblicher Geist sträubt sich unter dem Wort und siegt über den blinden Gedanken.

FRANZ: Ich will aber nicht unsterblich sein! – sei es, wer da will, ich will's nicht hindern. Ich will ihn zwingen, dass er mich zernichte, ich will ihn zur Wut reizen, dass er mich in der Wut zernichte ...

And the vain attempt to pray should, as in Schiller, surely follow this confrontation. Maffei has tried, for the sake of the design of the operatic scene, to keep back the lyrical formulation until the very last moment, by which time there is no genuine confrontation left. Franz is trying to browbeat God, and Moser, having failed in his redeeming mission as a priest, can only threaten perdition.

Notwithstanding such occasional failures, the odd loose end or missing link, there is no doubt that out of Schiller's play Maffei created a libretto that for poetic eloquence, thoughtfulness, psychological interest, and freedom from the habits of Romantic melodrama stands head and shoulders above the majority of those Verdi set in his early years. The mystery remains that it did not inspire Verdi to the composition of a great or even of an unusual opera. It may be that occasionally the poetic eloquence remains a literary grace of little use to the composer, as in Francesco's dream narration 'Pareami che sorto da lauto convito'. It may be that Maffei's thoughtfulness occasionally tempted him into metaphysical regions where Verdi was ill equipped to follow:

> Anche i malvagi
> Trovano il sonno ... ed io nol trovo! ... Oh vita,
> Tenebroso mistero! E voi non meno,
> Morte ed eternità, profondi arcani,
> Che vi sa penetrar? ...   (III.5)

But it is difficult not to agree with Budden that the crucial deficiency is the lack of confrontation in the dramatic design. As we have seen, two of the duets – Francesco/Amalia in Act II and Francesco/Moser in Act IV – are less effective than they might be; others – Massimiliano/Amalia in Act I, Carlo/Amalia in Act III – arising out of a virtual unanimity of sentiment are not really confrontations at all; in other cases again, scenes that Schiller designed as confrontations – those between Franz and Maximilian and Franz and Amalia in Act I – have been eliminated altogether in the work of compression. In his moods and passions, in his analysis of character, in his tableaux, Maffei provided Verdi with three-quarters of an excellent libretto. But for a composer of Verdi's temper it was perhaps the most vital quarter that was missing.

The music of *I Masnadieri*

In no other Verdi opera does the tenor hero assume quite such a dominant position in the dramatic scheme. Of course he is a romantic lover, and of course he is the leader of a group of comrades who together carry out bold and terrible deeds. But the real dramatic theme concerns Carlo alone, his emotional and moral response to the world in which he finds himself, and the challenge which he subsequently issues to that world. Carlo's centrality to the theme is aptly reflected in the form which Maffei and Verdi give to the opening scene. They take the unusual step of suppressing the traditional opening chorus and beginning at once with the tenor's *aria di sortita*.

It is in this scene that we witness the young idealist so embittered by his experience of the world as to embark upon a life of brigandage. The scena, with its allusions to the valour of Classical times and the decadence of the present, and with the banal and cheerful off-stage shouts of his 'companions in error', is brought into focus with the arioso in the last bars. At heart Carlo is the prodigal son yearning for reinstatement.

Homeland, family, the beloved are the burden of the cantabile too, and the D♭ tonality and the fluttering woodwind textures are the conventional imagery of such dreamlike, idealizing themes. But Verdi sustains the idea very effectively through into the following *tempo di mezzo*, where the inexpressive mechanics typical of such a section are twice suspended when Carlo is overcome by his feelings for home. There is a sudden flood of tender joy when the letter appears: 'Beato io sono! Questo, amici, è il mio perdono', and a spasm of heartbroken regret when he finds himself rejected: 'Così calde e pie preghiere ...'

What Verdi misses, on the other hand, is that element in Carlo's make-up that Maffei has suggested quite well at 'Ah, potessi il mar', the sense of his letting chaos loose upon the earth. Probably it is the kind of concept for which one needs an orchestrally orientated imagination, the imagination of a Weber or Wagner. Verdi's music, though fiercely passionate and endowed with a good gestic quality, is too formal, too centred on the articulating human voice to feed the imagination. As for the cabaletta, the music lacks any trace of the diabolical rhetoric which the words call for; it is merely energetic, and energetic in a way which makes Carlo indistinguishable from any other Romantic hero.

Maffei's depiction of Carlo again moves into regions where Verdi is ill equipped to follow in the Act III finale, at the recitative 'Ti delusi Amalia'. The matching scene in the play, with Karl's song 'Sei willkommen, friedliches Gefilde' and the soliloquy 'Wer mir Bürge wäre', is one of the critical episodes in Schiller's depiction of his central character. Reduced by Maffei to a vague and abstract pondering of the questions of mortality, it proves ill matched to Verdi's talents. The recitative that emerges is wholly lacking in evocative power, its merely dignified opening being succeeded by a merely vehement close.

Other aspects of Carlo's character, however, Verdi is able to reflect more convincingly. In the recitative and 'romanza'* of Act II for example, the fallen Carlo, surrounded by a horde of thugs and assassins, and loathing himself for the way of life that he has adopted, is yet moved by the beauty of the world, and by the dream of love that might have been. The slow moving, fluid recitative at 'Natura! oh sei pur bella' has something of the rapt entrancement of that sung by Elvira and Ernani in the summer night outside Silva's castle at Saragossa; disillusion and idealism are admirably set against one another in the aria. In the first half the ritenuti at the ends of the falling phrases impart a suggestion of weariness and self-disgust. The second half of the song is set in the relative major key; the grim broken-chord shapes of the melody are superseded by legato rising phrases, and the angry, shaking chords of the accompaniment by ethereal floating arpeggio patterns. For the sake of theatrical clarity Verdi keeps the emotional antithesis simpler than Maffei. Despite all the verbal emphasis on 'la mia pena', it is the music of the holier vision associated with Amalia that is sustained through to the end of the aria.

In the giuramento at the close of Act III Verdi again comes close to the Schillerian essence of Carlo. The movement is an impressive example of the standard responsorial form adapted from Guillaume Tell, to which the throbbing horns, rolling drums, and galloping trumpets lend a resplendent colouring. One cannot help suspecting that the blaze of spiritual and military exultation in which the scene culminates is at least partly intended for the risorgimento audiences back home. But this time the militaristic-cum-idealistic tone of the chorus really does match Schiller's dramatic situation beautifully too; for it employs the idiom of the 'padre del coro' to give a sense of holy mission to the terror and destruction on which Moor and his brigands are bent.

*Not so called by Verdi. In his autograph score the scene is counted as part of the Act II finale.

In *Die Räuber*, a foil to the formidable energy and vehemence of the Moor brothers is provided by the wholly passive figures of the father and the beloved. They too are recreated by Verdi in as authentic a manner as the medium permits. Massimiliano, an image of lachrymose, enduring senility, is embodied, very much like the elder Foscari, in a series of slow-moving cantabiles. At no point in the opera does he sing a cabaletta, or even participate in a cabaletta; the only energy of which he is capable are the passive energies of horror and disgust, as for example when, in his narrative cantabile 'Un ignoto, tre lune or saranno', he recalls the vision of Francesco leering over his coffin lid or ordering him to be thrown into a prison vault.

It is sometimes assumed that such deficiencies as the critics have discerned in Verdi's characterization of Amalia are largely due to the peculiar talents and limitations of Jenny Lind, the creator of the role. Incomparable in trills, *fioritura* and all the paraphernalia of florid song, Lind seems to have lacked the power, the range of vocal colour and the stage personality called for by the most memorable of Verdi's early soprano roles, Abigaille, Elvira, Giovanna, Lady Macbeth. As a result, Amalia's music all assumes a basically similar, monochrome colouring. The melodic lines are generally flexible and delicate, and both in cantabiles, such as 'Lo sguardo avea', and in cabalettas such as 'Carlo vive?', profusely ornamented in a manner that is decorative rather than expressive or forceful. The orchestral textures that accompany her are distinguished by string pizzicatos, and by trilling and fluttering woodwind patterns. Everything suggests that the role was tailor-made for Lind.

Equally, however, everything matches Schiller's Amalia. A character who never takes an initiative, who reacts sensitively but passively to every situation in which she finds herself, whose distinguishing traits are tenderness and emotional enthusiasm, surely does not call for the shrill brilliance of an Abigaille, or the blood-curdling chest notes of an Odabella. Sympathetically performed, the floating and dancing coloratura of her arias can sound very much like a musical image of that 'paradiso' which she has once tasted in Carlo's embrace, and where she may once again be reunited with him. Such an Elysium is as central to Amalia's thoughts as it was to be in Luisa Miller's – perhaps more so, since Maffei is so much more dutiful towards Schiller than Cammarano was to be. It is probably relevant to this question of the musical characterization of Amalia to recall the botched effect of the first scenes of Act II. In view of what follows – the lament for Massimiliano in her recitative, 'Un altra voce', and for Carlo in the duet 'Tu che pur dianzi a

morte' – it is impossible to believe that the recitative and cabaletta
'Carlo vive?' were part of the original considered dramatic scheme
for this act. In other words, the cantabile 'Tu del mio Carlo' would
surely have been a single-movement aria lacking its cabaletta, like
'Lo sguardo avea' in Act I. It looks as if initially Amalia's passive,
undynamic character, like Massimiliano's, was to be reflected in the
formal structure by a lack of solo cabalettas. But not even the
absurdity of 'Carlo vive?' can be described as merely a concession to
Lind. Verdi became uneasy about the original form of the act as soon
as he began work on it, and long before he heard what kind of singer
she was.

Of the four Schillerian protagonists that Verdi has taken over into
his opera, only the younger brother, Francesco, must be accounted a
total failure. That is not to say that the attempt to emulate the satanic
prototype did not have some interesting and worthwhile consequences. Verdi's repertory of horrific and macabre gestures was
extended, sometimes with electrifying effect, as at the end of the Act
I finale where, accompanied only by a timpani roll, Francesco
exclaims 'Morto? . . . signor son io!' (Ex. 1). Among the profusion of

Ex. 1

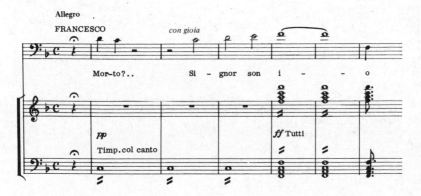

proto-Iagoish orchestral figurations, of slides, trills, and unison brass
fanfares, another interesting phenomenon is provided by the emergence of what one might almost call a Francesco motif. Unlike the
'mask'-themes of I Due Foscari, this can nowhere be observed in an
unmistakable, definitive form; but throughout the opera – in his Act
I scena, in Massimiliano's narration, in the 'dream' – his evil presence is suggested by rising arpeggio figurations based on the
diminished-seventh chord (Ex. 2). In some movements Verdi's

Ex. 2 (a)

(b)

(c)

attempt to get to grips with diabolism results in striking distortions of colour and musical form. A good example is provided by the cantabile 'La sua lampada vitale', where the bleating *legato* of the trumpets and horns transforms the conventional introduction into a hideous travesty of the lyrical style, and where an unforeseen formal feature, a kind of refrain which appears once between exposition and episode, and again between episode and culmination, imparts a superbly obsessional character to the aria, as if Francesco were chewing endlessly over his secret lusts.

The reason why Francesco must be accounted a failure of Verdi's dramatic imagination, notwithstanding a number of impressive and interesting moments, has already been hinted at in our discussion of Carlo. The Italian tradition to which Verdi was bred up was a humanist tradition of lucid and impassioned utterance. It was ill equipped to deal with metaphysics or with murk. Verdi's vision of the cosmic chaos which was Francesco's habitat was, at this stage, simply inadequate. Man is the measure of things in the dramatic world of Italian opera. He is perfectly aware of the emotions to which he is subject, and experiences neither difficulty nor diffidence in imparting them to his audience. He addresses them man to man, in a series of emotional confidences, which appeal to their sense of human fellowship without making any real appeal to their imagination. Faced with Schiller's image of the universe dissolving at the Last Judgement, such a tradition is helpless. Neither Verdi nor any other Italian of the period had the sensibility or the technique – as Wagner might have had – to build a sustained vision such as would make the imagination quake. All Verdi can do in Francesco's dream narration is to subject the nerve-ends to a series of shocks and bruisings, the kind of things which in conventional Romantic melodrama help set an audience on edge in readiness for an aria, but which in their own right are quite incapable of nourishing the imagination.

In the cantabile itself, 'Pareami che sorto da lauto convito', we find that the formulae tend to be built into symmetrical patterns, with the result that they lack even the power to shock. The treatment of the fire image at 'E dentro quel foco', for example, rapidly palls: it becomes merely a decorative pattern, incidental to the sense of the words, but treated in a way that contradicts their spirit (Ex. 3). Similar inadequacies are felt in the setting of the actual passing of judgement. The Last Judgement is the most appalling imaginative vision experienced by man. But Verdi, as yet unable to unleash the full evocative power of the orchestra, reduces it to a mere theatrical ritual, playing on the audience in a crudely physical way with his chromatic modulations and his shattering *tutti* outbursts. Never once does he fashion a musical image that was not a commonplace with every miserable hack of a maestro in Italy. The whole scena represents an extraordinary failure of the imagination: the limitations of the medium are mercilessly exposed.

Ex. 3

Surprisingly, the opera's most successful evocation of chaos is to be found among the choral movements; though not consistently, certainly, for in a majority of cases there is the same ludicrous

disharmony between the hideousness of their words and the in-
nocuous cheerfulness of their music. The brigands who sing 'Le
rube, gli stupri' are about as awe-inspiring as the Pirates of Penzance,
whose ancestors of course they are. Once, however, in the scena and
chorus 'Tutto quest'oggi' in Act II, Verdi does succeed in expressing
the dramatic meaning of the outlaw band. While for most of the
members it represents nothing more momentous than a roistering
camaraderie, for the world at large it constitutes a glimpse of anarchy
and terror.

Verdi does not seem terribly interested in the ostensible occasion
of the music – the report of Rolla's capture and rescue. Both the
opening and closing sections of the chorus – unconcerned, formally
patterned music – employ conventional Verdian narrative techni-
ques, the one in dialogue, the other a unison cantabile, with a
concluding refrain of Sullivanesque bonhomie. Between these two
sections, however, comes the evocation of chaos and the expression
of the awe which it inspires. Despite the traditionally decorative
nature of the chorus, nowhere in the opera does Verdi handle this
theme better. Like a real German he puts the burden of his vision in
the orchestra – an impressively conceived texture of flaming strings
and streaking woodwind – while the chorus itself is reduced to a
subsidiary, colouristic, and even percussive role. No less memorable
is his use of the chorus in a largely unaccompanied texture in which
high sustained chords and thrumming percussive chords are coun-
terpointed to suggest a sense of awe and breathless terror.

Although *I Masnadieri* was written for London, Verdi could
reasonably have anticipated that the greater number of its performances would occur in Italy. It is therefore not surprising that together
with this solitary awful vision, and the profusion of lusty banalities
that make up the opera's repertory of choruses, there should be some
that remind us of the *risorgimento* episodes in the earlier operas. The
giuramento at the end of Act III is one obvious example: another
might be the Act II finale, a quick march in praise of brotherhood and
freedom. And what is one to make of the extraordinary episode in
the Act III chorus, a setting of the words

> Gli estremi aneliti
> D'uccisi padri,
> Le grida, gli ululi
> Di spose e madri ...

in the style of a Strauss waltz? Is this conceivably a satirical allusion
to the Viennese, who, in the embittered view of an Italian national-

ist, waltz on heedlessly while their Empire resounds to the howls and groans of the slaughtered and the oppressed?

The libretto of *Luisa Miller*

Having discovered Schiller during the summer weeks spent at Recoaro with Maffei in 1846, Verdi was eager to translate his admiration into a practical act of homage by making a further operatic adaptation of the great playwright. While Maffei was still busy shaping *Die Räuber* into a libretto, Verdi had already taken fire from *Kabale und Liebe* and wrote to Cammarano expressing his admiration: 'it is a magnficent drama, passionate and very effective theatrically, but it would need two women principals'.[6] Its passion and its theatricality are perhaps not those aspects of the play which the higher critics would choose to emphasize, but they are typical preoccupations of Verdi. And at least his mention of the need for two women principals suggests that he appreciated the dramatic and therefore the philosophical significance of Lady Milford's role. How far Verdi might have wished to incorporate Schiller's philosophical and social preoccupations into his opera we cannot now know, for Cammarano rather wrested away the initiative in the planning of the libretto and proved adept at countering most of the proposals and criticisms which the composer was moved to make.

Kabale und Liebe, written and several times revised between 1782 and 1784, is the last of the three prose dramas of the *Sturm und Drang* phase of Schiller's youth. Its historical significance in German literature is primarily due to the fact that it is the earliest example of a drama used to express direct critical involvement in contemporary political problems. Lessing, dealing with comparable issues in *Emilia Galotti*, had felt it necessary to lend his drama a certain distance and detachment by transposing it to a foreign country at a distant point in time. Schiller makes no such concession. The problems with which he is concerned belonged to his own country and his own day; they were the problems of tyranny, corruption and, above all, dehumanization, from which the petty principalities of late-eighteenth-century Germany suffered as did no other part of western Europe. In *Kabale und Liebe* Schiller avenges himself for the injustice and indignities he had suffered at the hands of one of the most characteristic of the monstrous monarchs of the period, Karl Eugen, Duke of Württemberg.

But a man with the soul of a Schiller, a man whose whole being was illuminated by the loftiest humanitarian idealism, is not to be satisfied with mere vengeful commination, no more in *Kabale und Liebe* than in *Die Räuber*. The real theme of the play is a philosophical and even religious analysis of varieties of human relationship, in particular those organized by social laws, and those inspired by the promptings of the heart. It scrutinizes social conventions, the actions of the characters, and the human relationships forged between them in the light of the highest moral ideals and in terms of their religious import. The love of Ferdinand and Luise is not merely a question of mutual inclination; if challenged it can uphold its claim theologically: 'Ich will sie führen vor des Weltrichters Thron, und ob meine Liebe Verbrechen ist, soll der Ewige sagen ...' (II.5). Even when Ferdinand makes the terrible resolve to poison Luise, he sees himself as fulfilling a heaven-ordained obligation: '... Die obern Mächte nicken mir ihr schreckliches *Ja* herunter, die Rache des Himmels unterschreibt, ihr guter Engel lässt sie fahren –' (v.6). In *Kabale und Liebe* humanity and divinity are one: it is by the promptings of the heart that the truths of theology are apprehended.

The complementary aspect of Schiller's theme is the thesis that social organization, in particular the hierarchy of class, destroys humanity. In one character after another he analyses the antagonism between the better instincts of humankind and the conventions of social organization, particularly in its upper reaches. At court, in politics, one can prosper only by opportunism, corruption and iniquity; in short by denying one's humanity. A dialogue between Ferdinand, who makes the idealist humanitarian choice, and Walter, who has chosen the unscrupulous path to political power, reveals the nature of the dilemma. The brilliant prospects which in Walter's view should thrill and enchant his son only appal him,

Ihre Glückseligkeit macht sich nur selten anders als durch Verderben bekannt. Neid, Furcht, Verwünschung sind die traurigen Spiegel, worin sich die Hoheit eines Herrschers belächelt. – Tränen, Flüche, Verzweiflung die entsetzliche Mahlzeit, woran diese gepriesenen Glücklichen schwelgen, von der sie betrunken aufstehen und so in die Ewigkeit vor den Thron Gottes taumeln – Mein Ideal von Glück zieht sich genügsamer in mich selbst zurück. In meinem *Herzen* liegen alle meine Wünsche begraben ... (1.7)

It is in the character of Lady Milford, however, that the dilemma is most memorably embodied. Supposed by Ferdinand to be the unprincipled and pampered mistress of a dissolute and tyrannical prince, she proves in fact to be no less nauseated by court life than is Ferdinand. Her ideals are not sensuality and luxury, but passion, intelligence, sensibility; for the sincere love of such a man as

Ferdinand she would turn her back on her privileged position at court in a moment:

Lass mich aus seinem Mund es vernehmen, dass Tränen der Liebe schöner glänzen in unsern Augen als die Brillanten in unserm Haar, und ich werfe dem Fürsten sein Herz und sein Fürstentum vor die Füsse, fliehe mit diesem Mann, fliehe in die entlegenste Wüste der Welt. (II.1)

The counterpart to her scene with Ferdinand in Act II is that with Luise in Act IV. Perceiving that there can be no spontaneous happy outcome to her dilemma, Lady Milford is tempted to enforce a solution by the standard high-society, power-political methods of intrigue and tyranny. But the world to whose principles she is about to resort is stripped bare, exposed in all its rottenness, by the uncompromising, searing glance of Luise, thanks to whom Lady Milford is finally moved to renounce the prerogatives of privilege:

In deine Arme werf ich mich, Tugend! – ... Gross, wie eine fallende Sonne, will ich heut' vom Gipfel meiner Hoheit heruntersinken: meine Herrlichkeit sterbe mit meiner Liebe, und nichts als mein *Herz* begleite mich in diese stolze Verweisung ...(IV.8)

The theme of *Kabale und Liebe* is, then, that dilemma with which Ferdinand challenges Lady Milford: 'Wir wollen sehen, ob die *Mode* oder die *Menschheit* auf dem Platz bleiben wird' (II.3). It is not a dilemma that Schiller scrutinizes with dispassionate objectivity. For him there is no question where one should stand: *Mode* is the world's most loathsome tyranny, *Menschheit* its loftiest ideal. The idiom of the play is therefore based on an alternating pattern of indictment and idealization.

This pattern is clearly established early in the play. In three consecutive scenes of the first act (I.5–7) Schiller savages three of the vices he associates with the privileged strata of a hierarchical society – sensuality, imbecile servility and the unprincipled carrying-out of deeds of shocking iniquity. The picture is filled out early in the second act with a servant's description of an exportation, and Lady Milford's of sexual debauchery:

... wie uns die gellenden Trommeln verkündigten, es ist Zeit, und heulende Waisen dort einen lebendigen Vater verfolgten, und hier eine wütende Mutter lief, ihr saugendes Kind an Bajonetten zu spiessen, und wie man Bräutigam und Braut mit Säbelhieben auseinander riss und wir Graubärte verzweiflungsvoll dastanden und den Burschen auch zuletzt die Krücken noch nachwarfen in die neue Welt – Oh, und mitunter das polternde Wirbelschlagen, damit der Allwissende uns nicht sollte beten hören – (II.2)

.. Die Wollust der Grossen dieser Welt ist die nimmersatte Hyäne, die sich mit Heisshunger Opfer sucht. – Fürchterlich hatte sie schon in diesem

Lande gewütet – hatte Braut und Bräutigam zertrennt – hatte selbst der Ehen göttliches Band zerrissen – hier das stille Glück einer Familie geschleift – dort ein junges unerfahrenes Herz der verheerenden Pest aufgeschlossen, und sterbende Schülerinnen schäumten den Namen ihres Lehrers unter Flüchen und Zuckungen aus ...   (II.3)

Against these appalling images of tyranny Schiller sets an idealization not of bourgeois life – as the subtitle 'ein bürgerliches Trauerspiel' might seem to imply – but of the heart. The bourgeoisie is, after all, no less a product of stratification and convention than the aristocracy, and its coarseness and silliness are characteristics scarcely more amiable than theirs. For the man of passionate feeling and refined understanding the world of the Millers offered a no more adequate refuge than that of President von Walter. The tragic catastrophe of the play is rooted in the fact that society as constituted has no refuge for those whose law is the prompting of the heart. Inevitably the idealization of feeling, the apotheosis of *Menschheit*, leads Schiller to those Arcadian or Elysian realms he hymned so sublimely in his lyrical poems. There is, however, a difference between the ideal worlds of the poems and that of *Kabale und Liebe*. For in a play so committed to the realistic depiction of contemporary life, there can be no place for the Antique grandeur and beauty of his lyrical Arcadias, no place for the sublime and distant landscapes of his lyrical Elysiums. Only in death, a condition naively yet nobly romanticized by Luise in a Christian sense, can the values of passion, sensibility and goodness really prevail:

Ich entsag' ihm für dieses Leben. Dann, Mutter – dann, wenn die Schranken des Unterschieds einstürzen – wenn von uns abspringen all die verhasste Hülsen des Standes – Menschen nur Menschen sind – Ich bringe nichts mit mir als meine Unschuld, aber der Vater hat ja oft gesagt, dass der Schmuck und die prächtigen Titel wohlfeil werden, wenn Gott kommt, und die Herzen im Preise steigen. Ich werde dann reich sein. Dort rechnet man Tränen für Triumphe und schöne Gedanken für Ahnen an.   (I.3)

The grave, in Luise's idealizing vision, becomes 'ein Brautbette ... worüber der Morgen seinen goldenen Teppich breitet und die Frühlinge ihre bunte Girlanden streuen', and Death itself 'ein holder niedlicher Knabe ... ein stiller dienstbarer Genius, der der erschöpften Pilgerin Seele den Arm bietet über den Graben der Zeit, das Feenschloss der ewigen Herrlichkeit aufschliesst, freundlich nickt und verschwindet' (V.1)

I have already had sufficient occasion to remark that authenticity was one of the qualities Verdi ranked highest in making operatic adaptations of literary models. It was when working with Cammarano that he found this most difficult to achieve. Cammarano was one of the most experienced and accomplished librettists in Italy, but his experience and accomplishment had been acquired primarily in Naples, the most old-fashioned, convention-bound opera centre in the peninsula. Skilful as his work was, Cammarano's real forte was the transformation of almost any kind of subject into a traditional melodramatic libretto; the very reverse of what Verdi had begun to achieve in such a work as *Macbeth* in collaboration with the much less able Piave. Cammarano was good at what Italian opera had traditionally demanded: wild passions in orderly array, strong situations with no dramatic significance beyond their own thrillingness. He could perhaps appreciate and reproduce the passion and theatricality of *Kabale und Liebe*, but his talents were ill suited to making a genuinely authentic adaptation of the other levels of the play. Its social preoccupations, even if they had interested him, would have been unacceptable to a Neapolitan censor; its philosophical and religious dialectic was quite outside the range of his competence; and the intricately woven structure of the play, the manner in which each scene prepares for or leads inexorably towards the next, required more from a librettist than adeptness in the self-sufficient, tableau-like scena of the conventional opera.

Obviously, though, unless some trace were left of Schiller's *Mode/Menschheit* antithesis the drama would be meaningless. Cammarano does indeed touch upon the matter in at least a few scenes in the opera – the dialogue between Miller and Wurm in 1.4 and in Walter's scenes, 1.5 and 11.3–4. In the first of these, Wurm, besides embodying the hostile passions of jealousy and anger that disrupt the idyllic opening, prompts Miller to a fairly full statement of his libertarian idealism. For a moment Wurm represents the worst aspect of the *Mode* of marriage –

> ... non potevi forse
> Alle richieste nozze
> Astringerla? non hai
> Dritto sovr'essa tu? ...

– and Miller the best aspects of its *Menschheit* –

> Sacra la scelta è d'un consorte
> Essere appieno libera deve ...
> In terra un padre somiglia Iddio
> Per la bontade, non pel rigor.

In Walter's scenes – which would originally have formed a more compact unit, in that the cantabile now in 1.5, 'Il mio sangue, la vita darei', belonged to 11.3* – Cammarano seems to suggest that his

* Cf. letter of 13 August 1849, quoted above, p. 245.

relationship with his son has been destroyed by the intrigue inseparable in a corrupt society from political ambition as surely as Miller's love for his daughter is threatened by it. Walter's aria is full of tensions and paradoxes – 'felice'/'possente', 'voti'/'ordini' – of which he is apparently unaware: Walter is helpless in his failure to see the fallaciousness of his equation of power with happiness, and the reason for the loss of all that really matters to him. 'Il mio sangue, la vita darei Per vederlo felice, possente', and the *tempo di mezzo* that originally followed it – 'L'alto retaggio non ho bramato Di mio cugino che sol per esso!' – are the passages in the opera that come closest to grasping that *Mode/Menschheit* dilemma with which Schiller's Walter wrestles in his dialogue with Ferdinand: 'Wem zu Lieb' hab' ich die gefährliche Bahn zum Herzen des Fürsten betreten? Wem zu Lieb' bin ich auf ewig mit meinem Gewissen und dem Himmel zerfallen? . . .' (I.7)

In general, though, the passages in which Cammarano comes closest to Schiller are not those in which the dramatic essence of the play is most concentrated, but those in which the playwright anticipates the idiom of Romantic melodrama. Verdi himself noticed that the thrilling acceleration of incident at the end of Schiller's second act would provide an excellent pattern for his own Act I finale, and insisted that Cammarano 'must do it exactly like Schiller'. In a different way the sustained emotive dialogue of such a scene as that between Miller and Luise in Schiller's v.1 provides an excellent pattern for Cammarano's operatic duet; the richness of language and idea in the play enhance rather than embarrass the work of the librettist. Given the firm, sustained design of the scene, almost every detail of the play can be matched in the libretto: Miller's alarm at his daughter's stillness, his reading of the letter to Ferdinand/Rodolfo, Luise's explanation that the sojourn which she refers to is the grave, and the extended lyrical apostrophe to the grave:

Es liegt ein Brautbette da, worüber der Morgen seinen goldenen Teppich breitet und die Frühlinge ihre bunte Girlanden streuen. Nur ein heulender Sünder konnte den Tod ein Gerippe schelten . . .

> La tomba è un letto sparso di fiori,
> In cui del giusto la spoglia dorme:
> Sol pei colpevoli, tremanti cori
> Veste la morte orride forme . . .

And so the parallels continue throughout the scene.

Despite such close verbal parallels in a handful of scenes, little of the real character of Schiller's work remains in the opera. The action has been transposed out of the here-and-now into a rural community in the Tyrol in the first half of the seventeenth century. Partly this was done to facilitate the use of the chorus as picturesque rustics,* and to give the enchantment of distance so congenial to the operatic medium. But partly, too, it was a matter of drawing Schiller's political sting. Cammarano must have recognized, the moment he read the play, that many of its facets were uncompromisingly hostile to the conventions of *ottocento* melodrama especially as practised in Naples.

In Cammarano's libretto virtually all the play's political implications are eliminated. The scenes that show this most clearly are those set in Walter's castle in Act I (1.6–7). In the dialogue between Walter and his son, neither the extent to which Walter has been compromised morally by his political rise nor Rodolfo's contempt for the values of court life is really suggested. Moreover the nature of the marriage that father is urging upon son has been wholly changed. In the play, marriage with the prince's mistress, the 'privilegierte Buhlerin', Lady Milford, is seen as the stepping-stone to a brilliant career at court – 'privy council – embassages – extraordinary favours'. In the opera a similar court career requires only marriage to the widowed Duchessa d'Ostheim, a long-standing friend of the family, who had been romantically attached to Rodolfo before her first marriage. Though Walter insists on obedience in both play and opera, in the one he is, without a flicker of conscience, condemning his son to abject dishonour, in the other making what, under different circumstances, would seem a very reasonable fatherly proposal.

Cammarano's unwillingness or inability to re-create the social world of Schiller's play is shown most blatantly in the way he deletes the character of Lady Milford altogether, and makes the respectable but shadowy Federica d'Ostheim the court lady Rodolfo is to marry. The motives for this change, admittedly, seem mixed. In explaining it to Verdi, Cammarano seemed worried not about censorship, as one might have anticipated, but about the question of casting. Operatic roles were expected, especially perhaps in Naples, to conform to certain character-types. Lady Milford – at once an idealist, a fallen woman, a woman who finally renounces all hopes of happiness or power – was in terms of these usages a sheer impossibility. There was, Cammarano explained, 'not one leading lady (among singers) who would have taken on the role'.†

* Cf. Cammarano's letter of 11 June, quoted above, pp. 241–2.
† Cf. above, pp. 241–2.

The atmosphere of the scenes involving Lady Milford is inevitably quite transformed when Federica d'Ostheim steps into her shoes. Every suggestion of moral impropriety or of court corruption is eliminated from the libretto. Under the circumstances there can be no trace of Schiller's tremendous confrontation between Milford and Ferdinand. In the play both characters had prepared themselves emotionally and philosophically for the encounter, and during the course of the scene their moods evolve from idealistic and noble hopes to fatalistic despair on the one side, and from angry scorn to fatalistic despair on the other. For both characters and, thanks to Schiller's storming eloquence, for the audience too, the scene is a tremendous emotional and spiritual experience. Expurgated and reworked by Cammarano it amounts to little or nothing: an encounter between old friends – one embarrassed, one entertaining romantic hopes – is turned, by the revelation of Luisa's claim on Rodolfo's affection, into a conventional operatic jealousy scene, with gentlemanly apology on one side and hyperbolic indignation on the other.

The conventional operatic scene was of course Cammarano's speciality, and the way in which he fashions such scenes out of the play does generally provoke admiration. Though his technique varies in detail from scene to scene the fundamental principle underlying it is that dramatic action and dramatic dialogue must yield pride of place to emotional expression. Cammarano sees opera as a medium in which characters are interesting not for the ideas they embody, nor for the actions in which they become involved, but for the feelings to which they are subject. It is therefore not the impassioned philosophical dialogues nor yet the tangled intrigue in *Kabale und Liebe* that concern him – though these are perhaps the qualities which make the play most memorable; it is the effect which these dialogues and intrigues have on the characters involved, the extent to which they can be manipulated to provide openings for outbursts of passionate feeling.

Probably the best example of Cammarano's operaticizing is provided by his reworking in the second act of the opera of the intrigue by which Walter and Wurm compel Luise to renounce her love for Ferdinand/Rodolfo. The scenes are approximately equivalent to Act III of Schiller's play.

The gist of this act is that Walter and Wurm, frustrated in their first attempt to persuade Ferdinand to marry Lady Milford, decide on a new approach to the matter by way of Luise. Her father is to be arrested, and she to be blackmailed into writing a letter admitting that her love for Ferdinand was a pretence, and professing in reality to love another (von Kalb in the play, Wurm in the opera). This letter is then to fall into Ferdinand's hands. In *Kabale und Liebe* three things chiefly impress us in this act: the careful detail with which Wurm prepares the intrigue; Schiller's masterly dramatic manipulation, which ensures that the effect of the intrigue on Luise and Ferdinand should be absolutely plausible; and, as in every other section of the play, the searing humanitarian rhetoric, the sheer weight and passion of the ideas.

Wurm's preparations involve persuading Walter that such an oblique approach is a better way to achieve their objective than any further attempt to browbeat Ferdinand; it involves allusions to the diplomatic resource with which Walter had risen to his present position, and the appropriateness of such skills in the present instance:

Sie haben, dünkt mich, der biegsamen Hofkunst den ganzen *Präsidenten* zu danken, warum vertrauten Sie ihr nicht auch den *Vater* an? Ich besinne mich, mit welcher Offenheit Sie Ihren Vorgänger damals zu einer Partie Piquet beredeten und bei ihm die halbe Nacht mit freundschaftlichem Burgunder hinwegschwemmten, und das war doch die nämliche Nacht, wo die grosse Mine losgehen und den guten Mann in die Luft blasen sollte – Warum zeigten Sie Ihrem Sohne den Feind? (III. 1)

The particular stroke of dramatic cunning by which Schiller ensures that the blackmail scene shall have its full dire effect and remain absolutely plausible to the audience is that he precedes it with a scene (III.4) in which tensions and even mistrust begin to arise between the lovers. Ferdinand tries to persuade Luise to elope with him. But duty to her family and the conviction that to separate son from father is morally wrong deter her: 'Wenn nur ein Frevel dich mir erhalten kann, so hab ich doch Stärke, dich zu verlieren.' After a long, gloomy silence of an authentically *Sturm und Drang* wildness – Ferdinand gnaws his lip, grinds his teeth, attempts to play a violin and then smashes it to pieces – he turns on Luise accusingly: 'Schlange, du lügst. Dich fesselt was anders hier.' The lovers around whom we have already seen Walter and Wurm weaving their intrigue are thus at the crucial moment weakened by dissension, deprived of mutual support, rendered temptable. As for the ideological rhetoric it is scarcely ever still: provocative, savage, or sublime, it does its work of persuasion and inspiration in every episode in the act. The same scene in which Walter and Wurm plan their intrigue is the occasion for a report on Ferdinand's contempt for the court. That dialogue between Luise and Ferdinand whose dramatic purpose is to weaken their resistance to Wurm's intrigue furnishes besides grand speeches that idealize passion, and others that reflect the spiritual anguish for which class-consciousness is responsible:

dein Herz gehört deinem Stande – Mein Anspruch war Kirchenraub, und schaudernd geb' ich ihn auf ...

... Lass *mich* die Heldin dieses Augenblicks sein – einem Vater den entflohenen Sohn wieder schenken – einem Bündnis entsagen, das die Fugen der Bürgerwelt auseinandertreiben und die allgemeine ewige Ordnung zu Grund stürzen würde ...

Of all these wonderful features nothing remains in Cammarano's libretto. By reordering the scenes in the pattern of chorus (report of Miller's arrest), aria (Luisa blackmailed by Wurm), duet (memories of Walter's rise to power assisted by Wurm), he deprives the drama of that sense of an intrigue constricting inexorably around the lovers, and because he has eliminated the scene between the lovers he cannot suggest their vulnerability. The news of Miller's arrest is not carefully motivated, prepared, and made the more effective by the preliminary weakening of Luisa; it comes as a sudden blow at the start of the act. Even in the Luisa/Wurm scene, which comes closest to the parallel scene in the play, Cammarano has shifted the emphasis significantly. Its dramatic object is of course, as in the play, to lead directly to the final catastrophe, but its more immediate purpose is expressive: to depict Luise racked by spiritual anguish and finally succumbing to fatalistic despair. It never becomes a real duet, as Verdi had originally proposed; it remains a scene exclusively concerned with the emotional consequences of the blackmail on the heroine, with sweet memories, vanishing hopes and mental torment.

Finally the scene between Walter and Wurm follows that between Wurm and Luise instead of preceding it. It is a scene not of dramatic preparation but of emotional revelation: here as nowhere else in the opera Walter's sinister past is uncovered. And because the object of the scene is the exploration of Walter's soul, Cammarano elaborates the allusions which Schiller had made to the murder of a predecessor. He does not leave it vague and mysterious – one particularly evil incident in the whole unsavoury background of political machination – he brings it into the open to haunt Walter, and he wrings it for shudders.

WURM: Varcar dovea
         L'irta foresta notturno il Conte ...
         Noi l'appostammo, e ...
WALTER: Non seguir ...
         Sento drizzarsi il chiome in fronte!
         Tutto il mio sangue rabbrividir! ...   (II.4)

Cammarano's libretto is based on the traditional principle of the set-piece in which a character or group of characters express the emotions by which they are stirred, uplifted or oppressed. But a corollary of this principle is that the range of emotions experienced by the characters should be as wide as the subject matter permits, and this leads Cammarano to make a further drastic modification of the play. In *Kabale und Liebe* the love of Ferdinand and Luise acts as a focus for that contest between *Mode* and *Menschheit* with which Schiller is principally concerned. His drama shows a noble example of the love which is the finest faculty of humanity threatened, corrupted and finally destroyed by the most abominable manifestations of class habit. The process of destruction and the openings which this gives for philosophical and moral rhetoric are Schiller's chief interest. Cammarano on the other hand sees the relationship simply as a tragically doomed love affair; and is equally interested in every phase of its development, its primal naive raptures as well as its tensions and its despairs. In order to vary the emotional colours of this love he transforms the character of the opening scenes of the opera. Schiller, bent at once on his dramatic theme, shows Luise and Ferdinand already threatened: their felicity belongs to the past, to the 'damals' which Luise recalls with such yearning eloquence –

Damals – o damals ging in meiner Seele der erste Morgen auf. Tausend junge Gefühle schossen aus meinem Herzen, wie die Blumen aus dem Erdenreich, wenn's Frühling wird. Ich sah keine Welt mehr, und doch besinn' ich mich, dass sie niemals so schön war. Ich wusste von keinem Gott mehr, und doch hatt' ich ihn nie so geliebt. (I.3)

At the time of the action of the play a happy outcome to this love has already become an impossibility. Both in the uncouthly cynical terms of Miller and in the philosophical resignation of Luise herself we hear the tyranny of *Mode* exerting itself at the expense of *Menschheit*. At no point in the play do Ferdinand and Luise spend a happy moment together, for their relationship has been poisoned by social taboos even before the action of the play starts.

For Cammarano to have adopted such a pattern in his libretto would have been to deny himself one of the most operatically emotive phases of such romantic love, namely its first rapturous avowals. And so, while Schiller – first by means of Miller's cynical vulgarity and Frau Miller's *bieder* sentimentality, and later in the memories of Luise herself – describes the love of Ferdinand and Luise, Cammarano embodies it. He devotes the opening scenes of the opera entirely to an expression of Luisa's first youthful happiness. She is, in these early scenes, positively engulfed in love – the 'dolce amistade' of the villagers, the fatherly tenderness of Miller, her own naive and confident adoration of Rodolfo, and his of her. That a world of feelings separates Schiller's heroine from Cammarano's at this stage of the drama may be shown by comparing the already quoted 'Ich entsag' ihm für dieses Leben' with the text of the cabaletta with which Cammarano closes the scene:

> T'amo d'amor ch'esprimere
> Mal tenterebbe il detto! . . .
> Né gel di morte spegnere
> Può sì cocente affetto:
> Ha i nostri cori un Dio
> Di nodo eterno avvinti,
> E sulla terra estinti
> Noi ci ameremo in ciel!

where some of Schiller's most passionately proclaimed metaphysics have been reduced to conventional literary graces.

So far, our examination of Cammarano's libretto has tended to emphasize what has been lost: the intricate, tightly woven cunning of Schiller's dramatic design, and above all his moral, social and philosophical ideologies. But we must not forget what Verdi's dramatic priorities were. His primary concerns were not form and style and ideas, but character and passion, and in these respects Cammarano surely served him better. He can perhaps be debited with two black marks: his total failure to endow Wurm with a touch of macabre humour as Verdi had urged;* and, more gravely, his suppression of the brilliant character of Lady Milford in favour of the entirely uninteresting Duchessa d'Ostheim. Certainly in the latter case, and probably in both, he allowed his dramatic imagination to be overridden by his too-acquiescent understanding of the conventions of operatic casting. With the youthful lovers, however, Cammarano was in his element. Although the scenes in which Rodolfo and Luisa are involved have generally been recast into conventional operatic scenas, both retain enough of their Schillerian pedigree to live in the imagination as dramatic characters, not just operatic types.

Though he is obviously neither an outsider nor an actual outlaw like Karl Moor, Ferdinand, the hero of *Kabale und Liebe*, does share with the heroes of Schiller's other early plays a propensity to confuse the heroic and the criminal; to pursue the loftiest ideals, to demand the highest standards, so uncompromisingly that idealism shades into egoism, and egoism into a solitary and destructive

---

* Cf. letter of 17 May 1849, quoted above, pp. 239–40.

defiance of God and His universe. In this particular play the source both of Ferdinand's idealism and of his downfall is romantic love. This passion Ferdinand hymns with an impassioned eloquence in the early scenes of the play. His love for Luise is of a superhuman intensity, all-obliterating, and God-willed:

Wer kann den Bund zwoer Herzen lösen oder die Töne eines Akkords auseinanderreissen? – Ich bin ein Edelmann – Lass doch sehen, ob mein Adelbrief älter ist also der Riss zum unendlichen Weltall? oder mein Wappen gültiger als die Handschrift des Himmels in Luisens Augen: ... An diesem Arm soll meine Luise durchs Leben hüpfen; schöner, als er dich von sich liess, soll der Himmel dich wiederhaben und mit Verwunderung eingestehn, dass nur die Liebe die letzte Hand an die Seelen legte – (I.4)

But as the drama develops, this easy assumption that the love-match is God-willed is more difficult to sustain, and the immoderation and lack of humility in Ferdinand's passion prompts him rather to challenge the divine plan than to seek to understand it:

Ich will sie führen vor des Weltrichters Thron, und ob meine Liebe Verbrechen ist, soll der Ewige sagen ... So wahr mich Gott im letzten Hauch nicht verlassen soll! – Der Augenblick, der diese zwo Hände trennt, zerreisst auch den Faden zwischen *mir* und der *Schöpfung* ...   (II.5)

Inevitably, as catastrophe strikes, as Ferdinand falls to the temptation of Walter and Wurm, the progress of such a passion leads one stage further, to blasphemy, to the defiance of God, and the determination to do His work for Him:

Richter der Welt! Fodre sie mir nicht ab. Das Mädchen ist mein. Ich trat dir deine ganze Welt für das Mädchen ab, habe Verzicht getan auf deine ganze herrliche Schöpfung ... Sollte der reiche vermögende Schöpfer mit einer Seele geizen, die noch dazu die schlechteste seiner Schöpfung ist? – Das Mädchen ist mein! Ich einst ihr Gott, jetzt ihr Teufel! ...
  Eine Ewigkeit mit ihr auf ein Rad der Verdammnis geflochten – Augen in Augen wurzelnd – Haare zu Berge stehend gegen Haare – Auch unser hohles Wimmern in *eins* geschmolzen – Und jetzt zu wiederholen meine Zärtlichkeiten, und jetzt ihr vorzusingen ihre Schwüre – Gott! Gott! Die Vermählung ist fürchterlich – aber ewig!   (IV.4)

And these tones of reproach towards God, and a contemplation of Luise's damnation that is compounded of terror, despair and ecstasy pervade the last act, until, almost at the end, the truth of her innocence is revealed.

Ferdinand/Rodolfo's fall, due as much to emotional pride as to an iniquitous social system, obviously cannot be analysed in such detail by Cammarano. Nor can it be denied that there is a tendency to moderate the blasphemies and the challenges he issues to Heaven. A typical example would be in Rodolfo's Act II aria, the scene that embodies the poisoning of his heart and maddening of his soul, which matches scenes 1–5 of Schiller's fourth act. The first part of Cammarano's scene is linguistically quite close to Schiller. Hypothetical witnesses to Luisa's fidelity, whether heavenly or earthly, are denied in view of the fact that the letter is in her handwriting – 'es ist ihre Hand' – 'son cifre sue'. But for the sake of operatic effectiveness and emotional contrast, Cammarano's dispenses with the bitter abuse of Luisa and lingers instead over the sweet memories of the 'sguardo innamorato' and the 'placido chiaror d'un ciel stellato'; only to snatch them away in the simple, heartbroken refrain 'Ah! . . . mi tradia'. What one might describe as the mediterraneanizing of the hero is even more apparent in the cabaletta. Not for Cammarano the images of damnation of Ferdinand's appalling speech in Schiller (quoted above); instead, the manipulation of the plot to introduce a planned wedding with the Duchessa d'Ostheim provides the cue for a more frank and extrovert confusion of passions, a fatalistic launching into revenge and despair.

> L'ara, o l'avello apprestami.
> Al fato io mi abbandono.
> Non temo . . . non desidero . . .
> Un disperato io sono . . .

In the duet of the last act Cammarano matches Schiller rather more precisely. After the poison has been taken the parallels are indeed very close, Rodolfo's mood modulating from vicious anger – 'Ah, quel che m'offre Par che sappia l'infame!' – through reproach to the creator – 'Fattor dell'universo, Perché vestir d'angeliche sembianze Un'anima d'inferno' – to despairing grief, as in Schiller. It is this moment, when Rodolfo weeps, that the adept Cammarano makes the point for the cantabile; and though he gets slightly lost in the second part of Luisa's verse (for by then Schiller's words are exhausted and he is able to think of nothing more plausible than Luisa's anticipating her appearance at the judgement-seat and her appeal for Rodolfo's lot to be made 'men funesto'), Rodolfo's tone remains entirely authentic. Luisa is a lost soul, and these are comfortless tears, icicle-tears, tears of blood. In the cabaletta which follows the revelation of Luisa's innocence, Cammarano draws together the strands of Luisa's God-fearing and Rodolfo's God-defiance that run though the whole of Schiler's last act:

> RODOLFO: Maledetto il dì ch'io nacqui . . .
> Il mio sangue . . . il padre mio . . .
> Fui creato, avverso Iddio,
> Nel tremendo tuo furor! . . .

LUISA: Per l'istante in cui ti piacqui ...
Per la morte che s'appressa,
D'oltraggiar l'Eterno, ah! cessa ...
Mi risparmia un tanto orror ...

One might in fact say of the whole of this duet scene that it comprises a dramatic dialectic between the simple, bourgeois God-fearing soul who has learned to accept suffering, and the proud, passionate aristocratic soul who, denied that human joy on which he had set his heart, seems bent on spiritual suicide. For the first time in the opera it expresses the contrast in Luisa's and Rodolfo's reactions to the assaults on their love, which Schiller had been analysing virtually throughout the play.

Cammarano's most considerable success in terms of characterization is Luisa herself. Though at a purely formal level his treatment of her role is quite conventional, he does succeed in bringing out those Schillerian elements of humility, naivety and incorruptible bourgeois honesty that so distinguish her from most of the heroines of *ottocento* opera. In particular her two scenes at the start of Acts I and III suggest that she is part of a simple rural community, not someone exalted above it by rank or heroic accomplishment, and that the ties of family affection mean as much to her as the searing passion for Rodolfo. The choruses that open each of these acts are, if one will, a conventional formal requirement of opera, but Cammarano uses them with great skill to characterize his heroine. In both Luisa is surrounded by dear and solicitous friends; in both Cammarano expresses not the homage due to a prima donna but the affection which she inspires in her compeers.

Ti desta, o Luisa, regina de'cori;
I monti già lambe un riso di luce:
D'un giorno sì lieto insiem cogli albori
Qui dolce amistade a te ne conduce ...

The duet following the Act III chorus runs as closely parallel with the play as anything in the opera, and provides its fullest expression of that wholesome, bourgeois family affection which contrasts so poignantly with the mad passion of Luisa's relationship with Rodolfo. Every essential detail of Schiller's scene is found in the libretto: Miller's alarm at his daughter's calm, his reading of the letter to Rodolfo, Luisa's explanation that the sojourn of which she speaks is the grave, her enthusiastic apostrophe to death. But above all Cammarano seizes on the point that where tyranny and the terrors of divine judgement have failed to bring Luisa to renounce Rodolfo, love for her father can: Schiller, launched on a grandiose metaphysical disquisition on death and judgement, makes the point in a confused delirium of emotions:

LUISE: Halt! Halt! O mein Vater! – Dass die Zärtlichkeit noch barbarischer zwingt als Tyrannenwut! – Was soll ich? Ich kann nicht! Was muss ich tun?
MILLER: Wenn die Küsse deines Majors heisser brennen als die Tränen deines Vaters – stirb!
LUISE: Vater! Hier ist meine Hand! Ich will – Gott! Gott! was tu' ich? was will ich? – Vater, ich schwöre – Wehe mir, wehe! Verbrecherin, wohin ich mich neige! – Vater, es sei! Ferdinand – Gott sieht herab! – So zernicht' ich sein letztes Gedächtnis. (*Sie zerreisst ihren Brief.*)

(V.1)

Cammarano, necessarily more economical in his evocations of Luisa's bourgeois values at other points in the opera, is admirably lucid at this critical juncture:

MILLER: Ah! nella tomba che schiuder vuoi
        Fia primo a scendere il genitor!
LUISA: Ah no, ti calma, o padre mio . . .
        Quanto colpevole, ahimè, son io! . . .
        Non pianger . . . m'odi.
MILLER: Luisa . . .
LUISA: Il foglio
        Lacero . . . annullo . . .
MILLER: Vuoi dunque? . . .
LUISA: Io voglio
        Per te, buon padre, restare in vita . . .
MILLER: Fia ver?
LUISA: La figlia, vedi, pentita
        Al pie' ti cade . . .
MILLER: No, figlia mia . . .
        Sorgi . . . deh! sorgi . . . Qui, sul mio cor . . .

(*La rialza, e se la stringe al seno con tutta l'effusione della tenerezza paterna*)

a 2   In questo amplesso l'anima oblia
           Quanti martiri provò finor! . . .

Music and drama in *Luisa Miller*

Tamed and decently veiled though he has been, faint as his eloquence and idealism have become, Schiller nonetheless remains the presiding genius of *Luisa Miller*. Not even Cammarano could eliminate all the resonances of the play from his libretto and Verdi's music does from time to time come to grips with some at least of its issues. The antagonism of *Mode* and *Menschheit*, the tension between the delirium of romantic passions and the sacred bonds of family affection, the relationship between the individual and society are just three such issues which contribute to the complexity of feeling and richness of musical resource in some of the opera's most impressive scenes.

Since Cammarano has virtually eliminated those indictments of the upper reaches of society that ring out in so many scenes of the play, the conflict of *Mode* and *Menschheit* comes to be expressed not so much in argument or explicit denunciation as in the soliloquies of the characters most affected. Particularly good examples are provided by the arias for Miller and for Walter in Act I.

Miller's aria is addressed to Wurm; it is the climax of a scene designed to point the contrast between malicious tyranny and benevolent humanitarian idealism. Force is the only language Wurm understands. Even in discussing his claims on Miller's daughter as a bride, his words are permeated by the vocabulary of oppression – 'astringerla', 'dritto sovra essa' – an attitude that pricks Miller to a full statement of his own libertarianism. Though Verdi uses only conventional methods in the recitative, the pair are nicely characterized. Wurm's music is punctuated by a brusque snapping figure (Ex. 4); on a couple of occasions – at 'furor di gelosia' and 'or che il

Ex. 4

novello signor . . .' – it swells up in an almost physically threatening manner. The sudden, quite extended row of *tutti* chords marks the point when Miller takes the initiative, thrusting aside the nagging, niggling style of Wurm with one grand gesture.

The cantabile 'Sacra la scelta' is a beautiful expression of the triumph of *Menschheit* over *Mode*. As so often in *La Battaglia di Legnano*, Cammarano has put the most eloquent expression of the 'affect' in the last couplet, and Verdi designs the whole aria in such a way as to culminate in a magniloquent lyrical phrase matched to this (Ex. 5). Indeed the phrase is repeated to give it still greater weight within the scheme of the movement. Compared with this stirring line, the opening of Cammarano's text is a bit sermon-like. Verdi matches it with rather dry, square phrases which nevertheless

Ex. 5

accumulate impetus enough to lead to a strong rhetorical emphasis at the central cadence. Expressively the interest of this opening lies in the fact that its didactic straight-speaking comes from someone who is quivering with fury. The relationship between Miller's avowed and suppressed feelings is clearly reflected in the contrast between the firm, clear-cut melodic style and the turbulence of the orchestral accompaniment. At 'Non son tiranno', in a context of rich harmonic movement, and melodic phrases that arch more widely, the turmoil of these accompaniment rhythms seems to recede into the background. The mood of indignant contempt for Wurm is slowly transmuted into one inspired by the noblest impulses of Miller's heart.

At the end of this scene, Miller, the father who in Cammarano's adaptation represents *Menschheit*, makes way for Walter, the father who represents *Mode*. There is a tension in the plight of both men, but while Miller embodies an idealism clouded by anger and dismay, Walter is portrayed as a man already spiritually destroyed. The most powerful figure in the state is tormented, frightened and deeply unhappy; his better self is expressed only in intangible and fleeting yearnings. Cammarano's text is good. The fragmentary dark hints, the sense he gives of Walter being always pursued, evoke the impression of a sinister man with a guilty conscience. And as I observed above, the aria text is full of paradoxes and false equations – 'felice'/'possente', 'voti'/'ordini' – which reveal the blinding of his insight.

The turmoil of sorrow, tenderness and bullying rage in Walter's heart is evoked both in the quality of the musical materials and in the way they are laid out. The cantabile's first impulse is one of profound unhappiness, expressed in the dragging vocal line, the heavily beating minor chords in the strings, and the shuddering under-trills in the bass. But almost at once this mood is dispelled by a twist into the major key as the tormented heart fills with tenderness for his son. Grief returns, this time not to be relieved by gentler feelings but to swell up into anger. And because Walter is a man corrupted by power, a man for whom tyranny has become a way of life, this mood is emphasized and sustained with an ugly vehemence until it occupies nearly as much space as the other moods put together.

These contradictions of mood are stylized structurally in the latter part of the aria, where, twice in succession, musical sentences expressive of the frustrated tenderness of 'paterno affetto', and of the 'supplizio d'inferno' which it is his lot to endure, are starkly juxtaposed. Unlike Miller, whose noblest sentiments have the last word and are consequently impressed most vividly on the minds of the audience, Walter is finally overcome by a frenzy of despairing rage. After the bluster and wildness in which his aria closes, his tenderer moods remain merely as dim memories, partial glimpses of the man that might have been.

Walter's cantabile 'Il mio sangue' was originally designed to form part of the second scene of Act II. There, in conjunction with a preliminary recitative soliloquy and the following duet with Wurm, it would have constituted the opera's most extended examination of the *Mode/Menschheit* dilemma. With the removal of the cantabile to Act I the conflict is all but eliminated from this Act II scene; it is the subject of a preliminary recitative, and is fleetingly mentioned in the opening phrases of the duet. In his music, however, Verdi contrives to reinstate something of the psychological complexity that was originally envisaged for Walter in this scene. At this stage in the drama he has delivered himself up irrevocably to a life of evil and deceit; but the original motive for his fall, as Schiller had insisted, and as Verdi now insists, was his love for his son. As a musical reflection of the streak of humanity in an irrevocably corrupted figure Verdi begins the scene not with an independent prelude, but with a reminiscence of the cantabile from Act I. Accompanied by a shuddering off-beat figuration and dissolving into a stream of chromatic syncopations it sounds even lonelier and more tormented here than in the aria.

The emotional complexity which Schiller's *Mode/Menschheit* antithesis lends to certain scenes in the first two acts of the opera is succeeded in the last act by a more formidable type of complexity. Again it takes its origin from the play, specifically from the daunting array of passions that Schiller relates to the central idea of 'love'; the warm orderly affection between Luisa and her father, romantic passion, embittered love by which the moral frame of the universe is unhinged, forbidden love which attempts delusory escapes into Elysian imaginings. It is because of Schiller that the third act of *Luisa Miller* contains the most emotionally complex music Verdi had yet written, notably in the two duets for Luisa and Miller and for Luisa and Rodolfo.

By the third act Luisa's passion has been bled of all the optimistic ardour of Act I. The 'mown lily', over whom her friends have sighed in the introductory chorus, is calm; she appears to bow herself to destiny. Her romantic passion has been transmuted, *Liebestod*-like, into a blissful vision of an Elysian after-life, to evoke which Verdi uses the musical imagery developed for Amalia in *I Masnadieri* – a timbre dominated by flutes and clarinets and pizzicato strings, floating and dancing coloratura. Thematic metaphors for rest – at 'in cui del giusto ...' – and for aspiration – 'è dessa un angelo ...' – are incorporated into the line, but the prevailing atmosphere is of disembodiment. Is there perhaps also a suggestion of frivolity in the music? For Luisa's resorting to the consolation of Elysium is not in fact a submission to destiny at all: it is an irresponsible delusion, for she proposes to take her own life.

The peculiar pathos which the character of Luisa acquires in the latter stages of this duet is due to the fact that she allows herself to be recalled from the contemplation of this mirage. She is brought back to earth by shame and fear, and especially by compassion for her father. It is a figuration that Verdi has clearly designed to express Miller's tears that runs like an *ostinato* through the bars in which Luisa resolves to live for his sake (Ex. 6).

Ex. 6

While neither Cammarano nor Verdi succeeds very well in dif-
ferentiating filial from romantic love in the *tempo di mezzo*, the
cabaletta 'Andrem raminghi e poveri' becomes an exquisite image of
quiet domestic affection. When Miller has sung the first sentence of
his song, Luisa repeats it, but gives it a brighter, more serene
colouring by conducting it to a cadence in A♭ rather than one in C
minor. She sings phrases in antiphony with him, as an image of the
concept 'sempre al padre accanto', and most memorably – an inspiration Verdi was to recall in *Rigoletto*, his next father/daughter
opera – she hovers 'appena sensibile' in descant over the reprise of
his song like a guardian angel. Finally Verdi had the brilliant idea of
closing the movement with a suggestion of a cadenza: not a flamboyant one, but one that serves as an emblem of the absolute
simplicity and harmoniousness of their relationship, even in naked-
ness and need (Ex. 7).

The key to the characterization of Rodolfo in the second duet in
this wonderful scene is his sense of loss. Cammarano plays down the

Ex. 7

sarcasm and the viciousness of the matching scene in Schiller's play, and both he and Verdi intensify the sense of loss by the eloquence with which they express such things as his farewell to a life of service – at 'Addio, spada' – and his reviving wonder at Luisa's beauty – at 'Ah! lungi, lungi quel volto lusinghier'.

The confrontation of the duettists – Luisa, who has entrusted herself to God's providence, and Rodolfo, who arrogates the right to do God's work for Him – is thus less extreme than in Schiller. Indeed it is based on the common ground of compassion. Luisa is compassionate from a pure heart and a tender love, and thus sings serene lyrical phrases in the major key, supported by the simplest accompaniment patterns in the characteristically clear colouring of pizzicato strings and woodwind. All the phrases, sinking gently through the octave, and occasionally brought into focus with more naturalistic touches, seem analogous to the flowing of tears. Rodolfo's compassion, on the other hand, is coloured by spiritual torment. He believes Luisa to be a lost soul, and has taken it upon himself to send her to judgement. Moreover, because he has for so long taken his passion to be the measure of all things, he feels that God has betrayed him. He is alone, heartbroken, despairing of a universe that seems to be falling apart round him. The phrases with which Verdi evokes Rodolfo's passion are not only more strained and tormented in themselves: they are overshadowed – or undershadowed – by quaking trills in the low strings, or by the hollow, reedy colouring of high cellos and low clarinets and bassoons (Ex. 8).

Ex. 8

It was a happy touch to hold back the second quatrain of Luisa's verse until Rodolfo had sung all of his; because this quatrain, 'Se concesso al prego mio ...', is about that God of whom Rodolfo has been tempted to despair, an aspirational hymn of faith in Him by whom Rodolfo feels deserted. By setting out the verses in this way, Verdi turns the duet into a kind of discourse, not merely an effusion of mood. The element of discourse is heightened when, after Luisa has finished, Rodolfo comes back with just one of his lines, the blasphemous 'Dio mi lascia in abbandono', which he reiterates ceaselessly through to the end of the movement. Unusually, the moods of the singers become more antagonistic as the scene evolves, a sequence of compassion – selflessness – prayer on the one side, against a sequence of compassion–self-pity–blasphemy on the other. The tension inherent in this antithesis is worked up to a superb cathartic climax, in which Luisa's song of love engulfs and, one would imagine, 'redeems' the erring Rodolfo. In fact, though, enlightenment has not yet come to him; the blindness and the despair remain. To express this becomes the function of the cadenza –

another of Verdi's dramatically distorted cadenzas – in which, in gloomy, muttering *parlando*, Rodolfo perseveres in his blasphemy even in the face of Luisa's transparent purity of heart.

In the scena that follows, Rodolfo's recitatives are primarily concerned with the more-than-human rights which he continues to usurp. We hear music for a judge, at 'Donna, per noi terribile'; music for an executioner, at 'Pria che questa lampada si spenga'; music for a confessing priest, at 'Al ciel rivolgiti'. Nor does the recognition of his error at once restore his outsize passion to a measure that becomes a mere man. The quasi-theological confrontation which had developed in the cantabile remains the stuff of the cabaletta, now in a still more desperate form. Musical imagery and analogy is, however, less prominent in 'Maledetto il dì ch'io nacqui', probably because Verdi recognizes the limit to which such themes can be operatically useful. It is the *frisson* of terror that he seeks to impart in the howling and plunging melodic line and in the racing pulse of the accompaniment. Luisa's music expresses not a counter-argument, but the effect on her of Rodolfo's words. She is thrilled and appalled. Her music is close to frenzy: she senses with awe the threat of eternal perdition that is looming over him. And while there is perhaps no direct expressive sense in the unison repeat of Rodolfo's theme, there is good theatrical sense. It is surely designed to ensure that the audience tremble to Rodolfo's song as Luisa herself had done. The music no longer paraphrases the sense of the words. It has gone beyond their sense to their effect, setting the nerves tingling with the desperation of its momentum, where Schiller had relied on the savagery of his dialectic.

Paradoxically the musical reflection of Schiller's concern with the relationship between the individual and society is clearest in two scenes which have no real parallels in his play; the introductions to the first and third acts. Schiller had depicted Ferdinand and Luise as victims of the false values of a corrupt society; and he expresses the tension between the lovers and the world of the court in a series of antagonistic confrontations with representative figures of that world – notably Walther and Lady Milford. Cammarano and Verdi tackle the problem in a diametrically opposite manner. Even had they wished, they would hardly have been allowed to make of their opera so savage an indictment of court life; so that end of the social spectrum recedes into the background. On the other hand, they possessed in the chorus a resource for embodying a community – a society in a rather different sense – which Schiller lacks. In *Kabale und Liebe* corruption and injustice are the fruits of social organization which Schiller most vividly impresses on our mind: in *Luisa Miller* it is the sense of community, embodied in Verdi's choruses. Because of this the tragic drama of the doomed lovers acquires a slightly different emphasis. They are vulnerable not only because of the intrigue of evil men in positions of power, but because Luisa so clearly belongs to a different world from Rodolfo's and is becoming alienated from it.

The introduction to Act I is one of the most perfect in the whole Verdi repertory. It combines extraordinarily happily the functions of scene-painting, dramatic action and characterization. The tranquil rural scene, the awakening of nature, the assembling of the villagers, their relationship with Luisa – all these things are beautifully depicted in the music.

As he was to do more than forty years later in *Falstaff*, Verdi suggests the stillness of sleeping nature by a distant solo instrument playing improvisatory, dream-like phrases, to each of which, at its cadence, is added a short gracing figure in the violins. From this material Verdi builds up a musical image of awakening, of growing brightness and busyness. To the solo clarinet and violins other string and woodwind instruments are slowly added. The clarinet melody evolves into a tiptoeing figuration of repeated chords and uprising melodic shapes; the violin graces evolve into an *ostinato*, scattered over the underlying musical structure like drops of dew.

During this music, the villagers have assembled to bring greetings to Luisa on her birthday. The expressive burden of 'Ti desta, Luisa' is their affection for her. Luisa is clearly the prettiest, best-liked girl in the village; but she is not in any sense a creature apart, on a higher plane. Consequently the chorus do not remain in the background as an adjunct to the scenery; they come forward and fill the theatrical frame with the warmth of their feelings. And what they say about Luisa is not merely formal homage to a prima donna, it really does tell us what manner of girl she is. For the time being, the instrumental imagery which Verdi had matched so carefully to the stage scene recedes. The chorus sings a warmly-textured, fully harmonized, almost hymn-like tribute, except that by virtue of its lilting $\frac{6}{8}$ rhythm and its drone bass it avoids ecclesiastical or civic pomp and retains a pastoral character. In the later stages the rhythm and textures of the prelude begin to reappear, giving a sense of naturalness to the return of the preludial material in an interlude, before a repeat of the chorus with sparkling woodwind and string textures derived from the same material. This repeat serves two purposes: its contrived intricacy suggests the art which the villagers have bestowed on their tribute, and its fuller texture sustains the impression of awakening, of the scene becoming progressively more brilliantly illuminated, more full of busy detail. A last expressive point is the grand lyrical theme that begins the coda, and serves to place the expressive emphasis on the crucial line 'meno è soave, men pura di te'. The chorus bring not just friendly greetings, adorn the occasion not just with poetic graces: they do genuinely feel that Luisa is a creature fair and dear beyond all else in their little world.

The scene that follows begins with another *crescendo*, far more precipitous than that of the chorus, during which the relationship of Luisa and the villagers is confirmed. At the first stage of the *crescendo* Miller presents his daughter to them; at the next she greets them as 'care amiche'; at the last they call blessings down upon her. And she modulates into the recitative with the promise to go with them to church. Even Miller's recitative plays into the same central theme. Until 'Né giunge ancor' sets the action in motion, the whole introduction is concentrated on depicting the central position of Luisa in the affections of an idyllic rural community.

Even her aria is designed in such a way as to suggest the same idea. Her description of how she fell in love with Rodolfo is not an intimate confession, made only to the audience or to a confidante. It is a frank and public avowal, in which she expects her father and friends to rejoice. And the friends, at least, do. Cammarano, instead of leaving them with sweet nothings to mouth, closes the cantabile with a modest ceremony in which the chorus presents Luisa with bunches of flowers. Verdi brings back the principal theme of Luisa's aria once more in the orchestra, and uses it as the background against which the chorus makes its gracious speech. In this way he suggests a community of feeling, a happiness shared.

The introduction to Act III is likewise an expression of comradely affection, serving primarily to characterize Luisa, this time in the state of frail, passive suffering to which she has been reduced. Shorter and less developed than the Act I chorus, it is no less refined, its texture of solo voice, female voices and orchestra being used to suggest the layers of feeling contained in the scene.

The prelude is built on an alternation of two themes, a gloomy unison theme for strings, from the sinfonia, and airy fragments adapted from 'T'amo d'amor' for clarinets and flutes. While it is always difficult to assign precise significances to such movements, the citing of Luisa's Act I aria justifies the assumption that this prelude is a rather detailed evocation of her state of mind. Two acts ago, the words to which she had sung those scraps of melody had seemed mere metaphorical adornments of the central passion of romantic love.* Presented now in this fragmentary form amid the gloomy, impassioned unison of the strings, they seem to demand that we take the metaphorical graces seriously. Caught up in a tragic and ineluctable destiny, Luisa's tormented vision glimpses the serene Elysian where the love gainsaid for this life may be found again.

The string unison theme, the theme that Verdi seems to use as an emblem of tragic destiny, is employed as an accompaniment to the main part of the chorus. And with the aid of this theme to express the smiting of Luisa, Verdi creates a vignette in which the observed object (Luisa) and reactions to it both subjective and objective (Laura and the chorus) are depicted simultaneously. On the face of it, nothing could be more simple or formalized than the antiphony of chorus and choryphaeus, though in fact Verdi has rarely used it. But the choryphaeus does not lead the chorus; indeed she sings music of a different character: the chorus merely syllabizes the underlying harmony, while Laura sings deeply felt cantabile phrases. The music embodies both the corporate anonymity of neighbourly sympathy and the emotional involvement which any individual within the neighbourly body really feels.

One last feature of the score merits examination: the way Verdi used the musical opportunities provided by the reworking of Schiller's Act III in the first three numbers of Cammarano's Act II. It will be recalled that while Schiller's act takes the form of a continuous intrigue, plotted and executed, Cammarano presents a series of self-contained and contrasting episodes, each with a distinct dramatic and expressive function: the chorus bringing the news of Miller's arrest, the arias showing Luisa reacting to Wurm's blackmail, the duet expounding the vile history of Walther's rise to power.

The act begins then with a chorus describing the beating-up and carrying-off of Miller. Essentially Cammarano's idea was to provide a formal act-opening, and Verdi – rather unusually at this stage in an opera – employs for it one of the conventional narrative styles, the unison cantabile. The form and the idiom would have provided him with precious little scope for his art had Cammarano not had the happy idea of setting the narrative in the middle of a number of naturalistic details – the chorus coming in search of Luisa, her cries of dismay as she listens – which prompt the finest points in the scene. The recitative-like phrases at the start are superimposed upon

* The text is quoted above, p. 603.

a formal introduction made up of agitated orchestral figures; Luisa's cries of dismay upon what begins as a second verse and is then deflected by sympathy into an exhortation to trust in God.

It is in the following scene that the nature of Wurm's intrigue becomes apparent, and the emotional effects of the intrigue are explored. Although there can be no question of a long-term building-up of tension as in the play, Verdi does express a sense of Luisa's mounting horror and disgust as she perceives the plight she is in. He achieves this by concentrating the whole scena on the writing of the letter; the rest of the recitative is thrown away almost casually. Wurm's dictation, on a series of barely inflected monotones, is set against a wonderfully suggestive instrumental texture – the broken octaves image the beating of Luisa's heart, the sustained lines in the bass something of the mood of Wurm, brusque, menacing and mocking. Evocative as this material is, its cumulative effect is much enhanced by the pauses between its phrases: each successive phrase becomes longer too. But the finest point is that the pauses are filled with pantomimes expressive of the conflict of contemptuous indignation and grieving submission in Luisa's heart, fragments of unsung arias replete with sighing appoggiaturas (Ex. 9). Finally Luisa can endure no more and attempts to break out of the web which Wurm is spinning about her.

In her cantabile 'Tu puniscimi' Verdi shifts the emphasis of Cammarano's characterization markedly. As he had explained to the librettist, he regarded 'terror and desperation' as Luisa's dominant passions in this scene.* We find a curious situation here, then, for there is no doubt that, for once, Cammarano is more authentically Schillerian than Verdi is. His lyric comes close in tone to 'Helfe dir der Allmächtige, Vater. Deine Tochter kann für dich sterben, aber nicht sünden.'

Verdi's setting concentrates to an extraordinary degree on the most fearful couplet, especially the line 'Non lasciarmi in abbandono'. It is not Luisa's spirit or virtue which he chooses to emphasize but her vulnerability. The normal aria form is distorted out of recognition. He creates a coda out of the 'Non lasciarmi' line at the end of each half, and to this coda he gives a harrowing emphasis by breaking down the lyrical style into a near-hysterical *parlando*. Not defiance but frightened prayer is the essence of the aria. Verdi presumably felt this to be more in harmony with the image he wished to give of Luisa as a victim of fate.

* Cf. letter of 17 May 1849, quoted above, p. 239.

Ex. 9

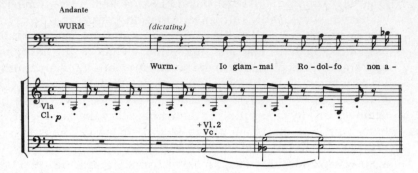

The scene most affected by Cammarano's reorganization is the Walter/Wurm duet. This too acquires an expressive purpose uniquely its own, and really quite unrelated to the intrigue that had been its theme in *Kabale und Liebe*. Its purpose is in fact to evoke that atmosphere of evil which in the play is exuded by virtually all the scenes dealing with life at court. Here, however, the atmosphere of evil clings not to a whole society but to a pair of corrupt individuals.

Their rise to power is exploited dramatically, to furnish not a sweeping political indictment but merely a shuddersome history.

The duet is interesting principally because of the way in which the horrific elements in the narrative are used as a touchstone of character. 'Con mistero' seems an odd description of how the opening is to be sung. The unimpassioned mildness of the music presumably reflects Walter's insistence on being only human – a mild fellow who, on his own account, would do harm to no one. When Wurm takes up the theme, it is to give it an air of quite light-hearted sprightliness. But this cool, matter-of-fact tone is suddenly dispersed. As the narrative approaches its first climax, Wurm crescendos and the orchestra plunges into the minor key with a new figuration incorporating trembling semiquavers and a sinister new element in the bass. Throughout this next section, Walter is trying to evade responsibility – 'I was afraid', 'You suggested' – and the rhythmic reiterations and the movement of the harmonies suggest his mounting terror. While Walter retains enough of his humanity to be tormented and appalled by what he has done, Wurm continues his description of the dastardly deed with blithe uncon-cern, During his suave G^b major cantabile, only the throbbing bass figure suggests an element of thrill or tension. Walter cuts him short. He has lost all self-control and vents his terror with blood-curdling vehemence and in an idiom conspicuously similar to that which he had used in the coda of his Act I aria; the same *tutti* chords over bass arpeggios, the same syncopation into the cadences. Still Wurm remains undismayed. Perhaps the cold-blooded indifference with which, having listened to Walter, he resumes the nonchalant cantabile from the start of the duet is one of Verdi's attempts to endow him with humour as we know he wished to do.

Cammarano's notorious proficiency in taming the manifold idiosyncrasies of vision of the world's great writers to accommodate them to the melodramatic requirements of the Neapolitan stage proved too much even for Verdi to resist. He could not have denied that Cammarano's dramatic action was in several ways more fluent and plausible than Schiller's, nor that he had provided a whole series of tableaux and dramatic encounters of immense theatrical promise. Indeed Verdi could not fail to see that Cammarano had written him an excellent libretto, 'concise and very passionate', as he had requested. Nonetheless, because of the extent to which the form, the content, the language and the characterization of Schiller's play had been conventionalized, it was not a libretto that challenged Verdi the way that *Macbeth* had done. By unravelling the constricting intrigue of *Kabale und Liebe* and presenting the action in a series of discrete episodes in the traditional pattern, Cammarano failed to stimulate Verdi to investigate afresh that question of the relationship between dramatic action and musical continuity that had already begun to fascinate him. By suppressing the character of Lady Milford, and all but eliminating the representations of corruption in high places, he deprived Verdi of the opportunity of cultivating some hitherto unexplored resources of his art. With the libretto's intimate dependence on *Kabale und Liebe* limited to the sequence of events in the Act I finale and a handful of verbal parallels and analogies in the duets in Act III, Verdi's genius could not be fertilized by that of Schiller in the way the composer would surely have wished. *Luisa Miller* becomes a work of refinement rather than of exploration: perhaps the most beautiful opera of Verdi's early years, but not the most eloquent or imaginative.

The originality of *Rigoletto*

'*Rigoletto*', wrote Verdi to Piave in October 1854, 'is a somewhat more revolutionary opera, and so a more youthful one; and it is more original in form and in style.'[1] Verdi was comparing *Rigoletto* with *Ernani*, but the comparison would have been as valid had it been made with any of the earlier operas. *Rigoletto* is the opera in which Verdi decisively breaks free from the mere habits of the *ottocento* operatic tradition; or perhaps it would be more exact to say that it is the opera in which he shows that he has reached the point of understanding through and through the meaning of every detail of form and style within that tradition.

Only in his very earliest apprentice scores had Verdi been content to work unquestioningly according to the routines of *ottocento* opera. Throughout the 1840s, from *Nabucco* to *Stiffelio*, he had become more critical and imaginative in employing these routines. His questing dramatic imagination had drawn him to plot sources of sharply differentiated character, which in turn had stimulated him to explore certain resources of his art more deeply and to play down others. Faced with themes of national and religious rejuvenation in *Nabucco* and *I Lombardi*, challenged by them to find a medium for expressing corporate concerns, he had discovered the dramatic potential of the chorus and the popular repertories of march and hymnody; spellbound by the monstrous egocentricity of human passions in *Ernani* he had shifted his emphasis and begun to explore the scope of musical characterization in soliloquy and in confrontation; wrestling with the psychological depth and sheer density of poetry in *Macbeth* he had first begun seriously to question the authority of the traditional patterns of *ottocento* operas, to pack them fuller with music, to distort them almost beyond recognition, to look for new alternatives. Each of these experiences, not to mention the engagements with Byron and Schiller and the Paris Opéra, had prompted him to cultivate different facets of his genius, had taught him to take a more self-conscious, sceptical view of the conventions of Italian opera. He had come to see that many of its habits, stylistic and formal, not only had little or nothing to do with dramatic expression but actually inhibited such expression.

By the time Verdi came to compose *Rigoletto* none of the conventions of *ottocento* opera was sacred to him. But one must at once add that the fundamental principle of the Italian tradition nevertheless remained inviolate: that opera was drama, and that the primary medium of this drama was song. Nor was Verdi disposed to dispute what Italian composers had traditionally regarded as a corollary to this principle: that opera was therefore a type of drama in which the ongoing action had to be expressed in self-contained, lucidly architected 'numbers'. It was not the privileged status of solo aria, ensemble, and grand finale that Verdi was challenging in this 'somewhat revolutionary' work – though as a matter of fact *Rigoletto* has no grand finales – nor was it even the statuesque formality of such movements. His target was rather the lazy habit of assuming that only certain types of formal design, such as the double aria with cantabile and repeated cabaletta, were proper to opera; that each and every dramatic theme could be expressed in a basically similar sequence of movements; that clarity and balance of musical design involved a kind of detachability of the aria or ensemble from the dramatic action. And of course beyond all this, and in many ways the source of much of the innovatory boldness, was Verdi's conviction that opera could and should deal with a wider range of character-types than had traditionally been allowed: with jesters and philandering noblemen, with silly infatuated girls, with assassins and harlots.

The formal constituents

In one of his most interesting critical pronouncements on *Rigoletto* Verdi once commented that he had 'conceived [the opera] without arias or finales, as an unbroken string of duets, because that had seemed . . . appropriate'.[2] As we shall see, this is a somewhat partial description, but it does suggest that Verdi felt that the time had come to place the burden of the drama on the most dynamic of the traditional operatic forms, on the ensemble; that he wanted to play down the elements of effusion and tableau in favour of confrontation and dramatic dialectic. The mere statistics of the index of movements are not uninteresting. There is indeed no finale in the usual sense of the word. Apart from subsidiary appearances in the opening scenes of both Acts I and II, there is only one formal choral movement (for men only – the opera has no female chorus). There are no fewer than five duets, three of them substantial scenes in several movements, together with a quartet and a trio belonging together rather like a cantabile and cabaletta. But there are also five solo arias. The number is not exceptional – *La Battaglia di Legnano*, for example, has five, *Luisa Miller* four, *Attila* six – but what is exceptional is the fact that only one of them, the Duke's in Act II, employs the traditional double-aria form. Of the rest, three are single-movement arias, two of them ('Questa o quella' and 'La donna è mobile') of very modest proportions.

The proportions of aria to ensemble and of ensemble to 'tableau forms' such as grand finales and choruses are, then, unusual. So too is the order in which these ingredients are arranged, particularly in the first act. After the introduction, which in the usual way is entrusted almost entirely to the male voices, Italian audiences were accustomed to expect one or more 'cavatinas' or *arie di sortita* in which the prima donna at least, and probably one or two of the other principals, made formal and extended solo appearances. But in *Rigoletto* the colours, orchestral and vocal, darken still further for the gruesome *parlante* duet of Rigoletto and Sparafucile. Not only Rigoletto and the Duke, but more surprisingly Gilda too forgoes her *aria di sortita*. Instead she makes her appearance in two duets, one each with Rigoletto and the Duke: and her first and only aria, the one-movement 'Caro nome', is sung in reaction to her experiences in the second of these scenes. The act ends with rapid and violent stage action, accompanied by quasi-symphonic orchestral music and a single exclamation from Rigoletto. None of these outrages against the decorum of *ottocento* opera is committed in a spirit of wanton iconoclasm. But the kind of purposes that Verdi had in mind, the conservative principles on which his revolution was based, only become clear when we examine the design in more detail.

Musical continuity

Of all the scenes of the opera it is probably the introduction that has undergone the most striking transformation. Certainly the traditional function of the introduction, that of suggesting something of the atmosphere in which the drama is to be played out, is preserved: indeed the off-stage *banda* playing a medley of dance music creates such an atmosphere with more directness and precision than usual. But in *Rigoletto* the introduction does not remain at the level of scene-setting, with the chorus reduced to the capacity of vocalizing *décor* and with soloists lurking in the wings, awaiting their formal entries so that the action can get under way. Instead Verdi gradually brings this piece of atmospheric scenery to life, adding to the continuing music of the *banda* details that suggest more specifically the hedonism and corruption that prevail in the court, introducing us to some of the characters, bringing to life the tensions and animosities within this society. The working out of the *banda* material, against which these various *parlante* episodes are set, culminates in a final *tutti*, 'Tutto è gioia, tutto è festa', in which, for the first time, the chorus, traditionally a protagonist in the introduction, masses into a texture of some solidity.

Though it is this *banda* music that gives the scene its momentum, it is not sustained with schematic relentlessness. Verdi plays down the stylization, provides a realistic dimension, by having a stage band of strings which varies the Terpsichorean fare with minuet and perigourdine. And though there is no *aria di sortita* for him, the Duke does have his *ballata* – a dance-song, be it noted – deftly fused into the texture of the revelries. In this song, strophic in form and absolutely regular in rhythmic pulse, Verdi can already set about his work of characterization without disturbing the momentum generated by the revelries. Such a disturbance can be reserved to make a real dramatic effect at the appearance of Monterone: the musical continuity becomes more precisely analogous to the dramatic action.

From the start Verdi had been a composer of rare rhythmic directness and energy. At first this quality had been shown within the single cantabile or cabaletta: in his tendency, for example, to avoid the clouds of *fioritura* in which such a composer as Bellini had so often dissolved the impetus of his arias. Later it affected the whole scena. Recitative or free-rhythmed music rarely intervened between cantabile and cabaletta; Verdi preferred a *parlante* based on a regular and energetically articulated pulse so that once the momentum of the scene had got under way in the shift from recitative or arioso to cantabile it progressed with one single accelerating impetus through to the end of the *stretta*. By the time we reach *Rigoletto* this quest for musical continuity has progressed further; Verdi is attempting to match it to the continuity of whole sections of the dramatic action. He approached this problem in a variety of ways, but his concern for it is clear in every section of the score. The technique used in the introduction of superimposing everything – stage action, dialogue, even an aria – on a continuous background of orchestral dance music, a technique which Verdi has apparently evolved out of the *parlante* passages common in the *primo tempo* and *tempo di mezzo* sections of ensemble scenes, is employed in very different forms in two other scenes of the opera. Almost the whole of the so-called duet of Rigoletto and Sparafucile is in fact a *parlante* dialogue superimposed upon and propelled by an orchestral 'aria'. Much the same could be said of the first part of the scena preceding Rigoletto's Act II aria, though here the course of the orchestral music is realistically suspended at phrase-ends to give due weight to the bitter exchanges between him and the courtiers. In neither of these cases, however, is the use of the orchestral aria and *parlante* a mere device to aid the continuity of the music: in both it is made to serve an expressive dramatic purpose besides. The spectator of the Sparafucile scene will react first at a pretty basic level to the ghastliness of the scene, the callous viciousness of the dialogue, the evilly glinting colour in which the orchestral texture drenches it. In this atmosphere the formality and understatement of the underlying orchestral aria is a brilliant psychological stroke. For Sparafucile is not a pantomime villain leaping melodramatically out of dark corners and cackling blood-curdlingly: he is a far more appalling figure, one able to live in a world of evil quite naturally, even with good humour and a sense of decorum. Rigoletto's scena is perhaps a more obvious example of the way the composer uses a technical device to express different layers of meaning simultaneously, here the contrast between real and simulated feeling. In themselves Rigoletto's 'La rà, la rà's might sound convincing – at least they might if singers put 'Vesti la giubba' out of mind, sang it at the proper speed, and avoided the 'Simian crouch' that Budden justly deplores. But threaded on to the fuller statement of the same theme in the orchestra, with its monotonous reiterations, its slow, heavy, dull accompaniment, and the pervasive minor-key harmonies, the pathos is unmistakable and irresistible.

Act I of the opera and 'La donna è mobile' in Act III provide examples of another means of enhancing the continuity of the opera which Verdi had become interested in in recent years. This is the device of introducing into the final stages of a fully rounded-off formal structure an element of tension, something which omens unexpected developments, and which therefore deprives the movement of that complete harmoniousness and finality which traditionally it had had. In the duet of Rigoletto and Gilda in Act I, the cabaletta is interrupted by the arrival of the Duke (hidden from the singers) so that, although the music is resumed and formally concluded, the audience senses all the time that the scene is threatened by someone waiting to pounce or to be discovered. There is, albeit on a somewhat naive level, an element of dovetailing between two movements of the opera. A similar effect of dovetailing is achieved in 'Caro nome' and the following chorus by introducing into their codas disruptive lines and colours which, while they do not prevent formal cadencing, do signal a renewal of the dramatic action.

In other parts of the opera, notably in Act II, it is the virtual elimination of recitative that contributes most to the sense of musical continuity. Once the scena preceding the Duke's very old-fashioned aria is concluded, there is in fact no real recitative in this act. Rigoletto's scena begins, as we have seen, with a kind of orchestral aria, out of which evolves the figuration of the following *tempo di mezzo*. And at the end of his aria, a movement closing in cantabile style and hence without the gratuitous noisy emphasis that ends most large-scale solo scenes, the following duet scene is launched directly on another *tempo di mezzo*. Throughout the act the pacing of the soliloquies and dialogues is dictated by orchestrally impelled themes and texture; nowhere is it relaxed into the limper movement of free recitative. The overall driving impetus that Verdi had long applied to the scena is now applied to the whole act.

Apart from the introduction to Act I the most imaginatively sustained example of musical continuity is provided by the scena, trio and tempest in Act III. Verdi returns to the recitative idiom here, but it is a recitative punctuated by a variety of orchestral figures alluding to the approaching storm, which become more obtrusive and continuous and finally develop into a miniature tone-poem, the *tempesta* proper. Such tiny lyrical passages as occur during this scene – the reprise of 'La donna è mobile', Maddalena's arietta, the two verses of the trio – scarcely suffice to delay the gathering momentum of the storm music. Indeed the relationship of trio and tempest is so close that the latter could, without too much exaggeration, be said to function as a *stretta* to the former. The degree of musical continuity in this scene, the density of the working of the storm figures, mirrors the movement of the drama to its catastrophe. That is why the recitatives carefully avoided through so much of Acts I and II are needed again here. They match the atmosphere of stillness and secrecy out of which the horrific moment of Gilda's murder rears up, and without them the sense of impending doom would be far less vivid.

The transformation of convention

One detail of the score which shows particularly clearly the stage Verdi has reached in reappraising the tradition of Italian opera is his treatment of what one might describe as the merely conventional. As we have seen, there were a number of features in the operatic language of the period which had nothing to do with the claims of either drama or music, but which had become habitual as a result of the style in which operas were performed or the circumstances under which they were produced: things like the rasping reiterated chords, generally on the dominant, quite literally calling for attention in readiness for the start of an aria; things like the orchestral introductions to the arias, which presumably allowed a singer to disengage himself from the action and strike an appropriate pose near the front of the stage; things like the *stretta* or *più mosso* at the end of an aria or ensemble, with bludgeoning cadential repetitions to provoke the audience to louder applause: all those features, in short, that might be described as the framework of the lyrical movements.

It is clear that Verdi, even at this 'somewhat revolutionary' phase of his career, conceived no doctrinaire detestation of these features of old-fashioned *ottocento* opera. Indeed it seems likely, to judge from the Duke's aria at the start of Act II, that he regarded them as quite seemly incidentals to any kind of solo scene for which it was still appropriate to adopt the classical form of scena, cantabile, *tempo di mezzo*, and repeated cabaletta. No 'conventional' feature is lacking here – the instrumental prelude, the arioso climax to the scena, the cadenza and full close at the end of the cantabile, the crashing dominant seventh to signal the cabaletta, and the introduction and *più mosso* to frame it. Elsewhere in the opera such features are used in a new way; in a way that shows that Verdi, having rid himself of them as habits of mind, was approaching them with an imaginative awareness of their dramatic or musical usefulness.

The three movements with formal instrumental introductions – 'Caro nome', 'Tutte le feste' and 'La donna è mobile' – provide good examples of how an old habit, once broken with, can be taken up again with real psychological or dramatic point. 'Caro nome' is an aria whose form, a series of embroidery-like variations, is prompted by its dramatic function, which is to depict Gilda musing over the declaration of love just received from 'Gualtier Maldè' – 'the whole is to be sung *sotto voce*', insisted Verdi:[3] its mood is intensely inward, its subject 'engraved on her heart'. Nothing could better express the point than the song-less statement on the flutes of a complete period of the theme over which Gilda is to muse in the 'variations' that follow. No less nicely observed is the oboe introduction to 'Tutte le feste' which, following after the recitative exclamation 'Ciel, dammi coraggio', subtly suggests that Gilda is trying over in her mind the words with which she is to break to her father the awful news of her seduction. With 'La donna è mobile' the flamboyant presentation of the theme against the strumming $\frac{3}{8}$ accompaniment makes no psychological point; it simply asserts that this is not aria but popular song.

Verdi is no less resourceful in modifying or putting to new uses the conventions that had grown up around the close of a movement. Clearly his sense of the dynamics of a scene did not allow him to find fault with the habit of ending it loud and fast. But he did seek to remedy the musical fatuity and dramatic incongruity that had so often disfigured the scene's concluding *più mosso*. In the trio, for example, the formal verses dissolve into the music of the tempest; while the final duet of the opera is cut short by Gilda's death just at the point where its form might have been expected to become conventionalized, and wild, grim cadences expressive of Rigoletto's despair round off the design. In other duets, 'Veglia, o donna' and 'Sì, vendetta', Verdi takes up in a less tentative form the scheme he had first adopted in the 'Andrem, raminghi e poveri' movement of *Luisa Miller*. In such movements he preserves the long-established habit of commencing with solo verses: thereafter the genuine, duetted section and the *più mosso* become one and the same thing. So the gathering momentum is not merely a matter of cadential material tacked on at the end once the real music is over; it is co-existent with the richest textures and harmonies of the movement. Likewise modelled on the *Luisa Miller* duet are the orchestral postludes which recapitulate the principal theme instead of merely reiterating tonic chords. It is a striking demonstration of the deeply conservative instincts that informed Verdi's art that his 'revolution' should beget movements that are not less lyrical but more so, not looser in design but tighter. It was not formal song that had inhibited the full blossoming of Italy's opera in the early nineteenth century, but the parasitic accretions that had battened on to that formal song. In the whole opera, despite all the originality of design, all the unfamiliarity of sequence, all the dovetailing, there is really only one movement – the trio that stands at the dramatic climax – whose formal outlines are dissolved into the musical surroundings. Even this is a symmetrical form, but instead of being set in a frame it simply looms up out of the storm and is swallowed up again into it. This, of course, is the kind of procedure Verdi preferred in the works of his full maturity such as *Aida* and *Otello*. The clarity of the musical design is unimpaired, but it is not emphasized by elements extrinsic to itself.

The arias

The unfamiliarity of the overall pattern of the opera, its unprecedented dynamism, its total elimination of mere convention do not in fact upset the traditional priorities of Italian opera in the least. Within this urgent and flexible drama the musical forms remain song forms, as carefully shaped, as balanced, sometimes even as symmetrical, as ever. The difference, as we see when we come to examine the arias more closely, is to be found in the variety and dramatic purposefulness of the designs.

Of the five arias, no fewer than three are sung by the Duke: it is perhaps one formal manifestation of the fact that he alone of the characters is afflicted by that consuming emotional egoism that had hitherto been characteristic of the genre. Moreover, while the single arias of Rigoletto and Gilda are both unique structures, those of the Duke all adopt standard forms, the strophic song in Acts I and III, the double aria in Act II. But that is not to say that they have been thoughtlessly adopted. Indeed in each case the choice can be seen to be the result of the interacting of the two considerations that had become so crucial to Verdi at this stage of his career: the psychologizing of the character and the overall structure of the drama.

For some years Verdi had tended to trim down the proportions of such lyrical movements as appear in the introduction, so that the opera's first double aria should be the prima donna's *aria di sortita*. The tendency is clearly illustrated, for example, in both *Macbeth* and *La Battaglia di Legnano*. In *Rigoletto*, where Verdi's concern for the continuity of the music came to a head, it was to be expected that such a tendency should be intensified. 'Questa o quella', with its strophic form and dancing rhythms, does indeed become part of the unbroken sequence of periodic forms that make up the ballroom music of the opening festivities. But as always in this opera, there is another consideration in mind. It is in this aria that the Duke proclaims that philosophy of faithless hedonism, that contempt for passion, which is to dictate his action throughout the opera. And while this state of mind is utterly repugnant to the whole tradition of Italian opera, it is quite in keeping with that of French operatic comedy. There the pleasure of inconstancy had been a pervading motif. From the time of Lully's *Thésée* onwards, light-hearted gallants had sung wittily and winsomely of the 'coeur qui change chaque jour'; had avowed, like Damon in *Les Indes Galantes*:

> Les fidèles amants font la gloire des belles,
> Mais les amants légers font celle de l'amour.

Seen in this light Verdi's use of a strophic dance-song redolent more of the *opéra comique* than of romantic melodrama acquires a further measure of fitness.

Ostensibly similar, 'La donna è mobile' really constitutes a quite different type of case, since it is a *canzona*, that is to say a piece that would have been sung even in the original spoken form of the drama. It is Hugo's 'Souvent femme varie', not so much an expression of the Duke's character as his favourite song, though it does of course restore him to type after the more complex feelings of his scene in the second act. The most interesting thing about it is its use; fused nicely into its context at the first appearance by its long fade-away coda, and haunting the Duke's mind throughout those scenes in which the falseness of its sentiments is being so drastically demonstrated by Gilda's action.

On the psychological aptness of the Act II aria little can be added to the admirable paragraphs of Budden.[4] It is, however, perhaps worth recalling that this uniquely formal scene is a non-Hugoesque interpolation, substituted for the notorious 'key scene' at a late stage in the evolution of the opera (cf. above, p. 272). Also, it is surely not fortuitous that besides being in the traditional double-aria form this scene is actually old-fashioned in style. The substantial reprise in 'Parmi veder le lagrime', not of the melodic incipit, but of the continuation and cadence phrase, has a distinctly Bellinian air, as if the Duke were turning to a more decorous, old-world manner in his attempt to express the unfamiliarity of his state of mind. Still more old-fashioned is the cabaletta with its thematic introduction, the episode schematically derived from the principal theme by inversion, the snatch of reprise and the quite distinctive dissolving cadence theme. The point of all this is that while Verdi continued to cherish tender feelings for the old fashions of the cantabile, he had come to regard the old fashions of the cabaletta as representing all that was coarsest and most unfeeling in the tradition. The one expresses the Duke's reversion to type as infallibly as the other had expressed his self-deluding aspirations to real humanity.

The most original of all the arias is certainly Rigoletto's 'Corti-

giani, vil razza dannata', for there was among the traditional resources of Italian opera no form to which Verdi could turn to achieve
the reversal of the normal kind of psychological development that is
called for here. It is at the beginning of this movement that Rigoletto
speaks with greatest energy and authority; by the end, exhausted and
frustrated, he withdraws into a world of private despair, tearfully
beseeching the pity of those he had been accustomed to hector and
harry. Where the operatic scene normally gathers momentum, normally modulates from a delicate, almost chamber-music-like texture
to a strident *tutti*, here the process is reversed: the momentum flags,
the textures become more chamber-music-like, the cantabile instead
of initiating comes at the end of the scene. Characteristically Verdi
controls the unprecedented boldness of the design with a number of
age-old disciplines. For all the broken declamation and ranting
figurations of the opening, he composes the first half of Piave's lyric
into a standard short-aria pattern with a tonic-key exposition, a
modulating sequential episode, and a culminating phrase returning
to the tonic. A comparable short-aria pattern underlies the final D^b
section, though the fact that it is not an independent movement is
suggested by the absence of modulation. Finally there is the orchestral figuration, magically transformed from the wild, menacing
agitation of the start, first into a pattern of sighing slurs and tolling
pedal notes, and then into a solo cello obbligato (Ex. 1).

Ex. 1 (a)

(b)

Ex. 1 (c)

Gilda's only aria is likewise a single-movement design scrupulously matched to the dramatic context. A more sentimental age might have called it a reverie, for the whole aria comprises a series of rapturous, palpitating variations on a single melodic figure. After this figure has been presented in a concise aria design, the episode and reprise sections are twice repeated, adorned with ever more dreamlike fioritura. This fioritura gives rise to a coda theme, pervaded by a figuration that is clearly designed as a musical metaphor for the 'sospiri' of which Gilda sings. During this, in the usual manner, the harmonies move more rapidly, and in the cadence phrase they become positively kaleidoscopic, evoking by the scoring and rich juxtapositions, the flavour of the introduction. The coda leads to a postlude, formed by another pair of variations, this time on the exposition. During the first, the orchestra bears the thematic burden, while Gilda's musings become more inward; when she resumes the theme for the final variation a sinister touch of chromatic countermelody in flute and bassoon marks the point where the dramatic action is resumed. Hardly less remarkable than the postlude is the prelude. It seems to be a derivative of the transitional woodwind harmonies so often used to link into a cantabile. Here, though, they are given a kind of dreamlike, aspiring character by the flute figurations, and Gilda uses them to accompany an arioso-like intonation of the subject of her aria: 'Gualtier Maldè!'.

Gilda's music

With the suppression of the *aria di sortita* and its replacement by 'Caro nome', not to mention a final scene in which Gilda is dragged on stage in a sack, hers became a role which left many a prima donna with feelings of unease. Even Teresa De Giuli-Borsi, a personal friend of the composer and an artist he had admired for many years –

she had taken over the role of Abigaille in *Nabucco* in Autumn 1842 from Strepponi, and had created that of Lida in *La Battaglia di Legnano* in 1849 – even she was provoked by *Rigoletto* to get her husband to write to Verdi asking him to add an aria of the traditional cast. Verdi's reply, dated 8 September 1852, may serve as the text for the final section of this chapter:

My dear Borsi,

If you were persuaded that my talents were incapable of doing better than I have done in *Rigoletto*, you would not have asked me for an aria for this opera. Miserable talents! you will say . . . Agreed: but that is how it is. And then, if *Rigoletto* can stand as it is, a new movement would be one too many. In fact, where would one find a position for it? Verses and notes could be written, but they would always be ineffective since there is not the right context. Actually there would be one, but God deliver us! We should be flagellated. One would have to see Gilda and the Duke in the bedroom!! You do see? In any case it would be a duet. A magnificent duet!! But the priests, the friars and the hypocrites would howl at the scandal. Oh, happy were the times when Diogenes could say in the public square to someone who asked him what he was doing: 'Hominem quaero!!' etc. etc.

As to the first-act cavatina I don't see where agility comes in. Perhaps the tempo has been misjudged; it must be an *allegretto molto lento*. With a moderate tempo and the delivery entirely *sotto voce* there cannot be any difficulty. – But to return to the first proposal I would add that I conceived *Rigoletto* without arias, without finales, as an unbroken chain of duets, because I was convinced that that was most suitable. If someone remarks, 'But here you could have done this, there that' etc. etc., I reply: that might be excellent, but I was unable to do any better.

Meanwhile convey my affectionate regards to your wife . . .[5]

Verdi's observation that he had 'conceived *Rigoletto* . . . as an unbroken chain of duets' applies primarily to the role that De Giuli-Borsi was proposing to sing: Gilda is a participant in all the duets, except the *parlante* duet between Rigoletto and Sparafucile. And this formal pecularity is, as we might expect by now, a reflection of her character. Unlike most prima donnas Gilda is a mere child, passive, submissive and wholly unegocentric. All her emotions, all her actions are prompted by the more obviously forceful and dynamic figures of the Duke and her father. The duet form is Verdi's way of expressing the fact that it is only in communion with those she loves that she really flourishes.

Until the last act of the opera there is about almost all Gilda's music an air of girlishness, a certain propensity to florid agitation. It is only when she is being demure and deliberately appealing, as at 'Se non volete di voi parlarmi' or 'Già da tre lune', that she expresses herself simply and quietly: elsewhere her music lacks the firmness of line that characterized the more mature prima donnas that had preceded her. The tone of Verdi's characterization is set unmistakably in the big duet with Rigoletto in Act I, where the excitability of her reactions is vividly suggested both in cantabile and *tempo di mezzo*.

The cantabile is a movement dedicated to Rigoletto's memories of her dead mother. It is Gilda who has requested these recollections, and yet, witnessing her father's emotion, his tears, his gradual loss of self-control, she is overcome by an agitation of regret which Verdi expresses in the change of mode, the more rapid movement, the repetition of words and melodic figures which, far from comforting Rigoletto, rather sweep him along into her own fluster. A similar kind of over-impetuous reaction comes in the *tempo di mezzo*, where she seems to fall over herself in her eagerness to assume the roles her father's love has assigned to her (Ex. 2).

In the cabaletta Rigoletto sings in a quieter mood. And the first line of Piave's text, 'Quanto affetto! quali cure!', suggests that it is a mood absolutely in harmony with her own wishes, or perhaps one which she sees it her duty quietly to submit to. For the pattern Verdi adopts – based, as we have seen, on 'Andrem raminghi e poveri' – of a simple repetition of her father's melody and, after some naturalistic digressions, a delicate descanting embellishment, is clearly the musical analogy to an idealized father–daughter relationship. It is not Gilda's role to act or think independently but to provide a harmonious assenting and a tender adornment to Rigoletto's perception of the issues.

Perhaps still more sensitive in its depiction of Gilda's responsiveness is the cantabile of the love duet that follows. At the end of the Duke's magnificently extrovert apostrophe to love, 'È il sol dell'anima', we watch Gilda expectantly, but for a moment hear only the delicately nuanced palpitations of the flute and strings. Then, *sotto voce*, she takes up one of the Duke's phrases, repeats it and adorns it with that dreamy, caressing fioritura that in the next movement is to form the whole substance of 'Caro nome' (Ex. 3). As with Rigoletto in the previous movement, once the Duke has resumed the burden of the music, Gilda engages not in dialectic but in descant. Nowhere here or in the cabaletta that follows does she sing music that is genuinely independent of the Duke's.

The next duet, sung again with Rigoletto, comes immediately after her seduction in Act II. Again the cantabile in particular is an exquisitely observed piece of characterization, with its preliminary essay at the theme on the oboe, and the hesitant, broken rhythm of the opening phrases. When, despite herself, her love for the Duke

Ex. 2

gives the music a sudden radiance and confidence, turning the music to the major key, shifting the rhythm to fall on the main beat, the oboe returns to act as her admonishing conscience, turning the mood of the music back to remorse and regret. The process is repeated in the second verse, this time followed by a series of 'Caro nome'-like embroideries on the single phrase 'Partì, partì', and the agitated cadence phrase in which she recalls the abduction. To Rigoletto's answering verse Gilda responds characteristically, at first with hesitant interjections, then in agitated, breathless effusion.

The cabaletta is more conventional: the identity of material is perhaps less obviously right than in other cases in the opera. Verdi apparently takes his cue from the first lines of Gilda's verse. Of course she does not experience Rigoletto's 'gioia feroce' herself, but she does behold and describe it, and though it appals her she is unable to resist or offer it any dialectic countering. Such dissuasion as there is in the verses Verdi ignores. His sense of dramatic momentum told him that Rigoletto's lust for revenge could not be braked at this stage; the passion must impel the drama relentlessly forward to the catastrophe.

So far Gilda's music has been all of a piece, a characterization extraordinarily subtle and convincing. In Act III inevitably a change comes, for it is here that she comes of age emotionally, determining to assume individual responsibility for her actions and to make the supreme self-sacrifice for her lover. We can observe the musical reflection of this in the quartet and trio. In the former, the style of her music is wholly consonant with what we have heard before: at first little flurries of eager sentiment evolved out of stylized weeping and

637

Ex. 3

sighing figures; later a florid melody developed from this same material but now sustained over whole periods of music. It is in the trio that the change comes, at the moment when she decides to cut herself free from all ties. The excitement and horror of the movement, moods she had herself partaken of, are at this redeeming decision transformed in a radiant cantabile phrase, which momentarily floods with light the gloomy turmoil of the scene (Ex. 4).

The independence that Gilda asserted in the trio is ratified in the

final duet, the one movement in the opera whose tone she dictates.
One observes something of the quiet narrative style of 'Tutte le feste'
in the opening section, something of the noble and simple cantabile
of the trio in the 'Lassù in ciel' section; but it is Gilda's serenity that
is most impressive here, the emotional maturity that she has at last

Ex. 4

Ex. 4 cont.

arrived at, and it is expressed most clearly by means of the tonality.
Throughout the duet her passionless, disembodied D♭ music,

floating above delicate textures purged of all rhythmic drive or harmonic tension, is set in contrast to the burning humanism of Rigoletto's. He, still swept by gusts of tenderness and compassion, wrestles defiantly with fate and its decrees, and his music, still throbbing with inner life, tosses to and fro – to the dominant, to the mediant minor, to the tonic minor. All these impulses Gilda quietens, restoring the music with gentle inexorability to her own serene tonality. In this duet, a duet of ultimate farewell, there can be no such reconciliation as normally distinguishes the form, and there is accordingly no ensemble singing. The singers can scarcely even comprehend one another's words. While Gilda fades away into paradise, Rigoletto's earthly anguish remains, as the final cadences clearly assert, unassuaged.

Verdi and 'realism' – *La Traviata*

Dumas *fils* and French realism

Hitherto, almost all the subjects that Verdi himself had selected as the bases for his operas had been taken from works which can be regarded as classics of European literature. In the case of Shakespeare or Schiller he had worked with established masters of superlative quality; in the case of Hugo or Byron with near-contemporaries whose style and whose literary values were exemplary for the age. The best of Verdi's early operas vividly reflect in their music the qualities of their literary models. He had striven to enrich and to vary his own art by emulating those characteristics which he admired in Shakespeare or Schiller or Hugo.

At first sight *La Traviata* seems to be a product of the same habit of thought. Like *Hernani*, *La Dame aux Camélias* (on which *La Traviata* is based) was, in both its novel form (1848) and its dramatic form (1852), a major work of modern French literature. Moreover, like *Hernani* again, *La Dame aux Camélias* inaugurated a whole literary movement, that of 'realism', from which Verdi might well have felt that he had something to learn. Certainly Basevi, writing in 1857, had no doubt that *La Traviata* had introduced 'verismo' into the Italian theatre.

There is no doubt that the extended visits Verdi paid to Paris between 1847 and 1852 provided him with sufficient opportunity to study and absorb the earliest manifestations of the Realist movement. It was during these years that such paintings as Millet's 'The Sower' and Courbet's 'Stone-breakers' and 'The Funeral at Ornans' were exhibited; the same period marked a peak in the career of the great popular *chansonnier* Pierre Dupont, and in the activities of the open-air Funambules theatre, where Jean Deburau's company had abandoned the traditional pierrot-style costumes for those of the modern working classes. In a different way, a protest against artifice and the high style was registered by those 'Bohemian' artists in the shadow of Courbet, who met at the Café Momus, and who are immortalized for us, if not by their paintings, at least by the preserving sugars of Murger and Puccini. Wherever Verdi went on those strolls about the city with which, he reported to Giuseppina Appiani,[1] he filled his time in Paris, he must have come across reminders of (to quote Baudelaire) 'how great, how poetic we are in our cravats and our patent-leather boots'. Was it not Baudelaire's dictum 'faire du vrai', one of the proudest mottoes of the Realist movement, that Verdi himself was echoing when, many years later, he enunciated his own artistic credo: 'To copy the truth may be a fine thing, but *to invent the truth* is better, far better.'[2]

The search for the 'true' and the 'real' undertaken by French artists in the middle years of the nineteenth century affected both the subject matter and the style of what they did. Elegance of manner, polish of form, anything that could be regarded as the mere trappings and appurtenances of the presentation were discarded. These things were seen not as aids to make a work more vivid and effective, but as a kind of pose, a species of artificiality that stood in the way of directness and honesty of expression. The point is well illustrated by a familiar anecdote told of Courbet. Finding himself one day seated by Corot and painting the same scene, he is said to have observed, 'I am not as clever as you, M. Corot. I can only paint what I see.'

This emphasis on direct observation necessarily went hand in hand with a new interest in everyday contemporary life. The idealizing, mythologizing effect of historical distance was the last thing that was wanted. And even in dealing with the modern world the realists naturally enough concentrated their attention on those strata of society where they felt there was least pose and least artificiality, on the working classes, on social outcasts, on the underworld. The more commonplace, vulgar and sordid the subject matter and style of a work of art, the more surely was its sincerity guaranteed.

This artistic concern with the frank recording of unvarnished truth, reflects, or at least is wholly consonant with, the dominant position in French intellectual life of the ideas of Auguste Comte: for Comte's search for the values on which an orderly and stable society could be founded took as its starting-point a systematic review of the aims and methods of modern science, and the establishment at the very top of the hierarchy of sciences of 'la physique sociale', the new science of sociology. Courbet and Millet, Flaubert and Balzac, Dumas *fils* and Augier, all share Comte's passionate interest in the structure of society. A thematic dimension which in the imagined worlds of Romantic literature had been hardly more than an element of the décor becomes a central and deeply problematic concern. To be a worthy hero in a novel or drama one no longer needed Napoleonic achievements to one's credit; it was enough that, like Emma Bovary, or Marguerite Gautier, one should be a victim or even merely a symptom of the social order.

The element of sociological observation is a pronounced feature of *La Dame aux Camélias*. In his play Dumas was the first writer of his generation to face up to a theme which more than any other was to preoccupy French dramatists of the 1850s and 1860s – the social problem of sex. The courtesan in any number of forms – *grisette, lorette, demi-mondaine, femme entretenue, cocotte* – became the anti-heroine of a huge number of plays during these decades. Some evoked the squalor of the brothel, others the attic idylls of irresponsible youth, others again the sumptuous debaucheries financed by the noblemen and *nouveaux riches* of Parisian high life: all were concerned with the impact of these aberrations on society, and specifically on the institutions of marriage and the family. Though concern with these issues may have been anticipated both by Hugo and by the earlier vaudeville comedies and dramas, it was *La Dame aux Camélias* in which for the first time they become a central theme of the drama.

The note of objective sociological realism is sounded in several scenes. During the party scenes in Acts I and IV of the play Dumas depicts the world of coarse and hollow gaiety inhabited by the *femme entretenue*. The heartlessness of the women, the insane extravagance of the men, the easy acclaim of a philosophy of fickle lewdness is exuded on every page and periodically jolted into focus by a *mot* of some frankness:

OLYMPE: Donnez-moi dix louis, Saint-Gaudens, que je joue un peu.
GASTON: Olympe, votre soirée est charmante.
ARTHUR: Saint-Gaudens sait ce qu'elle lui coûte.
OLYMPE: Ce n'est pas lui qui le sait, c'est sa femme! . . .

In the last act the darker side of the picture of the courtesan's world is revealed, albeit markedly less starkly than in the novel. As Marguerite's health fails and her beauty fades, former friends desert and exploit her, creditors and bailiffs move in.

Prominent too in *La Dame aux Camélias* is that preaching note that was to become all-pervasive in Dumas's later plays. Duval *père* is the prototype of the 'raisonneur', the middle-class moralist through whom Dumas expresses his views on the threat that the courtesan offers to organized society. In Act III scene 4 he first comes face to face with Marguerite and, notwithstanding the fact that he is obliged to recognize in her qualities far more admirable than he could have anticipated, embarks on his philosophical exposition. It is immense-ly weighty and profuse in saws, probably the classic statement of the problem of the erstwhile *femme entretenue*:

DUVAL: Vous êtes prête à sacrifier tout à mon fils; mais quel sacrifice égal, s'il acceptait le vôtre, pourrait-il vous faire en échange? Il prendra vos belles années, et, plus tard, quands la satiété sera venue, car elle viendra, qu'arrivera-t-il? Ou il sera un homme ordinaire, et, vous jetant votre passé au visage, il vous quittera, en disant qu'il ne fait qu'agir comme les autres; ou il sera un honnête homme, et vous épousera ou tout au moins vous gardera auprès de lui. Cette liaison, ou ce mariage qui n'aura eu ni la chasteté pour base ni la religion pour appui, ni la famille pour résultat, cette chose excusable peut-être chez le jeune homme, le sera-t-elle chez l'homme mûr? Quelle ambition lui sera permise? Quelle carrière lui sera ouverte? Quelle consolation tirerai-je de mon fils, après m'être consacré vingt ans à son bonheur? Votre rapprochement n'est pas le fruit de deux sympathies pures, l'union de deux affections innocentes; c'est la passion dans ce qu'elle a de plus terrestre et de plus humain, née du caprice de l'un et de la fantaisie de l'autre. Qu'en restera-t-il quand vous aurez vieilli tous deux? Qui vous dit que les premières rides de votre front ne détacheront pas le voile de ses yeux, et que son illusion ne s'évanouira pas avec votre jeunesse?
MARGUERITE: Oh! la réalité!

Nevertheless one should not exaggerate the extent to which Duval's interpretation of social problems dominates *La Dame aux Camélias*. Whatever may be true of Dumas's later plays, this one is far more than a mere sociological treatise. And so in this scene of confrontation Dumas goes on from the philosophical statement of the dilemma to explore the workings of 'la réalité' on the characters and on their relationships with one another. He shifts his attention from the philosophical abstraction to the human consequences. Duval, increasingly impressed by the integrity of Marguerite's char-acter, puts it to her that, in the situation in which fate has placed her, only renunciation can, in the end, be a source of pride and pleasure to her. Marguerite acknowledges defeat, embracing suffering and despair as her portion, She experiences the social problem from an opposite angle, taking as the theme for her effusion the thought that 'la créature tombée ne se relèvera jamais!'

The attraction of the play for Verdi

The reputation of Dumas's play rested in the first instance on the frankness with which he portrayed the world of the 'kept woman', and on his compassionate and honestly ambiguous feelings for the social problem posed by her. Basevi, as I have mentioned, thought that it was this element of 'verismo' that had appealed to Verdi in the first instance and that, in La Traviata, constituted a large measure of the opera's individuality. He was not alone in this view. A number of influential voices in mid-Victorian England felt that La Traviata reflected all too vividly the detestable world of French realism. At early productions of the opera at Covent Garden the English genius for compromise manifested itself in a particularly humbugging manner when the management refrained from providing translations of the libretto, out of consideration (it was implied) for the patrons' moral well-being.[3] Chorley's familiar reflections on the early London performances also imply quite clearly that the values and concerns of Verdi's opera were the same as those of Dumas's play:

> . . . By way of adding to the excitement, there arose – or, it may be said, there was got up – a controversy concerning the good or bad morals of La Traviata as a piece to be accredited or condemned. – That there is an unwholesome interest in the story, is evident from the fact of its having been the first of a series of bad dramas, which have since taken possession of the Parisian theatre for the exhibition of simple and compound female frailty in modern guise . . . It was the commonplace nature of the sin and shame and sorrow, which revolted such persons as were really revolted, and which absolutely provoked a Manager's defence of the tale, as conveying a salutary warning to the young men of our times! The serviceable hypocrisy of such a plea was inevitable, . . . a wretched expedient to pique the jaded palates of play-goers: though but in harmony with that state of French society, which could delight in the dreary, morbid social anatomies of Balzac's novels.[4]

No one would seek to deny the realist or sociological dimensions of La Traviata altogether. Two extended scenes are devoted to that extravagantly gay and amoral world in which Violetta/Marguerite was accustomed to move; and if the gambling and drinking in the first of these, at the start of the opera, seems discreet, there is no mistaking the aura of that at the end of Act II. Carnal liaisons are casually discussed, the 'morals' of the masquerading choruses acclaim infidelity in men and complaisance in women, while one whole movement of the finale is concentrated on evoking the relentless monotony of the gaming-table.

Nor, when it is dramatically necessary, do Verdi and Piave evade the problematic moral questions posed in the play. In the great scene between Violetta and Germont the libretto depends closely on the play for its sequence of moods and ideas, and frequently borrows heavily from Dumas's actual language. Germont, like Duval, bases his appeal for Violetta's renunciation of her claim on Alfredo first on a sentimental idealization of middle-class life, then on reasoning prompted by religion and the real values of society: Violetta's youth will pass and her beauty will fade; young men are inconstant; there can be no lasting joy in a liaison that has not be sanctified by Heaven.

But when all this has been conceded, one must still beg leave to doubt whether Dumas's realism or his social philosophizing was really significant, in the way that, ten years earlier, Hugo's 'Romanticism' or Byron's stance of rebellion had been, in prompting Verdi to choose *La Dame aux Camélias* as the subject for an opera. The real secret of its appeal lay in the passion and tenderness of the relationship between Armand and Marguerite, a relationship which acquires a quite exceptional measure of intensity and sincerity from the fact that it is so palpably autobiographical, that Dumas had 'secreted his novel' – and by extension the play – 'from a personal sorrow'.[5] Most of all *La Dame aux Camélias* was irresistible because the story of Armand and Marguerite had a unique and peculiar relevance to Verdi's own private world at the time.

For it was probably in 1847 that Verdi had fallen in love with the long-admired Giuseppina Strepponi and begun to cohabit with her. And Strepponi, like Marguerite, was a 'fallen woman', a *Traviata*, the mother of two illegitimate children by 'il tenore della bella morte', Napoleone Moriani. From what Frank Walker has reconstructed of her early life,[6] one can imagine how often its drudgery, its sheer ineluctable problems, and the remorse that continuously haunted her must have moved her to feel, as Violetta was to feel, that

> . . . alla misera – ch'è un dì caduta
> Di più risorgere – speranza è muta.

And yet, like Violetta again, throughout these agonizing and despairing years she cherished in her heart the dream of a redeemer, of a man who would not simply use and exploit her, but one who would restore to her the possibility of a real relationship of mutual devotion, the 'gioia Ch'io non conobbi, essere amata amando!'

The extent to which the story of Armand and Marguerite (Alfredo and Violetta) reflects that of Verdi and Strepponi was first spelt out in detail by Luzio in his 'La "Traviata" e il dramma intimo personale di Verdi'.[7] It was not simply a question of a loose parallel in the unhappy past of one of the characters involved. Strepponi too was stricken with a near-consumptive illness which in the early years of their life together often brought her close to despair of ever regaining her health. She too found herself confronted with a Duval-like father-figure in Verdi's father-in-law, Antonio Barezzi, who – for all his magnanimity and his affection for Verdi – found it difficult to reconcile himself to this irregular liaison; who suffered from the ostracism of Strepponi by the people of Busseto that resulted from it, and felt moved to speak out about it in what Verdi himself described as 'very pungent phrases'. One wonders what Barezzi must have felt to have heard Germont exclaim to Violetta 'Ah, il passato perché, perché v'accusa', a sentiment perfectly in harmony with the conflict of moral and affectionate feelings that he seems to have experienced when faced with Strepponi.

Drama and real life did not, of course, remain strictly in step, though as a matter of fact Piave's libretto comes closer to real life than either of Dumas's two versions. The novel had closed in an atmosphere of pitiless harshness, with the dying Marguerite deserted by virtually all her friends and associates, despairing of ever seeing Armand again, attended in her last agonies only by the faithful Julie Duprat. In the play Dumas seeks to render the tragic conclusion at once more emotional and less painful by bringing back Armand in time for a passionate and tender reconciliation on Marguerite's death-bed. Piave goes further, adding Germont to the scene and making of Violetta's death-throes almost a family reunion. But real life was the fairy tale. Not only was Barezzi rapidly and fully reconciled to the presence of Strepponi in Verdi's house, but she slowly recovered her health, living to enjoy almost half a century of quasi- and actually conjugal happiness.

Nevertheless, the happy-ever-after cliché must not distract attention from the compelling intensity of Verdi's and Strepponi's relationship at the time of La Traviata. They were indeed living out a dream that had haunted both Dumas and Hugo before him, in which a fallen woman, corrupted and apparently destroyed by the lusts of men, is redeemed morally, if not reinstated socially, by the true love of one man. The best-known expression of this aspiration is to be found in Marion Delorme's words to Didier, 'ton amour m'a fait une virginité'. Dumas, in novel and play, and, following him, Piave in his libretto, give due weight too to 'celui que j'appelais du fond de ma bruyante solitude', and to the 'signor dell'avvenire'. But none of these writers could match the eloquence of Strepponi, who had actually experienced what they had merely dreamed of, and who as late as 1860 could still exclaim: 'O my Verdi, I am not worthy of you, and the love which you bear me is charity, balsam, to a heart sometimes very sad, beneath the appearance of cheerfulness. Continue to love me; love me also after death, so that I may present myself to Divine Providence rich with your love and your prayers, O my Redeemer!'[8] La Traviata, the opera Verdi created out of Dumas's realist, sociological drama, is really the most explicit of his offerings to Giuseppina Strepponi. It is their private opera, an artistic sublimation of their relationship.

From play to opera

The most typical characteristic of most of the librettos that Verdi had had written for him during the previous ten years was as close a degree of fidelity to the literary model as was compatible with the reformulation into an opera. Such fidelity remains characteristic of Piave's libretto for *La Traviata*. The scene of confrontation between Germont and Violetta provides a sufficient example of the way in which the dramatic climaxes of the opera are modelled absolutely faithfully on those of the play, imitating their form and, in this instance, exploring the same conflicts of sentiment and reason. We find Piave dutifully imitating Dumas in scene after scene of the opera – that part of 1.3 in which Alfredo confesses to Violetta the long history of his devotion to her; the fragmentary dialogues that embody the mounting tension of the gambling scene towards the end of Act II, the transfiguration of Violetta in the moments before her death – these and countless other details of the libretto, down to such tiny and insignificant-looking scenes as that between Annina and Violetta in III.5, are hardly more than translations of the equivalent passages of Dumas's play. Marguerite's and Violetta's last words in play and opera may be quoted by way of illustration:

MARGUERITE: . . . Ah! c'est étrange. (*Elle se lève*)
ARMAND: Quoi donc? . . .
MARGUERITE: Je ne souffre plus. On dirait que la vie rentre en moi . . .
    j'éprouve un bien-être que je m'ai jamais éprouvé . . . Mais je vais vivre!
    . . . Ah! que je me sens bien! . . .

VIOLETTA (*rialzandosi animato*): È strano! . . .
TUTTI: Che!
VIOLETTA: Cessarano
    Gli spasmi del dolore.
    In me rinasce . . . m'agita
    Insolito vigore!
    Ah! io ritorno a vivere,
    (*trasalendo*) Oh gio...ia! . . .

In general such shifts of emphasis and modifications of form as are necessary in translating Dumas's work into the operatic medium have been made by Piave in a competent if scarcely dazzling manner. At the start of Act II, for example, the opening three scenes of Dumas's Act III have been transformed into a solo scena for Alfredo. The actual sequence of events bears little resemblance to that in the play, save that in both Alfredo learns the secret of Violetta's accumulating debts by questioning a confidante – here Annina, in the play Prudence. But Piave has built the scene round the two emotional focuses of the Bougival scenes of the play, romantic idyll and harsh reality. It is, so to speak, an embodiment of Prudence's lines 'Ah, vous croyez, mon cher, qu'il suffit de s'aimer et d'aller vivre, hors de Paris, d'une vie pastorale et éthérée? Pas du tout! A côté de la vie poétique il y a la vie réelle.' Both the 'vie poétique' and the 'vie réelle' have been emotionalized somewhat to create a formal diptych of tender love and violent shame.

The scene is not without its incongruities. The hunting accoutrements of the opening recitative seem singularly inept – presumably they were suggested by a detail in chapter 23 of the *Dame aux Camélias* novel, where hunting is one of the pastimes with which Armand attempts to restore his spirits after the breach with Marguerite. And some degree of distortion is certainly brought about by making Alfredo the central figure. In the Bougival scenes of the play, it is Marguerite who is tormented by memories of the past and sees the present as an opportunity for regeneration, her lover as a redeemer. Here Alfredo paints an absurdly idealized picture of Violetta's past, speaking of 'agi . . . onori . . . pompose feste', and suggesting that it is he who is 'dal soffio d'amor rigenerato'. The intrusion of reality in the *tempo di mezzo* is characteristically abrupt and sketchy, and the lyric of 'O mio rimorso' a shambles of stale imagery:

> . . . Ma il turpe sonno a frangere
> Il ver mi balenò.
> Per poco in seno acquetati,
> O grido dell'onore;
> M'avrai securo vindice;
> Quest'onta laverò.

Notwithstanding its technical limitations, however, and the fact that it really matches no mood in the equivalent scenes of the play, the cabaletta text does serve to provide an operatic typification of the many outbursts of self-reproach and remorse that disturb the Bougival idyll in Dumas.

Other deft touches in Piave's transformation of play into opera are to be found in the songs given to Germont in Act II, 'Pura siccome un angelo', from his long duet with Violetta, and 'Di Provenza il mar', from his scena. It is by means of these that the librettist gives Verdi the chance to endow with emotive force the social and moral values of the bourgeois world on which the argument of the drama so heavily depends. In both movements Germont gives to the honest, dependable world which he has left behind a dream-like idealization. What might seem drab, narrow and repressive, if subjected to merely rational analysis, is transfigured into an image compounded of tender and loyal devotions, of serene joys tasted in the sight of God; and these things are given a further intensity of beauty by virtue of the fact that Alfredo has deserted and, by his conduct, threatened them.

> Di Provenza il mar, il suol – chi dal cor ti cancellò?
> Al natio fulgente sol – qual destino ti furò?
> Oh, rammenta pur nel duol – ch'ivi gioia a te brillò;
> E che pace colà sol – su te splendere ancor può.
>   Dio mi guidò.

Undoubtedly, however, the most impressive testimony to the dramatic power of those conventions with which Piave was by now so entirely at home is provided by Violetta's scena in Act I. Elements of the recitative at the start of the scena come from II.5 of the play. It was there that Piave would have found expressed Violetta/Marguerite's sense of wonder at what has befallen her, and her definition of the hitherto-unexperienced joy 'essere amata amando', which may be compared with Dumas's 'Nous autres femmes, nous prévoyons toujours qu'on nous aimera, jamais que nous aimerons, si bien qu'aux premières atteintes de ce mal imprévu nous ne savons plus où nous en sommes'. But the nearest thing in the play to this superb scena is the speech in which Marguerite tells Armand of the meaningless luxury, the deathly, heartless gaiety of her existence, and of her longing for a redeemer:

. . . au milieu de notre existence turbulente notre tête, notre orgueil, nos sens vivent, mais . . . notre coeur se gonfle, ne trouvant pas à s'épancher, et nous étouffe . . . tout autour de nous ruine, honte et mensonge. Je rêvais donc, par moments, sans oser le dire à personne, de rencontrer un homme assez élevé pour ne me demander compte de rien, et pour vouloir bien être l'amant de mes impressions . . . Alors, je t'ai rencontré, toi, jeune, ardent, heureux; les larmes que je t'ai vu répandre pour moi, l'interêt que tu as pris à ma santé, tes visites mystérieuses pendant ma maladie, ta franchise, ton enthousiasme, tout me permettait de voir en toi celui que j'appelais du fond de ma bruyante solitude. En une minute, comme une folle, j'ai bâti tout un avenir sur ton amour . . .

Piave's scene likewise contrasts the idealized glimpses that Violetta has sometimes momentarily caught with the frivolous abandon of her normal style of life. In the cantabile Alfredo is seen as the tangible realization of the fondest dream of her lonely heart: he who had watched over her in her sickness has now awoken her longing for 'quell'amor ch'è palpito Dell'universo intero'. He has become the hoped-for redeemer, the 'signor dell'avvenire'.

If Alfredo is the hero of the cantabile, the *tempo di mezzo* and cabaletta centre on what Violetta has come to regard as a realistic assessment of her plight. To place her hopes in a 'signor dell'avvenire' or in 'quell'amor ch'è palpito ...' is sheer self-delusion: perpetual debauch is acclaimed as the only answer to solitude and sadness. The hysterical urge to have fun sweeps away the despair with which she is threatened by her sincerest feelings. In the stylized antithesis of cantabile and cabaletta Piave furnishes an operatic paraphrase of those passages in the novel and play in which Dumas subjects Marguerite's changes of mood to rational analysis. The scene also parallels those frequent veerings from rapture to despair, the tempestuous scenes of jealousy and reconciliation that give the Marguerite/Armand relationship such a torrid and vulnerable intensity.

A last detail of the libretto that is worth a brief examination is the change in the tone of the drama which Piave sometimes achieves, and which sometimes goes beyond what has been strictly necessitated by the change of medium. Quite early in the first act, at the *brindisi*, one begins to sense such a transformation. Dumas's drinking song is rendered by Gaston:

> Il est un ciel que Mahomet
> Offre par ses apôtres.
> Mais les plaisirs qu'il nous promet
> Ne valent par les nôtres.
> Ne croyons à rien
> Qu'à ce qu'on tient bien,
> Et pour moi je préfère
> A ce ceil douteux
> L'éclair de deux yeux
> Réflété dans mon verre ... etc.

Piave, naturally enough, transfers the song to Alfredo, whom for the occasion he dubs a 'maestro'. Then he eliminates what we may call its wit, and transforms its trivial enthusiasm for 'les plaisirs' into a veritable hymn to love and beauty.

> Libiam ne' lieti calici
> Che la bellezza infiora,
> E la fuggevol ora
> S'inebri a voluttà.
> Libiam ne' dolci fremiti

Che suscita l'amore,
Poiché quell'occhio al core
Onnipotente va.
Libiamo, amor fra i calici
Più caldi baci avrà . . . etc.

And this exaltation of tone becomes more prevalent as the act progresses, the idealistic panegyric of 'quell'amor ch'è palpito Dell'universo intero' translating Alfredo's avowal of love to a quite different plane from Armand's. Later in the libretto we find Piave suppressing or transforming the sordid details that form the background to the drama. The transfiguration of the homage paid to a courtesan into 'agi . . . onori . . . pompose feste' in Alfredo's Act II *scena* has already been mentioned. Another perhaps clearer demonstration of the subtle change of tone in the libretto is to be found in III.3, a scene paralleling the fourth and fifth scenes of Dumas's last act.

It is New Year's Day. In the play Marguerite, on her deathbed, is visited by Prudence, a superannuated lady of pleasure and a sycophantic friend. She comes not with New Year's greetings, but to borrow money in order to buy some presents for other friends. Marguerite, struck by the irony of Prudence's promise to repay her at the end of the month, lends her the required sum. Afterwards she sends Nanina to sell the bracelet that she herself has received as a New Year's gift.

At this stage in the opera Piave and Verdi are no longer interested in the context of Violetta's life, only in the quality of her own sensibility. This little scene is characteristic of their preoccupation, emphasizing the loneliness that Violetta feels at this time of public festival –

Ah, nel commun tripudio, sallo il cielo . . .
Quanti infelici soffron! –

and replacing the grubby transaction with Prudence into a demonstration of the impulsive generosity of Violetta's better nature, the decision to give half her worldly wealth to the poor:

VIOLETTA: Quale somma
        V'ha in quello stipo?
ANNINA: Venti luigi.
VIOLETTA: Dieci
        Ne reca ai poveri tu stessa.

Throughout the opera, as is only appropriate in a work tacitly dedicated to Giuseppina Strepponi, it is in the idealization of the character of Violetta that its tone most differs from that of the play.

653

All the warmth, generosity and latent idealism of Dumas's Marguerite are retained and intensified, while much of the sordid, mercenary, and amoral environment of the play is discreetly suppressed. Piave's last transfiguring touch is especially appropriate to an opera for Strepponi, for he weaves into the final act a thread of religious sentiment and imagery.

There is something of this in Dumas. In v.3 Marguerite tells the doctor how the previous evening, despairing and fearful, she had summoned a priest, who had been able to bring her much comfort. Later in the act, after Armand's return, she proposes that they go to the church where two friends are being married 'de prier Dieu et d'assister au bonheur des autres'. But Piave works out this motif far more thoroughly. The refrain of Violetta's despairing 'Addio, del passato' is a prayer:

> A lei, deh, perdona; tu accoglila, o Dio,
> Or tutto finì.

At Alfredo's return Violetta proposes a visit to church, not, as in the play, to witness their friends' wedding, but to render thanks for their reunion. Finally, the motif recurs in the trio that acts as the last finale. After Violetta's death, when Alfredo marries another, he is not to destroy the portrait which Violetta now gives him. Instead she urges him

> Le porgi questa effigie:
> Dille che dono ell'è
> Di chi nel ciel tra gli angeli
> Prega per lei, per te.

Realism and formality in the music of *La Traviata*

In one respect at least Verdi's music for *La Traviata* is wholly alien to the philosophical tenets of French realism. While the realist disliked and mistrusted elegant, poised and cleanly articulated forms, Verdi remained devoted to them. The knowledge that he was making an opera out of a contemporary sociological drama did not tempt him to abandon the traditional patterned structure of the Italian melodrama in favour of something rougher-hewn, or more scruffily accoutred; on the contrary, *La Traviata* is the most formally perfect work of that period in the early 1850s when Verdi's grasp of the formal principles of *ottocento* opera was at its most assured and affectionate. For all the wonderful vividness with which he realizes the drama in his music, it is quite clear that his sense of musical structure, his Latin instinct for proportion and harmony, is as fully engaged as it had ever been. *Luisa Miller* and *Rigoletto* seem almost uncouth in comparison.

The several strophic arias all bear witness to this. In 'Ah! fors'è lui', in 'Di Provenza il mar', and in 'Addio, del passato' alike, the music is matched with extraordinary vividness to the mood and language of the first verse. In all of them, however, this word/tone relationship is altogether slacker in the second. The repetition of the music is not a dramatic necessity in the sense of being closely analogous to the text: it is a musical desideratum; it marks the point where the musician throws over the props provided by the librettist and becomes himself the dramatist, determining how heavily weighted, how long-drawn-out, the moods need to be.

The extent to which Verdi remains a composer who creates beautifully proportioned artifacts in sound out of musical ideas prompted by analogy with the libretto can still best be seen in the ensembles. In the duets and finales no trace of *verismo* disturbs the masterly, euphonious development of the material. As he had always done, Verdi begins his ensembles by embodying in distinctive solo cantabiles the passions or states of mind of the protagonists. These constitute the themes with which he works, and beyond this initial congruousness of mood and music, or situation and music, his primary concerns are the spinning-out of the lyricism, the euphony of the ensemble, the swaying symmetry of the phraseology.

A good example is provided by the *largo* of the Act II finale. Dramatically it is dominated by the states of mind of the three protagonists, Violetta, Alfredo and Germont. The emotional experiences through which father and son have recently passed have changed the character of the music of both of them. Germont, hitherto self-assured, somewhat bland and sentimental, has never quivered so with passion, never been so close to speechlessness as he is in his opening phrases. Alfredo, normally so eloquent, has been reduced to a guilty, muttering self-reproach. Morally broken, unable to face the public world before which he has disgraced himself, he is capable only of broken-backed, whispering scraps of melody. Violetta's lyricism, on the other hand, though at first fractured by weakness and distress, has the same sustained, simple serenity that it had acquired in 'Dite alle giovine', and which Verdi uses to express the dignity and truthfulness of her better self. But all this dramatically inspired music, wonderfully apposite as it is, is but the raw material of the *largo*. Once expounded, it is worked into a grand, sustained composition in which the details have no specifically dramatic or psychological function.

Even Violetta's scena in Act II, the one movement in the opera in which Verdi makes no use of the traditional forms of *ottocento* opera, replacing them by an apparently more naturalistic musico-dramatic flux, proves in fact to be an example of the same phenomenon. The whole scene is organized in such a way as to give maximum expressive impact to the opera's supreme expression of romantic love, and in a manner appropriate to the fact that it is made at the moment of separation, apparently for ever. This outburst 'Amami Alfredo' is the dramatic datum on which the musical composition is focused. But everything else, if we look at it in terms of theatrical naturalism or even expressive appropriateness, is an irrelevance; everything else is simply a part of the process of musical composition. The preliminary material is composed not in a manner that gives vivid expression to every phrase of the text; on the contrary, much of the word-setting – at 'Ai piedi suoi', for example – seems arbitrary, even pointless. What Verdi is seeking is a steeply intensifying expression of nervous excitement, achieved by means of the repetition of breathless melodic and rhythmic figures and the near-hysterical word-repetition. The process gains potency from the fact that it is once interrupted and then again suspended in the last moments before the orgastic outpouring at 'amami Alfredo'. Of course the effect is overpoweringly dramatic. But it is a dramaticism that has certainly not been acquired by discarding formal disciplines or subjugating musical values to those of naked theatricality. The disciplined composer, the craftsman trained in working his musical materials into tightly patterned structures, has never been more in evidence.

One last point, already discussed in a different context in Part III of this book, must be reiterated in connection with this question of how the traditional musical priorities of Italian melodrama prevail even in a score partially inspired by French realism. Verdi is at this stage of his career extraordinarily adept at matching the dramatic situation to the traditional musical form, or distorting the musical form slightly in order to give more vivid expression to the dramatic idea sublimated within it. Simple examples of this facility are even to be found in the link between first and second statements of the cabaletta in some of the solo arias, as for example in Alfredo's 'Oh mio rimorso'. The sudden plunge into a cataclysmic *minore* for the full orchestra no longer gives the impression of a mere convention devoid of expressive meaning. It sounds more like a miniature tone-poem suggestive of the possession of Alfredo by an all-pervasive black passion.

But the supreme example of this kind of interaction of a traditional form and a specific expressive purpose, to which one is bound to return, is Violetta's Act I aria. In general terms one may say that the conventional double-aria scheme is very well matched to the fundamental dramatic idea of this scene, which is the contrast between the nobler aspirations of Violetta's better self, expressed in the cantabile, and the attempt to reassert the amoral philosophy of the 'kept woman' in the cabaletta.

The music of the cabaletta consciously scintillates and titillates in every bar. Trilling and wheedling woodwinds and prancing cellos are prominent in the orchestra, while a controlled virtuosity, compounded of trills, grace-notes and scale-passages, tripping staccato and gliding chromaticism, is to be heard in every phrase of the singing voice. Its most remarkable feature, however, is the reappearance of Alfredo as a voice off, singing 'Amor è palpito' (cf. p. 421 above). Looked at realistically this cannot be said to be entirely plausible, for 'Amor è palpito' is hardly a favourite song of his as 'La donna è mobile' is of the Duke in *Rigoletto*. But psychologically it is just the way to remind Violetta of his presence in the street outside. The mere sound of his voice, which, realistically, is all we could suppose Violetta to hear, grows into a recollection of his avowal of love which she sublimates rather as Leonora sublimates Manrico's farewell in the 'Miserere' scene of *Il Trovatore*. With its harp accompaniment it sounds like a visitation from, or a vision of, a better world. And emotionally that is exactly what it is; the transfigured memory that makes absolutely necessary a repeat of the cabaletta. The whole idea of the conflict between Violetta's idealistic and professional selves finds a last brilliant presentation in the coda, where Alfredo's theme continues to sound, now assimilated to Violetta's own metre, like an obsession in her own mind which she attempts to dispel with a progressively more scintillating assertion of her wit and brilliance and charm. Modestly but genially varied in this way, the conventional aria form proves capable of expressing the juxtaposition of the external and the internal, the conflict of social façade and human necessity at every level and through to the very end.

The social dimension

If the ideals of the French Realists have left little tangible mark on the formal qualities of *La Traviata*, their interest in society certainly does affect the musical idiom in several scenes of the opera. As we have seen, two extended sections of the opera – the introduction to Act I and the Act II finale – are in great part devoted to an evocation of that Parisian high-society milieu in which Violetta had been at home, and in both cases the dramatic preoccupation with society has interesting musical consequences. In the introduction the scene is an extravagant party, a party so extravagant in fact as to verge on being a public entertainment. This would seem to be the reason for the style of the orchestration, which with its oompahing brass and shrill woodwind melody verges on that of the *banda*. But to create a *banda*-like sound in the orchestra is tantamount to bringing it forward from the background into the centre of the musical activity, just as the pastimes of Parisian society are brought forward in Dumas's play to form an integral part of the drama. The subsequent addition of the strings to round off the initial statement of the 'society' music completes the process of normalization. These clamorous and jubilant formalities are not designed to provide a mere dash of garish colour in the background of the drama: they become for the time being the focus of attention.

We are reminded of this introduction at the start of the Act II finale. We find ourselves in the same *mondaine* atmosphere, which Verdi evokes in the same way, with square-cut, jolly music orchestrated in a conspicuously tinny manner. And again a process of normalization seems to be suggested in the gradual softening of the colours.

On two further occasions Violetta's solo music adopts the idiom of this 'society' music. The association is clear in the introduction to 'Sempre libera sarei', where, in readiness for Violetta's acclaim of a life of mad gaiety, the orchestral sound is focused on unison woodwind melody and energetically strumming accompaniment figurations. Poignantly and ironically, the same idiom appears again in the *tempo di mezzo* of the Act III duet. Violetta's last despairing attempt to be cheerful prompts a resumption of the shrill, trilling manner of her Act I cabaletta, long after she has learnt to confess the hollowness and the emptiness of the world which this idiom was designed to evoke (Ex. 1).

Dramatically of far greater interest than this infiltration of 'social' music into the idiom of the opera is the question of the ways in

Ex. 1

which Verdi's expresses the growing alienation of the protagonists from 'society'. In the Act ɪ introduction the reversal of the process (already described) of bringing society into the foreground is simply accomplished. The receding of society out of the centre of interest is effectively symbolized by the appearance of a real *banda*. The opening bars of the duet – the invitation to the dance – mark the last point in the drama where protagonists and society are really at one. Thereafter the social music does become a mere background, a tapestry of sound against which Violetta and Alfredo heedlessly converse.

Other examples of this distancing of the protagonists from the social environment are more complex. It is in the Act ɪɪ finale that Verdi is perhaps most obviously and primarily concerned with evoking the pleasure-seeking, frivolous atmosphere of Parisian 'society'. This he does with two masquerade entertainments, choruses-cum-ballets, one of gipsies and one of matadors. They are, like most of Verdi's ballet music, gaily coloured and pretty, in a cool, decorative kind of way. But by using the device of an entertainment to evoke a world that is central to the dramatic theme, and which Dumas had taken pains to evoke realistically, he does suggest how remote from it the real concerns of Violetta have become. Even for a dramatic purpose, he cannot bring himself to portray her playing an integral part in such a world after the emotional and spiritual awakening she has undergone in the early part of the act.

The most eloquent expression of Violetta's alienation from the society that had once idolized her occurs in the central *agitato* section of the same finale. The music here is designed to accompany the gambling and thus has a darker and quieter character than the 'society' music hitherto. Nonetheless the basic idea is drawn out into highly formal and repetitive patterns which suggest something of the mindless monotony of the sport and provide the musical continuity on to which the conversations are threaded. What concerns us here, however, is the way Verdi has released Violetta from the spell of this music, held up its relentless momentum from time to time to express the stricken passion of one who can no longer come to terms with the inane frivolities of the world in which she finds herself. The gambling music is three times interrupted by a refrain which owes nothing to Piave's text, but which Verdi himself compiled from odd phrases here and there in the scene, to express a lonely grief welling up inconsolably in the midst of a heedless world.

Such superimpositions and juxtapositions are not Verdi's only resources for suggesting these ideas of alienation or of distancing. Characteristic of *La Traviata* is the way he uses shifts of tonality to express the idea of a shift of dramatic focus from one world to another, from past to present, from present to future, from reality to dream, from society to soul.

The origins of this device are probably to be found in those recitatives and ariosos in which a conspicuous change of emotional tone is matched by a striking tonal shift. A good example is found in the arioso preceding 'De' miei bollenti spiriti', where Alfredo, having reflected on the luxury that Violetta has sacrificed to be with him, goes on to express the emotional rebirth that he himself has experienced. As if at the wave of a wand, the music is simply removed from the key of F to that of D♭ (Ex. 2).

But because in *La Traviata* such ideas as rebirth, the conflicts between society and the interior world of the emotions, between *la vie poétique* and *la vie réelle*, play such a central role, we find this commonplace expressive device used with considerable frequency in a variety of ways. The last act in particular provides some splendid instances. In the prelude, for example, the pervasive atmosphere of melancholy stillness is once dispelled by the serenely palpitating D♭ episode, which, by its harmonies, its eager melody, its pulsing textures, gives a vivid impression of reawakening life. Its precise connotation is made clear only in the scena that follows, where, in simplified arioso form, it is associated with the other-worldly comfort given Violetta the night before by a priest. Between the *primo tempo* and the cantabile of the duet, too, the change of orchestral colouring from accentuated *fortissimo tutti* to sustaining *pianissimo* woodwind, and especially the enharmonic change of key, is designed to suggest removal to an imagined, longed-for world. Here the dream is of escape from Paris, the city of disease and corruption, to some idealized retreat where a shared life will restore Violetta to health and happiness.

This question of contrasting worlds, of alienation between one level of reality and another, may profitably be examined a little more

Ex. 2

closely, for it is no mere incidental detail in *La Traviata*. On the
contrary it is one of the central themes of the opera, perhaps *the*
central theme, permeating the drama at all levels, in any number of
forms. Thus, in the first act, where Violetta stands at the centre of the
action we witness the contrast between her inner and outer selves,
between the frivolous, amoral abandon of her public *persona*, and
her deep, yearning need for a redeemer; and we witness Alfredo's
arrival perhaps to fill this need. In the early stages of Act II we hear
from Alfredo that redemption has apparently been achieved: the
dream of love has become a reality. But already the world of
emotional reality is being threatened by realities of a different kind,
the petty realities of material need. And in the scene that follows,
between Violetta and Germont, the 'real' world breaks in earnest, as
a moral and social force which, given the inescapable data of the
characters and situations the drama is built on, can only enjoin and

prohibit. If Act I explores an antithesis between a world of superficial social games and deep psychological necessity, Acts II and III explore an antithesis between fond dream and harsh disillusion. The world of the heart, the world of our better selves, has become a fantasy world, a dream world, which can only be wretchedly compromised, or brought harshly back to earth in the awakening demanded by organized society. Just as the double aria of Violetta's Act I scena expresses the characteristic antithesis of Act I, so does the double aria of Alfredo's Act II scena express that of Act II.

But Verdi uses infinite variety and resource in illuminating such contrasts of worlds in his music. On occasion he does it in greater detail than would be possible simply by such structural devices, and actually incorporates the conflicts and the distances into the style of his lyrical music. It is for example clear that the emotional progression incorporated in the threefold tonalities of 'Addio del passato' – A minor, C major, A major – matches the three worlds of present reality, lost happiness, looked-for redemption (now in a religious sense). The somewhat cryptic cabaletta 'Gran Dio, morir sì giovine' is perhaps inspired by a comparable idea. Does the C major marching rhythm represent the irresistible forward sweep of destiny, the sudden *pianissimos* and the strangely dissonant slurs Violetta's attempts to brake the inexorable progress? With the addition of woodwind in the second half the effect of alienation between successive phrases of the song becomes even more striking. The irreconcilability of what delirium and sobriety expect, of what can passionately be longed for and what can reasonably be expected, seems to be what Verdi is aiming to suggest here.

Germont

The conflicts and antitheses of such worlds of feeling and perception, the experiences of the individual as a victim of society, are the most important dramatic elements that *La Traviata* has inherited from *La Dame aux Camélias*. A more modest but still interesting relic is Germont, a re-creation of Duval *père* in his role of *raisonneur*, the moralist who stands for and speaks for the values of bourgeois respectability. We have already had occasion to note the blend of sentimental and rational traits in Duval's role. In the opera Verdi, admirably assisted by Piave, redistributed these qualities in a manner carefully calculated to create a distinctive kind of musical rhetoric.

This rhetoric can be observed in each of the three solo cantabiles that Germont sings in Act II: 'Pura siccome un angelo' and 'Bella voi siete' from the duet with Violetta, and 'Di Provenza il mar' from his solo scena. In each of them Verdi employs a basically similar pattern. He begins the cantabile with detached, equable phrases in which no especial pathos or emotion is perceptible and which provide the musical analogy of rational argument; and he proceeds from these to vehement and impassioned climaxes in which Germont plays on Violetta's or Alfredo's feelings, and which provide the musical analogy to Dumas's sentimental and emotional appeals. The most convincing masterpiece of such rhetoric is the first verse of 'Di Provenza il mar'. The aria begins typically, with bland, repetitive phrases, apparently nothing more than an objective reminder of the familiar and trusted world of which Germont speaks: nothing could be calmer, nothing more reassuring and sweetly lulling. And here we may pause to admire Piave's work; for in his lyric the objective statement is followed by the catch in the throat, the intimation that Germont is emotionally involved himself, and from that stage he works himself into a kind of spiritual exultation, in which mind and heart and spirit are all fully and inextricably engaged. These developments Verdi traces first by playing on the expressive contrast of major and minor modes, and finally by building the initially cool and square-cut melody to an unexpectedly vehement climax, intensifying and dislocating its square rhythmic patterns, and replacing the impassively rocking harmonies by rich and rapidly shifting progressions that finally debouch on to a tonic 6-4 chord, in Verdi's favourite manner.

The *raisonneur* and his particular brand of rhetoric are really only in evidence in the second act of the opera. Thereafter merely reasoned attitudes are swept aside, dissolved in the flood of passionate feeling released by the love of Violetta and Alfredo. In the third act we find ourselves back in a world of pure emotion threatened and finally destroyed by a malignant destiny that is perhaps more typical of Italian Romantic melodrama.

But before the drama moves into this final stage, those themes that have dominated the first two acts, and which have been most consciously expressed by Germont – the conflicts and counter-claims of society and private life, of reason and emotion, of duty and inclination – are brought to a splendid climax of complexity and ambiguity in the Act II finale. The inadequacy and vulnerability of the *raissoneur* is as clearly demonstrated as that of the society figure, or the man of passion and instinct. Germont, hitherto the representative of bourgeois propriety, has been won over by the heart of the courtesan to defend her against the kind of insult he had himself once offered her. Alfredo, Violetta's redeemer, torments himself more than he does his beloved, by abandoning her again to the spiritual desert from which he had rescued her. Violetta herself, the erstwhile apologist of venal love, of amorality and of mere pleasure, has become publicly, in the face both of the bourgeoisie and of high society, the self-confident, idealizing hymnodist of life's supreme passion in its noblest form.

The music of Violetta

In the last resort it is the music that Verdi made out of the Violetta/Alfredo relationship that has made *La Traviata* one of the half-dozen best-loved operas in the world. In one general sense at least it is typical of the love-relationships in Verdi's operas, for the love scenes do not constitute a still centre around which the action of the drama rages. On the contrary they are themselves under strain, a fact which imbues them with a measure of that dynamism so characteristic of the composer. All three love scenes in *La Traviata* acquire a tension and a greater measure of poignancy from the fact that Violetta can participate in them only in an incomplete way. In the Act I duet, she feels herself morally unworthy to enter into a full relationship; in the *scena* of Act II, she knows the relationship to be doomed, yet has to conceal the fact from Alfredo; in Act III, after the reconciliation, she is mortally ill. Really only in the cantabile of Alfredo's Act II aria can the relationship be described in tranquil, wholly beatific terms.

The musical analogy to this quality of tension is perhaps to be seen in the unusually hectic quality of some of the *primo tempo* and *tempo di mezzo* sections. An excellent example is provided by the *primo tempo* of the Act III duet, which acquires an extraordinary impetuous intensity from the racing accompaniment, from the phrases of lyrical melody hurled backwards and forwards from one protagonist to another, and from the upward-pressing chromatic appoggiaturas. The *tempo di mezzo* that follows and the scena preceding 'Amami Alfredo' in Act II have a comparable quality of pulsing emotional steepness.

The opera's greatest strength and most enduring beauty is to be found in Verdi's musical realization of the character of Violetta, a study of remarkable range and sensitivity.

Verdi and 'realism'

We first become aware of Violetta as a musical characterization in the Act I duet with Alfredo. As the brilliant hostess in a frivolous, high-society environment, she sings music that is strikingly differentiated from Alfredo's earnest and passionate song. Her verse acquires an aura of calculated frivolity from the prancing and gliding coloratura, the utterly insouciant harmonies, the touch of shrillness in the orchestral colouring. And this differentiation Verdi sustains throughout the duet, even in the cadenza, using the lighter voice to weave embellishments around the firmer one.

The profounder recesses of Violetta's character begin to be revealed in the cantabile of her Act I aria. Whereas Alfredo had been, however tentative in public, confident in his heart of the rightness of his passion, Violetta is brazen in public, but doubtful at heart. The uncertainty with which she confesses her aspiration to experience the 'gioia ch'io non conobbi, esser amata amando' is beautifully suggested in the broken descending delivery of the opening phrase; the glides and grace-notes heard in such profusion in the duet have been transformed from ornamental frills into deferential hesitations. And nothing could better express Violetta's weakness at this stage in the drama, her dependence on others, her doubts as to whether what she longs for could ever become real in her own experience, than the fact that when she does finally come to sing her idealizing hymn to love she simply borrows the music from Alfredo's part in the duet. The remainder of the aria, as we have seen, expresses with growing vehemence the conflict between the two aspects of Violetta's character so far revealed.

If the great emotional experience for Violetta in Act I is the discovery of a 'redeemer', that in Act II is the realization of the fact that the mores of bourgeois society demand that she renounce the aspirations to 'redemption'. During this act, and specifically in her duet with Germont, her music vacillates between the emotional poles of despair and submissiveness to destiny.

After Germont's 'Pura siccome un angelo', the orchestra briefly assumes the leading role to suggest the hesitation, the fluster of her sensibilities which his words inspire. From a sweet tunefulness redolent of Violetta's modesty and tenderness it modulates into a more conventional agitation as she gradually appreciates the full purport of Germont's words, and by the time she breaks into her own verse, 'Non sapete quale affetto', she is close to panic. It is only in thinking of Alfredo that her heart is warmed again and she finds eloquence and control, loading the phrase with caressing appoggiaturas. But Violetta's inability to formulate a refutation of

665

Germont's words is best expressed in the final C major section where she sobs out her words on a monotone while the rising and falling chromatic phrase in the orchestra suggests the overpowering churning of emotion that afflicts her (Ex. 3).

Ex. 3

Against this movement one may set 'Dite alla giovine', which marks the point where Violetta resolves on following the socially proper course. In the context of passion and brilliance created by her earlier music, the controlled, classical austerity of this is overpowering. Violetta bows before the dictates of fate in humility and selflessness, to a melody of Gluck-like simplicity and intensity. Only the style of the accompaniment prevents this movement from straying from the sphere of popular melodrama into that of classical tragedy: only the touches of colour in the oboe and cello suggest subjective pathos. Otherwise it is a melody of wonderfully controlled line, rising slowly to the central cadence as if in ritual procession to the sacrifice, lingering there for a moment, and then falling down to rest in a grand gesture of self-annihilation. The line is unperturbed by rhythmic self-assertiveness or by devices of harmonic intensification such as chromaticism or appoggiaturas.

In the third act, Violetta's music is concentrated on expressing the way in which she struggles to reach acceptance of her mournful destiny, first in religious terms, and secondly – inspired less by Dumas, one suspects, than by the Verdi/Strepponi/Barezzi saga – in terms of a reconciliation of human relationships.

Her aria 'Addio del passato' is expressive of the very depths of desolation. An introductory theme on the oboe, sinking down over detached string chords in the most elementally sorrowful key of A minor, leads into a principal theme that focuses on the minor third and that in essence represents simply a slipping down from that to the key-note. The semiquaver quiverings of life in the end of each phrase only fall back where they began, to sink still lower. Thoughts of the absent Alfredo are matched by a change of mode and the addition of warm thirds and sixths in the woodwind; but this 'conforto . . . manca', and the warmth of the music is chilled again, dropping back to A minor with the reedy sound of the oboe. At last Violetta turns to God: the music begins to vibrate as it had in the D♭ episode of the Act III prelude; the quivering semiquaver phrases, now in the major key, become more urgent, reaching upward in a gesture of supplication. But only the melancholy voice of the oboe answers, turning the music back to the minor key, and sinking down again through the octave.

The religious fortification that she seeks here in vain comes only after the return of Alfredo and Germont has enabled Violetta to put herself right with the world. Once reconciliation there is complete, she is able to enter the presence of death with serenity. The death *topos*[9] at 'Prendi . . . quest'è l'immagine', which had moved her heroic predecessor Leonora to terror and dismay, is acknowledged by Violetta with quiet dignity. Later, at 'Se una pudica vergine', with one of these enharmonic steps typically used for the expression of distancing or contrasting worlds, she raises herself up to contemplate her role in paradise.

Finally we may note that the prelude is exclusively concerned with themes associated with Violetta. Its first theme is melancholy and morbidly sweet, the music associated in Act III with her deathbed, music which here casts a shadow as Verdi often liked to do even before the opera is under way. The 'Amami Alfredo' theme follows, the theme which expresses her feelings at their most romantic and passionate. Later the same theme returns, decked out in a superficies of frivolity and prettiness, of staccato runs and patterings. Even for those who are new to the opera the prelude plants a couple of important themes in the memory. Those who know the opera well may sense in it a miniature tone-poem evoking Violetta's condition of morbid sickness, the warmth of her heart, and the foolishness of her way of life.

La Traviata, is, then, minimally affected by the stylistic ideals of Realism, and shares only incidentally its sociological interests. Its central concern is the human passion of romantic love; if, as Gianandrea Gavazzeni has somewhat provocatively averred, *Il Trov-*

Ex. 4

atore is the Italian *St Matthew Passion, La Traviata* is the Italian *Tristan.* Because of this emphasis, Verdi employs throughout the opera a recurring theme to express and symbolize 'quell'amor ch'è palpito Dell'universo intero'. The theme has a certain kinship with Violetta's 'Amami Alfredo' and consequently with a whole series of Verdian themes which express desperate engulfing passion in phrases that spill down through the octave. But what is crucial to this phrase is that it is not a mere spending of naked passion. Verdi suggests too an element of mystery, by the horn note and the minor mode harmonies at 'Misterioso, altero', and he suggests the conscious tasting of the experience of romantic love in the appoggiaturas and *coloratura* at 'croce e delizia' (Ex. 4).

The dramatic and expressive significance of the recurrence of this theme in Violetta's aria has already been discussed, but a word must be said about its use in Act III. It is heard as Violetta reads a letter from Germont. This letter brings the news of Alfredo's return from abroad to seek her pardon, and explains the role which Germont himself has played in bringing about this return. It could be said in fact to act as an emblem of love's triumph over middle-class social and moral prejudice: in its concentrated, symbolic way it reasserts the situation that had been held in tableau form in the *largo* at the close of Act II. It is wholly appropriate that the theme associated with love as a sublime passion should be played in the strings as Violetta reads: for the emotion that fills her heart the while is that which has both raised her up from the demi-monde and enabled her to overcome the prejudices of the bourgeoisie.

The context for the final reprise of the theme at the end of the opera is Violetta's sudden sense of being released from the world of pain; a *Liebestod*-like vision of health, life and beauty beyond the world. It is a problematic concept in the humanist world of Italian opera, and Verdi can hardly be said to have acquired a Wagnerian relevance and artistry in his execution. Strangely enough, though, the machinery for this excursion into metaphysics is a little Wagnerian. Verdi takes the theme that has been associated with the supreme cleansing passion of romantic love and subjects it to a process of giddy, dissolving development. Unlike Wagner, however, Verdi returns to earth in the last bars of the opera, expressing in the elemental *minore* that sense of devastation and loss which the Italian humanist, for all his toying with the *Liebestod* idea, felt to be the essence of tragic drama.

Notes

Chapter 1. Verdi's Italy

1. G. Procacci, *History of the Italian People*, transl. A. Paul (London 1970), p. 272.
2. Santarosa, 'De la révolution piémontaise', cited and transl. D. Mack Smith, *The making of Italy, 1796–1870* (New York 1968), p. 39.
3. Cited C. P. Brand, *Italy and the English Romantics* (Cambridge 1957), p. 201.
4. D'Azeglio, *Things I remember*, transl. E. R. Vincent (London 1966), p. 311.
5. L. A. Garibaldi, *Giuseppe Verdi nelle lettere di Emanuele Muzio ad Antonio Barezzi* (Milan 1931), p. 259.
6. D'Azeglio, *op. cit.*, p. 174.
7. Manzoni, *Sul Romanticismo* (1823).
8. S. A. Nulli, *Shakespeare in Italia* (Milan 1918), p. 170.
9. *I copialettere di Giuseppe Verdi*, ed. G. Cesari and A. Luzio (hereafter cited as '*Copialettere*') (Milan 1913), p. 450.
10. Cited A. Rutherford, *Byron, the critical heritage* (London 1970), pp. 334 and 336.
11. F. De Sanctis, *Storia della letteratura italiana*, 2 vols. (Naples 1870–1), ch. xx.
12. D'Azeglio, *op. cit.*, p. 116.
13. A. Momigliano, cited and transl. A. Colquhoun, *Manzoni and his times* (London 1954), p. 213.
14. D'Azeglio, *op. cit.*, p. 199.
15. *Ibid.*, p. 25.
16. D'Azeglio, *I miei ricordi*, G. Torelli's posthumous completion, 2 vols. (Florence 1867), ch. xxxiii.
17. *Ibid.*
18. Hübner, *Ein Jahr meines Lebens, 1848–49* (Leipzig 1891), p. 122.
19. *Ibid.*, pp. 25–6.
20. Stendhal, *Rome, Naples et Florence en 1817* (Paris 1817), entry for 14 December 1816.
21. D'Azeglio, *Things I remember*, pp. 310–11.
22. A. Ghislanzoni, 'Storia di Milano dal 1836 al 1848' in *In chiave di baritono* (Milan 1882).
23. Stendhal, *op. cit.*, entry for 29 November 1816.
24. Hazlitt, *Notes of a journey through France and Italy* (London 1826).
25. Stendhal, *op. cit.*, entry for 20 November 1816.
26. Nicolai, *Otto Nicolai's Tagebücher nebst biographischen Ergänzungen*, ed. B. Schröder (Leipzig 1892), entry for 21 June 1834.

27. Stendhal, *op cit.*, entry for 3 November 1816.
28. Hayez, *Le mie memorie* (Milan 1890), p. 64.
29. Cited R. Barbiera, *Il salotto della Contessa Maffei*, 11th edn (Florence 1915), p. 98.
30. Lady Blessington, *The idler in Italy*, 3 vols. (London 1839–40), entry for 3 May 1823.
31. Dickens, *Pictures from Italy* (London 1846).
32. *Ibid.*
33. Stendhal, *op. cit.*, entry for 25 September 1816.
34. D'Azeglio, *I miei recordi*, Torelli's posthumous completion, ch. xxxi.

Chapter 2. Theatrical censorship

1. Stendhal, *Rome, Naples et Florence*, entry for 2 April 1817,
2. C. Di Stefano, *La censura teatrale in Italia (1600–1962)* (Bologna 1964), p. 78.
3. *Copialettere*, p. 487.
4. Di Stefano, *op. cit.*, pp. 60–2.
5. *Ibid.*, p. 72.
6. *Ibid.*, p. 71.
7. Gnoli, cited Di Stefano, *op. cit.*, p. 57.

Chapter 3. The operatic experience

1. Mendelssohn, *Briefe aus den Jahren 1830 bis 1847* (Leipzig 1899), p. 117.
2. The memoirs of Hector Berlioz, transl. and ed. D. Cairns (London 1969), p. 209.
3. Dickens, *Pictures from Italy*.
4. Letter of Donizetti to Gaetano Melzi, 31 October 1843: G. Zavadini, *Donizetti: vita – musiche – epistolario* (Bergamo 1948), p. 696.
5. Bellini, *Epistolario*, ed. L. Cambi (Verona 1943), p. 404.
6. 30 September 1851: British Library Add. MS 33965.
7. Spohr, *Selbstbiographie*, 2 vols. (Kassel and Göttingen 1860), II, p. 16.
8. G. Radiciotti, 'Teatro e musica in Roma nel secondo quarto del secolo XIX (1825–50)', *Atti del Congresso Internazionale di Scienze Storiche*, VIII (Rome 1905), pp. 157–8.
9. Stendhal, *Life of Rossini*, transl. R. N. Coe (London 1956), pp. 435–6.
10. Letter to Verdi, 3 January 1853: A. Luzio, *Carteggi verdiani*, 4 vols. (Rome 1935–47), IV, p. 264.
11. Cf. (e.g.) the full details of the performances at La Scala given in G. Tintori, 'Cronologia completa degli spettacoli ...', vol. II of C. Gatti, *Il Teatro alla Scala nella storia e nell'arte*, 2 vols. (Milan 1964).
12. F. Walker, *The man Verdi* (London 1962), p. 63.
13. Spohr, *Selbstbiographie*, I, p. 277.
14. Berlioz, *Memoirs*, p. 196.
15. Stendhal, *Life of Rossini*, p. 436.
16. *Ibid.*, p. 435.
17. Gatti, *Il Teatro alla Scala*, I, p. 44.
18. Cited A. Cametti, *Il teatro di Tordinona* (Tivoli 1938), p. 245.
19. Gatti, *op. cit.*, I, p. 61.

20. Spohr, *op. cit.*, I, p. 301.
21. Stendhal, *Rome, Naples et Florence*, entry for 29 August 1817.
22. Cited Cametti, *op. cit.*, p. 245.
23. Stendhal, *Life of Rossini*, p. 428.
24. Stendhal, *Rome, Naples et Florence*, entry for 12 November 1816.
25. Stendhal, *Life of Rossini*, p. 429.
26. *Storia di Milano* (Fondazione Treccani degli Alfieri), vol. XIV (Milan 1960), p. 761.
27. Stendhal, *Rome, Naples et Florence*, entry for 20 March 1817.
28. Dickens, *Pictures from Italy*.
29. D'Azeglio, *Things I remember*, pp. 288–9.
30. Lady Blessington, *The idler in Italy*, entry for 3 May 1823.
31. Letter of 13 August 1821: G. Meyerbeer, *Briefwechsel und Tagebücher*, ed. H. Becker, vol. I (Berlin 1960), p. 434.
32. Stendhal, *Rome, Naples et Florence*, entry for 2 March 1817.
33. Letter of Bellini to Florimo, April 1828: Bellini, *Epistolario*, p. 76.
34. Spohr, *Selbstbiographie*, II, p. 15.
35. Garibaldi, *Verdi nelle lettere di Muzio*, pp. 344–5.
36. Mendelssohn, *Briefe*, p. 80.
37. Pacini, *Le mie memorie artistiche* (Florence 1865), p. 43n.
38. Nicolai, *Tagebücher*, entry for 14 February 1840.
39. Zavadini, *Donizetti*, p. 343.
40. G. De Napoli, *La triade melodrammatica altamurana* (Milan 1934), p. 223: cited and transl. A. G. Mooney, 'An assessment of Mercadante's contribution to the development of Italian opera', unpublished M.Mus. dissertation, Edinburgh 1970.
41. Spohr, *op. cit.*, I, p. 276.
42. Mendelssohn, *op. cit.*, p. 116.
43. Berlioz, *Memoirs*, p. 196.
44. Lichtenthal, *Dizionario e biografia della musica* (Milan 1826), entry 'Capo d'orchestra'.
45. F. Abbiati, *Giuseppe Verdi*, 4 vols. (Milan 1959), I, pp. 467–8.
46. Spohr, *op. cit.*, I, p. 276.
47. O. Tiby, *Il Real Teatro Carolino e l'ottocento musicale palermitano* (Florence 1957), p. 89.
48. G. Bottevi, 'Cenni storici', *Il Comunale di Trieste* (Udine 1962), p. 80.
49. Spohr, *op. cit.*, I, p. 308.
50. Berlioz, *op. cit.*, p. 196.
51. Mendelssohn, *op. cit.*, p. 116.
52. Berlioz, *op. cit.*, p. 196.
53. Spohr, *op. cit.*, II, p. 13.
54. *Ibid.*, I, p. 276.
55. Berlioz, *op cit.*, p. 186.
56. Spohr, *op. cit.*, I, p. 330.
57. Mendelssohn, *op. cit.*, p. 116.
58. Berlioz, *op. cit.*, p. 186.
59. Cited Radiciotti, 'Teatro e musica in Roma', p. 160.
60. Stendhal, *Life of Rossini*, p. 327.
61. H. F. Chorley, *Thirty years' musical recollections* (London 1862), I, p. 73.

62. Cited and transl. H. Weinstock, *Vincenzo Bellini, his life and his operas* (London 1971), p. 99.
63. Les frères Escudier, *Rossini, sa vie et ses oeuvres* (Paris 1854), p. 225.
64. Spohr, *op. cit.*, I, p. 306.
65. Walker, *The man Verdi*, p. 88.
66. *Ibid.*, p. 65.
67. Meyerbeer, *Briefwechsel und Tagebücher*, I, p. 547.
68. Hazlitt, *Notes of a journey through France and Italy*.
69. Spohr, *op. cit.*, I, p. 279.
70. Garibaldi, *Verdi nelle lettere di Muzio*, p. 329.
71. Cited L. Gamberini, *La vita musicale europea del 1800, Archivio Musicale Genovese, I: Introduzione: Opera lirica e musica strumentale; Documente e testimonianze* (Siena 1978), p. 79.
72. *Copialettere*, p. 57.
73. Tiby, *El Real Teatro Carolino*, p. 91.
74. Berlioz, *Memoirs*, p. 160.
75. *Ibid.*, p. 186.
76. *Ibid.*, p. 196.
77. Cited M. Rinaldi, *Felice Romani, dal melodramma classico al melodramma romantico* (Rome 1965), p. 196.
78. Meyerbeer, *op. cit.*, I, p. 325.
79. Gatti, *Il Teatro alla Scala*, I, p. 24.
80. Stendhal, *Life of Rossini*, p. 438–9.
81. *Ibid.*, p. 438.
82. Gounod, *Autobiographical reminiscences*, transl. W. Hely Hutchinson (London 1896), p. 76.
83. Gatti, *op. cit.*, I, p. 120.
84. Stendhal, *Rome, Naples et Florence*, entry for 22 November 1816.
85. Dickens, *Pictures from Italy*.
86. Ghislanzoni, 'Storia di Milano'.
87. Berlioz, *Memoirs*, p. 208.
88. Meyerbeer, *Briefwechsel und Tagebücher*, I, p. 361.
89. *Ibid.*, p. 578.
90. Mendelssohn, *Briefe*, pp. 80–1.
91. Dickens, *op. cit.*
92. Ghislanzoni, *op. cit.*
93. Glinka, *Memoirs*, transl. R. B. Mudge (Norman, Oklahoma 1963), p. 61 (I have substituted 'maestro' for Mudge's 'conductor').
94. Heine, *Reisebilder, III: Italien 1828* (Hamburg 1830), 'Eine Reise von München nach Genua', XXVII.

Chapter 4. Dramatic principles and musical form in early *ottocento* opera

1. Bellini, *Epistolario*, p. 400.
2. Mazzini, 'Filosofia di musica', *Edizione nazionale degli scritti di Giuseppe Mazzini*, VIII (Imola 1910), pp. 136–7.
3. Michotte, 'Souvenirs personnels: La visite de Wagner à Rossini', cited F. Lippmann, *Vincenzo Bellini und die italienische Opera Seria seiner Zeit (Analecta Musicologica, VI)* (Cologne and Vienna 1969), p. 91.

4. Ritorni, *Ammaestramenti alla composizione di ogni poema e d'ogni opera appartenente alla musica* (Milan 1841), I, paragraph XLVI.
5. Cited M. F. Robinson, *Naples and Neapolitan opera* (Oxford 1972), p. 60.
6. Stendhal, *Life of Rossini*, p. 106.
7. G. B. Rinuccini, *Sulla musica e sulla poesia melodrammatica italiana del secolo XIX* (Lucca 1843), p. 27.
8. Cited Lippmann, *op. cit.*, p. 34.
9. *Ibid.*, p. 47.
10. Ritorni, *op. cit.*, I, paragraphs XLI and XLII.
11. A. Basevi, *Studio sulle opere di Giuseppe Verdi* (Florence 1859), pp. 114–15.
12. Mazzini, *op. cit.*, p. 127.
13. Ritorni, *op. cit.*, I, paragraph LIX.
14. Mazzini, *op. cit.*, p. 128.
15. Bellini, *Epistolario*, p. 400.
16. Cited Lippmann, *op. cit.*, p. 46.
17. Mazzini, *op. cit.*, p. 156.
18. Letter of 17 July 1849: *Copialettere*, p. 473.
19. Ritorni, *op. cit.*, I, paragraph LXI.
20. The phrase is Pacini's, in *Le mie memorie artistiche*, p. 8.
21. Letter to Pacini, 27 January 1866: cited Weinstock, *Rossini: a biography* (New York and London 1968), p. 471.
22. Pacini, *op. cit.*, pp. 64–5.
23. Stendhal, *Life of Rossini*, p. 53 n. 1.
24. Ritorni, *op. cit.*, I, paragraph LIII.
25. *Ibid.*, I, paragraphs LIV and LV.
26. E. Branca, *Felice Romani ed i più riputati maestri di musica del suo tempo*, cited Weinstock, *Bellini*, p. 38.
27. Stendhal, *Life of Rossini*, p. 112.
28. Abbiati, *Verdi*, I, p. 606.
29. R. Schumann, 'Neue Sonaten für das Pianoforte', *Gesammelte Schriften über Musik und Musiker* (Leipzig 1914), II, p. 14.
30. Spohr, *Selbstbiographie*, I, p. 338.
31. Mendelssohn, *Briefe*, p. 79.
32. Spohr, *op. cit.*, I, pp. 281–2.
33. 'Einige Bermerkungen über die italienischen Opern' by 'a German Singer', *Allgemeine Musikalische Zeitung*, XLVIII (1846), columns 433f.
34. M. Nordio, *Verdi e la Fenice* (Venice 1951), p. 40.
35. Cited Bellini, *Epistolario*, pp. 293–4.
36. F. Walker, 'Mercadante', *Grove's dictionary of music and musicians*, 5th edn (London 1954).
37. Bellini, *Epistolario*, p. 439.
38. Cited and transl. Weinstock, *Bellini*, p. 66.
39. *Ibid.*
40. Ritorni, *Ammaestramenti*, I, paragraph LXVII.
41. Mazzini, 'Filosofia di musica', pp. 158–9n.
42. *Ibid.*, p. 120.

Chapter 5. Launching a career

1. Milan, Museo Teatrale alla Scala.
2. A. Pougin, *Giuseppe Verdi, vita aneddotica*, with notes and additions by 'Folchetto' (Jacopo Capponi) (Milan 1881), p. 41.
3. Cf. Walker, *The man Verdi*, pp. 24–5.
4. Letter of 28 July 1835: cited and transl. Walker, *op. cit.*, p. 25.
5. C. Sartori, '*Rocester*, la prima opera di Verdi', *Rivista Musicale Italiana*, XLIII (1939), p. 99.
6. *Ibid.*, p. 100.
7. C. Gatti, *Verdi*, 2 vols. (Milan 1931), I, p. 135.
8. Sartori, *op. cit.*, p. 100.
9. Cited and transl. Walker, *op. cit.*, pp. 26–7.
10. Pougin, *op. cit.*, p. 41.
11. Walker, *op. cit.*, p. 24.
12. D. Lawton and D. Rosen, 'Verdi's non-definitive revisions: the early operas', *Atti del Terzo Congresso Internazionale di Studi Verdiani* (Parma 1974), p. 192–4.
13. Cf. letter of 21 September 1837, p. 93 above.
14. Walker, *op. cit.*, p. 28.
15. Sartori, *op. cit.*, p. 103.
16. Pougin, *op. cit.*, p. 26 n. 2.
17. Cited Gatti, *Verdi*, I, pp. 150–1.
18. Walker, *op cit.*, p. 27.
19. Pougin, *op cit.*, p. 41.
20. *Ibid.*, p. 42.
21. *Ibid.*, p. 42.
22. A. Soffredini, *Le opere di Verdi, studio critico analitico* (Milan 1901), p. 23.
23. A. Loewenberg, *Annals of opera, 1597–1940* (Cambridge 1943), p. 406.
24. Transl. J. Budden, *The operas of Verdi*, I, From 'Oberto' to 'Rigoletto' (London 1973), p. 71.
25. Rinaldi, *Felice Romani*, p. 392.
26. Cited and transl. Walker, *op cit.*, p. 33.
27. Abbiati, *Verdi*, I, p. 347.
28. *Cenni storici intorno alle lettere, invenzioni, arti, al commercio ed agli spettacoli teatrali*, Bologna, no. 865, vol. XXXIV, 17 September 1840.
29. *Copialettere*, pp. 556–7.
30. Transl. Walker, *op. cit.*, p. 34.
31. Tintori, 'Cronologia completa'.
32. Abbiati, *op. cit.*, I, p. 359.
33. To Molossi: cited Abbiati, *op. cit.*, I, p. 368.
34. Transl. Walker, *op. cit.*, pp. 34–5.
35. Lessona, *Volere è potere*, 2nd edn (Florence 1869), pp. 297–8.
36. Letter to Arrivabene, 7 March 1874.
37. Cavicchi, 'Verdi e Solera. Considerazioni sulla collaborazione per *Nabucco*', *Atti del Primo Congresso Internazionale di Studi Verdiani* (Parma 1969). Budden, *The operas of Verdi*, I, p. 92.
38. Letter to Brenna, 15 November 1843: quoted Nordio, *Verdi e la Fenice*, p. 24.

39. For a sceptical analysis of this anecdote see Cavicchi, *op. cit.*
40. Transl. Walker, *op. cit.*, p. 35.
41. Cited and transl. *ibid.*, pp. 166–7.
42. Transl. *ibid.*, p. 94.
43. Transl. *ibid.*, p. 92.
44. Lessona, *op cit.*, p. 299.
45. Walker, *op cit.*, p. 169.
46. Abbiati, *Verdi*, I, p. 446.
47. Quoted *ibid.*
48. *Ibid.*, I, p. 431.
49. *Ibid.*
50. Luzio, *Carteggi verdiani*, IV, p. 78.
51. Transl. Walker, *op. cit.*, pp. 173–4.

Chapter 6. The genesis of an opera – *Ernani*

1. Letter of 11 June 1843: *Copialettere*, p. 423.
2. Sandro Della Libera (ed.), '*Ernani* di G. Verdi, Cronologia': typescript, Archive of the Teatro La Fenice, Venice (hereafter cited as '*Ernani* Cronologia').
3. Letter of 9 April 1843: Abbiati, *Verdi*, I, p. 463.
4. Letter of 19 April 1843: '*Ernani* Cronologia'.
5. Letter of 28 April 1843: Abbiati, *op. cit.*, I, pp. 464–5.
6. Undated letter: *ibid.*, p. 463–4.
7. Undated letter: *ibid.*, p. 464.
8. '*Ernani* Cronologia'.
9. Abbiati, *op. cit.*, I, p. 465.
10. '*Ernani* Cronologia'.
11. Letter of 25 May 1845: Abbiati, *op. cit.*, I, pp. 465–6.
12. '*Ernani* Cronologia'.
13. *Ibid.*
14. Letter of 11 June 1843: Abbiati, *op. cit.*, I, p. 469.
15. '*Ernani* Cronologia'.
16. A. Benedetti, *Le traduzioni italiane da Walter Scott e i loro anglicismi* (Florence 1974).
17. Letter of 16 June 1843: Abbiati, *op. cit.*, I, p. 470.
18. *Ibid.*
19. '*Ernani* Cronologia'.
20. Letter of 26 June 1843: Abbiati, *op. cit.*, I, pp. 470–1.
21. '*Ernani* Cronologia'.
22. Pacini, *Le mie memorie artistiche*, p. 101.
23. Letter of 11 August 1843: Abbiati, *op. cit.*, I, pp. 471–2.
24. '*Ernani* Cronologia'.
25. *Ibid.*
26. Letter of 19 August 1843: Abbiati, *op. cit.*, I, p. 472.
27. '*Ernani* Cronologia'.
28. *Ibid.*
29. Letter of 27 August 1843: Abbiati, *op. cit.*, I, pp. 472–3.
30. '*Ernani* Cronologia'.
31. Letter of 5 September 1843: Abbiati, *op. cit.*, I, pp. 473–4.

32. 'Ernani Cronologia', 17 September 1843.
33. *Ibid.*
34. *Ibid.*, 22 September 1843.
35. *Ibid.*
36. *Ibid.*, 26 September 1843.
37. *Ibid.*, 29 September 1843.
38. Letter of 2 October 1843: Abbiati, *op. cit.*, I, pp. 474–5.
39. 'Ernani Cronologia'.
40. Letter of 10 October 1843: Abbiati, *op. cit.*, I, pp. 475–6.
41. 'Ernani Cronologia'.
42. *Ibid.*, 23 October 1843.
43. *Ibid.*
44. *Ibid.*
45. Letter of 10 November 1843: cited and transl. Budden, *The operas of Verdi*, I, p. 144.
46. 'Ernani Cronologia'.
47. Abbiati, *Verdi*, I, pp. 476–7.
48. 'Ernani Cronologia'.
49. *Ibid.*
50. Letter of 30 November 1843; Abbiati, *op. cit.*, I, p. 478.
51. Letter of 12 December 1843; *ibid.*, pp. 478–9.
52. *Copialettere*, pp. 424–5.
53. 'Ernani Cronologia'.
54. 1 January 1844: *ibid.*
55. Cited and transl. Budden, *op. cit.*, p. 145.
56. Harvard University Library, Theatre Collection.
57. Abbiati, *op cit.*, I, pp. 481–2.
58. Cf. note from Brenna to Mocenigo of 31 January; cited Budden, *op. cit.*, p. 146.
59. 'Ernani Cronologia'.
60. *Ibid.*
61. *Ibid.*
62. *Ibid.*
63. *Ibid.*
64. 21 February 1844, *ibid.*
65. *Ibid.*
66. Zürich, Max Reis Collection.
67. Abbiati, *op. cit.*, I, p. 497.
68. *Ibid.*
69. *Ibid.*, p. 482.
70. *Ibid.*
71. *Ibid.*, pp. 497–8.
72. *Ibid.*, p. 498.
73. *Ibid.*
74. Letter of 15 March 1844: Abbiati, *op. cit.*, I, p. 483.
75. *Ibid.*, p. 499.

Chapter 7. Two overcrowded years

1. *Copialettere*, p. 425.

2. Letter of 18 April; Abbiati, *Verdi*, I, p. 513.
3. *Ibid.*, p. 516.
4. *Ibid.*, p. 514.
5. *Ibid.*, p. 515.
6. Garibaldi, *Verdi nelle lettere di Muzio*, p. 162.
7. *Ibid.*, p. 166.
8. Letter of 24 June 1844: *ibid.*, p. 167.
9. L. Escudier, *Mes souvenirs* (Paris 1863), pp. 91–2.
10. Letter of 28 August 1844 to Giuseppina Appiani: *Copialettere*, p. 427.
11. *Ibid*, p. 8.
12. Abbiati, *op. cit.*, I, p. 521.
13. *Ibid.*
14. *Ibid.*, p. 522.
15. Cited and transl. Walker, *The man Verdi*, p. 124.
16. Letter of 16 November 1844: Garibaldi, *Op. cit.*, pp. 173–4.
17. *Copialettere*, pp. 427–8.
18. Letter of 2 December 1843: *Copialettere*, p. 428.
19. Harvard University Library, Theatre Collection.
20. *Copialettere*, p. 428.
21. Letter of September 1844; Abbiati, *op. cit.*, I, p. 534.
22. Garibaldi, *op. cit.*, p. 175.
23. Garibaldi, *op cit.*, p. 178.
24. *Ibid.*, p. 179.
25. *Ibid.*, p. 180.
26. Letter of 12 January 1845: *ibid.*, p. 181.
27. Letters of 22 and 29 December 1844: *ibid.*, pp. 177–9.
28. *Ibid.*, p. 179.
29. *Ibid.*, p. 183.
30. Luzio, *Carteggi verdiani*, IV, p. 80.
31. Garibaldi, *op. cit.*, p. 212.
32. *Ibid.*, p. 225.
33. Letter of 26 October 1846: *ibid.*, pp. 286–7.
34. *Ibid.*, p. 303.
35. *Copialettere*, pp. 34–5.
36. Luzio, *op. cit.*, IV, p. 80.
37. Letter of 27 February 1845: Garibaldi, *op cit.*, p. 184.
38. *Ibid.*, pp. 195 and 198.
39. Letter of 17 March 1845: *ibid.* p. 191, transl. Walker, *The man Verdi*, p. 131.
40. Letter of 21 March 1844: *Copialettere*, pp. 3–4.
41. Letter of 3 July 1844: *ibid.*, pp. 5–6.
42. *Ibid.*, p. 429.
43. *Ibid.*, p. 430.
44. Garibaldi, *op. cit.*, p. 195.
45. Letter of 14 April 1845: *ibid.*, pp. 195–6.
46. Letter of 17 April 1845: *ibid.*, p. 196.
47. Letter of 18 April 1845: *Copialettere*, pp. 8–9.
48. Letter of 21 April 1845: Garibaldi, *op. cit.*, pp. 197–8.
49. Transl. Walker, *op. cit.*,p. 133.
50. *Copialettere*, p. 9.

51. *Ibid.*, p. 10.
52. Letter of 28 April 1845: Garibaldi, *op. cit.*, p. 199, transl. Walker, *op. cit.*, p. 133.
53. Letter of 10 May 1845: *Copialettere*, pp. 429–30.
54. *Ibid.*, p. 10.
55. *Ibid.*, p. 11.
56. Letter of 14 May 1845: *ibid.*, pp. 11–12.
57. Garibaldi, *op. cit.*, pp. 200–2.
58. *Ibid.*, p. 202.
59. Letter of 29 May 1845: *Copialettere*, p. 12.
60. Letter of 2 June 1845: *ibid.*, p. 13.
61. *Ibid.*, pp. 13–14.
62. Letter of 9 June 1845: Garibaldi, *op. cit.*, pp. 203–4.
63. Letter of 30 June 1845: *ibid.*, p. 205.
64. Cited and transl. Walker, *op. cit.*, p. 135.
65. Letter of 12 July 1845: *Copialettere*, p. 431.
66. Letter of 16 July 1845: Abbiati, *op. cit.*, I, p. 564
67. Cited and transl. Walker, *op. cit.*, p. 138.
68. Letter of 23 November 1848: *Copialettere*, p. 58.
69. Letter of 30 July 1845: *ibid.*, p. 431.
70. Letter of Muzio to Barezzi, 13 September [August?] 1845: Garibaldi, *op. cit.*, p. 217.
71. Abbiati, *op. cit.*, I, pp. 563–4.
72. *Copialettere*, p. 431.
73. Garibaldi, *op. cit.*, p. 215.
74. *Ibid.*, p. 217.
75. Abbiati, *op. cit.*, I, p. 566.
76. *Ibid.*, p. 567.
77. Cf. Walker, *op. cit.*, pp. 138–9.
78. Letter of 5 November 1845: *Copialettere*, p. 432.
79. *Ibid.*
80. Letter of 21 December 1843: M. Nordio, *Verdi e la Fenice*, p. 24.
81. *Ibid.*, p. 31.
82. Abbiati, *op. cit.*, I, p. 515.
83. *Copialettere*, p. 438.
84. Letter of 12 January 1845: Garibaldi, *op. cit.*, p. 181.
85. Abbiati, *op. cit.*, I, pp. 553–4.
86. *Ibid.*, p. 585.
87. *Ibid.*, I, pp. 579–80. Both Abbiati and the *Copialettere* place this letter in 1844, but it is difficult to see how it could antedate the two letters to Piave already quoted. Muzio's letters to Barezzi also suggest that *Attila* was a subject determined upon in April 1845 (Garibaldi, *op. cit.*, p. 199).
88. *Copialettere*, p. 431, n.3.
89. Garibaldi, *op. cit.*, p. 215.
90. *Ibid.*, transl. Walker, *op. cit.*, p. 142.
91. *Copialettere*, p. 439. The date given, 12 September 1845, must however be wrong. By then Verdi was in Busseto and composition had been commenced.
92. Abbiati, *op. cit.*, I, pp. 586–7.

93. Cited and transl. Walker, *op. cit.*, pp. 180–1.
94. *Copialettere*, p. 432.
95. *Copialettere*, p. 439.
96. Abbiati, *op. cit.*, I, pp. 590–2.
97. Cited and transl. Walker, *op. cit.*, p. 113.
98. Letter to Clarina Maffei, 3 April 1861: cited Luzio, *Carteggi verdiani*, IV, pp. 246–7.
99. *Copialettere*, p. 440: a slightly fuller version is cited by Abbiati, *op. cit.*, I, pp. 593–4.
100. Luzio, *op. cit.*, p. 245.
101. Letter to Clarina Maffei: Abbiati, *op. cit.*, I, p. 599.
102. *Ibid.*
103. *Copialettere*, p. 441.
104. Abbiati, *op. cit.*, I, p. 601.
105. Collezione Eredi Maffei, Milan-Chiaro.
106. Letter to Piave, 14 January 1848: Nordio, *Verdi e la Fenice*, p. 33.
107. Letter to Marzari, 5 December 1850: *Copialettere*, p. 108.
108. Abbiati, *op. cit.*, I, pp. 606–7.
109. Cited Nordio, *op. cit.*, pp. 33–4.
110. *Ibid.*

Chapter 8. Verdi the idealist – the Florence *Macbeth*

1. Abbiati, *Verdi*, I, p. 515.
2. *Ibid.*, p. 636.
3. Walker, *The man Verdi*, p. 148.
4. Garibaldi, *Verdi nelle lettere di Muzio*, p. 252.
5. Abbiati, *op. cit.*, I, p. 639.
6. Garibaldi, *op. cit.*, p. 258.
7. *Copialettere*, pp. 25–6.
8. Letter of 25 August 1846: Siena, Archivio dell'Accademia Musicale Chigiana.
9. Letter of 2 September 1846: Abbiati, *op. cit.*, I, p. 642.
10. Rovigo, Accademia dei Concordi.
11. The sketch was sent to Piave on 5 September, Lanari's assent was received only on the 10th (Garibaldi, *op. cit.*, p. 269).
12. Letter of 15 October 1846: *ibid.*, p. 283.
13. Letter of 11 April 1857: *Copialettere*, p. 444.
14. Abbiati, *op. cit.*, I, p. 643.
15. Letter of 22 September 1846: *ibid.*, pp. 644–5.
16. Garibaldi, *op. cit.*, p. 278.
17. Letter of 15 October: Abbiati, *op. cit.*, I, pp. 650–1.
18. *Ibid.*, p. 651.
19. Letter of 28 October 1846: *Copialettere*, pp. 444–5.
20. Letter of 2 November 1846: *ibid.*, p. 445.
21. *Ibid.*, p. 446.
22. Abbiati, *op. cit.*, I, p. 651.
23. *Ibid.*, p. 652.
24. *Ibid.*, pp. 656–8.
25. *Ibid.*, p. 667.
26. This is a continuation of the letter of 10 December: *ibid.*, p. 668.

27. *Ibid.*, pp. 668–72.
28. *Ibid.*, p. 675.
29. Garibaldi, *Verdi nelle lettere di Muzio*, p. 285.
30. Letter of 5 November 1846: Abbiati, *op. cit.*, I, p. 654.
31. Garibaldi, *op. cit.*, p. 300.
32. *Ibid.*, pp. 302–3.
33. British Library Add. MS. 33965.
34. Letter of 24 January 1847: Abbiati, *op. cit.*, I, pp. 676–7.
35. *Copialettere*, p. 444.
36. Garibaldi, *op. cit.*, pp. 289–90.
37. Abbiati, *op. cit.*, I, p. 652.
38. Letter of 28 January 1847: Garibaldi, *op. cit.*, p. 308.
39. *Copialettere*, pp. 34–5.
40. *Ibid.*, pp. 446–7.
41. *Ibid.*, pp. 447–8.
42. Letter of 27 January 1847: 'Jarro', *Memorie d'un impresario fiorentino* (Florence 1892), p. 47.
43. Undated letter: *Copialettere*, p. 448.
44. Giulia Cova Varesi, 'L'interpretazione di *Macbeth*', *Nuova Antologia*, CCCLXIV (1932), pp. 437–9.
45. *Copialettere*, p. 449.
46. Garibaldi, *op. cit.*, p. 311.
47. Cited G. Monaldi, *Verdi* (Stuttgart and Leipzig 1898), p. 82–4.
48. Cited Abbiati, *Verdi*, I, p. 687.
49. Letter of 21 March 1847: Collezione Eredi Maffei.
50. Abbiati, *op. cit.*, I, p. 689.
51. Monaldi, *op. cit.*, pp. 84–5.
52. Garibaldi, *op. cit.*, pp. 312–13.
53. Letter of 19 March 1847: Abbiati, *op. cit.*, I, pp. 690–1.
54. Letter of 27 March 1847: *ibid.*, p. 691.
55. *Copialettere*, p. 451.
56. *Ibid.*, pp. 59–60.
57. *Ibid.*, pp. 61–2.

Chapter 9. Opera as a business

1. Luzio, *Carteggi verdiani*, IV, p. 264.
2. Garibaldi, *Verdi nelle lettere di Muzio*, p. 227
3. Letter of 29 October 1845: *ibid.*, p. 232.
4. *Copialettere*, p. 16.
5. Abbiati, *Verdi*, I, pp. 598–9.
6. *Ibid.*, p. 591.
7. B. Lumley, *Reminiscences of the Italian opera* (London 1864), p. 142.
8. Undated letter: Abbiati, *op. cit.*, I, pp. 599–600.
9. Letter of 24 February 1846: *ibid.*, p. 601.
10. 6 April 1846: *Copialettere*, p. 19.
11. Letter of 9 April 1846: *ibid.*,, pp. 19–20.
12. Letter of 14 April 1846: *ibid.*, p. 20.
13. Letter of 13 May 1846: *ibid.* pp. 21–2.
14. Letter of 22 May 1846: *ibid.*, p. 22.

15. Maffei's preface to the printed libretto.
16. *Copialettere*, p. 32.
17. Garibaldi, *Verdi nelle lettere di Muzio*, p. 268.
18. *Ibid.*, p. 274.
19. Cf. *ibid.*, p. 283.
20. Muzio to Barezzi, 4 October 1846: *ibid.*, p. 279.
21. *Copialettere*, p. 30.
22. *Ibid.*, p. 31.
23. Letter of 3 December 1846: *ibid.*, pp. 32–3.
24. Letter of 4 December 1846: *ibid.*, p. 33–4.
25. Lumley, *Reminiscences*, p. 192.
26. Letter of 12 January 1847: British Library Add. MS 33965.
27. *Copialettere*, p. 32–3, n. 2.
28. Abbiati, *Verdi*, I, pp. 705–6.
29. Muzio to Barezzi: Garibaldi, *op. cit.*, p. 314.
30. *Ibid.*, p. 318.
31. Cf. Muzio's letters of 22 April and undated: *ibid.*, pp. 317 and 319.
32. *Copialettere*, p. 35.
33. *Ibid.*, pp. 35–6.
34. Letter of 23 February 1847: Abbiati, *op. cit.*, I, pp. 709–10.
35. *Ibid.*, p. 700.
36. Garibaldi, *op. cit.*, p. 245.
37. *Ibid.*, pp. 321–5.
38. *Ibid.*, pp. 325–6.
39. *Copialettere*, p. 457.
40. Muzio to Barezzi, 16 June 1847: Garibaldi, *op. cit.*, p. 328.
41. *Ibid.*, p. 329.
42. *Ibid.*, p. 334.
43. Lumley, *Reminiscences*, p. 188.
44. Garibaldi, *op. cit.*, p. 335.
45. Letter of 27 June 1847: *Copialettere*, pp. 457–8.
46. Letter of 17 July 1847: *ibid.*, pp. 458–9.
47. Garibaldi, *op cit.*, pp. 338–9.
48. Letter of 18 July 1847: *ibid.*, p. 341.
49. *Ibid.*, pp. 343–4.
50. Muzio to Barezzi, letter of 23 July 1847: *ibid.*, pp. 344–9.
51. Letter of 23 August 1847: *ibid.*, p. 352.
52. *Athenaeum*, nos. 1030–1, 24 and 31 July 1847.
53. Lumley, *Reminiscences*, p. 193.
54. Letter to Emilia Moresini, 30 July 1847: *Copialettere*, pp. 460–1.
55. *Ibid.*, pp. 42–3.
56. *Ibid.*, pp. 44.
57. Letter of 8 August 1847: Garibaldi, *op. cit.*, p. 350.
58. *Ibid.*, p. 234.
59. *Ibid.*, p. 353.
60. Letter of 22 August: *Copialettere*, p. 462.
61. Letter of 6 September 1847: Collezione Eredi Maffei.
62. Cited and transl. Budden, *The operas of Verdi*, pp. 342–3.
63. U. Günther, 'Documents inconnus concernant les relations de Verdi avec l'Opéra de Paris', *Atti del Terzo Congresso Internazionale di Studi*

Verdiani (Parma 1974), pp. 566–7.
64. *Copialettere*, p. 464.
65. Collezione Eredi Maffei.
66. Garibaldi, *Verdi nelle lettere di Muzio*, p. 358.
67. *Histoire de l'art dramatique en France depuis vingt-cinq ans*, 5e série (Paris 1847) 29 November 1847.
68. *Copialettere*, pp. 44–5.
69. Letter of 4 November 1847: Abbiati, *Verdi*, I, p. 734.
70. *Copialettere*, pp. 45–6.
71. Abbiati, *op. cit.*, I, pp. 734–5.
72. *Copialettere*, pp. 87–93.
73. *Ibid.*, pp. 93–4.
74. Letter of 5 January 1851: *ibid.*, p. 112.
75. Letter of 6 June 1843: 'Ernani Cronologia'.
76. Letter of 27 August 1846: Rovigo, Accademia die Concordi.
77. *Copialettere*, p. 461.
78. Letter of 2 August 1847: *ibid.*, p. 42.
79. Letter of 22 September 1847: *ibid.*, p. 461.
80. *Ibid.*, pp. 461–2.
81. Cited and transl. Walker, *The man Verdi*, p. 185.
82. *Ibid.*
83. Garibaldi, *Verdi nelle lettere di Muzio*, p. 361.
84. *Copialettere*, pp. 46–7.
85. *Ibid.*, p. 47.
86. Abbiati, *Verdi*, I, p. 764.

Chapter 10. Collaboration with Cammarano

1. *Copialettere*, pp. 14–15.
2. Budden, *The operas of Verdi*, I, p. 389.
3. *Copialettere*, p. 26.
4. Letter of 4 July 1846: *ibid.*, p. 23.
5. Letter of 31 August 1846: *ibid.*, pp. 26–7.
6. *Ibid.*, p. 27.
7. *Ibid.*, p. 38.
8. Abbiati, *Verdi*, I, p. 752–3.
9. Letter of 19 March 1846: cited Budden, *op. cit.*, p. 389.
10. Garibaldi, *Verdi nelle lettere di Muzio*, p. 361.
11. Letter of 20 April 1848: Abbiati, *op. cit.*, I, pp. 746–7.
12. *Copialettere*, p. 53, n.1.
13. Letter of 24 August 1848: *Ibid.*, pp. 49–50.
14. *Ibid.*, p. 52.
15. Letter of 23 July 1848: Abbiati, *op. cit.*, I, pp. 751–2.
16. Letter of 24 August 1848: *Copialettere*, p. 51.
17. Letter of 15 September 1848: *ibid.*, p. 52.
18. *Ibid.*, pp. 53–4.
19. Letter of 21 September 1848: *ibid.*, p. 54.
20. Abbiati, *op. cit.*, I, p. 769.
21. *Copialettere*, p. 55.
22. *Ibid.*, p. 55–6.

23. Abbiati, *op. cit.*, I, p. 771–2.
24. *Ibid.*, pp. 772–3.
25. *Copialettere*, pp. 60–1.
26. Brescia, Biblioteca Quiriniana.
27. *Copialettere*, p. 469.
28. Letter of 21 November 1848: Abbiati, *op. cit.*, I, pp. 775–6.
29. Letter of 14 December 1848: *Copialettere*, p. 64, n. 1.
30. Letter of 6 January 1849: Abbiati, *op. cit.*, I, p. 781.
31. *Ibid.*, p. 782.
32. *Ibid.*, p. 781.
33. Garibaldi, *Verdi nelle lettere di Muzio*, p. 362.
34. Cited and transl. Budden, *The operas of Verdi*, I, p. 393.
35. Letter of 19 September 1857: *Copialettere*, p. 562.
36. *Ibid.*, pp. 55–6.
37. *Ibid.*, pp. 56–7.
38. Abbiati, *op. cit.*, I, p. 770.
39. *Ibid.*, p. 774.
40. Luzio, *Carteggi verdiani*, IV, pp. 217ff.
41. Letter of 23 November 1848: Abbiati, *op. cit.*, I, p. 777.
42. *Ibid.*, p. 781.
43. Letter of 18 January 1849: *ibid.*
44. *Copialettere*, p. 69.
45. Abbiati, *op. cit.*, II, pp. 4–7.
46. *Copialettere*, pp. 71–2.
47. Abbiati, *op. cit.*, I, p. 772.
48. *Copialettere*, p. 58.
49. Letter of 12 December 1848: Abbiati, *op. cit.*, I, p. 779.
50. *Copialettere*, p. 69.
51. Bologna, Accademia Filarmonica.
52. *Copialettere*, p. 69.
53. Letter of 8 March 1849: *ibid.*, n. 2.
54. *Ibid.*, p. 76.
55. Reprinted Abbiati, *op. cit.*, II, pp. 10–16.
56. Letter of 17 May 1848: *Copialettere*, pp. 470–2.
57. *Ibid.*, pp. 78–80.
58. *Ibid.*, p. 472.
59. *Ibid.*, pp. 473–4; Abbiati, *op. cit.*, II, pp. 20–2.
60. Letter of 1 June 1849: *Copialettere*, p. 80.
61. Letter of 15 June 1849: *ibid.*, p. 82.
62. *Ibid.*, p. 83.
63. *Ibid.*, n. 1.
64. Letter of 23 July 1849: *ibid.*, p. 475.
65. Letter of 28 July 1849: *ibid.*, p. 476.
66. *Ibid.*, p. 477.
67. Letter of 13 August 1849: Abbiati, *op. cit.*, II, pp. 26–7.
68. Walker, *The man Verdi*, p. 198.
69. *Copialettere*, pp. 84–5.
70. Abbiati, *op. cit.*, II, pp. 35–6.
71. *Ibid.*, pp. 36–7.
72. Letter of 17 October 1849: *ibid.*, p. 37–8.

73. Marchesi, 'Gli anni del *Rigoletto'*, *Bollettino dell'Istituto di Studi Verdiani*, III.8 (Parma 1973), pp. 849f.
74. *Ibid.*, p. 857.
75. *Copialettere*, pp. 85–6.
76. A Pougin, *Verdi, an anecdotic history*, English edn (London 1887), p. 126.
77. Cf. Walker, *op. cit.*, pp. 198–9.
78. Garibaldi, *Verdi nelle lettere di Muzio*, p. 363.
79. Abbiati, *op. cit.*, I, p. 591.
80. Abbiati, *op. cit.*, II, pp. 47–8.
81. *Ibid.*, p. 49.
82. *Copialettere*, p. 478. The full text of the scenario follows on p. 478–82. An English translation is given in Osborne, *The letters of Verdi* (London 1971), p. 70–3.
83. Abbiati, *op. cit.*, II, pp. 56–7.
84. Letter of 18 June 1850: Marchesi, 'Gli anni del *Rigoletto'*, p. 860.
85. *Copialettere*, pp. 482–3.
86. Letter of 19 July 1852: Naples, Museo di San Martino.

Chapter 11. Bouts with the censor

1. Letter of 28 December 1849: Abbiati, *Verdi*, II, p. 47.
2. *Copialettere*, pp. 93–4.
3. Abbiati, *op. cit.*, II, p. 60.
4. *Ibid.*, p. 48.
5. Letter of 28 April 1850: *ibid.*, pp. 59–60.
6. *Ibid.*, p. 62.
7. *Ibid.*, p. 65.
8. *Copialettere*, p. 106.
9. Letter of 28 April 1850: Abbiati, *op. cit.*, II, p. 60.
10. *Ibid.*, p. 66.
11. *Ibid.*, p. 65.
12. *Ibid.*, p. 67.
13. *Ibid.*, pp. 69–70.
14. *Ibid.*, p. 72.
15. 'Stiffelio', *Quaderni dell'Istituto di Studi Verdiani*, III, (Parma 1968), pp. 101–2.
16. A full selection is printed, *ibid.*, pp. 101ff.
17. *Ibid.*, p. 114.
18. *Ibid.*, p. 115.
19. *Ibid.*, p. 116.
20. Letter of 5 December 1850: *Copialettere*, pp. 108–9.
21. *Ibid.*, pp. 112–13.
22. 'Stiffelio', *Quaderni* ..., p. 17.
23. *Copialettere*, p. 85.
24. Letter of 8 May 1850: Abbiati, *Verdi*, II, p. 62.
25. *Copialettere*, pp. 96–7.
26. Abbiati, *op. cit.*, II, pp. 56–8.
27. Nordio, *Verdi e la Fenice*, p. 36.
28. Abbiati, *op. cit.*, II, pp. 58–9.

29. Letter of 10 April 1850: *Copialettere*, pp. 100–1.
30. *Ibid.*, p. 101.
31. *Ibid.*, p. 102.
32. *Ibid.*, p. 103.
33. Nordio, *op. cit.*, p. 38.
34 Budden, *The operas of Verdi*, I, p. 477.
35. Abbiati, *op. cit.*, II, p. 60.
36. *Ibid.*, pp. 62–3,
37. Letter of 3 June 1850: *ibid.*, pp. 63–4.
38. Marchesi, 'Gli anni del *Rigoletto*', p. 873.
39. Cf. *Copialettere*, p. 486.
40. Nordio, *op. cit.*, p. 39.
41. *Copialettere*, p. 106, n. 1.
42. Nordio, *op. cit.*, p. 39.
43. *Ibid.*, p. 40.
44. *Ibid.*, p. 40.
45. Abbiati, *op. cit.*, II, pp. 71–2.
46. Letter of 11 November 1850: *Copialettere*, pp. 485–6.
47. Nordio, *op. cit.*, pp. 40–1.
48. *Ibid.*, p. 41.
49. Undated letter to Piave: Abbiati, *op. cit.*, II, p. 84.
50. *Copialettere*, pp 486–7.
51. Letter of 5 December 1850: *ibid.*, pp. 108–9.
52. Abbiati, *op. cit.*, II, pp. 86–7.
53. *Ibid.*, p. 88.
54. *Copialettere*, pp. 488–9.
55. Abbiati, *op. cit.*, II, pp. 90–1.
56. *Copialettere*, pp. 489–90.
57. Letter of 4 January 1851: *ibid.*, p. 490.
58. *Ibid.*, pp. 490–1.
59. Abbiati, *op. cit.*, II, pp. 97–8.
60. *Ibid.*, pp. 98–9.
61. Letter of 24 January 1851: *ibid.*, pp. 104–5.
62. *Copialettere*, pp. 491–2.
63. Letter of 21 January 1851: Abbiati, *op. cit.*, II, p. 100.
64. Abbiati, *op. cit.*, II, pp. 102–3.
65. *Ibid.*, p. 103.
66. Letter of 29 January 1851: Nordio, *op. cit.*, p. 43.
67. Abbiati, *op. cit.*, II, pp. 105–6.
68. *Copialettere*, pp. 494–5.
69. *Ibid.*, pp. 495–6.
70. Letter of 4 February 1852: *ibid.*, p. 135.
71. Varesi, 'L'interpretazione del *Macbeth*', p. 440.
72. Verdi to Piave, October 1854: Abbiati, *op. cit.*, II, p. 110.
73. Nordio, *op. cit.*, p. 44.
74. *Ibid.*
75. *Copialettere*, p. 496.

Chapter 12. Giuseppina's operas – *Il Trovatore* and *La Traviata*

1. Letter of 3 January 1853: Luzio, *Carteggi verdiani*, IV, p. 264.
2. Second letter of 3 January 1853: *ibid.*, p. 265.
3. *Copialettere*, p. 69.
4. Quoted in full *ibid.*, pp. 81–2.
5. Letter of 26 July 1849: *ibid.*, pp. 83–4.
6. *Ibid.*, pp. 84–5.
7. Marchesi, 'Gli anni del *Rigoletto*', p. 860.
8. Monaldi, *Verdi*, 2nd edn (Turin 1926), pp. 118–19.
9. Letter of 29 March 1851: Abbiati, *Verdi*, II, p. 121.
10. Letter of 4 April 1851: *ibid.*, pp. 122–3.
11. *Copialettere*, pp. 118–21.
12. Cf. Verdi's letter of 25 June to Cammarano: Abbiati, *op. cit.*, II, p. 135.
13. *Copialettere*, p. 125.
14. *Ibid.*, p. 124.
15. Letter of 23 September 1851: *ibid.*, pp. 126–7.
16. Letter of 1 October 1851: *ibid.*, p. 127.
17. Abbiati, *op. cit.*, II, pp. 192–3.
18. Letter of 25 November 1851: Ferrara, Biblioteca Comunale Ariostea.
19. Letter of June 1852: Abbiati, *op. cit.*, II, p. 167.
20. Letter of 3 July 1852: Milan, Archive of the Teatro alla Scala.
21. Letter of 24 August 1852: Modena, Biblioteca Estense.
22. *Copialettere*, p. 128.
23. *Ibid.*, p. 148.
24. Naples, Museo di San Martino, Collezione Archivio Storico.
25. Letter of 19 July 1852: Naples, Museo di San Martino. The rest of the letter is quoted above, p. 252
26. Abbiati, *op. cit.*, II, p. 169.
27. Letter of 29 September 1852: *ibid.*, pp. 170–1.
28. *Ibid.*, pp. 172–3.
29. *Ibid.*, p. 177.
30. *Ibid.*, pp. 180–3.
31. *Ibid.*, pp. 188–9.
32. *Ibid.*, p. 190.
33. Letter of 4 February 1852: Nordio, *Verdi e la Fenice*, p. 46.
34. *Ibid.*, p. 46.
35. Letter of 14 April 1852: *ibid.*, p. 47.
36. Cf. Verdi's letter to De Sanctis, 3 May 1852: *Copialettere*, p. 147.
37. Budden, 'The two *Traviatas*', *Proceedings of the Royal Musical Association*, XCIX (1973), p. 47.
38. Letter of 9 May 1852: Nordio, *op. cit.*, p. 47.
39. Abbiati, *Verdi*, II, p. 214.
40. Nordio, *op. cit*, p. 47.
41. Abbiati, *op. cit.*, II, p. 174.
42. *Ibid.*
43. Letter of 26 October: *ibid.*, p. 177.
44. Paris, Théâtre de l'Opera.
45. Abbiati, *op. cit.*, II, pp. 183–4.

46. *Ibid.*, p. 189.
47. Letter of 17 January 1850: transl. Walker, *The man Verdi*, p. 210.
48. Letter of 30 January 1853: Nordio, *op. cit.*, p. 48.
49. *Ibid.*
50. *Ibid.*, pp. 48–9.
51. Abbiati, *op. cit.*, II, p. 217.
52. Transl. Walker, *op. cit.*, p. 296.
53. Budden, 'The two *Traviatas*', p. 43.
54. Cited F. Schlitzer, *Mondo teatrale dell'ottocento* (Naples 1954), p. 156.
55. *Gazzetta Privilegiata di Venezia*, cited Nordio, *op. cit.*, p. 50.
56. Abbiati, *op. cit.*, II, p. 229.
57. Schlitzer, *op. cit.*, p. 156.
58. Walker, *op. cit.*, p. 297.
59. Luzio, *Carteggi verdiani*, IV, p. 259.
60. *Copialettere*, p. 535.
61. *Ibid.*, p. 536.
62. *Ibid.*, p. 536.
63. *Ibid.*, pp. 536–7.
64. *Ibid.*, p. 537.

Chapter 14. Italian grand opera – *Nabucco* and *I Lombardi alla Prima Crociata*

1. Muzio to Barezzi, 19 November 1845.
2. Letter of November 1845 to Piave.
3. Giuseppe Giusti, 'Sant' Ambrogio'.

Chapter 15. The early 'galley' operas – *Ernani* to *Attila*

1. Cf. P. Petrobelli, 'Verdi e il *Don Giovanni*', *Atti del Primo Congresso Internazionale di Studi Verdiani* (Parma 1969), pp. 232–3.
2. Letter to Cammarano, 4 April 1851.
3. Letter of 17 July 1845: Garibaldi, *Verdi nelle lettere di Muzio*, p. 210.
4. Chorley, *Musical recollections*, p. 154.

Chapter 16. *Macbeth* and its satellites

1. Letter to Barezzi, 23 July 1847: Garibaldi, *Verdi nelle lettere di Muzio*, p. 346.
2. Noske, 'Ritual scenes in Verdi's operas', *Music and Letters*, LIV (1973), pp. 415–39.

Chapter 17. *Verdi à la parisienne* – *Jérusalem* and *La Battaglia di Legnano*

1. Zavadini, *Donizetti*, p. 495.

Chapter 19. 'The popular trilogy' – *Rigoletto, Il Trovatore, La Traviata*

1. Donald Jay Grout, *A short history of opera* (New York 1947), p. 438.

Chapter 20. *Nabucco*, a risorgimento opera

1. Heine, *Reisebilder, III: Italien 1828*, cited above, pp. 60–1.

Chapter 21. Verdi and French Romanticism – *Ernani*

1. Letter to Bancalari, 11 December 1843: Abbiati, *Verdi*, I, p. 469.
2. Nordio, *Verdi e la Fenice*, p. 34.
3. Transl. Walker, *The man Verdi*, p. 467.
4. Hanslick, *Die moderne Oper* (Berlin 1875), p. 222: cited L. K. Gerhartz, *Die Auseinandersetzungen des jungen Giuseppe Verdi mit dem literarischen Drama*, Berliner Studien zur Musikwissenschaft, 15 (Berlin 1968), p. 370.
5. Abbiati, *op. cit.*, I, pp. 473–4.
6. Letter of 2 October: *ibid.*, p. 475.
7. Gerhartz, *op. cit.*, pp. 3of.
8. Budden, *The operas of Verdi*, I, p. 147.

Chapter 22. *Byronismo* – *I Due Foscari* and *Il Corsaro*

1. Swinburne, 'Wordsworth and Byron', cited Rutherford, *Byron, the critical heritage*, pp. 468–9.
2. Mazzini, 'Byron and Goethe', cited *ibid.*, p. 330.
3. J. P. Eckermann, *Gespräche mit Goethe*, 5 July 1827.
4. Cited M. Simhart, *Lord Byrons Einfluss auf die italienische Literatur* (Leipzig 1909), p. 30.
5. Dickens, *Pictures from Italy*.
6. Rutherford, *op. cit.*, pp. 338–340.
7. Letter of – January 1846.
8. Byron, Preface to *Marino Faliero, Doge of Venice*.

Chapter 23. The impact of Shakespeare – the Florence *Macbeth*

1. A. Graf, *L'anglomania e l'influsso inglese in Italia nel secolo XVIII* (Turin 1911), p. 317.
2. F. S. Quadrio, *Della storia e della ragione d'ogni poesia*, III (Milan 1743), p. 149.
3. Cited M. Praz, 'Shakespeare translations in Italy', *Shakespeare-Jahrbuch*, XCII (Heidelberg 1956), p. 220.
4. R. Davril, 'Shakespeare in French garb', *Shakespeare-Jahrbuch*, XCII (Heidelberg 1956), p. 198.
5. Cited Nulli, *Shakespeare in Italia*, p. 170.
6. *Copialettere*, p. 624.
7. *Ibid.*, p. 559.
8. Cited Rinaldi, *Felice Romani*, p. 182.
9. Cited Weinstock, *Rossini*, p. 66.

10. Letter of 3 March 1818 to Samuel Rogers.
11. Weinstock, *op. cit.*, p. 310.
12. The synopsis is printed in Abbiati, *Verdi*, I, pp. 656–8.
13. C. B. Young, 'The stage-history of *Macbeth*', *Macbeth* (The New Shakespeare) ed. J. Dover Wilson (Cambridge 1947), p. lxxiii.
14. Wilson, 'Introduction', *ibid.*, p. xxxix.
15. *Ibid.*, p. xxi.
16. Carcano, 'Sul dramma fantastico', cited Nulli, *Shakespeare in Italia*, pp. 173–4.
17. Noske, 'Verdi and the musical figure of death', *Atti del Terzo Congresso Internazionale di Studi Verdiani* (Parma 1974), pp. 349f.
18 Noske, 'Ritual scenes in Verdi's operas', pp. 415f.

Chapter 25. Essays with Schiller

1. Schiller, 'Rheinische Thalia', 11 November 1784.
2. A contemporary review, cited B. von Wiese, *Schiller, eine Einführung in Leben und Werk* (Stuttgart 1955), p. 16.
3. *Copialettere*, pp. 32–3.
4. Schiller, 'Selbstrezension: Die Räuber', in *Dichter über ihre Dichtungen, Friedrich Schiller* (Munich 1969).
5. Budden, *The operas of Verdi*, I, p. 321.
6. Letter of ?31 August 1846: Abbiati, *Verdi*, I, p. 770.

Chapter 26. The originality of *Rigoletto*

1. Abbiati, *Verdi*, II, p. 110.
2. Letter to Borsi, 8 September 1852: *Copialettere*, p. 497.
3. *Ibid.*
4. Budden, *The operas of Verdi*, I, p. 499.
5. *Copialettere*, p. 497.

Chapter 27. Verdi and 'realism' – *La Traviata*

1. Letter of 9 March 1848: Abbiati, *Verdi*, I, pp. 737–8.
2. Letter to Clarina Maffei, 20 October 1876: *Copialettere*, p. 624.
3. N. St John-Stevas, *Obscenity and the law*, p. 68: cited V. Godefroy, *The dramatic genius of Verdi. Studies of selected operas*, I (London 1975), p. 251.
4. Chorley, *Musical recollections*, pp. 238–9.
5. P. E. Charvet, *A literary history of France*, IV (London 1967), p. 351.
6. Walker, *The man Verdi*, ch. 2.
7. Luzio, *Carteggi verdiani*, IV, pp. 250–76.
8. Letter of 5 January 1860: transl. Walker, *op. cit.*, p. 226.
9. Cf. Noske, 'Verdi and the musical figure of death'.

Bibliography

Abbiati, F. *Giuseppe Verdi*, 4 vols. Milan 1959

Barbiera, R. *Il salotto della Contessa Maffei*, 11th edn. Florence 1915

Basevi, A. *Studio sulle opere di Giuseppe Verdi*. Florence 1859

Bellini, V. *Epistolario*, ed. L. Cambi. Verona 1943

Benedetti, A. *Le traduzioni italiane da Walter Scott e i loro anglicismi.* Florence 1974

Berlioz, H. *The memoirs of Hector Berlioz*, transl. and ed. D. Cairns. London 1969

Blessington, Margaret, Countess of. *The idler in Italy*, 3 vols. London 1839–40

Bottevi, G. 'Cenni storici', *Il Comunale di Trieste*. Udine 1962

Brand, C. P. *Italy and the English Romantics*. Cambridge 1957

Budden, J. *The operas of Verdi*, I: From 'Oberto' to 'Rigoletto'. London 1973

'The two *Traviatas*', *Proceedings of the Royal Musical Association*, XCIX (1973)

'*La Battaglia di Legnano*, its unique character with special reference to the finale of Act I', *Atti del Terzo Congresso Internazionale di Studi Verdiani*. Parma 1974

The operas of Verdi, II: From 'Il Trovatore' to 'La Forza del Destino'. London 1978

Cametti, A. *Il teatro di Tordinona*. Tivoli 1938

Cavicchi, A. 'Verdi e Solera. Considerazioni sulla collaborazione per *Nabucco*., *Atti del Primo Congresso Internazionale di Studi Verdiani*. Parma 1969

Cenni storici intorno alle lettere, invenzioni, arti, al commercio ed agli spettacoli teatrali, XXIX–XLIII. Bologna 1838–45

Chorley, H. F. *Thirty years' musical recollections*. London 1862

Colquhoun, A. *Manzoni and his times*. London 1954

Davril, R. 'Shakespeare in French garb', *Shakespeare-Jahrbuch* XCII. Heidelberg 1956

D'Azeglio, M. *I miei ricordi*, with posthumous completion by G. Torelli, 2 vols. Florence 1867

Thing I remember, transl. E. R. Vincent. London 1966

Dean, W. 'Some echoes of Donizetti in Verdi's operas', *Atti del Terzo Congresso Internazionale di Studi Verdiani*. Parma 1974

Della Libera, S. (ed.). 'Ernani di G. Verdi, Cronologia', typescript in the Archive of the Teatro La Fenice, Venice (cited in the notes as 'Ernani Cronologia')

De Sanctis, F. *Storia della letteratura italiana*, 2 vols. Naples 1870–1

Dickens, C. *Pictures from Italy*. London 1846

Bibliography

Di Stefano, C. *La censura teatrale in Italia (1600–1962)*. Bologna 1964

Donizetti, G. *See under Zavadini, G.*

Escudier, L. *Mes souvenirs*. Paris 1863

Escudier, Les frères. *Rossini, sa vie et ses oeuvres*. Paris 1854

Florimo, Francesco. *La scuola musicale di Napoli, e ic suoi conservatorii*, 4 vols. Naples 1880–2

Gamberini, Leopoldo. *La vita musicale europea del 1800, Archivio Musicale Genovese*, I: *Introduzione: Opera lirica e musica strumentale; Documente e testimonianze*. Siena 1978

Garibaldi, L. A. *Giuseppe Verdi nelle lettere di Emanuele Muzio ad Antonio Barezzi*. Milan 1931

Gatti, C. *Verdi*, 2 vols. Milan 1931

 Il Teatro alla Scala nella storia e nell'arte, 2 vols. Milan 1964 (*see also* under Tintori, G.*)

Gautier, T. *Histoire de l'art dramatique en France depuis vingt-cinq ans*, 5ᵉ série. Paris 1847

Gerhartz, L. K. *Die Auseinandersetzungen des jungen Giuseppe Verdi mit dem literarischen Drama* (Berliner Studien zur Musikwissenschaft, 15). Berlin 1968

Ghislanzoni, A. 'Storia di Milano dal 1836 al 1848', *In chiave di baritono*. Milan 1882

Glinka, M. I. *Memoirs*, transl. R. B. Mudge. Norman, Oklahoma 1963

Godefroy, V. *The dramatie genius of Verdi. Studies of selected operas*, I: *'Nabucco' to 'La Traviata'*. London 1975

Gounod, C. *Autobiographical reminiscences*, transl. W. Hely Hutchinson. London 1896

Graf, A. *L'anglomania e l'influsso inglese in Italia nel secolo XVIII*. Turin 1911

Grout, D. J. *A short history of opera*. New York 1947

Günther, U. 'Documents inconnus concernant les relations de Verdi avec l'Opéra de Paris', *Atti del Terzo Congresso Internazionale di Studi Verdiani*. Parma 1974

Hayez, F. *Le mie memorie*. Milan 1890

Hazlitt, W. *Notes of a journey through France and Italy*. London 1826

Heine, H. *Reisebilder, III: Italien 1828*. Hamburg 1830

Hübner, A. Graf von. *Ein Jahr meines Lebens, 1848–9*. Leipzig 1891

'Jarro'. *Memorie d'un impresario fiorentino*. Florence 1892

Kimbell, D. R. B. '*Il Trovatore*: Cammarano and Garcìa Gutiérrez', *Atti del Terzo Congresso Internazionale di Studi Verdiani*. Parma 1974

 'Verdi's first *rifacimento*: *I Lombardi* and *Jérusalem*', *Music and Letters*, LX (1979)

Lawton, D. and D. Rosen. 'Verdi's non-definitive revisions: the early operas', *Atti del Terzo Congresso Internazionale di Studi Verdiani*. Parma 1974

Lessona, M. *Volere è potere*, 2nd edn. Florence 1869

Lichtenthal, P. *Dizionario e biografia della musica*. Milan 1826

Lippmann, F. *Vincenzo Bellini und die italienische Opera Seria seiner Zeit* (*Analecta Musicologica*, VI). Cologne and Vienna 1969

Loewenberg, A. *Annals of opera, 1597–1940*. Cambridge 1943

Lumley, B. *Reminiscences of the Italian opera*. London 1864

Luzio, A. *Carteggi verdiani*, 4 vols. Rome 1935–47

Bibliography

Mack Smith, D. (ed.). *The making of Italy, 1796–1870*. New York 1968

Marchesi, G. 'Gli anni del *Rigoletto*', *Bollettino dell'Istituto di Studi Verdiani*, III.8 (Parma 1973)

Martin, G. *Verdi, his music, life and times*. London 1965

Mazzini, G. 'Filosofia di musica', *Edizione nazionale degli scritti di Giuseppe Mazzini*, VIII. Imola 1910

  Scritti di letteratura e di arte. Florence 1931

Mazzuchetti, L. *Schiller in Italia*. Milan 1913

Mendelssohn-Bartholdy, F. *Briefe aus den Jahren 1830 bis 1847*. Leipzig 1899

Meyerbeer, G. *Briefwechsel und Tagebücher*, 1, ed. H. Becker. Berlin 1960

Mila, M. *Giuseppe Verdi*. Bari 1958

Monaldi, G. *Verdi*, 2nd edn. Turin 1926

  Verdi, German edn. Stuttgart and Leipzig 1898

Mooney, A. G. 'An assessment of Mercadante's contribution to the development of Italian opera', unpublished M.Mus. dissertation, Edinburgh 1970

Morazzoni, G. *Verdi, Lettere inedite*. Milan 1929

Nicolai, O. *Otto Nicolai's Tagebücher nebst biographischen Ergänzungen*, ed. B. Schröder. Leipzig 1892

Nordio M. *Verdi e la Fenice*. Venice 1951

Noske, F. 'Ritual scenes in Verdi's operas', *Music and Letters* LIV (1973)

  'Verdi and the musical figure of death', *Atti del Terzo Congresso Internazionale di Studi Verdiani*. Parma 1974

Nulli, S. A. *Shakespeare in Italia*. Milan 1918

Osborne, C. *The complete operas of Verdi*. London 1969

  The letters of Verdi. London 1971

Pacini, G. *Le mie memorie artistiche*. Florence 1865

Petrobelli, P. 'Verdi e il *Don Giovanni*', *Atti del Primo Congresso Internazionale di Studi Verdiani*. Parma 1969

Pougin, A. *Giuseppe Verdi, vita aneddotica*, with notes and additions by 'Folchetto' (Jacopo Capponi). Milan 1881

  Verdi, an anecdotic history, transl. J. E. Matthew. London 1887

Praz, M. 'Shakespeare translations in Italy', *Shakespeare-Jahrbuch* XCII. Heidelberg 1956

Procacci, G. *History of the Italian people*, transl. A. Paul. London 1970

Quadrio, F. S. *Della storia, e della ragione d'ogni poesia*, III. Milan 1743

Qvamme, B. 'Verdi e il realismo', *Atti del Terzo Congresso Internazionale di Studi Verdiani*. Parma 1974

Radiciotti, G. 'Teatro e musica in Roma nel secondo quarto del secolo XIX (1825–50)', *Atti del Congresso Internazionale di Scienze Storiche (Roma, Aprile 1903)*, VIII. Rome 1905

Rinaldi, M. *Felice Romani, dal melodramma classico al melodramma romantico*. Rome 1965

  Gli anni di galera di Giuseppe Verdi. Rome 1969

Rinuccini, G. B. *Sulla musica e sulla poesia melodrammatica italiana* ... Lucca 1843

Ritorni, C. *Ammaestramenti alla composizione di ogni poema e d'ogni opera appartenente alla musica*. Milan 1841

Bibliography

Robertson, J. G. 'Shakespeare in Italy', *Cambridge history of English literature*, v. Cambridge 1910

Robinson M. F. *Naples and Neapolitan opera*. Oxford 1972

Rutherford A. *Byron, the critical heritage*. London 1970

Sartori C. 'Rocester, la prima opera di Verdi., *Rivista Musicale Italiana*, XLIII (1939)

Schiller, F. von. *Dichter über ihre Dichtungen, Friedrich Schiller* ... Munich 1969

Schlitzer, F. *Mondo teatrale dell'ottocento*. Naples 1954

Schumann, R. *Gesammelte Schriften über Musik und Musiker*. Leipzig 1914

Simhart, M. *Lord Byrons Einfluss auf die italienische* Literatur. Leipzig 1909

Soffredini, A. *Le opere di Verdi, studio critico analitico*. Milan 1901

Spohr, L. *Selbstbiographie*, 2 vols. Kassel and Göttingen 1860

Stendhal (M.-H. Beyle). *Rome, Naples et Florence en 1817*. Paris 1817
  Life of Rossini, transl. R. N. Coe. London 1956

'Stiffelio', *Quaderni dell'Istituto di Studi Verdiani*, III. Parma 1968

Storia di Milano (Fondazione Treccani degli Alfieri), XIV. Milan 1960

Tiby, O. *Il Real Teatro Carolino e l'ottocento musicale palermitano*. Florence 1957

Tintori, G. 'Cronologia completa degli spettacoli . . .', vol. II of C. Gatti, *Il Teatro alla Scala nella storia e nell'arte*. Milan 1964

Varesi, G. Cova. 'L'interpretazione di Macbeth', *Nuova Antologia*, CCCLXIV (1932)

Verdi, G. *I copialettere di Giuseppe Verdi*, ed. G. Cesari and A. Luzio. Milan 1913 (cited in the notes as *Copialettere*)

Walker, F. *The man Verdi*. London 1962

Weaver, W. *Verdi: a documentary study*. London 1977

Weinstock, H. *Rossini: a biography*. New York and London 1968
  Vincenzo Bellini, his life and his operas. London 1971

Whitfield, J. H. *A short history of Italian literature*. Harmondsworth 1960

Wiese, B. von. *Schiller, eine Einführung in Leben und Werk*. Stuttgart 1955

Wilson, J. Dover (ed.). *Macbeth* (The New Shakespeare). Cambridge 1947

Woolf, S. J. *The Italian risorgimento*. London 1969

Zamboni, G. *Die italienische Romantik*. Krefeld 1953

Zavadini, G. *Donizetti, vita – musiche – epistolario*. Bergamo 1948

Index

Note: Verdi's works are indexed under Verdi.

Index

Index

Index

Index

Index